CONTENTS

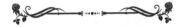

FOREWORD

A foreword is usually written by a well-known person, but I have found that ethicists are seldom at the forefront of literary or social discourse. Why? Because in addition to speaking truth to power, we speak logic to societal naiveté—and this is not appreciated. I want to express my profound admiration for what the author has courageously presented to the world in this compelling memoir.

The boundaries we set as a society are restrictive and unforgiving. In the name of "morals" and religious constraints we create the so-called "deviant," whose behaviors we isolate and excoriate—no matter if they are helpless children or powerless young girls. What this book will do is open the minds as well as the hearts of readers to an understanding that the cards we are dealt are not evenly or fairly distributed, but how we play them is based on inner forces developed as we evolve as individuals.

The trajectory is uneven and the path circuitous when we are guided more by our innate character than by good fortune. This is the story of a woman brutalized as a child, taken advantage of as an adolescent, and objectified as an adult, who rose above the abuse of systems and individuals and created a life of integrity and standards seldom met by those who have not faced true adversity.

Pope Francis wisely said in 2013, when queried about people outside the margins, "Who am I to judge?" But we do judge, all of us. Libbe Leah Siskind is determined to present to us a world we have never really seen to bring to light the urgent need to save the children and young women who are brutalized and enslaved to this day, this hour, this moment.

We have free will and need to examine our place in the world and fight, as Ms. Siskind would have us do, to end the exploitation that still exists. Read her story and ask yourself—could I have withstood all that? Then ask this: what can I do, how can I help affect change, make the world safer for the "deviants" set aside by the self-serving boundaries of society? Holocaust survivor, Nobel Laureate, and educator Elie Wiesel said, "The opposite of love is not hate, it's indifference." Be it a child tied to a bed or a girl sold on the streets, do not judge or behave with indifference—take action.

Allyson T. Woolf

PREFACE

*I*f you pick at scars, the wound will never heal. But if you leave them alone and forget they are there, they will go away. If I fed on all the bad things that have happened to me, there would be no food left for the good things—none. I filled those small, unscarred areas that were left with as much positive impact as possible so that there was little left over for the ravenous darkness of my mind and body. I never forget, but I put it all aside as memories, not living and breathing entities. We all want to live and learn, but so many cannot get past one awful thing that happens to them. It's like watching a bad program on TV; you must teach yourself how to change those channels and make everything work for you in a positive way. Move on!

The phrase "in the room" comes out of the world of streetwalkers and in-house prostitution. How a girl performs "in the room," what happens "in the room," is the measure of her ability and the site of her job description. If a madam describes you as being great "in the room" it means you can handle a client well; you are a performer on the mattress who uses the theatrical veil in a creative way. In the room that houses my spirit, I have always been the loved child of my adoptive mother. I am strong and unshakeable today because I remember my mother, Rose.

My best memories come from my experiences as a young child in Rose's care. I have collected letters from adoption agencies, foster care workers, psychologists, and the Department of Social Services that describe me from the earliest times in my life. One letter describes me at thirty-five weeks old: "She is a pretty baby with large, dark brown eyes and curly brown hair. Libbe has high social qualities and is very responsive, lively, and playful. [...] Libbe shows security and contentment in this home. Mrs. Siskind has given her excellent care and she is like their own child, accepted by the family circle. [...] Libbe is very active. She can pull to her own feet on the sofa and stand holding on. In block play, she seems to prefer the left hand, is alert in manipulating and grasping."

Now imagine me as a grown woman, a woman who is wheeling her bicycle and sits down next to you on the banks of the Charles River. She is friendly, bright, and articulate. You like her. What if you knew she had been a street whore? A woman who so violates the status quo that she has been legislated against and condemned by every generation in history, whether politics and society are in a morals and ethics phase or totally decadent. Whores are women who have forsaken their rights. Do you stand and apologetically leave, saying that you can't possibly be friends? What's in the heart of a whore? If you got to know me, perhaps you'd use different labels—like mother, caretaker, lover of dogs, author of novels and children's books, faithful friend, and a fan of Elizabeth Taylor, old movies, and cartoons. My heart is the same heart that beats in all of us. I was that vibrant thirty-five-week-old child described in my papers, like any other healthy young child of the same age.

The phrase "in the room" also refers to the boiler room in the house where I grew up, where my adoptive father's new wife, Anita, locked me up and tortured me. When my mother Rose was alive, the basement was my favorite place, a room where I took refuge and played—a space reserved for fantasy. My dad, Fred, built the basement out of knotty pine, with velvet-padded benches for sitting and storage, a tile floor, a bar, and a bathroom. Both doors in the boiler room and bar could be locked from the outside with those old slide locks made of brass, but they couldn't be opened from the inside.

Fred crafted the boiler room in his careful way, and it could be a scary place if he wasn't there working with his tools and labeled jars of screws and nails. With Fred, it was warm, and thc sound of the boiler flue whispering in the little room was soothing. Once Anita became my evil stepmother and jailer, the dark, locked room became my cell, and the concrete floor my bed in the bad room.

"In the room" is also the safe place I created far away from Anita. I had a bold persona on the streets when I ran away from my adopted family, foster homes, pimps, and abusers. I picked myself up from being a street whore to establish my own business in the high ranks of in-house party girls and call girls; someone who was, by far, sober and clean throughout sixteen years on the streets in Boston's Combat Zone, only taking small hits of cocaine and an occasional drink with my men. Finally, I had my dream house—my attempt to build a childhood I never had after my mother died, to protect me from the bad memories of the past. How did I end up here? Odds say I should be among the detritus, the wasted sisterhood of streetwalkers, whores, and hustlers whose bodies and souls have been beaten down, polluted, and sometimes stamped out. Whatever is left of them—if anything is left—shivers and shakes, pulls on itself in hurt and agony, and hungrily grabs for any chemical or substance to soften and dull the constant pain. I became a person of many interests and talents. I did not want pain and death. Untouchable. No one knew that I was there, only a couple of people knew what I did. I had a son to be proud of and who was proud of me, and a home for us both. What follows is the introduction to my story.

INTRODUCTION

To begin…I was an abused and mistreated child, a prostitute, and a madam. But even more importantly, I am a woman and a human being. My story is often happy, brutal, and unnerving. It is also one of subtle and clear triumph. It is ultimately hopeful.

My book describes much of the terrible reality of adoption, foster care, prostitution, and the system. It goes in depth into an existence that should have killed me prior to reaching the age of twenty. What I endured and overcame seems remarkable to other people. I never viewed my life that way as I was living it. To me, it was my daily life. Today, in my seventies, I am known as a compassionate, industrious, and warm woman—and this defies the odds.

Everyone who has heard even a partial account of my story finds it very intriguing. I began my life being given up for private adoption by a birth mother who was married to a man other than my biological father. I was only seven when stomach cancer took my mother from me: the mother who had adopted me and whom I loved. I sustained myself beyond the wicked stepmother and being molested by the gardener. I made it through the foster homes to which I was sent and my pregnancy at sixteen—giving birth to a healthy girl given up for adoption in 1967. In 1970, I gave birth to a baby boy who was also given up for adoption for reasons that will be explained further on. I never forgot them—it has taken over forty years of searching, letters, phone calls, lawyers, and working with the bureaucracy and agencies. One child I have met and connected with, the other did not want to meet with me at that point in time. I lived through torture, child rape, and gang rape. I stuck it out and dealt with sadistic and controlling pimps, and a decade of selling myself on the streets of Boston and cities with truck stops in the Northeast. These were men I pleasured for money. There were more rapes! In 1969, I gave birth to my son R. Lee, whom I adore, always supporting him and never abandoning him no matter what occurred in my life on the streets.

I stayed alive as my sisters on the hoe stroll died and disappeared. Kara was butchered and carved up in an apartment in the Back Bay. Marcie, a madam and close friend who owned an old brownstone in Back Bay, Boston, couldn't stay away from alcohol and freebasing. She overdosed and her heart froze. Katie shot up junk with her lover, caught AIDS, and ended up as dead as Kara and Marcie. And although I didn't know them personally, there was Melodie Stankiewicz, Holly Davidson, and Kathy Williams—all found murdered north of Boston within a year. So many other street sisters. Gone. Dead. Most were never mentioned in the newspaper because they were prostitutes—a sub-human species—unlike other women.

Then there was Ruthie, a few years younger than me, my tightest friend in the sisterhood of prostitutes. She was, like me, a Jewish girl from the Boston suburbs who had a dysfunctional parent. Ruthie was not like me in that she did not grow to trust her own opinions and perspective. She was fickle and insecure. Ruthie, known as Robin, danced in the Zone and did tricks as well. She constantly longed for a true feeling of belonging to something. You will read her story and learn her destiny.

I moved on and then, if not in the estimation of polite society, I started to take control. I figured out and acted on my transition away from the enslavement of pimps in Boston's Combat Zone to establish myself as a madam, an operator of my own enterprise. I felt as though I was respectable. I built a business that provided quality companionship, and whose ladies of the evening had to be twenty-one years or older, alcohol and drug free, pretty, well-kept, and could at least affect a semblance of sophistication—in fact, many had a college education.

Later on, in 1978, I met David, my soul mate and the second love of my life. He didn't like what I did, but he had to learn to deal with it. Soon after, I left doing tricks behind and was exclusively a madam. My business grew, and it was not long before I became a leading madam on the decades-old national high-end sex network called "The Circuit." We were a clique of highly successful, authentic madams; none connected in any way except to trade our girls with each other.

Even as I lived an underground existence, I ensured that my son had faith and a spiritual background. I enrolled R. Lee in Hebrew school and impressed upon him the importance and value of Judaism. After I had a near-death experience, I made plans to take R. Lee to Jerusalem so that his bar mitzvah ceremony could be at the Wailing Wall.

I bought a rundown Victorian house in 1982, and commenced the twenty-year-plus rehabilitation and restoration of the home into a gorgeous "painted lady"—my "Pink House." I leveraged the equity in the Pink House and invested in other properties; a passion of mine that continues to this day.

With the credit backing of a wealthy client, I opened up several small retail stores. The businesses were profitable, as was my in-call enterprise. Not enough time in a day, but the money rolled in. I started to think, *Could I? Could I leave the life of a madam one day and operate totally on the right side of the law?* This was something I wished for every day. I made the choice to go for it, to go for the life of a "square." David was happy. I, on the other hand, was not! My plan was to sell off the businesses (no more shoe stores) and open one store in the high-rent section of Boston, which I did.

I cut off my telephone number. I tossed the black book with my clients' phone numbers. To me, it was like losing a part of myself. It was my lifeline. I launched an accessory boutique. I even had a small florist shop adjacent to the boutique. Things went well; the businesses made money. I did not have to be a madam. But my business partner was going bankrupt. All the money I had saved went to my partner to buy out his interest so that I did not lose my home.

I returned to what I knew. I returned to the life. Applying my business sense, I quickly regained my standing by using ads selling myself in the edgy section of the Phoenix. Later, I opened and ran a small collectibles and jewelry store that specialized in antique dolls—this time without partners. I loved both my enterprises. I ended up, as I always did, back on my feet. I vowed never to give up my client books again. David wasn't pleased.

I continued as a madam and store owner, compartmentalizing each business in my mind. Answering the phones to schedule the girls restricted my participation in social causes that first year. Somehow, someway, despite the abuses I underwent—or maybe because of them—my constitution has been one of empathy, laughter, smiles, and devoid of self-pity.

None of my fine and affluent friends could ever guess what goes on in the room. No one knew I was running a high-class brothel, part of a soon-to-be infamous nationwide network known as The Circuit. To them, I was simply Libbe, the woman who owned a raspberry-colored Victorian in Brookline, an affluent town next to Boston, Massachusetts.

And yes, I got caught up in the circus of the federal sting to take down madams. It made the papers, magazines, and TV news across the country. FBI agents were monitoring madams' phone calls while Osama bin Laden and the Islamic terrorists of Al Qaeda were plotting to make their attack on September 11, 2001. Some calls were made on that fatal day in our history that were apparently of great interest to the feds and received prime attention—what could be as important to national security as prostitution?

My highly visible 2002 FBI arrest was traumatic, and I will never forget it—since then, I have no secrets. *The Boston Herald* headlines on April 6th and 7th, 2002, were "Fed brothel bust ID's Brookline woman as alleged Hub madam," (written by Jose Martinez) and "Neighbors shocked at charge of catting under hot pink roof" (written by Doug Hanchett). Ironically, hanging on a wall under the "hot pink roof" was an original poster from the movie *Cat on a Hot Tin Roof*, starring Elizabeth Taylor. The article on April 6th identified me by name as an indicted madam living in Brookline, making a point that my house was a pink Victorian brothel. How dare they! It said that I was part of a prostitution state-to-state Circuit bust and would have to face a grand jury in Louisiana on a count of "prostitution conspiracy." Further, it stated that I had not yet been arraigned on the potential five-year imprisonment charge and that no one had been able to reach me for a comment on the situation.

I pleaded out, and the judge handed down a relatively light sentence as I stood in federal court in New Orleans. I guess he realized that being a madam was not the only thing I did and that they wanted to shut the case down for everyone involved, and for other reasons due to political involvement. I returned to the Boston area and the Pink House, and my collectibles and jewelry store. I was about to begin another chapter in my multi-faceted life.

Above and beyond what others may have expected of me, I have had to prove my worthiness to myself. Fires burned inside me to stay alive and succeed. I pushed myself every inch of the way from the beginning. Now that I'm older, I continue striving in order to leave something of true value to my son—the legacy of my story, which I hope will be of help to others, a special part of myself for him to treasure not derived from my past but from what the future holds. I will always have a plan; what is life without one? Giving up—never!

As I wrote this book, I could feel the past like a knife piercing through my chest. The pain of recounting my life was more excruciating than I imagined, but I approached it step by step in an effort to write my entire story, looking at my life the way an outsider would. As difficult as examining the truth of my existence has been, I have the satisfaction of completing my own story after years of others attempting to write it for me. I see myself quite clearly. I am thankful I did not get caught up in a trap of substance abuse or succumb to demonic people who would have destroyed me. I hope my former life does not affect my loved ones or friends; the scars I bear are mine alone, not theirs.

CHAPTER ONE

Busted (April 6, 2002)

Oh no, the day I hoped would never come is here…in a room—all white, cement walls surrounding me like hands squeezing my throat. My god, I dreaded this day and now it's happened.

****

I owned a big Victorian, colonial-type, two-family home near the trolley that runs to Boston and Cleveland Circle in prestigious Brookline, Massachusetts. In 1980, I made an offer to an attorney at an estate sale. The house was a dump no one had been in for years, destitute except for the bats that inhabited every corner of the eaves. It had belonged to two sisters. One died in the first-floor unit on the couch; a neighbor who would bring food to her became worried and called for help. They found her body. The other sister was in a nursing home. Their nephew put the house on a private estate sale for one hundred fifty thousand dollars, as is. It should have been condemned, but I thought it was beautiful. I knew it was worth saving—an ugly duckling with the potential to grow into a swan—and I attached my heart and soul to it. I too was an ugly duckling! I had some cash stashed away from the flea markets I went to on weekends that were strictly cash exchanges. My client/sugar daddy (friend and partner-to-be) suggested that he'd sign and I could give him the money and the deed would go in both names. I believed he was trustworthy, and I agreed. The neighbors were happy to get the eyesore on their street cleaned up, and I was ecstatic to own a home.

Years went by. The house was beautiful, but there were still so many things to do. My store was closing, and I was going to get a larger location to sell more collectibles. I bought investment property in Boston's South End with my partner. I bought and sold stores to make money to put back into my home, travel, and for my son's education. There were many good things between the difficult years. And just when things were going well…

One of the girls who worked for me said she got busted in New Orleans, and the madam there left her in jail. "Close your apartments and put your stuff up, just in case," she warned, panicked. When I heard the name, I became uneasy and rightly so: the New Orleans mini-madam, as it turned out, was my epic mistake.

I was supposed to go to the house I bought in Florida in April for two to three weeks with Russ, the man I was dating. We were packing and had lots of stuff to take. I was stressed because I had gone ahead and taken in a Circuit girl turned mini-madam. I said yes because I do understand how it is to be in a rut. I should have listened to the sound advice of Russ, but, more importantly, I should have listened to that inner voice that was money in the bank for me for so long, that inner street voice that told me something wasn't quite right. In fact, nothing was right. Miss New Orleans was straight-up, low-down, bare-bones bad news. I was about to learn just how bad—it was a set-up.

When Nana called me from Manhattan in October 2000, it was to ask me for a favor: to help out Ginny, a mini-madam from New Orleans who I knew had recently been a working girl. Nana was a big-time madam. She had no trouble funneling a steady flow of high-class clients who would provide serious money for the services of this woman in addition to her other girls. Nana said she was recommending Ginny, who was hot for an older girl and good in the room but was in a serious cash crunch. Stating that she was too old for her place, Nana persuasively noted, "But you like 'mature' there, and I like 'the babies' for my clients." I should have said, "No way."

To myself, I was thinking if Ginny needs to make money and she can't do it out of her home base it means she has a big problem down in the bayou, and owes serious money to probably more than one person. I asked myself what else the issue might be. I was told that Ginny had a track record of getting into trouble. I told Nana, "I have a few problems with taking her in." But Madam Nana managed to talk me into it, reminding me of how many girls she had referred to me. Guilt trip time! I fell for it.

Why is she in such a rush to get out of New Orleans to make the cash? I'm a smart businesswoman, but I do have a good heart, a quality I usually channeled in a way that helped my bottom line. I took good care of my girls, my most valuable resource. I helped out lots of madams, even wrote a newsletter for them to read for their amusement. In the case involving Ginny, I did not practice smart business, and my good heart torpedoed my better judgment. I kicked myself in the ass because of it for years afterward. A little down the road, she sure as hell became a problem. I should have known better about Nana after watching her rip off her own girls, always looking out for herself before anyone else. During the Canal Street case, she let a man take the blame for her, and she had just sold him the business!

According to an article in *Newsweek* by Arian Campo-Flores (*Newsweek*, 9/02/2002, Vol.140, Issue 10, 59), "A Crackdown on Call Girls: The Feds Bust a Prostitution Ring with a Franchise Near You," the Circuit was nationwide. The article explains how the Circuit worked, that it eliminated the need for pimps by having madams keep their base brothels, shifting the prostitutes from place to place across the United States. Ginny, a madam, testified that in 1996, she was accepted into the Circuit, and it was one of her clients who tipped off the feds, allowing them to gain information that they had been unable to access previously. There were many indictments, Ginny's being one of twenty-four in numerous cities around the country. The article states that among those thirteen cities were New York, Chicago, Miami, and New Orleans, and further, that due to the numbers—the extent of how many brothels were involved—many had not been discovered, were still in operation, and likely to remain so, but no thanks to a newcomer who took down what we all worked for, our privacy. Although it is mentioned that there were rivalries between the madams and problematic issues relative to both the madams and the prostitutes, it is also emphasized that the prosecutors were impressed by the system that the Circuit madams had set up and acknowledged the skill and ingenuity of the enterprise.

Everyone kept working until the last minute. Madam C. (in her sixties in Chicago) got a visit from the feds and locals early one morning, and they left after questioning her. She called everyone with a sigh of relief, and we figured that's all—they just want to ask questions. *That's all?* I wondered and continued to pack for Florida with a pit in my stomach. I needed to get away. In the old movies, they would drink a glass of milk for stress: I needed gallons! Okay. I can take a breath. Or should I? We are going to Florida in a couple of days. But being away from Boston would not change this picture.

I felt no real urgency. I was not shaking and trembling with worry or concern like I did at first when I had closed up shop. Then, early in the morning, about a week after Madam C. had visitors, the situation was clear. The sons and daughters of J. Edgar Hoover came calling in New York, Atlanta, Miami, Pittsburgh, Chicago, Houston, Biloxi, Grand Rapids, and Brookline—my home. Yes, they came to my house. They rang the bell. We were caught unaware, unprepared, all of us, some more than others. When they busted her in Chicago, Madam C. was already up, having coffee, ready to take on the day. But all the rest of us were in bed, none of us alone. No one likes to get woken abruptly and certainly not to get arrested! By the local police—and the FBI, no less.

The madam in Pittsburgh had it the worst. She was home recovering from plastic surgery, in a deep snooze aided by the anti-inflammatories and painkillers, with her face all bandaged up when it happened. No self-respecting madam likes to get caught without her makeup on, never mind getting dragged out of bed, handcuffed, with gauze stuck to her forehead, cheeks, and chin!

At six o'clock on the morning of April 6th, 2002, from my bedroom on the third floor, Russ and I could hear the dogs yapping and loud pounding at the inside hallway door. This was unusual, but

I wasn't terribly alarmed yet. My downstairs tenants were in their twenties, and were already up, and answered the outer door where the bells are located.

My cocker spaniel barked like crazy. Russ got up and looked outside. And my dachshund followed, yipping.

"It's the police."

"The police?" I freaked.

I was in shock; it was so early, then the knock. "FBI. Open up." My heart sank as I froze for a minute or two. This is not good at all. I'm not getting a wakeup call by the FBI just to have a talk, or am I? This is bad—very bad. And the worst of it was not what was going to happen to me, but how much hurt would be dumped on my son, and Russ too. I thought to myself, *My son is the only family I have, stomping on myself is forgivable, injuring him is not.*

I went down to confront the day wearing my pajamas, my heart in my stomach! We never walk in shoes in my home, and everyone takes theirs off before they enter. Not this morning. There were four FBI agents, one was a woman who was assisting, and two Brookline police officers, both men. These were the authorities. The feds wore those navy blue windbreakers with the oversized FBI logo on the back and one on the right breast. Russ was up on the third floor stair landing, off to the side, where I told him to stay. I knew it would be a big no-no: black man, white girl. Yeah, my auto thought was that he'd be classified by white men as a pimp of the house. A broad-shouldered FBI agent, about six-one, with a full head of brown hair, stepped in front of me and asked, "Are you Libbe Siskind?"

"Yes, I am. What's going on?"

"You are under arrest for conspiracy to travel in interstate commerce in aid of a prostitution enterprise out of New Orleans."

Conspiracy? Prostitution? New Orleans? Me?

"Conspiracy?" I said. "I don't know what you're talking about. I've never conspired against anyone."

The agent was unsmiling.

"Do you know anyone in New Orleans?"

"I know lots of people in a lot of different places. But I don't know anything about a conspiracy there." Conspiracy? In New

Orleans? At that moment, I had totally forgotten about Ginny and drew a blank.

"Well, you are under arrest and we have to take you in for questioning."

"Something's all messed up," I pleaded. "This is a big mistake."
"No, 'fraid not. We're looking for you. You are under arrest, Ms. Siskind. We have to take you in."

As I looked up at Russ, his scowl hardened into pain and concern. Within those few seconds, I understood that I was being arrested, and I was going to be taking a ride downtown, or wherever the authorities had decided to settle this matter. The good thing was that they didn't harass Russ; he said he had a job and was unaware of all this. Had the arrest taken place outside of Brookline or a number of years ago on the streets, that would be the first thing they would have done. I was shaking inside. Then again, getting arrested was not exactly a novel experience for me, considering where I came from. I knew cops, and Miranda, and cuffs, and the back seats of cruisers well. But I was never used to it—and not at my age now. That was so long ago, and this was the FBI, not the local police. Standing in my dining room, I felt so invaded.

"You're not going to take me out of here in my pajamas," the voice that was still Libbe, and a proud woman, said. "Please, let me get changed."

"Yes, that will not be a problem," answered one of the FBI agents. "Our female agent will have to accompany you, though," he said and nodded to the woman.

The female agent stepped forward. "Ms. Siskind, this is procedure and protocol. We have to follow it."

"Okay," I reluctantly answered.

It was clear by the expression on my face that I was embarrassed and distressed. The idea of being watched brought back memories of my evil stepmother Anita insisting on being my witness every single time I went to the bathroom as a little girl. Imagine not even having the dignity of privacy for that most personal of matters. I turned around and headed for the stairs, to go up, Ms. Federal Agent on my heels to make sure that I wasn't going to escape. Ha ha…to where?

In my closet, my head swimming, I rummaged through my drawers for a pair of panties, jeans, and a sweatshirt. The agent stood in the doorway watching, an attractive young woman with porcelain skin and brown hair pulled back into a ponytail. She kept her eye on me as I yanked off my pajamas and pulled on my clothes. She knew I was no threat and not about to try anything. I could tell she liked my closet by the way she looked at it, and she said with a smile that it was like a store, with so many things everywhere.

After brushing my teeth—under the supervision of the government—I took my inhaler (my weezer), just in case nerves jump-started my occasional asthma. The agent and I went back down to the second-floor landing where everyone was still in place—Russ, who had been questioned, still stood on the stairway.

Eyes scanning the rooms around him, and not looking at me, one of the Brookline cops said, "You have a nice place here."

"Thanks," I said with a nod.

I don't know what they expected, but I was thinking they were probably surprised by my stately and well-maintained home. Even in the cold, the gardens in front were beautifully manicured. The interior boasted fine custom woodwork, nice rugs, and extensive framed movie memorabilia on the walls from the downstairs hall to all the upstairs floors. There were custom-made pink velvet Austrian shades on all the windows and a floral tapestry couch with tassels in the living room.

"This place is so clean," said the other officer.

"Yes, I like to keep a clean home."

Mr. FBI pursed his lips, nodded, and said, "Ms. Siskind, I have to put the cuffs on now."

I looked around my house, all pretty pinks and soft greens, velvet Australian shades on the windows, and the thought that my house could be misconstrued as a bordello flashed across my mind. It had that rich Victorian flair. All Victorians look just like bordellos. *If and when I get the chance,* I decided, *I will rip it all down.*

One of the officers noted that there were no mattresses around on the floor. Funny! Good joke! At first, I thought that was a crazy thing to say, then I realized why he said it. "Yes, you're right, sir. This is my home, where I live." I told them they could look around, that I had nothing to hide, but they didn't have a warrant to search so they briefly toured the house. They were in shock to see a spotless house, all in order. And I was happy that the outside of the house had just been painted a couple of years ago so that it looked perfect. At least if I go down I won't be known as a lowlife, a person living in a messy house with an unkempt exterior—I have a great deal of pride. Believe me, they would have talked about it even more if it hadn't been so orderly.

The handcuffs went on as Mr. FBI said, "Please turn around."

I had a really bad feeling, a sick-to-my-stomach feeling. "Do I have to have these on? I won't run, please, I don't want my neighbors to see me like this, please." Uncle Sam was not about to budge. My stomach churned as I glanced over at Russ, who was obviously feeling fear. I felt like throwing up.

From all my years on the streets, I knew the cuffing drill well; you never forget, even if the most recent time was twenty years ago. Now here I am again, at age fifty-one, turning my back to the man and putting my arms behind me. The cold press of metal on my wrists, then click, and the sound of a watch being wound as the bracelets constrict. I felt horrible!

"Libbe Siskind, you have the right to remain silent…" He began reciting my rights—the Miranda.

The cuffs were on so tight I felt like I had just been put under a death sentence, lightheaded, couldn't think straight, in total shock. And the questions that ran through my head were, *why me, why me, what did I do that was so bad? I am not trafficking or conspiring. My girls don't have pimps. They're not underage, they don't do drugs. Okay, calm down, Lib. What do they have on me? Who had I talked to? How did they know? I thought I was so careful!*

Russ's face was frozen. "This man is just my roommate," I told them. "He has no part in this. I don't want him in any trouble. He has no role in my affairs." As I was being ushered away, I told Russ, "Call Alan, my attorney. His number is in my phonebook by the desk."

"Libbe, sure, I'll get hold of him," Russ said. "Everything is going to be fine."

"Look after Oscar and Perrii. Don't forget the dogs!" "Yes, of course, Libbe."

"Please call my son. His number is in my phonebook too."

Walking down the stairs, I could feel the rhythm of my heart beating in my neck very fast, trying to catch up with my breath. Oh my god! I was really worried; I sensed bad, really bad things were about to happen!

The agents helped me out and put my jacket over my shoulders, hiding my cuffed wrists. With an agent on my left and the other on my right, each grasping one of my arms through the coat, we stepped out my front door into the early spring. The sun was warming up, no more than a cloud or two in the sky, temperature approximately fifty degrees, birds conversing with song, and the fragrant promise of moist and fertile earth. It was a beautiful day to be alive and a shitty day to be me and arrested. I was overwhelmed by a sense of doom that washed over me, the fear of never returning home.

So now I was out the front door and scared to death about who was going to see me. How could they not notice me with this big, puffy jacket over my shoulders, without my hands sticking through the sleeves, being escorted (no pun intended) by these men with FBI written on their jackets as large as the sun coming up? I know someone is bound to see me…shit!

As I walked across the street to their car, I glanced up to see if any neighbors were watching. The folks who lived on my street, a side street with an eclectic architectural mix of high-priced homes on small parcels of land with only twenty to thirty feet between them, were still sleeping or readying themselves for the day. I figured that with the neighborhood laid out the way it was, a resident or two must have taken in the curious, yet not unrecognizable, sight of a bust going down. With the Brookline cops trailing behind us, I was put in the FBI car, a dark blue sedan parked on the street. *Yup,* I thought, *it's like a Hollywood movie, except it's my life.*

I could not spot any neighbors at all peering out of a door or window, which brought a bit of relief. But later, I found out that they did see Mr. FBI push my head down and into the back of the vehicle.

The cuffs were cutting off the circulation to my hands.

"Can't you loosen these cuffs? They hurt. Please?"

"Just don't move or they'll pinch," said the agent.

"If I start having trouble breathing, am I going to be able to use my inhaler?"

The pretty young woman turned to me with something approaching sympathy, and as her face softened, she said, "That won't be a problem. Just tell me if you need it."

Before we drove away, the agent in the driver's seat gazed up at my house, turned to me, and said, "That's some house. What's it worth?"

He looked away, back toward the house, and rephrased the question. "What did you have to pay for this, a million dollars?"

I was silent for a moment, looked at him, and said, "No, not at all. I could never afford a million-dollar home, money down, and payments. I paid eighty-five thousand dollars, which I could afford to pay."

He laughed and said, "Eighty-five thousand dollars, yeah, right."

Yes! "I bought it in the 1980's. It was rundown and condemned. I fixed it up with my boyfriend. He was a contractor."

"So what's it worth today?"

"Conservatively, almost seven hundred thousand dollars or maybe eight hundred thousand."

I thought that would end it. Perhaps they couldn't get over what I'd told them or they thought I was lying. There are people in this world who envy what I have and probably think I don't deserve it. Guess what? I've earned every bit of it, and not the easy way either. I deserve it; yes, I do. Not only from the street and my business as a madam, but I worked hard in my legitimate businesses as well. Coming from nothing with no one to help me, if anyone deserved a home, I did. And I wished for many others to have one too. My son had a home as well, a place he would inherit at some point in the future—that was my goal. I needed to know he was safe.

It was a mostly quiet, twenty-five-minute drive from Brookline across the town line into Boston, and then through the city to the seaport south of Boston, where the federal courthouse is located. The driver again asked if I knew Ginny, and again I told him that I knew lots of people. He asked me if I had ever been to New Orleans, and I said, no, never. I had enough personal experience and had seen enough TV shows to know I should talk with my lawyer before being too generous with information. I felt smaller and smaller the closer we got to the courthouse.

A guard cleared us at a security booth about seventy-five yards from the front entrance, then we passed through to a driveway that connected to an underground garage. Suddenly, it reminded me of a visit I made in 1996 with David just before he died to a network of brothels in Panama, where you entered the motel by car, through a parking garage that had a similarly whitewashed interior and exterior. And the doors shut automatically behind the cars there, just like here. The agents walked me out of the garage and down a long hallway, then into an elevator that climbed a couple of floors.

I was a wreck, though I maintained a calm front.

And then, I met the real bad men.

U.S. Marshals, finger printers, bad cop, good cop—just like the shows on TV.

I wondered if they smiled when they left their jobs.

At this point, I took on the hard-edged demeanor of my younger self, brash and strong. *Hold tight,* I told myself, *don't say a word.*

The female agent directed me into the booking room. There were just the two of us in there. She fingerprinted me and took my picture; a horrible one, of course, worse than a driver's license one. Another agent entered and left as abruptly as he came in. She administered a strip search. The fact that she had watched me dress at the Pink House should have made it clear that there were no concealed guns, knives, grenades, drugs, or missile launchers, but procedure must be followed. Lady FBI was a little cool about it, just had me take my clothes off, then she quickly looked me up and down, front and back, and okayed me to get dressed again—again. Embarrassed but not blushing.

Then I was in a new confined space: a room with no windows. It had a rectangular table and a chair, and across from that seat were two more chairs.

"Please, take a seat, Ms. Siskind," the lady said, pointing to the chair that stood alone on one side of the table. I sat.

The agent sat across from me and placed a blue folder on the table. The female agent opened the folder and began to separate and study a stack of typewritten pages.

After watching this for fifteen seconds, I asked, "Is that all about me?"

"Most of it."

My records. What a surprise! A long time ago I had paid good money to have my records sealed. Guess what? They weren't. Another one of those incidents where the man tells you, "I will take care of it; you know how much I really like you," and, of course, all he wants to do is to go to bed with you any chance he can. A Boston cop, no less. And I paid him, too! He swore my record was sealed, said he checked several times, and even gave me an old mugshot I still have. All those people from my past needed to be closed out of my life for good, the same way I did with all my so-called friends after Dave died. I believe in life we have to close lots of doors and open new ones with not so much baggage. Set goals for what is important. Set them real high. If you don't reach the top one, it's okay to achieve smaller ones along the way.

I asked, "May I please make a phone call? When can I make it?"

"Any time you want."

"Well, please, may I make it now?"

I was escorted out of that room and across the hall to another room, dark and gloomy, where there was a phone. It was now barely eight in the morning. I hoped Russ had been able to get a hold of my attorney, but I needed to hear his voice myself. Lady FBI stood there, ever watchful, as the call was placed. The other lawyer in my attorney's office, John, answered. When he learned who it was on the other end of the line, he started talking excitedly, saying he had already spoken to Russ, and "The wheels are already rolling to have you released from custody. It may take some time, Libbe. Lots of paperwork. Please be patient." Patient…guess so. I can't go anywhere—yeah, that's a fucking joke.

That sounded good. What didn't sound good was that my attorney and his wife were away on vacation, but John was going to take on the role of legal general for the day, and Alan would be leading remotely. John was handling a number of important cases in court that morning and afternoon, but he would be sure to be on it.

"Don't worry," he said, "everything is being taken care of. Everything will be all right."

I was exploding inside. *Everything is very definitely NOT all right! I knew that!*

"Don't be difficult. Don't provide any specific information other than basic personal facts." This was the attorney's advice. I was so scared.

"No problem," I said. "Just get me out of here, please!"

I put down the receiver and the agent brought me back across the hall where I was greeted by two standing men: the agent who had cuffed me, now with his jacket off, wearing a starched, white-collared shirt and a tie, and a new guy. He was tall, at least six-one or six-two, sharp-featured, square jaw tightly clenched, with unblinking eyes that fixed cold and penetrating pupils on me. His arms were crossed above his pumped-up chest, just under the shoulder holster that held a firearm down by his hip.

"You can sit down," the marshal said. I resumed my spot in the seat I held earlier as two agents established positions across from me while one agent remained standing behind them. He loudly dragged air into his nostrils, and then asked, "What do you do for a living, Ms. Siskind?"

"Until recently, I had a store where I sold collectibles, jewelry, and antiques. But I shut it down. I mostly buy and sell just jewelry and antiques now."

"Do you own any vehicles?"

"Yes, a car."

"What kind of car?"

"Ah, it's a Volkswagen. I call it my puffer."

The agent frowns, half-incredulous, half-confused. "A puffer?"

"That's what I call her. She's a Jetta, a 1987 Jetta GL."

"Please, an explanation for 'puffer'?"

I said, "It has smoke coming out of the tailpipe, that's all."

"Do you own any other vehicles?"

"No."

"Are you sure you don't own any other vehicles?"

"Yes."

I thought that perhaps this was a trick question, and I repeated myself. "I don't own any other vehicles."

The agent can't leave it alone.

"Do you transport people in your car?"

"Well, yeah, people go with me to places sometimes." "Do you transport people across state lines?"

"No. The only things that go across state lines with me and my car are antiques."

The agent hardened his stare, narrowed his eyes, and furrowed his brow in disbelief.

"You transport *antiques* in a Jetta?"

"Yes."

"You can't load much into a Jetta."

"Oh, yes, I can. So I taught myself how to pack it in and tie things to the roof, whatever works." Time for me to shut up, I could tell. I didn't want to piss off the people who had me there against my will and under arrest. As it was, they were finding it hard to believe me. The attorney told me to only answer basic questions.

"I don't wish to be difficult, but I really would like to speak with my attorney before I answer any more questions."

The agent said, "That's your right. It would be better for you if you cooperate with us."

It sounded as though this agent might be on my side. Yeah, right; I knew otherwise.

The agent said nothing, and instead of talking he made a stern face—then turned around and walked out of the room. Lady FBI stepped up, took me by the elbow, and walked me down the hall to my holding cell, one with some kind of shatterproof glass instead of the bars I was more familiar with from "time done" many years ago.

The walls were white cement, and there was a toilet in the back corner with only a half-wall—exposed for everyone to see. "Have a seat, Ms. Siskind. It's going to take a while." As I was sitting there in the new room, hunched over, with my hands cupped over my eyes, I was thinking, *What's going to happen to me? Let me ride out this nightmare. I can't allow myself to freak out!* A shiver traveled down my spine as I recalled every moment in my childhood, teen, and adult life, all leading to the point where I was now—alone and locked inside a cold cell. Yet another instance of being "in the room."

CHAPTER TWO

A Curly-Haired Girl

"*I* was loved, me, a curly-haired girl who liked to sing and tap dance."—Libbe Leah Siskind

****

"Ms. Siskind, we will let you know when your lawyer calls." *Time... All I have is time to sit and think. There's no paper to write on, no pen to write with, so I'll just sit here and think—even though I feel like my heart is going to explode, I can't let my emotions show—go way back, back to the very beginning when my strong, inner core was just forming.*

****

I was born in Boston on November 10th, 1950, to an unmarried couple, Goldie P. and Joseph C. My mother, the daughter of Russian immigrants, and my Sicilian father put me up for adoption, and within several months, a private adoption was arranged. They both were married, but not to each other. Rose and Fred Siskind, a childless, Jewish couple, were older than conventional adoptive parents, and Rose, who suffered from diabetes and was eventually diagnosed with terminal stomach cancer, certainly wasn't an ideal choice for motherhood by today's standards. Although the adoption wasn't entirely legal, it was pushed through by Rose's cousin Sadie, who was a judge in Malden, Massachusetts. I was in a temp home until it all went through. The papers were drawn up and signed, and off I went to live with Fred and Rose in Stoneham, a small town fifteen miles north of Boston.

One of my earliest memories was when I was five years old. Rose was shaking me awake. I was having a terrible nightmare. It felt so real—the snake slowly constricting around my neck. "It's choking me—it's choking me!" I screamed, and I couldn't pull it off my throat. I was saved by my mother waking me. I was shaking, chilled to the bone, and she patted my forehead and neck with a dampened towel. She held me tight to her bosom as she whispered, "It was only a dream, nothing more. You have a little fever, Libbela...that's all. I'm here." Rose was matronly and full of love. I felt safe as long as my mother was holding me in her arms. Mommy Rose would often console me when I was scared. She protected me, and I believed she would always be there for me. The dream stayed with me, though, and throughout my life, whenever I think about it, I have difficulty swallowing. The fear of dying while choking haunts me. Especially when I eat; several times I have choked on food.

I remember only the best things about my mother, Rose. Oh, how I miss her. She doted on me. I could cry just thinking about her now. She would sit for hours and lovingly, one by one, twist my long, auburn hair into banana curls. She loved to dress me up in taffeta dresses with velvet bows and my favorite Buster Brown patent leather shoes. To this day, I am fond of black patent leather shoes and handbags. Mommy Rose signed me up for dance lessons that were held in a studio in Malden, one of the next towns over. She didn't drive, so she had a friend drive us. Because she knew how much I loved it, she made certain I had the opportunity to learn about dance and performing. When I sang, my heart poured out. Shirley Temple was my ideal performer. Mommy Rose told me I had a voice like an opera singer and promised she would take me for singing lessons soon. She wanted me to go on the TV show *Community Auditions*, a talent show that ran in the Boston area every Sunday morning from

1950 until 1987 and was revived in 2007 as *Community Auditions—Star of the Day.* My Mommy Rose praised me all the time and made me feel like a star even if I didn't have the opportunity to go on the show. I was her star.

Rose was a heavy-set woman with dark brown hair. She owned a few dresses and some housecoats, which were the kind with round balls and made from terrycloth, like the old bedspreads. I thought they were pretty back then and still do. Her nightwear consisted of long, cotton nightgowns and large slippers—at least they looked that way to me. Yes, Mommy Rose was old-fashioned, but she had a great smile, a smooth voice, and the warmest brown eyes. She was the center of my life, and I loved her. My dad, Fred, was a tractor-trailer driver for the M&M Transportation Company. He was short and balding with a powerful build and muscular arms like Popeye's. His arms were developed from working the steering wheel in a truck without power steering and by doing mechanics on the side. We were an observant Jewish family. They lit candles on Friday night, walked to temple on the Sabbath, and sent me to Sunday school, where I learned my Hebrew.

Fred had no clue about little girls. Rose knew how to dress me nicely and do up my hair. I looked forward to her gentle touch every day; I was Mommy's little girl. Fred wanted me to do boy things with him, like cutting the grass and handing him small tools. He liked doing physical labor and kept busy. I've retained the things he taught me to this day. In the basement, he had a workspace where he tinkered with things. His tools were down there, and I actually liked playing with them. I played with trucks—anything that was part of my daddy. Always organized and efficient, he also kept nuts, bolts, screws, and other little pieces of hardware in jars that he screwed into caps that were nailed into the underside of a shelf. It was a smart bit of innovation that saved space and time. It fascinated me. You would just reach up and unscrew the jar, take it down, and the lid remained in place. I recall those jars whenever I store beads and broken jewelry in containers.

My dad was handy. He built the storage units down in the basement, which we used to put things on. All the walls were knotty pine as were the built-in storage benches that went around the entire room. That wood was very popular in the fifties and gave the room a warm glow. There were navy blue vinyl cushions to sit on. He built a bar with knotty pine wainscoting, a padded vinyl top, and bar stools with chrome and padded seats that swiveled. I would climb up on the seat, lie on my belly, and twirl around until I was dizzy. There were two doors that opened into the boiler room, one was behind the bar, with a small ship's porthole in it, and the other was a solid pine door to the right of the bar. On the shelf area above the wainscoting wall was an old Emerson radio in an ivory-colored plastic case with brown knobs. There was a good-sized mirror on that wall too. I played music and would sing and dance to it, imagining that I was a star in the movies. Back then, I thought that when I grew up, I would be a professional singer, dancer, and actress. There was a small closet by the stairs, and a doorway to the laundry area where there were two sinks with deep basins. There was a bathroom to the left with a toilet and shower.

I loved watching my dad do things. He would wash his hands with Lava or castile soap in the basin sink, the grease and dirt funneling down the hole into the pipes. Yes, he was a tinkerer, and he had a brain for machinery and engines, whether car, truck, plane, or lawn mower. He was frequently under the hood of our family car, a Desoto, or other cars the neighbors brought over for him to look at. Fred was the "go-to" guy in the neighborhood to have anything with a motor or engine fixed. I don't think he ever received a dime for his labor. While working on his car in the garage, Fred would point out various components to me and explained what they did. Much of what he said was beyond my understanding, but it sunk in and never prevented him from trying to teach me. He never stopped giving me lessons in auto mechanics, and eventually, I totally understood what he was saying to me.

Fred and Rose loved me deeply. I loved my daddy, but I loved my mommy more because she touched me lovingly and was there for me every day. With Mommy Rose, I was living in the world of a girly-girl. With Fred, I would be more of a tomboy. Both were ingrained in me, and remain, in large part, aspects of my personality today.

I think, deep down, Fred wanted an attractive wife, slender, who didn't smoke. Rose was matronly in all ways. She could just sit in her kitchen and revel in cooking kosher meals and smoking her cigarettes, surrounded by neighbors and her large family, whom she would visit and invite over for the holidays. He wanted glamour, not a billowy, heavy peasant woman who looked sixty when she was forty and would always look that way. And he found the sight of the syringe injections for her diabetes unpleasant. He cared for her, and probably loved her too, but because she wasn't fashionable, he did not desire her like a man does when he is in love. She did for everybody but herself. He was mellow when he was around Rose, except for the fact that every time he'd come home from one of his truck runs, he would scream at her for smoking. If it wasn't the cigarettes, it was her weight or that the house was too dark and gloomy from the drawn curtains and dark-colored furnishings, or the kitchen was untidy because of her cooking. He thought that Rose would suddenly become who he wanted by giving up the cigarettes—a wife, not a mother; a woman, not a pillow; a fancy showpiece to hang on his arm. And Rose was the type who would just "yes" him, and he'd keep yelling. I didn't understand, so I'd hide or go upstairs and cry for my mommy. To me, she could do no wrong, and Fred's nitpicking baffled me.

Fred's job as a truck driver for M&M involved runs in New England and the Mid-Atlantic states. Most of the time, he was gone for an entire week, from Monday through Friday, and sometimes longer if he took overtime, which seemed to be always. He never failed to bring me back Hostess Cupcakes, the chocolate ones with white swirls on the top and cream centers. I ate the chocolate frosting off the top first. I can still recall the taste and texture of the sweet icing. Then I'd eat slowly around the creamy center and wait until last for that cream to melt in my mouth. Today, the cupcakes don't taste the way they did back then; the cake is dry, and the frosting is thinner. Perhaps my adult taste buds don't respond in the same way they did then. Rose could accurately estimate within an hour or so when Fred would return from his time on the road, and I would wait for him anxiously, sitting by the window in the living room, which only gave me a partial view of the street in front of our house because of the thick bushes in front of the windows. Instead, I'd go wait by the wooden front door until I saw his car drive up, then I ran to the back door to greet him. After parking, I'd pounce on him for a hug and my treat. I knew my daddy loved me—he never forgot to give me my cupcake or a hug. Mommy always told Daddy how good I was. That made him so happy. My house was full of love for me.

The house I lived in was a Cape-style Colonial with a driveway and garage. There was a short walkway that led from the front door to the driveway. The front walkway was used only when company came over. Mostly, we entered from the side walkway to the back door that went into the garage in the rear of the house, which was attached to a walkway where Mommy Rose's trellis of red American Beauty roses was—so amazing and the smell, beautiful. Inside the house, she had decorated with a mix of Colonial and Victorian furniture, runner rugs, and wall-to-wall carpets throughout. She loved antiques! In addition to vintage items, Rose liked dark-colored floral patterns and tapestries. Upstairs on antique mirrored gold trays was her personal collection of lipsticks, perfume bottles, and filigreed compacts. She had paintings and figurines, menorahs, and symbols of Judaism everywhere in the house. She was especially attached to her kosher kitchen. Downstairs was Dad's space, with the boiler flue whispering in a soothing way and his tiny workshop. He cherished the bar he had made. Above the bar was a collection of old bottles and a picture of him on the wall standing next to an airplane and wearing his pilot's wings from the war. I have kept the photograph of him with the wings all these years.

In the living room of our home was a large Victorian couch with a coffee table in front of it. There was a Philco radio and record player cabinet in the corner. It was a dark mahogany floor unit that lifted on the top left side to play old vinyl records—78's, 33⅓'s, and 45's—and underneath the cabinet were slots to store the records. I recall trying to carry a record or two, but I was small and the records were heavy. There was a long window behind the couch that looked out over the front bushes and yard, with dark curtains hanging to the sides of it. The dining room was opposite this room, and you passed through a swinging door to go from there into the kitchen. It had a linoleum floor (like so many kitchens in the 1950's), a window over the sink, a kitchen set made of metal, the chairs padded with shiny, white vinyl. The white stove had a clock built into the back panel. And there were two doors, one for the basement and another that led out to the garage.

I loved the basement; it was like being in an old knotty pine cabin. It was a happy place where my dad invited family down to have a drink at the bar he'd built. I remember his voice asking them, "A glass of Schnapps or rye and ginger?" Every inch of the house was a happy place. Dad loved his basement.

Rose had an area that adjoined the living room. She had an original Art Deco floor lamp, and above her desk hung an oil portrait of me. Rose had an artist come to our house to paint the portrait. I sat for him a couple of hours a day for weeks. The sitting was, of course, difficult and I didn't like it; it was impossible for me not to move, and I squirmed constantly. Mommy Rose never yelled at me. She would say softly, "Try to stay still, okay?"

On the landing, just before going up the stairs to the bedrooms, there was a funny little closet like the door in *Alice in Wonderland.* It was for storage and shoes and was extremely dark inside. Then you'd walk up to the second floor, where straight across there was a pink and gray tiled bathroom. And when you walked in there was a sink to the left, a tub to the right, and the toilet was near the window on the back wall.

My mom and dad's bedroom was next to the bathroom, and it was the largest room on the top floor in a house with three bedrooms. They had a double bed and dresser. There were ornate, gold trays on the top, and on them were beautiful perfume bottles (Shalimar was one) and Rose's favorite lipstick—it was made by Revlon in a dark, reddish-wine color. I can still smell the scents of the perfume and lipstick, and I have one of those lipstick tubes, given to me later in life by my mom's sister-in-law Rose. There was a fairly good-sized closet in their bedroom. The guest room had a rug and heavily patterned burgundy curtains and bedspread. There was a double bed and a tall, wooden dresser in the room that housed fancy linens and keepsakes. The dark, oversized furniture loomed large in the relatively small room.

My room was small and across from the bathroom. The twin bed was covered with all my dolls: Chatty Cathy, and my two favorites, Tiny Tears and a cloth doll from Israel that my Aunt Fanny (my dad's sister-in-law) gave me that lit up and glowed in the dark—that doll was so beautiful to me! I had an Annie Oakley outfit with brown suede fringe on the arms of the jacket. I had the entire outfit, including a holster with a gun and boot spurs. I would watch Annie Oakley on TV all the time along with *The Howdy Doody Show* with Clarabell the clown, my favorite. I also had plastic high heels with elastic straps and dresses that I would put on when I wanted to play Elizabeth Taylor or dance and sing like Shirley Temple. And there were other dolls and all sorts of toys in my room and the basement. Oh, how I loved my house and my mom and dad!

The driveway of our house was narrow and on a slight incline. At the bottom were cement lions. There was a white picket fence around the front yard, but the driveway was open. Rose's prized American Beauty roses grew on the trellises to the left of the house for everyone to see. They were her pride and joy, and I can still smell the sweet fragrance. Rose's other pride and joy, besides me, was her dog, Buddy, a cocker spaniel mix. She adored him and dad did too. I loved Buddy—he kissed me all the time!

Rose was a frugal woman. She would spend on others but not on herself. She'd bake all day and then wrap up the goodies, and walk them over to an old-age home that was less than half a mile from our house. She also read to the residents of the home, who were elderly and could not read on their own any longer. Rose loved to give. She donated all the money she saved to help build the Stoneham Temple. The congregation honored her and her contributions with a bronze tablet set on a wall in the front hallway of the temple. When I grew up and understood what that plaque meant, I felt proud that so many others appreciated her as I did. Later, I found out that the temple had closed, and the plaque had been moved to their archives.

****

As I sit in my cell, I think about my mother Rose. She passed, and then my nightmare began. Rose and Fred were in their early forties when they adopted me. Back in the 1950's, that was considered very old. Rose was diabetic even before I was born. She was afraid of giving birth. Then, when she came down with cancer, my life changed. Her decline was rapid. Now more than ever I wonder what my life would have been like if she hadn't passed away.

CHAPTER THREE

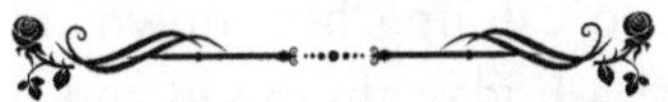

Haunting Memories

There are several memories from my childhood that stand out from the rest. I was in first grade at the Robin Hood School in Stoneham. During after-lunch recess, we went back to our classroom. A woman showed up at the school. She was very short and trim, sharply dressed, with dark hair cut in a pageboy, and sunglasses that kept me from seeing her eyes. She told the principal that she was an assistant to my dancing instructor and that she wanted to take a few photographs of me for a pamphlet for a dance rehearsal I was going to participate in. Of course, she would take the photos of me right there on the school grounds. I was called out of class, and the woman took me outside and explained what she was about to do and the reason for it, and I felt so proud! She sat me on the hood of her shiny, black car, half of which was parked directly in the sunlight. It burned my behind, and I cried out for her to get me down! "Sorry, dear," she said and placed me on the shady side of the car—gently, like she was someone I knew for a long time—then began photographing me. She didn't speak much as she clicked one photograph after another and told me my mother would be so proud of me. I don't know how she got away with it, but she did, and she was allowed to take the photos without written consent. People in the 1950's were more trusting than now; unlike today, abductions were virtually unheard of, and if they did happen, it was a rarity. When she was finished, she jumped into her car and drove away.

I was so excited! Someone wanted my picture! I couldn't wait to go home and tell that to my mommy and daddy. When I got home and told my mother, my dad was home and overheard us and became furious, swearing and ranting. Rose just sat there looking nervous. There was no calming him down. He could not call the teacher because it was a Friday afternoon and the school was closed. The only other time I heard Fred scream like that was when Rose was smoking. Even though he smoked a pipe, he hated for her to smoke. After his fury about the woman taking my pictures had subsided, my parents made phone calls and I was sent off to play. I didn't understand what was going on. Why were they so mad at that lady when she was nice to me?

Mommy Rose loved animals, and Buddy was a good dog, except for when he was running around the farms in the neighborhood. He smelled blood from the chickens on the farm and would get the heads to bring back to Rose as an offering. The farmer knew Mom and Dad, and he warned them several times to keep Buddy off his land or he would shoot him. In those days there wasn't a leash law, so Buddy was free to run to the scent. Even now, if a dog or other animal kills another animal or pet on your property, you have the right to shoot it. Of course, I wasn't aware of what territorial rights were back then. One day, the farmer did shoot Buddy. He made it all the way back to the garage door, where he lay down, bleeding. Rose ran outside when she heard Buddy yowling in pain. She was crying and told me to go into the house. I didn't know what was going on, and she told me that Buddy had to go to the doctor. But Buddy wasn't moving anymore, and his coat was drenched in blood. Rose was kissing his head and hugging his body. Why did I have to stay in the house? Mommy Rose said he had to go away because he had gotten so sick that he wouldn't be coming back. Buddy just lay there; his eyes didn't blink once. Mommy Rose had blood on her dress; she went into the house to fetch a blanket to cover him. When my dad came home, he put Buddy in his car and drove away. I didn't see Buddy after that. My mother cried and cried. I will never forget her sorrow. I was a bit shocked and didn't fully grasp what "not coming back" meant. I only cried when Mommy did. I missed Buddy.

Fred and Rose did not mention Buddy again. I knew my mom missed him; he was her shadow. As time passed, my mom got two more cocker spaniel mixes. They had to be taken together as a pair. She named one of them Buddy; I can't recall the other's name. It was not too long after that that she had to give one away. I did not understand when two people came to get the dog. Rose kept the one she had named Buddy. We loved both dogs so much. Why did we have to give one away? He wasn't hurt like our first Buddy. Rose was very upset, and again, I didn't understand what was happening. Things did not make sense anymore. The dog was not sick, or was it? Didn't my mom and dad care? Where did he go? When I asked they said not to worry and that the dog was going to a good home.

I remember that it wasn't long after the mixed spaniel was given away that Mommy found a big black raven on the front walk that couldn't fly because of an injured leg. She fixed the leg and fed the bird until it regained its strength. She kept the bird in a covered box at the back of the house for a couple of weeks or so. Then Rose said, "We have to let the bird fly now, Libbe—he has to go." I wanted to keep him. I didn't want her to let him loose. "Please," I begged. But she did, and he flew away. I really liked the shiny black raven. Mommy told me the bird was wild and didn't belong with us. I missed the bird. I felt so empty. From my point of view, it was yet another animal gone from our home. It seemed to me that once I was attached to an animal and didn't want to let it go, I had to. I wished that I would never have to give an animal up when I got older.

Rose was never a highly energetic person. She was heavy and she smoked. I knew she used to go to the doctor frequently for "check-ups." What I didn't know was that Rose had lived with diabetes for some time and was now having an unrelenting bout with stomach cancer. She wasn't a healthy person. These thoughts sadden me, thinking how I was so young and was never told all the things that were going on. When I think back, it would have been a lot easier for me if the grownups had explained what was really going on.

When I was six years old, I was introduced to the needles that Rose used to inject herself with insulin. Until that time, she kept them hidden from me. She explained that she needed extra sugar, and that she put the sugar into her body with the needle. I stared at her bruised skin. Why couldn't she eat a cupcake? She smiled and told me her skin was used to the needles and it didn't hurt, but I could tell by the strain of her facial expression that they must have pinched. At about the same time, I learned about Rose not having enough sugar, I noticed that she was getting very tired all the time and vomiting her food. She rarely went upstairs to her bedroom. She slept more, and she took a lot of naps on the couch in the living room, getting up to bring damp washcloths from the kitchen for her headaches. I was frightened and wanted to be close to her, to get hugs. When I sat next to her, she would brush my hair, but she no longer made banana curls. Her hands were weak. Sometimes she would read to me. She wasn't doting on me the way she used to, and I sensed that something wasn't right. There was a distance between us, and I needed my mommy. Daddy wasn't there, and no one came to help at first. Rose said she did not want others there.

Fred and Rose sometimes went away for the weekend, and on those weekends I would stay with the Heber family, who lived three houses down from us on the street. What I didn't know was that she was actually in a sanitarium in Stoneham, getting treatments. Grace and Al were the parents of Kate, my neighborhood friend. They were always smiling and seemed to like their martinis. I mean *loved* their martinis—with extra olives—they were always high. I really enjoyed going to their home. They had two daughters, Kate and an older sister, Mary, who, with her black hair and blue eyes, people said looked like Elizabeth Taylor. Mary would draw a black beauty mark on her face—just like Liz—and would dress like Elizabeth Taylor. I considered that actress to be the epitome of beauty, and I still do.

One day when I was over at the Heber's, Rose called Grace and told her that she was going to be home in ten minutes and that I could walk home because the gardener was there. So I headed home, anxious to see Mommy and Daddy. I didn't think anything when the gardener said hello to me because he helped tidy the yard when my dad didn't have time, probably because Dad was working too much. He was an old man who was thin and short with dirty, gnarled hands. He wore a cap on his gray hair. He asked me if I wanted him to read a story to me, and I said yes—I was excited! It didn't occur to me that he didn't have a book. He told me to come in to the garage with him so he could sit down. We walked around the garage to the back door, and he pulled it closed after we went in. A few rays of light came through the dingy window at the top of the garage door. It was dark and cold inside. As he sat on one of steps that led up to the door to the kitchen, the gardener gestured for me to sit on his lap. I sat on his lap. He didn't have a book but started to tell me a story anyway. He was pulling closer to me, and his body was leaning into mine. I started to shiver. He said it was cold in the garage and he would make me warm. Telling me everything would be okay, his hand reached for my leg. Then he eased it up under my dress and said that he was rubbing my legs to make them feel warmer. When his hand went under my panties, I panicked and told him I had to pee! "I have to go to my daddy!" I said. I told the gardener I didn't want him to put his hand there. I begged for him to stop! To *please* stop! Those were my private parts, but he did not take his hand away. He pulled me toward him even tighter, and I could not break free! I started to cry! This was not right! I was sure about that! I tried to stand, but he held me in place. He was too strong, and I couldn't get away. I was terrified! But he seemed to like it and had a weird smile on his face. He told me that if I said anything to anyone, my mom and dad would die, and it would be my fault. Then I would be all alone. I was so frightened that something was going to happen to my mommy and daddy that I sat there quietly as he touched me with his rough fingers, rubbing me so badly that it hurt!

Then I heard my parents' car coming into the driveway. The gardener let go of me. My panties were stuck between my private parts, and I ran out the back door to the walkway and over to the driver's side of the car even before my mom and dad got out. I could feel the cold on my skin underneath my dress where my panties were crooked. I was crying, "Daddy, Daddy…" Rose and Fred quickly got out of the car. They had their arms around me, and Rose told me to calm down. "What's the matter?" she asked me. "We're home now. Were you scared?" Again she asked me what the matter was, and although I was reluctant, I knew my mommy wouldn't be angry with me and I told her about the gardener and what he did. Mommy Rose quickly took me inside the house. My dad stayed outside for a while talking to the gardener, asking him questions. My mom was upset and crying. She called my father's sister, who was also named Rose. Aunt Rose rushed over, and she and Mommy Rose got into a discussion. Both of them asked me about what the gardener did. Still afraid to speak, I managed to tell them again. My dad got involved in the conversation. I never understood why Fred had questions about whether I was telling the truth. Why would I lie? My mom and aunt didn't seem to doubt me. And that was the last I saw of the gardener. Even with the gardener gone, I was afraid and I never wanted to go inside the garage again—it was not a happy place anymore. Maybe he would come back, hide in the garage, and take me away! My mom and my Aunt Rose believed me but, as he told Mom, when Dad confronted the gardener, the man denied it. My dad told Mommy that he had known the gardener and his family for years, and he didn't believe that the man would do such a thing. A long time afterward, Dad still would bring up the subject and how he could not believe that the old gardener did what I said that he had done. I always wondered why my father didn't believe me. Why would I make up a story like that?

I remember the drives in the car when Daddy came home. He would put me on his lap and let me steer the car. Those were good times—I loved driving with my daddy. Mom, Dad, Buddy, and I would take a drive in the car to get an ice cream cone. Mommy Rose couldn't go out much now because she would become car sick sometimes on long drives to visit family. She was getting sicker by the day. I didn't know what to do to help her feel better except to sit with her as she lay on the couch. Mom wasn't holding her food down at all now and was throwing up all the time. She was going to see the doctors constantly. I remember it all so clearly.

Once, Daddy said Mommy had to go to the hospital to get better. There was a storm brewing, the dark clouds hanging heavily in the ominous sky. My dad told me to stay in my room and not to go near the windows. I remembered long ago when I was really little, about four years old, a huge hurricane with ferocious winds hit. I could hear the sound of the wind howling and the shutters banging against the house. I was so frightened, but Mommy held me while I was shaking—a relief—and it seemed to take a long time before Dad came in and took us to the safety of the basement. I didn't know at the time what he was doing outside, but afterward, it was obvious that he was trying to secure the house. The whole house above us seemed to shake. When the storm had gone, it left a chaotic scene behind. The awnings were ripped off and the shutters were hanging by a thread. The trees had splintered and some were completely down. This was the first time I'd experienced a hurricane. Until this one, there were rainstorms—none as bad as when I was really little… but Mommy was there then. Mommy Rose was not there this time, but my daddy was there for me. There weren't many bad times when we were all together, but we were not all together as much anymore, and lots of bad things were happening.

I longed for the spring and summer when Mommy Rose and I would sit outside in the sun eating lunch. Her roses meant the world to her, and she cared for them with a gentle touch, watering and feeding them the way a mother cares for a baby. She would cut them and put them in water to decorate the indoors with their beauty. I recall breathing in their scent and feeling the velvety petals with my fingers.

Mommy was absent from the house more and more often. Where was the hospital she went to? And why couldn't I go? I began staying a few days a week with Aunt Fanny, my dad's sister-in-law, and at Aunt Eva's, my dad's sister. Aunt Eva had an apartment on Beacon Street in Brookline. The building had a gilded birdcage elevator and a neon sign outside. Inside the apartment, there was dark wainscoting and shiny, dark hardwood floors. The contrast between the dark wood and ivory walls was dramatic, unlike in our house where the sameness of the dark walls could be dreary. Aunt Eva had a Jean Harlow wardrobe, and I would try on her sparkly costume jewelry and satin dresses, dreaming that someday I would have all of that too. The way the light played off the rhinestone earrings and bracelets fascinated me, as baubles and beads still do, though Aunt Eva didn't wear only costume jewelry but had a collection of real diamond jewelry she wore as well. Mommy Rose was far too conservative to flaunt herself wearing a wardrobe like Aunt Eva's.

Aunt Fanny was a good cook and made delicious mohn cookies, and my Aunt Rose and Uncle Uggie were my favorite relatives. Uncle Uggie was Aunt Rose's husband, my mom's brother, and I always liked staying with them because playing with Aunt Rose was like playing with a friend my own age. She appreciated children. Aunt Rose would come over to our house to help out Mommy Rose; when she was feeling ill she hardly got up. She was coming over more often, and that was okay with me, but it was only because my mom wasn't feeling well enough to come home as often. Aunt Rose would call me Little Lizzie or Lizzie Tish. After a while, I ended up at Auntie Rose's house. She would cut out paper dolls with me, and we colored them in together. The dining room hutch at Aunt Rose's house had drawers that were filled with paper dolls, real dolls, toy figures, games, marbles, gimp, yarn, and all sorts of craft materials. Aunt Rose and Uncle Uggie loved me as if I was their own; at least that's how I felt when I was with them. They used to say to Mommy that they should take me to live with them, and Mommy would answer, "No, she stays here with me." I didn't know until later that Uncle Uggie's son Les had wanted to adopt me first, even before my mommy did. There have been moments when I have wished he had adopted me considering all that I suffered as a result of Mommy's premature passing. But I would not ever want to change having had Mommy Rose in my life as my mom, as short as that time was.

Mommy went away again, this time for longer than all the other times. Aunt Rose took care of me either at our house or at her house in Newton. She treated me with great care and kindness, as did Uncle Uggie. Aunt Rose would tell me stories and hold me, but it wasn't enough to quell the ache in my heart. I wanted my mommy. Where was she? And where was my daddy?

Mommy was not home at all, and we didn't speak on the phone. Days would go by without her. Our house felt empty, and I felt lonely. Dad was taking off time from driving his truck, but he didn't stay home with me. He didn't bring cupcakes for me anymore. Then Mommy finally came back to the house for a couple of days, and I went home to be with her. Oh, how I had missed her! Her stomach was round and bigger so that it protruded. I could tell she was in pain because she expressed it. A man came by to take away Buddy while Mommy was home, and she cried and held him, but finally had to let him go. Tears fell from my eyes and dropped on my cheeks. "No, please, don't take him away too, please!" I protested, but nothing worked. I didn't want another dog to be taken away! I cried so hard I couldn't breathe! All our dogs were gone now—and Mommy would be gone soon too. The dogs paled in comparison to Mommy.

Aunt Rose told me that Mommy Rose had to stay in a house down the street by the water and that we could go there to visit her soon. This time she would not be coming home, ever again. My mom was the center of my life. I was feeling so lost inside that I stopped eating. I was taken to a doctor who said to give me what I liked to eat regardless of what it was to make sure I had food in my stomach. I was missing my mommy, my dad, and my dog—that was a lot! I was overcome with sadness. Finally, one night my Aunt Rose told me that when Daddy went on the road she would sneak me in to see Mommy. I was so excited that I actually wanted my dad to go back to work!

Children were not allowed to go inside the sanitarium, the building I called the "white house," but Aunt Rose was going to break the rules. I didn't know why Mommy would want to live there and so I asked Aunt Rose, who answered that Mommy's stomach hurt her and she had to stay there until she got better. I begged Aunt Rose to tell me when Mommy would be coming home, and every time I asked she answered, "I don't know, Libbela, I don't know." And then the night came when we went to see Mommy Rose. I couldn't stop fidgeting in my seat. We drove for only a short time, and when we arrived at the huge, white Victorian home and got out of the car, I saw that we were across from Spot Pond in Stoneham, near the zoo. It was dark out—and it was gloomy. The house looked scary—and the facade of the white house was foreboding. Aunt Rose was a big woman, and she wore a large mink coat that almost touched the floor. She concealed me inside the coat as she opened the front door. I held close to Aunt Rose's leg as we shuffled down the hallway. I looked down and could see the wood floor moving past. Someone said hello. Then Aunt Rose opened her coat a bit and I saw a hallway with several wooden doors to each side, and a window at the end of the hall. We kept shuffling, and as we turned to the left, there was a large door with a brown doorknob. Aunt Rose opened the door and we went into the room. There was an unpleasant odor I had never smelled before. I never knew death smells until much later in my life.

Aunt Rose opened her coat again, and in front of me I saw a white sheet hanging from a chrome pole curving from the ceiling in an "L" shape. Aunt Rose pushed the sheet aside and there was Mommy! I sprang over to her without a care in the world. "Careful," Aunt Rose told me. "Be careful." Mommy Rose hugged me hard, and tears rolled down both of our cheeks. "Libbela," she said, "I missed you so!" I gave her the drawing of a clown I had made. I loved to draw. Mommy smiled and said she would hang up the drawing and keep it forever. "Mommy, I miss you! Are you coming home tonight?" "No, not tonight," she replied, gasping with every breath. Then she hugged me again and held on. Mommy smelled different, not like the musky Chanel perfume she normally wore or the Shalimar she dabbed on her wrists for the holidays to smell sweet.

Mommy Rose had a hard time sitting up and Aunt Rose helped her. I looked around this all-white room with its sheets, walls, and tall windows that showed the darkness outside. There weren't many lights on, and it was dim and bleak inside too. I could feel the queasiness of a different fear in the pit of my stomach. I asked Mommy if I could stay with her in her room and she said no. She said she would be seeing me soon and for me to do what Aunt Rose told me to do, that I had to be at home and go to school, and do what Daddy says too. "Okay, I will." Aunt Rose said the nurse would be stopping by the room soon and that we had to leave before she returned. Mommy said something to Aunt Rose about me getting her diamond ring and all her jewelry. I didn't know why she said that. Mommy and I kissed and hugged. We cried as we said our "See you soon"s. Even then, as a young child, I sensed that something was terribly wrong. Was I ever going to see her again? Was this her new home? I was scared to death.

We left quickly and skipped down the white hospital corridor. As Aunt Rose and I got in her car and drove away from the house, I looked back to see if I could locate the window of my mom's room. I watched the house until I couldn't see it anymore. The sheer size of the house inspired awe, yet at the same time instilled fear. Later in life, I understood that sanitariums were places where terminal patients spent their last days. Whenever I watched movies about sanitariums for the terminally ill or the mentally ill, I would think about my mother lying there in her bed, surrounded by white sheets and waiting to die. How horrible it is to be alone and have no one to be there to hold you until your last breath.

Aunt Rose drove us back to our house in Stoneham. We weren't far from Mommy at all. Auntie Rose said we were going there rather than to her apartment because she wanted to be closer to Mommy Rose and school. I was so sleepy. Auntie Rose gave me a bubble bath and told me funny stories. I asked her when Mommy was coming home. She seemed like she didn't want to answer my question. Instead, she asked me, "Are you happy now that you know where your mommy is and that you got to see her?" I was happy that I was able to see my mother, but seeing her wasn't enough. I told her yes, but I wanted Mommy home, and it had been such a long time since she had been here that I didn't even care if she stayed on the downstairs couch forever—just as long as she was home with me. Auntie Rose helped me into my pajamas, and I knelt to say my usual prayer. "Now I lay me down to sleep, I pray the Lord my soul to keep. Please, God, teach me how to pray, and make me better every day. Amen." I asked Auntie Rose why I said a prayer, and she answered that it was to keep me safe. She had tears in her eyes, not what you call "happy tears," like when something I did was cute or we went to a bar mitzvah. On this day, she hugged me close to her and looked at me lovingly but with tears of sorrow.

Days later, I came home from school and found that there were cars in the driveway, in front of our house, and lined up all the way down the street. We never had company over this early, usually just on the Jewish holidays. There were cars that looked familiar because they were close family. My aunts, Rose, Fanny, and Eva, were there at the door to greet me. Everyone wore black. Their eyes were red and swollen, and they carried hankies in their hands. As I walked farther inside, I saw that the mirrors and pictures were covered with stark white sheets, just like the ones around Mommy's hospital bed. Some people were crying; others were eating the food set out in the kitchen and on the dining room table. If it were a holiday then people wouldn't be crying. Dad was crying and blowing his nose so hard that it sounded like a horn. I asked, "Where's Mommy?" and a hush came over the room.

Aunt Rose came over and held me tightly, crying "Oh, my Libbela," but I wanted my daddy. Daddy stood by my side and held my hand. "Is Mommy coming home?" I asked, and he said, "No, Libbe, she can't come home." The house and all the family and guests were scaring me, and I didn't want Daddy to let go. I looked around and did not understand, nor did anyone tell me why the sheets were up. It was almost quiet, just a couple of background voices. Strange people were coming to the house, and now there was an inordinate amount of whispering. Aunt Rose took me upstairs to my room, and Daddy followed to sit with me, bringing a paper plate with some goodies. I wasn't hungry. I was curious and frightened.

What else was going to change now that so much was different? When Mommy Rose comes back it will be okay, and not until then. But Mommy Rose was never coming home—that's what they told me. Both Daddy and Aunt Rose said she was gone. Gone to heaven! Shocked and confused, I sat and cried with my Auntie Rose. Daddy left, sobbing.

Aunt Rose was always close to me for the next week or two, and would speak about how good Mommy was, and that if I looked up at the night sky I would be able to see her because she was the biggest and brightest star. I said I understood what she was saying, but I really didn't. What did she mean when she said Mommy was the brightest star in the sky? Mommy always said I was the biggest, brightest star—now she is? I already knew how good my mommy was. I saw her in the white house. How did she leave there? And why?

I cried, and asked, "Mommy doesn't love me anymore—is that why she went away?"

"No, no, Libbe, God had to take her away. Your mother will love you forever," Auntie Rose said. "Don't worry, Auntie Rose will be here. I will always be near." "But why did He do that?" I asked. "Please…can you take me to see her again? Please? Please?" *Gone* did not register to me, and God taking her really made no sense.

I wanted my mommy, and would look at the sky every night for her star, and believed it was her. So I talked to her, asking her when she would come down and come home. I cried myself to sleep, begging Mommy Rose to please come home. I asked God to please give Mommy back, but hollow silence followed. "We all go to heaven when we become too old or sick," Auntie Rose told me.

I was told that Daddy was not home because he needed to find someone to take care of me. He told me I had to stay in school and behave for my aunts. Sadly, my aunts could not stay all the time and Daddy had to find someone. He told me there would be a lady and her little boy staying here when he was at work. Finally, both he and Aunt Rose sat me down and told me bluntly, without tears, that my mom had died and that she was laid to rest in Sharon Cemetery. I couldn't grasp it. I did not understand what death was. No one had ever explained death to me. Mommy had told me that when animals died, they went to heaven and didn't come back. That's where Buddy was. So now I believed that she was in heaven too. I had seen her alive for the last time at the white house. But she said that she would see me soon, and she never broke her promises—but this time she had no choice. Mommy may be the biggest star in the sky, but she will be back. I believed that. I had to believe that. I did not want to understand death. I believed she could see me from heaven. "Come home, Mommy, please! I love you and miss you!" I cried and begged her all the time.

I was not doing well. I did not eat, talk, or play much. I was taken to doctors and psychologists. Everyone seemed to be so worried about me. I was just sad and missing my mommy. When Mommy comes home, I will be okay. No more dogs, Daddy said. There wasn't enough time or anyone to care for them. I felt as though my world was empty. Auntie Rose told me to pray, and that if I prayed hard enough, my prayers would come true. All the things in my life that I loved were going away. My mother had been the one to keep me warm and safe from harm, and now I was alone, adrift. The fear of abandonment was new to me. Would everyone else I loved leave me? Dad remained, and Auntie Rose and Uncle Uggie. I did pray, but nothing changed.

The new lady finally came to the house. She was a "colored" lady, as black people were called back then; that was how my father described her to me. Her name was Mrs. Talbet and she would be my nanny. Mrs. Talbet had a little boy named Michael, who was two years younger than me. She was heavy-set and happy like Mommy Rose. Sometimes I felt like my mommy was back at home when I was with her. She was an exceptionally good cook, and I began to eat more. I looked forward to her baking cakes and rolls—the house smelled warm and inviting like it used to. She held me the same way Mommy Rose did, and I loved her. Michael and I were best friends, and it was like having a brother. We were so happy! Daddy came home on Friday evenings and stayed until Sunday afternoon. During that short period, Mrs. Talbet and Michael went to their own home, and I missed them terribly. When they came back on Sunday afternoon, it wasn't soon enough for me. When Daddy came home on Fridays, he brought chocolate Hostess Cupcakes for me and Michael, who looked forward to Daddy coming home too. Mrs. Talbet often talked about my mommy in such a comforting way that I would feel safer after she did. Together, we would look at photos of Mommy and me. It was almost as if Mommy was home with us and had never left.

****

To this day, I still ache inside when I think about her, especially at times when I am in dire circumstances such as I am now, sitting in jail waiting to be released. I still ask for her help.

****

I was getting used to my nanny and I loved her so. Mrs. Talbet read books to us. She talked with me and listened to what I had to say. She encouraged me to speak about Mommy all the time and didn't avoid my questions like everyone else did. She explained what happens when someone dies. Aunt Rose had also spoken to me about death, but not in the same way. Nanny said Mommy was a spirit in heaven and could not come back to me. She was the brightest star and a spirit, but what was heaven? Mrs. Talbet said that a lot of good people went there if they had been very sick and could not come back because God needed them more. Heaven was for good people. I hoped God loved her as much as I did. Missing Mommy was natural, Nanny said, and Mommy would have been with me if she could. I did not have to be afraid now because my nanny was here with me. Her son and I would eat, play, and even take baths together with our toy boats in the water. I was happy again. We were a family now. I wished that Daddy would marry Mrs. Talbet. I watched Nanny as she lovingly took care of my mommy's belongings, cleaning her perfume bottles and dusting her pictures. When Nanny sang, it was so soothing.

Mrs. Talbet's son slept with her in the guest bedroom. I slept in my room, holding Tiny Tears, with one of Mommy's bathrobes tucked beneath my head; Nanny told me it would help me sleep, and it did. Just when I thought everything was okay, the heavens opened up and dark clouds suddenly appeared. Daddy told me that my nanny was leaving and a new one was coming. "I want my nanny!" I protested. I was angry! "Mommy left, and now you're taking Nanny Talbet and Michael away! Why?" I screamed and cried, took a fit. "I want my nanny!" The resentment I felt toward my daddy bordered on hate. I wanted to leave with her and never come back. I later learned that Nanny had to leave after Mrs. Broder from next door told my daddy that the colored lady was giving her son a bath, naked, in the same tub with me, and that my father ought to investigate because it was not proper. My dad fired her on account of that prejudiced, spiteful neighbor and I never saw my nanny again—I was devastated. My hurt turned into fear, and I hated that neighbor. Later, I learned that the real reason had been race! My bleak future began when my dad hired an older white lady, a haggard-looking woman, to take care of me in Nanny's place.

The new white lady was skinny, smoked cigarettes, coughed, and had a raspy voice. I cannot remember her name. Today, I would describe her as trailer park trash. She was weird and scary-looking—no smiles and stern as stone. Dad said she was good and to behave. He was losing his patience with me and my questions about where Nanny Talbet was. Why didn't he give me to Aunt Rose and Uncle Uggie? He had nobody to watch me now, and so she was hired. She didn't read to me, she didn't cook, and she didn't clean. She stunk of cigarette smoke. I hated her. I wanted my nanny back, and I missed Michael. She watched TV all the time and spoke loudly on the phone, sitting at the very desk where my mother took her calls. I wasn't allowed to talk to her at all. She cooked only hot dogs for lunch and supper, and she never made breakfast, just gave me a bowl and a spoon for Kellogg's Frosted Flakes cereal. She was boorish and crude. I told my dad I didn't like her, but he said that she had to stay because he had to work and there wasn't anyone else to watch me. I wasn't eating again. I wasn't getting cared for. My hair went unwashed, and she constantly yelled at me to go to my room. She took my soft blanket for herself and replaced it with a woolen one she took from the linen closet, one that I couldn't use because I was allergic to wool. I would curl up in Mommy's robe with a sheet and a bedspread. But then, she took away Mommy's robe! Nanny had told me it would help me to sleep! She said I wasn't a baby anymore. I hated her! I was back at the psychiatrist's office again. I wanted to run away to find Nanny Talbet, but I didn't know where she lived.

One day, the white so-called nanny put me in the bathtub and pushed me in the water so that I slipped and banged my back and head on the faucet. I was bleeding, and she took me to the local doctor. The doctor was concerned and talked to my dad. She covered it up by saying I had pushed *her* in the tub, and that she got hurt when she tried to lift herself, and then I fell when I tried to help her. Such lies! She sued my daddy because she said I was at fault. The lady lost her lawsuit. I told my dad what had really happened in the tub and that I was the one who was hurt, not her. I was glad the mean lady would not be back. I wanted my first nanny, I begged him, "Please!" But Dad said she had another job. I think he was probably embarrassed to ask her to come back now. Had she stayed on, I would have had a brother and a good life. She would have been like a mom to me. I stayed upset with my dad over that.

Then Daddy broke the news that he had an old friend he knew before Mommy and that she might want to come live with us and be my new mom. "No, I hate you! I don't want anyone except Mommy Rose or Nanny Talbet!" I prayed to my star in heaven, *Why is Daddy saying he's getting me another mommy? Please, God, I want* my *mommy back!* There was only a deafening silence. The next surprise was about to come, and so for a short time my aunts watched me. What would happen to me this time? It was clear to me later that my dad had no idea what he was doing when it came to taking care of a child. Aunt Rose told me, "Libbe, try it. She may be a nice lady, and I'll be here if you need me…" That's what she said, but the truth was she didn't want to take me in. I would have loved to be with her son Bobby, but although we got along really well, he was too busy to take me in. And being adopted by Bobby's older brother Les at the time of my birth, when he wanted me, would have averted in the first place the tragedy that was about to occur.

CHAPTER FOUR

Haircut

I was only seven years old and growing up fast. My fears seemed to make me more aware. The trust I had in people was a given until my experiences with the gardener and the bad nanny. After that, I became aware of everyone and everything around me because I felt so alone. At school, the children I considered my friends were making fun of me and getting me into trouble. During class I was inattentive and distractible, easily misled by the other children, and the teacher constantly had to tell me to pay attention. Concentrating on my schoolwork was nearly impossible. I was starved for the kind of attention and approval I had once gotten from Mommy Rose.

Dad and I went for a drive from Stoneham to Boston, where I had only been a few times before. We were on Newbury Street, he said. It was, and remains today, an upscale area for the wealthy with brick and stone buildings, galleries, salons, and high-end shops. Even back then it was a busy street; there were cars, trolleys, and people everywhere. Dad parked the car. He opened the door, and held my hand as he helped me out. "I can't park here long," he said. I looked up at a stone building maybe three or more stories high with a large picture window shaped like a half-moon. It was so impressive and beautiful that I never forgot it, but little did I know that the Devil was waiting up there for me—the beginning of an uncertain existence, a dark life, without any means of escape or turning back.

My dad held my hand the entire time, and I held his back, not wanting to let go. This was all new for me. I had not been the same girl since Mommy Rose died. My banana curls were droopy now, and my hair was unkempt. My clothes did not look or feel the same, and Daddy didn't know how to put them together. I was frail and timid. We walked up the sidewalk to the front door of the building; it was such a big, fancy front door! We went into the hallway to an elevator that was bigger than Aunt Eva's in Brookline. It opened like an accordion instead of like the wrought iron door in her building. We entered the elevator, and the door behind us clanked shut—a bit scary. Dad pushed the round button and off we went. I listened to the clanking and groaning sounds as we went upward. Then the elevator stopped, and since it was not level with the outside floor, I was too frightened to step near it. Dad needed to lift me out so I wouldn't trip on the edge. We went down the hallway that led to the door of a beauty salon, which was the room with the curved window I had seen from the sidewalk. I held Daddy's hand tighter now, and we went in. There was a strong smell, a mixture of perfume, hair-spray, and other malodorous chemicals I was not familiar with. It was unpleasant.

A woman with a fancy dress was approaching. She had bluish-gray hair and cat eye Lucite-framed glasses with glittery jewels sparkling on the edges like Aunt Eva's costume jewelry. Her dress was a pearl gray color with thick, wide straps at the shoulders, and tight at the waist. She had on pearls and high heels. She looked like my aunts did when they went to a bar mitzvah or some other special occasion. Dad was so happy to see her; he let go of my hand and went to her. She gave him a peck on the cheek and they hugged briefly. I was feeling left out and abandoned, standing there alone. I could tell he was pleased to see her.

Daddy turned to me. Standing so still and feeling outnumbered and unsure at that moment, my stomach felt queasy. I sensed something about her and wanted to run away. He said, "Libbe, say hello to Anita." I looked up at him and then to her, and paused. Her eyes looked evil even though she was smiling at me. Her smile was crooked, not like the smiles of Auntie Rose and my other aunts; those were warm smiles that lit up a room. Daddy repeated, "Libbe, say hello to Anita…please?"

Softly, I said hello and stepped behind Daddy, who was encouraging me to come back in front of him. I was ready to go now, but Daddy was talking to her, not budging an inch. I guessed he was not pleased with my reticence. This was my introduction to Anita to see how we would get along, and I hoped I wouldn't have to see her again. I didn't want the lady talking to Daddy anyway—he belonged to my mommy, always.

Then, out of nowhere, Daddy said, "Libbe, I have to move the car and I'm going to leave you here with Anita for a while. Daddy has an appointment to go to, and it's very important. You and Anita can become friends while I'm gone."

"No, no, Daddy! I want to go with you! I don't want to stay here with the lady! No, please, Daddy!" I was having a full-blown temper tantrum.

Daddy grasped my shoulder with his outstretched arm to keep me from going with him, and Anita was trying to get my hand so that she could hold on to me. I pulled away. "Stop, Libbe," Daddy said, "behave yourself."

"Please, don't leave me! I want to go!" I pleaded with tears streaming down my face. "Daddy, you can't go! I don't know where I am! I don't want you to leave me! Mommy's gone away and now you're leaving me with this strange lady!"

He turned, and with a frown on his face said, "Libbe, please… stop!" and walked out the door. When I went to go after him, Anita took me firmly by the arm. Her hand gripped me tightly, and I turned with her. I wrenched my arm away and ran to the window, where I saw Daddy standing on the busy sidewalk below. I became quiet and still. I didn't want to stay, but where could I go? I didn't know where I was, and the lady scared me. She was like the bad witch from *The Wizard of Oz.*

Anita asked me questions about school and my mommy, but I didn't answer. She asked me if I wanted to look pretty for my daddy when he came back, and she told me she could brush and curl my hair. Quickly, I remarked, "Only my mommy makes me Shirley

Temple curls. I am going to tap dance just like her one day." Anita said she could do the same curls and, pulling my hand tightly, she brought me over to the chair. She put me in the chair and raised it up high to see in the mirror. She wrapped a robe around me that hugged my neck a bit too tightly. I squirmed to try and get down; it reminded me of the snake coiled around my neck in my dream. The silky robe covered my entire body. Anita was intent upon doing what she wanted to do. "Sit still or you will fall down and hurt yourself." She took a brush to untangle my hair, and as she brushed, I felt tugging at the nape of my neck. I thought she was giving my hair a good brushing, but as I soon learned, she was doing more than just taking the knots out—I couldn't see behind me that she was cutting it off in clumps! I saw the scissors behind me, and could feel something was different about my head, like a breeze around my neck. "Stay still, Libbe, or all your hair will be off," she said. I started to cry and tried to put my hands back to touch my hair. Anita pushed them down and kept cutting the back and then started on one side. She stopped and looked at me, saying, "You want me to stop? You'll look funny and everyone will laugh at you. I am doing this for you; this is what's in style."

I pleaded, "Please, give me back my hair!" I was crying so hard I could barely speak or breathe. My hair was disappearing! She held me tight to the chair as she turned it to cut off the rest of my hair. I felt exposed as if I was no longer myself. The lady, Daddy's friend, had cut off all my hair—all of my hair! *She is evil,* I thought. She cut it to the tops of my ears. She was a witch; I knew it all along. The haircut was called a pixie cut, she said. This was not a good beginning. My eyes were red and burned from crying. There was another lady hairdresser who saw my hair on the floor and said, "Oh, dear. This is your first haircut. You'll be okay, honey, it'll grow back." They were both against me. I cried so much I felt breathless.

I had no hair left. Anita had cut off the hair Mommy Rose loved so much. *I hate this lady*! I said to myself, but when I looked up at her from the chair, what I felt was fear. I was scared to death of her, scared of her face and eyes. Since that time, I have experienced anxiety whenever I have my hair cut, worrying that the hairdresser will cut off more than I want and leave me with short hair. And believe me, scissor-happy hairdressers have happened several times in my life. I often cut my own hair when it's needed.

Daddy had been gone for what seemed to be a very long time. Why isn't he here to take me away? I looked at the mirror to see myself and was sinking in the chair. While she was cleaning off my neck, she poked my shoulder to sit up straight. She pulled the long, silky cover off, and when I started to get away from her she said to wait, that the chair was up too high. Oh, she cared? She lowered it, and I climbed down as she took off the kids' seat.

****

I wanted to be as far away from there as possible, just like I want to escape from the cell where I now find myself. I don't want to be here, I want to go home.

****

I huddled over by the crescent window. Tears silently fell from my eyes and dropped off my face like a waterfall. Anita asked me if I felt hungry. I shook my head no, my hair short, wet, and matted to my head, my face damp with tears. I wouldn't eat her food—I couldn't stand looking at her. No, even though I was hungry, I'd rather starve than eat her food. The back of my neck was itchy and cold. *Oh, Mommy Rose, where are you? I miss you, I wish you were here, please come get me!* I repeated over and over to myself.

It was late afternoon, and I looked out the window at the dimming sky. Daddy was still gone. Maybe he was not coming back either. My insides felt so sick. Anita tried to talk to me, asking lots of questions, but I had my hands at the bottom of my neck, feeling for the hair that was no longer there, tears still trickling down my cheeks. I tried not to listen to her voice. I didn't want to turn around and look at her; she made me so uncomfortable. She got busy with customers, and I was so relieved she didn't have time for me. Then Daddy finally came through the doorway and walked into the salon.

I ran from the couch to him. He was stunned. "Oh, god, what did you do?" he asked me. "I didn't do anything, Daddy. She cut my hair off! She did it!" I said. Angrily, he turned to Anita. "Why did you do that without my permission?" I was crying again and trying desperately to hold onto his hand, but he had raised his voice and was moving about and gesturing with his arms flailing.

Anita, as cool as a cucumber, told Daddy that I had wanted a new haircut. "Didn't you?" she asked me. I didn't reply. "Freddy, this is the style all the young girls wear."

I just stood there, frightened, close to his side, watching as he completely ignored me. He kept talking to her, and Daddy went from being super angry with her to being awfully nice. She had gotten him to believe that I wanted a new hairstyle. I didn't want it at all. Couldn't he see my eyes? I hadn't stopped crying.

Finally, Daddy said, "You will get used to it, Libbe. Stop fussing." I was very confused. It was time to go. Dead silence came over me. He told me to say goodbye to Anita and thank her for my new haircut. I did not want to. I lifted my hand to make a short wave without saying a word. Why would I thank her? Not even wanting to look in her direction, I turned my head away to ignore her. My dad took my hand and said, "Libbe, that was not nice, not saying goodbye to Anita. She was nice to you."

I said, "No, Daddy, she was mean to me! She cut off my hair and pulled my arm and neck! I didn't want her to cut my hair! Mommy wouldn't have cut my hair. I don't like my hair now! I don't want anyone to see me!"

Daddy said, "Please, Libbe, Mommy's not here anymore. Anita did that because she knows the latest look, and this is a better hairstyle for you." Tears filled my eyes. I was defeated. I did not look "better." I was skinny and looked weird!

I knew then that I had no right to speak anymore—Dad listened to her, not me. *I hope I never see her again,* I thought. I hated my hair and I hated her. Everyone at school made fun of me now and called me "Siskinitis," as if I were a contagious germ. I was ashamed of myself. No one knew how to dress me, and making friends was difficult enough as it was. I wasn't the confident little girl Mommy

Rose had as a daughter. My spirit had been broken and my confidence was completely gone. When I awoke the day after Anita cut my hair, I had forgotten all about it until I felt the coolness of the pillow on my neck, not the warmth of my curls on Mommy's robe. (I had reclaimed the robe as soon as the lady who pushed me in the tub left.) It wasn't the worst thing Anita ever did to me, but it was the first bad thing she did to me. I was being shuffled from aunt to aunt, had nannies and sitters, and to me, a child with no sense of the future, it seemed like such a vicious thing to do. Mommy Rose had kept my banana curls so beautifully wrapped around her fingers. She would tell me how much she loved me and what beautiful hair I had. And now it's all been cut off because of Anita the Witch.

My Aunt Rose suggested to my father that I go to a hypnotist to see if they could help me with the great loss of my mother. She set it up, but Freddy did not want to go, so Auntie Rose took me there. I was scared, and when we got to an old building in Boston, she said we were there. Inside, a lady greeted us and we went into a huge, dark room with long, heavy drapes pulled closed. Mommy Rose would have loved them. The furniture in his office and the reception area was all oversized antiques. As I look back, I can see in my mind how beautiful it was, but then, the room scared me. The doctor hypnotized me not just that one time, but during several visits back there. I never could remember what difference it made, but Auntie Rose said it helped a lot. Well, I will never forget that dark, vintage room.

CHAPTER FIVE

Surprise!

Shit, I wish I could skip this part of my thoughts, but it's my past and memories can't hurt me. Little did I know that Anita was in my life to stay. Even if someone had given me advanced warning, the shock would have been the same. It wasn't too long before my dad sat me down to tell me that he was going to marry Anita, the lady who had cut off my hair, twisted my arm, and choked me with the nylon cape. And she was the one who would take care of me. "No, Daddy!" I pleaded. "I'll run away!" Then I asked him, "Don't you love Mommy? Don't you?"

Daddy's reply was, "Yes, I loved your mother, but she's gone now and can't come back." I was hysterical. My dad had to call Aunt Rose to help me understand. I tried to tell Daddy I was frightened of that mean lady, but he kept saying that her cutting my hair was in my best interests because that was the current style and easy to care for. Dad said the haircut was in style because Anita said it was, and he took her word for it. Auntie Rose pointed out that I had beautiful hair and asked why anyone would cut it so short? At least *she* was on my side.

I was staying here and there until Daddy got married. I missed having my own room, surrounded by my toys and dolls. He got in touch with the Jewish Family and Children's Services to get me some psychological help and to refer me to temporary homes, but while he was waiting he had to work, so he sent me to some homes his friends recommended. One of the homes I was sent to was the Taffees, friends of my father. I stayed at their house two days a week before Daddy married Anita, and I was uncomfortable there. He shifted me to the Heber's home when Mrs. Heber—whom I adored, and loved the family and their "Lassie" dog—could take me. And, occasionally, I went to the Gray's, a very strict Catholic family, on the next street. They were so kind to me, but I couldn't stay with them all the time so I went to stay with a lady in Malden. My dad knew someone from the M&M Trucking Company who knew the lady. She had no husband. There were two children: a boy about four or five years old, and a baby girl. She needed money badly, so she said I could stay with her for a few weeks, maybe longer. My dad was thrilled and told me he was sure I'd have fun playing with the other children there. I cried, but it made no difference. Dad packed me up and drove me over. He rang the bell, and when the lady opened the door, Daddy said goodbye to me. He didn't even come inside the house. He just told me to be a good girl for the lady, a woman he had never met. He said goodbye and handed her an envelope. As he drove away, I called out to him, but the car didn't slow down. The sting of his rebuff hurt like a sharp slap across my face. Dad left me standing at a stranger's door, all alone.

It was summer and there was no school. I felt abandoned and terrified. How could he leave me at this apartment that had no furniture? It had no rugs, and the wood floor smelled of pee, just like the cat lady's house in Nahant Beach across from Aunt Fanny's summer place. The cat lady's house was not pleasant. She had about thirty cats, but at least she was kind to me. The lady at the house in Malden didn't strike me as an adult; she looked more like a teenage girl. She did not look like a mother at all. You could hear an echo from the empty rooms as we walked through them. We were in a narrow hallway that led to the kitchen, and she was talking to me, holding the money she had taken from Dad's envelope in her hand. The kitchen was white with a junky metal table and two chairs in the corner. There were baby bottles on the counter, garbage overflowing the sides of the barrel, and unwashed dishes in the sink, smeared and caked with the remains of food. Would Daddy have left me here if he had seen this? Thinking back now, my guess is that he would have because he was desperate to get rid of me.

So here I was in this dirty, smelly house. And because I was very timid, I would never say anything about that. The lady took me upstairs to a small room that had clothes and boxes on a twin-sized bed and crumbs and empty soda cans all over the floor. It stunk so badly! Everything in this house was broken, torn, or old. She said this room would be mine except for when she wouldn't be home, and when that happened, "You can all sleep in the baby's room together, next to the crib. Do you understand?" I nodded my head. I asked, "Will there be anyone staying with us?"

She replied, "No, you are old enough to stay alone."

"I have never stayed by myself," I said. My voice rose an octave as I added, "I'm only seven years old!"

She walked away. "Hmm," she sighed.

I was feeling hungry. Even though Daddy said we would stop and he'd get me something to eat and bring with me, he never did. Lately, he would promise me something and then break his promise as if he had forgotten what he said or did not care to remember. I waited in the dirty room for her to tell me what to do. Then she stormed back through the door and told me to follow her. I walked with her down the narrow hallway to the bathroom, where there were blackened white tiles, clothes, and dirty towels covering the floor, hair, dust, and a dark ring around the inside of the tub. My mommy's house was never dirty, and I had never been in this type of house before. Then we went into the next room where a little boy was sitting beside a crib. The baby was dirty and her diaper was hanging off. The room smelled awful, like urine and feces. She showed me the baby's clothes in the drawer and told me to pick up the baby if she cried. I was overwhelmed and did not speak. I guess she expected me to know what to do because I was a girl, but I didn't. Did my daddy know about this? I thought someone was supposed to be watching *me*—I am just a kid too!

The lady said she was going to make supper and then go out. This was my first night, how could she go out? There was no TV, just a radio. I was so scared. I guessed she was poor. There were coloring books and broken crayons in my room, and there were toys and some other stuff in the baby's room. As it turned out, the room wasn't only mine. The little boy and I would share it, but we were all going to sleep in the baby's room tonight. I guessed I could be a helper like I was for Mommy when she was sick. She always told me to pick up my room and help out when she couldn't get up because she was ill, and when I did, I was her very special girl. Maybe this lady had a lot of house jobs for me to do to help her. She yelled for us to come down to the kitchen to eat. I was so hungry I hoped it was a big dinner. Daddy had told me that when I got there the lady would make me breakfast, lunch, and dinner every day—but she hadn't even made me a snack yet. I was starving!

I went downstairs to the kitchen, where the boy was already sitting at the table. A peanut butter sandwich was on each plate, and next to the plates were glasses of water. I asked if I could please have some milk, and the lady answered, "No, there is no milk. And if there were, it would be for the baby, not you." I ate my sandwich quietly. The peanut butter stuck to the roof of my mouth, there was hardly any jelly, and I drank my water with each bite to wash it down. She removed my plate before I had finished chewing. I didn't ask for anything else but followed the lead of her little boy, who was quiet. I wasn't sure of what to do or say. She didn't seem to be very nice.

Unlike when she first came to the door, the lady's face was all made up; her eyes had this black stuff around them and her lips were bright red. She had on the highest heels I had ever seen. My mommy didn't wear those types of shoes, even when she dressed up. I wondered where she was going. I didn't want to stay alone, but at least the other kids were there for company. She gave her son the baby's bottle and sent him upstairs to feed her. Then she told me to leave the table and put the rest of the dishes in the sink. I did, and there were a lot of them in there. I thought she was going to say something about washing them, but she didn't. She said that I was excused and to go upstairs. I went into the room where her son was feeding the baby sugar water. The baby was gulping the water very fast. The little boy finally spoke, and said, "You can help me change my sister's diaper, okay?" I said I'd never done that before but would try. He told me how easy it was. I noticed there were sharp pins in a pile, and he showed me how to push them through the cloth diapers by putting my fingers next to the baby's skin when I was inserting them so that I wouldn't stick her. The baby had a red rash, and her brother poured a ton powder over it. Then he told me that his mom went out all the time and had lots of boyfriends. I wasn't sure what all this meant. I asked, "Where is your daddy?"

He said he didn't know and hadn't seen him in a long time. The lady never said goodnight or goodbye, but just left; the only sound I heard was the door shutting behind her. I ran to the hallway, confused, and could smell the trail of bad perfume that lingered behind her. The little boy said, "It's okay. She'll be back later. I stay alone all the time."

"You do?" I asked. It was beyond my understanding. I told him I would clean the kitchen. The boy said I could use the bar of soap from the bathroom, and I stayed in the kitchen washing the piles of dirty dishes. After that, I washed the dishes daily. Without a dish drainer, I had to set them out on towels all over the kitchen counter.

We were by ourselves now. I was frightened but the boy was not; he was used to it. There were lots of noises coming from the neighborhood. He said I would get used to them too. I was still hungry and asked him if we could have another sandwich. He said no, we couldn't because his mom didn't want us to touch any extra food and that we had to be sparing with it because it cost a lot of money to eat. I knew my daddy gave the lady lots of money because I saw it. I asked if I could have more water and he said, "Yeah, all you want." We were hungry and tired. I drank enough water to feel full, and then I saw the box of sugar on the counter. I mixed the sugar with the water like he did for the baby; at least now the water had some flavor. We fell asleep in the baby's room, curled up on the on the floor in dirty blankets. When it was morning, I didn't hear the lady come in but heard her at the door letting someone out. She was not in a good mood and yelled and screamed at her children that she hated them and that they were in the way. I was okay because she was being paid for me, she said. She never even mentioned the clean kitchen.

The lady slammed our door. She went up and down the stairs in a frenzy, and there was loud music playing. We were quietly waiting for something to eat when she finally called us to the table. It was rather late for breakfast. She must have gone for food, I thought, because there was milk. We got a bowl without much in it, but it was milk and cereal. I ate like I had never eaten food before. I was so hungry. I didn't ask for more. I knew better.

This went on day after day—one or two small meals if we were lucky. It was warm outside, but we were not allowed to open the windows downstairs, only in the bedrooms upstairs. The little boy and I would count the minutes until we got our meals; it was like a game we would play while we were waiting. We cleaned the baby's room, picking up the clothes and folding them neatly. I showed him how my mommy cleaned the floor with an old washcloth. We washed our clothes and the baby's in the tub and hung them to dry. He said that if we did certain things we would be all right. For example, if the baby cried late at night and we gave her water or milk, sometimes she would quiet down and go back to sleep. The lady was getting more forgetful about feeding us. She was tripping and falling, and slurring her words when she spoke. Her son said she was drunk. I didn't know what "drunk" was! She would have fits of anger and throw things around, messing up what we had neatened. I thought she might be sick. I was too young to understand that she was an alcoholic and a drug addict.

There was one boyfriend who came over often and would bring us snacks from time to time. I thought he was nice. Once when I was asleep he came in my room and gave me a snack, but said I had to be good to him for me to get more. I agreed, but didn't know what that meant. The lady was asleep. He kissed me on my mouth and stuck his tongue in so deep it took my breath away and I choked. He tried to stick his fingers in my bottom. It hurt, and when I screamed out from the pain, he covered my mouth with his hand. He called me a brat and said, "Shut the fuck up or I'll beat you!" It felt like a razor had cut me. I felt something wet between my legs and saw that there was blood on my panties. Then the light went on, and the lady was shrieking at him. He called her an old drunken cunt and pushed her away. She leaned over me and said, "You'd better not tell anyone about what happened, you little bitch—not your daddy, not anyone. Do you hear me?" I nodded my head, scared to death. "Yes, yes!" I said. The way she looked and acted reminded me of that lady, Anita. She left the room and went downstairs. I was trembling and crying. My bottom hurt so badly that I felt like I had to go to the bathroom. Why did the man do that to me? Why did he hurt me? The gardener had touched me down there too. I could hear the lady screaming and banging things around. I heard the sound of glass breaking. I was curled up at the edge of the bed, shaking. The little boy came in and asked in a soft voice if I was okay. I said, "I think so." Then his mom came running up the stairs, screaming at him to go back to his sister's room. She grabbed me, pulled me up, and said it was my fault her boyfriend got thrown out and that I was to blame. I wondered what I'd done. Then she took me to the bathroom, took my pajamas and undies off, washed me, and asked, "What did he put inside you?"

"His finger in my bottom," I said quickly. I was frightened and did not understand her questions. "He held me down! I didn't want him to, I swear! Please, it's not my fault, please!"

In a low voice, unlike her normal tone, she said, "Just promise you'll never tell. It won't happen anymore. He was drunk."

What was drunk? How did they get drunk? I bled for a short time but was swollen for quite a while. I was not taken to a doctor. She put ice in a rag for me to put on my bottom and said not to talk to her son about what happened.

****

I will never forget that night. I ask myself all the time why men like him aren't locked up for life? Why are the laws for pedophilia so lenient? Hopefully, there will be a truly severe sentence for this horrific offense someday, but in the meantime, I am in jail for selling sex between consenting adults while the pedophiles run free. Our judicial system is upside-down.

****

Days went by with no real food at all. The boy stayed close to me, and we drank sugar water together, hoping his mother wouldn't notice the level of sugar in the box going down. She would bring company back home constantly. When I heard these men in the apartment I would stay in bed, frozen, with lots of covers pulled up around me, and always as close to her son as I could get. If I had to pee, I would hold it.

The next few days, the lady did not come home and there was no more food. We had eaten the rest of the bread and there was no more milk for the baby. She cried day and night, and there were no more clean diapers. Although I tried washing them, they were still stained and damp. Her rash was inflamed and swollen. We didn't know what to do about not having food, so I sucked on my own shirt, the way the little boy showed me, to taste some flavor. We drank lots of sugar water, and the baby did too. Soon, there wouldn't be any more sugar. We were told never to go outside, and we were both afraid to leave. My stomach felt like it was touching my back. The boy was so hungry that he cried out at night, and we held each other for comfort. "Why doesn't my mom come home?" he asked me. She was not a good mom; I refer to her as "lady" but, really, she was just a girl with kids. "Where is my daddy? He doesn't care about me either. Please, someone, come!" he would cry out. At night, I prayed to my mom to come rescue us or send us someone! Nobody called on the phone, and even if the phone had rung, we were too afraid to answer it. She had warned us about touching the phone.

I had to call someone, but who should it be? I didn't know anyone's number. I told the boy I would call my Aunt Rose. "My Auntie Rose will come and bring us food," I said. I didn't care if the lady punished me. I picked up the receiver, and a kind voice said, "Hello, operator. May I help you?"

I said, "Yes, can you get my Auntie Rose, please? We're hungry."

"You're hungry?" she replied incredulously. She asked, "Where are you?"

"I don't know. I am at a lady's house," I answered.

"What's the lady's name? You have to tell me or I can't help you. If you don't know the name of the street go out and look at the number on the house where you are or look at the address on the mail."

I replied, "I can't go out. I'm not allowed. Please, call my Auntie Rose!"

"Okay," she said. "What is your aunt's name? What's her last name?" "Aunt Rose Levinson," I said. "She lives in Newton." I gave her a partial address, or what I though the street name was. At least I had remembered the name of the street. The operator told me to stay on the phone, to not hang up. "Please!" I begged. I think she was calling my aunt while we waited. The boy was too nervous to tell what his last name was or the address of where we were. He kept saying "We'll be in trouble!" and "My mom will spank me hard!" My mom had never spanked me.

Although waiting seemed like it took forever, they had our number and said, "Hang up now; we will call you back." My aunt called just a few minutes later. "Hello, hello? Libbella, is that you? Where are you?" Aunt Rose sounded excited.

"I don't know, but Daddy took me here and we're hungry, so hungry! Please, can you bring us food?"

"Of course, but where are you staying?" I told her I didn't know. "Okay, go outside and look for the mail, and then tell me the address on the letters. I give you permission. Now, go!"

I went outside right away. I collected the mail from the box and read the addresses to Aunt Rose, who said she would be over to the house soon. Before Aunt Rose arrived, shortly after I hung up the phone, the police were at the door. They banged at the door and ordered me to open it. "No," I said, "I can't. I want to wait for Auntie Rose." They tried to persuade me to open the door, but I was waiting for my aunt. It occurred to me that one of the lady's boyfriends could be at the door and I froze. The police gave up, and then for what seemed like a very long time, I waited for Aunt Rose to knock on the door. Finally, I heard her call my name. This big, beautiful woman, with her sunshiny smile, was here! The little boy was smiling, but he was scared to see anyone. Aunt Rose had crackers and candy in her hand. She came in and looked around. "Oh, god, how could he do this to you?" Tears rolled down her cheeks. The little boy went to the policeman and asked, "Please, mister, do you have crackers too? Please? Please?"

"No, but I'll get you some food on the way," the officer assured him. Aunt Rose gave the boy a bunch of crackers to eat, and he hugged her. They got the baby, and as he looked around the house, one of the officers said, "We know this girl. She has a long record. She is a drug addict and an alcoholic," he told Aunt Rose. "Let's get these kids out of here. We didn't have cause to enter before, but this is clearly a case that calls for the state social services to get involved."

I was so happy to see my aunt that I stuck to her like glue. "Do I have to go back there later, after we eat, Aunt Rose?" She looked at me. "Never, ever. Your daddy and I will talk. Let's get you back home with me. We'll get you some food, and you can take a bath to wash away the dirt, poor dear."

"What about my friend and the baby? Where are they going?" I asked.

"Don't worry," Aunt Rose reassured me. "The officers will feed them and help find them a good home."

"What about their mom?" I asked.

"She will be fine," she replied.

We got back to Aunt Rose's house in Newton. I was so relieved when we pulled into her driveway. I wanted to go to my house, but Daddy wasn't there. Aunt Rose said Daddy was working. I told her that I had asked the brightest star for help when I said my prayers, but it did not help. Auntie Rose explained that all my mommy could do was watch from above and that the rest was up to me. And I guess that's what happened—a wish is what you make it. Uncle Uggie was waiting for me with a warm hug and a kiss. I felt safe and knew I would eat supper. Her home smelled like cakes and baked cookies. Aunt Rose scurried into the kitchen and said, "Libbe, we *have* to give you a bath first."

I said that I had washed at the lady's house but without using soap. I told her that when Daddy's check came in the mail the lady would wave it in the air and tell her son that it was her payday from my dad, and then out the door she would sail. Auntie Rose was speechless!

Uncle Uggie took me upstairs to the spare room I used whenever I visited. Auntie Rose's house was eclectic and somewhat disorganized, but I was relieved to be in the warmth and coziness of the house with all her dark, antique furniture and things. I thought that this was good, that I was safe again, and that no one would touch me anymore. But where will I go? Who wants me? Maybe now I will be able to stay here forever, even though Daddy said I could stay with my aunts only a couple of days. I hoped they would change their minds and keep me. After the Malden home, I would remember everything people said and did. When we finally came downstairs after my bath, I asked again about the lady's kids. What would happen to them? I still wonder to this day. Aunt Rose never did explain. Instead, she asked me lots of questions about the house, the living conditions there, and what had happened. She wrote down what I said on a sheet of paper. I told her almost everything, leaving out the part about what the man did to me. I was ashamed and afraid. When I was upstairs in the tub with all the bubbles, I told Uncle Uggie that I was older now and could wash my own bottom (which was sore and still hurt). Even though I trusted my Uncle Uggie and knew he would never hurt me, that's what I told him. Now I felt embarrassed and protective about my private parts because of what those other men had done. I didn't want anyone touching me there ever again. My dad never believed what I told him about his friend, the gardener, and I was afraid that telling him about the lady's boyfriend would only cause more problems. He wouldn't believe me anyway!

Aunt Rose put such an array of food on the table that I didn't know what to eat first. I forgot what it looked like to have meals. She said, "Don't eat too fast because you'll get a tummy ache. I am sure your tummy has shrunk. Take just a little at a time. You're skin and bones!" I shoveled food in my mouth, swallowing almost without chewing it. I remember the dark rye bread and butter—it tasted so good. There was beef with vegetables, and I drank two glasses of milk with the cookies that Aunt Rose made. My stomach was full and sticking out. I was so tired that I could hardly smile, and my eyes were closing. Aunt Rose and Uncle Uggie walked me upstairs to their guestroom, where they tucked me in and stayed with me while I said my prayers. They kissed me goodnight and shut off the light in my room but left the bedroom door ajar because they knew I was afraid of having the door shut, that I did not like the dark. I fell asleep in the warmth of a familiar and loving home. I knew Mommy Rose was watching over me and had guided me.

Morning arrived, and I awoke to the smell of food: eggs, bagels, hot cereal, and cinnamon buns. I couldn't wait to go downstairs to the kitchen! No longer did I have to suck on my shirt or drink sugar water instead of milk. I came bursting into the kitchen, breathing in the smell of food. There were some people there who had come to visit. Aunt Rose took me in her arms and hugged me, saying, "You'll never go hungry again, not as long as I am alive." I thought of the time Mommy Rose discovered that I was allergic to fish—I had touched and smelled the whitefish on the table and my face swelled up and my throat started to close. I was itchy. Mommy called the doctor to come, and I remember taking a tiny white pill. She was afraid for me after that and never put fish near me again. Neither did Aunt Rose. But today I got a bit of a smell of fish and, yes, it was fish she had in the fridge for later.

After breakfast at Aunt Rose's, I was so content that I played for hours without bothering anyone. I wished I could stay forever and that Daddy could come to visit me here when he had days off. I had forgotten all about how empty my stomach had been before. Mommy Rose had heard my prayers when Aunt Rose came to rescue me, and I was certain she would hear me again. Before supper the phone rang, and by the excited way Auntie Rose was talking I could tell it was someone asking about me. Auntie Rose said that the lady who was supposed to marry Daddy had called. I could tell that my aunt and uncle were angry with Daddy and couldn't wait to see him.

A couple of days later, Dad came to Aunt Rose's house, and I listened to him trying to reason with her, trying to wiggle his way out of trouble. She was very angry. "Freddy, if you ever have Libbe in a home without food or proper care, I will call the police on you!"

He admitted that he didn't know anything about the lady and was very, very sorry. "How would you know? You didn't even bother going inside that filthy house before you left her there!" she screamed. I thought Daddy might feel too embarrassed to face me after Aunt Rose's tirade, but he turned to me and said, "I won't send you to strangers again." That was the extent of his apology. "You surely won't, Mr. Siskind!" she yelled. Wow, I knew Auntie Rose was really mad.

I didn't want to leave my Aunt Rose's house, but Dad said there was an older couple in Melrose who had a small home and would like the company. He had known the man for as long as he knew the Taffees, maybe even longer. But I didn't like the Taffees, they were so old. Mr. Taffee frightened me because of the way his hands trembled, and their Boston terrier was nervous and barked all the time. Aunt Rose didn't have authority over me, but she wasn't shy about asking when I would have a normal home again. Dad answered that he and Anita would be married before September and that then I would be able to go home and back to school. Auntie Rose and Uncle Uggie had smothered me with hugs from the day they took me away from that lady's horrid apartment.

"Can I stay over with you again soon?" I asked.

"Yes, Libbela, but you must always ask Daddy first. And remember that if you ever need help, you can call the police. Right, Freddy? But there will be no next time. I promise!" We were ready to leave, but I felt uneasy and didn't want to go. Daddy didn't even give me a hug while he was at their house. I was feeling empty.

When he and I went off, we didn't talk much. The only thing he did say was that I would be back home soon, sleeping in my own bed, and I asked him if I would be staying by myself in this new place—be left alone—like I did at the lady's house. He interrupted me and said never to bring up the lady again, ever. Daddy didn't like hearing about upsetting things that had to do with me or him.

"Where are we going, Daddy?" I asked.

"I will take you home to get your clothes, then drop you off at the new house today."

"But I want to stay with you!" I insisted. "I don't want to go!"

"Please, Libbe, I have to work."

"I don't want to go anywhere else, please!" I begged and pleaded, over and over. I concentrated as much as I could, and repeated, *Mommy Rose, please help me,* over and over again in my mind, but she didn't answer me. And who could I call now? I wanted to stay at home with my dad! I wondered, *Did Auntie Rose know?* She thought Daddy was taking me home, at least that's what I thought.

Daddy skillfully pulled the car between the two lions at the end of the driveway, like the expert he was when it came to driving. We went around to the back door of the garage—the door that had haunted me since the time the gardener touched me against my will. It was the first of many sexual situations I found myself in throughout my life when a man, even a man of my own choosing, has insisted on doing what he wanted to me even though I clearly said no and protested. Daddy went upstairs, taking two steps at a time, and put all kinds of things in my bag. "Daddy, how long do I have to stay there?" "Just a short time, until Anita comes home," he said.

"What do you mean, Daddy? Anita at home?" Fred answered, "I told you already, Libbe, that Anita will be moving in after the wedding." I couldn't speak. How could I have missed that? Anita hated me, I could tell, and I certainly didn't want her living with us. I disliked her from the first moment I saw her. Dad didn't care about how I felt. Nor, despite my begging and crying, did he listen to me. I asked, "Daddy, where will Anita sleep?" He didn't answer me.

It was nighttime when we drove to the new home. On the way, it was quiet in the car except for the Amos and Andy Show on the radio. I didn't feel the same being around Dad now that Mommy Rose was gone; there was a great distance. We arrived at a house that was smaller than ours in Stoneham; it didn't have a second level like the houses I was familiar with. It seemed dark, with only one light on in the front living room, and I felt scared. We knocked at the door and a small-framed, gray-haired woman answered. "Mr. Siskind, please come in. My husband has told me all about you." Dad introduced me. "This is my daughter, Libbe." I always felt proud whenever he introduced me as his daughter. "Please come into the living room and sit down," she said. We walked in and an old man, her husband, was sitting in an armchair. Dad had told me he knew the man from M&M, but that he was sick and wasn't able to work anymore. They talked about trucks for a little while. I sat quietly. The house was stuffy and had a peculiar odor. There were many decorations scattered around the room: pictures of flowers, doilies on the tables, candy dishes, and a TV. At least there was furniture, I thought.

The woman asked me for my bag and if I had any books or toys. I peered at my dad who said no, he had forgotten but would bring them on his day off. "We were in such a hurry…" he attempted to explain but stopped.

My new room had two twin beds. It was gloomy. My mommy had liked dark flowers and patterns, but this small house was dark and plain without patterns. It wasn't like my house at all. There wasn't even a radio. The house had two bedrooms, a living room, a small dining/kitchen area, and a bathroom. At least Dad had come inside this time and did not rush off.

Daddy asked the lady and her husband if they would please feed me three meals a day. "Of course, Freddy," the man said. My dad handed the lady an envelope and said goodbye to them. Then he turned to me. Tears filled my eyes and flowed down my face. "Please, Daddy, please take me with you! I'll hide in your truck so no one can see me. Please take me!"

"Libbe, stop it!" he said. "These are nice people. Behave yourself. I'll see you soon, when I bring your dolls and cupcakes."

"You promise, Daddy?" He promised me and patted me on the head. Without hugging me, or at least giving me a kiss on the forehead, he walked out of the house. Once again, I felt lost. The lady shut the door, then asked if I was hungry. It seemed like she felt bad for me. I told her I wasn't (even though I was, sort of) and that I wanted to be by myself. I went to the room that had been set up for me, and she softly closed the door. I pressed my damp face into the pillow and sobbed. After a while, I stared out the window into the darkness. The sky was pitch black—no stars. My sadness washed over me in waves. I cried myself to sleep, still in my clothes. I wouldn't have known if the lady or her husband had come into my room to check on me.

The next day when I awoke in the Melrose house, the lady told me I should wash up and come to eat. Yes, eat…oh boy, was I hungry! I was relieved that they were at home and had soap. When I asked if I would get food later, she looked puzzled by my question and said, "Yes, of course. For breakfast you'll have toast, one egg, and a glass of milk." What an improvement over Malden, my frame of reference. I noticed how old the husband and wife were, that they moved slowly and didn't speak much. The man devoured his breakfast without saying a word. I spoke to the lady, who really didn't talk much either. She told me I could go to my room if I wanted to read. Read—I had no books! Then I asked her if I could go outside, and she said, "Oh no, we have to watch you, and unless we go outside, you have to stay inside too." I asked if I could watch TV and she said no, and explained that her husband didn't want anyone in the living room while he was up, but if he went to bed early I could watch if it wasn't too late. Because I didn't have my books, I decided to use pencils and paper to draw pictures with and doodle. I loved to draw, so that was okay. And so began a series of long days sitting in my room, coming out only to wash and eat. Sometimes I sat at the kitchen table, but when I stayed in my room I couldn't tell if it was daytime unless I raised the shade. The lady always kept the darkening shade down because she said the room would be cooler. I wanted to see sunlight—not be in the dark!

Where was Daddy? I knew it had been more than six days because the husband told me it had already been a week. I thought, *I'll ask the lady to call Daddy to bring my toys, books, and bracelets.* I missed my books and all my things—they reminded me of Mommy.

It was during this episode of my life that I began defending myself against the emptiness I felt. *Yes,* I said to myself, *until Daddy comes back, I'll be Elizabeth Taylor.* Mommy was always saying that I would become an actress one day, or a tap dancer and singer. *I'll just act in my room, this will be my stage,* I told myself. My world changed. I was no longer in a dark room and envisioned myself dressed in beautiful clothes, like the actresses in the movies. I knew my Mommy was watching me and loved it; she was the audience I played to. All the actors and actresses I knew from TV came alive in the space of this bedroom, and I wasn't alone anymore. When I tried to sing, though, the lady would come in and tell me, "No noise, please."

A few more days passed by, and I couldn't wait any longer; I had to ask the lady if she would call my dad. "Oh please, oh please, can you call him?" I begged. Without emotion, she firmly stated, "Your dad is busy and won't be home until Saturday. We'll call him on Saturday, not before." I was extremely anxious and prayed hard every night until it was Saturday. I thought Daddy was working, but as I later learned, he was with Anita.

The lady told me to get washed and dressed, and I assumed that Daddy must be coming soon. I wouldn't be housebound anymore! I saw that the lady and her husband were dressed to go out, and I was thrilled to be going outside also. Then she said, "I've already talked to your dad, and he said to go to the store to buy you a doll to play with because he is too busy helping Anita with the house."

I didn't understand what that meant, and so I asked the lady, "Is Daddy going to come and visit me? What is he doing at the house? I want the toys Mommy bought me." The old lady's only response was that we were going to the store and that she didn't know anything more than that. I said I wanted to go to my room, but they replied that I couldn't stay alone and that this would be my only chance to go to the store. I went to the store with them. Finally, I was outside! The lady and her husband ordered me food she knew I liked, but a doll and a toy were never mentioned again. Why didn't we go to a toy store? We just went out to eat. I continued drawing pictures every day in my room. When I wasn't drawing, I was an actress performing for my mommy. I knew she was proud of me.

Daddy never came to visit me during the three months I stayed with the lady and her husband. We went out to buy groceries, and I watched TV a few times when the old man went to bed early…and that seemed like never. If I went outside, I had to stay near the front door. Then the lady told me my daddy had called and said that I needed some time with Anita before I started school in September. I was so excited to be going home that I didn't care about my daddy's friend Anita! When Daddy came that weekend, I was happy to see him, but I didn't run to him like I used to; I felt different. He didn't hold out his arms to me either. He said, "Say goodbye to the nice people who took such good care of you." I said goodbye without giving them a second thought. The lady told my dad that I was no trouble and could come back any time. I thought, *Of course, she would say that. All I did was stay in that room, talking to and performing with my imaginary friends.*

Daddy told me to hurry because Anita was waiting for us. He seemed to be happy about that, but I wasn't. I was disappointed that Daddy never came to visit me or bring me my toys, but I kept that to myself. He had made many promises since Mommy went away, and he had not kept one of them. Why is Anita so special that he forgot all about me? "Why is Anita going to live with us?" I asked. "Does she have to? Doesn't she have a home of her own?" He replied that he would explain it to me later and turned up the volume of the talk radio program he was listening to. I was beginning to feel happy about going home to my room and my toys until Daddy turned and said, "Libbe, there are lots of new things at home now. Anita made the house look pretty. You'll love your new room."

"My *new* room?" I asked. I was confused.

"Okay, Libbe," Daddy said in a stern voice, "I want you to be nice to Anita. She is your new mother and will take care of you."

"No, Daddy, she is not! I don't want your friend Anita! I don't want her to be my mother!" Tears were rolling down my cheeks.

"I don't want to hear that; stop your crying. Be quiet and do as Anita says. She lives with us now, and it's for your own good!" He didn't say anything more. When we arrived at the house, Anita was waiting at the door. The last time I had seen anyone in the front doorway was the day Aunt Eva, Aunt Fanny, and Aunt Rose stood there like three dark shadows with their arms open wide.

CHAPTER SIX

Anita, Anita, Anita

I used to feel happy and eager whenever we turned into our driveway. This time, even though I was excited to be going back to my own room, my stomach felt queasy. Daddy gathered my things and was first at the door. He was so happy to see the mean lady, the one who now lived in Mommy's house. I stood outside, next to the car. Daddy called to me, "Libbe, Libbe, what are you doing?" Slowly, I went to the front door.

Anita looked at me and said, "Hello, dear." I didn't answer her, and looked beyond her into the hallway. There were thick, plastic covers on the floors, and the rugs weren't the same; they were a beige color. My mom's mahogany telephone table with the black phone and old telephone book that popped up when you pushed the button was still in the hallway near the door to the kitchen. I took a step or two inside and saw that the living room was totally different. Except for my mom's desk, floor lamp, and Philco record player, everything was gone. The chairs, the Victorian couch, the coffee table, and the curtains weren't there anymore. I began to panic and asked Daddy, "What did you do with Mom's couch?" He didn't answer me, and I fled up the stairs toward my room. I wanted to be with the dolls Mommy bought me and away from them.

I walked into my room—it was gone! The twin bed against the wall had a puffy, white terrycloth bedspread with a design on it of a lady in a long, full-petticoat gown, holding a parasol. The dresser was different and had a large mirror attached to it. And on top of the dresser was a vintage vanity set, all placed on a white doily. The walls were painted antique white. I opened the closet, expecting my toys to be there, but it was empty! I was shocked, and I let out a bloodcurdling scream! "Daddy, where are my toys and dolls! Where are my books! I want my things back! Give me my dolls!" I shrieked.

My father came upstairs and yelled at me to stop making a scene in front of Anita, who had worked so hard to make a beautiful room for me. "Anita says that you're becoming a young lady, and you've out-grown your dolls," he said. I sat on the floor and cried inconsolably for all my losses. "I am not a grownup!" I wailed. "I want my toys!" Daddy walked away without even giving me a hug. I sat and sobbed alone. I wished that Aunt Rose would come and get me.

I suspected that my toys were put away in the basement, so I got up and went downstairs, past Anita and Fred, who were sitting together on the new plastic-covered couch in the living room. I felt left out and displaced in my own home—not even my *own* room belonged to me. No room looked the same! Everything I loved had been taken away…no one cared about my feelings and what I wanted anymore. I walked through the kitchen and saw that the kitchen set was still there, but the room looked and smelled different. The walls were another color and the linoleum floor was new. I put on the light and ran down the stairs to the basement. The built-in bar and the seats were the same, but there were other things on the shelf where the radio used to be, the same radio I listened to and would sing along to during more happy times. I looked everywhere, but my stuff and Mom's things were not there. I rushed back upstairs to see what happened to Mom's room and the guest room, and on the way Fred and Anita asked me what I was doing. I said, "Nothing. I'm not doing anything," and I sprinted past them up to Mom's bedroom.

Everything was gone—all her pictures, her bed, all her clothes and perfumes, the deep wine-colored lipstick that had a fragrance I loved—all gone, gone, gone! I peeked into the guest room and it, too, was different. And the closet where Mommy stored things was empty…all those pretty linens. Where were her pictures? I went downstairs and positioned myself directly in front of Daddy. "Give me Mommy's pictures, Daddy! Please, I want them!"

"Libbe, I have never seen you act like this before," he said. "Go to your room and stay there until you're ready to say you're sorry to Anita. The pictures are put away, and when you're old enough you can have them."

"I want Mommy's pictures for my room, please!" I was crying so hard I choked on my words.

"Go to your room," he said. "And no dinner until you can behave!"

I could tell he didn't feel badly for me, Daddy had never told me no dinner! He was a different man; he belonged to Anita now, not me. I walked upstairs to the room that really wasn't mine anymore and shut the door tight—something I'd never done before. Mommy always kept my door open, but I didn't want to see anyone or have them see me. I wanted to die. I sat by the closet door and cried for what seemed like hours until I fell asleep on the floor.

It was late when Dad came in my room and said, "Libbe, Libbe, wake up!" He shook me a little, and I woke slowly, hoping that he would hug me. Instead, he said, "Libbe, I'm so ashamed of you for behaving the way you did. And why are you sleeping on the floor?"

"I don't want to sleep in that bed," I told him as I cried.

"If you can act nicely, you can come downstairs. We saved you some dinner."

I said, "No thanks," and told him I wasn't hungry. He said I had to wash and change into my pajamas even if I didn't eat and that Anita would help me. "No, Daddy. I can do it myself," I replied. "You said I am not a child. I don't want her to!" For the first of many times to follow, I heard him say, "Libbe, I'd better hear good reports about you when I come home from the road."

Anita came upstairs anyway. "I'll lay out your pajamas," she said. I thought that at least my clothes would be the same, but no, they were not. I didn't speak at all until she said, "I'll help you."

"No," I said stepping back away from her. "My mommy showed me how to dress, thank you." I thought for a moment that maybe she cared. "Please, can I have my Tiny Tears doll to sleep with? And my blanket and Mommy's robe?"

She looked at me as if she were looking through me and replied, "No, you cannot have your old toys back—or anything!" It was clear she meant what she said. I went to bed hungry that night, after staring out the window for a long time as I prayed to the biggest star in the sky. When I went to the bathroom, I drank a lot of water from the sink to fill my belly.

Days went by. Dad did not go on the road. He stayed at home, saying that it was important for Anita to feel comfortable with me. I knew it was a lie. He really wanted to be around Anita. I was sent to my room several more times before Dad went back to work. When Daddy returned home, he and Anita went back-to-school shopping for me. The clothes she picked out for me were somber grays, dull browns, navy, and black. None of the other kids at school wore clothes like these.

Although Dad told Anita I was allergic to fish and wool, most of the clothes she bought for me were wool or had some wool in them.—She told him that my allergies were in my head and that I was only saying I was allergic to these things to get attention. Daddy didn't entirely agree with all of it and told her the doctor said that if I ate fish my throat would close up and I could possibly die. The wool stayed, however. Daddy told me, "You're making it up, Libbe. You are not allergic to wool. You'll do as Anita says and wear the clothes." The wool made my skin itchy and gave me a rash, but I didn't have a choice…at least I wouldn't die.

Daddy was getting ready to go back to work again, and it seemed to me that Anita was trying to be nice whenever he was around. I wasn't sure of her yet, and I didn't like staying in my room all the time. I hated it now, especially with the door shut. Usually when Daddy was preparing to go on the road, he would hug and kiss me and tell me he would bring me back cupcakes. Now he said, "Behave yourself, Libbe, and be good for Anita. Do everything she tells you. I don't want to hear any bad reports."

I could tell he was serious and meant every word he said. But I was so frightened to be alone with her that I grabbed his coat and told him, "Please Daddy, don't leave me with her! Please!"

He gave me a little pat and then pushed me away. "Libbe, I don't want to hear this. I am going on the road, and upsetting me is not helping. Go upstairs!" He gave Anita a nice goodbye with a long kiss on her lips, something he never did with Mom. I was overlooked completely. I ran to my room and shut the door. I didn't care if I stayed in there forever. I prayed for Mommy to come get me.

I stayed in the room and cried. When I quieted down, I could hear Anita walking around. I was hungry, but didn't want to leave this uncomfortable room until she went to bed. Finally, I went downstairs to the kitchen. I thought she was asleep because her door was shut. There was a small light on above the stove, and as I walked in there, I saw her sitting on a chair as if she were waiting for me. She was staring at me, and the light reflected on her face in a way that horrified me. She looked like a wicked witch. "You scared me!" I said in alarm.

In a soft tone, Anita replied, "Did you think I was sleeping?" Her demeanor suddenly changed and she barked, "Don't you ever leave your room unless you ask me!" Then she said, more gently, "Are you hungry?"

And although I was petrified, I said, "Yes, please."

Then she raised her voice again and said, "You will eat in the morning! Go to bed and don't come out of your room!" I went back to my room in a hurry. Remembering what the little boy had taught me, I sucked on my shirt. It took a while, but I finally fell asleep.

Anita came into my room in the middle of the night. She told me, "Get up! Get up! Look what you've done to your bed!" I was startled. I'd never been awakened like that before. "Look at what a mess you've made out of the bedspread!" she snarled. I got up, groggy, and she pulled all the sheets and covers off the bed and dropped them onto the floor. A shiver came over me. She turned to me and said, "You'll learn how to make your bed and how to sleep in it!" I didn't know there was a way to sleep in a bed. Half asleep, I watched her make the bed as I tried to memorize how she did it. Then, in the harshest of tones, she said, "Take it apart and make it yourself!" I did, but wasn't sure if I remembered correctly. I wished the time would go by faster so I could leave to go to school. I had to make the bed three times, and then she told me that when I came back from school, she would teach me again until I learned. I could feel Anita's evil presence in my room and stood silently. Going back to bed was out of the question. In the morning, she laid out my clothes, and I wore them even though I hated them. And I itched. Soon I would be meeting my friends, Smelly Diana and Kat. I didn't know what was in my Howdy Doody lunchbox (at least she hadn't tossed that out).

On my way to school, I spoke with my friends but didn't mention a word about what happened over the summer. They asked about the ugly clothes I was wearing, if they were old ladies' clothes from a rummage sale. Feeling awkward enough as it was, I didn't respond to their sneers. I had to tough it out. I wasn't even apprehensive about going back to class. It didn't matter to me if my teacher hit my hands with a ruler like Miss Zane did in the first grade; at least I wasn't home with Anita.

When I opened my lunchbox, there was a cream cheese and olive sandwich on dark bread and that was all—no cupcake or dessert. I thought that maybe Anita didn't know what to give me or what children liked, so I planned on telling her what Mommy used to make for lunch and how she used to read me stories. I was hoping she had changed during the time I was at school. When I got home, I opened the back door to the garage to let myself in and there was Anita, waiting for me at the back door. I walked past her to go to the playroom in the basement, but she stopped me. "One minute, young lady. Before you do anything, come into the kitchen."

I looked at her and said okay. I was about to tell her about the sandwiches my mommy used to make me for lunch, but Anita started in on me and said in a low, tense voice, "I am in charge now, and your mommy is not to be brought up again, ever! Do you understand?"

"Yes, but my sandwich wasn't the kind Mommy used to give me and there was no cupcake."

"What did I just say!" she threatened. "What you get for lunch is what you eat, and every day when you get home from school, you will do chores and homework."

I asked softly, "May I have a snack?" and Anita flatly declared, "No snacks! You will eat supper later, but now you have work to do." I was too young to say anything in reply, and she scared me. So every day for weeks, it was learning how to make beds with hospital corners, sew hems, wash clothes on a scrub board in the big sink in the basement, and the proper way to clean the bathtub and toilets, using Borax soap and "elbow grease," as she put it.

Anita ordered me to tell my dad that we were getting along fine. The control she wielded over me was so absolute that I told him exactly what she said, even though I knew it was a lie. When Daddy came home for one day a week, he was too tired to talk to me, but he was sure to mention that Anita told him how happy I was. Happy? I wished I could tell him how unhappy I really was. When I asked my daddy, "Where are my cupcakes?" he replied, "I gave them to Anita, and she says that she gave them to you."

Of course, it was a lie, but I stayed silent. All I could do was shake my head, wanting—but not able—to speak up for myself. *Where did Anita put my cupcakes?* I wondered.

At the time they were married, Daddy and Anita didn't have a wedding party, so they decided to make one afterward. I resisted the idea of attending the celebration, and when the day of the party finally arrived, things could not have been worse. I was dressed up in one of my taffeta dresses that Anita hadn't thrown away but had hidden somewhere. She was all dolled up with a pearl choker and earrings. We traveled a considerable way to where the party was being held. Her family and Dad's side of the family were there. We sat in a hall at a large table, and it was after dinner, when the coffee and cakes were being served, that the accident happened. I was happily anticipating eating a big piece of cake, even though Anita had stipulated that I could have only one piece because there was too much sugar in cake, and I wouldn't be able to sleep that night. The coffee was being passed around, and Anita's cup was full to the brim. As I turned to get up from the table, I accidentally hit her cup and the hot, brown liquid splashed all over the skirt of Anita's beautiful dress. She gasped, and Daddy yelled at me and called me clumsy. "Look at what you've done!" he said in exasperation.

I apologized to Anita, and as I did, she stared at me—with daggers in her eyes. She said, "Come with me to clean my dress." I didn't have a choice. She took my hand and squeezed it so tightly it hurt. I didn't dare talk back.

Nobody was in the bathroom when we went in. She put her skirt under the faucet in the sink to wash it, and said, "From now on, young lady, you are to do what I tell you to do. When I say to sit or stand, you are to do it, and when I say jump, you jump. You do it, or else when your daddy leaves, I'll lock you up in the closet and throw away the key! Do you understand me?" I stood there in shock and told her yes, even though I wanted to run out of the room! I wanted to tell Daddy, but she said, "I will take the belt to you if you misbehave or talk without my saying so! If you ever tell your daddy anything, you will not live to see another day." After she finished rubbing the material of her dress, she had me put water on it to rinse it off. Curtly, she said I couldn't even do that right. Scared to death now…

When other ladies started coming in the restroom, Anita's voice softened and she smiled as if we were happy. I was puzzled and thought how this woman had two faces, each one the opposite of the other. We returned to the table, and I resigned myself to just sitting there, knowing that I wouldn't be allowed to eat even one piece of cake. I thought fast and told the lady serving the cakes that my stomach hurt from all the food I had eaten. I lied, and from then on, I would continue to lie out of fear. I knew I had to behave or else something bad would happen to me. I had to keep my mouth shut. I studied Anita's face, watching the twitches for what to do next. Daddy was so in love with her, he was completely oblivious to what was going on. This was the beginning of my having intrusive thoughts, nightmares, and wetting the bed with regularity. I withstood her daily beatings and having to listen to the foul language that spewed out of her mouth. It was a living hell. I will never forget

Anita and Fred's wedding party, to the point where I avoid going to all weddings—and certainly not one my own.

Daddy went back to work. Every day for lunch I ate a cream cheese and olive sandwich; it never changed! When I would get home from school, it was torture. Anita had me strip down to my underwear at the back door and go down into the cold basement. There, she would make me shower with lye soap and cold water, never warm or hot water. It was the end of using the bathroom upstairs. She would take a scrub brush and say, "You are a dirty, filthy girl." The brush was so stiff and hard that it made my skin sting! Things got worse by the day. Anita started to scrub my private parts until they turned beet red, and when I peed it burned so badly that I would try to hold it as long as I could. My bedwetting became a frequent occurrence. Every time I tried to tell Daddy what was happening, he would fluff me off with hand and facial gestures that clearly indicated he didn't want to hear it—at all. I thought, *Why is this happening? I want to go away, far away!*

The days and nights seemed so long, and I looked forward to Daddy coming home because Anita had to put on an act in front of him. She didn't punish or beat me then, and she had to serve me the same food she'd made for him. She got around this by giving me smaller portions and explaining to Daddy that my little stomach couldn't hold more. When he wasn't home, she did her best to hurt me. She would shove me down the stairs when I least expected it. It wasn't carpeted and there were about ten stairs, including the landing. I went limp, thinking that I wouldn't get as hurt that way. Thank god I was an agile child, but my back and neck hurt constantly; my body was always bruised. And I knew it was in her to do worse. *Here goes another day of it,* I'd think. It didn't matter if I was good or bad—she hated me. She loved to shame me.

As time passed, Anita became more comfortable mistreating me, and that caused her to get worse. I was starved for warmth and attention and I began acting out at school. I wasn't allowed to go to my friends' houses anymore, and if I didn't come directly home from school, I was punished. It seemed as though I was being punished every minute. At night, I was afraid to sleep; Anita would come into my room and wake me to make the bed, or to beat me and make me sit in a corner for an hour because of something I'd done earlier, or for no reason at all. My anxiety increased, and it was not surprising that I now wet the bed every night. My mind harbored unsettling thoughts and I had nightmares about Mommy Rose. Anita told me that dead concentration camp victims lived in the closet where my dolls and toys used to be, and that they would come out and kill me if I slept in my room with the closet door open. I never, ever again left the door open! I would watch the door even when it was closed because I was so frightened they would come out to kill me. Anita told me that the people were starved and killed without deserving it, but there were bad people like me who *did* deserve what happened to them. I wondered why I was among those people who deserved to be killed. Was I so bad? It was only because Anita wanted it that way, that's all. No one else ever said I was so bad I should die!

Anita moved me to the basement to sleep. My bed was a metal cot with a mattress covered in plastic, a white sheet, a wool blanket, and no pillow. In the winter, it was much cooler in the basement than upstairs, except for the boiler room, which was always warmer. I rarely got to see the upstairs anymore. Even on the day Daddy was home, Anita would tell him I had homework to do and that was the reason I couldn't leave the basement.

Anita became worse still. I had to stay in the basement and write specific sentences over and over: "I will not lie. I will do well in school. I will do what I am told. I will do my chores. I won't pee my bed." I became so tired from writing night after night that I often fell asleep on my papers. Anita would come downstairs and throw me into an ice-cold shower to wake me. Once the shock of these tortures dulled, Anita would ramp up the severity of whatever her sick mind could come up with. "You have it easy," she would say in her Romanian accent. "You should have been in the camps. That's what you deserve, torture until you become a good girl or die."

The shower of notes from school continued to come. The contents of them all were variations of: "Libbe does not pay attention in class and is disruptive. She might benefit from extra help at home." Anita began to beat me with anything she could find. She would have me get undressed, bend over a chair or bench, and beat me with a strap across my back, the buckle always striking my lower back. The pain was excruciating. The welts stung and ached to the bone. The rubbing alcohol she put on afterward burned, and I knew she did it intentionally to cause me more pain. Then she would pour cold water on my back and scrub until I was red and couldn't stand the pain anymore; it felt as if I had no skin. I could hardly walk or sit when I was in school, but I was too embarrassed to tell my teachers, and so I kept it to myself, never showing my deep pain.

I was only eight years old, almost nine. I wanted God to take me to Mommy Rose. I didn't want to be with Anita and Freddy. I was convinced they hated me. Even though I couldn't see the stars from the basement, I prayed to my mom every day. I could not remember having good days in my life anymore. I thought it couldn't get worse, but then, just when I got used to the routine, Anita would ramp it up and become even more brutal. My crying stopped because I had developed a tolerance to the abuse and pain—it was so high that the more she hit me, the tougher I became. My mind went someplace else. I would think of Mommy Rose's garden, the silver scissors with the black handles, how she taught me to cut the stems at an angle and then would neatly lay the roses down on her dishtowel. It wasn't the pain that made me fearful, it was the anticipation. By the time Anita was through beating me with the belt buckle—degrading me, and not giving me food—she would be almost crazy with anger because I wouldn't cry or show emotion. When I realized that, I thought it would be better if I cried. It was at school, when I was free of her presence, that I suffered the most pain and humiliation. I was so sore and tender I couldn't even touch myself, yet I still didn't cry. That stoicism has remained with me since childhood and kept me alive when I was on the streets. It has helped me on so many occasions when my life was at stake. As a child, though, I was under Anita's control and always felt frightened.

There was no end to the bedwetting; I still couldn't control it. Anita would come downstairs to check on me several times during the night. She startled me as she dragged me out of my cot by the arm. Her eyes were demonic as she pushed my face and hair into the urine that had saturated my sheets. Half awake, it was then I cried. Her unpredictability was frightening. I could never get warm enough in the basement. When I would pee the sheets, I tried not to move so I could stay warm from the heat of the urine.

Anita began saying strange things to me, that she would cripple me so that no one would ever want me or marry me. She said I would never have children because I was a tramp. I didn't understand what she meant, and she called me many other vulgar names and used crude words that I had never heard before. By the time I was nine and a half, Daddy still didn't see the things that were going on. I was sent to counseling at Jewish Family and Children's Services. The social workers I initially saw thought that I was the problem because the stories I told them were so strange.

Anita's derogatory name-calling escalated. She told me I couldn't go to the bathroom alone, and that she needed to be present whenever I used the toilet. She would force my head into the dirty toilet water before flushing to show me what would happen to me if I lied. I was crushed by the indignity of what she did. She would make me sit on the laundry room floor while the foul water from the toilet dried on my face. I hated myself. When I walked anywhere, I stared at the ground and rarely looked up. I didn't want anyone near me—to kiss my face or to touch me in any way. My haircut had grown out some, and I let my hair fall over my face and cover my eyes, thinking no one would be able to see me that way. In my prayers, I constantly asked God to let me die, but there were more times I did not say any prayers out of sheer exhaustion and disbelief.

I hardly saw my aunts. When I saw them on the holidays, I did whisper to Aunt Rose a few times that I hated Anita and that she was doing bad things to me. She asked me to explain what I meant, and I couldn't find the words to tell her what was going on so I just shrugged. I knew I would get a beating if Anita even suspected I had spoken to Aunt Rose, and that is exactly what happened. Aunt Rose told Freddy she was concerned about me, and Freddy told Anita everything. After that, things became even worse.

I could no longer sleep on the cot. She put me on the floor in the boiler room with no blanket, no pillow, and the doors shut tight.

It was warmer, yet cold—like being locked in a dark cell. Before Anita closed the door and locked it for the first time, she said, "Now you can lie in your pee on the floor just like the animal that you are, and every day you will scrub the floor clean with a wire brush, you little bitch. You'd better hold it in." I couldn't control what happened while I was sleeping, and I cried so hard out of frustration that I could hardly breathe.

The space was claustrophobic, and the boiler flap made a scary "shoo-shoo" sound, like a ghost. I didn't like being in there and wanted to get out. It had once been a happy place where I spent time with my dad. But now I hated it because I was alone, locked in the room where the fires from hell would ignite. When the boiler flue went back and forth I thought something was going to come out of the wide pipe and grab me. I would sit on the cold floor until I finally lay down on my side and curled up, sometimes next to a pool of my urine if I couldn't hold it. And I was terrified to move from the spot by the door. One time, Auntie Rose took me to the movie where a gigantic tarantula sat on a house, which gave me nightmares for months. I always became frightened if I saw a spider anywhere, especially in the boiler room.

It's a good thing I had my imaginary friend, Elizabeth, to play with, and in my mind, I was in a movie with her. I dreamed that when I grew up I would have lots of horses and dogs, and I would meet Elizabeth in person. That never did happen, but my son met Elizabeth Taylor and stood next to her in her home a few years before she passed. It was a deeply spiritual moment for me when he told me about it. And since then, he has wanted to keep all her original movie posters I acquired at our home.

The boiler room was my bedroom the rest of my days with Anita. When I had to scrub the floor, sometimes she would have me use ammonia and other times bleach. The fumes were so harsh that my eyes burned and my breath taken away. I suffered constant headaches from so many blows to the head during Anita's beatings that it was seriously difficult to perform at school. I remember one evening in particular when Anita served me fish knowing I had a severe allergy, and after refusing to eat it, she forced it down my throat until

I gagged and vomited. She made me eat the vomit, and I became sick again and again. My lips were swollen, my eyes were puffy, and my throat felt tight. And when she saw that I was having trouble breathing she said, "Get out and go downstairs, you filthy bitch! Get out of my sight!" I cried all the way down the stairs. Trying to rinse away the fishy taste in my mouth and throat, I swallowed handfuls of hot water from the faucet and I threw up what I could. I had such a hard time breathing from what little fish stayed on the lining of my mouth and throat!

Anita meted out another punishment. When I was hungry, she would have me sit for hours in front of the clock on the stove in the kitchen. She would put all sorts of food on the table where I could see and smell it, but I could only sit and listen to the *tick tock… tick tock…tick tock* of the clock. If I couldn't tell her the exact time when she asked for it, then I wouldn't get supper. Once, Aunt Fanny came to visit and said I looked undernourished. She told Dad, who took me to the doctor and confirmed that I was, in fact, severely undernourished. To avoid taking responsibility, Anita told the doctor I didn't like a lot of foods and refused to eat. It was a lie, but I was too afraid to contradict her; I told the doctor what Anita said was true. The doctor prescribed One A Day vitamins for me to take. He suggested that she give me foods I liked to eat and to make sure I ate as much as possible. Anita ignored the doctor's advice and did as she pleased.

One night, when it was freezing cold, Anita locked me outside in the yard and told me to stand where she could see me. Otherwise, she said, she would tie me up in the garage, a place I hated. After a while, I became so numb to the cold that I felt warm and tired. Finally, she let me in, and it felt great to lie down on the boiler room floor…a luxury. That week I came down with a fever and a cold and had to take medicine the doctor prescribed. The saving grace of being that ill was that I got to sleep on the cot; it felt so comfortable I thought I was sleeping on a cloud. After I convalesced, Anita said I had made her sick by causing her so much trouble, and that I had to take Maalox every day because she had to.

There were a few playthings Anita didn't throw away because she didn't want to encroach on my dad's territory and that included anything in the garage and boiler room. My ice skates, my bike, and my roller skates were still there; I was good at all three. One day when I came home from school, I quietly took my roller skates before she could see me. She didn't hear me in the back at the garage door. I crept in, swept them off the shelf, and ran back to the sidewalk, where I put them over my shoes and tightened the key to lock the skates. As I rolled down the street, I felt free and experienced the pleasure I used to feel when my mom watched me play. I would have played with the other kids if I were allowed to. The neighbors, who hadn't seen me for a long time, waved as I rolled by. "Libbe!" I heard Anita's shrill voice call out. "Libbe, get in this house right now!" Oh my god, she saw me!

Although she saw me, I don't believe she saw my skates. I took them off and put the skates on the front steps so I could get them later, before Anita could find them and throw them away. I was anticipating the pain that awaited me, and as I ran around to the back door, scared to death, I saw Anita at the kitchen door with the belt in her hand. She beat me all the way down the stairs to the basement. She told me to lay face down and look at the floor, and not get up until she told me to. Then she said I would have to write sentences for an hour. After I finished writing the sentences, I could have a glass of milk for supper. I told her I had homework. "You are stupid anyway," she said. "Why bother with homework? Either get up early at five a.m., or when she asks for it, tell your teacher that you didn't do your homework." I begged her to let me do my homework, but she said if I did it that night, she would add to my punishments, so I stopped asking. Years later, I found out that Anita had told one of my father's nephews that I had put my skates on the front steps to kill her. I wish I had, and that she would have died, but I didn't have the type of brain that worked that way then. Even later, I may have wished her dead, but as an adult I still would not do it unless it was in self-defense.

I met Anita's brother Carl and his wife Alice. They were kind and considerate people, and when Anita was around them she was a different person. She was so quiet and sweet that I looked forward to her being nice to me. This was how she behaved around my dad's family too. But I knew by the way her eyes looked and her body moved that it wouldn't be long until the other Anita reappeared. Carl owned a beauty salon on Fifth Avenue in New York City. Anita also had a sister named Rose. While she was with them, I overheard her say how much she loved them and it confused me how a woman who had so much hate could love at the same time. Carl fenced professionally, and Anita had photographs of him in tournaments. I went to watch him fence a couple of times in New York with my dad and Anita, and he gave me the sword and let me try. His wife, Alice, was slender, tanned, and very attractive, always dressed impeccably, and with tons of diamond jewelry. I thought she was beautiful. I wondered how they could be related to Anita. Carl died when he was relatively young of a massive heart attack, and Alice moved to Belmont, Massachusetts, on the Watertown line. They had no children.

Anita's sister Rose lived in in a spacious home Connecticut, where I stayed for a couple of months. Anita would have shipped me out to wherever she could to be alone with Dad. I was grateful and went gladly; I just hated leaving my dad. I enjoyed myself with Rose. I was fed, and when I felt cold, she'd give me a soft cotton sweater to wear. She would come in my room at night when the air was getting cool to cover me with a soft, warm blanket. Everything was good at Rose's in Connecticut. She gave glowing reports about me to Fred and Anita. My dad was glad to hear something other than derogatory remarks about my behavior. I hoped the good reports would make Daddy like me again. But it never happened…

During the time I stayed with Rose I went to three musicals. My favorite was *The King and I* with Yul Brynner. I could sing all the words to the songs, and like my mommy, Rose encouraged me to sing. Anita's sister told my dad he should arrange singing lessons for me. I dreamed I would be in musicals—maybe even opera or classical music—someday, just like Mommy Rose said I would be. Anita never would ever think of exposing me to music and was more likely to remove my vocal chords if she could. After Mommy Rose died, I never went to dancing lessons again.

There was an accident that happened in the neighbor's yard behind Anita's sister's house while I was there. I was playing with another kid and was high up on a seesaw when the other kid suddenly jumped off, and I came down to the ground with a jolting thud, hit my head, and suffered a mild concussion. Even then I appreciated the irony of the situation—with Anita, I was beaten many times over but to my knowledge never had a concussion. Except for that, everything else at Rose's house was wonderful, and I learned many new things. I learned how to set a table with good china and flowers just like my mom would do. Not so in Anita's house, where it was impossible to have a desire for culture and the beautiful things in life. She covered everything, even the floors, in plastic. I wanted to stay with her sister, where Anita wouldn't be able to hurt me.

Fred and Anita came to pick me up, and I knew the ride back would be the same as the ride to Rose's—no talking would be allowed. How I dreaded seeing Anita again. Before we left, I wanted to tell Daddy about the musicals, and I thought that perhaps he would listen to me rather than allow Anita to tell me not to speak. I kept asking, "Daddy, can I talk to you please?" I told him we could sit on the window seat in the middle of the stairway, which was my favorite place to be. He finally walked with me up the steps, and I pulled him by the hand over to the window. Anita was enraged. He was sitting with me—not her—as I proceeded to tell him all my stories about my stay with Rose. Infuriated, Anita stormed halfway up the stairs. Her sister had told her that I was such a pleasure that I could stay longer if they allowed me and that I was welcome to come back anytime I wished. Imagine that, *I* was a pleasure! That was all Anita had to hear; she was so angry that I was happy. She began yelling at Freddy, asking him if he had any backbone. She said all this "Daddy, Daddy" stuff had to end. She wanted me to stop talking. He said, "Please, Anita. Be quiet and let me talk to Libbe. For god's sake, go downstairs and don't make a scene!"

Anita didn't care what he said. Then she screamed, "That's not your daddy! You are adopted! Do you hear me? He's not your daddy! Do you understand me, you tramp? You're illegitimate!"

Her sister Rose was yelling at her to leave me alone. Freddy said, "Anita, why? Why did you say that?" I got up. "Please, Libbe, come here," he said. I was crying so hard. I wanted to know why I wasn't Daddy's daughter. He was trying to calm me down. "Libbe," he said, "Anita was upset. She didn't mean what she said."

"Daddy, what does 'adopted' mean? Tell me!"

Finally, with Anita screaming and cursing me from downstairs where her sister had dragged her away, he explained, "You are my daughter. Mommy and I adopted you when you were a baby, and you are like our real daughter."

"I am not your real daughter?" I asked.

I watched Daddy intently as he was speaking to me. His words rolled off me like the marbles between my books, a game I used to play to escape. Freddy told me, "Your mommy could not have children…she was afraid…I can't go into all this now. Anita, please! Shut up!" (I later learned that Mommy Rose's sister had died in childbirth.)

Tearfully, I asked, "You're not my real daddy? And Mommy's not my real mommy either?"

"That's right, Libbe," Fred replied, "but you're part of the family and you have the Siskind name." He couldn't explain further with Anita screaming in the background. "Then I don't want to go with you or her!" I said, stomping my feet. "I am not yours! Just leave me here!"

Anita continued to yell, "Get rid of her! She's no good!" Her sister Rose came upstairs to try to calm me down. While Freddy and Anita argued, she began packing my things, talking to me, trying to soothe me. I was crushed to find out that I didn't have a real daddy and that Mommy Rose wasn't my real mother. Mommy Rose, not mine? If I didn't belong to anybody, then who was I? Where were my real mom and dad? Why did they leave me?

I asked Anita's sister, but she said she couldn't tell me anything because it was my father's responsibility to tell me. I was crying, and she held me. I didn't want to drive with my "dad" to go home. I wondered, *Does Auntie Rose know?* I was in shock. Daddy tried to talk to me, but I didn't say a word. It was bad enough living with Anita, now I feared even worse that Daddy didn't love me because I wasn't his child. Anita was satisfied; I heard her say that Freddy should have told me long before she did. Her sister replied, "Not like this, Anita. What is wrong with you, she's just a child! This isn't the right time. She's already confused and won't understand." Rose hugged me and told me that everything would be okay. I wasn't comforted by her words. I knew that things weren't going to be okay.

On the way home in the car, Freddy and Anita argued even more. It was scary. I felt carsick and remained silent. In any case, I wasn't allowed to speak, and looked out the window, feeling sad and empty. I had no dad, no mom. I was preoccupied thinking about who I was, and I wasn't sure if my mommy really loved me. It seemed as though I had become a stranger to myself. Although it was confusing that he was closer to me before Mommy left, now I understood why Daddy was staying away from me. It was because I wasn't his. And the home Mom said would always be mine was surely not. What would happen to me now?

After endless arguing, Anita and Fred finally fell silent. Fred turned to check on me in the back seat a couple of times. He could see my puffy, tear-filled eyes. I wondered if he really cared. By the time we arrived home, I had finally drifted off to sleep. Freddy must have picked me up and carried me into the house to my bed. All the other times when I'd fallen asleep in the car, he would wake me and say, "Libbe, wake up, we're home." But this time, he must have felt guilty and didn't wake me. I woke startled and sat right up in bed to see Anita's cruel face looking at me from the doorway. Curling up, I tried not to mess the covers. I knew I would be in trouble the minute Dad left to go to work because Anita had to get me back for her sister liking me. The next day, Freddy left for work, but it was still too early to start back to school. Although I dreaded staying home, at least the basement would be cool during those long, hot summer days and nights.

I was afraid I wouldn't get a meal until Dad came back. In the summer, I would become skinnier because I didn't eat lunch at school. I would get hungrier whenever I smelled food Anita was cooking for herself. I wished they had sent me to camp for the short time left. Anita said if I kept busy sewing and cleaning I wouldn't feel the hunger pangs, but being busy didn't stop my feeling empty and hungry all the time. She couldn't wait to get to me after Freddy left. She began calling me "dirty bitch" and "ugly face," and said that I came from filth! She spit out names in Romanian; I knew she was cursing. Then she had me go down to the basement, get out my paper and pencils, and take off all my clothes. She accused me of humiliating her in front of her sister. And that her sister had lied when she praised me for being such a good guest and had told Anita that she just didn't want to get me in trouble with my dad. I knew that was a lie! She told me that I needed to be taught a lesson, that I didn't learn—but I would!

I was standing naked in the middle of the floor with my hands above my head. She warned me not to move an inch. She spit out more names at me: "ugly tramp," "little bitch," "harlot," "stupid," and many more. While she was calling out names, I remembered the story Auntie Rose had read to me about the ugly duckling that turned into a beautiful swan. I was wishing that would happen to me, and when Anita saw me daydreaming she whipped the belt so hard across my waist and back that I fell to the floor! She kept saying, "Get up, you tramp, get up!" and continued beating me until I knelt on the floor crying, not just from pain but because of the realization that I belonged to no one. My heart was crushed!

I couldn't get up, so she grabbed me by the hair and pulled me to the bathroom, screaming at me the entire length of the floor. "Crawl into the shower, you filthy girl!" Anita ordered. It was hard crawling in there, and I could tell by the feel of the air that the water was cold. She left for a moment and returned carrying a pail. There was something in it—bleach—I shut my eyes and she splashed it over my body. It burned so badly, I screamed in pain. My skin felt weird. The odor was overpowering, and in a curled up position I couldn't avoid getting the bleach in my eyes and mouth. When I tried rubbing my eyes, they burned even more. "This is not your home! Do you understand?" she screamed at me. Anita ran the freezing cold water over me, and when the bleach washed away I was bright red and in pain. She walked away and left me at the bottom of the shower, wondering what was coming next.

Even though I had to pee, I was afraid to ask to go to the toilet. I could have peed in the shower, but she would have killed me. Then she came to the edge of the shower with a plate that had a sandwich on it. In a different tone of voice than she had used before, a teasing one, she asked if I was hungry and if I wanted to eat before I did my writing. "Yes, I am hungry, Anita, please." She told me to sit on the toilet cover and dry off. I did, and then she took the towel away. She told me to stand up, lift the cover, and sit down on the toilet seat. I asked her if I could go to the bathroom, and she said, "Not yet." Then she picked up half of the sandwich and started to eat. She told me to not look away, to watch her. My stomach was growling. When Anita finished eating, she told me I could go to the bathroom. I was relieved and happy, even with the humiliation of her watching me. I was about to flush when she blocked my arm and stopped me. As my eyes widened in disbelief, she dropped the other half of her sandwich into the toilet bowl. The sandwich! It was floating in the yellowed water. "Eat it if you are so hungry," she said. I could not, and would not, do it. She said, "Then you aren't hungry enough, but you will be soon!"

Naked and hungry, I sat at my desk with my pencils and paper and wrote sentences for hours. I wrote the sentence, "I will not talk back to Anita," a hundred times over. I fell asleep a few times, my head resting on the desk—then I was awakened by a slap of the belt across my back! Startled, I jumped up and continued to write. After many hours, Anita gave me a glass of Hood's milk, the best taste in the world, but by then I would have been happy with any scrap of food. I would have been happy with sugar water! That night I had to sleep on a towel on the boiler room floor. Somehow, I managed to wrap the towel tightly around myself. It felt good to sleep and not to have to see Anita again until the next day.

Over the next few days, the beatings and food deprivation became worse. My aching stomach was always growling. Anita would hold my head under the water in the sink until I couldn't hold my breath any longer and my arms would flail wildly about. I began having a recurring dream of Mommy Rose standing at the top of a staircase, wide at the bottom and narrowing as it reached the top, beckoning me to come up. I couldn't make it more than one step—always one, and not a step more. She would talk to me, telling me that I could do it and she was up there waiting for me. "Come up, Libbe. Come up. You can do it," she encouraged me. I don't know what kept me from going higher up the stairway.

Anita made sure I was upstairs in my bedroom just before Dad came back from being on the road. I had to sleep on the floor, and if my dad asked me about it, I was instructed to say that I had fallen out of bed while I was sleeping. And then there was some good news! Anita had convinced my dad to ship me off to camp for the remainder of the summer. I couldn't wait to go…the degradation was never-ending. Anita would spit in my eyes whenever I asked her a question. Mommy was in the sky, and Elizabeth was with me all the time—I had a friend—but it was becoming increasingly difficult to be with Anita in the house at 11 Dewitt Road.

CHAPTER SEVEN

After Camp, Back to School

I would have a little less than a month at camp before school started. Despite my protests, Anita packed for me; things I would not have chosen to wear at camp. Daddy said that Anita knew what she was doing. She decided not to give me money for canteen because I would just buy candy with it like the other kids did. On the way to Pine Hill Camp, I experienced a feeling of dread in the car as I recalled the first time I went there, sitting under a tree, and a boy threw a daddy long-legs spider at me. I was petrified of spiders, especially daddy long-legs. I made it through camp again, however isolated I felt there this time, and when I returned to the house on Dewitt Road, I felt like a stranger visiting for the first time. I was struck with fear—now I was "home" to stay. Oh no!

The first day back at school was a nightmare. The other children made fun of me, calling me "Toothpick Siskinditis" because I was so skinny and still had very short hair. After the school year, I felt like I never wanted to go back to school again. I was made fun of all the time.

Anita spoke on and on about how at my age I should be doing more housework. And although I was a bad child, I would get better before my next birthday. I didn't know what she meant. That night was odd because Anita did not beat me or make me write sentences as she usually did...I thought that perhaps she was sick. I sat in the kitchen at the table and she gave me some thick soup and didn't take away the plate. Next, she gave me a glass of milk and a small plate of food. I couldn't tell what the food was but I thought it was chicken and peas. I ate a piece, and it was fish! I coughed it up. "Please, Anita, I can't eat this—it's fish!" My throat was itchy, but this wasn't the first time she had served me fish, and I had a trick now too. I stuffed the fish into the bottom of my chair through a hole I'd made in the fabric. The other times I used my trick I assumed Anita didn't notice so she served me fish again because I didn't have a reaction or die. I was too young to make the connection between not dying and lying about having an allergy to fish. I didn't understand that eating the fish made it seem as though I must have been lying all along. I knew I didn't want to die and was afraid that would happen because Anita wouldn't call the doctor.

Anita told me to clean up and go downstairs and she would be there later. I quickly rinsed my mouth in the sink and sat down at my desk, with my lips and tongue swollen from where the fish had touched me. There was a knock at the back door. It was Kat, Mrs. Heber's daughter, who came to see if I could go to her house. She had asked me over countless times, but Anita would say no and that I was busy. Anita let her come downstairs to see me, which was a first. Out of fear, Kat and I were whispering. Then, after a few minutes, I could hear Anita's footsteps slowly coming down to the basement. She said, "Libbe has been very bad and she can't go out. She can not have company until she straightens out and becomes a lady." She asked Kat, "Do you understand?"

Kat answered, "Yes, but Libbe doesn't come out anymore except for school."

"That's right," Anita said. "And when she listens, she will go out one day."

Kat turned to me and said, "I'll meet you in the morning to walk to school with you."

I nodded because I felt too scared to speak. I had already let her know that Anita was mean to me but didn't ever give her any of the details. I was going to ask Anita if I could walk Kat upstairs, but before I had the chance, Anita jumped at me and said to Kat, "I will show you what bad girls get!" She began to spank me with the belt and pulled up my dress in front of Kat, who ran up the stairs and out the door! I was so embarrassed and later heard that Anita was the talk of the neighborhood. They said she was crazy. But Anita wasn't even half-done after Kat ran out of the house. She pulled me by the hair to the chair, the one I had stuffed with fish. She must have smelled it, or found out some other way, and she made me get it out, put it in a napkin, and take it to the backyard. She told me to dig a hole to bury the fish and then to put my face over the hole. She shoved my face into the dirt, and with both hands on the back of my head, she pushed and rubbed my face into the dirt and spoiled fish while screaming, "Eat it! Eat the filth, damn you!" I couldn't help crying. I couldn't hold back the tears, and I was gasping for air because of the dirt and pieces of dried-out fish in my mouth. Then she brought me inside, covered in soil, to sit in a corner of the garage. I hated sitting there, but was grateful for the light that filtered through the door's square window like a ray of hope. I stayed in that corner until dark, looking at the steps to the inside door and remembering the old gardener, on guard for spiders crawling near me. One day I would run away; I wished to be any place other than where I was. That was a long, uncomfortable night: she beat me unmercifully, gave me milk for a meal, and then sent me to the boiler room, hungry, to go to sleep. She said that if I made it to my next birthday, I would be lucky…very lucky. I did not care anymore.

For the next few months, I planned to run away. I had only two friends at school: Diana, from the end of the street, and my best friend, Kat—at least I thought she was my best friend. Sometimes on my way home after school, I would see Kat's beautiful sister waiting at the door for her. Since Anita moved into the Stoneham house, I wasn't able to watch Elizabeth Taylor on TV or see any of my favorite programs. When Daddy was home he would watch *Dragnet* or sports programs, especially the Red Sox during baseball season, and wrestling with Killer Kowalski and Haystack Calhoun. Before, he used to take me to see the wrestling with his brother Abe, who lived in Chelsea. He'd watch programs Anita suggested, whatever she wanted to see. Anita said I was not to watch TV. Instead, she had me doing chores like cleaning and scrubbing the entire house. Anita had it all covered. She got just what she wanted.

It was getting colder out, as it does in October and November. My birthday was coming up, and I knew it was going to be another bad one, so I was prepared. Anita said she had a surprise for my next birthday. She had never told me she had a surprise for me before, and I hoped it was some cookies or a cake like Mommy Rose used to make, although in my heart I knew better. Still, I thought, *maybe.* She hadn't hit me for a couple of days. Certainly, I wasn't anticipating what happened next.

Anita told me to shut my eyes tight and wait. I was wearing a pair of pajama bottoms and an undershirt. She said to put my hands behind my back to be tied, and that she would lead me. I was afraid she was going to hit me. Then I heard the boiler room door open. *It was too early for bedtime, so why was I going in there now?* I thought. I wasn't eager to open my eyes. She told me to sit down, and I felt the concrete floor under my bottom. My hands were tied with a silk stocking and my eyes remained shut. "Surprise!" she shouted. "You've made it to ten years old!" And there, on the floor, was a plate and a cupcake with an unlit candle in it, and a glass of milk. My eyes were wide open, and Anita said, "I'm going to tie your legs together. See if you can get your gift." *How can I get my cupcake?* I thought. I didn't dare ask. She said, "If you can get it, you can eat it. Happy Birthday, slut. Goodnight."

There I was—alone in the dark, cold, with no towel, and hungry. One thing was clear: I wanted that cupcake! I squirmed on the floor until I reached it. As I stuck my face into the top of it to take a bite, my breath was taken away! It was not sweet, but tasted like salt and pepper! I spit it out and lapped a little of the milk from the top of the glass; that was the best I could do to wash away the bad taste with my hands tied. I curled up to go to sleep, but I had to go to the bathroom. I held it as long as I could…and then I passed out. When I awoke, I was saturated with pee, and my stomach was empty. Anita came downstairs. "Guess you weren't that hungry after all," she said. She grasped me by the hair at the back of my head, pulled me over to the puddle of urine, and rubbed my face in it, scratching the skin on the cement floor. She untied my legs and wrists, then said, "Clean it up, tramp!" Then she asked, "What happened? You didn't like your baking soda and salt cupcake?" She was angry I had made a mess by spitting out the mouthful of cupcake. I didn't even understand what she was telling me and kept cleaning, trying to get rid of the odor with the scrub brush and bucket she gave me. I couldn't wait to go outside in the fresh air and daylight with Kat to talk on the way to school. I hoped she wouldn't leave without me.

My arms and legs hurt badly, but that was okay because Kat had given me a card for my birthday with money in it. Last year, I told Kat that no one had given me a gift. It was a good thing I had an extra sweater with me because it was cold, and I pushed the money up the sleeve of my jacket. I had five dollars! Wow! That was a lot of money to me. I told Kat I wanted to run away, and that I didn't want to go back to Anita ever again. I confided in her, and told her that Anita beat me every day—she was trying to kill me! She said that I could come over to her house and stay with her family, that her mother would know what to do. I told Kat, "No, it's our secret. I don't want Anita to find out what I said. Please don't tell, please? You're my only friend. Please Kat, please tell me you won't say anything?" She promised, and when we got to school, I couldn't concentrate and was sent out of class twice for not paying attention. I figured that the school's front office must have called Anita to tell her. She will kill me, for sure! I'm not going home, I'm going to run away to Aunt Rose's house today.

I walked home as usual, and after leaving Kat at her door, I cut through the yards to the next street. I was free! No Anita! No more boiler room, beatings, or taking freezing cold showers! It was cold outside, and I was happy I had my sweater on underneath my winter coat. I wore gloves, but my fingers were still numb. I walked past a small store and in the direction of the Weiss Farm—an old, large white house with cows and chickens. My daddy and mom knew them, and I had even stayed with them once when I was very young.

I decided to go into the little store for food that I hadn't eaten for a long time: candy, crackers, drinks, my Hostess Cupcakes. I even had change left over. I needed to find Aunt Rose's house, and I thought that if I kept walking, I would get there. I had no clue that I was walking in the wrong direction, not toward Newton. It was getting darker and colder. All that mattered to me was that I was free and had food, yet I felt scared and alone. No one was ever there at the house for me except that witch Anita, who waited every day to lock me up, beat and torture me. I longed to go to sleep among the stars above. I talked to my friend Elizabeth Taylor and made up stories as I ate my snacks. There was a big hill ahead. I went up and sat down, then got some leaves and stones to build a fort up against a large rock. I was unaware it was public property. It was warmer, and I curled up on my bed of leaves with my bag of candy. I counted the stars and made wishes; I hoped that just one would come true, especially my wish that Daddy would care about me again. And if not, please just take me to heaven. I didn't want to go back to my house where Anita was…ever. I fell asleep.

Then the next thing I knew, I was being shaken. I must have dozed off. "Wake up, little girl! Hey honey, wake up!" When I opened my eyes, I saw two policemen. One of them was helping me up. I guess I had fallen into a deep sleep. They asked for my name. I told them my name and that I was walking to my Aunt Rose's house. I couldn't go home because my stepmother had a rare disease. I didn't know a missing report on a girl of my description had been issued. I told them my daddy was away, and that I couldn't go home because he wasn't there. I had to go to my Aunt Rose's house until my daddy returned home in a few days. "Please take me to my aunt's house," I begged. "My aunt is waiting for me." The officer told me that they had to speak to my mother first. "She is *not* my mother, she's my stepmother!" I pleaded, "No, no, she is contagious!" He said there was a missing report on me and it would take just a minute to get to my house. Then he would take me to my aunt's house in Newton. If only he had phoned Auntie Rose first!

We drove to my house, and I stayed in the car with the other officer while the one who had talked to me went to the front door. He rang the bell, and then backed down the stairs to be away from my stepmother who was, as I told him, contagious. He told Anita he would take me to my aunt's house while she was sick. Anita was furious. "Sick?" She let them know I was a habitual liar and that she was not sick. She said I was a disturbed child. As the other officer opened my door, I held my bag with the rest of the candy tightly. He told me to come out and that I had to go inside my house. Tears rolled down my cheeks. As I approached the front door, I sensed the beating that was inevitable. It occurred to me to tell the officers about what was awaiting me, but I was too timid. Plus, the officer said, "That was not a nice thing you said about your mom."

I spoke up and replied, again, "She is not my mom! My mom's in heaven!"

The officer said to Anita, "She appears to need some discipline. A spanking will teach her not to run away from a home with such a caring parent."

Caring parent? I thought. I am starved and live in fear every day of my life and cannot tell anyone because she will kill me! Anita had convinced him how worried she was. Why couldn't anyone see I wasn't a bad girl? Even as I grew to be a young adult I was treated the same way—as if I was a "bad seed."

Anita was so pleasant to the officers; she waved to them like they were good friends as they were about to drive away. Once they'd left, she pushed me down the hallway, through the kitchen, clutching me by the neck, and shoved me down the basement stairs. I hit my back against the last step and wall, and it hurt! I couldn't move right away. Some of the candy spilled out of my pocket…and I knew she was about to become worse. She seized the torn bag from me, and as she emptied it all out on the floor she said, "Is that the kind of shit you buy with money stolen from me?"

I raised my shoulders and used my hands to make a point. "No, I did not! I didn't steal anything!" I argued. "It was my money, Anita! It was my money, I swear!"

She screamed at me, "You liar, you tramp, you no good bitch! You have no money!"

I didn't want her to know that Kat and her mother had given me the money for my birthday. Anita's diatribe continued. "I'll show you to how eat shit! I'll teach you not to lie! And to not speak unless spoken to!" She slapped me until my cheeks were red—they stung like when she beat me with the strap.

I was stripped of all my clothes, then put in an ice cold shower with lye soap. She beat me all over my back and legs, and I had welts and stripes that were worse than before because this time she hit me all over my body. I cried out "Please Anita, stop!" so many times, promising her I would never run away again. Rather than hitting me on the knuckles with a ruler like my teacher Miss Zane, she whipped my palms again and again until I couldn't move my fingers, insisting that I stole money from her. She told me to bend over, and then she beat me some more. She hurt me badly. She ranted vehemently in Romanian, and then said, "I will cripple you!" I was suffering and could not help screaming out in pain. She said, "That'll make you think twice!" If only someone could hear me from the basement—she always saved her worst brutality until we were down there, where no one could hear.

Next, she told me to go upstairs and get into the bathtub. Then she ran the cold water until it was freezing and the tub was full. Every part of my body stung. I sat there shivering until she told me to get out. I couldn't tell if I was numb or in pain, like the time Mommy and Dad brought me to a pond to skate and I fell onto my rear on the freezing ice; this felt like the freezing cold through the tights covering my bare bottom that day. I was shaking and turning bright red. Finally, she let the water out. She ordered me out of the bathroom and told me to go to the boiler room. I was naked with no towel. "Get out of my sight, you dirty girl!" she said. "I'll deal with you later." She locked me inside the boiler room and left. I was safe. Freezing, I laid down, feeling very tired and sick to my stomach. I couldn't find a comfortable position no matter how I twisted and turned. Every inch of my skin hurt. I was thankful to have Elizabeth beside me in the dark; it made me feel warm. I thought to myself that I would never run away again unless I could go so far away that I wouldn't be caught. After I talked to myself, and Elizabeth, for a while, I drifted off to sleep in a fetal position while listening to the sound of the boiler flue flapping back and forth.

Anita did not forget that night. She was going crazy at me every day, and at night she would wake me yelling and screaming, slapping me, spitting in my face, and—of course—calling me every derogatory name she knew. Anita was so infuriated by the bag of candy I bought that she referred to it as the "bag of shit." One night, after I wrote hundreds of sentences, Anita told me, "Since you like to eat shit, that's what I'll give you every day for supper." I didn't understand. What did that mean? She never gave me sweets? And the little bit of food she allowed me to eat was so small; plain boiled peas or beets. If and when I got a piece of chicken—wow!

I hadn't been upstairs on a weekday for some time, why was today different? She told me to wash up before I came upstairs for supper, but after I cleaned myself and went up to the kitchen, she told me to go back to the basement and wait until I was called. I was so hungry. I'd only had milk at school and half of a cream cheese and olive sandwich. Kat gave me cookies on the way home a few times, and I was so grateful. I was no longer embarrassed to say I was hungry. I told Kat not to say anything to the other kids. Kat said she'd have her mom put extra food in her lunchbox for me. "You should have told me sooner," she said. I was always afraid for anyone to know and I hoped Mrs. Heber wouldn't say anything to Anita. When I told Kat that I hadn't told Anita about her birthday money, she understood; Kat was afraid of Anita too.

I was down in the basement waiting when I heard her awful yell, "Libbe, get up here, tramp!" I skipped up the stairs and into the kitchen. On the table there was a glass of milk and a large plate of what looked like sugar or salt in a pile, like a small pie. I sat down and Anita ordered me to eat. I was enthusiastic about eating, but as usual, I was afraid because I didn't know what was on the plate. Maybe there was fish underneath! There was no fork so I took the spoon, scooped up the sugar with some breadcrumbs, and put it in my mouth. It was sweet, but somehow strange. I took another spoonful of sugar, and what looked like chocolate pudding under the layer of crumbs and sugar. As I dug in, the odor was foul, but I put the concoction in my mouth again. And immediately, I identified the sour smell and bitter taste—under the chocolate pudding was real shit, doo-doo! I threw up and was heaving and gagging. Anita stared at me and said, "Eat it…you like shit. Eat it, or I will shove it down your throat!" I didn't care! I could *not* eat it! I said, "Please, Anita! I promise! I swear! I'll never run away or eat candy again! I promise! Please, please! I promise to be good!"

She came over to my side of the table and said, "Promise?"

I said, "Yes, I do! I will do everything you say!" She patted me on the top of my head. I took a breath, and then she grabbed my hair in her fist and shoved my face in the plate, rubbing it into the filth! The breadcrumbs, pudding, and sugar couldn't mask the putrid odor. As she pulled me back, there was a foul taste in my mouth and my eyes were burning. Even though I should have known something worse could always happen, I hadn't expected her to do that! She was hateful. Her message was clear. She was not capable of being, nor would she ever be, decent toward me. I couldn't breathe as she shoved the shit and sugar farther into my mouth, and screamed at me, "Swallow!"

I vomited again. I felt like I was what she continually accused me of being: a dirty, filthy girl. She shook me by the shoulders and told me, "Clean it up, you bitch, clean it up!" Gagging and heaving, I wiped it up. My eyes were swollen, and though I kept trying to spit it out, the rancid taste stayed in my throat. Anita pushed me away from my chair while I was still, essentially, vomiting. I was choking. I felt that I couldn't get up. Yelling and screaming, she kicked me repeatedly. I was overcome with exhaustion and wanted to die. Finally, she pushed me down the stairs. As she screamed at me to get out of her sight, I braced myself for the landing. She shrieked, "I hate you, you no good tramp! Wash your dirty body!" I was convinced she was trying to kill me. Once I was safely in the washroom, I scrubbed myself, then I entered my boiler room. I wondered why she didn't force me to clean the kitchen. Whose shit was it? Was it hers or a dog's she'd picked up? *Oh god,* I wondered, *what kind of person is Anita?*

I couldn't get the taste of the shit out my mouth, and for the next few days, Anita would say that I stunk of it. I was afraid of eating anything she gave me. Now the olive and cream cheese sandwiches even tasted funny, so I would throw them away. I was afraid that I smelled and didn't want any of the kids at school near me. In fact, the idea that my mouth had an odor carried forward into my adult life when it came to being kissed. It scared the shit out of me—no pun! Thank goodness I got over that eventually, although it took until I was well into my thirties.

I was looking forward to lunch now that Kat had extra for me: real sandwiches, cakes, and cookies. I showed her the bruises and welts Anita had given me so she would know the truth. She wanted to tell her parents, but I was afraid of Anita and reminded Kat that it was our secret. She had been under the impression that olive and cream cheese sandwiches were my favorite, and I told her I despised them, but that it was the only kind of sandwich Anita would give me. Kat promised she would not tell, and we did "blood sisters" to seal it. I believed it was our secret, and that made me happy. I prayed Anita would never keep Kat from me.

Since that time, I had stayed in Connecticut with Anita's sister, I did not feel I belonged anywhere. The day Anita—out of sheer malice—shouted that I was not my mother and father's child, that I was adopted, my world turned upside-down. *I have no one, not even Freddy,* I thought. *Things are so different now.*

One day when Daddy was home (they spent every moment together when he was), I overheard him and Anita planning to go away to Florida for two weeks during the coming year or the year after, as they had done before. They were not sure, but I kept that in mind as something to look forward to, and I made a wish for that time to hurry up and come. Anita continued complaining about me to Dad. They spoke about me going to Florida to live with the Taffees for a few months. That confused me. I never thought Anita would let me go anywhere that far away. I really didn't like the Taffees, particularly Mr. Taffee, who was strange and trembled, but anybody was better than Anita. They decided I would go to Florida for the new school year, which started in September. I was old enough. I thought about the weather in Florida and, though I would miss snow, how it would be better than the constant cold and the wool Anita made me wear. I was happy and tried not to care if Anita didn't feed me. There was one day on the weekends when I got a full meal to eat. On his day off, after Daddy woke from his nap, we'd have dinner. He never asked me how I was. Instead, as though I weren't there, he would ask Anita how I was and if I was still bad. She always told him that I misbehaved. Then he'd scold me because he never got good reports. He seemed angry with me all the time. I could eat at the table with him, but Anita ordered me beforehand to tell him I was full, that I didn't want seconds—no seconds! I desperately wanted Daddy's love, and just being able to sit with him at the dining room table was wonderful. I didn't allow myself to smile because I was too afraid Anita would take away that time with him. I learned never to show happiness whenever I was around her.

The days after Dad left were always hellish. I spent my time washing clothes with the scrub board, bleach, and lye soap until my hands and knuckles were red and sore. It was always some work or chore—never playtime. I didn't know if I remembered how to play anymore; even at recess I wasn't interacting with the other kids. I just wanted to eat, sleep in a bed, and be warm. I told myself that if I ever had children I would sell my soul to clothe and feed them.

Hanukkah passed, and as usual, there were no presents for me. There were wrapped gifts that I never opened. Anita lit the candles. And she told my father I didn't want anything, just clothes. I never said a word. My father and Anita both said that I had to go to another social worker because I misbehaved in school, my eating habits were a concern, and I appeared ill-kempt. My dad worshipped Anita and always believed what she told him. They contacted Jewish Family Services to arrange counseling for me. I was told that I would have ongoing sessions twice a month and an evaluation every year. I wondered, *Why me? Why not them?*

As I was coming into the house from school, I saw Anita waiting at the door with a belt in her hands and a weird expression on her face, one that I'd never seen before…I was doomed. Before I could speak, she began to beat me in the doorway! As I moved backward on the step, she pushed me onto the garage floor! Stunned, I put up my hands to block the belt because yesterday's beating had been so brutal, and I was too sore to withstand another one. "You liar, you tramp! You told people that you were being starved, did you? You'll be starved *now*! You'll see what it's like to have 'no food'! Get in this house, right now!" I went into the house so fast it was as if I had wings. How did she know? Kat and I were blood sisters, she promised not to tell anyone. She must have told her mom. Oh god! Anita screamed, "How long did you think you'd be fed by your friend, huh? How long, you little bitch?" I shook my head, and Anita grasped my hair in her fist, pulled me to the sink, and poured black pepper in my mouth. The area of my head where she had pulled my hair the day before was sore, and throbbed with pain. "Liar, liar!" she said. I was choking and gasping for air! The pepper burned and I couldn't swallow! Anita told me I couldn't walk with Kat anymore.

"No, Anita!" I yelled out. "I promise I won't take food from her! Please, please, Anita—she's my friend!"

Anita slapped me on the back of the head and continued beating me. "Don't let me catch you near her!" she threatened. Needless to say, there wasn't any supper, not even a glass of milk. She only gave me water. It was difficult to walk because my feet hurt, and my back and body were so sore. What will I do? How can she stop me from walking to school with my friend in the morning? I could meet Kat at the end of the street. Anita wouldn't be at the end of the street unless she followed me. That's where I can meet Kat.

I spent the evening sitting up in the boiler room, listening to Anita loudly bang things around in the kitchen and angrily talk to herself. I was tired but too frightened to go to sleep. Eventually, I dozed off. That morning, Anita sent a note in a sealed envelope to the teacher. She waited for Kat to go to school before she sent me. Kat didn't wait for me at the end of the street or after school. I felt lonely because she wasn't there and hungry because there wasn't any food for me. I wondered if her mom was afraid of Anita too. At recess she told me I had gotten her in trouble because I had lied about the food to get extra, that Anita actually gave me food and I would hide it. She said Anita told her mom I was being treated by a psychiatrist and that I might be mentally disturbed, that was the reason for my lying, and she had documents from Mass Mental to prove it. She said that Kat needed to stay away from me. Anita was winning! She was convincing and had an answer for everything. Now Anita had me all to herself. I was totally isolated. No one was allowed to visit my house unless she gave the okay, not even family. She never allowed anybody to come close to me. I needed to protect myself. I made the decision not to talk with the girls at my school because they were cruel to me. Why try to be friends with anyone who doesn't like me? I didn't want the summer to come because I would not have the six hours a day at school where, even though the kids hated me, I was away from Anita. I was an outcast—alone, all alone.

Whenever we visited either Dad's or Anita's relatives, I had to sit in a chair and tell everyone that I was sick and couldn't get up. I didn't want to anyway because the wool clothes that Anita made me wear were itchy against my allergic skin. I never told my aunts anything anymore. I would just shake my head when they asked me if I wanted any food. I would politely say thank you and that I was not hungry. Everyone was convinced I needed mental health treatment. All I did was stare off into space and bite my nails. Inside I was pleading, *Help…help…doesn't anyone hear me?* After a while, I couldn't think of stories to share with Elizabeth, and I stopped playing with her too.

Freddy and Anita went away for a week to Florida again. While they were away, I stayed with neighbors, the Grays. I hadn't stayed with them for more than a day or two before, but Freddy said I was old enough now to go back and forth from my house to theirs. I knew the Grays as well as other folks I'd stayed with, though I didn't feel close to them because they were strict Catholics, and Dad had forbidden me to be involved in any of their religious prayers at mealtimes because I was Jewish.

It was warmer than usual when Freddy and Anita got into the car to go to the airport. Dad put an extra house key for me in the garage in case I needed it to take more clothes over to the Grays. As they left, he warned me to behave myself—no hugs or "I'll miss you." At least the Grays had children, and Mrs. Gray was a good cook. She always had her daughter and I pull our hair away from our faces at the dinner table to be neat, and then they all said grace. They prayed, but I didn't. I did fold my hands and say "amen."

At school, the Gray children had told the other kids that the Siskind house was empty. They wanted to have a party there, and told me that if I wanted friends I had to let them do it. I told them I was afraid of getting in trouble and refused. They said that they would keep the house clean. They understood it to be an odd place, everything covered in plastic, and that Anita had a sign in the kitchen that read, "Cleanliness is next to Godliness." They promised. Kat had promised and broken her word, but because I was desperate to have friends, I wanted to believe them. They said the party would be this weekend and they promised that after that, they would all be my friends. So, I believed them. I was apprehensive, but I said okay to the party. Just to be sure, I asked, "Just a few kids?" and they said yes. I didn't know them before, but the kids who knew about the party at my house acted friendlier to me, and that made me feel important. I was so naive! Mrs. Gray's daughter knew all of them and so it seemed it would be all right.

The day of the party arrived. So many kids came over that I couldn't control them. The bullies pushed me aside like it wasn't my house! They just called me a baby and told me to grow up. They were twelve years old and older, and they were wrecking Dad's house! If Anita ever saw this she would kill me! It was the first time I was happy that everything in the house had plastic covers. I knew I would have to clean up the mess after the party ended, and I wished with all my might that they would leave. It was so late when they did begin to go, and I didn't know where to begin…this was a nightmare! I'd been misled and lied to again! Mrs. Gray thought I was at a sleepover at her daughter's friend's home; what if she finds out? Days later, I learned that the nosy neighbor who caused Nanny Talbet to be fired, Mrs. Broder, didn't call the police to break up the party because she had no idea that my father had gone away on vacation. Freddy and Anita were due back either the next night or the day after—I wasn't certain which one. I was tired and there was no one to help me. As the kids were leaving the basement, they kicked over their cups so that their drinks spilled on the floor.

I tried putting things back in order, but I rarely went upstairs and didn't know where all the things belonged. When I took a towel from the linen closet, I saw that eggs were broken on the sheets and beer was spilled all over. The boys had peed on the closet floor. Everything smelled, and I could not move fast enough to try to clean up the mess and wash the sheets. I worked for the rest of the night until early morning. The sheets never dried; I had to put them back damp.

When Mrs. Gray's daughter woke from her nap on the floor, she smelled like beer. She said she was going to her house to eat and that I should come. She told me she would help me afterward. I told her that I had to finish. She didn't care, and said that she would tell her mom that I had stopped at my house to get something. When I asked her why she and her friends had done this, she told me that's what happened at parties, and I was a baby who was still scared of her mommy and daddy. She was right—I was scared. I yelled at her, saying that Anita was not my mommy. "Okay, okay. I'm leaving," she said. It didn't occur to me that if she had done the same in her own house she would have been in big trouble. I was alone in my dad's house, "Anita's jail." If she finds out, I'm dead! She would say that I held the party to spite her; Anita always called me a spiteful child.

I had never known any boy as a friend except for the Kessel boy who lived down the street from school. He would talk to me every now and then and belonged to the temple my mom helped build in Stoneham. The boys at the party were loud. They were drinkers who swore and kissed girls. The Kessel boy wasn't like that at all. I had never witnessed this kind of behavior before. I was cleaning as fast as I could, and although it looked passable to me, I could not get it all. I should have looked more closely at the areas that seemed okay; I assumed that there was nothing left to do. I rushed back to the Grays, hoping I could get some food. It was not until later in the evening that Mrs. Gray got a call from my father. We were all in bed for the night. He said it could wait until the morning, but that there was a problem at the house. I had one final, peaceful night before all hell broke loose.

The next morning arrived far too quickly. Just as I was about to sit down to breakfast, Mrs. Gray answered a sharp, continuous knocking on the back door. It was Anita, and she was boiling mad! "Where is she? Where is the witch?" Anita shrieked.

Mrs. Gray stepped back and said, "Anita, is everything okay? Calm yourself. She's right here, having breakfast with us, and then I was planning to walk her home. You're welcome to come in and have something to eat."

In her high-pitched voice Anita said, "No, no, she will eat with us. She is to come home now! She destroyed my house! She had people there! Did you know about this? The neighbor next door said there were lots of people, lots of boys."

Mrs. Gray turned pale as she looked at me, and said, "Libbe, is that true?" I was scared and remained silent. Then she asked her daughter what went on. Her daughter said it was my fault and I had invited boys and girls to a party. She said that she tried to break up the party. "I didn't want to get Libbe in trouble, Mom."

Her mother asked, "Were you there?"

She answered, "I went over to help her get the kids out and clean up."

I looked up. She lied! How dare she? I was speechless; I would never do that to a friend. But she's not my friend. I know that now. It wasn't my idea, and she lied to clear herself. It wouldn't matter—they would never believe me. I was going to get it from Anita whether it was entirely my fault or not. I was better off to say nothing and take the blame. It was not in me to squeal on anyone. Anita was dragging me by the ear as we went out. I could hear Mrs. Gray say to her daughter that she was not allowed to hang around with me unless it was at their house under her supervision. I wondered, because Freddy was home, what would happen. Would she beat me in front of him? Now he will be convinced beyond a doubt that I am as bad as Anita says I am, that I have "bad blood."

"She comes from bad blood," she would say to Freddy, "and you know it. She's a tramp like her mother." I was told my real mother was a tramp, so I assumed I must be one too. Freddy always agreed with her. He began to scream at me, saying, "Look at this! Look at that! Libbe, look what you did to Anita's house and things!" Anita's house? Really! "And now you're hanging around with boys! What's wrong with you? There better not be things missing from the house!" I was so unfamiliar with the house that I wouldn't have known if things had been taken or not.

Once my dad left, there would be hell to pay. "You'll be going to live with the Taffees soon," he told me before he went on the road, "and you'd better behave when you're there or next time it will be a detention center for bad girls! Maybe that's the best solution—for you to give Anita a break from your bad behavior." *Everyone hates me,* I thought. *Now Daddy hates me as much as Anita does.* Anita resumed her brutal beatings. I scrubbed all the linens by hand as well as the floors. Food was a distant memory. I couldn't wait to leave my dungeon room.

CHAPTER EIGHT

Florida

The Taffees were there waiting for me when I arrived at their small home in Stoneham. I hadn't seen them for a long time. Mr. Taffee still shook, trembling even more than the last time I visited. Mrs. Taffee looked the same with her short, bleached-blonde hair, trailer-park-trash appearance, and large hands. She smelled like Dove soap and stale cigarette smoke, and had a deep voice with a raspy cough, the kind that came from smoking too much. I wondered if the Taffees still had their old, pug-nosed dog, a Boston terrier that snorted and had long nails that tapped against the linoleum floor in the kitchen when he walked. He must have been hiding. I hadn't seen him during my last stay.

At least I would be away from the house that haunted and tortured me, although I was sad to think that I wouldn't see my dad for a while. I would be staying with the Taffees in Florida for an even longer stretch once they moved. It was going to be sometime soon. I didn't know what would happen then. I'd be staying for only two or three days while Anita packed all my things, and afterward, she and Dad told me they were sending me right away to meet up with the Taffees in their new home in Florida for the entire school year. As it turned out, it was me who ended up leaving Boston and going to Florida, not Anita and my dad.

On one of my trips to Florida with Daddy and Mommy Rose, I was far too little to know anything. I have a fond memory of driving in Dad's Desoto, wearing a new pair of patent leather shoes. The shift was on the steering wheel, and Dad used to let me sit on his lap and play that I was steering the car. We could actually drive on the beach back then and even park on the sand. Mommy Rose and Dad got out of the car to test the water. As my Aunt Rose and Uncle Uggie told it, they left me in the car playing with the wheel. I was small, and they must have thought I would be okay. When I threw my shoes out the window, I accidentally hit the shift on the steering wheel and the car rolled into the water! I was not scolded but hugged because I was safe—and that's what mattered. Aunt Rose told and retold that story about how, as little as I was, I wanted to drive. Every time I listened to her tell it I was reminded of how much my mommy and daddy loved me. Memories of moments such as these were what kept me trying to regain my daddy's love.

Anita had me all packed up, and Dad was at home to take me to the airport. The Taffees left before me. Their furniture was being transported by truck ahead of time. The plan was for me to meet them in Florida after they had arranged their new house. As we were driving to the airport, I thought about funny moments with Anita, scenes that made me laugh, although she certainly wouldn't think they were funny. I was afraid of flying alone, and musing about Anita distracted me while I boarded. One of the incidents I recalled happened after I had finished writing my sentences and crept upstairs into the kitchen to show Anita what I had done. She was washing the kitchen floor, and when I handed her the papers the bucket of soapy water tipped over, and as she kicked the bucket in a fit of temper, she lost her balance and fell onto her behind in the pool of suds on the floor. I hid the joy I felt inside. She was busy cursing in Romanian and didn't see me, with a slight smile on my face, skip down the stairs to the basement, away from her anger.

The stewardesses kept me busy with all sorts of goodies, and before I knew it, we had landed. Mrs. Taffee was there to greet me at the airport terminal while Mr. Taffee waited in the car. The sun was unusually bright, and I stared at the tall palm trees, which were fascinating to me. She told me we had a drive ahead of us. I looked out the window of the car because sometimes I became carsick on long drives sitting in the back seat. I laughed inside about the other time in the kitchen when Anita slapped me for something I'd done, and I fell off the kitchen chair onto the floor. She was hovering over me screaming, and her 1950's Lucite glasses slipped down to the tip of her nose, about to fall off. I had to hold back from laughing out loud; I could feel the laugh coming up my throat and filling my cheeks with air. Then she leaned back to slide her eyeglasses back up, and she pushed them so hard out of anger that they went right up her nose and beyond, all the way to the middle of her forehead. I burst out in laughter and spit at the same time. Even though Anita took the strap to me, I could not stop laughing. "Oh, you think I'm funny, do you?" she said. I was laughing so hysterically I couldn't even feel the pain, letting it all out. It wouldn't have surprised me if Anita had started to laugh. I could tell that she wanted to. That was a great moment for me, and my smile warmed me inside with the thought.

Then I recalled another time when I was still sleeping on the cot in the basement (before I had graduated to the boiler room) and I was hungry, thirsty, and wanted milk. I crept up the stairs without making a sound, and just as I was about to get water at the sink, I turned and there she was—Anita. It was like a horror film. It was her, but she looked different, almost like someone else: she had a towel wrapped around her head and another around her body, with a thick layer of white cream on her face like a mask. She yelled, "How dare you!" as if I were a stranger who had just broken into the house. She ran upstairs as I ran downstairs to my cot to hide underneath the sheets. It was funny to me that I had seen her almost without anything on when she never let anyone see her without full makeup, hair, and a dress on. She was unattractive to say the least, a terrible sight. She never came downstairs that night. Laughing at her was my way of distancing myself from the constant pain.

One of the best moments happened when, for a change, I scared her instead of her scaring me. It was during one of her frenzied beatings when she ran after me, chasing me down the basement stairs while shrieking at me. I tried to get in a corner to put up my arms and protect myself but ended up on bench near the door to the boiler room. I saw the latch was on, and I couldn't escape in there fast enough. There were two brass candleholders on the wall above me, and Anita was whipping me so hard that I was swaying from side to side, and with one of her swings her hand caught a candleholder and it dislodged from the wall, falling on my head. It hit sharply, and I screamed out in pain, crying and holding my head. Anita stopped hitting me, and it was as if the world had stopped. I thought, *Okay, I will tell her I can't see.* I pulled my hand away from my face, looked straight ahead, and yelled out, "I can't see! I can't see! Please, I want to see! Daddy! I want my daddy!" I watched her moving back and forth and looked up to the ceiling so that my eyes wouldn't follow her.

"I'll get a cold rag!" she said—it was then I knew I had her. I was so happy that for once I was in control and not her. *I* finally scared *her.* I played out the triumphant moment for as long as I could. I was an actress in the starring role. I sat on the bench cushion, leaning back against the knotty pine paneling. As she gave me the rag with cold water, she asked, "Do you want to go to bed?" *Bed,* I thought… *where would she put me to bed?* But her heart was still cold and mean, and she rolled out the cot. I wasn't satisfied with that, but it was better than being beaten all night. I continued crying out, "When will I see, Anita? Please call my daddy!" "Oh no," she said. "You are not to tell your dad because this was *your* fault. Do you understand? Or there will be consequences."

I paused…"Yes, okay," I said.

She made me a couple of pieces of toast. I knew that eventually I would have to tell her that I was able to see, but a moment like this was worth all the times she had been cruel to me—for once, this evil woman was frightened of *me.* Finally, holding my head where a big lump had appeared, I told her I could see out of one eye. She hadn't screamed or yelled but waited silently until I could see. Because it hurt when she pressed the flat side of a cold knife against my bump, I didn't believe her when she told me it was to reduce the swelling. Then she told me to lie down and go to sleep and didn't demand anything else. She gave me a glass of milk. "You will be fine later," she said. Of course I was…

The things Anita did were so bizarre that I didn't know what was right or what was wrong. Just about everything I did was deemed wrong, except for when I was asleep at night and couldn't do anything. Before I began wetting the bed, even when I was on the cot, she always found some reason to wake me in the middle of the night. Anita would make me sew for hours, hemming pants and skirts. The stitches had to be perfect, and even when I made them perfect, she would pull them all out and make me do them again. I despised sewing and knew that when I grew up, I would never sew or iron clothes again.

My head was pressed against the car window as I thought about all these things, like I was watching a movie of my own life in which I was the actress performing the drama. Mrs. Taffee turned to me and said we were almost there, just a few more streets. Phew, I hated the back seat! These houses were different from what I was used to. They were long, and only one level high, with no garages, just carports. She pointed out the coconuts at the top of the palm trees. My dad always brought coconuts home with us, and I would get a piece to chew. Older and more curious, I asked her about them, and she told me there was sweet juice inside them that was healthy to drink. I wondered how it would be living in Florida. It was hot all the time, and there was no snow, ever. No sledding or tobogganing.

****

Hmmm...right now I wish I was there at my Florida house and not sitting in this Hell of a cement-walled cell!

****

We arrived at their house. Mr. Taffee was quiet the whole way. She had to help him out of the car first. He seemed to stop shaking a bit once she got him safely into his wheelchair. She took my little suitcase from the trunk and told me to take the other one. "This is where we live now. It's bigger and better than our old house in Stoneham," she said, "it has more bedrooms." Mrs. Taffee was very neat, but there weren't any plastic coverings on her floors or new furniture like in Anita's house. She said, "I'll show you your room and you can put your clothes away." I could hear chirping coming from the living room and asked what the sound was. She said that it was a bird, a parakeet. "Can I see it?" I asked. Mrs. Taffee said sure. It was blue, green, and yellow; it was pretty, but noisy. She said I couldn't play with it, that it only responded to her. I said okay, and that I would not touch the parakeet. When I asked her about her dog, she said, "Oh, J.T. passed away. Sixteen years old is long for a Boston Terrier to live," she explained. Even though I never particularly liked her dog, I felt an aching sadness. She told me to wash my hands and face before every meal and also when I came inside. I told her I would do that; it seemed easy enough. Just to know I would be sleeping in a real bed and wouldn't be getting beatings was enough to satisfy me. And Mrs. Taffee was an okay cook.

Mrs. Taffee said that before she registered me in school, I would be gardening and pulling the weeds under the trees. I used to watch Mommy Rose weeding, and I thought, *I can do that myself without help from anybody.* When Anita gardened, she had me do the work she hated, so I dug holes for her plants and wrenched the weeds from the ground. Mrs. Taffee made a "Libbe list" of things for me to do after I got out of bed in the morning: make my bed, pick out the clothes I wanted to wear, go to the bathroom and brush my teeth, wash my hands and face, and at night, take a bath or a shower. I would have to help clean the floors, dishes, and kitchen. I agreed to everything. I asked her if I would get supper every night. "Yes, of course, you will—like I always gave you—and seconds if you like. You'll also get breakfast, lunch, and a small snack before bed." I was ecstatic! The only thing that scared me was her husband, who would always glare at me. Having men or boys stare at me made me feel uncomfortable and unsafe. She would tell me to give him a kiss goodnight on the cheek. I didn't like that. He smelled like Mommy Rose's room in the hospital. His mouth drooped on one side and his speech was impaired, and it took me quite a while to understand him because each time I tried, he was worse.

It was time to enroll at the new school and I was better now, not as bent over from pain in my back. The sun felt good, and I was able to sleep at night without fear. There was one thing that did scare me, and that was the way Mr. Taffee would sit at the side of my bed early in the morning, shaking uncontrollably, watching me as I slept. I would suddenly wake up—and there he was with a sly smile across his face. I didn't know how long he had been sitting there, and when I spoke to Mrs. Taffee about it, she told me he was harmless and not to pay attention to him. She said, "He's up before the sun comes up and rides his wheelchair around the house. He's watching over you." It was impossible for me to ignore his gaping stare.

The more work I did for Mrs. Taffee, the more snacks she gave me. I was able to be healthy and gain some pounds, but why do I have to do all these things? Why do other kids play and I always have to work? I wondered why I wasn't allowed to play with toys or watch TV more often. I was always tired from morning until night. I wasn't allowed to bring friends home from school because of Mr. Taffee's illness. Kids asked if they could come over, but I had to tell them no. Mrs. Taffee said that she was responsible for my whereabouts and that my dad had given strict orders saying I wasn't allowed to socialize at other kids' houses. She drove me to and from school. I had no friends in Stoneham and none in Florida either. I only spoke to the kids I was friendly with during class. My dark clothing set me apart from the others, who wore more vibrant colors. All the colors in Florida seemed brighter than in Boston.

Because I didn't have friends, adjusting to the new school was difficult. Mrs. Taffee would report to my father every couple of weeks. She always said I was not doing well in school and that I might need extra help or stay back a year. "Libbe seems to have trouble concentrating." I told Dad that I sometimes had a problem understanding. Freddy wasn't surprised; Anita had filled his head with her vile comments about how stupid I was. I resented him for not seeing me on my ninth and tenth birthdays. In fact, Dad hadn't been home on any of my birthdays since Mommy Rose died. I wondered how long I would be staying with the Taffees. Although life was much better without Anita, I missed seeing my father. To me he was my real dad—the only father I knew—and I wanted him to spend time with me. At least at home I knew I would see him once a week. When he called Florida, he asked, "Are you behaving for the Taffees?" I would say, "Yes, Daddy, I'm being good. I miss you and I love you," to which he would respond, "Okay, I'll call you another time. Be a good girl." I could hear Anita screaming in the background, "Freddy, get off the phone!"

Mr. Taffee would not only sit by my bed in the morning, he began to come into the bathroom when I took baths. He would stare and shake like crazy, so much that his wheelchair creaked and clanged. Mrs. Taffee said that he was making sure that I washed all over with the soap. I felt strangely enough about him watching me when I slept. I did not like him staring at my private parts. He reminded me of the men who had touched me and enjoyed it, and I tried to make foamy, thick soapsuds so he could not see my body in the water. I was swirling the water hard one time, and Mrs. Taffee asked, "What are you doing?" in an accusing tone, and gave me a harsh look. She told my father I was masturbating in the tub, and that I was a dirty girl to do that with her husband in the room. The only good thing that came from it was that she did not let Mr. Taffee in the bathroom with me anymore, which for me was a victory. I didn't know what the word "masturbating" meant, but I understood soon enough from a girl I asked in school. Now Mrs. Taffee thought that I was a dirty kid with a dirty mind, and her obsession of scrubbing her hands with Dove soap was worse whenever she was near me. She had me washing my hands all the time, and I could smell the distinctive fragrance of Dove soap in the bathroom even when I was not washing my hands. I hated that bar of soap, and when I smell that scent, I still think of her. They were a pedophilic voyeur and his enabling wife, old people who used me as their "house girl"—a position for which Freddy paid them. As I recall, I did some sort of work in all the homes where I stayed throughout my childhood. I felt like a slave.

One day, Mrs. Taffee said I was to stay at the house and do my chores while she took Mr. Taffee to a doctor, and that she would be back shortly. I was cleaning, and the boisterous little bird was chirping wildly so I went to its cage. The cover was on, and I whispered,

"Birdy, be quiet, please, shhh." The bird kept on making noise, so I said, "No more singing!" as loudly as I could and lifted the cover. It was swinging and tweeting. Even though I wasn't supposed to, I opened the cage door to pick it up because I wanted to calm the bird. It flapped all around and was hard to get ahold of. But I finally got it and, squeezing and shaking it a little, I said, "Be quiet you, be quiet!" When the bird became quiet I tried putting it back on the swing, but it fell over. I pushed the bird with my finger and it did not move. I picked it up again. "Hey, birdy, wake up!" It was then I realized the bird was dead. Dead! Oh, no! Mrs. Taffee loved that bird! I didn't mean to kill it! "What can I do?" I said out loud. I didn't know what to do. I positioned the bird on its swing, leaning it against the cage, and replaced the cover. My heart was beating fast, just like the bird's heart when I held it. I had killed a living creature; I did not mean to! If I told them it was an accident, they wouldn't believe me. Would they put me in jail? I knew from watching *Dragnet* with Dad that people who committed murder went to jail.

I heard the slam of a car door—the Taffees were home! I ran outside, gasping for breath, and busied myself in the backyard pulling weeds from under the red flower tree, a place where there were always black, furry spiders crawling around. Usually they frightened me, but given my state of mind at that moment, the spiders did not bother me. I listened for Mrs. Taffee and didn't hear anything…maybe she will not notice, or so I hoped. She is probably tying the bib around Mr. Taffee's neck, getting her husband ready to eat dinner. Oh no! There she was, shouting, "Libbe, come in this house right now!" I collected myself and moved toward the back patio doors to go inside. She stood in front of me. She had been cooking, I guessed, because she had a Pyrex dish in one hand and the cover to the birdcage in the other. "What happened?" she demanded to know with a mean look. "What happened to my bird, Libbe? What did you do?" I looked up with tears in my eyes. "I don't know what happened! I don't know! I wanted it to be quiet and didn't mean for anything to happen! I didn't do it, please!" "How *dare* you come into my home and kill an innocent animal!" I felt terrible, and was crying hysterically. Mrs. Taffee lifted the Pyrex dish high into the air and brought it down on my head! I didn't feel it at the moment of impact. I just heard the smash, and then my head started to pound in the area where the dish had broken. I saw that the thick glass dish had cracked in two pieces. I was dazed and did not think about the pain because she was so angry, swearing and screaming at me! Mr. Taffee had wheeled himself to the patio doors, trying urgently to speak, but couldn't and instead made short shrieking sounds. I was living in another hell!

Mrs. Taffee called my dad and said she was putting me on the next plane back to Boston, and that she'd send my school things later. She called me a "bird killer" and said that she wanted me out of her house before I could do anything else. That's also what she told her husband, who was shaking violently. I felt terrible. It was an accident. The incident was so traumatic to me as a child that I feel horrible about it to this day. She packed my clothes that night and, at my dad's expense, placed me on the first plane flying out the next day. I thought to myself, *She's like everyone else who believed I was bad—they really didn't want me, and I was only there because my dad paid them and I could do work of some sort. I am not my dad's blood, and one day he'll get rid of me too so he won't have to pay for me. Things have been so different since I found out he is not my real dad.*

Looking back, I regret not running away while I was in Florida where at least I could have lived outdoors. Oh no, back to hell again! Back to Anita!

CHAPTER NINE

Back to Boston

Mrs. Taffee couldn't wait for me to leave, but I was used to that. The stewardesses made the flight less stressful by giving me everything I wanted to eat, plus another pair of airplane wings like the ones they gave me on my flight to Florida. Even though I was worried about how he would react to my coming home, I was looking forward to seeing my dad. It wouldn't be too long before I found out how he felt. On the plane, I also thought about good things like Mommy Rose's cooking and how I wished I could feel the freedom of dancing again. I had the best tap shoes and ballet slippers but never saw them again after Anita came. Although she would use what happened at the Taffees as ammunition against me, maybe Anita would be different now. I always held out for "maybe." Maybe Dad would hug me...maybe he would say he missed me...maybe I would feel wanted again. I thought about how I would be starting in my school again with a new teacher, and whether anyone would talk to me now that I was older.

The plane was about to land, and my stomach felt funny. I did not want to go back to the house with Anita there. I shouldn't have touched Mrs. Taffee's bird. Living with the Taffees I had sunshine, food, and a comfortable bed. I was so ashamed of killing the bird that I never revealed it to anyone until many years later. I had to sit by the stewardesses while I was in the airport waiting for Dad, and then there he was! I didn't see Anita, and thought that maybe I could talk to him on the way home. "Daddy! Daddy!" I said, and he put his hand out to stop me. He said, "Wait. Wait, Libbe." He walked past me and up to one of the stewardesses and said something to her. She gave Dad a piece of paper. He took my hand and said, "Hurry up, Anita is waiting."

"Okay," I said. I was disappointed and my mood sunk further, but at least I got to hold Daddy's hand. I tucked my chin to my chest and looked at the ground as I walked. I was afraid of saying something wrong. We walked out the doors and there at the curb was Anita, waiting in the car, watching us through the window. As our eyes met, I could see hate written all over her face; I was back, and she didn't want me in her home. I felt alone for a fleeting moment, and then my stomach progressed from queasiness to nausea. I wished I had real wings to fly away, like the fairies and angels in all the stories. I believed they were real, but where did they live if not in this world? Aunt Rose told me they fly, and live in tree trunks and under the leaves in the woods. I believed that.

Daddy hadn't spoken a word. When we got to the car he opened the back door for me to get in. Anita turned to me and gave me a hard look. With her accent, she snapped, "So now you kill birds? You are sick and you need to get help! And don't you dare think about boys or having parties!" I wasn't "thinking" anything except that I wished I wasn't there.

Freddy said, "Anita, please, she is going to see someone. Wait until she gets home. Please, not in the car."

Anita rambled on to Freddy. It was worse now than before I went away; I knew I didn't belong, even more than I did before. I felt carsick again. I had to prepare for Anita's cruelty. Why didn't my father speak to me? If only he would ask me what happened. I felt so lonely and didn't understand his silence. I remember how it was before all these different places and people—no one was like my Mommy Rose. I thought how Freddy must have told Anita about all the things I loved before she met me, and she had gone about taking each one away from me. My dad talked to Anita while we were driving, but I couldn't hear everything they said because of the radio playing. I dreamed about sunshine, stars, and trees. I loved trees, the way they are rooted in the ground and grow into unique shapes with branches that sway and the individual movements of the leaves. How free they are! As a child I wondered if the trees and flowers felt pain when they were cut, and I worried about them. It seemed like the ride home was taking forever…

****

As I sit in my jail cell, I experience the same feeling as I felt then. When is this going to end? Where is everyone? I want to get out! I take a breath and think back to the car ride home.

****

I was anxious and frightened about what Anita would do to me now because I knew the time off from her beatings was over. My skin did not burn to the touch and my bones didn't ache. One of the things I liked about living with the Taffees was taking bubble baths in hot water, and I hoped I would be able to take more bubble baths one day. But there were many other things to think about now that I was home with Anita. I feared her, and that there wouldn't be an end to the agony. I wished I could have chocolate ice cream and cotton candy with Daddy.

My dad stopped at a store and he told Anita that he was going to buy some pipe tobacco. He stepped out of the car. I spoke up, "Daddy, can I go with you?"

Anita raised her voice and said, "No, you can't!"

But Daddy stuck his head out the window and said, "It's okay. She's been away for a while. She can go inside the store, Anita."

I jumped out of the car quickly with a smile across my face! Daddy finally said that he wanted me to go with him! Maybe everything would be okay when I got back home. I went into the store, which was small and had cigars, pipes, and an Indian head. I had been downtown before, and I knew the park across the street from the store was Boston Commons. I loved smelling the sweet scent of my dad's tobacco, a smell I identified with him like I identified the fragrances of the lipstick and perfumes Mommy Rose wore with her.

The man in the store knew my father, and Dad introduced me as "his daughter." His daughter…that made me feel proud because I wasn't sure whether he thought of me as his daughter or not anymore, and it had been a long time since he had spoken those words. After the fiasco in Connecticut at Anita's sister's house, we didn't discuss the subject of adoption again. Anita said I was nobody's and that I was left because I was a bad baby. How could an innocent baby be bad? Freddy and Rose took me because they felt sorry for me, she said. I didn't know any other dad; this dad would have to do. Freddy paid for his tobacco, and he took my hand as we walked out the door to the car. I felt safe and secure. I didn't look up at Anita because I knew the scowl she had for me, and I didn't want to see it—I would be seeing it soon enough. I got in the car and Anita was not happy with Freddy, she said I didn't deserve to go outside the car. Freddy said, "Anita, please," and we were all silent again. I was overjoyed, even if it was only for a brief moment. My heart always beat faster when I was excited, and my stomach churned. I was either hungry or nervous, or both; I couldn't tell which. In any case, I knew I would be fed because Dad was home. Maybe, I prayed, Daddy will stay for a while.

We got home, and Freddy took out my suitcase and small bag. Anita waved her hand in the air in disgust to signal me to go ahead of her. She said, "I don't want to look at your face." I didn't think Dad heard what she said. When I walked through the back door to the garage into the house the air was thick, and it felt like I was walking through a wall. I was terrified of being back. My lungs felt tight. It was hard to breathe. I didn't know what to do or where to go; I had to wait for Anita's commands. "Put her things in the basement so they can be washed," she said to Freddy.

He replied, "I can call Mrs. Taffee to find out whether her clothes are already clean."

"No!" Anita insisted. To me she said, "Go to your room. Get ready for supper. Why are you standing there?"

What room, I wondered? I started to move upstairs and Anita said, "Wait, tonight you'll wash downstairs because your clothes are dirty." Freddy didn't argue with her. She appeared so natural when she spoke, but I could tell she didn't want me upstairs. And, as always, Anita got her way. I went downstairs to get my pajamas, which were in the suitcase. I could hear Anita upstairs talking to Freddy, saying how she was not going to tolerate any of my nonsense. I waited to be called to be sure it was okay to go upstairs. Freddy yelled down, "Libbe, what are you doing down there? Come up."

"Okay Dad, coming," I yelled back. He didn't know the rules Anita had established about going upstairs and staying in the basement. When I went up, the food was on the table. I was really hungry and hoped that I could have seconds so I wouldn't have to feel hungry again later after Daddy left. I wasn't allowed to speak when we ate. Anita would say, "Children should be seen and not heard." I would get beaten if there were so much as a thread on the floor. I was in the habit of checking the floor for crumbs. When I ate I couldn't drop a crumb, and had to hold my plate or hand under my chin, and if I did drop a crumb I had to get down on my knees and lick it off the floor.

I went to sleep on the cot that night, and Anita told Freddy that I would be on the cot until she washed all my clothes and dusted the room upstairs. Freddy didn't know that Anita had lied, and as far as he was concerned, I was the liar, not her. I cringed each time I heard him tell his friends what a good stepmom Anita was. Imagine!

When Dad left the next day, what Anita said and did surpassed anything she had done before; the advance planning must have given her immense pleasure. She told me stories about how I would never have children and that I had an incurable disease and would die before I reached the age of sixteen. What disease? I wanted to ask, but I couldn't get my mouth to move. The thought that I would be with my mother made me less afraid, but she embellished the story even more, saying that I would be sick with high fevers and open sores. As she spoke, I felt like bugs and worms were inside me, eating my organs! I was beside myself because I believed her. I was helpless and hopeless without anyone to talk to.

If I was one minute late coming home from school, she would yell at me to take off my socks and—her new kick—she would strike the bottoms of my feet with wooden spoons from the kitchen. This was extraordinarily painful, and the pain would travel up my legs to my back. She said she would cripple me and then put me out of my misery. It hurt so badly I didn't want to walk. Other kids I knew were never treated this way; they were happy. Anita always took Maalox for her stomach. She had given it to me before, but now she began giving it to me every day. The chalky taste from the two tablespoons made me gag, but Anita told me I had to take it because of my disease. I wondered when I was going to die.

Anita had two faces: one for family and friends and another one for me. She also seemed to have several personalities. In addition to calling me a filthy tramp, now she would call me a murderer. I became so used to being called those names that I began to hate myself. The kids at school called me names so often I was used to thinking of myself as ugly. The terror Anita inflicted on me was bewildering. I tried to keep up with her deranged mind, but I was so confused. Anita would stare at me when I was in the basement writing my sentences or doing my homework, making it impossible to concentrate. I was considered stupid at school. Sometimes the homework from school was difficult because I was thinking about food or worrying about Anita and what she was going to do next. If I could hear her in the kitchen, I would wait to get water, milk, and some bread. If I had no food, I would go to the basement sink and drink lots of water to feel full.

When I finally saw the Kessel boy, I could tell he felt badly for me. He even stuck up for me when two boys threw a rock at my head. It hit hard and left me with a giant knot there and a headache. He shouted at them and they ran away. Then he said he'd walk me home (he lived on the main road in one of the newer, modern houses). I told him that because I had to go home alone, he could only walk me halfway down the street. He said okay—he knew from the other kids about Anita. He had also heard the rumors about the food, but I hoped that maybe someday he would share one of his lunches with me. He said he went regularly to the Stoneham Temple.

My dad seldom went to the temple in Stoneham anymore, certainly not as often as my mother used to. Instead, he went to the temple his family attended on Beacon Street in Brookline, especially for the high holidays of Rosh Hashanah and Yom Kippur. It was easy for me to fast because I was so used to not eating. It impressed my father and his family that at such a young age I was able to go for an entire day without food. They would use smelling salts to keep alert, but I didn't need any. They thought I was a dedicated Jew, not a hungry one. I was extremely skinny, and Anita continued to blame it on me, saying that I pushed my food away. "She was such a good eater when Rose was alive," they'd say, and Anita would give them the impression that I had an eating disorder, although there was no name for it back then in common usage.

The Kessel boy and I became friends. He began to give me an apple or a cookie from time to time, and I looked forward to seeing him. It didn't matter to me that he was a boy; I was just happy that he talked to me and didn't tease me. I wished Kat was still my friend, but she had never come back to my house because of the way Anita spooked her. All the other kids thought Anita was a witch, and instead of feeling sorry for me and comforting me, they just ignored me. I would try to hide the extra snacks I got from the Kessel boy so I could eat them when I went to the boiler room. I could hardly wait to go to school now.

I had to go to the Jewish Family and Children's Services for more help, and they sent me to Mass. Mental Health Center for an evaluation. They tested me, and one of the questions was, "Where do the parents in this doll house belong?" Even though I knew the answer, I said the opposite, putting the mother in the garage and the father in the kitchen. I was going to see social workers all the time, and just as I became used to one, the social worker would change. Change was uncomfortable for me. Mrs. Roman, the only one I liked, tried hard to help and support me. The endless questions of the other social workers were tedious and annoying, but Mrs. Roman's concern was genuine, and I could tell the difference. But…she ended up leaving.

One day, Anita had been looking out the window and saw the Kessel boy walking slightly ahead of me. She must have seen him talking to me. When I got in the house, she screamed, "What did you do with that boy? He touched you! And you had sex with him, didn't you!" I didn't understand what she was saying, and I told her, "No, no, no, Anita! He never touched me, I swear!" She made me strip off my clothes. She touched me down there, where I peed, and it hurt me where she pulled at my skin. I was screaming as she took the lye soap and scrubbed me with ice-cold water. She cut my hair as short as my ears. Then—she punched me in the stomach! I gasped for air! "That's for the babies you won't have!" she screamed. I almost doubled over. She slapped me on the head and pushed me to the floor, where I lay crying. *Just kill me,* I thought. *Kill me, please!* I felt like I couldn't take it anymore.

She made me write paper after paper of sex words, thousands of words—words I was hearing for the first time, but surely not the last. When my father came home late that night, Anita told him I'd had sex with the Kessel boy and he was to take me to my doctor in Chelsea to be examined. My father told her he didn't believe it, but he took the time off work to take me because Anita insisted it was true. I was sore from her pinching my skin down there but not bruised, and on the way my father asked me if a boy had ever touched me. I said, "No, Daddy, we just walk home from school. He's my friend."

My father said, "You're too young to have boys for friends."

"But he's my only friend. No one else will talk to me."

Fred hushed me and said, "Anita is right, Libbe, you don't listen, and you lie."

I was silent. I resigned myself to the fact that Daddy was never going to listen to me.

Freddy drove me to the doctor's office in Chelsea. We went into the part of his house where his office was, and the doctor took me by the hand and said to go with him. We entered a white room with a white sheet on a type of table, and he asked me to take my dress and panties off and to lie down. I was frightened. He put a sheet across my stomach and told me to relax, that he had to check me and it might hurt a little. Then he asked me if a boy had touched me there, and I replied, "No, never." I was frail, and my body was trembling. He asked if anyone else had touched me there, and I hesitated a moment because I didn't want him to tell my dad about the gardener again, or have him know about the girl's boyfriend—or Anita—and get myself in trouble with Daddy, who would say I was lying. So I said, "No, no, no." Then he put something in there with his hand. It hurt, and he stopped immediately and patted my head. He told me I was okay and to get dressed. He gave me a glass of water. It hurt down there as I put on my panties. He went out to talk to my dad. When I was dressed, the doctor took my hand and walked me out to the front office. He told me not to worry and that I was fine. "You're a good girl, Libbe," the doctor said. After talking with the doctor, my dad walked out and said, "I'm sorry, Libbe, for putting you through that." I was confused about what had happened. No doctor had ever examined me like that before. But I was happy to be called a good girl, and Dad saying he was sorry was worth it all.

When we got home, Dad and Anita had an argument about him taking me to the doctor. Freddy told Anita that I had not been touched and I'd never had sex with that boy. He was so upset because the doctor had said that I shouldn't have been put through that kind of exam with no proof. "Never again, Anita!" he shouted. Anita was angry because she knew I could hear everything, and that my dad was extremely upset and embarrassed by taking me there. He finally stuck up for me—not her. I was worried about what would happen when Dad left for work and wished I could do something to make him stay. What could I do? I went upstairs and spoke up.

"Daddy, can I talk to you, please?"

Anita snapped, "No, we are talking! Go downstairs where you belong."

Freddy said, "Anita, she can stay up here. Why does she have to go down? Her room is upstairs, that's where she belongs."

Anita was furious. She said, "You have homework now."

"Do you have homework?" Daddy asked.

"Yes, only a little," I replied. "Please, Daddy, can I talk to you?" He finally came downstairs with me, and I said, quietly, "I am scared. Please, can you stay home? I don't feel good. I want you to stay."

Freddy looked puzzled, and he said, "I'm sure Anita can make you feel better. I have to go to work later." I started to cry. I leaned toward him and he patted my back. "I'll be back next week."

"Daddy, please, just please. You don't understand." For once, he looked me in the face and said, "Okay, Libbe. This one time I'll call in sick."

I hugged him and got a quick hug in return. I had been waiting for this moment a long time, but I still didn't feel he was as close to me as he used to be. I said, "May I please have some food for my stomach? It's hungry."

Freddy said, "Yes, of course, you'll have supper now." I could hear Anita stomping upstairs, and although I usually tried not to look at her when she came downstairs, I will never forget the expression on her face. It looked like the face of the devil. I was happy that Dad stayed. She was furious. She had to let me sleep upstairs because there was no excuse. One day a week sleeping in a bed was better than none, and this was two days, Friday and Saturday. The only other times I got to sleep in a bed were the Jewish holidays unless Anita said I was wetting the bed and had to sleep on the cot. I could sleep easy and then after Sunday evening, I would be in for more of Anita's brutality.

CHAPTER TEN

Dad Loses His Temper

Usually Dad woke up at four or five in the morning to go back to work. I thought he was going to be home all day Sunday, but the company called and he had to go in. He said goodbye, and I watched as he drove away. I tidied up my bedroom so that it looked exactly as I had found it. Anita was quiet and hadn't screamed yet, so I went downstairs to get out of her way. Something was different. I could sense it. I sat down and read my book. But I couldn't pay attention to it because I was worried. This was typical of me—I had difficulty understanding anything I tried to read, I was always distracted. It was never this calm when Dad left. She usually hit me or punished me in some way, right away, or at the very least, had me write sentences. I heard her footsteps. She came down, pulled me upstairs by the hair, and told me to get on my knees and wash the kitchen floor. I did it over and over until my hands were red and sore from the Borax in the water. She had me do the toilets, and when I was done, she put me in the chair at the desk in the basement, took off my clothes, and put a sheet over my face that had a hole cut in it. She tied my hands and feet to the chair and said, "Sit here all night until you tell me the truth about that boy." I had nothing to tell. She shut off the lights, and I sat there in the dark all night long. She did not beat me, but my back hurt from the chair. I was cold and hungry, and my mouth was so dry it was hard to swallow. I fell asleep sitting up in the chair.

I woke to Anita untying me and dragging my limp, exhausted body into an ice-cold shower. "This will wake you up," she said. She threw my school clothes at me and told me in a threatening way, "I will deal with you later." She warned me to stay away from that boy forever. He was my only friend, and I wondered, *who I will talk to…*

I put my clothes on and felt warmer, but I remember feeling sick and going to the nurse at school. She said I had a fever and called Anita to bring me home. I asked the nurse if I could stay in her room at school. "No," she said sweetly, "you have to go home to your parents." Anita didn't drive, so the nurse took me home. I guess I had gotten a bad cold from sleeping without any clothes on. The nurse told Anita that I needed to eat lots of soup. I felt awful, but Anita didn't care. As soon as the nurse left, she began screaming, "Boys, boys, parties—you are a tramp and you are not sick, you are just playing around! So you will work your fever off! Work first, drink later!" I was thirsty and hungry and felt burning hot. I hadn't eaten my lunch, and Anita wanted me to wash the floors and toilets before I got a drink. I was feeling very weak, but I had no choice. The nurse said soup, but I wasn't getting soup, just suds… If I was lucky, I'd get a drink of water. I was slow, and Anita didn't whip me much because she knew I was really sick. I felt as though I was going to pass out on the floor. She kept pushing me and would hit me on the back to get me to move. I worked as fast as I could, and when I was done, I collapsed. She yelled at me to get in the basement and gave me pajamas. By then, I was cold and had the chills all over. I was shaking so badly my teeth chattered. She called me upstairs. I dragged myself up the steps, and on the table was a cup of hot water and some white rice. I drank the water and ate the rice, and then asked her for more. She turned to look at me, and for a moment I thought she might be sympathetic, but she shook her head no. "Can I be excused?" I asked.

She said, "Yes, go! Here, eat this first." It was gelatin, not sweet, but it had some flavor.

I was grateful and said, "Thank you so much." She shook her head with a smirk on her face as if she were heroic for caring for me. Maybe she did feel badly for me because she let me go with no other punishments. I went downstairs, and when I touched my forehead, it felt hot. I wished I could go to my bed upstairs, but Anita rolled out the cot and said, "Sleep on this, tonight only."

"Yes, yes, thank you," I replied. I remember shivering until I fell asleep, and when I awoke I was in a total sweat and thirsty. She gave me a week at home to improve in case the nurse examined me once I was back in school. But it was a housework week, not all bedtime. I did get tea, and Anita's idea of soup for me was hot water with a bouillon cube for flavor, and gelatin for desert. I realize now that when she didn't feed me at all she was projecting her starvation in the concentration camp onto me, making me the victim instead of her.

Anita's punishments became progressively worse after I recovered. She had to be careful where she hit me because I was going to the social workers more often. Her threats were frightening: she told me that if I said anything she would shove fish down my throat until I choked to death and that she would feed me my own shit from the toilet for supper. I never wanted to taste that again! These threats were more frightening than her routine abuse. Anita couldn't forget the Kessel boy and said something every day about boys and me and sex, sex, sex. Even when I found out what sex meant, I was still confused about it.

It was one of those days that I remember vividly. I was on my way to school and took my usual shortcut on a path that cut through tall weeds and grass. I was in a hurry to get there, and when I stepped on a rock by mistake, a snake appeared and slithered over my shoes. I lost my balance, fell backward, and went to the bathroom in my pants from fright. My father had shown me garden snakes before, but this had never happened. I didn't want to, but I smelled and had to go home! If I went to school, I'd have to go to the nurse. I didn't know what to do. I went home. I was standing in front of the house and was scared to death to enter. I bravely walked to the back door through the dark garage. Maybe she will understand. I hadn't prayed in a long time, but now I prayed to my Mommy Rose to help me. I opened the door to the kitchen, and there she was. She looked at me and gasped. "Anita, I'm sorry. I had to come home. I had an accident in my pants, and I can't go to school. I have to change!" I started running down the stairs, holding my backside with one hand. I was trying to get to the bathroom when Anita grasped me by the neck from behind. She practically pushed me through the wall, calling me trash names. She said I was so dirty she hated having me in her house. I was so embarrassed! When I got to the washbasin, she told me to remove my clothes and scrub them in the sink. She was wearing rubber gloves from the kitchen sink, as she always did when she washed dishes or hit me. When I took off my panties, she grabbed them and rubbed them in my face! The smell choked me. I was too shocked to cry. Anita was smothering me in my own mess, and I tried to pull away to breathe. She was screaming. I was panicky! Finally, she turned on the hot water and shoved my head in the sink. I sucked in air, and when I took that breath the water and crap went into my mouth so that the taste was horrible—I spit it out! I will never forget that. She held my neck down so I could smell the soap being put on my head. She said, "Wash your shit off, nasty bitch, you pig!" I was scrubbing all over, desperate to get it off. I hoped she would call the school so I could get out of the house. She did, telling them that I was late but to expect me. She said that she wanted me out of her sight or else. She called me a piece of shit. I sniffed at myself all the way to school, and went to the girls' bathroom to wash off one more time.

I wouldn't be seeing the Kessel boy again until I began junior high in September. I was told I would have to go to summer school. As usual, I did not get out with the other kids when school was over because I always needed extra help and tutoring. Fred and Anita couldn't wait to go away on vacation again. They were making plans. Anita was pounding on my back, legs, and arms whenever she felt like it. Hitting me and watching me starve gratified her. I was tired of living. I was going to the social workers all the time now, but just sitting there, listening to them try to open me up—me, the problem child from a loving home…

I kept wishing on my biggest and brightest star. The night sky was always so beautiful when I could see it. I felt pulled, like it was calling me to come up. Liz was a comfort to talk to, and I wished she were really there. I continued praying to my mom, but there was never an answer, just an empty silence. There was no one to help get

Anita away from me. Still, I believed my mom was up in the clouds and just couldn't see me.

Junior high in three weeks—wow, I made it this far! Freddy and Anita were planning to go away before school started. Anita made her phone calls about the vacation at my mom's mahogany telephone table in the hall. I hated it when she sat there. When Mom was alive, she sat there whenever she got a call. I would be staying at the Gray's house again, but this time her kids didn't have anything to do with me because of the party. Mrs. Gray said she would have to monitor me if I went home because I had behavioral problems. I asked my dad if I could stay with the Hebers instead, but Anita wouldn't allow it. She said I had too much freedom there. Apparently, my father convinced Mrs. Gray that I had learned my lesson and that as long as I was supervised, it was okay if I wanted to go to my house to get my clothes or to study. She agreed. Dad stipulated that there were to be no other kids at the house with me. It was usual for my father to talk to the neighbors, but Anita rarely did because she knew they suspected what she really was.

I went to my house with Mrs. Gray's permission. The Grays would be away for the day, and Mrs. Gray said I could sleep over at my house if I wanted…just no company. Mrs. Gray trusted that I wouldn't have any more parties. She gave me the key. I felt grown up, twelve years old and I could finally be alone. Anita believed I was crazy and bad. I had gone to the mental health center for two years. The people there based their opinions on the various tests they gave me, like the Rorschach tests, where I was shown inkblots and asked what I thought they were. I was never told the results at the time. Going to all those homes and then to Florida had not changed me. The incident with the parakeet bothered me. Freddy and Anita said that staying at home wasn't an option, and they would put me somewhere before school started. I wondered where I would be going and what would happen to me. I was nervous thinking about it. I thought, *What's the difference what I do now? I get beaten and punished no matter what I do!* I felt like I was a stranger in my own home.

I had observed Anita long enough to be able to imitate her, and I wanted to be just like her (except, be nice) for one day—a hair stylist with nice clothes and jewelry—even though I hated her. I went to Anita's closet, picked out one of her dresses, and put on her makeup. I wore her lipstick. Then I went to the telephone table and, using the local phonebook, called numbers that were under men's names until I finally I got one to talk to me. I think he said his name was John, and I invited him over. I told him I was nineteen years old, and although I thought I looked older all dressed up, I did not. I told him that I was a hairdresser. He told me he would bring something to drink with him. I paced back and forth…

When he came to the door, I was more nervous. He was so tall, and thick and muscular—he looked like a wrestler. I acted like Anita, using her mannerisms and speaking like her, and when he stepped inside and brought out a bottle, my eyes widened, nearly popping out of my head. It was the biggest beer bottle I'd ever seen! And even though I was frightened, I wanted company. I had never been told anything about boys or men and understood nothing about male/female interaction. He asked if he could kiss me, and I said okay. It was a quick tap on the lips. I was drinking, talking, and trying very hard to be Anita. He seemed to like me. That's all I remember. I must have passed out because when I woke, he was gone. The bottle, though, was still there—half full. I was sweaty and sticking to the plastic cover on the couch. Startled, I got up quickly, cleaned up, and put Anita's things back. I had a headache from the beer; but otherwise, I was unchanged and concluded that he hadn't touched me because my clothes were still on. Nothing was missing from the house as far as I could tell. I thought to myself that I was lucky, and I'd never do anything like that again! I wondered for years if he left abruptly because he figured out I was under age, and it remains a mystery to this day. I was also fortunate that Anita never had a clue I used her dress and makeup. Mrs. Gray never found out about my escapade, and the condition of the house was exactly the same as I'd found it.

****

Since the time of the party in my house on Dewitt Road, I learned to pay very close attention to detail, developing an almost photographic memory that serves me well to this day. Unfortunately, I missed all the signs this time. They were there, the ones that should have tipped me off that my business was being investigated by law enforcement—the reason I am locked in this cell today. I look around this cement-walled room… and plan to not make the same mistake in the future!

****

School started again. I met a girl who was a grade or two ahead of me. I must have had vulnerability written across my forehead because she kept coming over to talk to me for no real reason. She wanted to be friends and kept inviting me to her house. One day, she said her uncle was coming to pick her up and take her shopping. She asked me to come along and made it sound so great that I agreed. I certainly was in no hurry to go home to Anita, but could avoid it that afternoon because she had a doctor's appointment. I had told the girl about that. Her uncle drove up in a Cadillac convertible—that did it for me! But then things got creepy. We stopped at a little convenience store and picked out snacks. I got my favorite Hostess Cupcakes, a small bottle of Hood's milk, and a Charleston Chew, along with a bunch of other kinds of candy. Getting into the car, he wanted me to sit between them in the front seat, not in the back where I had been before. He put his hand across the seat, and it kept dropping onto my shoulders and back. I was becoming frightened of them both. They had said we were going to the beach, but he pulled over into a secluded park-like area. She kept telling me to be nice to her uncle, but I repeated that I had to go, I had to be home soon. He continued to get too close, both with his body and his hands. I finally screamed that I had to get out, and she nervously said that I could go in the back seat again. She was sitting way too close to him while he was driving to my house, and was trying to convince me that if I was good to him, that he would be really nice back to me. I was freaked out. I'd already had awful experiences with creepy older men, and my antenna was way up. I remember the time one of my father's relatives pulled my panties down in his house in Saugus. I screamed and ran outside. I avoided this girl like the plague after that. As an adult, I realized that she was probably getting goodies in exchange for his attentions.

Anita continued finding fault in every little thing I did. One afternoon, Dad was supposed to pick me up to go see the social worker. I was walking along Main Street with the Kessel boy. I was thinking about how Anita thought he was my boyfriend. Freddy drove down Main Street before I could get home! He was furious with me as he pulled over and called to me to get into the car. Anita must have mentioned something about how I was always lollygagging on my way home, and Dad got upset. The Kessel boy ran ahead when my dad stopped the car. I got in, and he was screaming at me. "What are you doing, Libbe, you knew to come right home! Anita said you were with the boys again! She was right, you never listen!"

I said, "Daddy, I did walk right home. I didn't go anywhere else. I'm not lying. He is very nice, and Jewish. Anita always fills your head with bad things about me." I had spoken up for myself. He was so angry! He couldn't reach me, so he took an ice scraper and hit me right at the corner of my eye! My eye hurt, but it was not nearly as painful as my father hitting me for the first time in my life—that hurt was far worse than any beatings I ever got from Anita. I was so upset that I opened the car door and rolled out onto the pavement. I got up and started racing down the street. He stopped the car, leaving the motor running, and jumped out, chasing me. "Libbe! Libbe, I'm sorry! Anita has me crazy! I didn't mean to hurt you!"

I stopped and turned to look at him. I was crying, my eye was cut, and blood was trickling down my face. Dad talked me into getting back in the car and kept repeating, "I'm so sorry!" He gave me his hanky to dab the cut. I wanted to be away from him and pushed closer to the door, yet I yearned for him to hug me to make it better. Neither of us moved, and the distance between us remained.

We had to see Mrs. Roman, my social worker. After the blood stopped staining the hanky, I covered the bump with my hair. I was uncharacteristically quiet with Mrs. Roman, whom I liked. She kept asking what was wrong. She could see something had happened, but

I didn't say anything. "Libbe, why is your hair in your face?" she asked. I shrugged my shoulders and kept my head down. She didn't pressure me, just said, "Let me know if you want to talk, okay?" I left. On our way back to Stoneham I told Daddy that I would never say he hit me to anyone but that I had bumped into the car door. He was apologizing all the way home, telling me that Anita had aggravated him by saying I was always late because of the boys. "I don't know what got into me," he said, putting his hand to his forehead, shaking his head in sadness. We parked in front of the Gray's house. I said goodbye to Daddy and told him not to worry, that I wouldn't tell a soul. I could see how badly he felt by the expression on his face, but he didn't hug me or tell me he loved me before I got out of the car.

I had my hair over my eye when Mrs. Gray opened the door. She told me to wash up for dinner. In the bathroom mirror, I could see that the bruise and cut were noticeable, and I covered the gash with my hair. Mrs. Gray was very proper at the dinner table: wash up, hair back off your face, and say grace before eating. She asked me to pull my hair back while we were eating, and when I didn't, she got up to get a rubber band and pulled my hair back for me. She saw the cut and a swollen bruise at the corner of my eye. She asked me what happened, and I told her that nothing had happened. "Libbe, tell me."

I told her that as I was getting into Dad's car after school I banged my eye on the door. She was very upset and called my dad's house to ask Freddy what happened. He told her the truth. He said that he hadn't intended to hurt me, but that he hit me. Why did he tell her? Mrs. Gray had my aunts' numbers for emergencies when Dad was in Florida. She called my Aunt Rose, and they decided to call the police because of stories they had both heard about Anita. The police, in turn, reported it to the state. The Jewish Family and Children's Services stepped in, and I was taken away because of one blow from my dad. After all the brutal beatings I endured for years from Anita, the irony astonishes me to this day.

CHAPTER ELEVEN

Foster Home in Sharon

A new kind of life was about to begin. I would be living in a foster home in a place other than Stoneham, where I wasn't familiar with the neighbors. Mom was gone. And now, without Dad, I had no idea what the future held for me. "Good riddance," was what Anita hissed at me as I left, and I felt the same about her. Since she moved in, it was Anita's home, not mine, not Dad's—and not my mom's. The social worker came to place me in my new home. Driving away, I knew in my heart that I would never return to the small Colonial home in Stoneham. I was feeling insecure, unsafe, and so empty…

On the way to Sharon, a nearby town on the South Shore, I was preoccupied with thinking about my mother's grave in Sharon Memorial Cemetery, that at least now I would be closer to her. Staring out the window, I looked at the trees. I was fascinated by how they were bare in winter and so beautiful when they blossomed in spring.

****

As I reflect on my life in this white-walled space, I realize that we pass by the beauty of nature every day without noticing because we rush from place to place and forget what life is. Freedom and beauty lie outside the bars of this jail cell. I can't wait to get out of this hell!

****

I asked the social worker if, since we were in Sharon, we could go by the cemetery to see my mother. "Please," I pleaded, "I want to see my mother's grave. Nobody ever takes me. Will you take me? I won't be long, just long enough to say hello." She told me I would have to ask the Madison family and that she didn't have the authority to take me. "It has to go before the board first anyway," and then she changed the subject. What did she mean by the board? *She doesn't care either,* I thought to myself. *Why did I bother asking?* The social worker told me that I would be living in a nice home, a ranch-style house, and that there was a daughter two years older than me. *Oh, just great...*I thought, imagining some strange girl who would bully me like the kids did at school. I was not thrilled. These people were complete strangers to me. I was sad on the ride and didn't want to go there. Feeling carsick, I opened the window to get some air. I wanted to puke but held it down and continued staring blankly out the window, holding my forearms across my stomach. I remembered that my dad had always told me to pay attention to buildings along the way when I traveled so that I would never get lost. I managed to look at the houses and small stores but forgot them immediately on this trip.

I thought only about my mom being buried in the cemetery and about how I had gone there a few times on the high holidays with Aunt Rose. After Dad married Anita, he stopped going to Mom's grave. If it were possible, I would have visited my mother every day. I considered getting into the grave myself, not altogether understanding what a grave was. I decided that if the cemetery was close enough to the Madison's house, I would walk to it. I recalled the times Aunt Rose took out the brass vase, and we put Mom's favorite red roses in it. I thought about all the years I looked up at the night sky praying to her, the brightest star. I never fully grasped how she could be in the ground and up in heaven too. Unlike other cemeteries I had seen, this cemetery reminded me of a park because there were no gravestones, only plaques with the person's name and dates on it. To this day, I don't believe that when we die we are fully gone. I think a part of our soul lingers on after death. I was so anxious, I worried that my new foster family might live too far away and not have a car to take me to see my mother. They were Jewish, so maybe someone they love is buried in the cemetery and they wouldn't mind making the trip. Although my stomach relaxed for a moment with that thought, my fear was growing, and the nausea and queasiness returned with a vengeance. My stomach was empty because Anita never fed me before I left. I was always worried about having food anywhere I went. I couldn't tolerate pangs of hunger; they only added to my distress. I thought that when I grew up, if any person needed food, I would give it to them whether I knew them or not. Then the car stopped.

"We are here," the social worker said. "This is your new home!" In my heart I knew this was not my new home. Why do they tell me what they think I want to hear? I didn't have a real home anymore. Home meant a place where you lived with your belongings, not a place where you stayed for a short time, not knowing when you would have to pack up your things and leave. Why don't they say the truth: this is a new place for you to stay temporarily.

We went up the walkway to a one story, off-white house with what appeared to be a large yard. The land between the houses on the street was wider than in any other neighborhood where I'd lived, including my father's house in Stoneham. This neighborhood was much more modern than what I had been used to up until then. The social worker rang the bell. My stomach dropped.

****

I was heading into the unknown, just like I am now. When they release me from my cell, I will be entering my future—an unknown one. I have to stop thinking about the "what if's" or I will make myself sick. I don't want to lose my home. That would break my heart, and leave nothing for my son. Then I took a breath, and in my mind, I was back at the front door, waiting to meet my foster family.

****

The wooden door opened, and a woman's arm pushed the metal and glass storm door open. "Hello, you must be Libbe." I looked up at her with a big smile. I did that not only to please the social worker but also to win the prize of staying in my new surroundings. I was sure I'd won. Later in life, I learned that foster care is a business, money being the overriding reason most families accept foster children as boarders.

In any case, the woman acted as though she liked me. She said, "Libbe, you are so quiet. Don't you speak?"

"Yes," I replied. My manners were impeccable. As Anita had drilled into me, I answered only when spoken to. In any case, it wasn't characteristic of me to speak up for myself. We seated ourselves in her living room, and I posed, as Anita had made me do so many times, sitting with my hands folded in my lap, back straight. My eyes wandered around the room. I was only half-listening to the conversation. The lady asked me if I wanted lunch or perhaps some cookies and milk. I smiled genuinely, out of happiness. Food! Yes! After suffering food deprivation, eating had become a sure way of getting to my heart. "Yes! Please!" I replied enthusiastically, hoping that I didn't appear too forward.

"Well, of course, would you like to see your room and your bed?" Again I answered yes, thinking that it was not *my* bed or *my* room that I was about to look at. The social worker must have thought that I was comfortable enough for her to leave at that point, and she told us she was going so that we could get better acquainted. No, I wasn't comfortable, and couldn't understand why she thought I was. It was true I was smiling, but that was because of the food. I asked the social worker to stay, please, but she assured me that I was in good hands and should not be afraid. "Libbe, this is a good fit for you. Their daughter will be like a sister." How would she know that? Has she ever stayed with them? Has she ever met their daughter?

Had she ever been left door to door? I was scared to death! Despite my fear, there wasn't any choice other than to stay—I didn't have anywhere else to go. The lady tried to take my hand, but I pulled away. I detested being touched, especially in a gentle way. That kind of touching meant that what followed might be trouble. I didn't get good feelings from others, and I kept my distance. I especially didn't trust men or boys touching me, nor did I like affection from women, an exception being the hugs and kisses of my mother and Aunt Rose. As much as I craved affection, I never experienced closeness with others.

Mrs. Madison said she understood, and that maybe later when we got to know each other better, I would feel more at ease. I nodded because I understood what she was saying, not because I agreed with her. That assumption was untrue. *No,* I thought, *I won't feel comfortable unless I'm living with my dad and without his bitch of a wife.* Anita's brutality had taught me to construct walls around myself for my own protection, and with each year that passed, I built stronger walls.

Time passed quickly for me that first day. Before I knew it, Mrs. Madison had emptied my suitcase and placed my things in a dresser next to the bed. She was unsure about whether the clothes I had were appropriate for school in Sharon, and she told me her daughter had some extra "old clothes" hanging in her closet that were too small for her that I could use those until I got new ones. Even though I hated them, I told her that my clothes were fine; I didn't like the idea of wearing somebody else's clothes. She insisted that I wear the more stylish clothes she was offering me, and I felt pressured to take them. Later on, I learned that Mrs. Madison was more concerned about her own daughter being seen with me. I couldn't *have* the clothes, but I could *use* them. That was not what I wanted—I wanted my own stuff. She told me that when she received my clothing allowance, I could buy new things. Her daughter's clothes had pretty colors and were different from the clothes I wore. Even though they weren't mine, and were a bit roomy because I was so skinny, I was happy to wear them because they were not wool. I didn't know about second-hand clothing until I went to classes and her daughter let everyone in the school know that I was wearing her "hand-me-downs," as she called them. She told her friends I didn't have a home, my parents didn't want me, and that when I moved in I didn't have anything but an old suitcase. I was ashamed and didn't want to mingle with the other kids. I wanted to rip the clothes off my body. I was learning that I was not good-looking, with a sad demeanor, and so skinny that after I wore the clothes even her mom said they weren't right for my type. What was my type? Because her daughter had big breasts and I had none, the clothes hung off me like a sheet on a clothesline.

I remember when her daughter came home that first day. She looked at me strangely as if something were wrong. I knew right there and then that she didn't like me. She looked at me in that same way every day after our first meeting, and during school she ridiculed me in front of her friends all the time. Although she was only two years older than me, she appeared more mature. She was also stuck-up, like some of the women in Dad's family. I didn't know how to act when I was around her. She was clearly upset that I was sharing her room. "Can't she stay in the den or on the back porch?" she asked her mom. Her mother was not pleased with that question, and reprimanded her, "Listen, young lady, this girl has no home, and for now, she will be staying with us in your room!"

I remember that first night when we all sat down to dinner after the father came home. I was hungry and accepted a second portion when it was offered to me. Her mom and dad said they intended to bulk me up. That was certainly okay with me. Later, the daughter told me I was a pig for coming to stay with her family and then accepting second helpings of food. But I didn't ask her mom, she asked me. Still, I begged for her forgiveness. "Please, I promise I'll never take seconds again." After that, I said nothing else to her unless she spoke to me first—it was obvious she despised me. That first night, when I helped Mrs. Madison clean up out of gratitude for the food, her daughter was pissed off at me once again. It was not the best of starts with Annie. I had no idea what I could do to make her like me. I was not good at making friends and horrible with schoolwork, but I could keep her room clean. I decided I would do what she asked...and stay out of her way. It wasn't long before she was throwing her things on the floor just so I would have to pick them up. She was bossy, and it was impossible to make her happy. I didn't fit in with her clique of friends, nor did I fit into the setting at her home—I was an outcast.

The family was Jewish, but Reform, not Conservative or Orthodox. Mrs. Madison lit the Sabbath candles, but they only went to temple on holidays. We finished filling out the enrollment forms at the junior high school. Annie, who was a ninth grader, refused to walk to school with me, so her mom drove me until I was ready to go by myself. It didn't take long before I was walking alone. Being alone was better than someone making fun of me. I looked forward to coming home for dinner. I spent time in Annie's room playing solitary games like rolling old marbles down the creases of book bindings. I cherished the ones I had because they'd belonged to my dad; it was like having a part of him.

At school, the kids called me all sorts of names—I was a "ragamuffin," "the hand-me-down kid," "skinny mini," "Siskinditis" (I made the mistake of telling Annie that's what they called me in Stoneham), and "the fosta' kid." I identified with the name "fosta' kid," this contributed to the desire I developed later to one day work with foster children, especially adolescents. In the present time, for and about foster kids, I have made a business plan, business cards, and created an app. If Annie didn't instigate the name-calling herself, she certainly participated in it. Their bullying was constant.

When I walked down the corridor, a girl named Lucy would always smile and say hello to me, but I didn't speak back because I wasn't sure if she was "one of them." Head bowed and eyes looking at the floor, I would walk much the same way I did when I was with Anita for all those years. I never looked behind me, fearing that I would turn into stone, as Anita had once told me would happen. If I ever wanted to turn back to look at something, I would stop, pivot, and walk in the opposite direction. That old superstition went by the wayside once I figured out that it was a lie, and my body wouldn't actually turn into stone. It was a while before Annie would talk to me, and when she finally did, it was only at the house, never at school. Annie was one of the reasons I didn't have any friends, and she gloated knowing that. She was an only child and had to be the center of attention, especially at home.

I remember walking up the stairs at school one day when I heard a boy's voice behind me saying, "Hey, hey there." I was afraid, so I didn't respond. He tugged at my shoulder. I pulled away. Then I turned completely around to face him. He was colored (as they said then), and was smiling at me. It was a warm, sincere smile, not a sneering smile like the other girls and boys. He whispered, "Listen, I know everyone makes fun of you, and I don't want them to laugh at you, but you've got blood on the back of your dress. I can walk behind you until we get to the nurse's office. Okay?"

Oh my god, I felt terrible! "Yes, thank you," I answered. I was so embarrassed, and I could feel the heat of my cheeks as I blushed, just like the day I got my period and Anita slapped my face saying she hit me to make my cheeks rosy.

"It's okay, I understand," he told me. "Girls get that." With my legs pressed tightly together, I tried to walk without losing my balance. While we were walking, he asked me what my name was and I asked him his name. "Robby," he said. "And I don't have any friends either. Do you want to meet me for recess?"

"Yes, sure," I said. "I will, thanks. But…I have to…"

"Yes, I know!" It was exciting to think I might have a friend. I prayed Robby wouldn't tell the others about the blood. I scurried into the nurse's room, and she was able to reach my foster mother, who came right away with a change of clothes. At least she didn't scream at me like Anita would have, and then beat me when I came home from school. Mrs. Madison said, "Accidents happen, dear." I was sure that somebody would notice I was wearing different clothes from the morning, but no one mentioned it. I asked my foster mom not to tell Annie about what happened, and I was grateful she never did. I was more thankful for Robby's kindness.

When I met Robby at recess that day, a new taunt was born. I was a "nigger lover," and he was a "white lover." I had never heard those words before, even though I was familiar with prejudice from the time the neighbor complained about my nanny. It was my first exposure to black/white prejudice that I could see and understand,

and it wouldn't be the last. Robby had to explain the reason the others called us names. I felt terrible. Why would they do that? What kind of people made these terrible rules? We were ostracized, but neither of us cared; they were the fools, not us. We just have different skin colors, but we are all the same—humans. We exchanged stories about our families, and he told me how hard it was for him to have friends. I never revealed to Robby, or to anyone for that matter, about what I had endured with Anita. Even though there was a connection between us, I couldn't do that, ever. Instead, I told him that I had a stepmother and we never got along. Robby said there were two Jewish boys at the school, one he saw at school only, and the other had a house on Sharon Lake where he visited them sometimes. He said they were a caring family and invited me to go swimming with all of them. "You'll love his parents, and you're Jewish like them," he said. "They were super nice to me when I moved in, and their other kids are cool. Otherwise, I don't have friends either. They won't associate with colored people. And I know lots of people who don't like Jews too. I was always told about that." He complained about how the kids teased him and called him "nigger" or "colored boy," and put him down by calling him just "boy." I told him that the kids at my school in Stoneham had always made fun of me, calling me names, and one particularly derogatory name: "kike." They would draw swastikas for me to see. I was among the small Jewish population in Stoneham, but not in Sharon, where there were more Jewish families. I told him the only other colored people I'd known were my nanny and her son. I had loved her as much as my mom, but they had to leave because a neighbor thought it was wrong for Nanny's son and me to bathe together in the same bathtub. What an awful loss that was. Like many issues in the fifties, it was swept under the rug—people just didn't want to rock the boat. In the reaches of my memory, I have always recalled the warmth and caring I received from Nanny. I will never get over the shock of her sudden disappearance from my life or my outrage once I understood the reason that she left.

My knowledge of black and white race relations had been nonexistent until Robby explained it all. My father told me that Jews were hated and to pay no attention to the kids calling me "kike" or drawing swastikas. It had been more than enough for me to deal with when the kids called me names because of the way I looked. Now they had another excuse for insulting me. I wasn't upset this time—I had Robby for a friend and didn't care what religion or color he was. I would snap back in his defense when he was called a name, and he defended me when they called me names. We drank from the same cup in front of the other kids. They made faces and gestures like they were going to puke. Despite their bullying, we hung out all the time. We protected one another's feelings from being hurt and shared a genuine friendship, unlike the other kids whose friendships were superficial, based on belonging to one clique or another. Robby and I were both outcasts; we had the experience of prejudice in common.

Robby and I became best friends, and I hoped we would always remain that way. I had a friend and felt as though I wanted to stay in Sharon now. The girl with short blonde hair who said hello to me in the hall several times began talking to both of us. She knew Robby, but hadn't really spoken to him much until I was in the picture. She told us not to be afraid of the kids who made fun of us. She said she lived in Sharon Heights and explained that there were other cliques in Sharon, like the Jewish rich kids, the middle-class Jewish kids, and the Catholics like her. She told me that her boyfriend went to Sacred Heart School, where the boys were tough types. They wouldn't hesitate to come to the high school and beat up anyone who messed with us. I was a bit shocked. I had never heard of kids beating up on other kids. I knew that there were Hebrew schools, but Catholic schools? Wow, did I feel naive…and pretty dumb. Her name was Lucy, and I will never forget her. I felt like a stronger person around her. She was a good friend; our small circle was complete. Even Annie stayed her distance from Lucy when the three of us were together. Whatever fears I might have had about walking to school disappeared. None of the kids at school wanted to tangle with Lucy.

I was getting used to my foster home. I was grateful for the good food, although there were times at the dinner table when Annie would glare at me and make me feel uncomfortable. When she did that, it was hard to swallow. Sharing a room with Annie was always tense. It was usual for me to pull the covers up over my face when

I went to bed to block her out. That was the best way to have some privacy. She always lied to her parent, and I couldn't say anything. Her free time at home was spent on the phone with boys. Robby mentioned that there were some rumors floating around about her at school, but he didn't say specifically what they were. What was worse was that Annie used to sneak out of her window at night. Though I pretended to be asleep, she needed a guarantee I would not tell her parents so she would wake me up and drag me with her. Robby and Lucy told me to tell her mother, but I was intimidated by Annie and swore my friends to secrecy. I knew I could trust them.

A couple of months passed. Annie continued dragging me into the woods, leaving me standing on a patch of dirt and rocks, exhausted and afraid while she went off. The dark bothered me, as did the bugs, but I could stare at the stars and watch the graceful movement of the trees as they swayed in the breeze. I loved shadows, and when the moon was bright the shadows of the trees showed on the ground. My promise to do whatever she wanted ensnared me in her sordid plans, and I recognized the feeling I was experiencing—it was the same as when I was a young child in the garage and in the boiler room. I felt unsafe and vulnerable in woods by myself, waiting for hours, not knowing where she was. I would talk to myself and make up stories. When she finally returned it was very late, and in the mornings when I woke up I was tired. My schoolwork suffered because it was even more difficult to focus my attention. Robby patiently tried, but failed, to help me with my work; I was even having difficulty understanding what he was saying. Lucy tried to help too. Annie threatened to blame it all on me if she was ever caught. Half believing her, I was silent out of fear. I was her servant, and I resented her for using me. I knew it would all end badly. I was so stressed every day that my nail-biting got worse. When the social worker phoned to find out how I was, I would tell her I was all right, never anything beyond that. Mrs. Madison said things seemed to be just fine so far, and I was getting along well, although my schoolwork was suffering.

On one of Annie's nights out, she waited with me in the dark woods until we saw a boy approaching us. She left with him. That was the first time I saw someone else. She was becoming more confident that I wouldn't tell anyone about what she was doing. There was one frigid night when Annie met two boys instead of the one she usually saw. One was her almost steady boyfriend, and she tried to pair his friend off with me. I wanted no part of it. Both had been drinking. When Annie and her boyfriend left, the other boy pressured me to drink. I refused and told him that I was going home. Grabbing the collar of my jacket, he pulled me close to him and said I was acting like a baby. Then he started kissing me on my mouth with his tongue nearly down my throat. I screamed, running in the same direction Annie had taken. I found them—without any clothing covering their bottoms. He was on top of her. *How can they be half-naked in this cold weather?* I thought. After she yelled for me to go away, I told her I didn't care what happened and that I was going home. I started to run away in the direction of her house. Annie stood up, trying to gather herself together. "Wait!" Reluctantly, I turned back. Her boyfriend pulled his shirt down over his parts. Annie's shirt was pulled up so that her huge breasts hung down over her bra. Staring, I was taken aback by the size of them. I was confused by what I had just witnessed. What were they doing? I couldn't stand there another moment. I sped home, ducked through her window, and lay in bed trying to catch my breath. After she got back, she hovered over my bed and threatened me, saying that I was going to go with her whenever she wanted. And even though I protested, she told me I would have to go or she would have me thrown out of her house. I didn't want to leave Sharon. That was the last thing I wanted to happen. I had just made two friends, and I didn't know what to do.

Annie talked to me and explained a little about what I saw. She said all her friends do it. I told her about the other boy forcing me to kiss him. She didn't care. "Just deal with it; you're not a baby now." I said it was not something I wanted to do, and I asked her never to bring that boy again. "I don't want boys touching me!" I protested. "Oh, but you like Robby, the colored boy, don't you? You would let *him* kiss you, huh?"

"It's none of your business," I snapped, trying to protect my friend. "He never touches me!" What I didn't say was that I did think about Robby in that way, and if I had a choice, I would take Robby any day. She told me that there would be no more boys coming along with her boyfriend. "They don't like you anyway," she added. "You're ugly!" I hoped she understood how serious I was. I did *not* care if she thought I was ugly and didn't dress like her and her friends, I had good friends.

Annie then went on to describe some things it was okay to let a guy do, like putting his mouth on your breasts and kissing you on the lips. She said that she and her boyfriend had "sex" in the woods, which didn't help me understand what sex was all about. My understanding of what sex meant was still unclear. I was told that only married people had sex and then they had babies. I had heard from other kids that the boy puts his penis in the girl's vagina. I remembered Anita telling me that sex was bad, and girls who had sex were tramps. Why did Anita call me a tramp if I never did things with boys? Maybe that was what Annie was—a tramp. It occurred to me that Annie wasn't particularly clean either. She had been lying in the dirt without her clothes on and then went to bed without washing. That was dirty…

During my childhood, Anita had spewed out names at me randomly, spontaneously, accusing me of doing such terrible things as I got older, and now, I was beginning to understand what she was saying. Boys could make you have babies by putting their private parts inside you, and that certainly wasn't something I wanted. But if I were the kind of girl who kissed a boy, I would want that boy to be Robby. He was nice to me, and he wanted to be with someone who understood him. Because he never pushed himself on me, there were nights I wondered what it might be like to have him kiss me and hold me close.

Annie continued to force me to go out the window with her night after night so she could meet her boyfriend and have sex. I was too tired to think during class, and despite extra help from my teacher, I wasn't able to keep up at school. She asked me what the problem was, and I told her, "Nothing. Just sleepy I guess." I disliked living with Annie more and more. My foster mother and father refused to drive me to the cemetery, deeming it too upsetting, and I resented them as well. They constantly praised their daughter, thinking that she was beyond reproach, someone I should model myself after. I don't think so! I felt like a shadow roaming through their house. Though I wasn't a tattletale, and it wasn't my place to tell them, I felt that they should know what their sweet daughter was doing at night. When I told Robby more about Annie's escapades, he suggested that I tell the social workers, but again, I was too intimidated by Annie. Robby and Lucy attempted to build up my courage every day.

One night, Annie and I went out to a place other than her usual one, a spot near the tracks next to Sacred Heart School. It was not far from the house, and when her father discovered we weren't in the bedroom, it wasn't long before he found us. He spotted me first, and I yelled out to warn her. She came running toward us, her hair and clothes disheveled. Even though had I tried to save her from her father finding out about her having sex with one of her boyfriends, she ran to him, hugging him and crying uncontrollably, accusing me of being responsible for the entire situation. She said I had grabbed her and pushed her to the ground. "Look at me and what she did!" she told her father. He looked at me angrily. Her boyfriend said he had broken up the fight between us. She said I was the one who had gone outside and that they followed me so I wouldn't get in trouble. Annie said she called her boyfriend before she left to help find me and that I was with a boy who had run away from the scene. She lied, lied, and lied. I stood there and never stuck up for myself because I was so stunned—I was speechless! This would be my last week with the Madison family because, of course, Annie's parents believed her, even though when asked I told them my side of the story, which was the truth. The mother said I was horrible for making up stories about her daughter, and the father yelled that I was a bad influence on his precious Annie, and I had to go! No one believed me. Mr. and Mrs. Madison simply didn't want to face the facts about their wonderful daughter. Robby and Lucy were right about telling the social worker about Annie all along, but I knew she wouldn't have believed me anyway, and as it turned out, she didn't.

Later in life, I viewed Annie as a princess who got away with everything she did. Robby knew about everything that went on in

Annie's house because I confided in him. He knew about Annie's reputation but chose to keep that information to himself until all hell broke loose. Despite the rumors about Annie, Robby said they probably wouldn't have believed him either because he was colored. Robby, Lucy, and Lucy's friends were genuinely sad that I had to leave. They told me Annie was a real flirt and had several boyfriends, not just one. Lucy's impulse was to destroy Annie, but, of course, that wouldn't have changed anything. Who would take the word of a fosta' kid, a colored boy, and a working class Catholic girl over the word of Annie's middle-class white parents? What she did do was tell all the kids about Annie's romps in the woods.

From the start, I knew that Annie didn't want me living in her house; I had been in her way from the day I arrived. But I had friends at school who liked me, that was the best! I didn't want to leave them. Would I ever see them again? They both chipped in to buy me a cultured pearl ring, for friendship. Annie never apologized. I hadn't done anything wrong, yet she still hated me. She had to be the one who appeared to be good. The Madisons made me feel uncomfortable until the day I left.

I had a smile on my face the morning I sat on the sofa waiting for the social worker to pick me up because I was leaving the Madisons. I'd cried for quite some time before I went to sleep the night before because I wanted so much to stay with Robby and hang with Lucy but certainly not with the Madison family. When we hugged goodbye, I felt a connection to Robby so intense, I wished I could stay in Sharon to be near him. He sensed it too. "I will miss you, Lib…"

****

I take a deep breath. There is so much to remember, I tell myself as I wait on the hard, wooden bench inside my cell. I wondered about Robby and Lucy and what they might be doing in life now. Did either of them ever marry? Did they have kids? In retrospect, as I think about my life, I look at what has taken place up to now, perhaps to find some meaning in it. What does my future hold after my release from this jail?

CHAPTER TWELVE

Leaving Sharon

I wished I could have stayed with a family that didn't have a child, but wishing has never helped me. I had a difficult time leaving—just when I felt comfortable, I was uprooted. Again, I had no sense of belonging. This was another tough time to get through. I was learning to prepare for the worst, never expecting anything good to happen; this put me ahead of bad times. Annie's parents said goodbye to the social worker but had only the queen's wave for me. I read the scowling expressions on their faces, and I saw disgust. Annie never said a word. She just stared at me with a look of sheer happiness on her face.

I had been tossed from home to home when I lived with Anita and Freddy, but this was different because I wasn't going back to Dad's house. My dad wasn't aware of where I would be placed until they had a home for me. He wasn't familiar with the homes where I lived and, as far as I could tell, he didn't care; he was satisfied just as long as my existence didn't infringe upon his world with Anita. The social worker said they were placing me in the first "suitable" opening. I didn't think it really mattered to them where they put me. No one informed me if Dad had ever checked on me, and I was curious to know about that. They always said they would be in touch with him at some point.

While we were driving, the social worker said, "Libbe, do you want to talk about anything?" As I had on the first trip with her to Sharon, I asked if we could stop to visit my mom. I explained that Mrs. Madison hadn't taken me to the cemetery. Again, no, "There were rules." My feeling of loss was palpable. I begged her to call my dad to ask him if I could go back home to live. Living with Anita would have been preferable to going from one home to another, leaving friends I liked behind. If only I was able to see my dad… "Please, please," I repeated, "can you call my dad?"

She said, "Libbe, I could call your dad again, but we've already spoken to him and he told our office you can't go to his home now, not while you have a behavioral problem. He said your stepmother wouldn't stand for it." Behavioral problem? I hadn't done anything wrong! I shrugged my shoulders. "Please understand, we have your best interests at heart."

"No one wants to believe my side of the story," I told her abruptly. "What do you care!"

She replied, "We care, Libbe, that's why we placed you in a good home. Annie had never been in trouble until you moved in. We have to take the parents' word."

"Well, they are not my best interests. No one asks me how I feel. How am I supposed to act? No one ever takes my side. None of this was my fault!" I pleaded.

"We are trying hard to find you a good home, to help you out," she said. "Homes will not keep you when you do things like this. You must control your temper!"

"But they didn't believe me!" I protested. "They believed Annie, not me, the foster kid!" Silence came over the space we shared.

The truth was simple: Annie didn't get caught before I came, but she was bound to be found out eventually, whether I lived in her house or not. My response was to feel contrary, to rebel. I was thinking how much I hated everyone. I had to shut up and keep my feelings to myself. I could see I wasn't getting anywhere with my temper. Why bother? If I became upset, I was viewed as a problem case with mental issues, not a child having a bad day. The disadvantage of being a foster kid was slowly dawning on me. Looking back at that time in my life, I'm glad that pills weren't used as liberally as they are today for kids with problems because I would have been drugged and, surely, they would have made another addict. I had my issues, but I wasn't mentally ill. It was frustrating working with social workers who had book knowledge, and perhaps sympathized with me from time to time, but really didn't understand how I felt because they had never walked in my shoes.

I had been silent for quite a while. The social worker was speaking about the new foster home. She rambled on, but I really didn't care about what she was saying. She said that the new foster mother stayed at home doing some sort of interior decorating, and the foster father was a plumber. They had a young son and a daughter a little older than me from the mother's first marriage. I would be sharing a room with the daughter, but she was getting married and leaving soon and then I would have the room all to myself. I heard *that* clearly—a room to myself! She had three other daughters who were already married, and I would meet them later. I wasn't looking forward to meeting them. I just wanted to be alone.

She said the name of the town we were driving to was Mattapan. My dad used to take me to the delicatessens on Blue Hill Ave., from Roxbury, through Dorchester, to Mattapan. He went there because they were the best Jewish delicatessens around, especially the G & G. On the high holidays, we would sometimes go to the temple on Seaver Street, and from there we went to Talbot Ave. to sit on the wall. The ride seemed short to me. I had been given back my old clothes and some of Annie's hand-me-downs to take. This time, I wasn't as worried about having clothes to wear. Annie said bluntly enough that she didn't want them because I had worn them, and they were spoiled.

Again, I felt afraid of what would be behind the front door. I knew my Aunt Rose and Uncle Uggie weren't going to take me. I wanted to run away, but running without any sense of where I was going had failed once, so I resigned myself to my new place until another solution came into view. *I am stuck there,* I thought. Still, I was tormented by questions about the reason no one from either my mother's or father's family came to see me. Were they that uncaring?

They were aware that I was in foster homes, so why didn't they try to see me, or at least call? Perhaps it was because I was not related to them by blood. I was dejected. What Anita had told me was true—nobody had ever wanted me. I found out later that they all knew where I was living, and thinking that no one cared wasn't melodrama, it was the truth. The times I did call Aunt Rose and Aunt Fanny, they wished me well and told me to call them to let them know how I was every so often. Sure, why not? I could tell by the tone of their voices and what they said that they were not interested in extending themselves beyond the exchange of pleasantries.

We arrived at the house. Compared to the ranch house in Sharon and my dad's house in Stoneham, this one was huge. I liked the way it looked. It had a long driveway and two large porches. It was dark brown with off-white trim. The social worker parked the car in the driveway on the right side of the house, and we walked to the front porch. We climbed several steps, rang the bell, and waited at the door for an answer. Thoughts came—starting a new school in the middle of the school year, new foster parents—I was overwhelmed! I wondered if the school would be like the one in Sharon, where they dressed so differently from the schools in Stoneham. The idea of turning and running down the steps occurred to me, but my feet felt heavy. I doubted the social worker had any idea of how I was feeling. The smile she wore was wide and long, and it didn't waver. She couldn't possibly imagine the rage I felt toward Anita or the abject sorrow of being alone in the world. Waiting to meet my new foster family scared me more than walking on eggshells with Dad and Anita. How I hated her for being happy living with my dad. I wondered if she would have killed me eventually. In any case, starting over was the most frightening prospect for me.

A smiling woman in a dress and high heels, with bleached blonde hair and long earrings, opened the door. Her face was so happy it appeared unreal. Except in TV commercials, I had never seen anyone so dressed up that early in the morning except for Anita before she married Dad. I thought that perhaps she was going to some special occasion later. She asked us to come in and sit down. The social worker introduced me to Esti, who then kindly served cookies and tea. She was different from Mrs. Madison and not like the mothers in any of the other homes I had been in, or in my dad's or Mommy Rose's family. I liked her because she was different. She appeared to be somewhat awkward and flighty, and dressed gaudily. My stomach didn't have butterflies like it did before. The social worker asked Esti to show me my room so I could put away my clothes. Then, after she spoke with Esti alone, we would all talk. There were two bedrooms and a bathroom upstairs in a small area. Esti showed me the house and told me that it was called a Philadelphia-style two-family. She explained that it was called that because there were bedrooms on the top floor in the split two-family home. I knew about Philly because my dad went there all the time. The ceilings were high like those in my Aunt Rose's house. I put my things away where she showed me, and I wondered where her son and daughter were. Just as I had that thought, Esti said her son would be home soon and that her daughter would be home late because she and her fiancé were making preparations for their wedding. I thought, *Great! I'm going to have my own room at some point, like the social worker said. It was true!* I won't get in trouble like I did with Annie—there wasn't any possibility of escaping outside through this window because it was too high up on the second floor. I didn't want to get into trouble anymore. What Esti didn't tell me was that her house was up for sale, and they would be moving as soon as it was sold. She also neglected to mention that I would be sharing the room with another foster kid sometime in the future. I wouldn't be the only breadwinner in the house; there was someone else coming. Esti went to speak to the social worker.

The adults were downstairs talking. I was worried that the social worker would say I was a "bad" girl, and that I had been in the woods with Annie and a boy. But why care? What's the difference what they say? They never believe me, whether it's the truth or a lie. Either way, I get punished. The psychiatrists and social workers who saw me thought they were helping me, but they made my situation worse by bringing up only negative subjects every time. I always felt worse when I left their office. Dwelling on my faults and the reasons I'd behaved badly emphasized the negative in my life—I did enough of that on my own. The more they told me how bad I was, the worse I became. I decided I would tell them what they wanted to hear, saying yes when it was called for and agreeing with whatever they told me.

I wondered how long I would be sitting in this plain room on the edge of the twin bed, unsure of whose bed it was. Was this going to be my bed or did it belong to their daughter? There was a night table between the two narrow beds. The floors and stairway were carpeted in beige, and there were large, heavy curtains on the windows. I don't remember the colors exactly because they blended into the beige so well. There was a lot of beige. Shit, I don't like sitting here alone in a new place. There was conversation downstairs, but I couldn't make out everything they were saying. Twenty steps or more separated me from them, the social worker and the new foster mother.

****

I always felt empty inside when I was left at a new home or had to sit by myself, just as I am sitting alone in this cell, waiting. How sad and empty it felt, as it feels now. Then it was Anita's fault, now it's mine.

****

Whenever I listened to the conversation of the social workers, I heard them say that I didn't have a family of my own. All because of Anita...why did she have to come into my life? I hate her! I constantly wished her dead. I had heard them say that I had no family so many times that I created an imaginary one, much the same as I had done with my make-believe friend, Elizabeth. To get the kids at school to like me, I made up stories about how my dad was rich but his new wife didn't want children so I had to leave. The kids would tease me anyway, saying that I was poor, a liar, and had no parents—look at your ugly clothes!

I anticipated seeing Elizabeth Taylor on TV more often now. As I got older, I admired her beauty and was awed by how prolific an actress she was. I idolized her, especially her style, and yearned to be like her in so many ways. I loved her jewelry and wanted to own lots of it when I could, even if mine would be all costume. I looked up at the white ceiling with its plaster swirls, and I thought how I didn't like this room I was supposed to sleep in. It was bland and the view from the window was the side of another house, mostly obstructed by trees and a tall fence. I was waiting for what seemed like an extremely long time when the social worker interrupted my daydreaming and asked me to come downstairs. The tall, narrow staircase was difficult to maneuver, and the height of it was scary to me at first. I hated heights because of the dreams I had of my mom calling me to come up to her as she stood at the top of a steep staircase, and of being left stranded on a rooftop holding on for dear life. Now, my stomach was empty and I was queasy. What are they going to ask me? My nerves were heightened.

CHAPTER THIRTEEN

Mattapan

I was afraid—really, really, afraid. I held in my tears as I waved goodbye to the familiar face of my social worker. I tried to understand that she had to leave. I hated her because she didn't take me to the cemetery to see my mother, but I was truly sad to see her go. I wished she could take me home with her. If all went well, the only telephone calls back and forth to my foster home would be to check on how I was adjusting. Would she find me another home if I disliked this one? Or will they find a reason to throw me out? It was an older and comfortable home with big rooms, except for the bedrooms. I had never lived in a city, only towns. I liked the city!

Esti closed the front door and asked me if I had lunch already. Even if I had lunch I would have wanted to eat more. I nodded slightly. "Okay dear, let me make something for you," she said. She went into the kitchen, and I followed. She started to prepare a sandwich and a glass of milk for me. While I was eating, she asked me questions about where I had been and what happened there. I shrugged my shoulders. Then I told her the last lady wanted me to leave. Esti said the social worker had told her I was with a boy, that I didn't get along with their daughter, Anne, and had almost gotten Anne in trouble because of what I had done "That's not true!" I said defensively in a raised voice, but she continued to speak without giving me an opportunity to finish. I didn't reply to most of her questions. It was obvious she wouldn't listen to me anyway. I put my dishes in the sink to wash as Anita had taught me, and Esti was grateful, as though helping her was not routine in her house; the same was true in all the homes. Esti was boasting about how wonderful her husband and children were... even her teacup poodle, Peanut, was the best. She mentioned that she groomed dogs professionally and sewed curtains and bedspreads for people. I was excited about Peanut because I loved dogs and, except for the Taffees, this was the first home I was sent to that had one.

Although I loved dogs, I was hesitant to touch any animal that lived at someone else's house except for Kat's house. I was absolutely in love her collie. He reminded me of Lassie on TV, and I loved that show. The reason I was initially reluctant to touch an animal in someone else's home was because of the time I accidently killed the bird at the Taffees by holding it too tightly—a trauma that held sway for quite some time.

Next, I heard the sound of a door slamming, and a boy came running into the kitchen. Esti said his name was Mason. She told him to say hello, but he ran past me, squinting and making a weird face. He had dark brown hair and brown eyes. She said that Mason was a sweet boy, but that I was a stranger to him right now, and he would have to get used to me. I could tell he didn't respect his mother or care about me, but as much as I felt like hiding, there was no place of my own to hide, not even the bedroom I'd be sharing across from his room. Esti took me outside to show me the backyard. It was small, unlike in the suburbs where the houses were not as large, but had enormous grassy areas between them. Esti's bedroom was on the first level. The kitchen looked out on the pavement in the backyard. This house was different from all the houses where I had lived because there were no plants, no grass except for a few blades that stuck out between the squares of pavement, no trees, only a border fence and bushes. There was a flagstone patio adjacent to the driveway but without potted flowers surrounding it. I was in the city, away from the house my father lived in with Mommy Rose's trellises full of red roses. There definitely weren't any rose gardens here, and I dreamed that one day I would have a pretty home with a rose garden.

Esti told me that she had my papers, and I would be enrolling in school in a day or so. The school was directly behind Esti's house, practically in her backyard. There was a tall fence on her property, then a footpath that led directly to the back of the Solomon Lewenberg School. While there wasn't a long walk to school to worry about, there were other concerns, like the brown corrective shoes the doctor said I needed to wear to support my ankles. The shoes were from Edwin Case, and the social worker gave them to Esti for me. My dad and Anita were convinced that I needed to wear these hideous shoes because of my high arches and an extra bone in my ankle. The Oxford shoes looked foolish enough with my skinny legs—these monstrosities were gross and unstylish, and I was nervous about being teased. I didn't have friends to protect me from the other kids' ridicule. Robby and Lucy would have agreed the shoes had to go.

I sat upstairs waiting, bored and frightened, with nothing to do. If I had paper and a pencil I would have doodled, my favorite pastime at that point in my life. Mason was making noise, banging things around, and rudely talking back to his mother, who cajoled him and spoke to him as if he were a baby. Esti told him, "Honey, why don't you go into my room and watch TV until Dad gets home?" He dashed into his mother's room. Finally, it was suppertime. Yippee! I heard a door slam downstairs. A man had walked through the back door into the kitchen. He had a deep, bellowing voice that didn't sound friendly. Esti called me for supper and to meet her husband. The man was large and gruff, not the least bit welcoming. He was rude, behaving much the same way his son did. Esti introduced me. I was really nervous and said a meek hello. He waved his hand upward, said, "Hmm," and walked abruptly past me like he didn't want to be bothered. He made me feel vey unwelcome!

I asked to be excused from the kitchen, but Esti said I could help her out by placing the dishes and silverware on the table while Mason and his father watched TV in her room. The arrangement here was the same as in Sharon, where I helped my foster mom while Annie and her father watched TV. It didn't really bother me, I enjoyed helping out. I figured that I would only be watching on special occasions because the set was in their bedroom. Whatever was cooking smelled so delicious that I forgot about them not liking me. I was thinking only about food and eating supper. After Esti called her husband and son into the kitchen, we sat down to dinner and she told me again that her daughter, Jennifer, would be coming home later. I was quiet at the table, studying my surroundings. Leonard reminded me of a lumberjack because of his broad shoulders and the extent of his appetite. He grunted when he ate. I saw him glance at me twice during dinner, like I was on display, but when I looked at him he turned away. His voice frightened me. Mason was ill-mannered, impolite, and ate and snorted like a pig. I could tell he was spoiled, a real brat. They were all speaking, and Esti explained about me to her family and told them that I didn't talk much. If people only knew I wanted to talk… I just didn't know what to say. I was wishing the day would be over soon; there were just too many changes to adjust to. I felt like crying, but held back my tears and choked up. Esti handed me a glass of water, and then I was okay. She was right. I didn't have much to say because I was uncomfortable and didn't fit in. When we finished dinner, Esti and I cleaned up. Then she showed me where the towels were so I could shower or take a bath and change for bed. She thanked me for helping her. She called Mason to get ready, and Leonard yelled, "In a while, Esti, he's with me. Leave him alone." Mason was whining about wanting to watch more TV and how he didn't want to go upstairs because I was a stranger. His dad cleared him to watch even more TV. Esti, who had been trying all this time to get me to speak, asked me if I wanted a cookie or some kind of cake before I went to sleep. Of course, the answer was yes to both. As I followed her into the kitchen, Jennifer and a man came into the room through the back door. Although her daughter seemed a bit dismissive, she at least said hello. Her boyfriend was friendly and even joked with me. I stared at Jennifer as she spoke with her mother. Her features and hair were like Elizabeth Taylor's! Even her clothes were like Liz's clothes, and I couldn't help staring at her. I thought she was beautiful and wished I could look like that. I was excited about staying in her room—her mannerisms reminded me of Kat's older sister in Stoneham.

Everyone was in the kitchen, talking in an animated way about Jennifer's wedding. She was boisterous, bubbly and vivacious, and a bit crude. I learned that Leonard was not Jennifer's father; that was the reason she called him by his first name, not Dad. I was told it was time to go to bed. Even though they were more interesting than the people in any other house I'd stayed in before, I was ready to sleep. There was so much going on. I said goodnight to everyone, and they all wished me goodnight, except for Leonard, who grumbled and walked out of the room without saying a word.

I went upstairs and stayed awake for a long time, curled up in a fetal position and holding tightly onto the blanket, looking at the window and wall. I wanted to be asleep before my roommate came upstairs. Mason whined every time Esti sent him upstairs, and so he was able to stay downstairs even longer. That's how it was in practically all the places I'd lived in—the children had special privileges and were spoiled, but I had to do what I was told without whining. I never got my own way. I lay in the bed and thought that if and when I had my own children, I would never allow them to be mean to other kids. Waiting to fall asleep, I thought back to a time when I was sick. I couldn't remember whether it was a cold or a stomachache. My mother Rose sat me outside in the yard in a lounge chair next to the rose garden and covered me with a blanket. She brought me some fresh fruit. Then, as I sat in the sunshine with the breeze touching my cheeks, she read out loud to me. Strands of my hair brushed across my face and Mommy Rose pulled my hair back ever so gently and clipped barrettes to keep my hair out of my eyes. That day was beautiful. I can feel the memory, always. I will never forget her tender touch for as long as I live. And then I went to sleep.

I spent my first weekend at Esti's home getting used to the layout of the house: what was where, and where I could and could not go according to everyone's rules. On Monday, she enrolled me in the school. It was an urban school and very different from those I was used to. Although I was teased and the school's students were hardcore, I felt more at ease with the kids who were black because they took to me. There were some white kids and a few other kids who spoke with accents. Black or white was less of an issue here, and a lot of the city kids had started using the term "black" instead of "colored." Martin Luther King, Jr. had interspersed "black" with his primary usage of "negro" several times in his "I Have a Dream" speech in August 1963. Both groups hung together, except for a few cliquey ones. They dressed in all kinds of ways, and I did not stick out as much as before, except when I was compared to the richer, Jewish girls. The Jewish and gentile kids were divided into cliques, but they used the names Collegiates and Rats no matter their religion because they based it on their inclinations. And then there were the girls who were Jewish princesses with pretty, in-style dresses and hair—real JAPS. They didn't want me around them because of my terrible clothes; however, there were kids less advantaged than me, so I didn't feel badly. There were hippie types. This was the city. It was an easier place for me to fit in socially. There were kids I hung around with after school, but at the time, I didn't know they were the "bad" kids, not yet. I was still so naive. I didn't fully understand the significance of all these cliques, and without guidance, it took some time to catch on. Esti wasn't much help as far as fashion was concerned, nor was she a role model with her overdone clothing and jewelry. The kids in the city school were totally different from the kids in the suburbs. It was a totally new experience for me, which was better in most ways.

Adapting to my new foster home took some time. Before long, between watching his Westerns and crime shows on TV, Leonard was cracking a smile or two in my direction. Esti spoke to me and was affectionate. I viewed her as rather motherly. She was liberal with me and allowed me to wear makeup to appear older, but once she saw what I was capable of doing in the house, she expected my help doing chores every day. She would watch a soap opera I detested, called "Days of Our Lives," and speak on the phone to a relative of hers who lived on Morton Street and gossip with other relatives every day. She told me she felt badly for her cousin because she was an obese woman and virtually housebound. When I met her, it was obvious that her size was what kept her from going out much, but she was nice to me. Esti gave me some of Jennifer's clothes, which were better than mine—especially on top! I was straight as a board and not even a size zero. I didn't feel as badly about myself when some people said I looked like Audrey Hepburn. Although I wasn't exactly sure who she was, and it was nice of them to say that, I did *not* see myself looking like an actress...no way!

At the new home, everything seemed to be going well. My dad even said he was coming by to meet Esti and see me. Wow, that was a switch! I had good food and was never deprived. Esti gave me second helpings after first asking her husband and children if they wanted more. It didn't bother me that she offered food to her family before me. I was used to being last. There were bullies at school, and I learned to avoid them as much as possible. I was catching on, learning the ways of the city. I would even take off my ugly shoes and hide them in the bushes until I came home. I would wear the black patent leather shoes I had for going out on special occasions instead. Still, I would have done anything to have a friend like Lucy or Robby. I missed them, and although I talked to Lucy a few times, we were losing touch. I kept the pearl ring in my suitcase and cherished it.

I must have worn a sign across my forehead that said "Sucker" because, once again, several of the kids convinced me to do something that was clearly wrong and for which I would very likely be punished, or worse. They asked if they could hang out at my house while my foster parents were out for the evening at some affair. And they were not scheduled to be back until the wee hours of the morning. It was not so much that I hadn't learned my lesson as it was a desperate need to be liked and to belong to the so-called "hip" crowd. Mason would be staying with a friend, and Jennifer was supposed to be staying at her boyfriend Silky's apartment for the weekend. I told four of the kids playing poker on the pathway stairs to the school on Walk Hill Street it was okay, and then they told some other kids from Blue Hill Ave., and from there it snowballed into a number greater than I could count. There were supposed to be about six kids coming over, not more. The others who showed up uninvited were white kids known as the Rats, who came from well-to-do families in Mattapan and Milton. Some were stuck up, with their noses in the air. They wore black leather jackets, but some were rich and wild. Now I was afraid of being a bad kid again. And I looked the part of the bad girl: I had lipstick on and eyeliner that one of the girls showed me how to use. I thought I wasn't bad-looking with the makeup on, and noticed the boys were paying more attention than usual to me and my new friend Amy.

The six friends I had originally invited came to my house, and then the party was crashed by a large group of kids who brought beer and liquor bottles in their jackets. At first, I tried as much as I could to get them to leave, and a couple of the kids I invited tried to help me. We were outnumbered, and at ninety-nine pounds, I was not successful pushing them back. It was a good thing no one went upstairs into the main house and that the party stayed in the basement. They called me a "little shit" and gave me a few drinks. When I became slightly intoxicated, the party seemed to be fun and I forgot about my foster family. I was living in the moment, and completely lost track of time. The basement was my space to do with as I wished, but that didn't include having parties, especially without permission. I focused on having a good time with my new friends rather than on what was going to happen when we were caught. I didn't even hear Leonard as he drove into the driveway. I had done the same thing when I was living in Stoneham, except now I was older and into the party scene. Obviously, I hadn't learned that there would be consequences. In Stoneham, no one saw or discovered the kids as they were trashing the house. This time I was caught red-handed. The voice of doom was about to descend upon me, and it was my fault. I was desperate for the other kids to like me, and I allowed the party to proceed to its ugly end.

These kids weren't my friends at all. Leonard and Esti came in through the bulkhead. As they descended the stairs, the kids shouted that they hadn't brought the beer they were holding. They said that I had invited them and already had the booze at the house. They shouted out that the party was entirely my fault. Leonard screamed, "Get the hell out now! Out! Out! All of you drop the damn booze!" They did. It was such a mess. Leonard was *really* cursing, and Esti was so upset with me that for the first time since I had moved in she screamed at me, "You've been here only a few months and look at what you've done! Your social worker is right, you *are* a troublemaker!" That name rang in my ears. Oh, god, I hope they're not going to throw me out. Anita constantly accused me of being a troublemaker, but I wasn't then. Leonard was so angry he couldn't stop swearing. *Oh, stupid, desperate me,* I thought. It was my fault for inviting those few kids without permission in the first place. All I wanted was to be happy and fit in. But I was going about it in the wrong way, and it wasn't helping. I worried about Esti calling my dad and the social worker. I wondered how the other kids managed to have parties without getting into trouble. Esti was fuming and told me she didn't trust me alone anymore. "Not in *my* house," Leonard firmly agreed. They didn't throw me out! I was surprised they let me stay. Instead, I was disciplined, "punished," Esti said—a word with which I was all too familiar. She didn't allow me to hang out with those girls anymore, even telling the teachers that I couldn't be friends with them. At first, I didn't understand why; those few girls were the only kids I knew. But then I was grateful she had done that because I did need to choose my friends more wisely. I thought Esti and Leonard weren't going to say anything, but the social workers and my dad were called. The troublemakers were the only ones who accepted me. What was my alternative? I did not want to be alone, sitting around doing nothing every day with no one to talk to. So, whenever I could, I would sneak out to meet them where they hung out on Walk Hill pathway. Bad once again, and desperate…

I learned about cars from my dad, not only how to fix them, but especially how to start one without a key—a talent that got me into trouble when I used it for the wrong reasons. The boys liked me because of my knowledge about cars, and even my foster dad liked me after some time had passed and the party was forgotten. I was even more of a son than Mason, helping him lift heavy pipes and tools. I enjoyed boxing matches and would watch them on TV with Leonard. His son, on the other hand, didn't like boxing or wrestling. I felt more confident when Leonard needed me to help him with his plumbing jobs. I was always eager to go.

I met a girl at school who reminded me of Lucy, and we became close friends. Her last name seemed Jewish to me, and I didn't know that a person could have a Jewish-sounding name but belong to a different religion. I just assumed she was a Jew, like me. She was my friend, and I didn't care who or what anyone was just as long as they showed an interest in me and would be honest and true. When Esti met her, I let her know that my friend's last name was Jewish and that made her acceptable in this Reform Jewish home. I loved my new friend's house with its large rooms and stained-glass windows. She lived on Pasadena Road in Roxbury's Grove Hall area. Though things seemed better having Pam as my friend, my schoolwork was still suffering.

No matter what book I read, I didn't understand what I was reading, nor could I remember any part of it afterward. The only exception, the one book I loved and will always cherish, was *A Tree Grows in Brooklyn*. It reminded me of Freddy, and the kind of relationship we had. I didn't grasp mathematical concepts, and couldn't solve the difficult problems. I felt like there was a wall in my head that blocked me from understanding. I would try to understand, but nothing sank in. My attention suffered in school when I was younger, and it had become even worse. Unless the subject interested me—I loved to draw and liked science—I was bored. I didn't respond to anything the teachers said, and I felt stupid when other kids knew the answers. In gym class, I experienced the usual anxiety and embarrassment when I had to undress in front of the other girls, and I had a bump on my spine where Anita used to hit me with the belt buckle. I couldn't handle the name-calling, and it was little comfort that I wasn't the only one being harassed or ridiculed. My anxiety was overwhelming because I couldn't compete with these girls.

****

Thinking back about the girl I used to be, I understand that what happened to me was beyond my control. The baggage I held onto and carried with me into my young adult years, and even beyond, has lightened since then. The walls I built have been slowly chipped away. I rest the back of my head against the cold white wall behind me. I am stiff from sitting here, not shifting my position an inch. The bench doesn't have cushions, and my butt hurts. What is there to do besides recall my past? I have no paper or pens, no magazines, TV, or radio. Thinking of the past helps time go by faster. I'm afraid that I will have an anxiety attack and my panic will trigger an asthma attack. I have to be calm. The federal marshals confiscated my asthma inhaler, and even though my asthma isn't chronic, I was relieved when an agent told me they'd bring it to me if I needed it. A hug from my son would go a long way at this moment.

****

Pam and I were together almost all the time. In her city slang, which was all new to me, she would say, "We hang tough." I was interested in a boy for the first time, someone with long blond hair and big blue eyes, whose family had emigrated from Israel. Every girl had a crush on Kappy, and when he spoke to me I wasn't sure whether he was returning my interest or teasing me. When he would try to meet me after school, I thought that he liked me. Or was this only wishful thinking on my part? We saw each other, and he didn't make obvious attempts to hide it from anybody, although, at the same time, he didn't tell his other girlfriends about me either. The guys at the Walk Hill Street schoolyard knew. He probably didn't tell the girls because compared to the Jewish American princesses, I was an embarrassment. He asked me to go to the Oriental Theater in Mattapan, where I was mesmerized by the ornate Asian motif surrounding us, and I was surprised because all his friends saw us there together. Once, when we were at a party on Wellington Hill Street, we made out pretty heavily. That was as far as things would go because when he tried to get me alone, I refused. Making out was enough. Another time, when we were at the Beatles' movie at the Oriental, he tried to feel me up. At first I was relaxed about it because I was taken away by his kissing, but then I panicked, and quickly excused myself to go to the ladies room. I had to remove the socks that were stuffed into each side of my training bra. It would have been too embarrassing to have him pull out a sock and make fun of me in public—shit, that was the last thing I needed! We kissed some more. I was self-conscious about the size of my breasts and never did let him touch them after that. We only kissed because I didn't fully understand what to do yet. I had discovered masturbation, and although it took me quite a few times to get used to this new sensation, I liked it and would do it when I needed to relieve tension. When I was close to Kappy, I felt a strange sensation, and my underpants would get damp. That was way better than masturbating, but I didn't know what it meant. No foster parent, not even a social worker, explained sex to me. Pam helped me through this bewildering time by explaining about boys and the sensations I was feeling. She didn't quite know what to say because I knew virtually nothing about sex, and her explanations were vague at times. Although what I learned stunned me, I was grateful to her for finally telling me what no one had ever ventured to tell me before. Still, I didn't want to do more than kiss—not yet. I would overhear girls talking about parking with their boyfriends all the time, making out and going to first base. When I asked Pam, she said it meant getting felt up under my clothes, and then the next step afterward was when sex happened. I clammed up whenever sex was mentioned.

The black girls at school adored Kappy and were always saying how handsome he was and what great clothes he wore. I felt like I was competing with all the girls who were attracted to him and wondered why he chose me. Perhaps it was because I didn't chase him. Looking back, that makes sense. Men don't like women who are easy to get, and women don't like easy-to-get men. Parents try to tell their kids that it's unwise to be too easy, but when you are young the feelings you have are so overwhelming it's impossible to grasp what they are saying. Maybe if those feelings were described and discussed openly by adults, there wouldn't be as much confusion, and kids would have an easier time controlling their hormonal impulses. I regret my lack of candor when the time came to explain sex to my own son. I distanced myself from the subject, not knowing how or what to say, even though I was in the sex business!

CHAPTER FOURTEEN

Friends

I was on my way home, coming down the path from school. I walked up the steps to the porch of my foster home, just as I was about to open the front door, I heard a girl yell out my name. "Hey, Libbe!" she said. Another girl with her called out, "Bitch, you stay away from Kappy! He's not with you!" *Why would they say that?* I wondered. There were four black girls in all. I didn't understand the reason the tough, heavyset girl said what she did. "Stay away from him because my girl likes him." They were coming closer. I wondered if Kappy knew this girl. Another girl said, "I'm going to kick your ass, got it?"

"For what?" I asked. I could never fight four girls. "You'll never see him again, sweetie…" Just then, Pam came running up the stairs. One of the girls said, "Oh, so you think you're gonna' protect this white Jew bitch? Bring your high-yellow ass to your own kind, and stop hanging with her silly white ass." I was puzzled. I looked at Pam, who said to them, "One by one, she'll fight you, hear?" I stared at Pam in disbelief!

"What? I can't fight!" I said. Before I had a chance to think, one girl came up the steps and snatched me down. She started to punch me in the stomach and face. I ducked. She punched my chest so hard I couldn't breathe. Shit, this beating was Anita times two! It hurt—I hadn't been beaten since Anita, but this was a different kind of pain. Pam called out to me to fight back. "Punch her! Punch her!" she shouted. She came to my aid, holding the others back as they yelled, "You mulatto bitch!" at her. I had never hit anybody before and didn't know how to punch, so all I could do was block her punches with my arms and hands the way the boxers did on TV. Shit, this girl was serious, and her friends wanted a part of me too! Then—as if out of nowhere—Esti, my angel, opened the door. "What are you doing!" she yelled. "Get off her, and get off my porch! What's wrong with you girls?" Softly, Pam said that it was just an argument. She wasn't siding with anyone. Esti ordered me inside the house, and Pam asked to come in to explain. I was doubled over in pain. Esti wanted to know what was going on, but we underplayed the episode so that it appeared to be mere fluff, and Esti, being as gullible as she was, believed it. "Fighting over a boy?" she said. "You stay away from those girls." I knew she wanted to say more about them, like "Stay away from those *colored* girls," but she didn't in front of Pam. Leonard and Esti only used racial insults when they were speaking privately.

We went downstairs to the playroom, away from Esti. My chest and back were killing me. I asked Pam what "high-yellow" and "mulatto" meant. She prefaced what she was about to say by telling me that she was not Jewish, she was Baptist. She was colored with a Jewish-sounding last name. She said she was "mulatto" and that meant light-skinned or both black and white mixed. "I am just light-skinned, like Lena Horne, the singer." I was familiar with her but never thought of her as being any color. High-yellow was slang for it. What bothered me more was that Esti would think I had lied about Pam after I promised to tell her the truth no matter what the circumstances. I didn't care what Pam was, but they would.

Even though I had visited Pam's house, I hadn't met her parents. Funny, they were never there when I came by, and it didn't occur to me that anything was strange. I asked Pam what her parents were, and she told me they were colored and had dark skin. I wondered how that could happen. No one bothered to explain colors to me. As a child, it didn't matter to me until I found out that others had issues with it. Now I couldn't help but notice her skin was tan, but I'd never given a thought to what the shade of her skin was before, I just thought she was pretty. I had heard Leonard making slurs about colored people on many occasions. I *hated* that, but couldn't say a word. Even some kids at school would bad-mouth the colored kids, and the colored kids would call the white kids "honkies." Why do we have such a separation?

Because Pam wasn't Jewish and was colored, I worried that Esti might not allow me to be her friend. Eventually, that was exactly what happened. They found out Pam wasn't Jewish and thought I had lied to them. All hell broke loose. Esti and Leonard told me that because Pam went with a rough crowd we couldn't be friends. I couldn't see her before or after class, and I certainly couldn't go to her house. They didn't know about her color yet—they would be really crazy when they did find out. I felt as though I couldn't withstand another loss, and I wanted my friend. Why did I always have to give up what I liked and loved? She was my new best friend now. I even gave her the pearl ring my friends in Sharon had given me as a symbol of our friendship. From then on, we had to conceal seeing one another. I experienced a sense of loss once again. Just as the pieces of my life were fitting together, another piece came loose. It looked as though Pam would be yet another loss.

The Jewish girls at school felt superior to me, and I never was comfortable with them. I tried to be friends with a few of them, but they rejected me. One girl, Amy, was okay; she had stuck by me from the first day. I was envious of these girls, and of their nice homes and beautiful clothes. They came from families with their own moms and dads. And, of course, on top of it all, I was intimidated by the size of their boobs. I had been an A-cup for so long I thought my size would never change. They acted like the bigger the boobs a girl had, the more desirable she was.

****

It was true then and it is no different today. The size and shape of a woman's tits and ass make her more sexually desirable. That's due to the hype on TV, commercials, and in movies. Yeah, I should know that, especially in my past and present business. If you don't have boobs or a big ass but you have the money, you can buy implants for top and bottom. It is this mentality that fuels my business.

****

Paying attention at school was becoming increasingly difficult, and I was getting into trouble more often. It seemed that I was being disciplined all the time. I was waiting for Esti to give up on me, but I was another means she brought money into the household. It was something Esti and Leonard discussed. I overheard them saying that they needed the money. Jennifer was frustrated with me and yelled and screamed whenever she spoke to me. She wasn't that much older than me, but my sense was she liked to boss me, and others, around. And the more I was criticized for behaving badly, the easier it became to be bad. The punishments were so much lighter than Anita's that they didn't faze me. I would hang out at the Oriental Theater, trying to fit in with the other kids. But most of the time, I stayed to myself, waiting for Pam and Amy to show. Pam appeared less and less frequently, but Amy always came through. And then Michael came along; of course, I thought he was tough and sexy. I must have looked like easy prey to him, something like a toy girl he could mess with—and I was. All I needed was any kind of attention.

Michael was an egotistical, rich, Jewish boy from Milton. He and his friend Rob were called Rats because of their leather jackets and Harley motorcycles. Michael also drove a Corvette or two. The one I liked was a 1965. Outwardly, he was handsome with dazzling blue eyes and a muscular build. But, as I was to learn later, inwardly, he was lacking in so many ways. He told me his father owned a car dealership on Morton Street, and his mother was paid just to sit there—a real JAP. He didn't like speaking about her; he said he hated her guts. I met a girl he liked named Anna, a pretty blonde girl with nice clothes. He liked to show her off. She wouldn't speak to me; she thought she was better than me. She was Michael's girlfriend, but he wanted to see me on the side. Maybe it was his money or his rebellious nature that attracted Miss Stuck Up. Whatever the reason, he said she was having sex with him, Mr. Tough Guy. I'm sure that the tomboy side of my personality was what attracted him to me. He told me he liked me. No one was supposed to know that he hung out with me, and he said it was our secret. I didn't care. Kappy liked me, but he had many girls falling for him. I was just thrilled that another boy liked me. When I went to his house, he played the drums and then we kissed. He drummed as aggressively as he did most other things. He would scream at his mother in such a derogatory way when she asked him to stop that it was clear he was either spoiled rotten or he simply hated her and was vengeful. It was obvious he ran that house. Either way, he didn't respect her. He had an older brother I saw only once or twice during brief encounters, and he appeared to be Michael's polar opposite.

Michael and I were a perfect pair—he could not express affection, and I was used to a lack of it. I believed his bad treatment was, at the very least, attention, and that it meant he was attracted to me. It was in his basement that he coerced me into giving him my first blowjob. I gagged and gagged. He made me practice until I could take his entire penis down my throat. He taught me the way he wanted it done, and there were many times I couldn't stop choking. I believed that making him happy was what mattered, so I did it at the snap of his fingers. It wasn't long before he didn't have to hold my head down and hit me. I sucked his penis while he played the drums, never tiring until he allowed me to stop. If I didn't swallow when he came, he would slap me. More often, whether I was gagging or not, he hit me with his drumsticks. How I felt wasn't a consideration—it was a matter of making him happy.

From time to time, Michael praised my skills, telling me I was the best. I studied every movement he made to anticipate how to sexually respond. I knew by his expression and body language that I was getting better at doing it. At least I was good at something, even if I couldn't brag about it. To this day, I don't like a man to hold my head down when he wants pleasure. I choke if I sense he might cum in my throat. This began a lifelong pattern of pleasing a man before myself—a pattern that has proven difficult to break.

CHAPTER FIFTEEN

The Wedding

I was getting used to this foster home, and in many ways felt comfortable there. My only complaint was having to listen to the constant arguing between Esti and Leonard, and even Jennifer's voice was harsh and sometimes got on my nerves. I liked Jennifer and Silky, and we definitely had a connection. Esti basked in attention and was funny, and I was learning more about Leonard's idiosyncrasies. By Jennifer's wedding day, the activity in the house was more hectic than ever. The pink bridesmaid gowns were classic and sophisticated. I wore one of the gowns with my hair pulled up into a French twist, and although I still didn't have an inkling of who Audrey Hepburn was and certainly wasn't familiar with her style, several people at the wedding told me that I looked like her. Later, when I had finally seen her in a movie, I noticed a kind of resemblance, especially the way I appeared in the formal wedding pictures. We were both skinny with big eyes and dark hair, but I would be flattering myself to ever say I truly resembled Audrey Hepburn. At the time, I didn't think I did, but when I look at the wedding pictures now, I see the similarity. If I maintained a weight of ninety-nine pounds and wore an elegant gown every day, then *maybe* it could be said.

I looked forward to the day of the wedding and had even stopped biting my nails beforehand so I would look more feminine. It was a nervous habit that began when I was eight years old and has stayed with me to this day. For the first time, I felt like a part of the family because I was not just an invited guest, I was a bridesmaid! I felt honored being in the wedding. Jennifer's sisters were bridesmaids too. Esti would refer to them as her real daughters, adding that I was her "foster daughter." Jennifer once told me she remembered other foster kids who stayed for a while and then left, but I was different—she felt that I had always been in the family. What she said comforted me. But I was hardened for a child my age and knew I could never mean that much. And later, I found that to be true. I was critical of the family in every home where I had ever stayed. I was always attuned to the hypocrisy in their lives. Even today, foster children are stigmatized. People consider at-risk children's problems too daunting to address, and medications are often used to cover up both physical and psychological issues. Then and now, people don't understand how little it would take to make a difference in a child's life.

Esti appeared to be happy while preparing for the wedding, but I sensed there was something sad about her, an expression in her eyes. All of her other daughters were married off, and Jennifer was the last to go. There was a sensual air about Esti, as if she longed for something else that was missing inside her. She loved showing off for Leonard, for men in general, but when she came on to him and flirted, he often pushed her away. She put on excessive makeup and jewelry to draw attention to herself, which I thought was way too much. The truth was that Esti and Leonard were middle-class Jews who, despite the reality of their financial situation, wanted to keep up appearances. There are so many people who do that. Perhaps one of the reasons I chose to live an "outlaw" way of life had to do with them. Leonard stole from the homes where he worked and was proud of it. He gloated but kept it within the walls of his own house. Esti flirted to get her own way—a mannerism I eventually made my own. If Jennifer hadn't been there, sharing in my perceptions and my opinion of the whole picture, my life with them would have been as much a travesty as it had been with other foster families. I was always the workhorse in my foster homes. It was more comfortable in Esti and Leonard's house than in other homes, though. I didn't have new clothes to wear, just hand-me-downs, but there was plenty of food.

And despite my negative feelings about their habits and their ways, I tried as best I could to feel as though I belonged.

Jennifer and Silky's wedding day was celebrated at the Aperion Plaza in Grove Hall in Roxbury. The building was a large, soft pink hall, filled with people that day. I enjoyed wearing the long gown, and I accepted all the invitations I received to dance. Guys actually wanted to dance with me! I used to love to dance when my mom was alive, but my confidence had been eaten away by neglect and Anita's brutality. Leonard's brusque behavior when I first met him was long forgotten by the wedding day, and he glowed with happiness for Jennifer as he walked her down the aisle in his dapper suit; it was tight around his belly, like if he laughed too hard the buttons would pop! I didn't want to lose Jennifer, but she was now married to Silky and they already had their own apartment.

I liked Jennifer's oldest sister Meryl from the moment I met her. Her husband Gary was handsome, but he held his household to very high, rigid standards. It was obvious he loved his family. Their house in Waltham was modern. It was spotless inside, and the yard outside was manicured perfectly. Their son, who slept in a padded crib, was sick with a blood disorder and required transfusions. His illness was a source of deep sorrow for them. When they first learned of it, Gary would tell Meryl not to let their son see her cry. He didn't want his son to be babied. He wanted Meryl to be strong for her son in order for him to thrive so that his life would be long and fuller. He wanted his son to play with other children and to be as normal as a totally healthy child. I admired their toughness. Gary was an amazing man, and it worked. Susan, the next oldest sister, lived one town over. She was involved in taking care of her children to the exclusion of any other interests. Her attitude at Jennifer's wedding had nothing to do with the wedding or her sister but was indicative of her bland personality. Michelle, the sister closest in age to Jennifer, though attractive, seemed stuck up. She was always showing off and had a good-looking husband who eventually divorced her; even as young as I was, I could tell why. Observing Jennifer's sister and her husband, and other married couples who were friends of Jennifer and Silky, was enough to convince me never to marry.

I wished Jennifer could stay, but I didn't allow myself to cry at her wedding. I was hurt because I had gotten too close to her, and by the end of the wedding, I swore I would never go to another one. I had a bad experience at Anita and Freddy's wedding, and now, even though I was experiencing joy for Jennifer and Silky, I felt sadness. I regretted her departure from my life. On her wedding day, Jennifer looked as beautiful as Elizabeth Taylor with her black hair and flawless complexion.

I missed the way Jennifer looked before she fell into the role of a stereotypical suburban housewife, whose time was spent gossiping on the telephone and lounging by the pool with her friends. I suppose she ate too much to compensate for her unhappiness, something she couldn't put her finger on until much later in life, and even then, it kept going the wrong way. Occasionally, she would refer to me as her sister, but most times she called me her foster sister. She and Silky would sometimes take me with them when they went somewhere—I loved that.

I was always shy, frightened to be in places where there were crowds of people. It felt overwhelming to me, almost claustrophobic. I still avoid functions. The happiness of the moment is too intense, along with the thought that time will alter the joy. I have given large parties in my own home and never been troubled by those feelings, only when I go to other people's houses.

Without Jennifer living in the house, I found myself relying on my wits to get along. Even when I didn't want to, I would stick up for their son, Mason, to make him happy. Leonard, who worshipped his son, liked and accepted me on account of my attitude toward his only precious male child. I hated doing it, but catered to both of them just to be accepted. My life depended on being perceptive.

Their house was still up for sale, and someone was interested in buying it. At first I was frightened, but once they told me I would be going with them, I relaxed. I didn't like change. Esti said we would be moving to a newly built home in Canton. There were daily conversations about how the old neighborhood was different now that all the Jewish people were leaving. I later understood that black families were renting and buying in the area more and more, pushing out the white families who wanted to leave because the neighborhoods were becoming rundown—and black! That's the real reason…the exclusivity of the neighborhood was being compromised. Blue Hill Ave., they would say, was changing from Israel into Africa. But I liked this home more than others where I had lived. It was a house built with character, and it was in the city, not the suburbs. I didn't want to deal with the stuffier white kids in the suburbs of all one race. When I purchased a large house in the city as an adult, I realized that my taste in homes was acquired when I lived in Mattapan. Suburban cookie-cutter houses all look the same and are built in a development. That says to me that the people living in these homes are as similar to one another as their houses. All the white families in Dorchester, Roxbury, and Mattapan were so afraid of their children mingling with other races that they sold and ran away. It has taken decades for them to realize that not all black people (by then also called African-American) are bad, but that, like all humans, there are good and bad in every race. Sadly, even in our time now, race is still an issue.

There were two boys who were interested in me, Michael and Huckie. Huckie said he loved me and tried hard to be my boyfriend. He asked me to marry him several times, but I didn't trust him because he was almost too nice, and that scared me. He was easy-going and would do anything for me. Even in my imagination, I couldn't envision myself married, and I continued to see Michael, the wild one. His mistreatment felt right somehow. I wanted to believe he loved me in his own way. What would I do with someone who actually did care for me? Could I return love when I wasn't certain what it was? "Bad" was what I was attracted to and understood. There would be more missed opportunities with good men throughout the years. The "what if's" still haunt me. Yet, I still push the good ones away. Am I capable of changing now, at my age? Perhaps I am too set in my ways. I realize that I could never be with a man who only wanted me for sex. And I could never be with someone just for his money! I will accept the future as it comes.

Other foster kids came to stay with Esti and Leonard, and my simple, ivory-colored room wasn't mine anymore. One foster girl came before we moved to Canton. Kara was pretty…and slick. She talked me into running away with her. I fell for it. She made it sound like we would go to another state. We really had nowhere to go. As we stood in a doorway in the Newton Centre area, shivering, cold, and hungry, we were caught and reprimanded by the police. I was disciplined more severely than she was because, I was later told, I'd been there longer and should have known better. We ran away again. That did it—I still hadn't learned! This girl knew what to say; she won the laying blame contest, always saying that I was the one who was responsible for getting into more trouble, not her. This time we were arrested and held over in jail until we were rescued. Leonard was irate. He screamed at me right in front of the police. It was true, I should have known better. He overlooked Kara and took his anger out on me. Admittedly, running away gave me a feeling of freedom, but as much as I liked it, I did not like going back home afterward to face my foster family and the social workers—the firing squad. They called my dad, and I had to endure his screaming…and Anita cheering him on with a string of profanities in the background. I didn't see that Leonard truly cared about me, so it felt like his discipline was motivated out of meanness. They sent Kara back to wherever she came from, and Esti and Leonard were happy to see her go. She really was a troublemaker. Leonard made his sentiments known to Esti by shouting, "No more foster kids in this house! She's the last one! Do you hear me?" There had been another foster kid before me, a Chinese girl who wasn't any trouble. She became friends with Jennifer. She wasn't there for very long.

It was almost time to move to Canton, and I was anticipating missing playing cards and dice on the stairs between Walk Hill Ave. and Duke Street path, spending time at pool halls on Blue Hill Ave., the Jewish Community Center, and devouring pickles from the G & G Deli. The city was exciting to me because of Blue Hill Ave. and the variety of attractions there. I would miss spending the Jewish holidays at "The Wall" on Talbot Ave.; it reminded me of Mom and Dad and all the good times. Most of all, it would not be the same without my friend Pam and my boyfriend Michael. I would even miss Huckie, who really cared about me. Just as I was feeling permanent,

I would have to adjust again. In my anxiety, I wondered how long I would be able to stay in the new house.

Just as we were getting ready to move to Canton, Michael started acting angry and possessive. He wanted me to meet him all the time. His demands were greater than ever. It seemed he cared even more for me or was he losing his servant? I couldn't tell which. One night, on the way home from Michael's house, it was late and he knew I would get into trouble, which was just what he wanted. He dropped me off at the corner of Blue Hill Ave. and Wellington Hill Street and sped away—that made me feel like shit! He got what he wanted from me. I felt loss, and guilt too. Leaving was terrible, and I knew there was no way I could use the phone later to call him. Leonard was in the habit of picking up the extension to listen whenever I was making a call. I had no privacy.

I was always acutely aware of my surroundings because of my childhood. Anita always snuck up behind me, so I had an inner antenna. On this night, I noticed a strange car parked at the bottom of Wellington Hill Street. All the cars were facing one way going up, and this one was facing the other way, going down. Inside, there was a man taking his shirt off and putting on a wig. Crouching down, I hid and watched him. The building was almost at the corner of Blue Hill Ave. and Wellington. He put on women's clothing and makeup, just as a woman would. I had never seen anything even remotely like this, except perhaps on Halloween. Then he put on a pair of dark glasses and stepped out of his car. He shook his body and pulled down his dress. He had become a woman. Why would he want to do that? I was late because of Michael, and now it was even later. I decided to tell Leonard and Esti about what I'd seen and use it as an excuse. I was not certain they would believe me and let me off the hook.

Leonard was friendly with a group of cops and detectives who sometimes would come over to the house and sit, sipping coffee and telling stories…among other things. He sold them merchandise he "acquired" from his jobs. I wondered if they knew the items were stolen, but at that time, I didn't understand what it was that Leonard did for a living besides plumbing. Later on, I figured out what he did by eavesdropping on conversations he had about stealing. His buddies' voices would echo up to the window on the top floor from the small pathway on the side of the house. Oh, well, anyway…I had to get back to the house fast to tell Leonard what I had seen so he could tell his police buddies. I raced up Wellington Hill Street to Duke Street. Breathlessly, I ran in the back door and, without missing a beat, told Leonard. I was so excited I rambled on and on, and he had to ask me to repeat myself. He immediately called his cop friends. It seems that there had been a series of break-ins where the robber had gained entry by posing as a woman. My observation led them to arrest the man. Of course, Leonard took credit because he was an adult and they would not, he said, have believed me, a kid. His smile was crooked, smug from being a winner. He told me he understood why I was late coming home tonight *only*. I thought that I should get some of the credit for what I'd done, but Leonard, whose ego needed rubbing in general, had to feel superior, if only for a few moments. I didn't care; I had no ego. I had gotten off without punishment, which would have been a sure thing had I not seen the caper in progress. Michael was surprised I hadn't been punished. I got to use the phone while Leonard, in all his glory, was in his meeting downstairs with the cops. I felt as though I had won my own victory that night.

Another weird incident happened in the alley pathway to the school one evening after I went to bed. There was a loud scream. It sounded like a male voice. Leonard went to investigate. I woke up, but Esti told me to go back to sleep. Mason slept through the entire episode. Leonard would take care of it, she said. Thinking of myself as a crime fighter since the Wellington Hill Street case, I snuck downstairs and listened for an echo in the yard. There was a boy on the ground, obviously hurt. Leonard and Esti were talking, and the cops came and stood towering over him. I heard one cop say that he was young. I stepped out and hid behind the bushes, then quickly went to the door so no one would know that I had been hiding. I wanted to tell Esti to call the doctor, but I thought twice and didn't because Leonard would be pissed. I called out to Leonard, and he yelled, "Go back into the house and don't come out! Mind your business!" I went to my room but couldn't see anything from the window. No ambulance ever came. Was he dead? Who was he? Maybe the police took him to a doctor, or he stood up and was arrested, or ran off. I never knew the outcome, and as far as I could tell, Leonard never mentioned him again to Esti. He refused to answer any of my questions and would tell me to "forget about it" whenever I asked.

I wasn't certain that Esti's house was the best place for me. I wasn't happy working all the time, and that's all I did there. But there wasn't any place else for me to go. I had a warm bed, good food, discipline, and kindness. My sense of hearing was excellent, and I listened to everything. Leonard was always bringing up the subject of "illegal goods." I didn't really care what he did, but if I ever did it myself, I would be sent to jail. I didn't have connections to cops the way he did. Oh, yeah, his wonderful son, Mason, never contributed anything to the household. I was the one who cleaned and helped by doing work with Leonard. I suspected that Esti, the stereotypical blonde, middle-class woman, didn't know half of what Leonard was really up to and that her ignorance was a matter of choice. Esti not only liked the money, but she also required the security of having a man around if she needed him. My background of hate and distrust sensitized me to other people's greed, particularly in this foster home. As good-natured and loving as Esti was, she dabbled in insurance fraud here and there, and whatever else she could do to make the bucks because dog grooming and decorating were not enough. I could tell she was an accomplished seamstress. I had some sewing experience myself but just enough to get by. I learned more from Esti, although I didn't like doing it. Collectively, all these skills, whether practical or illegal, helped me survive in later years. These small bits and pieces of the puzzle of my life were fitting together even then, setting me up to handle life's unpredictability.

Leonard would sometimes take me on jobs with him. Many times, he stopped by the house of a blonde lady. He had me wait for a couple of hours in his truck for him. He told me he was "fixing her pipes"...and after I caught on, I was sure that's exactly what he was doing. His excuse for being gone from the house was that he was with me on a job, and his excuse to me was that she was a good customer. It was obvious that he was messing around. It hurt Esti; I could tell she suspected. She and Leonard argued about it, but it did not become a source of contention for her. If it was, Esti hid it well. I never told her anything, and Leonard noticed my discretion and was kinder to me. No one outside the house knew, or at least it was never discussed in front of me. Jennifer didn't know about Leonard's flings until I told her many years later.

I still held onto my anger with Leonard because of the time he slapped me when Kara and I ran away. I never forgot. His cheating only added to my animosity toward him as a figure of authority. I still didn't know the difference between abuse and caring. At the time, I took Leonard's slap to mean he hated me. Maybe he didn't mean to hurt me, but I was scared of him and his slap. He never knew how much that slap affected me until my bad behavior at school became an issue in the house, and then, in a rage, I told him. My father and the social workers would listen to Leonard and Esti and then lecture me, saying I lived in such a nice home, what was wrong with me? Why didn't I appreciate what I had? Why was I causing problems? Of course, they didn't believe anything I said in my own defense. I was not appreciated for the good that I did by helping, only the bad. When I told my dad that Leonard was a thief, stealing from the homes where he worked, my father was appalled that I could make such an accusation. All I heard was, "Libbe, what's wrong with you? You are an ungrateful child!"

Everything was changing. Not only were we moving, but Pam had given birth to a baby at sixteen. I'd believed her when she told me that she was ill and couldn't have company for a few months, assuming all the while that maybe she didn't like me anymore, but that wasn't the case. When I first visited before we moved, she announced there was a new addition to her family—her mom had a baby. I thought the baby belonged to her mother. When she finally gave in and told me later that the baby was hers, I felt like I had lost my friend. I assumed she would get married and live somewhere else. I was so wrong. We would hook up again, and my new life would begin.

****

Sitting here, looking at these hellish white walls, I realize that my need to be liked and loved continued propelling me down a path that led me to where I am today. No one in my life was at fault for the paths I chose to take except myself. I made some good choices, but I made the bad choices as well. The doors opened in front of me, and I took my chances. I stretch back. Oh, man…when will they let me out? Did my attorney call back? My son, does he know yet? What will he think? The stress is so intense. It seems like I've been here forever. Paranoia is what I feel at this moment. Closing my eyes, I continue remembering my life, putting the other pieces of the puzzle together to form a larger picture. I am trying to control my breathing and coughing. My chest is a bit tight. Even though my heart is pounding to a military beat, I will take some deep, calming breaths. I fear for my future. What is my son going to say when I get out of here? I never wanted to let him down by having my name or face in the public eye. What if my arrest is reported in the Brookline newspaper? What if my son's friends, their parents, and his teachers hear? Oh my god! If his friends are true friends, they won't care. Or will they?

CHAPTER SIXTEEN

City to Suburb

The move to Canton took place. In what seemed like a very short time, we had gone from a racially diverse city neighborhood to an all-white suburban neighborhood similar to Sharon. I believed that going back to the suburbs where I had come from originally would be easy, but I found out that I had gotten into living in the city; I loved the different kinds of people and the shops and restaurants. I loved the hot dogs and French fries at Simco's. I loved Blue Hill Ave.—hanging out on the corners, at the delis, drugstores, and Duchess Hamburgers, where everyone went. I loved drinking vanilla Cokes from the soda fountain at the Fessenden Street drugstore and hanging out at the Chez Vous Ice Skating Rink. It was the "in" place to meet, but because I didn't have skates, I could only observe. Funny, I knew how to skate, but felt self-conscious and shy. My big brown eyes and my rare, but genuine, smile were my best features, and I noticed the boys watching me.

I didn't like starting all over again. Michael was angry with me and tried to make me feel as though the move was my fault. He belittled me constantly, and it worked—I felt badly about myself, each day I felt worse than the one before. I accepted the guilt he dealt out. Everything that went wrong was my fault. I was desperate to do anything that would make him care for me so that I wouldn't lose him. Making this cruel boy happy was my only wish.

Leonard was more successful with his plumbing business in this neighborhood because of his regulars and the number of new homes. He kept his connections in Mattapan and Dorchester. The first month after we moved, he scored big with authentic art deco and diamond jewelry from some estate in Newton. Leonard also had a new side business. I watched him from my bedroom window, which faced out to the street where the cookie-cutter houses of the neighborhood were in the process of being built. Leonard took the bay windows and building materials from the development—he even gave Meryl a bay window for her home. At the same time, he was hyperactive and high-strung, and getting worse with age. He was stressed all the time. He screamed at Esti, often calling her stupid in the same way that Anita had called me stupid all those years. Leonard tried desperately to teach Mason his trade, but Mason was weak and too young and lazy to want to learn. He preferred sitting around, eating and watching TV, to anything else. I avoided Leonard's anger by sharing his work ethic, lifting heavy pipes like a man. I worked without being asked, doing the traditional kind of helper work a guy would do. I did yard work constantly. I nearly dug the entire hole for the above-ground pool (I hated the look of pools like that), all the while thinking, "I'll show them I can do it." When everyone else was tired at the end of the day, I was the one who could wheel the wheelbarrow and keep going. I was useful to have around. Leonard had problems with his knees, and at night when we had finished working, I would rub them for him. "Higher, lower, that's right," he would say, "ah, perfect." His knees gave him considerable pain, and I acted as his geisha, performing massage therapy. I did every household chore imaginable, just as I had done for Anita—minus the beatings and starvation. I still clean my home as if she were standing over me, pushing me to get things done.

Canton, in comparison to Mattapan, was boring. I viewed the kids as snobbish and had only a couple of so-called friends, whose names I couldn't recall on a bet. The friends in Mattapan were more real. Canton was by far better than Sharon. Even the school was bigger and better. I had no idea where to find them, but because of the proximity to Sharon, I planned to be on the lookout for Robby and

Lucy. I didn't fit in at the junior high school. Their taste in clothing was conservative but pricey. There were very few blacks, maybe one or two, unlike in the city, and the Jewish kids were what I called the geeky type. There weren't as many bullies. Some of the kids were afraid of me because of my tough appearance. To some degree, I thought that it was good they stayed away from me; their facial expressions and whispering about me hurt.

There was an Italian girl whose family was in the construction business. She acted friendly toward me and invited me to her house on Sharon Lake. Soon after my trip to the lake, others at the school were whispering behind my back that I was adopted and a foster kid. I regretted meeting her. Why did I ever confide in her? The girl's family had also asked me questions. They shared my answers with their daughter, and she then told everyone my information at school. Once again, I found out that I couldn't trust people. I was angry with myself for trusting someone, and although she tried talking to me, I kept my distance. Would they have treated me differently if I had parents and money like they did?

It was difficult adjusting to my new environment. Math and homework were at the top of the list of things I disliked. I did, however, look forward to music class and couldn't wait to play my violin. I had taken it up toward the end of my time in Mattapan but put it aside because there was no way for me to practice at home. After Esti made a special request, my father agreed to buy one for me. I practiced and practiced, and finally performed on the radio for the Tremont Hotel Talent Show—my debut, and last performance. I also loved playing the piano. I couldn't read music, but I discovered I could play anything by ear. The music teacher reminded me of the art teacher at the Home for Little Wanderers. That was my first placement after I left Stoneham. I liked both music and art. My art teacher, Mr. Wilk, told me many times that my ability to draw was a talent that I should never waste. Despite his encouragement, I didn't listen. The music teacher also said that I had a talent for the arts.

The Home for Little Wanderers was a temporary stop for me; Jewish Family Services had to put me there while they found a home to place me in. Except for art class, that was a memorable and unhappy part of my life. I acted out and wanted to go away from there. I wanted attention so bad… The more I acted out the less attention I got, and the result was that I got lots of punishment again. And the worst nightmare was the isolation room I was put in to "calm down." No way! It made me crazy being locked up in a room, especially one that was like a small, narrow hallway. It had two doors. The first door was the entrance, a second door was at the end of the room on the right-hand side, and that opened to a bathroom, but it was locked when they put me in there to calm myself. They locked the doors, leaving me in there. I screamed, cried, and kicked the door like crazy! After what seemed like hours, I finally kicked the bathroom door enough that it opened! My escape route was a window in that bathroom, and I could open it! *Yes! Out! I will get away now*, I thought. Out of the room that scared me so much. I opened the big, heavy wooden window and out I went onto a cement ledge. I hated heights, but I did not care if I fell because then I would not have to go back in the room or stay at the Home anymore. I walked along the edge that faced the Jamaica Way and someone driving by saw me and called the police, and they went into the Home to see what was going on. Needless to say, I could not jump off or find a way to climb down. The height scared me so that when they came to get me I crawled back into that window to go inside—so happy to be off that high ledge! But I did not want to be put in that room again! Ever! Every day, my only happiness was my art class. Then, finally, a home opened up so I could leave. No more isolation room. Never again…or so I thought.

****

I didn't have the motivation to pursue anything, although I've used my creativity and artistic sense for enjoyment and projects throughout the years. I loved to draw and paint, then and now, when I have the time. And I love to write stories, now more than ever. After this ordeal with the court hearing and I leave this isolation room, maybe I'll take the time to give expression to my artistic side, something I have been waiting to do my entire life.

****

Michael drove his Corvette to Canton to meet me at school. All the girls wanted me to introduce them to him because of his expensive car and good looks. I felt special because he had come to see me. I believed he missed me. Michael would always call me from home, several times at first, and each time he would put me through a test. He challenged me to walk from Canton to Milton, approximately twenty-five miles, to prove that I loved him. I took him up on the challenge. When I finally arrived at his house—exhausted—he requested that I give him a blowjob! It seemed like that was all I did with him. I hoped that I wouldn't have to give blowjobs every day of my life (little did I know…). I questioned whether that was all I was good for. As he drove me home, he laughed at my stupidity for walking and said that I was being punished for moving away, and if I had spoken up and said that I wouldn't do it, he would have picked me up. Was I stupid or just naive? I carved an "M" in my arm to prove to him that I loved him. He asked me to do it with a sharp pin, and so, of course, I did it. I did everything except for one thing—have sex. I was too fearful.

Michael always tested my love for him, but it was never enough. Allowing me to wear one of his leather jackets was a testament to his feeling for me, even though it was one of his old ones. His blonde girlfriend never knew how much he was seeing me, but he would tell me whenever he went to see her. He said he was not going steady and could see whomever he wanted. His friends told me differently, that he was going steady. I had no concept of what the word jealous meant then. There wasn't a reason to feel jealous if no one and nothing really belonged to me. Despite the distance between towns, his frequent visits and our relationship continued. He was traveling to Canton more often, every chance he could get. Michael forbid me to talk to Huckie anymore because Huckie wanted me to be his girlfriend, and he was the type to end up with me, he said. I was tempted to go with him but didn't. One thing is certain: my life would have been different. I recall all these opportunities as they pass by in my memory, like they passed me by in my lifetime. Will I ever get married? That question is always in the back of my mind. Will anyone love me enough to take care of me?

Michael was so spoiled. He had Corvettes, a motorcycle, and money—virtually everything he wanted, including both his blonde Barbie girlfriend and me. What he didn't have was a sense that his parents loved him. He created havoc with his friend Rob, walked all over his mother, and didn't speak much about his father or his brother. We made a great pair, both afraid of love. I became aware of this much later, when it was too late to matter. The meaning of love eluded me most of my life. I couldn't define it then and was confused for many years to come. I was certain that Michael was my first love, or what was my definition then. I had never been close to anybody else in that way yet. He stopped hitting me with his drumsticks, and I knew something was different. When he would slap me unexpectedly and for no apparent reason, he would get on his knees to beg for my forgiveness. I didn't understand his new behavior, but I could feel him changing. Over time, he became less aggressive toward me. And he kissed me differently, warmly and romantically (like Huckie tried to) as if he had developed a heart. I, on the other hand, didn't change. Rather than pulling my hair when he kissed me, he kissed me passionately. I was totally unfamiliar with that sensation. He had never asked, but always demanded that I give him a blowjob. This time was different, he actually asked. I had always been accepting of his abuse, coming back to him each time. But things were different now. Later, he explained to me that, in his mind, behaving badly was a way of avoiding being in a relationship. He said he hadn't been ready for an emotional kind of relationship before. If I accepted his mistreatment, and now his love, then I must love him after all. He really hated his mother and acted the way he did to get those feelings out. But it seemed like he didn't want to take them out on me anymore. Michael would always tell me how much he despised his mother, and how the very sight of her irritated him. I stayed with this boy when there were others interested in me who would have been far better, though less exciting, than him. I was familiar with abuse, and in a strange way, it was comforting to me. I was truly afraid of sensitivity. What I missed, huh…

Michael and I became closer. The sense of danger I experienced whenever I was with him was compelling. To be involved with Huckie seemed too simple. Although he would have loved me, I believe I would have been bored with him and would have treated him badly. I didn't know how to be with someone who was so nice. Huckie and I both liked old cars and there was an attraction between us based on interests that I didn't have with Michael. Our chemistry felt right, and in retrospect, a relationship with him would have been much calmer and certainly healthier. He always wanted to hold my hand. My fear of experiencing those warm feelings kept us apart. It was uncomfortable and I held back. Michael called constantly, and started showing up without arranging it beforehand. He was extremely jealous now, and it showed. Huckie was kicked to the curb but still tried to pursue me. He was immature, sexually inexperienced, and clumsy like me. The hugs and stolen kisses we shared became part of my past.

The feeling of being isolated in suburbia lingered, but I began to appreciate the house in Canton more because it was new and I didn't have to climb a long flight of narrow stairs to get to my room. Although the house in Mattapan had more character, this house looked brighter inside, and there was a yard with grass that reminded me of my earliest years.

It was during my time in Mattapan that I took up smoking. I wanted to look cool and fit in with the other kids on the avenue. At that time, cigarettes were very inexpensive, and I managed to buy Marlboros or Winstons. Michael had progressed to sniffing glue more often and taking higher doses of pills, habits I did not share with him, particularly after I had gotten sick when he forced me to sniff the model glue he put in a paper bag. The terrible taste of glue stayed in my mouth for several days, and I was afraid of people smelling my breath. That was the end of experimenting for me. No matter how many times he made me do other things, I let him know that drugs were not for me.

Of course, there were good times with Michael, like when we would go up Blue Hill Ave. on his bike, over the line to Milton, and park by Houghton's Pond, or when we went to Revere Beach and Nantasket, where I would eat hot dogs heaped with mustard and relish—just like the hot dogs my dad used to make for me. Michael always bought me food and paid for small, silly gifts. And he paid for me when we played pool on Blue Hill Ave.

****

But trusting the wrong kind of people got me into trouble when I was an adolescent, just like now, when, as an adult, I sit in my cell fuming about the girl who trapped me with her seemingly innocent booking phone calls that were being tapped by the FBI—a rat! At this late stage, I swear I will not trust anyone ever again. I have believed so many people who have lied to me that I have come to the point where I don't trust anyone—only myself and my son. It seems that, in one way or another, all the men I was with lied, promises were always broken.

CHAPTER SEVENTEEN

Secret

I missed Pam. Sharing her knowledge about sex and the adult world helped me understand relationships between girls and boys. I wished we had never left Mattapan. I was allowed to talk to Pam but only for ten minutes at a time. Esti actually timed each call, not wanting me to tie up her phone line. Pam told me that her mother had claimed the child as her own, putting the baby in her own name until Pam was older. It was supposed to be a secret, but Pam said that her friends' mothers did the same thing, and sometimes the babies were even put in the names of their grandmothers. It didn't matter to Pam because the baby was still in the family—I thought that was really cool. Pam mentioned her plans about going to a trade school after she went back to finish high school. We didn't get to see each other and spoke only on rare occasions. I didn't have any girlfriends except for one girl in the neighborhood, but she was not really close to me. School was bearable only because I loved music class and my teacher. I also had a sort of attraction to him and an art teacher. It was an older man—a father image—attraction.

Esti decided to take in more foster kids, which meant that I'd be losing my privacy once again. Leonard was against it and yelled at the top of his lungs at her. I was becoming close to Cici, the daughter of one of Jennifer's sisters. She was really nice to me when I spent the night once and invited me to her birthday party. Esti gave me permission to stay over again for the weekend of the party. I was so excited, but that would be the last time I'd ever stay there.

At first, Jennifer's sister's husband, Archie, seemed so friendly, asking questions and taking an interest in me. I thought he was sincere, like Silky. His workshop reminded me of my dad's. Then Archie became too pushy, almost weasel-like, creeping up on me and brushing against me. He took on the persona of a father at first, but the squint of his eyes indicated another more sinister intent. I wasn't aware of what it meant at the time. He asked me if boys had kissed me, and if they did, where. I couldn't imagine any place to kiss other than on the lips. He wanted to know where I let them touch me and if I'd had intercourse. Intercourse? He made me feel uncomfortable. I had never spoken about the subject to anyone besides Pam. I was *totally* embarrassed.

He was an older man, and I didn't want to answer his questions. He said he was trying to help me, just giving me fatherly advice, so I would know what to do when I was with a boy, that I was getting older and should know these things. I couldn't figure out what he was up to. Later that evening, after the birthday party, I found out. When I was sleeping right in the same room with his daughter, he slipped in, dropped to the floor, and slithered over until he was next to my bed. He woke me with one of his hands over my mouth, pressing the other on my lower stomach. He said, "If you wake anyone up, it'll all be your fault. I'll tell them you did something bad and you'll have to leave, not just here but Esti's house too." He put his finger to his lips. "Shhh…" he said. The last thing I wanted was to leave; I would rather be beaten. I didn't dare make a sound after he shushed me. He was as much of a tormenter as Anita was, only this abuser was a man, touching me in a creepy way. I felt strange—jittery and dirty. He moved his hand away from my dry mouth. I could taste the fear. I wanted to scream, but I couldn't. While stroking my cheek to calm me down—I shook with fright—he moved the hand on my stomach farther down into my pajama pants. "Relax, relax," he whispered. "It will feel good, I promise. I'll teach you." He wore a constant, eerie grin on his face. How could he smile? How disgusting! Would he do this to his daughter? His narrow, beady eyes slanted upward as if they were smiling too. He was enjoying every moment. I didn't care as long as I didn't get in trouble, but how could I stop him? In a frightened whisper, I begged him to stop. "Please, I don't like it, please stop," and I turned my face away. "Shhh, shhh," he softly said. His fingers were down there between my legs, stroking me, playing with me, and I felt a weird pleasure, sensitive to his touch, yet feeling hate and guilt at the same time. My stomach cramped. I was confused about how to feel. This was totally different from my first experiences with masturbation. Although I could feel the tight squeezing of my vagina, I felt dirty and invaded, and I wanted to scream and get up and leave. Any feelings of pleasure were compromised by Archie touching me in the darkened room where his own daughter was asleep only several feet away. What kind of father does that! When Archie put his finger inside me at the edge of my vagina, I felt wet. I tried to push his hand away, but he wouldn't stop. He was doing something with his other hand beside the bed. "Relax," he said quietly. I couldn't see, and he was saying "shhh, shhh," over and over again. "Shhh, you'll wake up Cici." Even when Michael made me give him a blowjob, he knew not to touch me there. This man was doing what the gardener did to me when he put his fingers in my panties in the garage, but went much farther. Archie said, "That's all, don't worry. It's okay. I won't put my finger in all the way—just the tip. Relax… Stay still! Don't move!" He was touching his penis, moving his hand quickly up and down. I don't know how long he did this, but the minutes seemed like hours. He didn't stop. I was trapped and wanted to cry, but I lay there, frozen, my arms and legs stiff. I thought about his wife and whether she was aware he was gone. Does she know he does this? When he was finished and finally ready to go, he told me, "Don't tell anyone. It's our secret. Remember, you'll be thrown out." I shook my head to show him I understood. He was sure I'd never tell. I was shaking and so nervous! No, I did not want this secret! But, of course, I wouldn't tell—how could I! Who could I tell? I would be the liar. He would be the good guy who no one would suspect. My father would never believe me. I had to pee but held it in until it hurt. I never wanted to be in this house again. I hated him. I never wanted to see him again. Although I didn't want to stay another night, Esti said I had to because she and Leonard were going out. There was a wall of silence between me and everyone else. I felt isolated, alone with my fear. What would happen in the dark tonight? I considered asking to sleep in Cici's bed with her, but that would have been awkward.

The next night, I played as long as I could with Cici. We were told to go to bed, and he came into the room a couple of times to check on us. While he stalked like a predator waiting for an opportunity to attack, I pretended to be asleep. He came into the room again later. This time he kissed my mouth and said that he wanted to put his mouth down there and lick me. I held the blankets tight under my chin, but he pulled them loose. He pushed my legs apart, and after putting the covers over his head, he put his mouth down there between my spread legs and licked me like a dog lapping water. I was sickened by what he was doing, and afraid. This did not feel good! I pulled his head up to try to get him to stop, and attempted to push his arm, but it was too solid to move. I didn't want him down there, but I didn't yell out. I pulled and pulled, trying to lift his neck up, and he pushed down even harder on me with his heavy head. Why did he do that, and with Cici right there? I tried to push him off again and again, but he held my hands down. He was like a maniac. Then he stood up suddenly and left. He must have heard his wife going to the bathroom, or maybe he just got scared. I didn't care as long as he was gone. I wanted him dead at that moment, even more than I wished Anita dead. I wiped and dried between my legs with my PJ's and wrapped myself in the covers as tightly as I could, tucking them in all around my body.

The next day, I called Esti again to pick me up. "Please," I begged, "I want to go home!" Even though I insisted, she said she couldn't drive me until later. "Archie will drive you," she said. It was nightmarish! I didn't want to be anywhere near him. He knew I'd be quiet because I was the foster kid. I leaned against the passenger window and door on the ride home, but nothing was going to deter him. He tried to touch me with his hand. "Come on, you know me now…" Then he pulled the car over to the side of the road—and groped me! I was being assaulted, but I was too small to resist him physically. Although he wasn't a large man, he was stronger than me, and desperate for this encounter. He molested me by putting his finger up my vagina just an inch, playing at the edge. I was screeching, and even though there was no one around to hear it, he covered my mouth to muffle the sound. He wanted me to put my hands on his penis. "No!" I pleaded. "No! I won't touch it!"

"Oh, come on," he said again, "I won't hurt you." Immediately, I connected Archie with the man in Malden who had tried doing the same thing so long ago. But Archie was like a dog in heat, humping me like crazy, making himself cum. I hated him to the core. He said, as he had over and over, he was teaching me so when I was with boys I would know how to have sex. If that was having sex then I didn't want any part of it! I didn't want to have sex at all. He said that if I told anyone he would deny it, saying I came on to him. He said he would tell them I was a promiscuous girl, and a bad influence on Mason and Cici. Oh god, why me? I was always being threatened in one way or another and was always the one to pay a price.

I washed up the moment I entered Esti's house. There wasn't enough water or soap to wash him away; he was etched on my body like a notched gun. I told my foster mom I didn't want to go to Cici's house again, ever. She didn't understand why and asked me the reason. I told her that I didn't like sleeping in a bed that wasn't mine and that the house frightened me. Esti said I should never be afraid anywhere she sends me…little did she know. She never questioned me beyond that. Whenever Archie's family visited, or when we visited them, it was horrendous. I was perpetually scared. I didn't want to see his face, but he would seek me out and talk to me to be reassured of my silence. His leer haunts me to this day. Had I known then what I know now, I would have had him put in jail. My encounters with Archie were among my first experiences with men. Not wanting to jeopardize myself or make a scene because of Esti and Jennifer, I kept them a secret. During that year, I confided in Silky—and only him at the time—about what Archie had done. He told me to keep it to myself, not to upset anyone. I didn't really feel the full weight of it until years afterward when I saw Silky and Jennifer's daughter, in her underwear, sitting on Archie's lap. I totally lost control and pulled Jennifer aside, insisting that she take her daughter away from him and put some clothes on her. When I explained why, she was taken aback, but then admitted that she wasn't altogether surprised. She did keep her daughter clothed from then on whenever Archie was around.

It is ironic that Archie's wife was one of the first people who judged me later in life and referred to me as a tramp. She didn't want her daughter near me. She should have known what a dog her husband was, and what a path men like him set for young girls like me. After I told Jennifer about him, I swore to her that I would never reveal what had happened to anyone in her family. What he did shamed me for many years, and left me with another hole in my heart for trusting men, or anyone, who abused me instead of protecting me. I couldn't keep my promise to Jennifer, and I am relieved that the truth has finally come out. I shake my head in disbelief that only now have I come to realize why I could never relax with men one hundred percent. It has been easier to be an actress performing while having sex, feeling someone else's emotions rather than my own. I have learned how to express affection, but I still struggle with the damage done by all the Archies who have touched my life. It boggles my mind to know that he has never had to pay a price for what he did, as so many others with "secrets" have not had to.

CHAPTER EIGHTEEN

To the Brink of Murder

It took me a long time to get past Archie touching me. I didn't want Michael to come close to me, and I had to cover up how I really felt. I wanted to tell everyone what he had done to me, but I stuffed it down. I kept wondering if his daughter had ever experienced anything similar, but then I realized—of course not; I was a foster kid, I was easy prey. To this day, I detest it when men leer at me with ill intentions. The fear of being caught alone with one of these men still plagues me, and the thought of being cornered sickens me. Throughout the course of my sex career there have been men like Archie. I have allowed them to act out their perverted fantasies, with me playing the part of a child to keep them from attacking young children. Today, I can recognize a man who sexually desires children just by looking at him. I can see through pedophiles—to their very souls—an ability I wish I didn't have.

I wanted to be left alone, but Esti had a new little boy coming to stay. He was there for only a short time because he lit matches in the backyard, almost setting the porch on fire. The social workers never disclosed that he was a pyromaniac to any degree like that. Leonard called to have him removed. Right after he left, a girl came to share the room with me. When she arrived, I disliked her immediately. I could feel her bad energy. She acted as if she were Miss America, wiggling in her tight clothes, with her blonde hair sprayed stiff. Her face was uglier than anyone's I'd seen in a horror movie. She had a huge toucan beak of a nose, beady eyes that were set too close together, thin lips, and a weird voice. She looked crazed. Her odor was rancid; she didn't use deodorant, just inexpensive perfume. Simply put, Louise got under my skin. I had never reacted to anyone this way. Even though I detested basements, I asked to sleep down there. Fortunately, there wasn't a boiler with flaps I would have to watch. For me to ask to sleep downstairs was an indication of how desperately I wanted to get away from this person, but Esti's answer was an unequivocal no. After unpacking, Louise pointed to my bed instead of the vacant one near the window and said, "That's my bed by the dressing table." Esti, who was in the room, turned to her and said, "Yes, you can have that bed if you want."

"But that's where I sleep!" I protested.

Esti tried to convince me, saying, "Libbe, be nice; you can take the other bed, and when she leaves, you can have it back. You've been here longer, and Louise is a guest, and she has been through a lot." Great, what could I do? I knew that when Louise left I would switch the mattresses. I wouldn't sleep on the same mattress as she had.

Dealing with Louise was a true test of my patience. My stuff was taken from the top of the dressing table, stored in a cardboard box that was shoved under the bed, and replaced with her makeup, lipsticks, and hairsprays. Her bifocal eyeglasses were made from unusually thick glass, and when she took them off she could barely see. When she tried to put on her base makeup, an unsightly line appeared under her chin and across her cheek because she didn't blend it in…gross. *I never want to wear makeup*, I thought. And I never did until I was in my fifties! She also spoke out loud to herself, and from what she said, she considered herself beautiful. Also, she was awkward and uncoordinated, dropping things all the time. This was because her fingers were skinny and weak, and they shook, so she could not grip things. Her voice was so high pitched, and it was shaky and nasal. I will never forget the first night Leonard met her. He barked, "What the fuck is this?" Esti protected Louise by telling her that her husband was just kidding, but Leonard would talk under his breath, making comments about Louise. He was speaking the truth. Mason made fun of her, and Esti would yell at him. She was so homely and weird that she alienated people. It was apparent that both Mason and Leonard were on my side when it came to all matters pertaining to Louise. Leonard threw up his hands and ranted at his wife, "Esti, didn't I say I didn't want any more of those kids? It wasn't enough with that boy who was just here, lighting matches in the backyard and nearly burning us up, catching the porch on fire? The agency didn't tell you about his pyromania? And now you bring in another freak? What crazy things does *she* do?" Esti paid no attention to Leonard. Well, if she was crazy, then I was the one stuck with her. She had to share my room; they couldn't inconvenience their precious Mason or put her in the basement. At the very least, for me, the fire boy was better than her. Esti didn't listen to her husband after the boy left—she just wanted the money and had Louise lined up immediately. I heard her on the phone with the social worker: "No more boys, and no one too young."

Eating at the same table with Louise was a challenge. She dressed in tight, straight skirts and high heels every night and day. She would cross her legs, shaking one for attention. She said that her legs were beautiful, and she knew it because other people had told her so. She looked much older than her actual age. Her nose was in the way of her mouth, and she would eat by picking apart her food and feeding herself with her fingers, otherwise the food dropped out. Her hands shook a little at the moment the food entered her mouth, and we would snicker. She couldn't hold a spoon or fork to her lips. It was obvious she was a weakling. Her nose was beaky, and her chin was long and weird. Leonard often left the table, asking Esti to bring his food into the bedroom so he could watch TV. However, we knew he left mostly because he couldn't stand looking at Louise. Despite her bird-like mannerisms, I stayed—even Louise couldn't stop me from eating. I turned my head the other way. Her nasal, whiny voice was more irritating than anything. She was planning to get her nose done in a few months, staying with us only for the amount of time it took her to heal and turn eighteen. That seemed a lifetime away. Every day there was another issue with her. Esti treated Louise like a princess, and the reason eluded me. Perhaps she was paid more money for taking Louise in for a shorter period of time, and because she was almost too old to be a foster child. One night, I overheard Esti and Leonard say that the state was paying for Louise's surgery because there was an obstruction in her nose that prevented her from breathing normally, and its extreme length hindered her from eating properly. That probably was the reason she sounded like she had a cold, snorted all the time, and found it difficult to eat with silverware. They also mentioned something about a mental problem. I had no doubt of that, but she knew what she was doing. The moment we were alone, she would act up, raising her voice and behaving like she was the bitch boss, but in front of Esti, she was so sweet. Louise's two faces reminded me of Anita's two selves, although, of course, her temperament wasn't as brutal as that of Anita. I had no fear of her.

Life with Louise was getting progressively worse. She was particularly annoying when she came downstairs to the den at night and changed the channel when Mason and I were watching TV. He would scream at her, but she didn't care. She did this one too many times and my patience ran thin. This had never happened before; I always allowed everyone to do as they wished. One afternoon, I was watching a program by myself. Even though I was very skinny, my arms were muscular and strong. During gym class at school I lifted weights and surpassed all the other girls and some of the boys. Whether it was from hard physical labor or something else, my muscle tone was great. I felt important because of my arms and worked them to be sure the muscles remained toned and would grow stronger.

Louise was not prepared for what I did when she switched the channel that final time. First, I told her to stop—and the bitch didn't. She was amused by me and laughed, saying that she would tell Esti that I changed the channel while she was watching TV, and I would be in big trouble. The hell she would! I yelled at her a few times and told her to stop switching the fucking channels, but she still wouldn't. We were going back and forth, from the couch to the TV, and from the TV to the couch. I didn't watch TV often, and I wasn't leaving the den because I was there first! She was on the couch and would not shut up. Without warning, I dove at her, crossing my leg over her body and choking the shit out of her. She shrieked, just like the parakeet at the Taffee's house. This girl had pushed me too far, and I really wanted to kill her! I let my temper go. I became Anita—enraged and out of control. Her scream was shrill and so loud! I choked her until she wasn't screaming anymore. The only sound she made was a gurgling noise. She tried to pull my hands from her neck, but her skinny hands were weak in comparison to mine. Esti and Leonard ran downstairs to see what the ruckus was about, worried once the screams that had started were extinguished. Leonard grabbed my arm to pull me off her, saying in a somewhat humorous tone, "Please don't kill her in the house!" Her voice tense, Esti said, "Please, Leonard, what's the matter with you? How can you say that? What? You're egging her on?" Esti's favorite saying to him was "What's the matter with you?"

Leonard said, "I told you no more kids, Esti, and now you see why. She's an aggravator." Mason was laughing. There wasn't any question that Louise would recuperate and be back to herself...she started talking shit almost immediately. But next time, she might think twice about pushing me too far.

Esti consoled Louise, but Leonard, Mason, and I were still laughing. Was I capable of choking her to death? Had I become Anita? Did I have that much rage in me? I supposed that anyone could be pushed to the edge. With Louise, I'd had enough. Maybe it was Anita who drew out this dark response from within me, and Louise just triggered my deepest anger. Louise was a temporary fixture in my life, a stranger passing through. I saw Anita's face in my mind and the faces of all the people who had abused me. Yes, I did want them dead then, but not by my own hand. Revenge had taken me over at that moment, and if Leonard and Esti hadn't intervened there was a slight chance I might have choked her to death. Fortunately, that didn't happen. The big ugly bird lived. I never felt badly then; and now, only a little because it was not her fault. She looked that way, but had she been nice she would not have seemed ugly at all.

There was a fight between Esti and Leonard about Leonard's siding with me and that I should be punished so I wouldn't do it again. Great, another punishment! Leonard won, and it was so special that he had stuck up for me that there wasn't anything I wouldn't have done for him. Her obnoxious behavior continued and escalated, and when she was intolerable, I would walk out of the room along with Mason, leaving Louise talking to herself. My temper was still not under control, but both Esti and the social workers had advised me to ignore her and just walk away. And as much as I didn't want to, I did manage to walk away, which seemed to infuriate Louise even more. Was this a new way to get back at someone? Lesson learned.

It was maybe a month or two later when Louise came home from surgery. She looked repulsive. Her glasses rested on the blood-stained layering of netting and bandages that covered her nose. She was swollen, and her nostrils were exposed so that she would be able to breathe. Esti was overly sympathetic. She pampered Louise, brought drinks to her bed, and Louise, of course, didn't have to do anything. I already did all the chores even before the operation, and Esti felt badly for her and told me that I should cater to Louise because I was the stronger one and Louise had been through so much in her life. Oh my god! Really? She told me that Louise's stepfather used to put out cigarettes on her skin, but I didn't see any scars, not a mark. Plus, I had caught her telling Esti lies many, many times. No one knew, nor would they have believed, what Anita did to me. I kept my past to myself. I didn't want sympathy based on Anita's cruelty; I just wanted fairness.

Had Esti known my history would she have babied me? I never needed nor wanted to be babied. Consciously, I didn't want pity, but simply wanted to be esteemed and loved. At least Leonard would say, "I want you to help me, not anybody else!" He valued me for what I was able to accomplish, and I would push myself even harder. I was self-reliant but needed to be recognized for the human being I was.

As a foster child, you eventually come to understand that the nice families taking you in are being paid to take care of you. So you never feel entirely wanted or welcome in their homes, where the belongings of the family are clearly theirs, not yours. I wished I had something I could call my own, even my own space, a space no one could invade or take away from me. I kept to myself as much as I could because I never knew whether I would be living in the same home the next day. Wherever I was, I always lived in just one room—*the room!* In the back of my mind, I was always aware that my situation was insecure, and I learned to live in the moment as much as I could. But I was worried about my future and wished I had a crystal ball to take the edge off my fears. Where would I go when I turned eighteen?

****

And now, waiting to be let out of my cell—a room of doom—I fear doing time because that would jeopardize my house and my son. Not paying the bills might render me homeless, and that thought is upsetting to me, especially at my age.

****

For the first few days, Louise stayed in the bedroom, just sipping soups or juice. One night, Miss Beauty Queen was resting in the bedroom with ice packs. Esti had dinner cooking. Mason and I were hungry all the time. I felt happy after I ate, even if it was something as small as a cracker. Food was my best friend and still is. Louise and other foster kids who stayed at the house took food without asking, but I was uncomfortable and unsure, and always asked first.

****

I empathize with people who don't have enough to eat. I certainly could go for a big piece of chocolate cake right now...some mashed potatoes with butter...or homemade spaghetti and meatballs. Sure, right—I don't think an FBI agent is about to bring me some made-to-order food, so I'll dream on.

****

Esti was ready for us to sit down to supper. She didn't have to ask me twice, but Leonard and Mason took their time. Louise, who was putting on a performance, moved with difficulty down the narrow corridor to the kitchen. Oh no, she was joining us! She was acting like an invalid. Anita would say, "I'll make you into an invalid, wait and see…" How I would have loved to say that to Louise. She also dramatized how much pain she was in and how weak she was for Esti, who ate it up. "Sit down you poor thing, are you all right?" Esti asked. Louise touched her nose with two fingers, shaking her head yes. There was fresh red blood and dried brown blood on the mesh bandage. It was nauseating. Mason came running in, propped his knee on the bench that was at the table, leaned back, and said, "I'm not sitting across from that!" He pointed straight at Louise with his index finger. She looked back at him with her beady eyes, which were almost crossed because they were so close together on her face. Then Leonard came in, and to make matters worse, said, "No! Shit no! Esti, are you crazy? Do you think for one minute I'm sitting across from her? I have to eat my dinner!" His voice was loud. "This is my dinner table!" he said. But then he relented, saying, "I'll eat in the other room." Louise was trembling as she looked at Leonard; it was not out of fear, but her usual shaking. Esti tried to calm him down without success.

"I'm not eating here either," Mason added. "I'm going with Dad." Esti couldn't fight with Leonard or Mason, so she made up their plates and took them to the den, Leonard grumbling all the way down the hallway. I hadn't said a word yet. It was me, Esti, and Louise, and I didn't want to sit across or next to her either, but I was stuck helping Esti with that creature. She snorted when she breathed, like a pug dog. With every bite, Louise's head and hand shook and her eyes peered up from her bifocals…all really weird. This is how I will always remember her.

When the bandages were removed, her nose was a little better, though swollen and crusty, and her eyes still had that bird look—they couldn't fix that. Her face was improved slightly; it was more her attitude that made her so unattractive. The surgery, which hadn't helped her appearance as much as they thought it would, did improve her ability to breathe through her nose, and she was able to put food in her mouth more normally with a fork, although she was shaking like a person with Parkinson's. Leonard told Esti, "No more foster kids here, ever again. This is the last. I mean it! If there's a next time, I'll be the one to leave!" I felt uneasy because of his dictating who could or couldn't stay; if I did something else wrong, I'd be gone too. Esti listened to him this time, knowing he meant what he said. Not having to share a room with her, or with anybody, made me ecstatic. She was nasty to me while she was packing on the night before she was scheduled to go. When she was leaving, she said goodbye to Esti but not to Leonard, Mason, or me. Leonard walked away. No one really cared. She made a slick remark, and I assumed it was meant for me, so I put my hands around my throat as if I were choking myself to send her a message—my own private joke. I whispered softly so that she could read my lips, "If you stay, I'll fucking kill you!" I was sure she understood what I'd said. She raised her uppity hand in the air, twisted around, and wiggled her ass out the door, following her social worker. That was the last I saw of Louise. I had the final word by joking about strangling her, and that was enough for me. But I doubt it had any effect on her. I occasionally wondered what happened to her, and if having the surgery helped, but either way, she had the biggest ego before and after.

CHAPTER NINETEEN

Freddy

My eyelids are heavy. I am tired after the shock of the police and FBI pounding on my front door this morning. I shut my eyes and yawn—a moment to clear my mind before I slowly begin to freak out. I am too organized for all this now. I'm not comfortable in this space. I never want to be in this position again. I recall more memories, trying to deepen my understanding of the long and complicated journey from the earliest years of my existence until now. Gee, it seems so surreal!

****

My dad hardly ever came to visit me at the homes where I stayed. I'd been at Esti's longer than any other foster home only because she was insistent that I stay there. I'd changed my ways in certain respects, but, as I learned, in others I remained the same. I was continuing to fail at school, always tardy in the morning and unfocused in class. I just didn't give a shit! Neither Leonard nor Esti had the know-how to help me with my work, and their lack of attention didn't give me any extra incentive to do well. And as far as Freddy was concerned, the saying "Out of sight, out of mind" applied to the situation. I was only thankful Anita never came with him to visit. This would be his last visit because he wasn't going to be living in Massachusetts anymore. It came as a shock to me that he was planning to move to Florida.

He had sold the Stoneham house, the home my mother Rose had loved…the home she said would be mine someday. I blamed Anita for taking my dad away and changing everything that had ever mattered to me. I was too young to understand that he wanted to live his life with his wife, not me.

My dad was extremely frugal. He was not a spender and never bought anything for himself. He just saved and saved. While I was living in foster homes, Freddy only bought me what was absolutely necessary, and as an adult, the message I took away from his stinginess was to enjoy the things money can buy. As I got older, I learned that he was more generous where Anita was concerned, and this only added to my animosity toward her.

Both Aunt Rose and my dad told me there was a will, and that when he died there was a lawyer who had all the information about my adoption and what I was to inherit, including my mother Rose's wedding rings and her personal items. Aunt Rose told me about money Mom had put aside for me at the Shawmut Bank. And she said the oil painting portrait of me was mine, as well as the house and its contents. Dad said that my mother Rose's brother had control over the money from her estate. It was being held until I was twenty-one years old, when they would contact me. I didn't understand all of what he told me. And when it dawned to go check it out, there was no money!

My dad gave my mother Rose's jewelry to that witch, Anita—the diamond rings that my mother promised me, and all her watches, pearls, and bracelets! It galled me that such a wicked woman with bad karma wore my mother's precious diamond rings. I hated Anita for wearing them! Sometimes when Anita used to hit me, I would notice them on her, and I wished that the rings would break and fly off her hand. When I was in my mid-twenties, I drove to Connecticut where Mom's brother lived. I called him from a pay phone, and he said, ever so politely, that he had used up all Mommy Rose's money over the years. He told me it went for legal fees, and only a few dollars kept the account open, an amount so small it wasn't worth speaking about. How dare he! I realized later that I should have hired an attorney to show me the account books, but I didn't know then what people were capable of doing for the love of money. The painting of me, a real keepsake, was being held somewhere by Dad's nephew. At the time, I believed that my mother's family would never interfere with her last wishes or harm me in any way, but they did, just as my dad's family did…every one of them. My painting—gone! I was *so* upset!

One of the last days Freddy visited, he took me to the cheapest store possible: Woolworth's. I was embarrassed with what he was showing me. If he didn't buy anything for me it would have been better than what he did buy. When I came back to my foster home, I told Esti and Leonard that I would never wear the boy's undershirts and the old-lady panties and shoes Freddy bought me. He showed little appreciation for the fact that I had grown into a young woman who didn't wear clothing like someone's grandmother. To me it meant that, still, he didn't see me. That night, I cried until there were no tears left because Daddy was leaving Boston. I had no one… Esti returned the clothes, and I never got anything to replace them. All I had to wear were hand-me-downs from her family. It wasn't surprising that I was not well-dressed and that the other kids at school thought I was a joke; this had always been the case, wherever I wound up.

It was always bittersweet whenever Dad visited. I would greet him with a big smile, hoping he would hug me, but no—he would say, "Hello, Libbe," without any emotion. He would address everyone else like royalty. It was almost as if he was afraid of acknowledging that I needed a dad or had one. It was always the same, whether the reports about me were good or bad, and I thought that if he didn't care about me, then what the hell, I could act badly and get more attention that way. Still, when my father left for home after his visits, I felt lost without him. Despite the fiasco with the clothes and all the other times, I still loved him.

I would say "Now I lay me down to sleep," the prayer that Mom and Aunt Rose had taught me so many years ago. I prayed for Mommy Rose to love me, to relieve the pain my dad's lack of feeling caused me. I prayed every day. Inside, I was always alone and scared, even though on the exterior I appeared to be tough. I would descend into depression and feel the deep, awful pain that accompanied it. I never smiled. I wanted to disappear. I wondered where my favorite cousin Bobby was or where Cousin Rebecca and her brother were. I had always assumed they liked me, but I felt isolated and didn't have any idea how to find them. I thought about Aunt Belle the last time I saw her in Connecticut and of her love of leopard and animal print coats—real fur! There was Aunt Eva's apartment on Beacon Street in Brookline, her satin clothes, and her beautiful jewelry. When I was very young, the pretty box on her vanity was filled with glittery costume jewelry that caught my eye, and I would dress up in her clothes and play make-believe. I wanted to have things like that one day—lots of those things. I recalled Uncle Abie and his rag business in Chelsea. I loved to jump into the piles of rags whenever Dad took me there. I remembered Aunt Fanny's cooking, especially the mohn cookies speckled with poppy seeds—so good! The drawers filled with special playthings in Aunt Rose's house were by far my favorite. I felt the sincerity of Uncle Uggie's affection whenever we were together, and I didn't need to be told he loved me, I knew it already. Where were these people? *Oh, yes…* I thought to myself. Anita drilled it into my head that I was adopted and these people were not my actual family, so why would they care? But who else do I have then? I didn't have any family to turn to. I resolved that I would make it by myself. I would just be with Esti and Leonard until I was old enough to leave. I didn't need clothes, and I didn't care whether Dad took me shopping—he probably wouldn't come back to visit me after he moved anyway. Why should he bother? As I learned later, my cousin Hilde in Florida was in touch with my dad and often asked about me. She was the only one, and I never knew that until I was an adult. She worked for a doctor Anita had gone to see before she and Freddy were married. The story she told was that Anita came to the office because she was experiencing problems having sex with Freddy. When I learned about this, it was mind-blowing! Anita didn't have sex except for that time she got taken by a gigolo. He took her money and left her after a short affair.

Dad came to Canton to say goodbye the day he was scheduled to leave for Florida. He wore a sport coat over his jersey, his usual attire, and Anita waited in the car, which was parked on the street in front of Esti's house. He stood back at a distance as he cordially said his goodbyes. After handing Esti some cash, he turned to me, and in a stern voice, told me to behave. There were no lighthearted words exchanged between us. I was hurt. He was leaving Boston, leaving me, and he wouldn't be coming back. If that weren't bad enough, he asked me to say goodbye to Anita! My first response was to say no. "Libbe," he said, "it's the least you can do." The least I could do was not go out there. I didn't want to budge, but I did it for my dad's sake. I went down the stairs to the walkway next to where the car was parked and stood at her door and open window. Before I could speak, she spit in my face. "Goodbye to rubbish," she said as nastily as ever. I wiped the spit away, turned, and walked back into the house. There was nothing more to say or do. For days afterward, I cried myself to sleep, feeling humiliated and abandoned by my father. The place of my happy childhood with Mommy was gone, and I felt its loss as much as I felt the loss of my dad leaving.

CHAPTER TWENTY

Stolen Car

The off-handed way my dad had so coldly left me behind put me in an angry state of mind. I didn't want to be near anyone. How could he leave me with no feelings of sorrow in his heart? Was love between a man and a woman so powerful that their children become secondary, or was that true only of adopted kids? I wondered for years about that. When I finally settled down after Dad had gone, I noticed that Leonard and Esti had become friendly with some of the neighbors, visiting each other's homes and talking. All the houses were occupied, and as a result, there was nothing left for Leonard to steal. One by one, the houses on the street had been sold. The Italian women who moved in across the street from us taught me how to cook. Tasting the food was the best part of learning, and the sauce I mastered was especially good.

I got nighttime babysitting jobs in the area. Michael constantly talked me into letting him come over with Rob. They would park down the street, where they wouldn't be seen, and then slip through the back door. Hanging out with them was torture—in addition to their usual delinquent behavior, they would scare me by threatening to have a party. Creating stress for me amused them. The boys would drink the family's liquor, watering it down so they couldn't tell that any of it was gone. Although I longed for Michael's company, relief was what I felt when they finally left. I knew it was wrong, but I took the chance of being caught because I wanted to be with Michael so much. Every time he asked me where I was babysitting, I told him. I started taking more jobs a few blocks outside the neighborhood. When Michael and Rob would visit me at the new homes where I babysat, I was never sure whether the stories they told me about urinating into bottles of juice were true or if they were just fucking with me. I would spill it out and pretend to them that I drank it. I wasn't supposed to have company, and I worried about what would happen to me if the people I babysat for found out. The anxiety of not knowing what might happen next kept me on the edge. Michael got off by making me feel like shit and then kissing me as if I were the most cherished girl in the world. He always stayed until the last moment before the parents returned, and eventually, I stopped telling him where I was because I would never get a job babysitting again. The torment of having him in the house so close to when they came home was too much for me to endure. I was becoming a nervous wreck. I told Pam everything that was happening, and she said that Michael was using me. "You need to toss him to the curb," she'd say. "But I love him," I would plead.

I became friendly with a girl who lived around the corner. I would go to her house fairly often and tell her stories about fixing cars with my dad, hanging out with the boys in Mattapan, and my friend Pam, leaving out the part about her having a baby. I told her I knew how to start cars without using the keys—a very bad mistake. She had that in mind when she came over one day to invite me to her house. Her parents were going out for the night and wouldn't be back until late, around twelve or one o'clock. She said we could watch TV. The car in the driveway belonged to one of her parents, and knowing that I could drive with or without keys, she asked me if I wanted to take it for a ride. Of course, I did. I loved driving. TV was out the door. Although she didn't tell me, she had the keys to the car in the house. I told her that I didn't want to get in trouble. She said they would never find out and if they did, she would tell them that it was her fault for talking me into it. Like a fool, I agreed. I figured we would take the car for an hour or two down Blue Hill Parkway. I hotwired the car just the way my father and Michael taught me, and it started without a problem. I loved to drive, and sometimes Michael let me drive his Corvette. The speed of the car was thrilling, and we would play chicken on the dark roads of the Blue Hills in Milton. My adrenalin flowed whenever I drove his car; I couldn't get enough of it.

This car didn't have nearly as much power as Michael's. I asked her if she wanted to go to my boyfriend's house. She said yes, and off we went down Route 38 to Blue Hills and to the parkway. I was concerned because the car started rattling and then, suddenly, it shut down completely. "Oh shit!" I shouted. "What's wrong?" Slowly, it rolled to the side of the road. When I asked if there was something wrong with the car, she answered, "That's why my mom stopped driving it." "Oh, great!" I yelled at her. "Why didn't you tell me before?" It was too late now. I opened the hood and checked for whatever the problem might be. The wires were tight, and it wasn't overheating. It wasn't out of gas. The pipes were not leaking. The ignition simply wouldn't turn over. "Maybe it's the starter," I told her. She had no idea what I was talking about. Rob's house was closest, maybe five blocks away. We walked, leaving the car there, locked. He was home, and—thankfully–he came with his tools and fixed the car by mickeymousing the starter. It started, but the other problem was that the hose had broken and there was a slow leak. It was simple enough to take care of, and he fixed it. Hours passed, and because he had messed with the engine for so long it was too late for me to go see Michael. We had to get back as quickly as possible.

When I pulled into the driveway of her house, her mom and dad were watching for us out the living room window. They had returned early. Did she know they might come home sooner? I expected my so-called friend to stick up for me. Instead, she blamed me entirely! She said that I took the car and wouldn't let her out. *Oh, man, what a snitch she is!* I thought. *How could she? I didn't steal it!* She insisted that I talked her into driving to Milton to see my boyfriend, and on and on she went. Although she told the truth about my friend fixing the car, she lied about everything else so she wouldn't get into trouble—and it worked. Her parents phoned Esti and Leonard. The police came and I ended up in the Canton Police

Station, arrested. Imagine, I was arrested…for a stolen car I didn't steal. Leonard and Esti thought that I needed to be taught a lesson, and I was charged with car theft. I took the blame, as usual. I had to go before the Youth Service Board. My history of running away from home, truancy, and now car theft followed me there, and the Board and Children's Services were prepared to teach me a lesson. But would Leonard and Esti have sent their blood children there? No, of course, they wouldn't have. I wondered why they didn't send me back to the agency. Was it the money? Would they still get their check if I were put away? I would have been better off running away. I didn't want to go back to their home after they had me arrested, not ever. No one ever believes me!

CHAPTER TWENTY-ONE

The Girls' Detention Center

I feel just as empty now as I did in that small jail cell in Canton. It doesn't matter whether the cell is big or small—they're all the same, with bars, doors, and locks to keep you in. I am locked in this stark room and cannot get out. I lost my freedom then and now. It is as claustrophobic in here as in the boiler room, and I am afraid I will panic and feel the same way I felt then. I don't even know what time it is. "Oh, god. Please, let me out!" I beg over and over again. I want to get out and to be free, free from my life of catering to girls and men for sex, always fulfilling everyone else's needs, building their egos, helping girls to think. They will be sorry they lost a good service, a discreet one. I know this, and I also know this style of business will continue. I would love to continue, but the stress getting caught again would be too overwhelming. No way, too old. They will all move on to the next service, whether respectful of their privacy or not—it's all about sex and money. Drifting back to when I had taken the car…

****

Now I did it, I thought to myself, *I am a real criminal.* I hadn't intended to do anything seriously wrong, but in their eyes I had stolen a car rather than simply taking it for a ride and returning it. My friend told me she couldn't find the keys when they were in the house the whole time—she knew where they were. A real friend would have defended me, not set me up. I could never do to her what she had done to me. I took the entire blame, whereas she absolved herself completely. One day I will learn not to be so gullible and to choose real friends. Nobody has ever told me the truth, and the promises people have made to me have always been broken. Did I learn my lesson? Yes, I cannot trust a soul.

Leonard and Esti were the ones who decided that I needed to be taught a lesson. When they called my father, he agreed; the social workers also agreed. The main person who thought I deserved a lesson, though, was my dad—my less than wonderful and understanding dad who, to my astonishment when I found out later, had skeletons in his own closet. His opinion was that I should be locked up and the keys thrown away. He had the witch Anita. If I died, he probably would experience relief and make up some excuse for not attending the funeral. Going forward, in 1980, when I lay in a hospital bed near death because of a horrific car accident, my father was called to come to my bedside and his response was chilling. "Tell me if she passes," he replied. Wow… The story was always the same: I didn't matter!

The adults spoke together, resulting in my going to the girls' detention center at 105 South Huntington Ave. Although by 1976, it would become the Boston Indian Council (later changed to the North American Indian Center of Boston), in the 1960's, it was a jail with deplorable conditions. But I didn't realize that until the doors locked behind me. Panic overcame me, and I screamed to be let out, begging over and over again to be released from the room, kicking at the door, beating at it with my fists. But it did no good; I couldn't get out. Only the staff and visitors could move freely. It looked like an old school with a large auditorium. This place had rooms with heavy institutional doors that were shut and locked. They each had bunk beds with wool army blankets that itched like the clothes Anita had me wear, and a tiny window that was darkened by a film of grime or blackout. It was impossible to see anything outside the window. I hated white sheets and curled up on the bed without covers, hugging the stiff pillow for warmth. I was claustrophobic in this place, and it triggered memories of my childhood and how Anita used to lock me in the boiler room. I still felt panicky. They told me I wouldn't be getting out for three months. I was all alone there.

The first day there, I was taken to the front desk. A social worker showed me around. We walked through what looked like a large gym or auditorium. I could feel the chill of the cement walls surrounding me. There was a hallway with wide stairs leading somewhere and heavy cell doors on the other side. The showering area was a row of cement stalls that had showerheads without curtains. We went down the stairs where there was a kitchen with huge Hobart machines. I had never seen such a large room full of gigantic kitchen equipment in my life. The stairways reminded me of the school in Mattapan, and I noticed there weren't any TV's.

I would be working during the day, the social worker told me. Working? Where? "Sometimes when volunteers come in on the weekend, you will be allowed to watch movies or play games," she said. The radio didn't announce the news, but played "Yellow Submarine" so frequently that the song got stuck in my brain. I despised hearing it then, and I could not tolerate listening to that song because of its association with that time in my life. Now, I just ignore it. I was afraid! Not only did I have a fear of being in a locked room, I was locked in a strange room at night, unable to see the night sky so I could not pray to the star that was my mother Rose. I asked them not to lock the door, but, of course, the rules had to be the same for everyone. Sometimes, when I stayed awake, I would stand in a corner watching out for any bugs—I was terrified of spiders. The cafeteria was like at a school, and at least I knew I would be fed. That first night, I cried and screamed. No one paid attention. They didn't come. Because I was allergic to the wool of the grayish-green army blanket, I couldn't use it. I was shivering. It was so cold in the room, and they told me that when I was cold enough I would use the blanket. Well, guess what? Instead, I froze. I was curled up on the white sheet, and I put the hard pillow over me as a cover. Frightened and alone, I watched a bug crawling on the floor and wall as a distraction. When the bug disappeared, I just stared at the blank wall, on alert for the bug to reappear. The white sheets brought me back to thoughts of Anita and of my mother in the hospital room the last time I saw her. I carried my past childhood traumas with me all the time (as well as the good memories), and looked back on them not to dwell on the bad in my life but to remember how to keep going to get through to the next point. I believe it kept me stronger as long as I used it to learn from.

I hated this place. I thought about my neighbor, my so-called friend, home with parents who loved her, having a pleasant family dinner in their warm home, and a good night's sleep in her beautiful room. She told me she had fun when we were driving in the car—all this discomfort for me for a good time for her. She probably isn't giving me a second thought. I swore to myself that I would have nothing more to do with her. And I was sure her parents told her to stay clear of me. I wanted to go to Esti's home just to be out of this place and free. I prayed until I fell asleep.

Adjusting to my new way of life was difficult. I didn't have any choice other than adapting to my surroundings; like a chameleon, I changed my colors. The morning was a bitch. We woke up at six a.m., then into the showers, which had only cold water. It was Anita all over again. No one could take hot showers because we might burn ourselves and have to go to the infirmary or hospital. I hated the feeling of stepping out of a cold shower into the cool air. There were strangers who watched me while I showered, and they would hand me a towel. I did not like being looked at.

We would eat breakfast and then do chores. Initially, I washed the halls and stairways—something I was used to doing—but it wasn't long before I found myself working in the kitchen at the Hobart machines, contentedly eating mashed potato leftovers. I was fond of mashed potatoes smeared with Land O'Lakes butter. The spaghetti with grated cheese and pie were delicious. Being in a kitchen was my type of work, and I could have just as easily become a chef as an adult rather than a madam. I missed that calling like I missed so many others, all due to a lack of confidence in myself.

There was a young girl who attached herself to me. Although I was uncomfortable at first, I felt badly for her and we became friendly. According to the older girls, she was there for suffocating her baby brother to death, yet I doubted she meant to do it. In fact, I doubted the whole story; I thought they were trying to scare me more than I was already. I asked one of the social workers about the girl murdering her brother, and she never gave me a direct answer. "Sorry, we do not discuss anything in here."

Jennifer visited me once while I was there to tell me her mother would be coming to pick me up when I got out. She said that if it were up to her, even though the others believed it was for my own good, she never would have had me arrested, just punished. I didn't want any more visitors because the sting of loneliness was worse when she left. At least it was reassuring to know someone came. I always felt abandoned and forgotten. One night, the elderly lady volunteers came to play games and we watched movies. That was so cool. I liked them and enjoyed myself, and they seemed to like me in return. My time would be up soon, the social worker said, giving me an update on my stay. And then I was assigned a roommate who was not friendly and, like me, didn't trust anyone, so it worked out fine between us—we never spoke. But I was a bit afraid of her because she offered to keep me warm if I was cold, to cuddle. No way. I just stayed cold.

Each day flowed into the next, and it felt like I had been there forever. Because of the time I spent sitting in my cell with all my fears, I learned to adjust to living behind the door with the barred window. I wasn't panicking any longer, and I kept thinking of when I would be free again to enjoy the sunshine and the stars. I wondered how I would feel about Leonard and Esti once they let me out. I didn't trust them and really didn't want to see them, but I had no other choice. When I asked my social worker to place me in another home, she told me there weren't any available and that it wasn't likely a family would accept an older child with my background.

Day by day and night after night, I waited. I felt like a caged animal. I vowed never to be put in jail again, never to be shut up in a room, whether in Stoneham, or in foster care homes, or jail. I vowed never to shut any doors in my own house when I became an adult and had my own apartment, and to this day, the doors in my home are left open.

****

But look at me now: I am in jail, the place I vowed I would never be in again. More than ever, I never want to be locked in any room! I am caged in this cell because I committed a crime knowingly, the offense of adults using their bodies as they choose. I do not believe that what I've done is criminal. The adults participating are of legal age and are consenting. Whatever they do is up to them, not me. The laws governing prostitution should be changed. Why do judges, lawyers, politicians, and other powerful men get away with their sex and drug crimes, and we do the time? The public needs to smarten up. That is my opinion, and who am I? Only someone involved in the backdrop of politics and the law who wants to have a voice in the future. I am someone who knows. There are others who share my point of view, but they are largely voiceless. I want to be the person helping others accept the rights of women of legal age who work in this profession, and the person who gets rid of traffickers! I always prayed that I would quit this business before anything happened. Damn, I wished I had! They know about the "The Circuit," they had for years, but couldn't find the link to bust it. So someone within the Circuit must have given the inside information. Who? New Orleans? I need to chill out. I can't change what happened. If only all people, inside or out, were exposed to the cover-ups in the system—what actually happens in adoption, foster care, juvenile justice, and prostitution along with the next step, crimes—they would then realize just how corrupt the system is, not just the criminals.

****

The experience of being jailed in the Girls' Detention Center changed me then. On the day I was let out, I had been waiting for quite a while with the social worker, who had all the release papers ready to go. Esti was late. I prayed she hadn't changed her mind because no other home was available to take me. I could feel my anxiety building. She finally arrived to sign me out. When I left Anita and my dad for foster care, I said I was free from them. Now I was being freed from a young adults' prison, but I wasn't free. Leonard and Esti were my jailers, their house my next prison. Although I would be able to go outside and to school, I came home to lockdown. My feelings had changed. I was plotting to leave the minute I was old enough—food or no food, shelter or no shelter. On the way back in the car with Esti, I felt so uncomfortable…in confinement without bars. I could see the green trees outside and feel the fresh air, and I knew I would have a comfortable bed where I could sleep, but that wasn't freedom. Even today, I experience a longing to be a free spirit before I leave this world—long drives, open spaces, and exploring. Esti tried hard to convince me that everyone had my best interests at heart, but why didn't they ask me how I felt? How could they speak for me? Best interest! Even the social workers would always say, "This is for your own good." Okay, when kids have come to you and then commit suicide, did you know and do what was best for them? For their "own good," huh? No crystal balls!

I considered running away every minute, but there was no way I could manage such a move yet. When we arrived in Canton, the house looked and felt surreal. I wasn't looking forward to going back to the Stepford foster mom, the bully husband, and the brat son. The only things I anticipated happily were food, taking walks looking at the trees and homes, and Michael. I wasn't even sure how long Michael would be a part of my reality either. I had spent hours thinking about how he treated me and had come to agree with Pam about his mistreating me. But I was still anxious to call him. Who else did I really have? Some torture was better than no one in my life. Going back to school was something I dreaded because of all the kids wanting to know where I'd been. What I didn't foresee was that they would already know. Canton was a small town, and rumors about my stealing a car and going to jail had already spread months ago, making my embarrassment all the more unbearable. I hated going to school. I avoided my tattletale neighbor so I wouldn't get into an argument. The neighbors squinted at me like I was a criminal. What if they knew the truth about the other girl? Then I wouldn't have been known as the adopted foster kid who stole a car and went to prison. The bad seed! Apparently, while I was gone, the Italian girl who talked behind my back heard the story about me and told the other kids I had stolen a car. She dramatized the story to such an extent that I appeared to be a hardened criminal. Her mom and dad knew someone who was related to me, and that created more problems. The two of them, the girl who drove in the car with me and the other girl from the lake, joined forces with the kids at school telling far-fetched tales about me behind my back. There was nowhere to hide. Esti and Leonard had changed their attitudes toward me and treated me like I was an outcast. I felt like I was walking precariously on a frozen lake of cracking ice.

CHAPTER TWENTY-TWO

The Mysterious Woman

I knew I would miss being in Mattapan and going to the wall on the Jewish holidays on Talbot and Blue Hill Ave. I hope Michael will come get me. That was such a fun time. I know that I won't have a wall to hang out on in Canton.

Shortly after I moved to Canton, I had the feeling that a woman was following me in a car, but I never spoke to anyone about it. I occasionally sensed her presence as I walked back and forth to school. It continued for some time and was becoming more frequent. When I finally told Esti about it, of course, she thought I was crazy, or fabricating an excuse for being late. The girl who had spread the rumors had relatives who lived in a big house on Sharon Lake. They apparently knew the woman who had been trailing me. Late one afternoon, after school, when Esti was in the kitchen, I answered the phone and a woman on the other end asked for me by name. I told her yes, I was Libbe Siskind. She then described my mom and dad, Fred and Rose. She said that she knew me very well and that I could come to live with her. "Who *are* you?" I asked. She went on to say that she had known me since I was born, and because I was of age, I could work for her. From her mouth to my ears, she told me she was my "real" mother…I was shocked! "My mother is dead, and her name was Rose," I snapped. "You are not my mother! Who are you?" I was really upset now! She was talking so fast, but I didn't want to listen. "I can prove it to you," she said. Who was this woman? She said she had photos of me. "I am your birth mother," she said distinctly. "I am your *real* mother."

"You're not!" I protested. She said that all I had to do was say "yes" and she would come get me. I didn't want to hear any more, so I yelled for Esti to pick up the phone. I handed the receiver to her. She spoke with the woman and gestured for me to leave the room. It didn't occur to me to eavesdrop. When the conversation ended, I came back into the room and Esti called my dad. I had many questions Esti couldn't answer: "Who was this woman? She wasn't my mother, or was she? Why did she call me? How did she know I lived here?" She knew Rose and Fred. "So my real mother is alive?" I asked. "I thought she was dead."

Esti couldn't answer my demanding questions. She said, "We'll find out." I regret not pushing the issue then because, good or bad, I could have spoken with her and gotten the truth. And because I didn't, it was years before I learned her identity.

My dad knew this woman who said she was my real mother. Esti told me that my dad called an attorney to run her out of Massachusetts. Why? There was no doubt she was my birth mother, and she had found me. The reason for my dad's extreme anger confused me. I had always wondered, silently, about her and why she gave me up and didn't search for me. I was never told the whole story about her. Dad's only comment to me was that she was "a no-good tramp," and as far as he was concerned, she was dead. Why did he say that? Was it true? Was she was a tramp? No one would tell me the truth. They told me she was "dead and gone" long ago, and Esti had to explain that it was a just a saying that meant my father wanted nothing to do with her. Anita called me a tramp, and I wasn't one; maybe he was saying she was a tramp when she wasn't one either. Everyone had told me that she was dead. She said she was my real mother and that she wanted me! Did I want to see her? Does she want me now—why? Did I really want to learn the truth? I didn't know her name, and if she left Boston where would she go? I tried to forget her. The only mother I wanted was my mother, Rose. I wondered what my life would have been like had I gone with this woman who claimed to be my biological mother. I wouldn't have been a foster child any longer. This woman was a piece of a bigger puzzle. I missed the opportunity to get to know her at that time. I was sad inside. I wanted so very much to have a mother, but I was not willing to give up my loyalty—I loved my mother Rose. I still do, forever.

I was not happy, and everything seemed to be getting more complicated. Silky and Jennifer had moved to Randolph, the new "in" place for young, middle-class Jewish couples. The wealthy Jews lived in Brookline and Newton. I was rebellious, running with the Blue Hill Ave. crowd every chance I got. I was in trouble more and more often because I was hanging out at Duchess, the burger place on the corner of Blue Hill Ave. and Wellington Hill Street, with all the roughnecks. I was punished constantly for coming home late. Michael had stopped doing as many pills and drugs. He wanted me to run away with him. Even though he seemed better, the idea of doing that frightened me. I could tell he still got high, just not as much. I wasn't ready to leave with no place to go, and then have to come back again to Canton. What if I went away and he left me? Huckie still tried to see me, calling constantly, and I would pull back from him whenever he became too sentimental. I was still friendly with the neighbors, who continued teaching me the art of Italian cooking. They were harmless; what could they do to me? Still, I never knew who to trust.

CHAPTER TWENTY-THREE

Rambler

Michael would drive to Canton often because I wouldn't call him back. Sometimes, he took his mother's car, a Rambler, to see me at my house so he wouldn't appear "rich and spoiled," as Leonard would say. He never ran into Leonard when he was driving the Rambler. I was so glad—at least if I took off in that car he didn't have the plate number. He disliked him because of his rich kid appearance and the look of rebelliousness that he had. Leonard said that maybe he would be more acceptable if he changed his attitude. Well, "maybe" Leonard should have changed his attitude! Esti, on the other hand, liked him because he spent money on me, and for her that was a big plus. And he was handsome and she loved to flirt with him. Everything was always about money with her.

One day, early in the evening, Michael and I told Esti we were going to get supper out, and we took off in the Rambler. We parked behind a building in Canton, off Route 138. We started making out in the front seat, with my passenger side seat all the way back like a bed. The kissing got really heavy, and the windows were steamed up. We were in a confined space, and it was the first time we had been this intimate. It probably took him by surprise as much as it did me. Michael was feeling me all over, not controlled like the other times, but crawling on top of me. I could feel him getting hard. I knew he would want me to give him a blowjob, he always did. I was afraid, and didn't want to be touched down there. I told him to stop over and over again, but I was getting into it from his touch and my defenses were down. My mind traveled back to sinister men and how revolting it was when they touched me with their fingers inside my panties. Somehow this sensation was different; I was letting my guard down. I wanted Michael to continue. Although I protested, I was excited. Michael was puzzled by my response as he tried to finger me: I pushed him away again, telling him, "No, Michael, please stop!" but my body was saying yes. He was insistent and wasn't listening to me. I was so wet that I think I wanted him to be aggressive. He told me, "Just let me rub it on you."

"Don't put it in!" I desperately told him.

"Pull your panties down, Libbe. I just want to feel, okay?" Then he unzipped his pants. I was willing—breathing heavily and moaning. I started to turn to go down on him, assuming that was what he wanted. He gently pushed me back and said, "No, just lay there. I promise I won't go inside. Trust me, okay?" Somehow I did trust him, and so I said okay. The single-minded expression on his face was intimidating. "I'm just going to rub the head against you, okay? I won't go inside, I promise. Relax." I did… Even though he said he wouldn't enter me, he tried, then immediately pulled back. Calmness washed over me. I'd never had the confidence to let a boy near me. I believed Michael when he said he wouldn't go inside. I could feel myself tensing and squeezing to prevent him from entering, yet I was almost willing to allow him to go all the way. We were behind the Morse Shoe parking lot; not the most romantic of places, but at least it was wooded and secluded back there. The windows were fogged up from sex steam.

The playing around became more serious. He put his penis between the lips of my vagina and rubbed intensely. We were both excited and in the moment. Michael was so hot that he came all over me. I could feel the warm liquid as it erupted. He never went inside me. I pulled back and, resting on my elbow, I saw cum on the lips of my vagina and on the dark, curly triangle of hair there. "Don't worry, we didn't have sex. I did not go in, it's okay."

"I know," I replied, feeling scared to death. Michael looked around for a Kleenex. I wiped the white sticky pools of cum between my legs with a small rag Michael gave me so that my clothes wouldn't be stained. I dried up all of it on the outside but stuffed a corner of the rag inside me to make sure nothing dripped out to my pants. I believed him when he said there was nothing to worry about. His penis was large enough to hurt had he pushed it inside. I did wonder how it would have felt. I really did want him. We both sat back to catch our breath. Then Michael said, "Let's open the windows to clear the steam out so I can drive you home." The smell of the woods outside mingled with the sex smell inside the car. The air was so refreshing. Cigarette smoke billowed above our heads, mingling with the aroma as I puffed away. I comforted myself with the thought that I really hadn't had sex yet. I vowed I'd never have sex until I had gone steady with a boy for a long time and was at the point of living with him. This was not like what happened with any of the other men who forced themselves on me. I was a willing body. My desire for Michael had surged inside me and made the encounter between us much more profound. Michael promised me he would not do that again unless he had something with him for protection. When I got home, Esti was angry that I was late again. I decided to wait to shower until after dinner so that I wouldn't be conspicuous. Perhaps the initial decision to put the rag inside me, and then to have a shower later was poor judgment on my part, but then I'd never made the best choices.

Despite the distance between Pam's house and mine, with Michael's help, I saw her more often. We were speaking on the phone frequently. She seemed to have more free time compared to when her baby was first born. Finally, I had my friend back to share the ins and outs of my daily life, and someone I could tell about my lock-up in the detention center. Michael never wanted to hear about it, and I needed to vent. Sometimes I used a phone booth to call her before school. I confided in her about what happened with Michael, and she said I was getting close to the real thing. She advised me not to run away just yet, that I had nowhere to go and I should just hold on, and to use protection the next time I was with Michael, just in case. She told me that I was always welcome at her house if I ran into a snag and that she might be getting her own apartment soon. I asked, "How can you do that? Won't your mom and dad be mad?" She explained that she was planning on moving in with a friend, and she had her mom's approval. I preferred running away to the embarrassment of staying back a year in school. The thought of living in an apartment with Pam stayed on my mind. I wished I could have my own apartment, maybe even with Michael, one day? That was just a dream.

The school had called Esti, and she said that they were keeping me back a year. Shit. It bothered me but there was nothing I could do about it. Esti phoned my dad, and he didn't seem to care one way or the other. "Do whatever you think is best," he told her. That took the responsibility off his shoulders once again. I was paying even less attention in class, and my grades were dropping much lower than before. The kids in Canton continued to make fun of me. I was hanging out whenever I could with my friends in Mattapan—they liked me better. They had graduated to stealing cars and whatever else they could take. Now I was picking up the ways of the street, learning how to steal for real. In retrospect, this was a move in the wrong direction, but at the time it made me feel special; unlike average girls, I hung out with the boys, fixed cars, played poker, and went off to the quarry in Quincy to jump in the water late at night. Which I only did once on a dare and never again—I thought I was going to die!

I was talking with Pam regularly; she was packing up her things to move out soon. Esti allowed me to use the phone more often in exchange for doing more chores around the house. I was their "house girl." She wasn't paying much attention to what I was doing because she was not interested. Michael drove me to Pam's mother's house on Pasadena Road numerous times, although he never came inside. I knew he wasn't the social type, and I noticed he wasn't such a tough guy when he was around her. I wondered if it was because he knew she was black or that she had a tough way about her. The white kids I knew in Canton were racist. Imagine, being scared of people just because of the color of their skin.

Even though I was noticeably hungrier and was eating more than usual, at school I would have to run out of class to either vomit in the morning or just gag. For some reason, I didn't feel nauseous until I was in school. Esti was completely unaware of it until one of the teachers finally called her to talk to the school nurse, who told her that I was too skinny and should go to the doctor to have a check-up. Esti told the nurse that I ate all the time but never gained weight. She made an appointment; they were thinking I had somehow acquired a tapeworm. I was hesitant to go, but I didn't have a choice in the matter. Even as gentle and caring as the doctor in Chelsea that my father took me to had been, since then I didn't like any doctor touching me. Every time I was subjected to an exam, I hated it. I wouldn't be seeing a doctor just yet, though. I missed a couple of days of school, and Esti became concerned and called the social worker, who didn't think it was serious enough to call my father or the doctor. She thought I had the flu or a stomach virus. Esti had a sense that something was out of the ordinary when I wasn't eating in the morning. She shared her concern with me, asking me questions like, "Did I feel exhausted all the time?" and "Did I feel hot?"

"No, no," I replied, "I'm just not hungry and I feel tired." I did like toast, which seemed to help me feel better.

When Michael came to school those few times, I was not there. Esti was screening my telephone calls so I wasn't able to speak to him unless I went behind her back when she went out. She said I was seeing him too much. I let him know I was sick and that I had an appointment with the doctor next week. At the exam, I got undressed, put on a johnny, and sat in a chair, extremely nervous. The doctor came into the cold white room with a nurse. I never liked clinical atmospheres, and this one felt even worse. They took blood and urine tests, and I had a pelvic exam, which freaked me out. The nurse was standing off to the side. Having the nurse there made me feel better, but the exam hurt. The concerned expression on the doctor's face when he was probing my abdomen troubled me. Esti left while I was getting examined. That was a blessing; I hated for people to see me undress. Then I was told to stay with her in the waiting room until the results from the tests were known. After some time, the doctor called Esti into his office by herself, which made me somewhat worried about what was wrong with me. I was thinking that I might be sick like my mom. She never left the hospital and was there until she died. I wasn't completely frightened yet. I wished my mother were with me for comfort. I didn't want to feel sick in the mornings anymore. Maybe the doctor could help.

The doctor and Esti were speaking privately in his office for what seemed like forever. They had been gone for such a long time that I was becoming anxious, nibbling away at my already short nails. I tried calling Michael on the payphone down the hall, but he wasn't there, so I called Pam, who was at home, and we spoke for a minute. "I'm nervous and I don't know why."

"It's just a routine exam," she replied, trying to calm me. I told her I would see her soon, hung up, and went quickly back to the waiting room. Finally, Esti and the doctor came out of his office. I was glad they didn't find me missing. She came over to me and said that the doctor wanted to talk with both of us in the exam room, which didn't strike me as unusual except for her facial expression. Foster parents had spoken in front of me with the doctor before for regular physical exams that didn't involve probing inside me. This time was different. Esti, who normally talked a lot, didn't say a word. And judging by her look, she was upset. Now I was seriously scared. I had the same jittery feeling in my stomach that I had when I knew Anita was going to hit me when I came home from school, or when I stepped into a new foster home for the first time. Now I could add physical exams to the list of situations that unnerved me. I hoped I never saw another doctor again.

The door closed behind us, and the doctor told both of us to take a seat. His voice was monotone, unlike when we first arrived and he was friendly and warm. I felt at ease then, but not anymore. I was twisting my fingers and biting my nails, nibbling them as if they were corn on the cob. I wanted a cigarette so bad. He leaned back against his table and looked straight at me, saying, "Libbe, you have a problem and we cannot correct it; it's too late." *What? A problem?* I thought, not understanding him completely. I looked at both of them, feeling utterly confused. "And you live in such a nice home," he continued. "How could you do this to your foster family?" Now he sounded just like Freddy. "What did I do?" I asked. "Esti, what's wrong?"

Then Esti spoke up, "You are three months pregnant, young lady!"

"I am?" I said. I was in shock. Did they say pregnant? No way! "No Esti, I am not pregnant," I said. "I didn't do anything, I swear! I never did!" She was so angry that I had done this to her, not that I had done it to myself. What about me? The doctor told me I couldn't get an abortion because I was too far along. Too far along? What did that mean, abortion? "You are three months and approximately two weeks pregnant," he repeated. I wondered how this could be possible when I had no belly, and I hadn't had sex. I kept on protesting, "I did not let anybody do anything like that to me, I swear! You have to believe me!"

Esti just looked…then asked, "Who did this? I want to know. I will have to tell your dad," she said.

"My dad?" I hadn't thought about that at all. No, not my dad! Please! There was enough on my mind, and none of it made sense. I was speechless. I had been reprimanded by Esti—and a doctor I did not even know! Tears rolled down my cheeks; I was so embarrassed. I swore to her I never allowed a boy to enter me. I imagined that the sour expression on the doctor's face meant that I was a tramp, just like Anita had told me all my young life. Who was he to judge me? Maybe the results of the test were wrong. I was carrying a baby with no husband? Oh, god! I could tell that Esti thought I was a slut too. "Your dad said that you were tramping around before you came to us, and now you've gone and done it. You're going to break his heart," she said. I listened and thought, *What about my heart?* It was traumatic for me just to know he was going to be told. I had already experienced enough heartbreak for a lifetime, and this only added to my pain. Another firing squad stood at attention, getting ready to shoot me.

Now I was more than scared. I had to go back to school. I couldn't let them know it was Michael's baby—it had to be. No one else had ever touched me there with their male organ. Michael was the only one who pressed his penis between the lips of my vagina, but that was before he came. How could I be pregnant? The doctor said I was three months along. He told Esti that sperm could swim from the lips of the vagina if there were enough of them. I was sure I didn't help matters by pushing the cloth with Michael's cum on it inside to dry myself. I understood that now. With the exception of the morning sickness, I felt fine physically. I was told to eat Saltine crackers to take the edge off my nausea. My sense of guilt, my loneliness and fear, were made worse to such a degree that I could hardly bear it. There was a baby inside me. I prayed every night for help, but none came. Maybe I am meant to figure it out for myself. Here I was, alone with the knowledge that I had caused others to feel ashamed. I was speaking to the air, expecting answers, when all along the answers were there inside of me.

Esti was on the phone the moment we got home, first calling the social workers and then my dad. Anita would know too. I could hear her in my mind—yelling. Her telling my dad was going to be awful. Anita already had him constantly upset by calling me a tramp, a liar, and a bad girl every day of my childhood, and the poison she spewed out had become progressively worse. My father had already taken on the role of Anita, calling me every name he could think of. He would never trust me again, not that he did in the first place. Esti was talking to the social worker about getting me into a home so that I wouldn't be seen by the neighbors, and embarrass them when I started showing. *Are they going to throw me out with a baby inside me?* I thought. *How could they? Don't they have any feelings?* I was more frightened than ever before.

Esti couldn't wait to spread the gossip about me to her family. A nice, Jewish girl, not to mention a foster kid, was an unwed mother in her house. When she told Leonard about the pregnancy, he erupted like a volcano, showing his true colors when he ordered me out of the house. "No babies here!" he said. "Get her out!" He obviously didn't care about me; his friendliness had just been a way to get me to do everything he asked. Then Esti got my dad on the phone. I was frightened to hear his voice. I couldn't take the constant abuse. He said that he was through with me, and if I kept the baby, he would never speak to me again. Ironically, he didn't speak to me now. What was the difference? There wouldn't be much! I could barely hear him with Anita in the background screaming that I was a no-good tramp. "I told you so!" she kept repeating. "I will disown you, do you understand me?" he shouted. "Get rid of the bastard!" I felt like shit when he called my baby a bastard. I knew what bastard meant; she called me that all the time. He went on, saying, "Anita was always right about you. You're causing us nothing but heartache! Now you've proven her right once again!" It sounded as though he believed I had done this intentionally. There was silence. "Don't you have anything to say? And what kind of scum did you find on the streets who did this to you?" Oh, god. Then he told me, in a softer tone, that if I gave up the baby and straightened out, I could come and live with them in Florida after I got out of the hospital, but I had to promise him that I wouldn't keep the baby. I thought, *What kind of choice is that?* Anita's harsh screaming drowned out my father's voice. I hadn't even given birth yet. *Promises,* I thought, *he broke them all the time.* "Dad, are you telling me the truth?" I was in tears and gasping as I asked him. I thought back to the time he said I could come back home if the reports he received were all good. That day never came. I waited for weeks and months for him to come and visit me at homes where I'd been placed. Promise after promise…lie after lie… Maybe this time he means what he's saying. Do I dare trust him? I could never leave my baby to someone else. I have no money and no home. Thoughts whirled inside my head. I was so confused. *Oh, god, what do I do?* I needed my mom more than ever.

I had to speak to Michael, but again there was no answer so I phoned Pam, who asked me if I was going to keep the baby. She told me to seriously think about it. I wanted to, but on the car ride back from the doctor's Esti said that I couldn't stay in her house with my baby. Pam offered her house for me to live in but changed her mind when she realized she would be burdening her mother with another child. Once I had the baby, perhaps I could move into her apartment. Pam said she would ask her roommate. The answer to that came back fast: her roommate said she didn't want kids in the apartment. "Sorry, Lib, I tried," she said. And I know she did.

What my future held became more frightening to me than my unspeakable past. I wasn't alone anymore; I had my baby to consider. I had to care about my unborn child. I didn't believe in myself, how could I take care of my baby? Where would I get the money to care for her or him? I just hoped the baby was healthy. I prayed for God's help and the strength to do the right thing. I must, at least, never think about what I want, but what is good for the baby.

CHAPTER TWENTY-FOUR

Baby Girl

As the weeks went by, I noticed changes in my body: my boobs were bigger and my back ached. At night, I could feel pressure when I lay on my side, and Esti said that it wasn't gas, it was the baby growing. The school told Esti that I had to leave the moment I started showing. I carried toward my back, and because of that, I didn't look obviously pregnant. I felt like an even greater outcast than I usually did. I now understand why student pregnancy was not allowed or accepted then. It is awkward and isolating going to school when you are the only one who has a growing belly, not to mention the moral ramifications of being a teenaged mother without a husband. Nowadays, you can do everything in public schools: dress like a hooker or be pregnant—anything goes! The acceptance makes it too easy to follow the trend. What the hell…no rules now. I wish I had been a pregnant teenager in this current time, now I would have kept my baby.

While I was still in school, some of the kids already knew about my situation thanks to Esti telling the neighbors and the faculty and word getting around. Canton was a small suburban town. Except for a few of them, no one talked to me, not even a word. Their parents wouldn't permit them to speak to me—the school tramp. They couldn't conceive of their own daughters having sex, not *their* precious girls. I wanted to crawl into a hole. Because no one discussed pregnancy with me, I went to the school library and read what I could find about babies. That was my sole interest at the time, but I would only choose books with pictures because I didn't like to read.

When I got in touch with Michael, before I told him what happened, I asked him not to get mad at me. He was impatient to hear what I had to say. When I told him, he screamed at me, "What the fuck, it's not mine! I didn't have sex with you!" He ordered me to get rid of it—and threatened to punch me in the stomach because it wasn't his baby! I told him what the doctor said. I believed he loved me. How could I have been so wrong? Why did he say those things? Why doesn't anyone love me? He said that his family could never know that I was pregnant, and I promised him I wouldn't tell anybody in Canton or Mattapan besides Pam, who already knew because I had confided in her. He kept on denying the baby was his. He insisted over and over again that he never came inside me, and accused me of lying to him. "Were you with Huckie?" he asked.

"I never had sex with anyone else, I swear!" I told him. Defending myself further, I added, "Never! I haven't even seen him." He then said that we could have sex now that I was already pregnant…is that all he thought of? That was how little he cared about anything besides sex. I felt like I was being used. Obviously, he wanted me for whatever I could do for him, nothing else. What about the baby? Our baby? No answer came to me. I put him off for as long as I could until he had a chance to think about the situation. And I thought I knew him but, clearly, I did not.

Michael continued calling me. He felt guilty. He had reconsidered and believed the baby was his. He knew that he was the only one I had ever been with. I wasn't lying! He wanted me around, but he didn't want to take any responsibility for the baby when it was born. Clearly, it wasn't the money; it was the embarrassment to his family. And maybe he was ashamed it was me. It was so apparent. I felt like an alien.

I was now showing, and Esti said I had to leave school. Before they notified me, I quit rather than being thrown out. I stayed at home with Esti for as long as I could, never venturing outside the house so that the neighbors could not catch a glimpse of my body.

Mostly, I stayed in my room. The nonstop kicking left no doubt that I was carrying life inside my belly. My own real live baby! It was time for me to leave Canton.

I was taken to the Salvation Army Home for unwed mothers on the Jamaicaway for an orientation visit. "Isn't this nice?" Esti said. "The girls are around your age." That didn't help me feel any better. She had little feeling for me or my situation. A couple of days after, I was dropped off there like a bag of old clothes. I felt abandoned. Jennifer sympathized with me, but she never offered to take me in, nor did she visit me even once while I was in the Home. That hurt. And later, even worse, she never visited me in the hospital either. Going from place to place wasn't as traumatic anymore. I told Jennifer that I would be going to my dad's soon, and she replied, "Won't that be great!" Did she really believe that, or was her enthusiasm an attempt to deny my pain? Did she already know that I would never be going there? Probably. I was young, and hadn't yet learned that others often don't want to help unless it benefits them in some way.

I didn't like this place. It felt cold. My bedroom was an empty, large room, like a classroom, shared by other girls who only talked about themselves and their boyfriends. There were beds instead of the usual school desks and chairs. I was uneasy about the place. Despite the company of the other girls, I felt alone. I called Michael that night from the phone booth. He said he really did feel badly, but… sorry, he couldn't do anything to help, "See you when you get out."

See me when I get out? What kind of comment was that? That hurt! My situation was pushing and prodding me to grow up. The other girls were sneaking out all the time at night to see their boyfriends. Why couldn't Michael be here like them? I wanted so very much to believe that Michael and my father cared for me, but as time went on I got older, my eyes opened wider. I was growing up and seeing things in a clearer light.

My baby bump was impossible to hide. My life was in shambles—a real fiasco. Leonard had been an ass since he found out I was pregnant, and Esti was her schmoozing self. "Oh, honey," she sighed, "I wish there was something I could do, but we can't have you here like that." No, of course not. Had I been her real daughter rather than her foster kid, she would have done anything for me and for the baby. Ironically, it was Mason who later in life stripped his own mother of her house and belongings. Karma. What an ass he was! As a child, he behaved like a prince who got whatever he wanted, and I couldn't cause problems for his majesty; as an adult, he became the bastard he always was and ended up treating his mother like shit. I always, from day one, recognized his real character and understood who and what he was.

I lay in bed night after night listening to stories the other girls told about their parents—some drug addicts, some alcoholics—most of them having experienced some sort of neglect and abuse. Occasionally, there were girls who were very young and simply had made a mistake like me, yet I seemed to carry more baggage than them. They all discussed sex. They told stories using words I had never heard before. Others were embarrassed and didn't want their friends to know they were pregnant. All of a sudden, my childhood had ended. We would go to classes during the late afternoon to learn how to breathe and pant like a puppy waiting to be fed. The puzzle of my life was becoming more intricate as I lay on my bed in the big room at the Salvation Army, praying for answers. I was going to have a baby and could feel my child turning and kicking inside me. My baby was the same as me when I was in my mother's abdomen, whoever she was. The thought that I might give up my baby like my mother gave me away pained my heart. Then a smile would dawn on my face as I reminded myself that my baby might be given to a mother as great as Mommy Rose. That was my only comfort, but how was I to know for sure where my baby would be placed? There wasn't another person on earth like my mom. Thinking about my baby's future was chilling. How could a girl as bad as me have a good child? I wanted the best for my baby. And in my innocence, I dreamed about someone marrying me and taking us away—my prince! Just like in the fairy tales.

The remaining time at the Home seemed to go by very slowly, and as it passed, the larger and rounder I became. Still, my frame was small. As mentioned earlier, I carried toward my back, so that even at eight months, I was not as big as the other girls. Because of the constant conversation of these tough girls, I was becoming even more streetwise about girl talk. They sounded like Pam and her friends. I spoke with Pam as often as I could, telling her how I had to manage with the little money I had for the pay phones, and I used it wisely, not for luxuries like smoking—especially during those last months. I didn't see or speak to anyone from school, although toward the end, the music teacher, who was aware of my condition, asked Esti to have me visit when I got back to school even if I didn't register again. He was different. There was no way I would do that being as embarrassed as I was, yet I wanted to give him my violin. I never wanted to play any instrument again. Everyone had done his or her part in making me feel like a failure, including myself. I didn't want to be around anyone unless they were in the same boat as me. I wanted to disappear by going to live in another state with my baby. I prayed that someone, anyone, would appear and help my dream come true.

I would be at the facility on the Jamaicaway until I delivered. When others screamed because of their increasing pain, even though they weren't my friends, I felt terrified for the girls and myself. I still daydreamed about someone coming along and taking care of me. Maybe Michael will! Like Snow White and Cinderella, I wished for my prince to come and my dream to come true. I wondered how girls knew when their boyfriend or man was the right one. When I asked them, they weren't always sure their partners were the right ones or if they had a commitment to them. All my experiences in the homes I'd lived in certainly didn't warm my heart enough to trust in another human being or to care very much about anything.

Michael and I had real sex a few times before I went to the unwed mothers home, but not often because it hurt. I always thought my first time would be romantic, but when we did it I was disappointed. I was too nervous, and he was too rough. At the same time, he was anxious about hurting the baby. My ideas came from TV and the movies—sex was supposed to be romantic and passionate, like the evening in the car when we kissed. I wanted to feel like Elizabeth Taylor does when she kissed someone. But movies were not real, and Michael was not the romantic type, especially when he felt the baby. When I discussed Michael with Pam, she said he mistreated me because he was insecure and immature, and had issues. She said that was not how sex was supposed to be. She said that sex was supposed to make you feel special, not hurt. I asked myself who would have me now after giving birth when I wasn't married. I realized that I did have a choice—Huckie, the gentle giant. But how could I be with him now? Was I too fearful to make that move? I didn't want him on the rebound from Michael. I didn't feel like I loved him enough. He said he would marry me several times, and I believed that he wanted to. He told me, "I'll take care of you forever." And the day he found out I was pregnant, he called Esti to find out how I was. Why didn't I see how sincere Huckie was? When he spoke with Esti, he asked if it would be okay if he married me and took care of me. She said yes but asked him if he wanted to make that commitment? I would only be sixteen when the baby was due to be born. I was naive about love because my love had never been reciprocated by anyone except for my mother Rose. When I asked Esti about Huckie wanting to marry me, she told me to do it. She said that he would be a great provider and that I should smarten up, but I was young and rebellious. I didn't consider that to be smartening up, rather, it gave me a place to stay—that's all. No doubt, Esti and everyone else were for the rationale to marry for money. But I couldn't return his love one hundred percent, and I didn't want to do that to him. I was too immature. I knew other girls married for security, why couldn't I? If Esti could have accepted Huckie's proposal for me, she would have. Even Jennifer said to marry him. My father had once told me he married Anita so I would have a stepmother to take care of me, and that turned out to be a nightmare for me but he really wanted her. In no way would I want it to happen that a man hated my child because it wasn't his.

There wasn't any doubt in my mind that I was attracted to the Marlon Brando type of bad boys, the macho kind who were not romantic. I was damaged by Anita's cruelty and by men taking advantage of me. I believed that was what I wanted and deserved. Michael hardly spoke about the pregnancy. He was totally uncomfortable with it and avoided the subject altogether on the phone with me. I didn't realize how frightened he was. Perhaps he feared that his relationship with his mother would be repeated in his relationship with his own child. Fatherhood must have been terrifying, especially given Michael's age and insecurities.

The boys who had gotten the girls pregnant were not allowed inside the Home to visit, and we were supposed to stay close to the others girls to watch for signs of contractions. We were only permitted to see our "men" for a short time during the day, and many of the girls went against the rules and slipped out to meet them late at night when they thought nobody knew. That was the term used to describe the partners of these girls: their "men," not boyfriends. The term was new to me. The girls told me about what was going to happen to me as the pregnancy progressed. It scared the shit out of me. Michael came up a few times to bring me money, then left quickly. He did not want to visit long and stayed away when I was almost ready to give birth. He didn't care how I felt. Soon, I would be taken from where I was and transferred to a hospital. I *hated* hospitals. They reminded me of bad things—my mom at the end of her life—and looked like the Youth Service Board, but without locks. Although the doctors told me I was healthy, my body was thin, and I could never get enough food. I was always hungry, even more than ever because the baby was growing fast. During the day, I was hyperactive, perpetually moving. I had been that way all of my life, and pregnancy didn't slow me down.

When I was still with Esti at her house, I had insisted on calling my dad despite the excuse I was given about not being able to call because of Anita. I couldn't call from the Home because it was long distance, so Esti agreed to call him for me and reverse the charges. She said she hadn't really talked to him, only long enough to say a quick hello from me. This was the last time Esti talked to him before the baby was born, and he echoed the same thing he said to me before about giving up the baby for adoption. Esti told me she could hear Anita in the background saying, "Hang up the god-damned phone, damn it! Hang up from that dirty tramp!" over and over, that I deserved getting knocked up like the scum on the street, and I would never amount to anything. She gave him the message to call me. When he did, the sum of what my father said was to make sure I signed the papers to give the illegitimate baby away, without any inquiry into my health or assurance that everything was going be okay. No mention of seeing me after the baby was born. He didn't say goodbye to me, just hung up. Why hadn't he said these things? I asked Esti. She told me that my dad had a lot on his mind because of me. Yeah, sure, only me, my fault…never Anita. The loneliness I felt was excruciating. The depth of that pain stayed with me throughout the time I was in the Home, and afterward, when I was on my way to the hospital to deliver. What I had wanted more than anything was his reassurance that I would be going home with him to Florida after the baby was born. Where else was I going to stay?

The feeling of wanting to keep the baby became overwhelming. "I want my baby," I cried at night as I went to sleep, rubbing my belly and telling the baby how much I loved him or her. I didn't know what I should do. I was so distressed. I called Esti a few days later and told her I wanted to keep my baby. That certainly didn't go over well. She called my dad. I hoped I hadn't made my father angrier than he was already. When she called him, Esti calmed my dad and told him not to worry and that she would call him back. Esti called the social workers several times, and through my barrage of tears, I was persuaded to take hold of myself and acknowledge the reality of my situation. That was so easy for Esti and the social workers to say. Sure, you guys should try it! Would they have done it? Yes, they were right, but I still wanted my baby. It was mine, and I had no one else to call my own. My baby would love me even if no one else did. Many telephone calls were made back and forth from Massachusetts to Florida. No one took the time to call me at the Home anymore to discuss keeping the baby. And my dad just ignored me. As far as they were concerned, it was a foregone conclusion that I would be giving my child away.

There was a spirit of being in the same boat with the other girls. One by one, the girls' cries and screams would come, followed by the sound of an ambulance, and then I would never see them again. I didn't have any calls or visitors unless I made the call out, and talking to Esti was disheartening. The baby was constantly moving inside me. I was resigned to giving up the baby to strangers and had nightmares about who these people would be. I loved my adoptive mother, and never gave much thought to my birth mother until the day she contacted me at Esti's house. I always thought of her after that and pondered the reasons my mother had given me up. Was her reason the same as mine, or was she a no-good tramp sleeping with whomever, like my father said she was? I didn't care what she was—she was my birth mother, and I wanted to know her reason. Being pregnant, I felt a bond with her. I flinched when I thought about how my dad had lied about her, just as he lied about all the other things he told me. The social workers lectured me, telling me that eventually I would feel differently because I was young and the baby would tie me down, to finish school and have a fresh start. I said that I didn't have much of a life, and raising the baby would give me a something to look forward to. They said no, I would have an easier time in life without raising a baby at such a young age, and they repeated that over and over. Every social worker always would drill and repeat things from my past, and that was depressing.

What did my dad tell Anita when he let her know that I was coming to Florida to live, that is, if he told her anything at all? I knew she would scream and rant the way she always did. There was no boiler room there, only one floor, so where could she possibly put me? Where could she beat me up? I never asked my dad whether he had an extra bedroom, and he never mentioned it to me. I didn't learn his home only had one bedroom until years later. Dad had retired and was home full-time. So Anita would have to hold her hands to herself! The only things he did were play golf and fix cars. I had it all figured out, yet at the same time I felt confused. Every time I felt a kick, I wanted the baby more. The girls' screams disturbed me because of the pain they were in. Who would be there for me when the time came for the baby to be born? Who would hold my hand when I yelled in pain? There would be no one other than the hospital staff—strangers—to share in the excitement of the baby's birth. My baby's birth!

It was hot and uncomfortable in late August. By September, I was anxious and paced the floor as my due date approached. I passed the time by discussing what was on my mind with another girl. She was giving up her baby for adoption but wasn't entirely sure about her decision either. The two of us were in the same position, and we shared our feelings. Dad had lied so many times, but the girl pointed out that maybe because I was older now, he might do what he said and let me come live with him in Florida. My hopes perked up. What did I have to do to be good in my dad's eyes? Never do anything besides go to school, get a job, and be an old maid forever?

I felt pressure in my lower abdomen as if I had to go to the bathroom, then a tightening across my belly. The ladies monitoring me were giving me an unusual amount of attention, and then the pain started in earnest. The contractions were more severe than any pain I had ever experienced before, but not more than I could handle. I understood now why the other girls cried out in pain. My fear was greater than the pain. And even though I had watched births in movies the Home had shown us, the thought of a baby traveling through my vagina intensified the fear. The intervals between the pains were getting shorter. Everyone was moving faster as the pain increased. My body felt like it wanted to push the baby out. I said goodbye to the girls at the Home, and then I was on my way to Beth Israel Hospital in the ambulance. The breeze outside was crisp, like a breath of fresh air.

The next thing I remember was getting an epidural to ease the pain. I was awake, and the doctor, a sweet woman from India, was gentle and caring. After the pain and pushes, my baby girl was born—I heard the doctor say, "It's a girl!" My baby girl! I could hear her crying, and then silence. The doctors were scurrying about. She was taken away. Gone! What? I didn't even have a chance to hold her! Where did they take my baby girl? After the pain of giving birth, they pushed on my belly and the placenta came out. Now the first pang of emptiness struck me. I felt hollow. There wasn't a baby there. All I could think of was that I wanted my baby back. When I was in the Home, the hospital social workers badgered me into consenting to the baby's adoption for the good of the child. I never said yes, and I didn't sign anything. The feeling of emptiness was so deep and vast that I could not tolerate it. How could I get my baby girl back? Saying yes didn't mean it was final. They said the papers were to be signed after the baby was born. I hadn't signed anything yet!

Why wasn't I allowed to see my baby? I couldn't even say hello or goodbye. When I asked the nurse if I could see her, she simply informed me that the social worker would be coming to the hospital to meet with me in a while. Softly, she said that when you give up your baby for adoption, it is better not to see the baby. Whose rules are these? The people eager to see a baby adopted. When I told the nurse that I may not give up the baby, she said she had her orders. "I am sorry, but I can't show you the baby. I'm so sorry," she said amid my tears, "that's what we're told. It's for your own good." Where have I heard that before? Even though I was sore, it amazed me that a baby had just come out of me and I was all right. Yes, as slight as I was I had produced a baby, skinny and bony me…something Anita said I would never do. She put a scare in me that I could never have a child—she lied! I felt proud of giving birth, and giving birth naturally without surgery. See Anita? You did not kill my insides!

They cleaned me up, and I was sent to recovery while they tried to locate a bed for me. Even though I was there for a matter of hours, it seemed like days, and I couldn't wait to get up and walk. The nurse told me it would be okay later in the evening or in the early morning. I was so eager. When I finally walked to the ward where the babies were kept, my name wasn't on any of the carts. I wasn't aware that babies up for adoption weren't tagged or put out in their carts for people to view. I went back to my cold, white room. So scared… Although the nurses told me they didn't know where the baby was, I knew they did but could not say. I felt detached from my surroundings. My sadness was profound—a sorrow deeper than when my mother died or when I was taken from my father. I felt this emptiness to the depths my soul. I thought about my mother Rose and how she'd have helped me take care of the baby if she were still alive. I know she would have put the baby in her own name the same as Pam's mother did so that the baby could still be part of the family. I wouldn't have been in this situation if she were here; I know that I would have had a somewhat normal childhood.

The social worker came into my room. She said the papers would be ready in a day or so. I half listened to her speech about how the best choice in my case was giving up the baby for adoption to a good home, although, she said if I truly believed I could bring up the baby by myself, that was another choice I could make. How could I judge which was the best choice then? I didn't have any answers. Today, I still wonder if I made the right decision. I beat myself up for not toughing it out. Never did the social workers say there were agencies that would have helped me, like Jewish Family Services, or that I could have relied on welfare before finding a job. I only became aware of these alternatives when it was too late. The social worker reassured me that the baby would be placed in a wonderful home where the parents were comfortably well-off. She also told me that Esti was coming to the meeting, and I would see her there. "What about my dad?" I asked.

"He hasn't called, and he was supposed to come from Florida to get me." The social worker evaded my question by telling me she had to check on it. I asked her to allow me to see the baby. I hadn't signed any papers yet. She replied that if I still felt the same way after the meeting, I could see the baby, but not until then. I asked again, "Will my dad be there?"

"We will talk soon. Think about it, Libbe. This is the best thing for your baby girl." She will be with loving parents…oh my god, *parents*, two people to love her! What can I do? What should I do? The social worker left without saying another word, not wanting to answer any more of my questions. Heartbroken, I just lay there, not knowing what to do. So I prayed to my mom in heaven, telling her my deepest thoughts. When I finished praying, there was only silence, absolute silence and white sheets, and an eerie sense of medicinal frigidity in the room. I didn't want to see anyone or talk. I was mentally exhausted, and so upset I couldn't eat. The lunch tray was left untouched as I dozed off to sleep.

I was so tired I was unaware of how many hours I slept, but I could tell it was past suppertime because the evening meal tray was next to the bed. I must have fallen asleep again because I was suddenly awakened by a nurse carrying my baby girl! She said, "Here's your baby," and I sat up, startled. "Yes, my baby. Thank you," I said with a smile that inflated my cheeks. Did they finally care? The nurse seemed to be confused by my surprise. She put the blanketed baby in my arms and handed me her bottle. "You're not breastfeeding, are you?" she asked. "No, no, I'm not." Of course, the baby wasn't being breastfed, I was giving her up for adoption—the nurse didn't seem to know. I cradled my baby gently yet firmly as if I had been holding infants my entire life. She was cute with dark hair and large eyes. She opened and closed her mouth as I caressed her cheek. I wanted to cry for joy. Just as I was about to feed her the bottle, two nurses came running in the room. "Miss Siskind?" one said.

"Yes?" I replied. "We are so sorry for the mistake. We'll take her now."

"No, no, she is my baby—I haven't signed the papers yet! She's hungry, wait!" Then one of the nurses took her from my arms. As it turned out, the new nurse who had gone on for the evening shift made a mistake by giving me the baby. "No, no, wait!" I begged. "Bring her back! Please give her back to me! I want to feed her!" I was weeping. I was so unhappy and lost. Despite the numbness and the pain of the stitches, I got out of bed and ran to catch the nurse who had taken right off, but she was nowhere in the hallway. I wondered where she took the baby. The other nurse who had come in to take her away stopped me and took me calmly back into the room, trying her best to be consoling. I brushed her aside. "Why can't I feed her?" I begged in a testy tone. I didn't want to look at her face or listen to her voice. Although she apologized, I knew she didn't care; no one did. The staff was concerned because the nurse had made a serious mistake by giving me my baby. They were worried about getting the new nurse in trouble. What about my feelings? The nurse told me I needed rest and that I shouldn't run because I might loosen my stitches, but I didn't care. All I could think of or see in my mind was my baby girl. I wondered what I could do or if I had anyone to advocate for me. When I closed my eyes, her face was there, tormenting me. Eating was impossible. I went to the nursery as quickly as I could to try to find her. I could recognize her now, but she was not with the other infants. The nurse saw me and told me to go back to my room. "Please, try to get some rest," she said. "We can't be noisy, there are patients trying to sleep. Please!" I ignored her and all the attending nurses. It seemed like this day would never end!

I cried, and kept crying long into the night. Tomorrow was the day we were supposed to sign the papers. I didn't want to sign any papers! I tossed and turned, and for the remainder of the night went wandering through the hallways, making sure to check when the nurses were changing shifts. I walked down the hallway by the nursery, where I looked through the glass, trying to find her…hour after hour. I tried peeking through the closed curtains, but she wasn't anywhere in sight. Maybe they put her in a corner somewhere because of what happened, or perhaps a separate room. Defeated, I shuffled back to my room. I fell asleep from exhaustion and woke up early. I decided I would talk to my father about the baby at the meeting. Maybe he would understand that giving up the baby would be a great loss for me. Perhaps he could find it in his heart to care and help me out. I wondered why Esti hadn't come to talk to me before the meeting. Alone, as always. The nurses were talking to me, but I hated them so much for taking my baby away that I blocked out what they said. I had images in my mind from watching TV of how special it is to welcome a new baby into the world. But no one came to the hospital. This was not a special day for me; it was a death sentence. The doctor came in and checked me, and she said that everything was great and I could go home. *Home?* I thought. *What home?* I told the doctor I had decided not to give my baby away. I wanted to feed her to be certain she was being fed. I didn't trust any of them. The doctor patted my leg and told me not to worry, that the baby was very healthy, drinking from a bottle, and well taken care of. "You will be just fine. I'm sure you'll make the best decision for your baby girl," she said. As I lay there, her words lingered in my thoughts.

By morning, I had made up my mind. I felt like a new person, ready for the world. I got up early, showered, and waited for breakfast. I was prepared to tell my dad, Esti, and the Jewish Family and Children's Service that I had changed my mind, that I wanted my baby girl, and I was certain about my decision. I vowed I would find a way to keep my child even if I had to starve myself to feed her. The only drawback to my decision was my dad taking me home. I had to control myself because no one would deal with me if I showed any signs of being angry or upset. I needed to be calm so the social workers wouldn't evaluate my state of mind as poor in any way or that I was mentally unstable, as they were quick to say when I became angry. What do they know—just their books. I wondered how they would react if they found themselves in my situation. I was sure that wasn't in their protocols or textbooks, which in my estimation weren't worth much anyway. The system likes to control you with doctors, pills, and psychiatrists. How could they go by any book when no two cases are alike because everyone is different? Weren't *my* feelings important? Or were their reference books all that mattered? I thought about school. Sure, my English and math weren't the best, but I knew how to read people, and that is education in itself! The warmth of the sunshine coming through the window was comforting. I asked the nurse to get my baby ready. She looked at me as if I were crazy and left.

The nurse said I had to go to a special conference room to meet with some hospital social workers, the social workers from the placement agency J.F.C.S., and Esti. My dad wasn't mentioned. Where will my baby go if Dad takes me from the hospital? Will she be tossed from place to place like me, or will she have a great mom and dad like I did until my Mommy Rose passed away? I am so confused. What do I do? My resolve weakened as I recalled my happiness as a young child. A nurse came into my room to take me to the meeting, and I began to feel nauseous. I was dizzy and my mouth was dry. The nurse talked to me on the way. Gently touching my shoulder, she asked if everything was all right. Then she stopped and went into a small room with a refrigerator. "You're pale," she told me, "but it's to be expected. Here, drink this orange juice; you'll feel better." We walked into a room that looked dark, with a long table and glass doors. The table was covered with papers, and there were mostly strangers sitting all around it. I recognized one person from the hospital, and there was another social worker I knew well. The rest of the people seated around the table appeared to be automatons, wearing blank expressions on their faces as they stared at me. They were, after all, part of the system and just doing their jobs—no minds of their own, robots limited by their training. There were no aides or advocates there to support me. I wanted to get away from the room, but everyone stood and greeted me with kindness. I relaxed and felt more at ease, but I was still mistrustful and wary. It was almost as if I were in a dream, like I had been in this room before, like déjà vu. The nurse told me she'd come back in a little while with some more juice.

Esti was not there, nor was my dad. I tried to pay attention to everything, but I wasn't able to comprehend or recall much of it—my mind was elsewhere. They wanted me to look at the papers, and the question "Do you understand everything?" was repeated over and over again. I answered, "I'm not doing anything until I speak with my father." Then Esti appeared with a social worker from foster care and told me she would stay right with me and that both of them would be there to answer any questions I might have. Where was my dad? They left the room to talk privately. Again…where is my dad? The social worker came back but not Esti, who had been absent throughout the whole ordeal and now wasn't there again. "Where is my foster mother?" I asked. "She'll be back. We're going to ask you some questions, Libbe." Perhaps this was the time to announce that I was keeping my baby girl. The meeting was about to begin. "How are you today?" they asked me. Really? "We have a lot of papers here for you to sign. You understand that once you sign these, that will make your decision final." Esti came back into the room with a slight grin, obviously hiding the facts. They spoke one by one about the reasons I should give up the baby. My heart was pounding! "Where will you live? How will you care for her? How will you feed and clothe her? What will you do when she gets sick?" So many questions… What was the best decision for my baby girl? They agreed with Esti, who said that no one would want me with a baby and that I would have a better life if I went back to school and graduated. How can they predict my future? Esti didn't mention Huckie and how he wanted to marry me. During a break, I told her I planned to call him. Esti advised me not to do that. She leaned in toward me, and in a lowered voice said it was wrong to marry him if I didn't love him. Later, she told me she hadn't said anything about him because he said what he did about marrying me out of pity. Pity? I knew better. He was in love with me and expressed that love by sticking by me from the beginning when we first met until the time he found out I was pregnant. Esti had tried crushing his feelings for me by telling him he was too good for me. Much later, when Huckie finally told me the truth—that he had always felt love for me, never pity—it was too late. Too late!

Once again, I asked for my dad and silence filled the room. Esti explained to everyone that my dad promised to take me home after the papers were signed, but what she didn't mention was that he had told her he didn't intend to follow through on his word. I was angry he wasn't there and didn't have a chance to express my feelings with the adults talking and answering for me. They asked Esti if she had my dad's number and if it would be possible to call him. My social worker said she would call Mr. Siskind for me even though she already knew his answer as well. Big secrets were being kept in this torture room. I told Esti that I wanted to keep the baby and begged her to let me stay at her house until I found a job or my dad could help me out. Then I would leave, I promised her. She said Leonard wouldn't allow the baby in the house because it would be disruptive, and it wasn't fair to Mason, who was too young to understand all of this. Yeah sure, imagine…their precious boy shouldn't be exposed to an illegitimate child. They wouldn't accept the baby because Mason was a brat and required their full attention. A baby would take up time. Nothing was about me, or my baby girl. The social workers said they wanted what was best for the baby and for me. They were overpowering, and maybe they were right. I wanted what was good for the baby too. I didn't believe them, but their arguments convinced me I didn't have a choice. Where was my dad! I was too young and naive. I knew I would suffer that day and for years to come. I just didn't know how much and for how long. As it turned out, I never forgave myself for signing away my daughter—never!

My dad was on the phone, and he didn't sound angry. He told me to sign the papers in a voice that sounded "too nice."

"Libbe, please!" he said. "Do this one thing for me; it *is* what's best for the baby." He told me not to think about myself, but to think about how the baby would suffer. I felt so guilty. Of course, I didn't want to harm my baby. He said to call him from Esti's house after I signed the papers and that then I could come home. I told him I wanted the baby safe and happy. "Let the social workers do their job," he said. "Promise me, Libbe, you will do what I ask." Maybe he was Right, and I was being selfish wanting to keep her. What could I offer a baby? I had nothing, and I didn't even know what love was. I knew that she would never be hungry, even if I had to steal food for her, but what kind of life would that be? "Okay," I replied. "Are you sure my baby will be in a good home?"

"Yes, Libbe."

"Daddy, I love you. See you soon." He didn't tell me he loved me too. There wasn't any expression of affection at all, but he had sounded so sincere. I should have known what was going to happen. My feelings were torn, and I wanted to believe his words. My heart was heavy, but I didn't want my little girl to end up like me…no way!

I signed so many papers with so many witnesses. While my heart was being torn apart, I could see they were all happy as I wrote my name. I was the only one in tears. They said it was in the best interest of the child, but all I felt was hurt—hurt and guilt. It stung! I would never see my baby's face again. How could I do the same thing to her that happened to me? I lost a big part of my soul that day. I was a bad person, just as bad as they said my birth mother was. I asked myself how I could possibly sell her out for my dad, yet that is what I did. It was over; the papers were signed. They made it sound as though she was going to be adopted by caring, well-off parents with a beautiful home waiting for her. What I see whenever I recall that day is the dark room, the table and the papers, and the outlines of my baby's face. September 16, 1967—that was the day I signed away my baby girl, a day that would haunt me forever. I was traumatized that day, and the date I signed her away was etched in my mind, not the date of her birth: September 14, 1967. The trauma of giving birth and then giving my baby away confused the dates in my mind for almost my entire life. This was not the end of my connection with my daughter.

CHAPTER TWENTY-FIVE

Broken Promise

I gathered my things and left the white, sterile hospital room and headed for Esti's house, carrying my small bag and nothing else—no Hallmark cards or bouquets of flowers like everyone else in the ward, no joyous tears. Even though my heart was heavy, I was trying to stay positive by thinking that I would soon be leaving my foster home. Esti hadn't brought me a change of clothes when she picked me up, and I was dressed in one of the same maternity outfits I had worn at the Salvation Army Home. I looked pathetic. The silence during the ride only made my feelings of emptiness worse. There I was without my baby, and Esti didn't know what to say except that she'd be fine and it would take a little time for me to get over it. Okay, over it! Really? I repeatedly asked her where my baby was taken, and she didn't have an answer. I knew that no one at Esti's house gave a shit about what happened. I came to the conclusion that I would be grappling with my problems all alone. I had to grow up and get out of there. It was harder than before because now I had to rely on others who did not want to help. I was always angry and in the habit of lashing out, not wanting anyone to get too close. Why should I love people who just used me? The car came to a halt…we had arrived. I phoned Michael the minute we got in, but he was playing his drums so loudly that I hung up on him. Although he called back quickly enough, I didn't have much to say and neither did he. His voice conveyed relief. He didn't want the baby. He said we would see each other in a while, after I healed. And after that conversation, I didn't think about him as much as I did before. He was only interested in me for sex now that I was healed and able to do it. During the last few months of my pregnancy, something had shifted. I had time to think and to prepare for a different life, one without him and without school. I never wanted to go back to school; I felt so dumb anyway. The humiliation of my situation was enough for me to handle without having to face the other kids. I was told that I could get my GED any time in the future, and that was encouraging. But the pressure was mounting and mounting. I waited for my dad to call me. One day passed, and then another and another. Esti warned me not to get my hopes up too high, that he might need some extra time. Extra time? He had enough time while I was pregnant. Why can't he simply pick up the phone and call me? I didn't want to wait. I had waited long enough. He had said that if I signed the papers I could go to Florida to live with him, not later, but now. I felt safe going there because he was retired and at home all the time; Anita wouldn't be able to torture me. "I am not waiting anymore," I insisted. "He said to call him." I pleaded with Esti to call my dad. "Yes, Libbe," she said, and then she hedged by telling me she would call him later. No call was made, another wasted day.

The social worker called me every day to find out how I was adjusting after having the baby, and I told her that I hated where I was living and asked if I would be leaving there soon. She said that we'd talk when Esti brought me to the office. I questioned her about where my baby had been placed, and she replied that she was in a good home and not to worry. She would give me an update soon, she said. I had put aside thoughts about my little girl for a short time, feeling relieved that she was taken care of. I was consumed by thinking about Florida and my dad. I thought about whether I would go back to finish school in Florida or get a job. I had learned how to do all kinds of work in my foster homes, from gardening to cleaning, especially cleaning. When I was pregnant, I spoke with the social worker about what I was going to do after the baby was born and told her that I wanted to be a hairdresser. I even surprised myself when

I said that because Anita had been a hairdresser for years and that should have been enough to keep me from considering it. I told her that I thought they made good money, and I liked doing hair. She said that the agency would pay for me to go to school for it. Maybe my dad would be prouder of me if I did that because hairdressing was what Anita did, and he loved Anita. I believed that the hairdressing would make him love me more. I wanted to please him, that's what I said to the social worker. She was indifferent and said that it was my decision. I wondered if there was a school in Florida. I'd had dreams of acting and singing professionally or drawing and becoming an artist, but I gave up those ideas as soon as it was explained to me that performers and artists had to be smart and talented, and that they rarely made any money. I didn't have enough confidence to perform or the talent to be an artist anyway. Everyone always shot down any ideas I had, and I believed them. How gullible I was, and still am in lots of ways.

Esti and Leonard were avoiding me because of my badgering them about calling my father. More than a week had passed. I was disappointed that he didn't call and decided to phone him myself. I found the telephone number in Esti's book. When I called, Anita answered and called me a string of names and wouldn't let Dad on the phone, so I hung up. I had heard his voice in the background telling her to give him the phone, but the bitch won. Esti came home and wanted to talk, but without me "flying off the handle." She told me she had talked with my dad the other day and that I should have waited and not called him. He told her that he and Anita were not ready for me to stay with them and that I should stay where I was, with her. I watched her mouth form the words. I was angry and didn't hold it in. "You're lying!" I shot back at her. "You knew all along, didn't you?" I didn't know whether to cry, scream, or throw something. I want to talk to Dad myself, without Anita! "You're lying to me! Everyone lies to me!" Esti assured me she wasn't lying, just protecting me from the facts. "This can't be true!" I couldn't hold back the anger and tears. "Why didn't you tell me? You want me to stay so I can clean for you and do work around the house—that's all, and to get your money!" Esti became flustered at what I said because it was the truth. Leonard came in the room and had an expression on his face that said he knew all along I wouldn't be going to live with my dad. Both of them had known. I looked at Esti and could tell by her face that she was busted. "You should have told her," he said. Esti told Leonard not to make it any worse than it was already. "Please shut up," she said. "Let me handle this!" Oh, yeh, okay, handle it?

My Aunt Eva was right. Not only did she say that her brother had no backbone, but she always said that Freddy was like an ostrich when he didn't want to deal with something—he buried his head in the sand every time. But this time was unforgiveable! I couldn't believe he had asked me to give up my baby for a lie! My baby! She was part of my blood and soul. They took away my baby girl and put her in a home that wasn't mine. She was the only being in the world who would have loved me. "I hate him and I hate all of you!" I shrieked. "Lock me up! Call the state! Tell them I'm crazy! I don't give a shit!" (And to think how the system handles young people who freak out—they are given pills and put away! Here you go, just shut up! I hated the system then and now. I feel helpless and wish I could change their horrible rules.) In my heart, I hoped that maybe my dad hadn't lied to me, but I knew he probably did. I hadn't spoken to him yet. "Call him, Esti, call him now!" She was upset, and I was lashing out to such an extreme degree that she had to call. Leonard didn't want to get involved, and as he walked away to his TV room, said to call the social worker.

Esti got my dad on the phone, and from the receiver I could hear Anita screaming my name and profanities in the background and that I had some nerve to call *her* house. Esti asked me if we could do this another day, and I gave her an adamant "no!" She asked Anita to get Freddy. Esti handed me the phone with Freddy on the line. Still crying, I asked him, "When are you coming to get me?"

"Libbe, please, stop your crying. You're upsetting me, and Anita is upset because you called," he said. They're upset, wow! Not me, of course, what did I have to be upset about? "This can wait, Libbe."

"No, it can't! I need to know from you now if I'm going to Florida or not." Anita was screeching at him to "hang up the god-damned phone on that tramp." Freddy answered, "No Libbe, you can't come here, not now and not ever! Anita won't stand for it, she will not have you! I'm sorry, but I did this for your own good. You don't need a baby." I could hear Anita shrieking. "I knew, and everyone else knew, that you would not have given up the baby unless you had a good reason. I had to do it for the baby's sake. You need to straighten out your life now. Anita, please! Shut up! Let me talk… I can't take you here, Libbe." He did it for his own sake, not for the baby's—how dare he do that! Shit! Shit! I could not believe my ears. I asked him if Esti knew, and he said that she did. "And did the social workers know too, Dad?"

"Yes, they did," he said. I couldn't listen to him or to Anita's screaming anymore. I dropped the receiver without saying goodbye to him. Esti ended the call. He lied! My dad had lied again! They had all lied… I will never believe him or anyone else again, ever! He had me believing him, and look what I gave up! How could I have given away my baby? What kind of person was I? A man who wasn't even my real dad had convinced me to give up my own child. I didn't care about anything anymore. I felt like I wanted to die. I did a terrible thing, and I didn't care what happened to me. I gave my baby up for that man, the man who had lied constantly throughout my life and turned his head the other way when Anita was brutalizing me. I wished for the worst to befall Anita and all the people who had used me. I knew that was wrong, but I didn't care. I was seething with hate for Anita most of all because she controlled my father, and he allowed her to do it. There was no turning back. I felt like my life was over. I decided I would run away, for good.

CHAPTER TWENTY-SIX

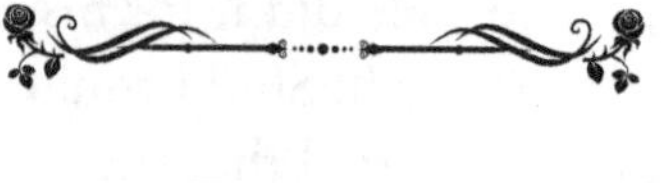

Runaway

I found out that Esti had lied to me on many other occasions as well—no surprise. The social worker had also concealed the truth. Liars! I had been set up. Pam said she wished she had been there with me. She would have told me to keep my baby. There was no way of getting her back. I asked. She was in her new home already. Once again, I later discovered that this was just another fabrication and it had taken a year for her to be placed. There had been a window of time when I could have gotten my baby girl back. Why wasn't I told? How I wished I had known!

It was intolerable in Canton, and staying wasn't an option for me given the way I felt. I had to get away. I wished I could live in my own space, outside in the fresh air, and be free from all the insincere and hypocritical people in my life. I started keeping a diary. Writing things down helped me get it out, even if no one ever reads it.

****

Now, in my cell, I hope I can live where waves hit the shore and trees sway in the breeze. I just want to sit in peace for the rest of my days on earth and write my stories. Since my last foster home, this has been my lifelong wish. That hasn't changed from the time of my younger years, but I've gotten trapped by a host of complications—the primary one being my habit of living for others' sake rather than my own. Oh, how it still hurts so, thinking of my baby girl who is grown now, how I lost out being in her life.

****

Finding out what had happened to my baby girl was going to become a lifelong mission. I couldn't speak with Jennifer and Silky about it because their response was the same as the others. Jennifer made a comment about my anger and how it would subside over time. My anger was fixated on what had happened. It was unwavering; it wasn't going away…and it never did. I was skeptical that she understood me, or the depth of my feelings of loss and betrayal. If she'd had to give up a baby of her own, she would have had a nervous breakdown. Surrounded by people who didn't care about the way I felt, I decided that living with Pam would solve my problems. She was the only one who understood.

I phoned Michael and told him I was planning to run away and that I would call him once I knew where I was going. We argued; he was against the idea. He tried talking me out of running, but I told him I was deeply hurt and offended by what was done to me. He sounded almost as if he cared. He told me that one day I might get the baby back and to hang in there. Really…I told him I wanted her now, not later, because I wanted to be the one who raised her. He asked me to come to see him and I refused, not wanting him to use me for a blowjob or sex, and then discard me as soon as he was finished. Why didn't he offer to get the money to find her? It was his baby too! I wasn't sure how I felt about him anymore. It was really going to happen—I was planning my move to leave Esti's home in Canton.

Pam had given me directions to her house. I had the clothes on my back and a couple of extra pieces of clothing, soap, toothpaste, and my favorite jacket. I realized that I didn't have any money to run away with, just a handful of quarters and some dollar bills. I put off going for a few weeks until I had saved over twenty dollars, enough to feel as though I was in a better position. The day I planned to leave arrived. Pam told me she would meet me at Grove Hall. I had to figure out a way of getting there. I considered taking the bus, but in the end I called Michael and convinced him I needed something to eat at Duchess Hamburger. I told him that maybe I could stay overnight. He came with his motorcycle, and I met him in Canton Center with my bag. I had slipped out when no one was at home, and the bag was so small Michael didn't even ask what was in it. We sped out of Canton to Mattapan and up Blue Hill Ave.

The ride was cold. Michael had on his thick jacket, and I was wearing a corduroy jacket with a long-sleeved shirt underneath. He must have assumed by the way I was dressed that we would be going to his house after we ate. I told him I was extremely hungry, all eighty-eight pounds of me. When we stopped at Duchess, I didn't see any of the crowd that usually hung out. I didn't feel much like talking to anyone anyway. He went in, and I stayed outside on his motorcycle to make sure no one messed with it. Michael took his keys with him, which was a first. Even though I didn't know how to drive the motorcycle, I guessed he was nervous about me stealing the bike knowing how good I drove cars. Michael knew from the last time I said I was running away and backed out that he could talk me out of it if we were face to face. I had to go immediately before he came out. I grabbed my bag, took off up Wellington Hill Street—running so fast—and cut down the first street behind Duchess, in the direction of Morton Street and the Brown Jug.

Michael was waiting in line, talking to people he knew. He never suspected I would have time to escape. Feet flying, I went down side streets because I knew that he would try to find me on Blue Hill Ave. Luckily, I caught the bus past Morton Street just as it pulled up to the curb. The bus driver let me out at Grove Hall. Pam had arrived a few minutes before me. I approached her with a smile, still gasping for breath. I had made it—perfect timing—I was so relieved. We walked the back streets to her place behind Egleston Station. It was a steep climb up Parker Hill Ave. Although I experienced a sense of freedom from the adrenalin surging through my body, I was tense because I had to stay hidden. Like a fugitive, I kept looking behind me to see if anyone was following me. Above all else, I didn't want to get caught.

I only had to wait until I turned eighteen to be free, but that seemed like forever to me!

It was a shock to Michael that I had actually run away, and he had no idea where I was or how to reach me. Esti didn't understand my reasons for running away from her dysfunctional family; I was just being "bad" again. My running away had a lot to do with her and her husband lying, as well as all the other things on my list. Also, "I've washed my hands of you," still echoes in my mind. That was what Freddy said about me having the baby. I beat myself up for getting attached to anyone.

Seventeen in November, I was able to read people's faces and body language so accurately I knew whether or not they were lying—or, so I thought, most people—thanks to my many experiences of having my dad and others lie to me. I felt as though I had the power of foreknowledge, and many times I thought that I had been to places I had never gone before, I seemed to know the surroundings. Of course, I was still immature, more so than other girls my age with normal childhoods, and was certainly naive compared to the girls at the home for unwed mothers. Pam never missed an opportunity to tell me I was a real square. Even today, after a life filled with brutality, I still enjoy watching cartoons. I can be naive, still wanting to believe. Fairy tales are such a better place to be. And even at the age I am now, people continue to lie to me. I understand that certain people feel compelled to lie. I simply move on. As a mature woman, I look back and see how dark my childhood was and know that staying optimistic is one of the ways I sustain myself and remain young at heart.

I had been quiet on the way to Pam's apartment. After climbing the steep hill, we were finally there. I crushed the rest of the cigarette I was having with my shoe in case she didn't allow smoking in her apartment, but, of course, she did—what was I thinking? She smokes! My nervousness prevented me from concentrating much on my surroundings at first. I had liked Esti's old, two-family house in Mattapan. Pam's house in Roxbury reminded me somewhat of Esti's, but not quite as big or fancy. Her apartment was in a small portion of a newly sectioned two-family house. We entered through the back door because Pam's bedroom was where the living room should have been, with French doors that opened to the hallway. She had blocked off the entrance so that there were two bedrooms in a one-bedroom apartment. The room where I would be staying was small, between the kitchen and living room. She told me the room used to be her bedroom, but because it was so small, she put her bed in the living room and a narrow couch bed in the original tiny room. There was a kitchen table with chairs, and a bathroom. It was a warm and cozy place with lots of detail.

I thought she had a girl for a roommate, but she told me her live-in boyfriend was at work. He was a few years older than her, and his nickname was Rosey because of his rosy personality that was so different and uncharacteristic of most men. Even though I thought it was an odd name for a guy, I liked the name simply because it brought up the image of roses and my mom. I told Pam not to worry about my telling anyone where I was, and if I got caught, I would tell them that I had told her I was just visiting. She knew my character, that I would never squeal. She knew she could trust my word. A promise was a promise, and staying true to my word was a way of compensating for all the people who disappointed me in life. I keep my word even now, though everyone else, with very few exceptions, still fails to keep theirs.

As I put away my things, I felt free. Pam was cooking something that smelled so good to me; I had never breathed in such an aroma before. I hadn't eaten since the morning, long before leaving Michael in the dust at Duchess. I asked about her baby. She said her mom was raising the baby while she finished school and that she had a job that paid her decent wages. We spoke about what had happened to me and my baby, and the longer I spoke, the angrier I became, an upsetting emotion that was immediately followed by an overwhelming sadness. I started crying. Pam consoled me the way a mother would. She told me it may take some time, but that it was not impossible to find the baby one day; I would need a lot of money. And if I went through the state it might be impossible. Unaware of all the obstacles I would encounter later, I was still hopeful. When she mentioned money, I began to worry that I didn't have a job. We even spoke about finding my biological mother. However, I wasn't quite sure if I was ready to do that yet—I didn't even know her name. Finding the baby came first, and I understood that attorneys were expensive and that my baby girl was placed by a private agency, J.F.C.S. At the time, I had no idea how hard it was going to be to deal with them. I had been sheltered from Pam's lifestyle and the kind of life I was soon to enter. Like a newborn entering the world, I was about to experience real life for the first time.

Pam's boyfriend came home from work. We said hello. He wasn't that tall and his skin was light, like Pam's. He was Portuguese, she told me. I had never met a Portuguese person before. He was thin and had an Afro. They kissed. Pam's lips were full, though not too thick, and her eyes were almond-shaped and sexy. I thought she was so pretty. Watching her expressions when they kissed so softly and when she spoke fascinated me—her whole face was talking. When we sat down to eat, Rosey asked me questions about my family, and I replied with scant details, only about my dad and the baby. I never mentioned my childhood in Stoneham because that was a deep, dark secret. Even though I had a place to stay, with people who were friendly to me, getting through the night was rough, especially because Rosey was a stranger and a man. Pam told me not to worry and said I was safe with her. She would take me to look for a job in a few days. We stayed up late talking and smoking cigarettes.

Pam told me things about life and men that I never knew. She spoke about the differences between young, white males who lived in the suburbs and white men in the city, and she compared young, black males in the suburbs to those in the city. She referred to everyone in the suburbs as "squares." We touched on black and white relations for a very brief time, but long enough for me to grasp the politics of skin color and the reason so many whites were prejudiced, particularly certain neighborhoods in Boston. She only said that it was easier for her out here because she was light-skinned, that it was tougher for her dark-skinned parents in the society they grew up in. Racial tension was never explained to me, and the only time I thought about it was when I went to school in Sharon with my friend. I never imagined that prejudice existed outside the school and town. There had been race riots on Blue Hill Ave. in June of 1967.

I recalled when my dad sent away my colored nanny because of the prejudice of the woman who lived next door. I would have remained naive about race if Pam hadn't spoken to me and I hadn't moved to the city. I was comfortable and felt safe staying with her. I was in the school of life, taking a course in people, learning more and more about what they did and why. So much to learn. Children do not conceive of prejudice until they learn about hate from their parents and peers. That hate lives on in the form of racial profiling and police violence against blacks to this day, as well as other races too.

We crashed after two in the morning. I slept soundly, though when I awoke I was still tired from the ordeal of the day before and was very hungry from the smell of toast that wafted through the apartment. Pam knew I could eat; she used to watch me pack away food at the house in Mattapan. I never drank liquor, but I'd had a drink the evening before and was mildly hungover. Pam said she'd introduce me to the man who owned ABC Linen at the bottom of the hill. According to Pam, he was a bit weird, an old Jewish guy, but cool with the ladies at work he liked. Weird…I didn't need more anxiety. The pain of leaving my baby girl behind was still fresh in my mind, as was my agitation about running away and my fear of getting caught. The last thing I wanted was to go back to Esti's house. They only cared about their own skins. None of them, my dad included, gave a shit if I lived or died.

People in his family didn't see how Freddy buried his head in the sand, and what an actress Anita was—the greatest actress I had ever witnessed with my own eyes. Not only did I learn how to sew, crochet, and clean from Anita, I learned how to hate, how to starve, how to feel ashamed, and how to accept beatings. All of this taught me to rebel, and clearly, I was rebelling now. I rejected the foster parents who stole, lied, and exposed me to sexual abuse. People like them never get caught behind their white picket-fenced life. I hoped Pam wouldn't harm me; she was my friend, and I believed in her. Maybe in helping a friend you are helping yourself just as much. How does anyone know for certain? And if friends let us down, do we continue trusting? I didn't know what a true friend was until later in life. I knew Pam from school and saw her only when I could get out, visiting her at her house or meeting her on Blue Hill Ave. She always had friends partying at her apartment, and for me that was exciting. But I never seemed to fit in. I was too private and shy, and never looked stylish enough. Because Pam and Rosey were in a relationship, staying with them was only supposed to be a temporary arrangement until I could afford a place of my own. I felt like an intruder. I dreamed every day about having a space where, even though I really didn't want to be alone, I could be free, and draw and put things I loved there.

We were both tired the next day from staying up so late, and it showed. The day after, we went down the hill to the ABC Linen Co. The huge, brick factory had many people working in it, mostly women, and I felt intimidated. It was hot inside from the steam machines. There were huge fans everywhere and rows of tables where women were folding laundry. Mammoth machines stood behind them. I wondered which job I would have. Could I learn to do this work? Pam went into the office to find the owner, and a stout old man with a cigar hanging out of his mouth came back out with her. I smelled the stink of the cigar smoke long before he was close to me. And as I inhaled it, I remembered my dad's friends from his truck driving days with their stogies and Dad with his sweet-smelling pipe. Pam introduced me as a sweet little Jewish girl, and he smiled as the cigar smoke billowed into the steamy air. "A Jewish girl, huh? So, are you ready to work, young lady?" he asked. His teeth were stained a faded brownish-gray. I nodded my head and told him yes. "Six a.m. tomorrow," he said, and he came even closer to me and pinched my cheek. "You're right," he said, "she *is* sweet." I didn't pay much attention to his comment at that moment. He would be paying me cash per day, and because of that, Pam said, no one would ever find me. I was happy. I could pay my way and help out. Then Pam told me she and Rosey were going to see some friends that night to play cards, and did I want to come? Again, my answer was yes. I certainly didn't want to be in my tiny room all alone. I was always frightened to be by myself, especially at night in a darkened, empty apartment that was not familiar.

After Rosey showered, he put on a sweet smelling men's cologne, Aramis, a scent I had never smelled on any of the boys or men I knew. Pam was snapping her chewing gum as always, wearing her oversized hoop earrings, the kind she always wore, and lipstick. She gave me some hot pink lipstick to wear and I liked it (it became my lifetime signature lip color). We hiked up to the top of Parker Hill Ave. to Pam's friends' apartment…another steep hill to climb.

When we got there and went inside the apartment, I immediately noticed there was something different about the girls. They were broad, masculine, and rough looking—not the kind of women I was used to seeing, but they were friendly. As Pam, Rosey, Sharley, Kathy, and four others sat down to play cards, I excused myself because I didn't know the game they were playing; plus, I was somewhat uncomfortable meeting these people for the first time. I knew how to play poker. My dad and mom's relatives would play pinochle, gin rummy, and poker. Most of the women played mahjong. I sat on a chair in the corner to wait. They told me that the TV was in the living room through the French doors and to make myself comfortable. There was a big couch and coffee table, but the only light in the darkened room came from the TV. It seemed peaceful where I was sitting compared to the next room. They were loud and boisterous, like Silky and his friends when they played cards for money.

They played gin for hours, drank, and ordered Chinese food. Pam brought me a plate because she knew I was shy around people I didn't know. I peered around the corner and could see they were having fun. I asked Pam if I could call Michael, and she laughed at me for asking permission. She did warn me to be careful about telling him where I was. I promised her I wouldn't say anything. I agreed it was possible he could betray me like the others. "Why would he?" I replied. "He doesn't care what I do, only what he gets."

Rosey yelled out, "He doesn't give a shit about you so why bother calling him!" Maybe he was right about that. I was so grateful when Pam offered me some more food. I didn't want to take seconds because I hadn't made any money to chip in yet. I gave her ten dollars, half of the money I had, not counting the emergency quarters. "Keep it," she said, "I'll take it later."

"No, please take it!" I insisted. Soon enough, I would learn "nothing for nothing" and "something gets something"...just not tonight.

Michael was still fuming that I had taken off that day without calling him right back. The anger in his voice frightened me, and I came close to hanging up. He asked me why I had run off from him like that. "I would have taken you wherever you wanted," is what he told me. I explained that I was afraid he was going to call Esti to warn her, and I didn't want to get him in trouble with the authorities. Also, I was scared that if I told him now where I was he'd come and take me back to her house, so I put him off by saying that I would tell him later. That kept him quiet. He knew that I was serious about running away now. At first, he thought I was kidding. He told me that Esti had called him several times looking for me, and he told her he hadn't seen me at all. He lied for me, so I felt that I could trust him. I gave in and told him that I was with my girlfriend in Boston and he could come by soon, being careful not to reveal more just yet. Michael said he would take me for a ride on any weekend I chose. I loved to ride free, with the wind blowing my hair all over. I agreed to it even though I was hurt by the way he ignored talking about our baby girl. If he had showed an interest in his child, I wouldn't have felt so alone. It was late, and I had fallen asleep on the couch with the phone beside me. Pam and Rosey woke me. "Let's go home," they said. I had work in the morning. The evening was cool, and as we walked home I was cold. I had no warm clothes with me. There were stars in the sky, reminding me that my mom was watching, and I thought about how I would still be in school if Michael hadn't met me that night in the old Rambler. We all went directly to bed as soon as we passed through the front door. I slept so soundly I never heard the alarm clock in the morning. But, believe me, Pam woke my butt up!

Rosey was up and gone by five-thirty a.m. Pam told me that because ABC Linen was a factory, there was a certain way to dress. I borrowed some clothes from her for the first day, and I looked presentable for work in a factory even though her black pants and shirt were a bit too big for me. We were right on time. The boss took me around, introducing me, parading me through the factory the whole time with his hand on my shoulder like a dead weight, all the while speaking with his foul cigar in and out of his mouth and breathing in my face between puffs. Listening to the sounds of the machinery in the background, I watched the steam rise high up to the tall ceilings like clouds in an indoor sky. He said I could start by folding and afterward I would be trained for other jobs. I followed the other women's lead as they worked, and he looked pleased as he watched me. He seemed to be so considerate and friendly, even paternal. By the end of the day, I had made a few dollars in pay. The boss patted me on the back and with his wide smile and smelly cigar said that he would see me in the morning. "Come in at five forty-five," he said. I was supposed to come at six-thirty, so I asked, "Why do I have to come in early, sir?"

He said, "Just come earlier. I'm going to train you on a machine." Okay. Then I was out the door with everyone else, and a girl winked at me. I hadn't the slightest idea why. I smiled and walked faster. I couldn't wait to get home to share my day's experience and contribute money to help out, giving Pam all my pay except for what it would cost me to maintain my habit of smoking Marlboro cigarettes. Pam explained she cooked for Rosey every night, and we went off to the grocery store to buy food for dinner. Everything was working out. Wanting to be punctual the next day, I went to bed early and got there on time. I was being trained on the press machine by an older lady who, as he put it, "would show me the ropes." She was there waiting for me with the boss man. The boss told me I was a great worker and learned fast. Like my time at the Youth Service Board when I managed the Hobart machines, I was quick to master this machine and was proud of myself. I was hungry for praise, something I rarely got.

I was speaking to Michael almost every night after work. When I asked Pam if she thought I should see him, she just shrugged her shoulders. Finally, Michael and I took a ride on his motorcycle. He met me at the bottom of Parker Hill Ave. I didn't tell him Pam's address, but I sensed he already had an idea of where the apartment was from seeing me walk down the hill. I would find that out soon enough. He didn't know I had a job, and we did not discuss the baby—the subject was far too tender for me to talk about. I tried to push the baby from my mind, but I dreamt about her face every night. I would wake up abruptly in a sweat, believing she was there with me. Pam and Rosey assured me that it would fade with time. I did not talk about Anita, or my past, or my baby girl anymore. That was too private. I held everything inside me. I concentrated on my new job and dreamed about what I would do someday. I visualized Florida, sitting on the beach next to the ocean while watching and listening to the waves break onshore. There were tall palm trees swaying in the breeze, like the ones that so impressed me when I first went there. Maybe I would have a chance to see them again someday—and see my dad?

Pam and Rosey were happy for me. They reassured me over and over that I was safe with them. I felt more confident and couldn't wait to go to work every day. Michael and I were speaking more and more, although there was something missing. The connection I had once felt wasn't there; I didn't feel the need to be wanted by him. Even though I didn't have experience with anyone besides him, I was growing up, and didn't feel like a little girl anymore. I wanted more, like the way Rosey behaved with Pam. They showed real love and tenderness, with romance… When I would hear them in their room, the sounds they made were gentle, not like Michael, who pounded away so hard during sex that it hurt, and I screamed out. When they hugged and kissed in front of me, they touched each other softly. I had seen that only in old, romantic movies from the forties, and I didn't know it could happen in actual life.

It was a relief when Michael told me that Esti wasn't calling anymore. I phoned Huckie to let him know I was alive, and he couldn't believe I'd stayed away so long. He said he never knew the details because no one had called. He begged to see me and told me we could get a place together next year. He said he would save up his money. That was the last time I called him for a while. By the time I was mature enough to appreciate Huckie, I was much older. The people at the factory seemed to like me. I concentrated on my work. The longer I was there, the more confident I became.

The old man at ABC had always been so friendly toward me; why didn't I see what was coming next? It had happened before… A man is "nice" to me and I hope that he is sincere, but there's an ulterior motive—and this time was no different than the others. Did Pam know how he was? Did she set me up? I wondered. Of course, she did, and I had trusted her. Every night for the past several days, he asked me to stay later to make a few extra dollars. I agreed at first, and then he got too comfortable, standing behind me at the machines with his body pressed against mine. When I stayed later, he would talk to me, asking me questions. Pam had let him know that I needed more money, something she never should have done behind my back. There were a couple of guys who worked late, so for the most part, I was comfortable staying until it was time for them to quit for the day. This one night, the others left, and he came out of his office asking if I was hungry and offering me part of his sandwich. It was from some Jewish deli, either pastrami or corned beef, piled thickly on dark rye bread with kosher pickles. I felt uncomfortable and moved as far away from him as I could; not even the food tempted me. Then he asked if I wanted to make extra money. In that instant, I understood—as he pointed to his pants and touched his crotch. How dare he! I was revolted by the old man's advances and tossed aside the sandwich he handed me. I didn't have an answer prepared for him and was frightened. Anxiously, I told him that it was late, and I wanted to go. I said I was happy with the extra time and money but didn't want any more, thanks, just my regular hours. "Oh come on," he said, "you're a big girl, and you know how this works." How what works, is this what jobs are? "A birdy told me that you had a baby, so you know what it's all about." He came over to me and, touching my shoulder, told me how much he liked me and what a sweet Jewish girl I was, that's why he was so attracted to me. He said he would help me climb the ladder and get to the top in the factory. I felt the same queasiness in my stomach that I did with the gardener, the man in Malden, Archie, and all the other men who had taken advantage of me up to that very moment. I thought, *No, not again!* I pulled away and took off out of the building as fast as my legs would take me.

That was my last day, and although I was owed a day's pay, I never went back to collect my money. I found out later that Pam was his "special" friend; she would see him after the factory closed. When I told Michael what happened, he said not to go back, and he gave me twenty dollars for food. I was grateful, but what should I say to Pam? I was angry, but I thought it would be better to stuff it down and keep it to myself. She was supposed to be my friend, but I couldn't count on her to have my back. The money Michael gave me would run out soon, and then how could I pay her to stay in the apartment? I had nowhere to go. I still wonder to this day why she sold me out. If I had stayed at the factory and made the extra money, where would I be today?

CHAPTER TWENTY-SEVEN

A Big Shock

I can hear lots of chatter from a group of FBI agents as they come closer. Two of the men and a woman enter my cell and speak to me for a moment. The female agent informs me they are waiting for my lawyer to speak to the judge. After they leave, I flash back to my thoughts. I had stayed at the same place I was when the agents came in, like I had paused a movie and then pressed the button to resume watching. I am thirsty, but I don't tell anyone. I take my mind off this white room with glass doors by going back.

****

I didn't speak with Pam about everything that happened at the factory that night, but I believed she knew the reason I quit. She said she spoke to the owner. When she asked me what happened, I didn't say anything except that it was awkward, and I didn't like it. I was leery now, unsure of whether I was living in the kind of place that was right for me. I didn't speak much to Pam and Rosey, and I felt that they were probably aware of my discomfort. My life was about to change completely and at a rate that was so fast I could hardly keep up with myself.

There was a card game at Pam and Rosey's friends' house that weekend. Michael had given me more money to help me out. It was

Friday, the day everyone had waited for to party. They were so over the top with drinking and drugging that night that Michael asked me to move out of there when I told him. Unlike Huckie, it never occurred to Michael to get a place. After Pam had picked up my money from the dirty old man, she mentioned that if she needed cash she could always get it from him, and he was like a second father to her. *Like a father?* I asked myself. No father would ever do what he did. "The old man is really cool," she kept repeating. "Give him another chance—you won't regret it." No thanks! It wasn't until later that I fully understood what was really going on. Michael tried to warn me that living with Pam and Rosey wasn't the best situation for me. And he pressured me to leave with him and go back to Esti's house until I was eighteen. But I stayed in their apartment, not wanting to go back to foster care and that hypocritical family. I could tell he was pissed off!

Rosey came home for supper and sat down while Pam was cooking and I set the table. I loved her spicy Portuguese dishes and hot soul food that was so rich in flavor. Jewish food was completely out of the question, and spaghetti was not on the menu either. We were all talking, and when we finished eating, Pam wanted her cigarettes and lighter from her dresser. She asked me to get them and, of course, I did as I was told. When I went into her bedroom, there was a package of condoms on her bureau and what appeared to be a rubber penis. It was shocking! I'd never seen anything like that before. I didn't know what it was called, and although I didn't quite know how to phrase the question, I was so curious that while we were smoking I asked, "Pam, what is the rubber thing on your dresser?" Pam and Rosey both looked at me in such a way I thought I was wrong for asking, but then Pam broke out laughing so hard she started coughing and Rosey joined in, gasping for air because his laughter was so raucous. "It's a dildo," Pam managed to say.

"What does that mean?" I said, puzzled. Rosey asked, "You don't know? We use it in bed. You're that green?" Still puzzled, I asked again. Pam said that Rosey sometimes used it on her during sex. "But why does he use it if he has a penis of his own?" They both looked at each other, puzzled and surprised. Pam told me that Rosey was not a man, she was a woman, and Pam thought I knew by now. "No way, how would I know that?" I had been there for over three weeks and it never occurred to me that Rosey was a girl. I stood up. "Are you serious? He's a girl?" I said.

"Do you want to see?" Rosey asked. Pam was laughing again. "It's okay, Lib, we're lesbians," Pam announced. Rosey lifted her shirt. She had breasts! I broke away from the conversation and immediately left the kitchen—I was shocked! Now I was even more confused. Lesbians? What the hell is that? I had never conceived of lesbians or lesbian sex before. Two girls together having sex…how did they do it? I locked myself in my room trying to sort all this out. Pam called to me to come out so that she could explain. "Why did everyone lie to me?" I asked through the door.

"How come? You had to be with a man to have your baby, right?" Rosey called, "Come on out. We're not going to bother you. You're being so immature!" It took me a while to come out, and when I did I felt stupid. My friend Pam was with a girl? I had her explain her baby and father bit, and she told me that she had a boyfriend then. All my questions, and there were many of them, were answered, even the one about the old man at ABC Linen Co. She explained that the old man gave her money in exchange for sexual favors. She said that the he liked being touched, and she would get fifty dollars each time. He would give girls extra money if they kissed him or let him feel them up, and more if they touched him. She told me that all her friends were lesbians.

"All of them? What about Kathy?" I asked.

"Kathy, too," she said. I was stunned, and frightened because I wasn't certain about how to act or where I fit in. I couldn't believe the old man gave Pam that much money. I was learning about female sex at a pace that was too quick for me, and I was about to learn even more. I kept my bedroom door locked that night and many nights after that. Although I hated feeling closed in, I didn't know what to expect from anyone. Because they hadn't told me about their lesbianism from the start, I felt as though they had lied to me, and I was uneasy about trusting them at all. Who could I trust?

****

I stretched my back. It hurt. Oh, what time is it? Is anyone going to get me out of here? I rested my head in my hands for a short while then sat up again as I've been doing from the start, back straight, almost motionless. I am not able to rest at all. My stress level is so high. Shit, I'm scared. They are probably watching my every move. I could try to listen to the jumbled conversation going on in the hall, but I choose to think about my past. I don't want to be sidetracked from my train of thought. I prefer to stay in the past rather than worry about my uncertain future. I worry that if I do not give up my business I can land in jail once more and do time for years. I can't afford that at my age. Do I want to risk my freedom again? I don't want to be locked up in the straight world either. So many people feel trapped. I hear that from my clients: trapped at home, trapped at the office, even business owners feel that way. Who is really free? I suppose society has us locked up in one way or another. We are in the womb until we are born, schooled for years, work until retirement if you can afford to—if you can't then you will probably work until you are in your eighties, still under the gun—or until you drop dead, only to leave all your money to your children and grandchildren after the few so-called golden years you have left. Those should be called the "gray years." Some smart and savvy people manage to have fun and relax in their retirement, but how many people really attain their dreams? All we are told is that we have to have money for retirement. That's it—money! Money is at the root of our loss of freedom. I see why some people want to live off the land somewhere, but that's not free either. To park yourself on the land you have to buy it, or live out in the wilderness. Is life really fair? Really being alive, if only for a moment, is when you are released from society's constrictions. We are all in an earthly bubble, beginning to end, supported until of an age, then released into the world to work and deal with it. So what is "free"...are we ever really free?

CHAPTER TWENTY-EIGHT

Meeting W.D.

I have spent enough time thinking about the power of the almighty buck. What if I get a long sentence and I have to go to prison? I would have ample opportunity to write about my life story as time passed. I could put all my diaries together to create an autobiography—that is what I want to do. My experiences with gay women turned out to have an enormous impact on my life. When I was introduced to them I was, as Pam constantly told me, a square. But nothing intimidates me now that I have seen so much. My life was not normal before or from then on. It's better for me to think positively. Maybe my angels will help me; they always have. It's what I want to believe. I want out of here!

****

Pam and Rosey went over what they had explained to me again and did the best they could so I would understand. After my initial shock, I was grasping things much better. Although I was more curious, my interest certainly did not extend to having sex with another woman. I had just started taking an interest in boys, and I was having sex regularly with Michael and using protection. The girls calmed me down by telling me that they would never touch me. That was a promise, unless, of course, I chose to. I was like their little girl, and they were watching out for me. Lesbians were not like men, they said. They reassured me they would never force themselves on me nor would any of their friends. I understood but kept my distance.

I liked them, but I stayed straight—I was only attracted to boys. That was the first thing they would explain to their friends. Now I understood why some of them were so masculine and Kathy and Pam were always waiting on them, bringing them food or a drink, the way a woman typically would serve a man. I usually watched TV in Sharley and Kathy's living room, but one night they taught me how to play their version of gin. It was cool learning how to play. It was a new challenge, and I was getting good at it. I was not quite confident enough to lose money yet. I needed to practice, so whenever I could, I played. Pam would get annoyed with me for asking so many questions all the time. Sharley had a brother who would be coming over soon, and they joked about what it would be like if he and I got together. I didn't care and never thought twice about it. No other man ever came there. "You like boys so much," they said, "but he is more of a man." I paid no attention to their teasing. They all spoke about him in such elevated terms I thought he must be a king. I went into the sitting room to get away from them; that was my comfort zone.

I saw a reflection while looking at the TV screen that night and quickly turned in the direction of the doorway. When he came through the French doors, I saw a tall, light-skinned black man wearing a long, black cashmere coat, shiny textured shoes, and a Stacy Adams hat like the one my dad wore to go to temple. He wore sweet cologne, even more alluring than Rosey's—I had never smelled anything like that before. I was mesmerized by his appearance and the way he carried himself. He looked like a movie star to me. Then he spoke to me so low and softly he sent shivers down my spine. He introduced himself as W.D. He asked who I was and where I came from. I told him willingly, leaving out the part that I had run away. He asked if he could sit with me. Butterflies fluttered in my stomach. In a shaky voice, I told him yes. He tugged at the lapels of his coat, putting them side to side neatly in place as he sat down. He said, "I think I'll sit with you for a spell. Do you mind?" I coughed, and without choking I managed to say no, I didn't mind. He stood and took off his coat, making himself more comfortable. He folded it in a refined way so that it wouldn't wrinkle. I was sitting next to this well-dressed, handsome man with an incredible scent, and the whole experience was something surreal. The mere sight of him made me light up inside. I asked him what cologne he was wearing, and he said, "Champagne. Only certain people wear it. Will you remember it?" Of course, I would. I would remember it always. I was used to Michael in his leather jacket, and though Michael was rich, he looked scruffy in comparison. Once in a while, Michael would splash on Old Spice, a scent I will never forget either because my dad wore it too.

W.D. told me how pretty I was and how he'd like to take me out sometime. Me? Out? I told him that I had a boyfriend, and I wasn't sure; maybe someday. He told me he would have to buy me something to wear if I went out with him. Buy me clothes? I didn't have a response to that. I didn't know what to say. I assumed he was rich and wondered what kind of job he had. Speaking in that hypnotic way of his, sitting close to me and almost whispering in my ear, made me feel like a queen. I thought of how many times in my life I had fought for the slightest amount of attention, and here it was flowing from the mouth of this man. Even though I didn't understand all the slang he used, I was enraptured by the sound of his voice. When he said he had to leave, he told me that he would see me soon. I missed him already. I had just met him. How could that be? I couldn't wait to share all this with Pam. No other boy ever had such a magnetic effect on me. The girls sitting at the card table chuckled and commented that I was glowing. I knew that the next afternoon Michael would be picking me up in his car because when it was too cold or snowy he didn't take his motorcycle. I considered cancelling because I didn't want to see him, especially not now, but refusing him would only pique his curiosity.

It was the time of year when the weather was changing and getting colder. Rosey approached me, just like a man would, and warned me to take it slow. She said, "Easy, girl. W.D. is too fast for you. Back off…" That made me more curious. I didn't understand what Rosey was trying to tell me. I couldn't get W.D. out of my mind. Rosey wanted Pam to talk me out of seeing him, but Pam said it was okay. "What's the harm?" she said. "He knows she's a square." Pam told me that there was a difference in me, that I lit up like a light bulb when I was with W.D. No one told me just who he was beyond Sharley's brother. Why was he a subject they weren't willing to discuss? Was he married?

When I talked to Pam about W.D., I was enthusiastic and she, in turn, initially seemed to lack emotion; on purpose, I guess, to stay neutral about my attraction. But then she said, "Libbe, he's too fast for you, and you're not ready for that kind of life yet. Rosey and I talked about it, and she's right." I really wanted to know more about W.D. Pam said she understood how I felt, but how could she possibly know? Did it ever happen to her? She told me she became excited when she was with someone she was attracted to, especially the first time she was with them. I had never felt this way before. "Be cool," she told me, "it's a physical attraction, nothing more. You have to learn the difference." She told me that W.D. visited sometimes, but she was certain that he would be coming around more often because of me.

"What should I do?" I asked her.

"That's up to you," she replied. "I can't tell you what to do. Just don't rush into anything until all the cards are on the table." I didn't understand what she meant.

Michael met me at the bottom of the hill the next day. He gave me money for Pam. We drove for a while, had some food, and then he wanted me to go back to his house with him to have sex. I didn't want to have sex with him. I felt different. I wanted to go home in case W.D. came around. I was obsessed, thinking about him all the time now, not Michael. It must have shown because Michael asked me what was wrong. "Why are you acting so weird?" When we were at the bottom of the hill, he revved his car's engine a couple of times, then went up the hill so fast I didn't have time to stop him. I didn't know that W.D. and his friend would be outside the apartment. When W.D. saw me, he approached me and said, "Hey, baby," which was all he had to do to set off Michael, who was furious. "Who the hell is that?" Michael asked. I was freaking out and told him that

I had only met the man twice. He thought I was lying. I could tell he wanted to hit me. Michael said that he was taking me with him and not bringing me back. We argued, and W.D. stepped in and told him to leave me alone. "You heard the lady. She doesn't want to go with you." It was true—I didn't want to go with Michael. "You heard her, she wants to stay." As he was speaking, W.D. grabbed my arm and pulled me to him, "You need to leave! You're out of your element, boy." W.D. meant what he said, and Michael could see he was not going to back down. Big shot Michael, who was always fighting someone, didn't challenge this black man. As he sped off, he told me he'd be back for me. I was sad, but at the same time this man, who didn't even know me, had stood up for me. I was totally infatuated with him and even more so now that I was under his spell.

"Thank you."

He smiled and touched my chin. "No problem, baby girl. For you, I'd do anything." I felt my knees buckling as if I were a 19th century lady about to fall to the floor in a faint. I still hadn't told him I had run away, and I wondered if Pam had told him yet. All I knew was that I was falling for this man who was a stranger to me. W.D. asked me if I was okay, and then asked me if Michael was my boyfriend. When I told him yes, he delivered a line I'll never forget. He said, "You need a man, baby, not a boy. He's not for you." What he said made my heart beat to his tune. I thought he was so sexy. All the hate I'd felt toward men for touching me washed away like sand at the edge of the shore after a turbulent storm. That was the first time I heard those words and not the last—I would remember them for the rest of my life.

****

I catch my breath. Just reminiscing about the first time meeting W.D. had that effect on me. I am getting hungry and thirsty. My stomach is growling and my mouth is so dry. I hate this room… This is not a hotel where I can call for room service. I am in a jail, and there is no Whole

Foods here. This is where my life will take a sharp turn. There was no going back…then or now.

****

I wondered what would happen next with W.D. This didn't seem like a usual night; my senses were acute from the encounter between he and Michael. He walked me into Rosey's apartment, stood at the door, and told me he would see me later that night when he came to visit his sister's apartment. "You *will* be there?" he asked me. It seemed like he was a master of fortunes, with special foreknowledge of where I would be. Then, pulling my shoulders to his body, he kissed my forehead and I melted as though I was sinking in quicksand. I had never felt this way before. I could smell the scent of his cologne on my face, permeating my pores and hair. I asked about the name and he told me, "Champagne, baby…" I was thrilled he would be coming by and wanted to look my best. Pam helped me find a suitable outfit to wear to Sharley's. They had all told Pam that I was like putty in W.D.'s hands. Rosey protested the way a parent would, pointing out that I was too vulnerable. I didn't care what they said to me. I wore pink lipstick and a touch of black mascara Pam applied. My brown eyes looked huge. I wanted to hear W.D.'s sexy, smooth voice talking to me. My dad and my baby girl were on hold. I was not thinking about how upset Michael was—I didn't care. Michael, well, had I been thinking about him I would have called him back to apologize. He didn't have my number, and there was no way for him to call and yell at me. Feeling so special, I didn't consider anyone or anything else. I couldn't wait to go up that hill to his sister's apartment, and Pam kept telling me to calm down.

When we got there, I was flitting around the apartment while everyone else watched, looking at the clock again and again. It was getting late and he hadn't shown. I was afraid he wasn't coming, and my heart hurt just like it did when my dad said he would come by and never showed up. Why did this stranger have such a compelling hold over me? I watched TV, trying not to care or get upset. I shouldn't have been such a fool because now it was so late we would be leaving soon. I was not as bubbly as I had been when we first arrived. Everyone told me that he would come another day and to stop freaking out. I sat quietly in the kitchen with my head bowed, listening to them making fun of me. W.D.'s sister said, "Poor baby, you miss your daddy?" I wasn't familiar with the term "daddy." She and the others were taunting me, and I figured Pam had told them about my dad. I had enough and was ready to leave.

"Please, can we go home now?" I asked Pam just as W.D. appeared, entering the room like royalty. He looked at me and said, "You're here. Come here, baby, let me see you." I stood clumsily at first, and as I walked over to him, I felt more confident. He touched me gently and turned me around. The hours of pain dissolved like specks of dust floating away. "You look good enough for me to take you out," he said and mentioned a place off Tremont Street. "But not tonight, baby," he said, "...soon." It was late. He told me the club would be closing. He explained that he wanted to be sure I wasn't still seeing my boyfriend before he put time into being with me. He had business to attend to and stayed for only a short time, just enough for me to want him more. "So what about it?" he asked. "Are you done with your boyfriend?" I stood there speechless. I wondered what kind of business he was in to be out this late at night, but I didn't ask him. "Yes, I will tell Michael goodbye." I was so struck by W.D. that I couldn't wait until the next time I saw him. I wanted to go to bed so morning would come sooner.

I wasn't aware that Michael was so furious and was not letting go of what happened. I had to break it off with him so I could see W.D. Change was hard for me. I imagined myself fading away, out of his life and my former life forever. I sensed the old familiar guilt I always felt when I didn't please Michael. I didn't want to call him, but I had to. When I was finally in bed and ready to sleep, I thought about how the different parts of my body would feel when W.D. touched me. I was happier than I had ever felt before. I was alive, totally infatuated, and unafraid. Michael was good looking, and within his group he was considered to be tough, but his reputation didn't follow him beyond Milton and Mattapan. That was his world. Like boys from other towns—whether North Shore, Stoneham,

Sharon, or Mattapan—they felt invincible when they were in their own territory. Michael hadn't gotten his way with me now because of W.D. coming into the picture, and that stoked his temper. He had been on W.D.'s turf, not his own. I was on W.D.'s territory now, out of my element.

The next day, the police were outside Pam's door with Leonard and Michael. Although he never gave the slightest clue, Michael knew precisely where I was living and had called my foster parents. Leonard was furious with me, and his friend from Station Ten, a policeman, was there with him—scaring me to death. He was arresting me for running away. I was outraged by Michael's betrayal. My own feelings of being special disappeared as quickly as they had come. I figured I would not be seeing W.D. ever again, and I wouldn't be let out of jail for a long time the way Leonard was talking. Since Michael broke my trust, Leonard changed his mind about him—they were buddies now.

I immediately started planning to run away again, and this next time, I wouldn't go back because no one would be able to find me. Leonard had his own plan. He told his officer friend to lock me up for the night to teach me a good lesson. That was not what I thought would happen, but it did. Station Ten had thick bars and concrete. Unlike the Youth Service Board, it was a real jail. I begged Leonard not to leave me there, but he refused and said he would be back as soon as I learned my lesson. Did that mean more than a day? I hated being claustrophobic, locked in a room, nowhere to go. Michael… how could he do this to me? My feelings were crushed. I prayed all night, especially to not go back to the foster home again, ever. Here I was, in jail until Leonard decided to get me out, with no one to call, not my dad or my social workers, Michael or W.D. (especially not him). Even Pam couldn't help me; she would implicate herself in the whole mess. I was still under eighteen years old.

CHAPTER TWENTY-NINE

Taken Away

Caged, a human animal having déjà vu. That night in the Station Ten jail felt like a lifetime. The run-down, seedy place was worse than the one where I presently sit, with its lights so bright you can see the smooth surface of its pristine walls. No one there was particularly kind either. Here the marshals have made it clear that they look down on me, and the two FBI agents play good cop, bad cop. What they said in Station Ten was meant to scare me to death. My skin grew thicker with time, but now I am not as tough as I was when I was younger. My responsibilities are greater, and I am far more realistic. With age came sensitivity to the contingencies of life and what can go wrong. Today I am frightened because I'm too old to be placed in a prison to live out any sentence that may be long. I can handle any situation, but being in this prison has taken me back to less assured times in my life. I have to believe that every experience, good or bad, is a lesson.

****

Leonard came to get me as late as possible the next day. I listened to his bellowing voice as he entered the station. I heard him but didn't speak at all. He and his buddies had made the point of scaring the shit out of me. I wasn't interested in their remarks, just in getting out of the damn cell. He said that my dad and the social workers were planning a meeting at Stoughton Court, and they were working out the details. I didn't think my father wanted to look at me. In fact, I was sure he didn't want anything to do with me so why was he coming to Boston? I hoped that the ride back to Leonard and Esti's house would be my last; it was nerve-racking anticipating going there. Why not let me do as I wished if no one wanted me? More torture, and just when I thought there was a spark of happiness in my life.

I acted as though I was apathetic. I didn't want to talk to Michael or see him again for any reason. He knew how I felt about trust, but he didn't care. I hated him as much as I had ever hated anybody. I learned later that he had called Leonard to turn me in not only because he was jealous, but also because he was genuinely concerned about me—I didn't realize that at the time. Pam was upset that I had to leave. She didn't get involved in my troubles because I told them she never knew I had run away, and as far as she knew, I was visiting before I went to live with my dad. Pam told me when I phoned her that she'd call W.D. to let him know what had happened and that I was welcome to come back anytime. She made that clear. Leonard overheard what she said about returning to the apartment and he said, "Don't even think about it. We know where she lives now, and next time, she'll get into trouble if you go back." Those were his words. Going back was out of the question because I didn't want her tangled up in my problem. I planned to take off again as soon as an opportunity presented itself. I wanted to see W.D. I imagined his spirit touched deep into my soul, and hormones coursed through my body whenever I thought about him.

Walking inside Esti's house felt worse than being in jail. It was a bodily sensation. I felt chilled even though the air wasn't cold. I didn't belong there anymore. Esti eventually told me that the meeting had been arranged in order to make a decision about what to do with me next. It was all hush-hush at the foster home. I had to wait it out. Leonard and Mason ignored me as if I didn't exist at all. My dad, Esti said, was angry and disappointed, which wasn't news to me. Even if I had done nothing, Anita would have poisoned him against me. That's what she did from the beginning, and now that I was acting

Out, I became an even easier target for her viciousness. I hated all of them and the feeling was mutual.

I was told that the meeting had been arranged around my dad's schedule, and he was coming to Boston to see his family, not me. Why does my dad push me away? I am not heard, just seen as a bad seed. I wanted my dad to love me the same way my mother Rose did, and even though I knew it would never happen, I still prayed for it. They said my dad had arrived in Boston, but I hadn't seen him yet. I was certain that after Esti, Leonard, and the social workers had gotten ahold of him he would hate me more. Why didn't he call? Why? I only saw him in negative situations.

Esti had grounded me. I had to sneak to use their telephone. I stayed in my room waiting for Leonard and Esti to go out so I could call my friends. They seemed to be glued to the house, not trusting me to be alone. Their piercing eyes were on me every moment. Jennifer said Leonard was wrong to leave me in jail overnight. He laughed it off as if it were some kind of joke. I didn't think it was funny. I thought it was nasty of him. I hated him. I was uncomfortable. The way they treated me was nightmarish, like I was a criminal who had broken into their home and was invading their space. I could hear them whisper about me at night. Mason, the little bastard, sided with his dad against me, saying I was bad despite all the times I took punishment for him. I took the blame for everyone. I vowed that the next time I ran away they wouldn't see me again. I was never going back, ever! Not to any one of them, in my family or theirs—and no more foster care system! No more social workers with the perspective of what they learned in college instead of social skills. Following a textbook would never get a true point of view from me or anyone in this system of rebellious kids or teens.

****

My brain is seething with unsettling memories, and I can sense my anxiety creeping up from behind, ready to wrench the breath from me. I tell myself to breathe... breathe... My chest is tight, and my mind is racing with thoughts of the past. I question myself: how did I ever make it through? The answer: I was determined to prove that I could.

****

The week before the meeting was extremely uncomfortable for me. I didn't want to eat their food so I took only the smallest portions at the dinner table. The house was quiet. The air was still, dead, filled with tension. It was obvious to me that I had disrupted the image they presented to others of having a perfect home. In fact, they were far from it. When we arrived at the Stoughton court for my hearing, my dad didn't look at me. He focused his eyes right past me. He had been doing that since my mother Rose passed away. Shit—Anita was with him! Why did he bring that bitch with him? He didn't speak to me until we were in chambers. Going near him was not an option with Anita attached to his side. The meeting reminded me of the day I signed the papers to give away my baby girl; that was branded in my memory forever. The time had come for me to have control over my life, no more adults telling me what to do. I was seventeen now. Each time I glanced at my dad, he turned away as if I were grotesque, some hideous person he couldn't bear to see, and I blamed myself for causing his reaction.

The conversation was about me but didn't include me, which gave me the sense of being invisible. My dad spoke with such rage against me that his words echo in my head to this day: "I want her put away in reform school, locked up with the key thrown away! That's where she belongs." That really hurt…way down deep. Locked up? I wondered what I had done that was so extreme to elicit this response. The social workers were startled. One of them, empathetically, tried to calm him down. "Mr. Siskind, please!" she said.

"Anita was right all along—once a tramp, always a tramp," he continued. Now Dad was joined to Anita's hate; she was aiming a long string of profanities at me while he spoke. The social worker admonished him again, saying, "Mr. Siskind, would you kindly compose yourself and your wife." I was humiliated, and the hate I felt for them was palpable at that moment. He had lied to me, and now he was doing his best to get rid of me, which was what he had done all along since Anita appeared on the scene. I wish I had seen that side of Freddy earlier. He should have let Auntie Rose's son Les adopt me when I was a baby. But then, I thought, I wouldn't have known my mother Rose. "Put her away!" my dad stood and shouted again, this time in unison with Anita. The social workers tried to quell their outburst. "You both will have to leave if the yelling doesn't stop!" Anita and Freddy sat back down. While the discussion was going on, the social workers came up with a plan that gave me some freedom that, considering my age, was acceptable to me. When they asked me what I thought about going to reform school as Freddy suggested, I told them, "Go ahead, lock me up. Do whatever you want. I don't care! But I will not go to any foster home, especially not back to that one." I was holding back tears. I was hurt, but I didn't want that vicious bitch to see me break down.

Finally, a decision was made for me to attend a trade school and live in a rooming house until I was eighteen. It was obvious to them that I didn't want foster care any longer. In the end, after much protest from me about the age issue and discussion about having given birth to a baby, the court granted that I could go to the Mansfield Beauty Academy on Boylston Street in Boston. It was a six-month certificate program, and as soon as I could get packed up, I would be staying at a rooming house on Littell Road in Brookline. There would be check-ins with the social workers regularly. Everyone, with the exception of my father and Anita, approved. Esti had no say in the matter; her extra money, gone… Much later in life, I learned that Freddy had done a short stint in reform school for hanging out with the bad boys in Chelsea, and I understood that some of his vehemence toward me must have been a response to his own experience behind bars. If only I had known that when he was alive! Why wasn't he more sympathetic? Maybe Anita didn't know. Imagine—he was a bad kid! He was in no position to be pointing fingers, but I didn't know about that back then; I just found out six years ago. Maybe he thought reform school would teach me the lessons it taught him. Or did it? Whatever it was he learned was not going to be passed on to me. I wasn't Freddy.

My father hid his past from everyone except his family. So many people have skeletons in their closets and won't come forward, too afraid of what others will think. I tried to shield others around me from knowing who I was—not a pleasant way to live. Now I don't care what people think. They don't really know me. I am more comfortable in my own skin as I grow older, and accept the person I used to be and the person I am at this moment. The genuine friends I have wholly accept who I am and was, and because the likelihood of finding such people is not great, I have only a small number who are close to me. I can count them on one hand!

I tried to adjust to Freddy's rejection by telling myself he loved Anita so much I was in the way from the beginning. In my estimation, he truly was a man without backbone. Despite the bad treatment I received from him, I was still stupidly compelled to try to win his affection. Although I wasn't conscious of doing it at the time, I chose to study hairdressing to please him because that was what Anita did. It was not for me.

I was allowed to start right away! A room had been assigned to me, and Esti made an appointment for us to see it. We drove to Brookline. *This is where I want to live someday,* I thought. The houses were beautiful, large older homes in the city, unlike suburban Canton. I liked the grander ones that had character. There was virtually no space between the houses, similar to Mattapan, Dorchester, and Roxbury in that respect. The rooming house had old-fashioned doors and woodwork. I loved it. Everyone shared the bathrooms and kitchen. I had my own tiny room that I could lock. *It's mine, a room to myself,* I thought as I played with the lock and keys in my hands. Esti could go now as far as I was concerned—no more Canton, Massachusetts. The trolley took me to Park Street, where I would get off right in front of the school. I hadn't called any of my friends because I was concentrating instead on getting good grades to prove to my dad that I was able to do something well. Then maybe he would be pleased enough to want to talk to me. W.D. was set aside for the next time I went to visit Pam.

Jennifer was a bit concerned about me being on my own, and we spoke often. No one gave me money beyond the few dollars I was receiving for food and trolley fare from the state. I was still smoking cigarettes, feeling more independent and mature. But, in fact, I was painfully lonely and broke. It had been over one month since I began school, and so I asked the social workers to call my dad. They arranged to have him call me one day after school. Although the social workers had given him a glowing report, he wasn't impressed by it. "At least you're not tramping around with your friends." And then he meanly said that doing well in school didn't prove anything. That did it. I thought, *What the fuck!* Anita had told him that I wouldn't ever amount to anything. According to her way of thinking, I could never become a hairdresser. I could hear her screaming, "That bitch! She can't do anything except find boys," in the background. Why did I care? I should have known he wouldn't like me as long as Anita was there, and the whole situation had been made worse by calling. There wasn't anyone else I could turn to. Dad's family sided with him. Suddenly, I didn't care about school anymore. Dad told me not to call because Anita became too upset, and I had to be sensitive to her feelings. *I* had to be sensitive to *her* feelings all the time? Fuck her! His last words were, "We don't care what you do, just stay out of trouble. Don't call me with your problems. Write if you have to. Anita doesn't want to hear your voice." Again, my response was that I didn't care either. Anita was trying to wrestle the receiver from his hand, and he hung up without saying goodbye. I was tired of listening to everyone. I wanted to see W.D. At least he made me feel good; his words made me feel wanted. Maybe I'll search for a good job, but then what would the social workers say if I didn't go to school?

I didn't feel like going back to school, but I went back briefly because two of the teachers were very kind to me, no hidden agendas...like other people had. I was no longer struggling to adjust, in fact, I was doing quite well, but I didn't care anymore. They said I had a knack for styling hair, but I was dissatisfied, broke, and hungry. I did learn how to look better. Fourteen dollars didn't stretch far enough after spending money for food and cigarettes. I didn't want to sit alone in a room all night, which was all I did. I doodled on blank pieces of paper and wrote down my feelings on the loose sheets, not having a locked diary to record my daily life. When I realized I could go out, I headed to Mattapan and hung out at Duchess. I called Pam again. We made plans for the weekend. I felt free. Hopefully, I would see W.D., and I could hardly wait. I was vulnerable and susceptible to the slightest expression of kindness. I was anticipating the weekend with excitement, and it wasn't far from Brookline to Parker Hill Ave., so I could get back in time for my curfew. I was so hungry. I had such a small amount of money to live on that I started to steal food from the grocery store. I was good at it, careful not to get caught. I had school to look forward to, but I was itching for the freedom to let loose.

Pam knew that I had fallen hard for W.D. and didn't give me any indication that I shouldn't see him now. It never occurred to me to ask him if he was seeing anyone else or if he were married. She thought it was cool that I was going to hairdressing school but pointed out that I didn't have a job. "How you gonna to make extra bucks?" she asked. Pam knew that my birthday had passed. It didn't bother me that no one had even mentioned it—I was just happy to have gotten past my seventeenth birthday. During those nights alone in my room, I had been hugging my pillow, thinking about W.D. and fantasizing about sex and love, the kind that was portrayed in the movies. I could hardly wait to see him; my body would become shaky and my sexual awareness was heightened, my panties soaking wet as I put my hands in there and gently stroked between my legs, reaching an orgasm. I went to Pam and Rosey's apartment first and then we moved on to W.D.'s sister's house. Everyone was pleased to see me and commented that I looked more mature since going to hairdressing school. They were planning to play cards, and there was some conversation about me going out to a club. I'd never been to a club before. Someone was covering for me at the rooming house, and if anyone called, they would say that I was sleeping. Being good or bad really didn't matter, so if I got caught what could possibly happen? Punishment, or jail? W.D. called, but it was very late. He explained that he had gotten tied up and would call in a week or two when he had taken care of his business. Another letdown…I was disappointed. *He doesn't want to see me,* I thought, *so back to reality and school.* Pam gave me money for a taxi to go home, adding that it was probably for the best that I go back and finish school.

I went back to school the next day, *not* in a good mood. I was afraid that W.D. didn't like me anymore, and he was just making an excuse. Again, I was worrying that a man didn't like me, just like I worried about my dad's feelings for me. I was sure W.D. had found a girl who surpassed me in looks and had less baggage. A couple of weeks had gone by and the cold weather chilled my bones. I didn't have enough warm clothes to wear, so I layered what I had. Pam finally called me at school and told me to come by on Christmas weekend. That meant W.D. was going to be there; I just knew it. With the holidays coming soon, I asked myself where I would go. No, not to Jennifer's apartment. I didn't want to be around her family, and anyway, I did not get an invite. I could go to Pam and her friends; otherwise, there wasn't any place for me to be. I had two months or so left of school and wanted to finish by next year, but I also wanted to hang out. I went with the tough kids who hung out at Duchess. They put me to the test, stealing cars with them every night after school. Michael and I were talking on the phone again; however, I tried to keep my distance. He had apologized profusely, but I wasn't moved by his words. I didn't trust him anymore, although I considered dating him if W.D. stood me up another time. All the girls at school had boyfriends. *Maybe I'll date Huckie,* I thought. I never gave him a fair chance. Would he still want me? Although I didn't realize it at the time, he would have jumped at the chance.

I was an emotional mess, starving for attention. My life felt chaotic. There was school during the day and stealing cars at night. I had some money though, from the extra I got for boosting clothes. I loved the high of driving new cars. I could pay for food now, not steal it, and when I went downtown I went to Jordan Marsh to buy their scrumptious blueberry muffins and to Filene's Basement for the their hot dogs with Gulden's mustard and relish—my favorite. I window-shopped at Filene's and Jordan's, especially during the holidays when they dressed the windows so spectacularly that my jaw nearly dropped, and my face lit up like a young child's. The sparkling diamonds in E.B. Horn's window mesmerized me. I stood in front of their window any chance I could to stare, thinking that maybe I would buy jewelry there one day. I dreamed of "one day." Me, walk into a fine store like that...imagine! I really did many years later, and still do!

CHAPTER THIRTY

Turned Out

My body is tired from sitting with my back straight for so many hours and my head aches from thinking. What I wouldn't give for big bowl of spaghetti right now with a pile high of grated cheese and Italian bread with butter. Food is all I think about when I'm depressed or trying to escape all the things that demand my attention in a day. I can't run away now; those days are long gone. I can see why people downsize, sell everything, just to have peace of mind and the leisure to search for what is really meaningful.

****

I was not concentrating on school, and there was only a month longer to finish and get my certificate. One of my teachers sensed that something was wrong and asked me several times if I wanted to sit down and talk with him. I had skipped a couple of days a week, which extended my hours on the other days. He knew something was up. Had I only known his concern was genuine, I might have saved myself, and perhaps my fate would have been different.

Still obsessed by thoughts of W.D., I called his sister's house and spoke with Kathy, who told me he would be at Sharley's apartment early that evening. He had asked for me, and I was thrilled. I was wary of being let down again, but I didn't allow that to dampen my high spirits. I walked to Parker Hill Ave., freezing cold but it felt so good. When I stepped in, everyone told me that I looked great; my cheeks were rosy, and I was wearing a bit more black mascara and a pretty pink lipstick. That lipstick had become my signature, my lifeline, like Chanel. They commented on how mature and sexy I looked; one of the girls at school had given me a hand with my eye makeup that day. Kathy was dressed all in black with black boots and a heavily made up face—more makeup than at any other time I had ever seen her. I knew that she worked nights, but I had never asked her what she did for a living because I wasn't as close to her as I was to Pam and Rosey. I had overheard some conversation and assumed that she worked in a bar, maybe as a cocktail waitress.

It wasn't long before W.D. walked through the door—my wish to see him had finally come true! My knight in shining armor, who had come to rescue me. The butterflies going around in my stomach and my knees made me weak. At that moment, I realized just how terribly infatuated I was with him. It was difficult for me to speak. Fortunately, W.D. did all the talking, telling me that I was pretty and looked sweet enough to eat. Going out, though, took money, he said as he sat close to me on the couch, our bodies touching so I could feel his energy flowing through me. I nodded eagerly, although I didn't have any money with me and had no idea what it cost to go to a club. He asked me if I wanted to go out and have a good time, and if I wanted to be with him permanently and make him happy. He told me he was letting me go out to work with Kathy and the two of us would meet afterward. I wasn't certain whether he meant tonight or tomorrow night—it was the holiday weekend after Thanksgiving. "Where am I going?" I asked him.

"Don't ask," he retorted, looking me straight in the eyes. "You are in good hands."

I understood he was serious about what he was saying, but he was so sexy when he spoke I didn't fully grasp the implications of what was going on. "Wherever Kathy goes, you will go," he stated flatly. "She'll take care of you. Don't worry, we'll hook up later."

I was hypnotized by him. I was listening to the sound of his voice, not paying attention to what he was saying or questioning what he meant. My need was to be wanted, and it compelled me to do whatever he asked. He grabbed me by the shoulders and then lifted my chin with his fingers. He put his lips on mine to kiss me. It was so erotic that my breath was taken away. I shivered, and the sensation between my legs was heightened and pulsing. I wanted his body on mine…I wanted him to enter me, to fulfill my needs. After he left, I could still smell his fragrance on me, just like the first night we met. W.D. knew exactly what to say and do, and I was unaware of what this shining knight in cashmere meant; I was already entangled in his web, and it never occurred to me to question his motives. Kathy and her friends knew, perhaps even Pam and Rosey were in on it. I thought it was odd that they hadn't arrived yet. Did W.D. put them up to calling me back to his web?

Kathy said that because I looked too young she wanted to put some more makeup on me. I refused to put on the false eyelashes, so it was another few applications of deep black mascara and deeper pink lipstick instead of the soft pink I was wearing. Then she had me put on a black dress she said was too tight for her and a pair of stockings. The stockings against my skin reminded me of the itchy wool Anita used to make me wear, and I pleaded with her to take them off. She insisted that I wear them. They were so awful! Once I was dressed, I was wavering between going out with her and waiting for Pam, but Kathy convinced me to go with her, saying that W.D. would be disappointed if I didn't. His scent lingered on my face, and as I smelled his cologne, my will weakened. I felt physical discomfort because of the clothes I was wearing, and detached, not feeling like myself and somehow out of place. Kathy gathered her things and hurried me along. "You look great; trust me." I felt like that little girl who dressed up in Anita's clothes that time in Stoneham to look older but, thankfully, the man left me because I was too young.

It was cold in Kathy's old, worn-down car and my legs were chilled. I hated the way I felt and wanted the clothes off. I asked her several times to take me back, but she kept saying no, blowing me off like I was a silly child. We spoke mainly about her girlfriend and how nice W.D. was. She didn't say where we were going. Her answers to my questions about him were vague, but what she did say was that many girls wanted him, yet he wanted me. As hard as that was for me to believe, I tried. I was so smitten I didn't think about it, thoughts of W.D. took precedence over my curiosity. Animal instincts clouded my thinking. I wish I had been taught that sexual attraction and infatuation distort our minds, what the big, bad wolf can do. Would we listen?

I was oblivious to the complete turn my life was about to take. *Totally* oblivious. Kathy drove the backstreets to Columbus Ave. toward Tremont Street and the South End of Boston. We smoked cigarettes in the car, which already reeked of smoke that had filmed the windows. She flicked her ashes out the window, and I watched them drift in the air and fall. I felt queasy, though I didn't know the reason why. Whenever I felt that way something bad always happened; I didn't know about premonitions then, but now I do. We were slowing down, looking for a place to park near a tall brick building standing alone with darkened windows as if no one lived there. She said we were near the clubs and bars. "Really?" I innocently asked, not knowing any bars other than the ones the girls at school talked about. I had never heard of or been to the area where we were. Kathy pushed the buttons down one by one to lock the doors. The smoke followed us as we stepped out of the car. I wished I had stayed to wait for Pam and Rosey at the apartment, but W.D. said for me to go, and I wanted to please him. I ached to be accepted by a man—a longing that persisted for years. The road was dark, only a streetlight shed a soft glow.

We walked through the oversized doorway into a hall marred by large patches of chipped plaster walls painted with horrid colors. There was a tall, broad Chinese man standing at the elevator who motioned to Kathy, without the trace of a smile on his face, for us to go up. Until then, I thought that all Chinese men were short like the waiters at Anita Chu's restaurant in Brookline, where I went to eat when I was small. We went there once a week. It was my father's favorite Chinese restaurant, and we never ate Chinese food anywhere but there. He loved Anita Chu, the owner. I remember her well. She was striking, with her jet-black hair, in the long, silk cheongsam dresses she wore. The man said nothing to me, unlike the friendly waiters at Anita Chu's. We went inside the heavy metal elevator, and the door clanked shut. It reminded me of the gilded cage elevator at Aunt Eva's apartment building on Beacon Street in Brookline. I felt nervous in elevators because I was afraid something would break and then I'd fall to the bottom, crushed. I was never comfortable with heights. Once, when I was very young and going to the Robin Hood Elementary School, I went to visit a friend after school got out. There was a ladder leaning against her house. The kids were going up and down the ladder, and they dared me to do the same. My dad was always climbing a ladder for some reason or another at our house, and I never hesitated to follow him up a step or two. There was a Chihuahua yapping incessantly on the ground next to the ladder. I went up to show them how brave I was. When I reached the last rung, they asked me if I could hold on to the top of the house and hang. It was a challenge, and they had dared me. I told them I could as I gripped the gutters at the top of the house, and it was then they pulled the ladder aside from underneath me. They weren't good friends! Panicking, I hung there. My hands froze. The dog barked louder. My hands were clenched so tightly they hurt, and I couldn't even scream. The ladder fell to the ground and I heard a thump, then the squeals of the dog and the laughter of the kids. Finally, a neighbor, who must have been alerted by the dog, put the ladder back in place and talked me down each rung. He stood right below in case I fell. I never told on the kids, but I said that the ladder had fallen over on its own. The neighbors felt terrible about it, and the parents somehow convinced Fred and Anita to let me stay over because I was so shaken. I didn't want to be near the kids who were so mean, but I stayed because the parents were nice to me and wanted to watch over me that night. They showered me with attention. After I got home, Dad left for work and Anita beat me not only for climbing the ladder and not coming straight home, but also for sleeping over my friend's house. Since then, I have been afraid of heights.

Kathy jabbed the button on the elevator. We lurched upward as the tired cables squealed and moaned. My stomach dropped. At that point, I knew I was in some sort of danger, a premonition of something awful that was about to happen. I turned to Kathy and said, "I want to go, please!" She just ignored my request.

The elevator came to an abrupt stop. The floor wasn't level with the elevator, and the gap scared me as we stepped over it, with Kathy holding my hand. "Come on, it's okay." When the doors of the elevator closed behind us, we were in a hallway. Foggy clouds of cigarette and cigar smoke stunk and billowed out a dingy doorway where another husky Chinese man stood. He knew Kathy. We entered a room filled with smoke, and the loud sound of the crowd struck us the moment we passed through the doorway. I couldn't hear any English being spoken. There were so many Chinese men in this room, and no females in sight. Their loud voices pierced my ears. They hovered around long tables, gesturing, shouting, and clutching cards and cash while holding shots of liquor and beer. I couldn't hear over the noise. Kathy led me to an old, torn couch with stains all over it. Everything in the large room was filthy. It looked like it had been abandoned years ago, and they had taken over the place to gamble and drink. I leaned toward Kathy and asked her where we were and what the men were doing. Again, I asked her if we could leave. Kathy tried to reassure me by saying, "I'm here with you. There's no need to be afraid. We'll be here for a while. These are my friends." The men were turning and staring at me. Why? I couldn't understand what they were saying with their Cheshire Cat smiles so wide their eyes appeared to be shut.

I had never seen so much money before. I recognized that they were playing poker, but it wasn't just poker. Kathy explained that they were playing high stakes poker and a dice game, and that this was what they did every night. It was hard to hear her over the yelling and screaming. I was a bit more at ease because this was the place where Kathy worked and they knew her, although I was confused about what it was she did. I wanted to ask her, but she was talking to different men, pointing over at me. At least the time was passing. I couldn't wait to see W.D. before it was too late to go out again. I had to get back to my room in Brookline before I got myself into trouble for being out all night; I was covered as long as it was nighttime. I was very edgy and kept poking her. Kathy told me to be patient.

"Aren't you supposed to be working here?" I asked. Before she could answer, some of the Chinese men walked over to her and handed her money. She didn't do anything to earn that money. What was up with that? They were whispering, and in the next moment, one of the men approached me, took me by the hand, and ordered me to go with him. "You, me, now!" he said, tugging at the sleeve of my dress. "You, me, now!" he repeated. Kathy motioned for me to go with him. She told me it was okay, she knew him, and she would be here when I got back.

"No, I don't want to go with him!" I told her.

"Are you crazy?" Her expression was stern. I felt like I didn't have a choice because there was nobody on my side—I was outnumbered. The man squeezed my hand tightly and dragged me about fifteen feet across the room to a doorway. I didn't want to scream and make a scene. Maybe it was a door to go out?

The linoleum floor was grimy, and a rancid and sweet smell of spoiling Chinese food hung in the air. When he opened the door, I could see a tiny, grimy room. It had a twin bed with yellowed, soiled sheets on it, and to the right was a sink, a tiny old-fashioned sink with a silver faucet, skinny legs, and black bugs crawling on it. "You go in, you wash now!" the man said.

"No!" I said, "I want to go!"

"No, no, you stay here! I pay!" he said with a heavy Chinese inflection, barely able to speak English. He pushed me in and closed the door tightly, making sure it was locked. He grabbed me by the arm. Then he pressed his skinny body against mine, and I pushed him away. He pushed against me again and said, "No speak! No talk! You take off!" as he pulled at the dress and roughly felt me up. I held the dress down. He kissed my mouth with his and I tasted garlic, liquor, and cigarettes. I was in tears and feared for my life. He pushed me down. "You fucky!" he said as I was trying to get away. *Fucky? Fuck!* My stockings ripped and my dress was pulled up. He held me down and entered me, kissing me with his foul tongue in my mouth, his sweat falling on my tear-filled face. "No, stop!" I pleaded, trying to push this boney man off me. No one could hear me with all the noise outside the door. I squeezed as tightly as I could to prevent him from penetrating me all the way, and though he was small, it felt as though he was big, and what lasted only minutes seemed like forever. He was so thin that his hip bones dug into mine as he thrust again and again. I felt wet, the same as when Michael came on my vagina in the car. Wet all over not only outside but also inside this time, an uncomfortable, sticky wet. He got up, washed with a cloth, and left the room. I was devastated! I was crying, and lay there numb and shocked when another man entered the room. He was even more aggressive than the first. He said, “Up, up, hurry! Wash now, you wash, get clean!” and threw me the cloth as if I were a servant. As I wiped, he pulled me by my dress and pushed me on the bed. “You take dress off!” He had my legs up like the first man had done and again it hurt, but worse this time as he thrust harder and harder. I cried and he loved that. “Please stop!” I begged. “You’re hurting me!” He did not stop and continued until he came, then he washed too and left the room as abruptly as he entered it. I was even wetter than before. The next one didn’t stop and neither did the thirty or so other men who followed him. How could they be this cruel! I was just a piece of meat to be used. As I stared up at the cracked ceiling, I hated myself. There wasn’t time to take a breath in between and it was impossible to leave. I felt like a dirty rag. My tears had stopped flowing—there were no more to cry. I had no time to reflect on what was happening; it just happened. In my mental state, I did not count exactly how many men there were at the time, but learned later by the amount of money they paid how many there had been. Over thirty men! It was fortunate I had taken the pills Pam gave me or I could have gotten pregnant. I felt nauseous and light-headed. The glare from the single, naked electric bulb dangling from the ceiling was blinding. It was hot in the room, at least ninety degrees. My body was wet with puddles of sweat. I hated this room more than Anita’s boiler room lockup.

There was a dark green, torn shade covering a small window that I noticed for the first time. I was ashamed and terrified. How could I walk out there? I tossed handfuls of water from the dirty sink onto my face and tried to wipe it clean. My lipstick was smeared off. And the thick mascara had bled down my face, mingling with the falling tears. My hair was in knots from thrashing my head from side to side. The rancid cum smell from the man who ejaculated on my face sickened me; that couldn't have been more ugly or obscene. The nasty cum inside me—how was I to get all that out? My hair smelled of Chinese food and booze. I was numb, drained of tears and emotion. I was so weak that I had to hold the wall for support when I stood. My vagina was red and dry, so swollen and pulsating that putting my legs together was painful. I was disoriented and lost. I had been "turned out," as they say in the business. I'd had no idea it was coming. I felt as though I had been turned inside and out and had lost my soul to many devils. How could Kathy let this happen to me? There was no turning back. I was tainted, truly the outcast I had thought myself to be, and who would want me now?

What was the reason for any of this? Why didn't Kathy tell me? Why did she trap me? She wasn't a friend like Pam, or was Pam as good a friend as I believed? And W.D.? Did he know? Is that why he told me to go with Kathy? Or did she set me up because she needed the money? The men had given her money for using me. They stopped only because I was so swollen and bleeding. They said, "No good. You dress and go." Later I learned that Chinese men won't have sex if the woman is bleeding. Had I known that, I would have cut myself. I was thankful to be out of that dank room, which I will never forget. I was trapped in rooms and subjected to fear for most of my life, but this was a living hell! The swelling was disfiguring, as if I had a tennis ball between my legs. I couldn't have put a Q-tip inside. I had to walk out into that smoke-filled gambling room with those men ogling me, and face Kathy—I hated her right then! I felt ashamed, and though they weren't actually laughing, they were gaping at me and grinned with knowing looks on their faces, nodding their heads as if they were tipping their hats. I wanted to die! The ones who came in the room had enjoyed themselves every moment because Kathy had told them I was a virgin. She smiled at me like she was a proud mother and I was a good little girl. I wanted to spit in her face like Anita spit in mine. She told me in a condescending way that I would understand everything soon. I had no words, just tears.

I walked out into the cold, gasping, sucking in breaths of fresh air. Kathy was telling me I would be fine after some rest. These men had attacked my very person! When she handed me my coat, she was so nonchalant that I didn't want it. "I don't want the coat!" I snapped. "How could you let those men do that to me?" I asked her, all freaked out, fresh tears streaming down my face. She told me that I had made lots of money, and I told her that I didn't want their money. I wanted to go home and insisted that she take me! Why would they pay her for me? I didn't ask her to help me out with money. I would have rather given the old Jewish man at ABC Linen what he wanted before this! "Why did you do that?" I asked, weeping and begging her for an explanation.

"I can't tell you," Kathy bluntly replied. I wondered if W.D. *did* know where she had taken me. The cold air reached under my skirt like a hand with ice chips, chilling down the inflammation between my legs. She tried to touch me in the car, and I stayed as close to the door as possible. I could hardly move because of the pain. I felt so nasty! I didn't want to be touched by any man or woman…ever, ever, ever. Kathy tried to reason with me, but I didn't want to listen to her. Men who were total strangers had used me for sex, and it occurred to me that Anita was right—I *was* a tramp now! I guess I was too easily led.

Kathy said we were going to W.D.'s house. I was totally embarrassed and didn't want him to see me like this, and insisted, "No! I'm not! Take me home to Brookline!" She told me I was W.D.'s girl now, and I had to do what he told me. "Now you're with him, Libbe, that's why you're going to his house."

"What? No I'm not!" I replied. "Kathy, I want to go to my house! Didn't you hear me?"

"That's the reason you did all that, for your man, W.D."

My man? He wanted me to do this for him? I was really messed up now. I didn't understand what she was trying to tell me, my pain was unbearable, and I wasn't able to think. We stopped in front of a brick house. "What do you mean, he's 'my man'?"

She said that it wasn't her place to tell me, and W.D. would talk to me. I wanted to kill her for what she had done to me and for refusing to take me home. Was all this W.D.'s idea? He did say I was going to be with him afterward, was this what he meant? I wasn't about to go anywhere with anyone. Kathy kept telling me to get out of the car, and I continued to refuse. Get out and go where? She stepped out of the car and went to the door of the brick house we had pulled up to. When W.D. answered the door she handed him the wad of money and a bag. He saw me and waved me in, "Come on baby, come on, I've been waiting for you!" I heard his voice and saw his face, and in that moment, the pain vanished like magic. What was wrong with me? I couldn't refuse. Was I this desperate? Yes, I was…

I could tell by his expression that he knew, and suddenly, for some reason, I didn't feel embarrassed anymore, just dirty. As I shut the door and walked away from the car the cold crept up my legs, and again I could feel the pinching pains caused by the lump of my swollen vaginal lips against my thighs. Before Kathy got back into her car she handed me my cigarettes. A Chinese guy had left five dollars for me on the sink, and I had folded it under the cellophane wrap—money to get home. I wasn't sure if I should just run away. Thinking back, maybe I should have walked, but I wouldn't be the same woman I am now had I done that. I didn't have a place to go at five a.m. I couldn't go home looking as disheveled as I was, and the main doors were locked at midnight anyway. I was familiar with the Grove Hall area from living in Mattapan. I could run, go to Michael's! No…no. I knew Dorchester and Roxbury, but Pam was on Parker Hill Ave., too far to walk in my condition. Kathy would not agree to drive me. She did what she was told. I thought, *With only five dollars, I don't have a choice.* Deep inside, I really wanted to see W.D. He was like a magnet, drawing me toward him even against my will.

I was standing there, trying to decide how W.D. fit into all of this. He came out of the two-family red brick house with his arms extended to greet me and said, "Come on, baby, I am gonna take care of you." He seemed to be so sincere. I went to him. I never felt that kind of hug before, and all that had happened seemed distant. He said he'd take care of me, and those words were crucial for me to hear. I wasn't thinking about the men taking advantage of me anymore. W.D. walked me inside the house into the back room, which had double French doors with curtains and a large bed with fluffy quilts on it. He asked me to be quiet because his mother was watching a baby and told me to take my clothes off. I was reluctant, despite what had happened. Even more so because it happened...I didn't want him to see my lower parts. He must have noticed my embarrassment. He handed me a terry cloth robe as he was leaving the room. "Take those clothes off, baby," he said. I took off my stained clothes and soiled underwear, and noticed the fresh red blood on my panties and the black and blue bruises on my arms and hips. Oh, god! Look at me! The robe overwhelmed my slight body, and I had to wrap the tie around my waist twice. I stood still in the middle of the room, looking at the fancy cologne bottles on top of the old wooden dresser. I stared momentarily at the French doors. I wondered about him. I was surprised that he lived with his mother. He didn't appear to be that type, like Michael, who lived with his parents. I wondered how old he was, maybe twenty-five, I guessed. Then I began to worry about going back to the rooming house and whether my absence would be reported to the lady who ran the place. I was trembling with fear, shivering uncontrollably from the trauma, my mind plagued by worries.

I felt terrible that W.D. was waking his mother to help me. I had been physically beaten and emotionally scarred. I wanted to sleep. I had to tell him that I needed to go back to Brookline, but then I thought that I didn't have my clothes with me. Where did he take the ones Kathy gave him in a bag she had in her hand? I was struggling to make it from one minute to the next. "Come, dear," said a voice in the doorway, "I'm going to help you. First a hot shower, then ice." She was heavy-set, with light to medium skin, and short dark brown hair. W.D.'s mother was a gentle and soft-spoken woman. She wore an extra-large man's tee shirt, pajama bottoms, and slippers like Pam's friends wore at night. On the way to the shower, W.D. said he would go get some of the clothes I had left at Pam's so I would have them while I was at his house. Why would she freely give him my things? She knew! That was the reason! I walked away with his mom, angry but relieved to know I would have my clothes. What was going on? Why did Kathy give him the money? I didn't dare ask him questions yet, but when he gets back… I had been turned out by my man—W.D. from Schuyler Street—and didn't have any idea what had just happened to me. I felt detached from reality, like I was in a fog. I recalled when Anita would beat me, and I withstood the pain by ignoring it. It's the same; I was drifting. Did I just have a bad dream or was my life unfolding? For a desperate moment, I wished that Michael would come to rescue me. My shame was so great, I wouldn't have prayed to my mom.

Things were happening with such speed that I couldn't make my own decisions. I let W.D. make them for me. I felt the steam from the shower as I walked through the bathroom doorway. I liked the style of the 1950's black and white tiles and the white shower curtain on a circular rod overhanging an ancient clawfoot tub with silver feet. Mrs. W. said she would wash me and be very careful. It struck me as wrong that a stranger was about to touch my body, however gently, but I allowed it.

There were basically two people in my life who had ever washed me: my mother Rose, whose touch was tender, and Anita, who scrubbed my body with a scrub brush until my skin bled. I was happy to have W.D.'s mother wash me because it was something I couldn't do myself. I did not want to touch my own body, and it burned as the hot water trickled down, with soapsuds touching my private parts. I began to sob. She apologized and explained that she had to check to make sure there weren't any open cuts or sores. "And I have to clean you out," she said. It was going to hurt. "Oh no, please!" I begged. "Don't put anything in there!" She had a hot water bottle made of rubber, kind of like the ones my mother Rose used to put on her stomach for belly aches, only this one had a hose attached to it. She filled it with warm water and inserted the hose inside me. "Oh, my god!" I cried out in pain. She examined me the way a doctor would, and reported that there weren't open cuts, just raw skin. She told me not to worry about the swelling because she had something to make it go down. She washed my hair with the small amount of Breck shampoo that was at the bottom of a worn bottle and rubbed Noxema over my face. I was cleaner on the outside, but on the inside, I felt as though I was still filthy. W.D.'s mother disappeared for a moment and returned to the bathroom with what she called a mustard douche. I was shaking all over from cold water combined with shock and fear. The inside of my vagina was so disfigured the nozzle of the douche wouldn't penetrate me without Vaseline, and the sensation of the warm liquid flushing up and down was agonizing. Smears of coagulated blood floated in the water. The energy I was putting into not thinking about what just happened was similar to what I would do when Anita tortured me: I would try not to think about it as it was happening, knowing that it would end soon enough, and I could take a break. I prayed that I would never see those men ever again, or any men at all. I didn't want to go back to Kathy's apartment either. I didn't trust her anymore. Mrs. W. was a mother, and somehow that made accepting her help easier. She touched my forehead and said I needed aspirin, that I was burning up. The bottom of the bathtub was filled with the pink sudsy water, and rose up even though the stopper wasn't in. The multiple rapes had devastated both my body and my mind.

As I shivered from the cold, Mrs. W. wrapped towels around me, held me, and asked me whether I was okay. I couldn't speak. My teeth were chattering and chills went through me like I was outside, exposed to the weather. "You poor thing," she said. Although Mrs. W. was tough in the same way as Pam's friends, she was different. I didn't dare ask her if she was a lesbian, although I sensed that she was. I glanced at the frosted glass window and saw that the sun had risen and was glowing through the steam. Mrs. W. asked me to sit on the toilet seat, but it was too painful to sit. I slid my bottom to the edge of the cracked, discolored toilet so the swollen mound between my legs wasn't touching anything. She explained that what she was about to do would hurt for a few minutes, but then it would feel cool and the swelling would go down after a few hours. She told me what to do, and I didn't have the energy to argue. As I sat, there was pressure from the swelling of the mound and stinging from the bright red lips of my vagina. I held myself up a few inches, using my arms for support, and opened my legs as she asked me to do. My eyes were full of tears. "Please don't touch me! Don't touch!" She insisted she had to, and after applying Vaseline to the inner lips of my vagina she took some Vicks VapoRub from a blue jar. I recognized the jar from the times I had a cold and my mother Rose would lovingly rub it on the skin of my chest. Mrs. W. rubbed it on the outside of my private area, not on the burning inside. I cried silently from the pain, tears streaming down my face. I could taste the saltiness as they entered my mouth. She told me the Vicks had to stay on for about ten to fifteen minutes and then she would gently wash it off and put Vaseline over the sensitive inner part around my vagina. As much as I wanted to, I could not move. It felt like tingling icicles.

W.D. knocked on the door. "I'm back! Hey, what's going on?" His mother called back, "You'll have to wait, we'll be done soon!"

I had to go to school—oh, god, I had to get home! I couldn't afford another day of being late for class. *Vicks VapoRub...who ever thought of that?* I wondered. I leaned back on my arms while the icy cold Vicks tingled on my inflamed skin. It felt as though the area was becoming even larger even though it wasn't. Mrs. W. said, "You'll be fine, honey. It will shrink," as she wrapped another towel around my shoulders to warm me. The memory of the men smirking flashed across my mind, and their grins became distorted and turned into grotesque smiles. I recalled the way they examined me, looking at my private parts like they were doctors conducting a medical exam. These men were horny monsters, not doctors. They were so disgusting. I doubted they treated their wives or girlfriends like that, and I wished all bad things to befall them.

The entire evening was so drawn out. It was the longest night of my life, and the morning hours seemed even longer. Not only did I learn that Kathy knew, but Pam knew as well. I couldn't fathom why Pam never told me what would happen if I went out with Kathy. I didn't want to believe that Pam could be that cruel because she was supposed to be my friend! Mrs. W. wiped away all the old Vicks and rubbed new cream on either side of the mound to make sure the swelling would subside. She put Vaseline on the inside again and then on my outer parts with her fingertip. Physically, I was much more comfortable. Mentally, however, I was in pain, even more so than when I was physically and sexually abused as a child. I had grown up and was able to think more critically than when I was younger. Still, to this day, I can't express all the emotions I experienced while I was hostage in that room. Words cannot describe the terror I felt. Those men forced themselves on me and groped me through my tears and pain, loving every moment of their "fucky-fuckies," as they called it.

W.D. was knocking at the door again. "What's going on?" he asked. "You should be done by now. Unlock the door!" "Wait one minute," his mother said, "she'll be out! Leave her be!" Then Mrs. W. handed me a pair of men's pajamas. I told her I needed my clothes because I was going home. "Okay, but at least put these on so you can go out there." The bottoms fell off but the top was long enough to cover me. She said that W.D. would talk to me, then she opened the door. I was still cold and tired, but there he was, looking at me. It was that simple—one glance and I was ensnared in his trap. W.D. massaged cream on my face and hands, and up my arms with gentle, circular motions. He was standing so close to me. He massaged my wet head with a towel until it was damp, almost dry. His touch was electric and passed through my body to my painful parts, awakening my sexual drive. He told me we would talk later and to try to relax. I desperately needed to sleep. I glanced at the top of the dresser where there was a thick wad of bills. Bobby Womack music was playing in the background, and though I was familiar with him from listening to Silky's albums, it was the first time I had heard the song that was playing. Later in my life, whenever I heard that song, I was brought back to that moment of listening to W.D.'s voice with the music playing softly in the background.

I was entranced, as if I were dreaming. Trying to grasp what he was saying as he rapped to me in a smooth soothing tone of voice, I barely understood what he was telling me. I responded sexually to his sweet murmur and kisses. Despite the ordeal I had gone through, he excited me. The swollen mound between my legs pulsated to the rhythm of his voice. He told me I had choices to make, and I had to make them that morning. "Do you want to be with me?"

"Yes," I answered automatically, even though I wasn't sure I should.

"Do you understand what you did?"

"No, I don't."

"Do you want to make your man happy?"

"Yes."

"Will you do whatever I ask you to do?"

"Yes," I said softly. He kissed my neck and licked my earlobe with the tip of his tongue. My passion was further aroused by this fine devil's kiss, and I felt caught between his touch and my desire. "You just made Daddy very happy!"

"I did?" I asked, flinching ever so slightly when he referred to himself as my "daddy."

"Will you do it again?"

"Yes, but do I have to?"

He put his finger over my mouth. "Yes, baby," he said, "if you want to stay and have me take care of you." He kissed my mouth and gripped my hair on both sides, firmly yet gently. My body ached for him. I could feel pulsations of pain mixed with ecstasy. I would have endured the pain to have him inside me at that moment. It was as if he knew exactly what to say. Did he know about my dad and how desperately I wanted him to be proud of me? W.D. would be my daddy, and I could make him proud of me. Was that it? I repeated yes as he put one of his fingers inside my mouth, draping it over my lip as Bobby Womack sang. Right then, I would have done whatever he asked, even if that meant suffering through the pain again. I wanted to know if I could get dressed to go home and to school. He said, "So I guess you don't want to be my girl?" He knew he had me.

"Yes, yes, I do, but…" I said. "Then you are staying here and will tell the school you can't go today. You're sick." As he held and caressed me, my soul was going to the devil. If I don't call in to the rooming house, the court or the social worker will be called. "I could get in trouble. Jennifer has guardianship of me, that's what the court said, until next November when I turn eighteen. One more year."

"What did you say? You're under eighteen? Why wasn't I told? Okay, baby. We'll figure this out. You should have told me when I met you."

I apologized.

"You get some sleep. My mom will make you some food. You can wear my pajamas until we get you your own."

I was hooked!

W.D. leaned over, turned me gently, and rubbed my back and legs. He told me he was going to train me after I got some rest. Train me? My eyes were closing…I was drifting off. Even though I was only half-awake, W.D. asked me about the court and Jennifer. He was nervous, I could tell. Sleepily, I told him that the boys from Duchess had taught me how to steal. "They called it boosting. Because I became so good at it, I continued boosting whenever I could until I got caught and was arrested. Jennifer bailed me out. My dad and the social workers weren't called, and the judge appointed Jennifer my guardian. I have to finish going to school. I didn't tell anyone about it, not even Michael or Pam." W.D. put his fingers across my lips and said, "Don't say his name to me again! Understand?"

"Yes," I said, frightened by the threatening tone of voice he used. "I won't, I promise." My sleepiness started to fade, and a second wind came—fear. "Judge Adlow told me jokingly not to come back. He wasn't stern like other judges are. I don't want to get in trouble and have to stand before him again; if I do I'll be taken back and maybe put away. And I have to find a place to go because I won't be living in the rooming house much longer." W.D. stood and said, "Let me think. Lie there and try to sleep. I'll wake you up so you can get back." Losing W.D. would have devastated me; he made me feel wanted. I lay on his sheets, taking in the scent of his body with every breath, and fell into a deep sleep.

When my eyes opened, I had chosen W.D. The decision was not a conscious one, but visceral. My days of hairdressing school were about to be over. I stuck with school a bit longer. I didn't want anyone else to suspect I was a "turn-out." Pam and her friends called me a turn-out like it was a special thing, joining a new lifestyle, but I refused to think of myself in those terms. W.D. told me to stay at the rooming house until my time there was up, and while I stayed in Brookline, I was to be with him every other night. I was to see no other boys or men. He talked to me about the large amounts of money I could make, and I was further convinced to choose him and the life. I was confident that I could be good at what I was about to do and make unlimited amounts of cash. I would be with W.D. and wouldn't feel alone anymore. For training, he swore by the book written by a pimp, Iceberg Slim, and he used it as his bible. He believed that all good pimps went by this book. He instructed me in a severe tone of voice never to tell the police about him or that I had a man, and never to use the term pimp! That was loud and clear! I shook my head in agreement. What was I getting into now?

Jennifer and I found the perfect place for me, an in-law apartment in Randolph separate from the main house. She was constantly asking where I was day and night. To go along with the changes I was making in my life, I altered my appearance to look prettier. I wore false eyelashes, lipstick, and cat-eye mascara. I was a working girl, not a sidekick car booster. The girls at school helped me turn the color of my hair from a classy chestnut brown to bluish black, which was a drastic change. Men were attracted to me like magnets. I never knew this existed out there in the world, or that I had it in me to do this kind of work, but I was hungry for money, success, and love. It was hard to swallow that I had chosen this for myself—servicing men I detested, like I did in Chinatown. Yet it was frustrating to sit inside the hairdressing school and watch the girls working on Boylston Street when I could be doing the same thing instead of wasting my time learning how to make short money. The "square" life, as W.D. put it, was working for the man, never getting anywhere, and it would never pay me what I could make on the street. He drilled this into my head. I could make twenty dollars in five minutes in and out of the cars and fully clothed, fifty in a half-hour, and seventy-five to one hundred dollars an hour. That was good money in 1968. Of course, W.D. was right; I could never earn that kind of money except, perhaps, if I owned a business. He taught me to repeat, "My man is always right." White men were considered to be tricks, black men, never. And the only black man I was allowed to talk to was W.D. This was my job. He was pleased that I was boosting fur coats and making money from selling them, but he didn't want to hear anything else related to the half-suburban life I was living. His conversation was limited to talking about hustling on the street and in bars. "Turning tricks and money are all I want to hear about," he told me repeatedly. Money, money, and more money. I had phony identification and was learning about street life, a life I had never been exposed to before. W.D. was particularly concerned about making sure I was not busted at seventeen years old; I was his meal ticket. All the white girls like me had black men as pimps. I suppose we were easier to entrap and turn out, and we were better moneymakers. That was what they said on the streets.

The days weren't long enough for me. Keeping up at school and pleasing everyone else was impossible so I began taking pills, an upper with a downer in it called "bombers." I was painfully thin. I weighed only eighty-five pounds and I was taking diet pills! Good thing I ate so much. I was always on the move. I would go to school and rush back to my new room in Randolph, then stay up all night working in Boston. I always could get rides to Randolph, either from clients living on the South Shore or the guys who hung around at Duchess. W.D. was not pleased I was living so far away and didn't approve of me hanging out with old school friends. He tried to reel me in closer after one of the parties I gave in the Randolph apartment. Nothing could stop me now. I felt confident and was braver, always pulling against W.D.'s tight reins.

CHAPTER THIRTY-ONE

The Road Takes a Turn

The intense light in my cell is causing the left side of my head to ache. My eyes are sensitive to the brightness of lights like these. I feel nauseous. It probably isn't so smart to rehash my past. I am becoming paranoid; I can feel it. I wish I had a pad of paper and a pen to write down the crazy thoughts passing through my mind. Not knowing the time adds to my sense of unreality. I look up then down, and relax a bit. Shit! What have I accomplished in my life besides accumulating material things? No, it isn't just material things that I have achieved—I have my son! Soon he will know the whole truth about me, both the good and the bad. Oh, man, taking a walk down memory lane is painful, as is the present. But if I think of it like reading a book of someone else's life story, then it's gone once I shut the pages.

****

Jennifer was becoming increasingly upset with me. She was also curious about what I was doing and with whom. My landlord complained about groups of boys coming around, driving their fast cars, and making too much noise at night. The small studio apartment was behind a single-family house and in a stuffy section of Randolph, but I thought it was cool and cute. One night, I was having a small party with my Duchess friends after we had been out boosting. Jennifer came in unannounced, screaming at them. She told me that she would report me next time and what I was doing had to stop. "Now!" she screamed. Lying to her was the only way I could account for the extra money and coats she saw. I told her I had a part-time job that paid cash, and even though she was dissatisfied with my answer, she accepted it. I was convincing; I'd developed a knack for lying. Thankfully, she didn't see the trunkful of furs. When I gave her a suede coat, telling her that I had bought it especially for her, she loved it. That took the edge off for a short time. Everyone liked getting gifts from me; it made them not care what I did to get it. How's that for deep love…I'd never had money, so now it was like a drug. I was addicted to it. I had learned how to do something well and didn't care if the way I earned money was legal or not. With the exception of the hairdressing school, no one had ever been willing to help me learn how to make a dime.

The road was about to take a turn. I was detached from my dad, from Esti, from Leonard, and even Jennifer and Silky were becoming more distanced from me. They had busy social lives, and I amused myself by picking out which of the husbands in their group cheated just by watching them. Jennifer was having a difficult pregnancy that kept her in bed all the time, and when I went to see her, I certainly didn't tell her about what was really going on. I didn't want to cause her grief by telling her I had gotten thrown out of my little apartment because of the noise. I was checking in with her regularly, and she'd always give me a lecture or two whenever I saw her. Finally, I had to tell her I'd been asked to leave my apartment and said I was living with Pam even though I wasn't—I didn't want to add to her already considerable stress. I was grateful she kept my leaving a secret from the court. I didn't have much longer until I finished school anyway. I was old enough to make my own decisions, but unfortunately, I was not mature enough to make the right ones. Although I wasn't aware of it at the time, I was changing. Everyone told me that. Days and weeks went by, and yes, I was growing up. It was already Thanksgiving. I worked on the holidays. Jennifer did not invite me to dinner, and even if she did, I would never go because Archie was supposed to be there. She knew I didn't like family get-togethers anyway. Instead, I ate dinner at the deli. I was harder now and didn't trust anyone. I hated what I was doing, but I did it for my man…and money. I stopped being friendly toward people and worked alone to avoid trouble. I didn't smile very much. I had been swallowed up by the street life.

****

Here I am, many years later, still at it but without a pimp. It's my choice now. That's the side I chose—to be on top of the game, not the bottom. What I've done has been accomplished by me alone. Life has been my teacher, and the street life doesn't award degrees or retirement benefits. I have learned the hard way. I didn't take the stereotypical route of finishing school and attending college to receive a degree, but opted to be taught by actual life, the day in and day out of living with people in various settings, some of them harsh, as reality tends to be. I had been granted greater insight into life than square girls my age but didn't have a piece of paper to show for it or downtime to relax. I was working constantly. Today, in this prison cell room, I have downtime. This is the best teacher…as long as I always learn.

****

My life was busy and complicated then. W.D. told me I had to choose between living a fast life or a square life. I chose the fast life. The apartment on Schuyler Street in Roxbury was dark and gloomy, yet beautiful with its woodwork and hardwood floors. I hated that all the shades were closed day and night, and money was the only light that shone in the darkness. I was completely broken into "the life," which would take me on to the next level: the streets of Boston, New York, Connecticut, Philadelphia, Chicago, Detroit and Florida—any place where there were cities, truck stops, hotels, or madams. These streets were paved with money. Even the smaller roads of a town were places to learn the back door sex lives of so many men and women. I became a hoe, a prostitute, a street whore, working girl, learning faster than any textbook could possibly teach me. If degrees were awarded in my profession, today I would have a doctorate.

I believed the choice I made would be permanent. I would have to quit school with just a few weeks left before certification. There were too many demands being made on me, and I was exhausted from working around the clock without any sleep. All that time and effort going to school was for nothing. I imagined my teachers would be disappointed and, of course, my dad, Freddy. The men out there on the street where I worked were mostly average guys, with a few bigwigs, looking for girls to please them as a way to cope with the stress of their lives, both at home and at work. I heard the refrain "My wife doesn't like giving me blowjobs" countless times, and a litany of complaints about headaches, menstrual and menopausal issues, and on and on...these were often cover excuses for not wanting to engage with a husband who was sexually selfish or no longer attractive to them. There were so many reasons, and in this sense I was instrumental in holding shaky marriages together. There were many men who had a hunger and were just looking for sexual experiences with somebody new all the time, and then there were those with kinky fetishes. There were also single guys hungry for pussy and a good blowjob.

W.D. eventually took me out for the night, as he had promised early on, dressing me up and parading me around like I was his prize—and I was. I was beaming like a beacon of light in the dark, and at the time, totally unaware that other fellas were gawking at me. W.D. had instructed me not to look at other men, so my eyes were fixed on him and him only. I felt proud that I was on his arm and enjoyed dressing up. He told me that if I did well and earned a lot of money during the week, we could go out to the clubs one night a week on Sundays. I was so excited! Yes! And believe me, I worked harder and longer than my other sisters on the streets.

I learned more quickly than I had ever done in a classroom because I was motivated by money—the money was key, like corporate ladder up. Had I been aware of my abilities in other areas would I have gone in a different direction? I don't think so, I sensed that the kind of work I did was in my blood; it was like second nature to me. Discovering that I could do something well was a vindication of everything Anita and others had thought and said about me—even if it was about sex! It didn't matter to me that sex was what I did, only that I did it well. I had to have something that made me feel worthy. I pleased others and made them believe that I loved what I was doing. That was what I was taught to do: be an actress and excel at it. I did just that, always wearing, and protected by, a theatrical veil.

I didn't know anything about W.D.'s world outside the life because, as I was told, it wasn't my business. In the morning and afternoons, he went out dressed differently, more like a straight man than he did at night. My job was to become the best working girl, not worry about what he did. I worked day and night to prove it. I learned lots of tricks from the other girls, like how to fake orgasms, and some moves from W.D. as well. It was obvious I was good and getting better. I was relentless. If there was one customer left, I didn't stop. The tricks were lining up to see me again and again. I was earning the reputation of being one of the best street girls in Boston. I would walk the streets, and instead of averting my eyes as Anita taught me, I looked up. As odd as it may sound, I was proud of myself. The people there liked me and I was accepted in this new world. The street became my home. The street people—liars, thieves, pimps, hoes, bartenders, businessmen, and gangsters—became my family; we were all in the same life. I had never felt like anything special before. Now men stopped in their tracks when they saw me. One look into my eyes and it was on. When I passed the other pimps, I walked by with my head held high. I could hear them say, "I wish she was my bitch," or "That's one dedicated hoe." I was young enough to feel good about what they said. I couldn't tell the squares about what I did because "the life" had to be secret, but you could tell the men working in the garment district in Boston and the ones working in other garment districts, especially New York City. All of them were tricks: hungry, sex-driven men, bored with life, who had wads of cash. You could smell the guys who wanted to pay; one look gave them away.

All the call girls, in comparison to those of us on the street, had an uppity attitude back then. They picked up men in bars and hotels and thought that was superior when, in fact, they were merely afraid of walking the streets. But they did the same things as the street hoes, and some even more because they had to for their steadies. There was no difference except for the help they got from their madams, bartenders, and hotel doormen arranging dates with traveling men. They still picked up men for money, the only difference being the amount of cash they received; they would tongue kiss and do everything else that was taboo for the street girls, and for bigger money. There was so much to understand, I wondered how I would learn it all, but I simply soaked it up, absorbing everything I could. The touch of the black pavement—the magic of the streets—was so alluring that it motivated me to be the best. I learned the ropes inside and out. Some of the other working girls and I would do "doubles" (which is two girls with their tricks having sex in one room), and there were pimp rules, like "Don't suck her pussy, fake it." I was a chameleon, changing colors at any given moment.

I worked twenty-four hours a day, for days on end, thanks to the bombers keeping me awake. I liked making money, and there was no downtime to think or reflect. I pushed aside the experience of being turned out. I had grown into a bona fide hoe and had developed a tough shell. Having sex with Asian men was something I detested, but I got over it. Some of the older ones would get gonorrhea and treat it themselves so it never went fully away. Without a doctor, they spread the disease, which I learned about from the other girls. I only worked in Chinatown when it was slow, and believe me, I tried my best to avoid it.

The Essex Deli and King of Pizza on Washington Street were my preferred places to hang out in the heart of Boston's Combat Zone. That's where I would get the everyday working guys, ninety percent of whom were married and wanted no trouble. My waitress at the Essex seemed genuinely caring. She always made me my favorite mashed potatoes saturated with Land O'Lakes butter every morning and homemade spaghetti and meatballs anytime of the day. I was always working outside in front of the Essex to give the five a.m. truck drivers and the six a.m. office workers their morning blowjobs. Early runs were, and still are, common and prevalent; men loved their early morning sex. I was paid a fast ten to fifteen dollars, and twenty to fifty if I thought they were not average working guys but professional men. I took care of them quickly; within five to ten minutes they were done. We knew exactly where to park in the garages so we could have privacy. It was actually safer than working when it was dark. The police wouldn't bother the girls during those early hours as much as in the evenings. The truckers were easy to do, always in a hurry and heading for the Haymarket area or downtown drop-offs. I was learning how to perfect my mouth movements to save my body for sex with my man.

Wives would be amazed if they knew what their husbands were doing at any given hour of the day, not just at night when they think they're fooling around in bars. These encounters often took place long before the men were out of work. Quickies at lunchtime were and still are famous! Full-time girlfriends and mistresses require more time and attention and can be problematic. They most definitely cost more in the end, when everyone finds out, causing family breakups. But don't worry, ladies, there are hardly any relationships in a working girl/client hookup, and love certainly isn't involved except in very few cases. Worrying about what your close girlfriends are doing with your husband makes more sense. A relationship is more likely to develop when the girl is not a street girl. In some instances, a call girl is looking for an easy way out by latching onto a rich client as a potential husband, or foreign girls are looking to become citizens. It took me a while to grasp the concept, but I did.

I was at W.D.'s home one morning, he had already left, and Mrs. W. was up with the baby boy. I was exceptionally tired from the bomber I had taken the night before and having been awake for two days and nights prior to that. I was always on the streets and in the house for only a few hours at a time to shower and get some sleep. I had been awake for so long I had forgotten what day it was. Mrs. W. asked me for money to buy food. She knew I earned plenty of money by eyeing W.D.'s take, but there was something about Mrs. W. I didn't know. She begged me, telling me that W.D. would never know how much money I had made. She wanted fifty dollars. "Fifty dollars! No way, I can't do that." I talked her down to twenty. I told her, "I can't give you any money, W.D. said so."

"Baby," she pleaded, "he won't know you took that out, trust me." I didn't want to get into any trouble. W.D. had told me not to give his mother money, anytime, ever, without explaining the reason to him first. It was only twenty dollars… I knew deep down inside that I was about to make a mistake. He said she had money for everything she needed, but she begged so much, I gave her twenty dollars on the condition that she would not tell W.D. "No problem," she said, "I will never tell, count on that!" She asked me to watch the baby for a few minutes while she went to the store and then she left. I hadn't held a baby since I was in the hospital cradling my baby girl. I didn't want to touch him, but he was so cute. This baby wasn't W.D.'s or his mother's, he belonged to one of the working girls who had left the baby and never returned to pick him up. How could she leave him? He was about a year old, a handsome, chunky boy. Playing with the baby took my mind off the streets for a while. I thought about how it would be to have another child, but in this business, I can't do that.

Finally, W.D.'s mother came back, stumbling, and without food. She pushed by me. I asked her what happened, and she put her finger to her mouth and whispered, "Shhh. It's all good." She was behaving strangely, as though she was drunk. I told her I could get into trouble. She fluffed me off. I went into W.D.'s room, closing the French doors behind me. Although the baby was crying, I left him with her and I lay down and fell off for a short time, assuming she was taking care of him. I was extremely tired and not yet fully asleep when the baby cried again, and this time did not stop. He was screaming. I couldn't sleep so I went out to the living room, where I found the baby on the floor with a diaper that was wet and messed. I picked him up and when I went into Mrs. W.'s bedroom, she was sitting on the floor leaning against the wall. It didn't look like she was breathing. Then I saw her arm. It was tied with a rubber strap with a needle sticking out of it. I took a breath, touched her, and then touched her again more firmly. "Wake up! Please wake up!" Maybe she was diabetic like my mother? I recalled my mom injecting herself in the leg, never her arm. Oh, shit, W.D. will never forgive me if his mother dies while I'm here! The baby was crying uncontrollably. I tried to get him to stop, but nothing worked. I had to get help. I didn't know what to do first. I pushed Mrs. W. and shook her shoulder. She moved her head and made a sound. I put the screaming baby down and ran to get a cold facecloth. "Wake up, please!" I begged as I held the dripping cloth over her eyes.

"I'm awake," she managed to say, slurring her words. The cloth had worked. She was drooling out the side of her mouth and her eyes rolled back as she attempted to focus, pushing the cloth away.

"I'll get help!" I told her.

She gripped my arm like a vice as she shook her head. "You crazy?"

"Okay, okay, I'll stay with you," I said. "What can I do?" "Nothin', baby girl, just be cool."

It was too late for me. W.D. was coming through the front door. I ran to tell him his mom was sick. He responded with the question, "Did you give my mother any money, Libbe?" I didn't say a word. "Did you give my mother money?" he said emphatically. "And I'm not going to ask again." He grabbed my arm. The tenor of his voice sounded like the devil from hell was speaking.

"Yes, for food for her and the baby."

"How much, bitch? How much?"

"Twenty dollars, that was all, I swear!" He hit me so hard I flew onto the floor. The baby was still crying. I went toward the baby to pick him up so he wouldn't strike me again, but W.D. continued shouting. He lifted the baby and put him in his crib. He kept on beating me for giving money to his mother. "My mother is a junkie! Do you know what that is?"

"No, I don't!" I said, crying hysterically.

"Girl, now you do!" he scolded me. "It's dope—heroin!" It was not something I had ever seen. The street girls did drugs, mostly pills, pot, and snorting coke. I had never witnessed someone using needles for street drugs before. I had heard about heroin but had no idea how it was used. "Look at her! Look real good. She has used heroin for as long as I can remember. She is an addict. Don't you give her any money again!" He slapped me so many times I bled out of the corner of my mouth. My face! Why couldn't he have hit me somewhere else? Anita was controlled enough to beat me where the marks didn't show, but he didn't care where he hit me and whether it showed. He picked up the baby, calling him his "little man," and the child stopped crying like magic. I was shaken from the beating and by what Mrs. W. had done. I was naive and wasn't aware she was a drug user. The beating reinforced my impression of drug users for life: never trust them. I had to stop trying to help people; it always backfired. I didn't blame W.D. for hitting me because he had told me not to give his mother money, and I hadn't listened. It was my fault! But I didn't need it to be taught in such a brutal way…or did I?

I questioned whether leaving hairdressing school and staying at W.D.'s house was a mistake. I could have had another career in hairdressing and a diploma. I thought it was too late to go back to Mansfield Academy; in fact, it wasn't. Why didn't I stay in school? I believed that I was already too deep into the life. I couldn't call Jennifer to tell her I had been beaten up by a pimp because she would send Silky to get me. In truth, I was even more attracted to W.D., and didn't want to leave him—not yet. I had to keep my life secret. I thought I was too bruised to go to work, and W.D. said that if I didn't make up the difference by boosting, I would have to work the streets whether I was bruised or not.

I had to prove how sorry I was by working twenty-four hours a day. I needed to make up for what I did wrong. I was tired. I kept on going, day after day, and I wasn't eating properly. When I began thinking about my first night—turned out—I realized that I would never get over it, the terror of being trapped in that small room with the bright light shining above me, my legs spread wide for strange men. Although I tried hard to push it out of my mind, having to work in Chinatown brought it all back, like a bad dream, and I hated it. I had to go there to work; they preferred young girls, and it was a continuous source of money. Like getting back up on a horse after you've been thrown, I walked the streets of Chinatown and the Combat Zone day and night. Unlike the other girls, I didn't drink or do cocaine. I was sober and alert, and there was nothing to mask the pain. Seeing W.D.'s mother slouched against the wall with a needle dangling from her arm was enough to turn me off to drugs. I serviced one man after the other in cramped, squalid, cockroach-infested Chinatown apartments populated by roaming groups of scraggly cats. I was not a woman; I was a sex machine, performing sex acts for my audience. I was paying for love by giving W.D. all the money I earned. Not only had I been turned out, and turning tricks, I was a trick myself.

W.D. had been pimping me hard for months. I knew all the rules of the life. My weight was a mere ninety pounds, sometimes lower but never higher, and despite a diet of mashed potatoes with butter and spaghetti, I was becoming run-down. I ate Hostess Cupcakes between meals, the ones my father always brought home to me. I tried to be tough and wanted to be the best at what I did. It was important to me that W.D. was proud of me every day. I was making more and more money and learning all the games of the trade. I could talk men out of money just by touching them in a certain way. I rapped sex talk, speaking low and softly, and this was long before rapping appeared on the public scene. I wanted to feel proud of something I'd done well. But I couldn't tell people, yeah, I'm an artist in sex! Even though people may have looked down on me because they didn't embrace or understand the life, my work ethic was strong. I never refused money. Working hard on the busy days made up for the slow days. I wanted to do every car that stopped, but I was new to the life and didn't always consider whether the client was normal. I didn't differentiate between who was crazy and who was crazed by the desire to have sex. But, slowly, by listening and watching them, I learned. I was driven. I wanted to achieve something, have nice clothes, jewelry, and homes like the rich people in my dad and mom's families. I had hopes and dreams. I wanted the same life my aunts and uncles had when I was a little girl, but I did not want to act like them—like a pompous ass. I wanted to be well off to prove to my rich adoptive relatives that I could have the same things they had without their help. They never offered me their support and never would, but I was committed to getting there, one way or the other. In time, I wanted to be respected by people outside the life.

I got dating offers and marriage proposals from the customers; lots of them asked me to marry them. I never budged. Marriage was a thorn in my side. I certainly didn't want anything close to Freddy and Anita's marriage or, for that matter, anything like the marriages I witnessed in my foster homes, where the husbands and wives treated each other badly or did things behind each other's backs. I didn't want marriages like my clients had—husbands getting blowjobs from women on the street because their wives refuse to do it, or having a girlfriend on the side. I didn't consider marriage as something better than what I was doing, and even now, I can look back and say I would have chosen my way of life as tough as it was. I wanted to leave the thorns in my rose garden behind one day. My education was every day, every minute, seven days a week. The social knowledge I gained was more profound than the lessons learned in the square life or from any textbook. I stored every bit of information I learned from my clients. I learned about drug addicts and what made them behave the way they did. I saw little black kids hustling for extra money on the streets and from the hoes every day. Why didn't anyone help them? I always gave them money. Having been homeless myself at times, I understood about homelessness, and as I walked the streets, I would give food to hungry people. I learned about the games people play, whether the people are in the life or straight. These experiences were gained at the expense of my life, which was at risk day and night. There was an excitement about the street, as well as a satisfaction in the same way a race car driver or a sky diver gets an adrenalin high from the risk. The streets were my high; life flowed, and I felt fully alive when I was there. I felt like I was someone important. I could accept or reject whatever came my way. Sure, it was tough, but is anything in life that damn easy? And if its too easy if and when any tragedy hits, you would not be able to cope.

W.D. was working me hard because he wanted me to "be correct," as the pimps put it, and make him lots of money. But I was becoming ill, even the girls on the street said I looked pale. One night, I felt so weak I couldn't walk the streets and nearly collapsed as I got out of the cab at the house on Schuyler Street. I had to go home. I had W.D.'s money on me. I was dreading going inside because he would be angry I had come in early, but where else did I have to go? I was *so* sick. When Mrs. W. opened the door she could see that I was not well. "Come on in, honey. What's wrong?" she asked. She placed the back of her hand on my forehead, and I felt like putty because I needed a mother or a connection to a caring being. I nearly dropped to my knees. Mrs. W. grabbed me. When she touched my skin, we both knew that I was burning up with a high fever. As she propped me up and helped me take off my jacket, she told me not to worry and that she would speak to W.D. She may have been a full-fledged heroin junkie, but she was a caring being between injections.

I sat on a wooden chair as she rummaged through the baby's things looking for the thermometer. My temperature read one hundred and three degrees. She was visibly upset. "You have to stay in," Mrs. W. said. She made several calls trying to locate W.D., and I heard his sister's name mentioned. She brought me a change of clothes; the flannel pajamas I'd had for ages, not the frilly lingerie I wore for W.D. I was shaking from head to toe. My temperature was rising, and although I was hot, I felt like I was freezing. I was exhausted, but she wouldn't let me fall asleep. "Please," I begged, "I'm so tired." As difficult as it was to swallow, she fed me cold liquid after liquid. I held onto the small amount of money I made. I was afraid to put it down and then fall asleep. I was frightened when I heard W.D.'s voice and the echo of his shoes walking across the hardwood floor—the shoes were the shiny ones from Crystal's Shoe Store, a hangout where all the players went to buy their shoes and socks, from pimps to musicians and slick black and white men. When W.D. saw me he did not yell, but his expression was unsympathetic. "We need to take her to the hospital or she is going to die!" Mrs. W. exclaimed. "Her temperature is almost up to one hundred four!" Die? Me? Oh, god…

"We can't take her to the hospital because she's not quite eighteen yet," W.D. replied. "I'll call the doctor on Hemingway Street." There were a couple of special doctors who had offices there. It was commonplace for them to make extra cash when the pimps or their girls needed medical attention, especially penicillin for the clap, and at any hour. I guessed they were doctors who made house calls for hoes. Imagine that! Hoe doctors! There were a number of strippers, as I learned from the girls, who would trick with them for pill scripts. W.D. wanted me better, and quickly, because no work meant there wouldn't be any money. I certainly couldn't hustle in my condition. At the time, his sudden attention made me feel special. He seemed to be concerned about me as he paced the floor while we were waiting for the doctor. His mom kept me cool with facecloths doused with alcohol. Perhaps W.D. was upset because I had just given him the money I had made, which was half my nightly quota. He sat with me and brought cool towels to place on my back. My fever had almost reached one hundred and five degrees, and I couldn't speak. Mrs. W. immediately put me in a cold shower, rubbing me with alcohol the whole time, then put me in bed and lay down next to me. My eyes ached. I could see that W.D. was becoming upset. When the doctor finally came, she got up. I was in and out of consciousness, but understood that the old doctor recommended that I go to the hospital immediately because my fever was too high to treat at home. Even though it was believed that I had pneumonia, W.D. refused, and said, "Give her some medicine, Doctor. I want my baby better now. We'll get her through it." Because the doctor was familiar with W.D. and other pimps, he did as he was told. W.D. told him I had a high fever when they spoke on the phone, and the doctor had a small amount of medicine with him when he came. "Give her double the dose," the doctor said. "We need to break that fever fast." The doctor recommended that W.D. and his mother keep me cool after the showers to help break the fever, and then feed me fluids. I was to take baths in tepid water as much as possible and sitting up in case I got drowsy. After the doctor left, Mrs. W. rubbed my naked body with alcohol and held me as if I were her baby, rocking me back and forth, telling me I'd be okay. "We have to keep you cool," she said as I shook uncontrollably. The medicine W.D. picked up as soon as possible at the drugstore was a reddish-orange liquid. Every part of my body hurt. It was hard to open my eyes. W.D. said I was not to go back to work until the fever broke. The room seemed as dark as I felt. Mrs. W. insisted that her son keep me home a few days more than that. "We'll see," he said. I wanted to get better fast so that I could go back to work and make him happy with me—even though I felt so weak

I thought I was going to die. I could tell he was unhappy I wasn't working, but at the same time he repeatedly said, "Baby, I want you better. I don't like seeing you sick." He cared, of course he did, I told myself. I wanted to believe that. We slept together. He held me and gave me my medicine on time. He caressed my hair, damp from sweat, and fed me ice cubes to keep me hydrated. He even ran out to buy me popsicles.

My fever broke in the early morning the next day, and I had sweat so much the pajamas were soaked. I was weak but still alive. One day off was more than enough, and on the third day, W.D. cracked the whip and said, "You need to get your ass up and dressed! You've had your time off! Your fever is down now, baby. You look back to normal to me. Come on, make Daddy happy." His mom tried to argue for another day off, and in response W.D. was probably aping Iceberg Slim's philosophy when he said, "Good hoes work sick or not!" I felt like the postman who delivers mail even in the rain and snow.

"Okay," Mrs. W. said, "but dead hoes can't work at all and make you money!" She slipped me a pill, and I was out cold. W.D. never found out about the pill but was under the impression I had passed out from being ill.

The following day, I tried covering up how weak and sick I really felt and went to work. The pill had made me feel like shit. Several days later, I finished the medicine and I was well. I was grateful to Mrs. W. for caring for me, in essence saving my life. She baked biscuits and cooked greens for me for the next week or so "to fatten me up," she said. A few days later, W.D. revealed to me that in addition to being a drug addict, his mom was a dyke. I wasn't particularly bothered by finding that out because of Rosey and Pam, and in comparison to the kind of life and death situations I was exposed to, it was an insignificant revelation and one that I had suspected for quite some time. Nothing really shook me anymore. I certainly didn't think worse of her. She was a good mother to the little boy, and W.D. No matter what, I liked her, but W.D. didn't want his mother near his hoes. She had given me one of her pills the night I was so ill, and because of her, I slept, giving my body a chance to heal. I felt indebted to her. I was living on the edge and really didn't care whether I lived or died.

I was working the streets seven days and nights a week and became very ill again. I went back out on the streets too soon after the pneumonia. I was told I had little resistance and probably had never fully recovered from the fever. My lifestyle of little sleep, work and then more work, and junk food eventually resulted in another high fever. W.D. took me to an underground doctor. I had the chills. I was bleeding vaginally and was in pain. The doctor told me that there was nothing he could do and that I had to be taken to the hospital. I didn't have any idea what was wrong, and I was frightened. W.D. drove me to Beth Israel Hospital, and we only had to wait a short time before I was examined. The emergency room doctor told me that I was approximately almost two months pregnant and had miscarried. I had stopped taking the pills because they made me sick. I wasn't one hundred percent certain whose baby it was. I couldn't calculate, and it could have been a trick's baby. Even though I was upset by the loss of the baby, I spent only one day in the hospital and pushed myself out on the street again, back to work. Because I was still seventeen, the hospital would have had to inform Jennifer or Social Services, so I just walked out before they did that to avoid winding up back in court.

CHAPTER THIRTY-TWO

The Rules

I heard all sorts of stories from the streets, and my dates were telling me I should go out on my own. I didn't know then why they said that. The pace of my life was so fast that I didn't have time to think about whether I was happy or not. It was a combination of the lifestyle and the pills that sped up my adrenalin. The tough rules and regulations of the street game kept me in line because I didn't want to make any mistakes. To make sure that none would happen, W.D. had a list of rules for me to follow, many influenced by his volume of the original Iceberg Slim book, *Pimp: The Story of My Life*, drilling them into my head while using my body for sex in order to control me.

1. Listen to your man.
2. Never talk to any other pimp or black man, ever.
3. Never have a black man as a customer. The only black man in your life is your man.
4. You cannot have girlfriends; no hanging around idle. Do not socialize unless it's with your man or your wife-in-law (one of his other women).
5. No drinking or drugs with or without your man.
6. Never have sex without being paid.

7. Work every day to reach your quota. Quota is no less than five hundred dollars a day. Making more is what you are supposed to do! Never refuse money.
8. Try to pull other girls that work well to make more money for your man.
9. If you are picked up by the police, never say who your man is; ask the bondsman on Mass. Ave.—he will find your man.
10. Never kiss or become intimate with a client, ever.
11. Use a rubber during sex unless the customer has "big money."
12. When you choose to go from one pimp to another you are considered a flaky bitch, and sometimes you get your ass kicked. If the pimp you choose is a step up from the last, he may do a payoff to the previous one to not have problems.
13. If you work for a madam, you follow your pimp's rules, not hers. Don't tell her you have a man. Madams usually do not hire girls with pimps—only the lower end houses do that.
14. Never speak until spoken to when out with your man. Never go to after-hours clubs alone.
15. You work in rain, hail, snow, and sleet, whatever (like the postman).
16. Walk between the raindrops.
17. Cash up front, then count your money and stash when not with tricks.
18. Stay away from bad reputation hoes. Association breeds simulation.
19. Never let a trick go down on you. It's not his job to please you, it's your job to please him.
20. Do not socialize with squares unless it's to pull a girl or a man to make money from them.
21. Don't get sick. There are no sick pay days.
22. Don't ever talk back to your man even if he's wrong.

And on and on…

W.D. despised drugs because of his mother's addiction. Although he didn't like me to take pills, I took them to be able to stay awake for days on end. He told me that was the only kind of drug I could take. I was getting more curious to know what he did during the mornings and afternoons, but I didn't ask him because I was afraid he'd beat my ass. W.D. was strict. Some of his beatings were harsh, and I tried to avoid them. If I was even slightly short with the money, he got all fired up. My money had to be correct without fail or hot coat hangers would be next.

CHAPTER THIRTY-THREE

Busted

I used to slip W.D.'s mother food; I never gave her money again, just sandwiches. She never squealed on me, but W.D. was still punitive for other reasons. He was worse with every passing day, and I took the punishment. In bed, he kissed me sensually and tried to please me as if he were trying to compensate for his cruelty outside the bedroom. The emotion I felt for him wasn't love. It was closer to lust, and respect, and my desire to please. His mom told me she was sure he loved me but wasn't able to show it because that meant weakness. It wasn't until much later in my life that I understood his real character. One night I came home without making close to my five hundred dollar quota. It was so slow; the police were everywhere. I still wasn't in great health or at a stable weight. My body hadn't healed since the miscarriage. W.D. beat me across my back with a pimp stick, a hot wire hanger covered with a rag, over and over again. I had never felt pain like that, a burning lash searing the exposed skin over every inch of my back and butt. I thought it would never end. I could see that his member was erect and hard, and he wanted me. He unzipped his pants and shoved his penis up my ass with one violent thrust, and continued assaulting me, stabbing at me with his big dick again and again. At times, he would withdraw entirely and then re-enter gently and erotically, but then he would thrust harder and deeper inside me. During normal sex, his penis was almost too big for me to take, but this was unbearable. He wouldn't stop. There were bloodstains covering the sheets. I was screaming, and my face was wet with tears. Like the night I was turned out, W.D. enjoyed brutalizing me even more when I cried. Was this the norm for men, to feel big and tough taking sex from a helpless woman or girl? He was punishing me more sadistically with sex than Anita had with her sticks and straps. My body burned and ached. I wanted to die. It was like my childhood wounds had been reopened tenfold, and the rules dictated that I couldn't even tell anyone. It was a secret I had to keep to myself, just like in my childhood. Mrs. W. felt badly but couldn't interfere; she just listened to my screams. I didn't want to be with him anymore. Later, he explained that the blood staining the sheets wasn't only mine, but his. He had sickle cell anemia. Although I hadn't any idea what that meant, I almost felt badly for him. When we had had regular sex again after he attacked me, he made a point of pleasing me. I was totally confused.

I was still hustling with the cars on the street and boosting, taking some questionable risks. I was in Filene's Department Store lifting small items again, sexy lingerie, stockings, and shoes—unaware that the store had just installed a new camera system. As I was heading out the door onto Washington Street, a man and woman grasped each arm and led me back inside, gripping so tightly it was impossible to break loose. Shit! They weren't letting go! Damn, now what? They sat me down, lecturing and threatening me about how much trouble I was in while I was thinking about how fortunate I was they didn't get me for hundreds of dollars of fur and suede coats. I didn't have any ID with me, and I didn't know whose address to give them, so I gave them my foster sister's. She was still my guardian for a bit longer. There wasn't anyone else I could call for bail money. W.D. always said never to mention his name, so I called Jennifer. I was busted. "It's going to be on your record," she said. "It's the second time, and I have to call your social worker." I pleaded with her not to call because I could become a ward of the state, so she agreed that she wouldn't. I would have to live with her in her apartment in Randolph. Since W.D.'s beating two weeks before, I had been trying to figure out a way to leave him without getting another one. Yes, this was my way out. Someone was watching out for me, I believed, and I knew it was my mother, my guardian angel. I believed in her more as I grew older because I had stayed alive throughout all sorts of situations when I could have been killed.

Jennifer and Silky came to the police station to get me and paid my bail. I left all of my clothes at W.D.'s—a small price to pay for leaving him. It was time to go, but "the life" was in me. I couldn't "square up," and I knew it. I didn't fit into the suburbs, and I wanted to go back to work. I was already scheming how to get out at night to make money for new clothes and to help out Jennifer. To my surprise, she did wind up informing the social worker about the theft. She said she had to because it would show up on my record and they would see it. We had to go back to court, and I was in front of Judge Adlow again. Jennifer gave him her word that I would be under her roof and in her custody until I turned eighteen, no longer under state supervision. Even though I understood she didn't have any choice because I had been arrested, I was a bit upset she had called the social workers. Going to another foster home was out of the question and living in Randolph posed its own complications. It was too slow for me; I was so bored, and I didn't like the lifestyle. Her friends were naive squares from the suburbs, even though many of them had originally lived in Mattapan or Dorchester. They were uppity middle-class Jewish girls whose husbands were dogs and cheated on them while they, the prima donna wives, shopped, and then stayed at home waiting for them, gossiping constantly either by the pool or on the phone, thinking that they had solid marriages. The life was in my blood. I would never become one of those white-picket-fence wives.

During court that day, Judge Adlow was funny, even more so than during our first encounter. The police showed him the items I stole—nightgowns, bras, stockings—and he joked that I could have done better. He held each piece of silky, lacy underwear in the air while everyone in the courtroom laughed. I shrugged when he asked me the reason I stole them. "Miss Siskind, I suggest you upgrade, and I don't want to see you back here again," he said, "especially with lingerie." The laughter in the courtroom sounded like a low rumble as the judge, at my expense, entertained them. It made me feel uncomfortable, and I wanted to get out of there. I knew that would be my last time; twice was enough. I went home with Jennifer. Although having home-cooked food and sleeping in peace was a respite from working, my body was itching for excitement, and I had to go. I wanted to make money. I would have to latch onto another pimp to survive. I wasn't sure if I wanted to work for a madam because I didn't want to follow their rules. I heard from the girls on the street that madams have their girls do everything, and I hadn't been trained that way. I needed to find another man, but which one? I called Pam, and she told me not to be afraid of W.D., he would be cool with it. I hoped so. It was Christmastime, trees were up, and there were lights everywhere.

Walter was a small-time hustler, a flimflam man I met on Morton Street, who aspired to be a pimp. We spoke often because he was a great source for hot clothes. I didn't know anything about him beyond that. He decided I could be an asset to him, bringing in a few bucks, and he would teach me the game. I took off from Jennifer's once again, but figured it would be better not to go back in town for a while. Pam said that W.D. felt badly that I had got-ten popped, but that wasn't enough to make me go back to him. No more beatings, I hope! While other girls were dressed in new clothes and jewelry, I had gotten nothing from W.D. except a night out here and there. I hooked up with Walter, and he took me on a bus to Columbus, and then Cleveland, Ohio to train in the art of money exchange scamming. He was not into the pimping game so much, and I was not considering choosing him; he was strictly a hustler. I just wanted to see if I could do what he asked. So there I was in Ohio for the holidays, having him show me again and again what to do. There were two envelopes, one in one pocket, and one in another pocket. One had three hundred dollars in it—all new twenties—and the other had cut up newspapers with a twenty-dollar bill at either end. Each envelope was sealed, but if someone held the envelope with the newspaper in it up to the light, it was possible to see the twenty-dollar bills. Walter said folks were gullible this time of year. We would tell the people they were buying counterfeit money that looked exactly like real bills: three hundred dollars for one hundred dollars. We would show them, and it worked. They believed me…it was like selling ice to the Eskimos. After a few days, it was getting hot out there, and just before we both were supposed to leave, he took the cash and booked out—leaving me to fend for myself without any money in my own pocket. I had been an asset to his business, and I didn't understand why he left me. Did he use me or did he have to run out? I had to catch a trick in an unknown city to get a ticket back to Boston. I hated bus stations, especially out-of-town ones. I only felt comfortable at the Greyhound station in Boston because it was home base. I caught a quick car date. He even tipped me.

I had learned the flimflam business but disliked the con of taking people's money for nothing, people who were not rich. I planned never to play that game again, not unless I was in dire need. When I got back to Boston, I was pissed. Walter was not at his house. I hung out around Morton Street and Blue Hill Ave., but no Walter. It was time for me to move on and go to work tricking. That was what I knew. I had nobody to be with on Hanukkah or Christmas, but why would that matter anyway?

CHAPTER THIRTY-FOUR

Choosing a Pimp

It was cold as hell out there. I thought about going back to Jennifer's apartment, but I couldn't get up the nerve to just go by her house. She wasn't happy with me because I left. I was on the streets again, and the girls knew I was a stray and a good score for their men. They were pulling me to go with their pimps. I was wary of getting caught and conned by W.D., but I wasn't as frightened of him as I used to be. I learned from the other girls who had been hanging out for a while that he wasn't one of the big pimps—he was a newcomer, a young-blood pimp from Grove Hall. I didn't know that before. I was okay with that news. The girls who had been working for years began hanging with me to get more clients and doubles, which meant more money for them. They saw how many tricks would stop and ask me out. They knew that I always made money and never got high. I was young and capable, happy to be out there helping them and myself. I found other streets to walk outside the Zone. In a strange way, I missed W.D. I stayed clear of Pam and Rosey and didn't speak much to them. I rented a room on Chandler Street, where I could stay and bring my tricks. But word was getting around to the pimps that I was solo. I did not want to work for the madams yet because I heard I had to stay on lockdown for at least one week.

Because I wasn't going to Mattapan anymore, some of the boys from Blue Hill Ave. came to the Combat Zone to find me. They told the other boys from Mattapan who went to the high school that I was hooking and all of them came to see me one night, curious to know what I looked like as a hooker, as if I was a stranger to them, like a clown in the circus. They were immature and awkward, and once they saw me, they wanted to pay to go to bed with me, probably out of curiosity and because I looked more attractive than I had before. They had never let on that they were attracted to me, and it was ironic that now they offered to pay me to have sex with them when before they never approached me. But I wouldn't have sex with any of them for any amount of money. Intimacy, no way, even for cash—that scared me to death. I backed away. I really wanted to give it a go, but I was too scared. I'm sure I would have been a lot more intimate if I was not in the life. If only I had a crystal ball then. The only times I really regretted not having a normal life was when I was feeling down and introspective or feared getting into trouble. Then reality would kick in. Now I want those things, but I waited too long to have romance, security, and peace of mind. The street was like my real home and comfort zone. It was a place of independence. And it gave me esteem as a person. I held my head high when I walked into the bars and they knew my name, and the same tricks waited in line for me to go to bed with them week after week. Some even fell in love. In my small world, hidden away from society's eyes, I was someone. I would never leave my job; it owned me and I owned it. I had to choose a man so I could work all night, every night. I wasn't the only one in the life who wanted what I did, I was sure of that. Other girls said they wished for a knight in shining armor, a sugar daddy. There are so many people who are in the same rut all of their lives, people who just have regular jobs but want to be recognized as someone big and important, and hang out in their neighborhood bars to be praised.

The rules were essentially the same, but not all pimps went by the word of Iceberg Slim's bible. They either added to the rules or didn't follow Iceberg's theories at all; they made their own rules. Because of my infatuation with W.D., the choice to be with him was made for me. I didn't have to think making that decision, but now I did. This time I had to listen to the 411 stories of the girls who had been on the streets for ten years or longer, who knew all the pimps right down to the bone—the bitch's choice was based on which pimp had the best sex with her or had the best car and clothes and bunch of bitches. A sharp appearance played a part in my decision, as did age. Although W.D. was young, he was older than me, and I liked the father image, someone with knowledge, so when he spoke I could learn from him. At the same time, I was also attracted to someone who talked shit, rapping softly into my ear so that my sexual arousal influenced me, not only to have sex with him but also to be fucked mentally—those were also the ones I fell for. There were the stupid pimps, the bums who drugged out and drank and encouraged their girls to get high too; some were known as Pepsi Cola pimps, a new term I learned. On the street, it was impossible not to be taken in by the ones who showboated with their fancy clothes, furs, diamonds and cars. I admired them then. As I matured, the ones who eventually attracted me invested their money wisely, the ones who bought houses and made their cash grow, but at the beginning, I had little experience making those decisions. My mentality then was that of a street hoe—all show.

I took my working friends' opinions and made a couple of bad choices. Then I went with a pimp who was many steps up from W.D. His name was Fats. It wasn't a hassle to go from one pimp to another, except that Fats pulled in the reins and held tight to the rules. I sensed that he was a bit weak because all he wanted to do was stay in bed with me and freak. It seemed like he was really into me…no pun intended. Once, when I was out with Fats we ran into W.D., and because of Fats' size and affiliations, he was so intimidating there wasn't any issue between them. I said who I was with, and there was nothing more to discuss. He had a reputation at all the after-hours places in Boston, particularly one place on Washington Street near the Dudley Station area where gamblers, cocaine hoes, pimps, gangsters, musicians, and street people hung out. Everyone knew and loved Fats, and the after-hours he frequented and ran. They said he owned it, but rumor had it that the gangsters backed him. I would meet him there every night. I wore clothes that were a step up from what I was used to and better makeup. My signature blue-black hair, false eyelashes, and pink lipstick were always on. My skin was flawless, so I never needed face makeup. I had big, brown eyes. I was skinny, a size zero, with long hair to my waist, and wore a small B-C cup size. I was hot. Fats raved about how good I was and how devoted to my work, but for me there was no attraction there, not like the way it was with W.D., my only frame of reference, and I guessed that was the way it was supposed to be—strictly business. W.D. stayed on my mind. I would have a drink or two but never indulged in cocaine or other drugs because of my reaction to Michael's substance abuse and W.D.'s attack on me after I gave his mother money for heroin. Anyway, I didn't like the burning sensation in my nose from cocaine when I tried it, and it made my heart race even faster than the bombers. I was hyper enough. The pimps liked their girls to get high so that they would get freaky in bed, but I refused drugs except when Fats dipped his finger into the coke dish and forced me to suck the white powder until it dissolved in my mouth. It had a bitter taste, a freezing sensation, and then I got high. Those were the only times I got high with my man. The working girls were always looking to cop; they said it helped them turn their tricks. W.D. always preached against using any and all drugs, and I was lucky he was my first pimp. The other girls on the street used drugs all the time, and there weren't many free from addiction. I wasn't attracted to that way of life and resisting it was easy for me as long as I stayed busy. I worked by myself to avoid contact with those girls. My pimp liked that about me. He said, "That's my bitch. She saves the high for me."

Fats' after-hours was swarming with pimps. No hoe was allowed to flirt or look at any other pimps, especially when she was with her man or she'd get her ass kicked for disrespecting him—that was the rule unless she was ready to choose. Abiding by this rule simplified being out at the after-hours or any place they went. During the time I was with Fats, I met a girl on New Year's Eve who was known as the expert booster in town. She and her pimp, Big D, were over at Fats' apartment one night, and after becoming friendly, I went with her to boost. I learned how to boost an item right in front of someone, looking at that salesperson with a straight face without getting caught. We went to the high-end Newbury Street shops and made out big time. I didn't see her after separating from Fats, but I continued boosting, even though it was easier when another person acted as a distraction. Fats wanted to stay in bed snorting coke all day. I didn't like the white powder enough to put it up my nose to feel the burn, and I liked him even less for forcing me to get high with him. The decision to split from him was made without a second thought—we were not a good match. I was gone, but I had to replace him fast for my own protection. Fats was in the life and knew its rules.

My train of thought has wandered for a few…into the now as I thought this: I have some life lessons I'd really love to give to the tricks' wives. Some men wouldn't have to pay for sex if their wives were more liberated in bed, and less distracted, although others are just doing it for sexual adventure or as a release from stress. And wives who have affairs are often willing to do it all because their husbands are too self-absorbed to care about mutual pleasure or are indifferent to how they present themselves. Conversations about aspects of "the life" could benefit those in the straight world by helping them to understand each other. I do feel that I was often able to offer what was almost a form of sexual therapy by explaining to my clients about how to achieve intimacy with their wives on the level they were seeking with me. I do know of many instances where it worked so well my tricks stayed home for their pleasure!

****

I've got to get out of here. I'm really claustrophobic. Time seems to be moving so slowly, and no one has told me anything. Where is my lawyer? I feel like I'm losing it, and I am afraid of saying a word. Take a deep breath…aah, that's better. Geez, my thoughts are speeding around. I just keep writing thoughts down in my mind like I would if I had paper. I tell myself every now and then that I can make it through this wait time. It's a big lesson to learn.

CHAPTER THIRTY-FIVE

More Choices

January 1968. I was happy New Year's was over. Months out on the streets felt like years. He was dressed like a movie star, not as flamboyant as a pimp, and rode in the backseat of a black limousine as it drove down the streets of the Combat Zone. His name was Green Eyes. He had traveled from New York looking for girls, and I knew at first sight that I wanted him as my man. Because I was still with Fats, I had to find out about Green Eyes on the sly so no one would tell Fats I was asking around. I figured out that after I was with Green Eyes, he could tell Fats. First, I had to find out what he wanted in exchange for my choosing him. I was more than ready to go with new blood. He was in Boston to cop a girl to work for him, and though there were other pimps I could go with, I wanted to see if he was the right one. I learned from one of the girls that when I chose I would have to give him money upfront—trap money. That was the correct way to leave a qualified pimp: pay-off.

I worked day and night, stashing away what I would need. I was working as hard as I could without getting caught by Fats, who would have taken my money away because I wasn't with another man yet. I didn't go up to the after-hours to meet him as I had been doing. I found Green Eyes in his car on LaGrange Street and asked if I could sit with him in the car to discuss things; I gave him five hundred in cash to show him I was serious. He asked why I left and if I owed anything extra. He was super fine, but seemed to be unfriendly, cold and plastic, like he was all about the money and a big front. Of course, he was aloof to make me want him more. I would have gone back to the streets, but the thought of running into Fats stopped me. Two days of not going back to his place—he knew something was up. There was no doubt he would take away my other money if he caught wind. I had to be straight first. Green Eyes understood and respected me for that. He told me to stay with his limo driver, Sam, while he met with Fats. The five hundred I had given him was toward choosing money, and it would cost me another five hundred for the changing fee to Fats. The balance would be five hundred more from me to Green Eyes to discuss what my new rules were. Altogether, choosing him cost lots of money—fifteen hundred dollars—bigger than anyone else, especially in Boston. He had a tight game and that worked on me, like having a business plan, and one I would never forget. Beyond that, my quota was seven hundred a night minimum, and he wouldn't accept any amount less than that from a Boston hoe. Money in Boston was too short for his style. Otherwise, it would have been a thousand a night. He said he took Boston hoes to New York to make real money. He gave Fats five hundred for me, and there weren't any hard feelings except that Fats was less than happy about losing his money-making white bitch.

Green Eyes brought me to New York, but I felt uncomfortable with his layout. He could tell I was unhappy, and he knew I would run off if he kept me there. Sam drove me back. He was very helpful. He clued me in to his boss's ego and that he had business in the straight world. Green Eyes stayed in New York, so I gave the money to Sam, who stayed on in Boston. I knew this long distance pimp/hoe relationship was not working out and would be over soon. I was living in a place one of my tricks gave me for work, a top floor penthouse apartment with a view of tree-lined Commonwealth Ave. The night Green Eyes came back to Boston and slept with me, there was no connection between us. I wasn't into him. This was not what I had in mind. He was just a pretty boy who was stuck on himself. I, at least, had to feel needed in order to do great work. It had cost me dearly to find that out. I had to choose again. Now I understood why the girls chose so often.

Green Eyes had a handsome, white acquaintance who was secretly in the life. Luca's cover was being a business owner; he had a shop on LaGrange Street. Green Eyes introduced me to this white boy when we first met, and I thought that he could be my way out. He would talk and flirt with me whenever his pal was gone. There was a definite connection. I didn't know there were white pimps, and he was a fine-looking man. He attempted to talk to me a few times when I was in his store. One afternoon, we made a connection. He said he had a place, a basement apartment in the South End, and I should make it a point to see him there. Luca told me that I should leave Green Eyes because he didn't have enough time for me and was a selfish man, and he would take care of me. I guessed that their friendship wasn't a close one. It was easy—no money was exchanged for me, just words. I went with him to his apartment, which was like a seduction pad. Instantly, the kiss was on. He was so good when we had sex that after two nights I paid him willingly; he never asked. We were in sync. I wanted to give him the money aside from the sex. He liked me, and I was happy sleeping with him at his place, an apartment in the basement, which I normally wouldn't want to go to but in his case, did. My apartment on Commonwealth Ave. had big windows to see the sky. His place had exposed brick walls and had a real cool feel to it. There was something comforting about him at first, so I did not feel intimidated. I felt needed. Luca didn't push me out of bed to go to work, but liked having me around him. He didn't give me a quota. And so I put one on myself, no less than five hundred dollars a night. Easy. He even bought me clothes—nice, classy clothes, and silk stockings with fancy garters that I loved.

I met him after work late one night. We got a bite to eat on Boylston Street, then we went to his apartment as usual. It was obvious he'd had a few too many. He gave me a sweet, mixed drink when we got home. I drank it, swallowing the entire glass in one long gulp. Not being used to drinking, I was really messed up. We were into some heavy, hot sex and my body was gleaming from his sweat, my long hair wet with perspiration. The soft skin of my rear end stung from him slapping at it with every thrust of his large, manly member. He asked me to stand against the wall with my legs spread apart. I was getting wet from the eroticism in his voice as he told me he wanted to watch me while he touched himself, and telling me to insert my fingers deep inside. I brought my fingers to my mouth and tasted myself. He placed his finger in my mouth as he talked, and as he walked away, he told me to keep my eyes closed. I shut my eyes…I could feel the pulsing inside my wet vagina…and then—the blast of a gunshot reverberated in my ears, and I dropped to the floor! I thought I was dead! He came back and lifted me to my feet. I was stunned by the sound of the discharge. It was terrifying and erotic at the same time. I knew he liked guns, but he had never shot one near me before. I thought the guns were for decoration. I asked him what happened. He casually replied, "I was practicing my shots."

"At me?" I asked.

"Yes, baby, don't worry. I'm a good marksman. See my bullet?" He was frightening me. He had been drinking; what if his shot was off the mark? I'd be dead.

Next, he asked me to stand with my back against the wall, facing him so that I could watch as he fired and he could see the expression on my face. Oh, hell no…are you for real? Sure was. There was a shot, and then one more. My body was shaking. I felt the panic; my breathing was hard and heavy. He got off on this—his dick was as hard as a rock. Pulling me closer to him and slowly bending me over, he entered me. The fuck was amazing. He talked and touched me, sucked my neck and breasts. Then we dropped from the bed to the floor in such ecstasy that I never even felt it as I hit the rug. I was putty in his hands, and then he stopped. My fear of not knowing if I would die was a rush for him. He asked me, "Wasn't that a high, baby?"

I couldn't speak and just shook my head yes. He handed me the gun, a .45 automatic pistol and told me to pull the trigger. It was far too heavy for me to handle, but I felt trapped in this insane game. Why hadn't anyone called the police? He told me his friend lived one floor above him, and the place had been soundproofed. It was funny he said that at the moment I thought it. His naked body stood behind me, and the sensation of his soft skin against mine eased my mind. I was aroused again. As he pressed against me, he put my finger on the trigger. I was thrust backward, nearly to the floor. Right then, I understood the reason no money was paid to Green Eyes. This maniac needed a girl to play his sex games with him…and his ammunition was real. Green Eyes just let me go to the crazy white boy with the guns—he had made enough money from me, the temp white bitch. I never returned to Lou, despite our physical attraction.

After work the next morning, I went to see him at the store where his legitimate business was. I made it clear that I would never go back with him. I apologized to him, expressing my regret that it didn't work out. I told him I didn't like guns. He understood but wasn't happy; he said we had a great connection. I wasn't intimidated by Luca because W.D. had drilled it into me that white men were tricks, and so in the back of my mind I didn't view this white guy as an authentic pimp—he was a con doing business ventures. But I did know tough white guys, and so I knew they existed, big time. Later, I learned that there were, in fact, white pimps, and hardcore ones at that. I had taken a risk leaving this one and was grateful I had made it out with no scars. I often thought of him and our sexual connection.

I had a new man about every two weeks or so, but no one I could relate to. In my own experience and from the experiences of other girls, I learned that it is a waste of time staying with a man you don't like. I was confused and lonely. I had to choose again, but I took time off to work for a madam in Columbus Circle, New York, a woman my friend and working street buddy Marcie suggested to me. I asked a few girls if they knew her. Only one did. She said she did not like working for madams because she had to do too much and pay the cut. Marcie loved to party, most of the time with her man. Both of them were into sex and drugs. She set it up for me with the madam. I needed to go. I phoned Jennifer, checking in with her, and she was fine. I told her I was going with a friend from Parker Hill Ave. to New York. I felt guilty about not telling her what I was doing, but she was having issues with her pregnancy, and the last thing I wanted to do was worry her. I was becoming a bona fide hooker, and knew the streets like I had been born on them. Marcie's connections led me to many madams' establishments in New York City, Chicago, Philly, and Connecticut. I learned valuable lessons from this experience, big ones. While I was away, Marcie looked for and found a new trick house on Parker Hill where we could both work. I hustled with her constantly, and we worked well together. She tried to pull me for her man, Hank, but I didn't like him. She liked women as well, but I wasn't attracted to her—not clean enough, kind of a nasty bitch, and way too into drugs. When we went down on each other during doubles, she was very much into it while I remained detached, totally… she went with too many men without douching.

Michael and Huckie heard rumors about me being in the Zone from the kids who kept coming down there. Illy, who had a crush on me, brought his brother. They all wanted me out of the street life, Huckie more than Michael, who kept his distance from the Zone downtown. I was long gone from the life I once lived in Boston's suburbs as a foster kid. These guys were just boys to me compared to the pimps. They will always remain so in my thoughts and heart.

When Marcie got high with her clients, she and I performed B and D (bondage) and S and M (submission) with them. I was learning all sorts of new techniques. There wasn't anything she didn't do, and I learned the tricks of the trade not only from the streets but also from her and some of the older girls and madams, like Les, Barb, and Charlie from New York, NY. I spent lots of time there. My education at the madams' houses in Connecticut, New York, Chicago, and Florida added new twists to my sexual repertoire, although not all my experiences with madams were pleasant learning opportunities. They were bitches who worked the girls like pimps and stole money from us. What could we say or do…there was no one to help us. I swore that if I ever had the chance to be a madam, I would not cheat my girls. The clients were deceitful, and I studied their ways both on the streets and in whorehouses. The black madam in Columbus Circle, who had bohemian beads for curtains, spied on the girls with their clients through peepholes. She was a drunk and abusive toward the girls, with a mouth on her like a truck driver. Her sexual preference was women. The rules allowed the clients to kiss and go down on the girls, do anal, and come two to three times. I knew she got off big time watching her girls work. To make money, I had to go along, even though I would have preferred doing things my own way. I would rather be on the streets than in the brothels, but I hadn't chosen a pimp yet and couldn't be on the streets without a hassle, especially in New York. Dominance came to me naturally, and I ended up at the houses where the madams specialized in B and D. I was becoming expert at it, and I had my own personal slaves. I even had a great German accent. I knew learning this specialty would go a long way at home. I went out after work to get away from the constant wake-up calls of the madams, who scheduled for three, four, five, and six a.m., and then all day and night; plus, some of them would drink and be bitchy. I learned the streets in New York where the girls worked. There were dicks in the morning for breakfast, and sex, sex, sex for the rest of the day and night. I needed only one or two outfits because the Jewish guys in the garment district would give the madams sample sizes, which fit me perfectly. So many Jewish customers went to the madams. I had been working solo, out of pocket as they would say, for weeks, changing from place to place and thoroughly enjoying the torture I meted out to the men. They pleaded for their balls to be tied until the blood stopped circulating, and I would tease and taunt them using dirty language to egg them on. I was learning more every day about their attraction to bondage, and why they derived pleasure from torture. The higher the office these men held at work, the more pain they required, and the better they loved it. The amount of stress that came with their position correlated with the severity and oddity of their requests. They truly wanted to be humbled by the experience and then go back to their so-called normal lives. It would have been a lot easier if some of the madams gave lessons, but most were brief in their explanations and let you figure it out. The few who did teach were well worth working for.

I still needed to go out and find a man for myself; I wasn't sick of working under one yet. One of the madams recommended the Turn Table on Broadway. She was right. There were plenty of players there, and a girl could be there solo without a problem. I met Mr. L, a pimp and businessman, and his young sidekick from Poughkeepsie, NY, his yes-man, who loved to please Mr. L and his girls. I ended up choosing him and went to work as a lot lizard at some truck stops in Philly and Jersey. Doing truck stops was a totally new twist but easy enough. I would tell them my dad used to be a truck driver and the tips came flowing in. The truckers were all waiting for me nightly, wanting a simple blowjob before they went to sleep. Word spread about me, and business was good. They told me stories, and the older ones reminded me of my dad so I wasn't afraid of being hurt by any of them. I was making twenty dollars for each blowjob, plus tips. The white madams' houses paid the best though, so I did not want to give that up: one hundred to one hundred fifty dollars for a regular session. It wasn't long before I realized that Mr. L and his gofer were not for me. His girls thought he was bitchin' because of his club and his notoriety for having made a hit recording. I was supposed to be with my man, Mr. L, earlier that night, but instead he snorted coke and got so high he watched his gofer boy fuck me into oblivion in a dark, sleazy hotel room outside the city. That was how he got his kicks. I wasn't happy about his young blood getting free sex, but I had to admit the kid could fuck! I had to go. I didn't give a shit who he was because I knew what he was behind his cover-up. Again, I had to choose. I caught some dates in Times Square, made some decent money; no cuts to the madams but not as safe. I knew that I would have no problem leaving Mr. L at all; he wouldn't follow me—it was just a thing to him. I made even more money on two outcalls from a madam, and took off when one of the truck drivers I met who had given me his card offered me a ride out of the city. He was going on a run to Boston. I was gone. I left New York on great terms with three top madams who wanted me to stay or come back and work a two-week stretch. But, at that moment, I declined.

CHAPTER THIRTY-SIX

The Essex Hotel

Back in Boston, Marcie and I dressed up to go to where all the pimps hung out: Paul's Mall, the Jazz Workshop on Boylston Street, and, of course, the Sugar Shack. One of the pimps I liked was Sess. He was so smooth! Even though he had a stable of girls, I had been watching him for some time, and now I was paying much closer attention. His build was slight, like the rock star Prince, and he wore the best threads, with a white mink coat and a custom-made white mink hat. He drove a white Cadillac and wore the best-looking diamond jewelry. He made an impression on me, and I liked the way he spoke, directly but not aggressively. His game was tight and all the girls liked him. He was considered classy and soft-spoken. His own girls stayed with him, his main one for years. Marcie gave him the message that I wanted to choose him. Then there he was—approaching me outside on Boylston Street just as we were about to see a coke and reefer man for Marcie. I liked the way he got out of his car, lifting his white mink so it wouldn't drag on the car floor runner or the ground. W.D. used to lift his coat in that same classy way. He was pleased when Marcie's man approached him with the news about me, one of the best white working girls in town. "Yeah, baby," Sess said, "I've heard she's hot." My girlfriend Katie (who I had just started hanging with) and her man came by. The fellas all shook hands, and were talking for a while before they left to party at the after-hours.

I told her I was choosing Sess because he was good to his women. When he fully understood that I was serious about choosing him, he told me to get into his car and drive him home. I was thrilled—that was it for me! Drive! Oh, yeah! Driving couldn't have made me happier; in fact, I was elated, and that was all he had to say for me to be his and choose. I longed to experience that sense of independence again. I bought my first car when I was living in the foster home in Canton, an old Caddy with standard drive that broke down after the first few weeks. Then they sold the car and I lost my first getaway vehicle. Now I drive a brand-new Caddy!

At his spot, he introduced me to the stable officially; I already knew them. And then he told me I belonged to him. These girls were all my "wife-in-laws," and each had a room at the Huntington Hotel on Boylston where he would have sex with them on their days off. When it was time for me to go to work, he took care of me and bought my clothes—suits with fur collars from the boosters—and everything was quality. It was a relief having Sess as my man, protecting me and being there for me if I ever got busted. I didn't need to give him any money up front; he trusted my word. That made me feel special; I would prove to be top money for him. Like the squares do when a man gives his wife a glitzy piece of jewelry or they get a pricey new car, players show off the same way when they by go out with their main squeeze or new girls, all flashing their gold and diamonds, dressed to the nines, and the pimps driving their fancy cars. That was all well and good, but there was still a void in my soul, a deep hole that caused me exquisite pain. This life was not real—it was like a storybook fantasy. But I was in it forever, I thought then… and even now.

None of the men I had been with loved me, nor had I loved them. It was all about sex and money and showboating. Most used and really abused me. Essentially, I was a trick to them, regardless of how they felt about me. The women choose the men; the men did not do the choosing. If I died no one would miss me; I could be replaced with another hoe. Maybe one day I'd meet someone who loved me for myself and would help take care of me without expecting to be paid sexually in return. After choosing, Sess told me I could take his car to go to the cemetery to visit my mom's grave every Sunday morning. Wow, that touched my heart for sure. I had told him about that when we were talking the first night I had chosen him, when he asked me to tell him one thing that I wished for. He made my wish come true! That was enough incentive to pay him big money and work 24/7. I didn't care if he went to bed with me; I didn't need that. I just loved driving him around and he loved being chauffeured by me. He paid me endless compliments on how well I handled a car. I realized from being among the others that sex wasn't going to be enough to keep me. Although Sess was fair to all his women, I knew he wasn't the right pimp for me and that I would be leaving soon. I was searching for what was missing inside me, and I was not sure what that was. I had improved my way of dressing by one hundred percent; I looked classy now, and that made more money for me. Each step I took was going up, not down.

I tried to work with Sess's girls but there were always jealousies, and I preferred working alone because I worked longer and made more cash. I brought in more money than the three others put together. They would come in early while I stayed out late on the hoe stroll. Making money was a rush, and I couldn't get enough. Driving his Caddy on Sundays gave me freedom; he let me go alone most times. My window was always open to fill my lungs with fresh air—I always have to have my windows open—that was my release and peace. But there was a schedule for freaking with Sess, and I was on the list for Sunday nights. My wife-in-laws were on for a one-night sex romp too, with the exception of his main hoe, who slept with him every night. The first two times were tolerable, we seemed to be into it, and by the third, I was totally indifferent and asked Sess if I could go to work instead of staying in on my day off. He refused, saying he wanted to be with me. "Come on, baby, you can work another night. Don't you want to be with your man?"

"Yes, oh yes, I do!"

"It's your night off," he said.

Once we started, I got into it. He was pumping hard on top of me, holding my hands behind my head, while the sweat rolled down his face and onto my neck. His small-framed body knew how to please, moving side to side, keeping his body elevated. My hair was damp as if I had just gotten out of a shower. He knew just how to gyrate his midsection to get into a groove inside me so that my juices began to flow, his hands tucking under my butt to pull me up so that he touched just the right area. There was a sharp knock on the door of my room at the Huntington Hotel—interruption! My body felt like a mating dog locking up on the hard member inside. Sess was sexing on top of me when he stopped and yelled out to whoever was at the door, "What the fuck?" It was one of his bitches. He pulled out of my tight pussy and stood up, his dick rock hard, leaving me to lie and wait, wet and starving for the finale, just like one of my tricks. He was still stiff when he put on his robe and approached the door. It was at that moment I fully realized the absurdity of the relationship between pimps and hoes: I get money to fuck the tricks, and then I give my money to a man to freak off with me, the trick bitch. *Wake up, Libbe!* rang in my brain. I knew I didn't want to be staying in this situation for too much longer. I thought how stupid I must be, making sex and money the priority in my life. After Sess spoke with the girl at the door, he said, "C'mon, baby, let's finish. I have to go take care of business. We'll hook up later, and I'll take you out, okay?" But it was not okay when he insisted I get him hard again. I had lost the mood. He fucked me until he got off, but I felt like a piece of meat this time, and I wondered if getting high like the other girls would sexually arouse me and deaden my emotional senses.

While he was showering, I turned on the TV and caught the clips from the war in Vietnam. When he got out, I told him I wanted to go to work, and he said I was his best worker and his other bitches would never use their days off to work. For me, working surpassed what just happened. During my last two weeks with Sess, I worked like a like a dog. And I said goodbye to my mom at the cemetery, knowing it would be a while before I had a car or ride to return. The cemetery was sacred to me. I never allowed a customer to drive me to my mother's grave. Sess wasn't difficult to leave, although he was upset because he liked me. "Baby, you got brains and looks, there's no exit fee, and you come back any time you want." He also said to let him know if I needed anything. That was cool…really cool.

We always talked after I left. There were no hard feelings. Sess was unique. He was not like the other pimps; he had a mind of his own, and it worked like a charm. He had a heart. I was so sorry to hear how it ended up for him later—shot and killed behind some bitch he cared about.

As much as I loved the life, the void in my soul informed me that something was sorely missing, and it nagged at me. What? Sex did not fill that emptiness. I had a profound yearning to be with one man for life, someone who loved me enough to take me away and care for me. Who? Where? It was a recurring dream I held onto throughout my life of working and choosing. I wondered if I was too mired in the life to change. Who would my prince be? One of my clients? And beyond that, who would want me if they knew my story?

Marcie and I hung out together all the time after I left Sess. She told me she wanted to leave Hank. He had been messing with her money and fucking around with square bitches, as she put it, without getting paid for it. He never brought the girls home to turn out; he was just having fun. She said that they had been together for too long and she was sick of his shit. It was time for a change. But the streets still wanted girls to have pimps. It was too much shit to go through if you were a renegade. Yes, it was possible for street girls to work in the shadows, but I would be putting myself in danger with the other hoes and their men unless I left the street to work the phones. I hated being stuck indoors.

I was invited one night to the Essex Hotel to meet Davey J. and his girl. Davey was a pimp from West Medford who knew the streets. There was another pimp there, Peppy, and all of them were really fucked up, sniffing cocaine and tossing down whiskey. Young bloods…a step up from Pepsi Cola. One of them suggested that we do a foursome, of course, with one of the girls going down on the other, and I refused. After about thirty minutes, give or take, I was firm about not partying with them. I turned and was about to leave when they came up from behind me, totally fucked up, and held me by the shoulders, the pressure of their grasp tight and threatening. They snapped handcuffs around my wrists! Then they wrapped my body and feet like a mummy, with ropes and cloth, and then they gingerly dropped me out the window of their room, dangling me upside-down out the window! I didn't know how they anchored me inside the room, they were so high, but I felt I was inching down lower against the red brick building, and I wasn't able to grip on to anything! Since the incident with the ladder when I was a child, I became petrified of heights, and now what I experienced was terror! I wanted to scream, but no sound came out—I was certain I was about to die! I thought, *Can't anyone see me?* They were laughing, telling me to choose over and over again. I didn't have a voice and couldn't say yes or no. My answer wouldn't have mattered anyway if I fell to the pavement several stories below—I would not make it! After they had enough entertainment, they hoisted me up and pulled me over the window ledge and into the room. My heart was racing…then I took a deep breath. It had felt like forever, but they made fun of me, saying that I was a punk bitch, that it had only been minutes. As they untied me I told them I would choose, but I knew that after I was set free I never would. I ran off, telling them I had to go to work to make my money. They were so high they believed me and knew I had a good track record. I never should have gone into that hotel room, even though the girl told me it was cool and no one would bother me. I knew better. The girls bring you along to their men to choose, and most of the time the pressure works. I wouldn't make a choice because as much as I had disliked them before, now I hated them. I had to get a good man to be with now, but who?

Good girls who paired up with me were hard to come by, and most of them had no hearts or were too scared to take chances. Then there were those who took too many chances and you would get popped. I had become apathetic and didn't care whether I was taken to jail. The paranoid girls always seemed to be the ones who got arrested. I was so lonely I became super friendly with the bartenders, and especially the owner of Izzy Ort's Golden Nugget (which had started as Izzy Ort's Bar & Grill); he was my favorite because he reminded me of my dad. Izzy liked me, and gave me good tips, pointing out the better pimps and clients. He was one of my favorite men, and he never tried *anything*. Sometimes I felt that I wouldn't care if I were killed because I had so little to look forward to; I didn't envision a future for myself. As badly as I wanted to be somebody important, it was hard to project myself into a better time in my life.

Katie, who also hung out at Izzy's, was a good worker, even though she partied excessively while constantly drinking her Miller beers, and Will, her man, allowed her to get away with too many things. She was a free spirit, spoiled and bratty. She was getting ready to leave Will for a square dude from down South. Both men were from down South, but he was her homey, not a pimp like Will. Before I knew it, Katie, Will, and his buddy Dandy were partying, having threesomes at Katie's apartment by Franklin Park. They would hang out at Izzy's club, get fucked up, and then get some blow and go freak. They all were cool about it—sniffin', drinkin', and freakin' all the time. She always invited me over, but I had no time. I was too busy working and wasn't into it. I made lots of excuses to avoid that situation. One day, they asked me and I went. They wanted me to join in and I told them I was about to go to work; Izzy had some good clients waiting at the bar. They continued pressuring me, trying to pull me in, but I chose not to because Katie was my friend, and I didn't want to share her men, or for that matter, her little dog Bootsy, who went down on her. Wow, that was a first for me to see! Not getting paid for sex…bump that shit! I needed to be at work, not get into her habits.

Robin was my other friend, a stripper at the Downtown Lounge who wasn't good with clients, but she got over. She was all about herself. She couldn't pass a mirror without looking in it, fixing up again what she never needed done. When she was with a date she had to have a mirror to watch her own expressions. Robin was one-of-a-kind; she and Katie were my best friends on the streets. I truly loved them both, flaws and all. Marcie and I were close when we were working, but not friends like they were. She was the best in the business, but not as a friend because she was too high to care about anyone or anything except her cocaine. She was always a mess. We talked about getting our own places. She wanted local girls and I didn't, so working with some more madams that I knew to get girls from the Circuit was for me. The Circuit was my in to a better world, to getting ahead one day. Marcie wanted local girls, I didn't. I did not want my clients to recognize each other or see girls they knew from Boston. I didn't want my married clients to get in trouble. Marcie never cared. "Fuck 'em," she would say. "Business is business. I'm about the money. It's their problem! Who cares if they get caught? There's a trick around every corner. If they end up with their cousin, it's their problem, not mine. They want to get laid so bad they wouldn't even notice if they ran into their daughters' friends or some college buddies. So what?" In the business, many men were afraid to run into girls they knew from here when they were out with their wives, always hoping the girls wouldn't speak to them. That happened to me several times, but I would look the other way. Any girl with sense knew better. I wanted safety for them. The right time to start a business hadn't arrived yet, though she began before me while she still was with Hank. Hank and his buddy Tommy hung tight, getting high and fucking all the girls. Hank tried to pull me, again and again, each time unsuccessfully, until one day when they kidnapped me outside of Izzy's place when I was leaving and took me to Franklin Park to rape me. I never told anyone except for Izzy. He said he could take care of it and get them out of all the clubs. I said no because I was afraid that they would come after me. Hank and Tommy never did bother me again. After that incident, when I was working out of the Golden Nugget, he watched out for me. He had taken a liking to me because I was a good Jewish girl working the Zone, and there weren't too many of us.

J.J. was a renowned pimp. All the bartenders knew he was a serious moneymaker and his girls didn't mess around—he was no one to fuck with, or his girl either. His girl wanted me as her wife-in-law because, she said, I had heart and made lots of money. She said her man would like me, and we could do doubles. I chose J.J. because of her, not him; she talked me into it, an unusual occurrence for me. I had to make five hundred to choose, which was easy for me with regulars waiting in bars for me to come out daily, with Izzy's and John's help (John was at the 663 Lounge), and the rest coming in from Chinatown with the late night pick-ups at the well-known restaurants. I would wait at a table with a bowl of white rice and a cup of tea; that was their cue. The girls would follow them to their dirty, unkempt apartments. I hated Asian tricks, particularly the way they would put me in bright lights, spread my legs apart, and look into my vagina the way a doctor would in an exam, thrusting their fingers inside and asking, "You like?" with a grin across their faces like they were *the man*. They mounted me and went at their "fucky-fucky" like a rabbit. Afterward, I always felt like shit. Their dicks were small, and they preferred young girls like me, especially the blonde ones. If their wives only knew that their fantasy was to have an underage Marilyn Monroe that would be the end of them. It was the same with black clients always wanting white girls—if their black wives knew even half of what they were doing… And the white men who wanted black women—if their white wives found that out, oh, hell! My pimp/hoe relationship with J.J. lasted less than two weeks. It was horrific. I couldn't handle his woman Nana pimping me for him, and then we almost got arrested and beat down when she peeled a trick (robbed a client) at the Sheraton Hotel. The poor man never knew what hit him; for real, she physically knocked his ass down.

We were on the twenty-fifth floor. She knew he had money and jewelry, and she set him up without telling me what she was planning to do. She hit him and knocked him down, and when he was on his feet again, he came for *me* and I pushed him away as forcefully as I could. I wanted out of there. It wasn't me who hurt him, but I was there. She had all his money, and she kept on striking him with her fist. I helped her hold him down while she tied his wrists and ankles so he couldn't follow us. I was just as guilty as she was. We raced out of the room and down the stairs. She said to separate—for me to go to my room while she went to J.J. with the funds and jewelry that I did not know about until later. I never knew at the time it happened just how much money there was, but later on when the pimps were drinking and snorting at four a.m. at the after-hours, where I was told to meet up with them, J.J. bragged that it was thousands of dollars and some real fine jewelry he would sell to a fence. I sat there thinking about how I had been so scared that I ran down the back stairs, all twenty flights in high heels, and when I reached the bottom my legs were like jelly. I did not want to be arrested; the crime was violent, and I knew that. I went to my room on Tremont Street where Nana showed up later and brought me out. I was surprised when she told me we had the rest of the night off and J.J. would be coming to see me after we got back from the after-hours. I wished I still had the apartment on Commonwealth Ave., but I had given it up after the shooting incident with Luca. I wasn't attracted to J.J. at all but it was his job to fuck his hoes; that was a nightmare to me.

When J.J. came to my room, he told me he was going to be with me first, then with his main woman later. I wasn't pleased that he was freaking me. I understood he could never stay over with me, the same way Sess would fuck me and leave. That had been fine with me, but never fucking me would have been better. J.J. was not my type at all. He was scary. He fucked me hard, like he was a boxer pummeling a punching bag, so hard I was sore. It totally felt like a rape. Before he started, when I was giving him head, I noticed he leaked out more than most men and it was a yellowy color. I never questioned it, but the taste in my mouth was bitter and sour. I gagged, but he pushed my head down even more. I didn't think too much about it until I went to work early the next day. Nana stayed in with her man. She loved him and would do anything for him, even kill. She was a short woman, but tough like a wrestler, hardcore all the way. She was the only girl in the Zone who scared me. When I left, I washed and washed but could not get the funk of him off me. I never wanted to see *him* again!

I worked all the next day, and at night I felt a burning down there I had never felt before and my throat was sore. I thought maybe I was getting a sore throat. I worked one more day, and after that, I couldn't do a thing I was so tender inside the walls of my vagina. After douching without any effect, and as dry as a bone, I knew I had to see a doctor. There was a nurse downtown. She had become a close friend, almost like a mother figure. The girls trusted me and would get their free check-ups from her—no need to pay crooked doctors on Huntington Ave. Mrs. Easterday worked at the Beth Israel Hospital, and we became close when she went to LaGrange Street on behalf of the Board of Health to educate the girls about venereal disease and provide them with free medical care. I paid attention. I would listen to her description and what could happen. I became her spokesperson on the street. My role was to prevent them from spreading the disease. She would always take care of me if I called with questions, but now I needed her because something was wrong with me. I went to see her without telling J.J. or Nana because I didn't want to get into trouble for taking time off work. But sure enough, I was sick with gonorrhea, not from a trick but from J.J.—he had infected me. She told me that the yellow discharge was a sign that a man had the disease and had it good. I thought I knew it all but didn't pay close enough attention, thinking that only my tricks could get me sick. I was so wrong. I learned afterward that he knew he had the disease for at least a week before he fucked me, and worse, Nana had known and didn't tell me. What the fuck! All the pimps screwed around but the hoes carried the blame for infecting their men, and it was often enough the pimps who infected the hoes because of their fucking around. I didn't want to share a pimp anymore and considered her attack on a trick to steal his money really low, lower than robbing stores. She was vicious, and I didn't want to involve myself in that kind of business. I loved the life but not to that degree. I could make money without doing harm. After Mrs. Easterday gave me my shots, I didn't go back to the hotel again, but left J.J. and Nana without taking anything besides the clothes on my back. I stayed away from them, going to other areas and calling Marcie to get some side dates. Mrs. Easterday gave me check-ups for the rest of the week, and I was fine. She offered me her private phone number to use whenever I needed her. I had a friend who wanted nothing from me except to help and to help anyone else she could. I loved her; she was like a street mom. She arranged free exams for me so I wouldn't have to deal with the quacks on Hemingway Street anymore. Those doctors were sexual nuts who would put their fingers deep inside me to get off while I was on the table; I pretended that nothing out of the ordinary was happening. So many doctors get off sexually when examining their patients, and no one ever knows. Mrs. Easterday got me paid exams. The exam was one hundred dollars an hour, unlike the doctors on Hemingway Street who bartered for sex and gave the girls bombers for free to get their thrills. This was legit. I was even in one of Mrs. Easterday's staff's hospital magazine articles.

I had run off from J.J. without giving an explanation and couldn't ask the girls on the street to recommend me to their pimps because Nana and J.J. would bust my butt. I began working around the bars where the gangsters hung out, and I knew the right guys. I worked there without a hassle while I searched for someone to deal with J.J. I was safe at the Garden of Eden on Washington Street—Nana wasn't allowed in there. I was powerful now. Everyone in the clubs respected me. They treated me to drinks, even brought me food sometimes. I was still scared when I would leave the clubs, but had to go with the tricks.

CHAPTER THIRTY-SEVEN

Rio

The Garden of Eden was located below street level in the Combat Zone. From the outside, it was just a doorway with a small sign. I crept down the stairs early enough so that the others girls wouldn't see me there and tell J.J. and Nana. If they found me, rather than me going to them, I knew I would get a double beating, and I was frightened. I had to choose a pimp who knew J.J. and was tough enough to pull me out. I was familiar with all the pimps who associated with J.J. They all had reputations, and the only reason I hadn't run into them was because it was daytime and they came out at night, like bats or vampires. I should have gone with Sess, but moving on seemed better. The boosters traditionally went in the afternoon to the barbershop hangouts to sell the pimps clothes for their girls. Sess used to go there to buy me the best suits. Eventually, I learned how to deal with the boosters myself. J.J.'s taste was the straight up trashy hoe look. I had to get him and Nana off my back so I could continue to work.

I was sitting on the bar stool when Johnny Mags' brother came over to me. He bought me a soda and asked, "Why so early today, Lib?" After I explained my situation, he said he had just the man for me, and he made a phone call. He told me the man was classy, extremely private, but well known like his brother, and he could definitely squash the problem I was having. But who was he? The wait for him was nerve-racking. I smoked butt after butt and drank

Shirley Temples like water. He finally entered the bar, and I had a sense it was him, Rio. I saw that he wasn't tall, maybe five feet nine or ten, and his skin was reddish brown and smooth. He wore Aramis, and the fragrance followed him, filling the smoky room with a trail of his sweet scent. As he leaned over the bar, he spoke with the bartender, who pointed me out. I was puffing on my Kool cigarette, Kools and Newports being the best street cigarettes, comparable to the Marlboros and Winstons of the straight world in the past. They said the menthol cigarettes were better for getting high on coke because the taste was more pleasant. I found it interesting to see the pimps empty out a cigarette casing, mix cocaine with tobacco and fill it back in, twist the end, and light it. That was before freebasing was a big thing.

The classy-looking man sauntered over to me. He was different, conservative yet sharp. He rubbed and turned the thin Dunlap lighter in his hand as he spoke to me, and then the rap became more serious. He placed his pack of cigarettes on the bar with the silver lighter on top, his silky hand covering them. He was much older than me by at least twenty years or more, the type I was attracted to. He told me what I needed to do and said he would meet me later. Not much game…just smooth. I was supposed to get a couple of customers then go to the LaSalle Hotel on Warrington Street and check in with the money I made. Sometimes, I used the LaSalle for my tricks or the Chandler on Chandler Street, with Whitey, the manager. At the Chandler, it cost me ten dollars for the room and two to three dollars for him when I brought clients upstairs. He had most of the girls coming to him, and the money he made was good considering he sometimes worked twenty-four hours a day. Katie's mom sang at the LaSalle, and although I never saw her up close, I could hear her voice down the corridor when I came in to meet the clients. The bellman there charged five dollars a trick, sometimes three dollars, depending on his mood, and he was there only on certain days of the week. But he looked out for me because I was catching quite a number of clients. The more you tipped them the better, and they would toss good tricks to you too.

I checked in at the LaSalle, paying for my room four days in advance. I stared at the heavy black rotary phone, anticipating the call from my new man letting me know I could work without problems. It was late and still bitter cold outside. I was hoping that Rio could get my clothes from J.J. because those clothes were the only ones I had left. I needed to have my warm jacket. Leaving things behind was a pattern of mine, and I suppose I was getting used to it even though it upset me; other girls did the same with their clothes all the time when they were on the run. There was one thing Rio said when we were talking that made me happy. He told me he had one other girl, and he would be seeing me half a week and her half a week. That gave me more time with him, which was a better arrangement than I expected. He was the image of the father I longed for. His style was so smooth and classy, and he knew people from outside the life, too. I thought that as a person he was well rounded, and these qualities made it easy to choose him. I was learning from each new pimp I chose, although they were unaware they were teaching me. I was beginning to see past their lies and the games they played every day. I would be able to play on these players one day at a bigger game called "never go back." I couldn't be played anymore unless they had a better game. I was learning their tricks. As the saying goes, never play a player or you'll get played. It's the squares that I really have to watch out for; they seem to be your friend, but only if you have no past.

Rio came to my room to celebrate, carrying a bottle of vodka. He said I was with him. It was as easy as that. I never had a chance to say yes or no. From the time he freed me, I was his. I didn't want to drink, but he made me one anyway, vodka mixed with juice. I was excited because he had gotten my clothes from J.J., even my personal items. Wow, he went there with no trap money first. I was very grateful. There weren't many personal items, but it was important to me to have things of my own. I felt slightly high from the drink he made me, and when he made love to me he was gentle, not mean. We didn't click though. He thought we did, but I wasn't sexually attracted to him. I put on an act to please him. He drank far too much, and I left him at the hotel to go to work. By the time I came back from working, it was so late he was passed out. One thing I really liked was his smooth style of talking, and I just melted whenever he called me "baby." His manners were what attracted me to him. Holding me was enough; I didn't want sex from him. He wasn't circumcised and giving him a blowjob when he was drunk was tough labor because he would not get hard. Although I liked and respected him, I realized that this was a phase of my life, a temporary arrangement that would lead to another. I learned that Rio was a bartender. After two-and-a half weeks, we were meeting on Newbury Street instead of the Zone, and once the money began rolling in I went out to clubs like Slade's on Tremont Street, Basin Street South on Washington Street, and Blinstrub's in Southie. We also went to after-hours where I'd never been before. We went to many of these places every week, where he showed me off. That was so exciting! I was meeting different kinds of people, and I enjoyed feeling important. Everyone knew him, and now I saw why he could squash J.J. Rio made it clear not to fuck around even though he didn't have me adhere to Iceberg Slim's rules. He was very possessive. My eighteenth birthday was approaching, and I looked forward to the end of foster care and guardians and being trapped in the whole messed-up system. I would be free. I was working hard. Rio always picked me up at the exact time he said he would, and because he kept his word, I felt as though he valued me. During this time, I came close to being busted for prostitution by two cops who, as it turned out, were both the lenient type and they didn't give me a case. I was working the Park Square area where the cab drivers waited by the bus stops, and the girls would gather at the breakfast restaurant getting early birds for sex. Rio was always precise with time, and he made it clear not to be late with him, not ever. There was a lot of hype about Nixon and the presidential elections then, and all my clients and the bartenders were talking about how he was about to become the next president. I did not care one bit about politics. To me, all politicians were on the take, and in that way they were no different from many of my clients. I heard the stories from the madams of politicians *being* clients, which I already knew because I'd had a few of them.

One night when I was working, one of the cab drivers, a Russian, offered me three hundred for an all-night date. It was after midnight, and I wanted the money. He told me he'd drive me back at five in the morning. I recognized his face; he was always in Park Square. It was late and he was a regular there so I accepted. I didn't feel anxious until we started to drive on the highway, far away from Boston. I didn't get a good vibe from him. He said he had a house in the suburbs, and we could stay there for the rest of the night. It was somewhere near Tewksbury. I had seven hundred dollars on me, but no knife, and that was something I was taught to carry without fail. We arrived after about forty-five minutes. His house was small and in the middle of the woods. We went inside. I asked him for the money up front, as usual, and he said, "C'mon, where am I going? For that matter, where are you going, huh? I'll pay you at the end. You know where you can find me every day." His heavy Russian accent did not resonate with me, nor did his promise. He put the money on the dresser, so at least I saw it. He had some drinks and then some more drinks, and I had only a few sips. I had to pay attention. I hadn't spoken with Rio since earlier that night. I'd be seeing him in the morning at my new room on Commonwealth Ave. He always brought freshly-cleaned clothes for me and orange juice, and vodka for himself—it seemed like he lived on his vodka.

As the night wore on, the cab driver was getting rougher and rougher, and he wanted to do everything without paying extra for it. When I first walked into his house, I saw that it was filthy, and I should have known better by the vibe it gave off. I had been there for two hours, and there were two more to go. I was tired, and he was getting in a bad mood, calling me a piece of shit in his Russian accent, pulling my face down to suck his dick and his balls. I sucked and gagged from him pushing my head all the way down. The belts strewn all over the floor were making me nervous. "You said you did everything! Bitch, whore—you lied!" he said. "Get the fuck out of my house! No money, you nasty bitch!" He threw my clothes at me and told me to give him my money or he would kill me. He fucked me to death, now this! He meant what he said; he grabbed his knife from an end table and came toward me. Standing behind me, he put one arm across my chest, and when he clenched me, I could feel his strength. I didn't want to fight him in his house because he might also have a gun or call the police on me. I just stood there looking at the mismatched pieces of furniture in the room. His size made it impossible to fight back, but for how long? I had to go! I pulled my clothes on fast. I was wearing my street clothes with a thin sweater. It was freezing cold and he kept my coat, which wasn't heavy but at least it would have been another layer. I was in pain and swollen from him violently screwing me, and my head hurt from his punch. As I got ready to leave his hellhole, I felt hate and anger. I was sick about him getting a free fuck, taking my money, and abusing me. I wondered what I would do if I had a gun and could shoot this arrogant bastard. Would I? He was a pig. My nipples were sore from his biting, and my ass hurt from him forcing himself in me as I screamed and fought him. He was a nasty motherfucker. When I was giving him a blowjob, he choked me by pulling my hair and shoving his hard penis down my throat. I wished I could have done the same to him. Shit! Shit! Shit…no money!

I had to walk all the way from Tewksbury back to Boston in the frigid weather. When I finally got back after getting a lift close to Boston—legs hurting, cold shivers, and no cash—I was afraid of telling Rio I had *no money*, but if I didn't tell him, I would have been in deeper trouble. I told him what happened without identifying the Russian as the one who assaulted me. Rio simply had me work harder during the week without going out on the weekend with him. It seemed like he believed me because I was such a mess but still punished me anyway. Eventually, the Russian asshole was no longer in the forefront of my mind, but to this day, I still get sick when I think of that man. And later in my life, I did see him a lot in the one town I never thought to run into him, Brookline.

I was working hard. I had a new client—a sugar daddy—who showered me with money and gifts. This man was my first sugar daddy client; others followed. He would pick me up and drop me off, and sometimes would wait outside the room for me. He was giving me hundred-dollar bills in bunches. As time passed, we became closer, and Rio was aware of it. For me, the relationship was all business. Rio was keeping his eyes on me wherever I went. After walking me to the door one night, my client gave me a quick kiss and told me he would see me soon. After his lips brushed against mine to say goodnight and he left, I noticed that the door was slightly opened. And there was Rio, waiting inside the room. He surprised me. I had a pocketful of money and my stash from earlier. He seemed so happy to see me. I took the money out of my boot and handed it to him. He didn't even count it. He asked me to sit on his lap and I did, anticipating a real kiss, which he was really good at. I had been with Rio longer than any other pimp because he had treated me like a human being until now. But instead of a kiss, he punched me in the eye and knocked me clear off his lap onto the floor! I didn't know what hit me, and I certainly didn't understand the reason for him slugging me. He told me to get up and wash my face and rinse my mouth out—blood had mixed with my saliva. "You kissed me after that trick put his mouth on you," he said in a tone I had not heard before. Then he spoke to me tenderly, calling me "baby." I remembered that one of the very first rules of street life prohibited girls from kissing clients on the mouth. I had broken the rule. Even though Rio didn't follow Iceberg Slim's bible, he had the street rules. With all pimps, kissing clients was strictly forbidden. No intimacy. How could I let my guard down and kiss Rio after the customer? When I insisted I didn't kiss him that way, Rio pointed out that the man's face touched mine, and that meant he was too close. He told me to get dressed, that we were going out for a drink and then he expected me to go to work. How could I? "And you won't be seeing that trick anymore," he said. I was so freaked out…my eye was shut tight and bruised, it was throbbing, but I had to go to work that way. At least the trickle of blood from my nose had stopped. That was my first ass kicking from Rio, and I hoped it would be the last. At the bar, he told me he loved me and that was the reason he hit me. He stopped me from seeing my sugar daddy; only he could touch me that way. I understood, and I stayed with him. But why does love hurt so bad?

My black-and-blue eye faded within a week or so. I successfully dodged my sugar daddy for a while, even though I didn't really want to. I did sneak a couple of times because I was more careful and slicker now. The ships were coming in and the opportunities to make money were endless. All the girls were talking about it. I had to find another girl to help me because there would be too many Navy guys for me to do them all. Only white girls were requested to come onboard, and they had to be young and cute. All my friends were busy. Robin was dancing, and Katie was in Detroit. Because Rio and J.J. were friends, all was swept under the rug, and Nana and I began speaking again. Despite her rough appearance, I asked her if she wanted some work. She complimented me on being such a good hoe and said there wasn't any reason we shouldn't get down and make that money. And we did. She had blonde hair, and they loved blondes.

I trucked on over to Chinatown, sensing the fear that always accompanied me when I was out before catching my first date—or, in street lingo, breaking luck. Like stage fright, once I broke luck I was good to go. I don't think there was one day I went out on the streets when I wasn't scared in some fashion or another, whether my fear was of the unknown, crazies, cops, or disease. If I was walking in a new area for the first time, I would become hyper. Either I was afraid of other pimps or leery of the wrong trick getting hold of me and beating, raping, or killing me. I had my share of beatings and rapes, and then there were the cops who could arrest me, belittling and scaring the shit out of me, like the two nicknamed by the hoes Starsky and Hutch, who harassed me and took me for harrowing rides in their paddy wagons. A hoe had cut one of them in the face. The word on the street was that's why he had it in for hoes. I had no way of knowing how true that story was. I had also been taken out of town and been dropped off on strange corners by my pimps to work pick-ups in places like Connecticut, New York, Jersey, and Philly, and in towns I wanted to escape from but couldn't because I was obligated to my man without other means to get away. I didn't have any choice because my pimps always threatened me by playing head games. I had to see it through. And each night was just one more instance of my body grinding out the minutes to fill my pants with cash. My brain would freeze and made it impossible to think about anything at all. When I wasn't idle and I was hitting the areas where the money was waiting to be made, my fears disappeared and my adrenalin rescued me, one date after another. The excitement made me bolder. And my other thought was, *Who cared anyway…*

To find hoes for the ships, I had to head down to where the younger girls were hanging. There were two famous restaurants in Chinatown, and I peered into the windows of both to see who I could grab to get to work. Where was everyone? I climbed the steps to the restaurant I frequented most, but none of the girls I knew were there, only a few new turn-out girls, and they were a mess except for one who was with her man. She was a real cute blonde, and both she and her man were young. He must have been new because I didn't recognize him. His hair looked processed, and I couldn't tell by the color of his skin if he was mixed race or all black. With his glasses, he looked like a square, certainly not a pimp. They almost looked like boyfriend and girlfriend, except for the bowl of white rice and tea, the signature come-on. I stood at the table in front of them, introduced myself, and asked their names. I told them I needed a cute girl to work the Navy boats with me and that there was a lot of money to be made. "Your man will be real happy," I said. "I can take you there and your man can wait here, and you'll come back with big cash."

"No thanks," was her reply.

"No thanks? Aren't you working?" I asked. "What about the rice and tea?"

"No, I'm finished," she answered. "Finished? Dinnertime? Or you like white rice? A good hoe never finishes when there's money to be made!" I blurted. "The guys are right there, you don't have to search for them. What kind of hoe are you, a turn-out? Or are you a lazy bitch!" My mouth was ahead of my brain. Her man puffed on his cigarette and didn't say a word—wow! Out of the corner of my eye, I could see him staring at me. I leaned in toward her and looked at the cup of tea and the bowl of white rice—the signal to Chinese men to call the girl out to trick. If she were done with work, the tea and rice wouldn't be on the table. Staring at the prima donna and her Pepsi Cola pimp, I asked him, "Are you sending your girl or not?"

When he turned to ask her if she wanted to go, she stood her ground and said, "No, I don't want to," and he turned to me and told me sorry, she was tired. Excuse the fuck out of me…tired? Bullshit! My temper flared. Tired of looking at the tea and rice, are ya? Who was the boss here? I couldn't wrap my head around that. Then I went off on him. "Your bitch shouldn't take up space. The girls here work, and real pimps don't ask their girls what they want, they tell them to go out and work. You need to quit and go home to your mommy and daddy and take your girlfriend with you. She's not a working girl!" I set it straight, the way I was taught. Another girl who had just started working heard me and said, "Hey, I'm game. Fuck that bitch, let's roll, I need to make money!"

"Come on, then!" She came with me. That was great! She was down for making cash and not sitting in Chinatown all night with her rice and tea, waiting for the last few stragglers to come in. In the three weeks the girl had been working, she hadn't made what she did that night. She made over fifteen hundred dollars working all night with me. Her man wanted her to work with me again to learn what she could, but I wasn't allowed to do that because she was a turn-out and wasn't a wife-in-law. I would get into trouble, and I didn't need the heat. That girl worked hard, though. I never saw her again after that night. She may not have stayed in Boston.

Rio told me he loved me numerous times. I almost believed him. There were twenty-plus years between us. So what… He tended bar at The Place, a well-known joint in Roxbury in the Dudley Street area. I'd always find him asleep in my bed when I got home from work, his vodka on the rocks beside him. Half-asleep and slurring his words, he'd say, "Hello, baby, come to bed." Then he would reach for me and pass out again. He always left at the crack of dawn, and I never asked him where he was going. He would kiss me sweetly on the forehead saying, "I'll be back before you go to work." Whether it was day or night, Rio's skin smelled like perfume. My attraction to him wasn't sexual. I felt affection for him, and that he would protect me. I wondered why he left so early in the morning and where he went every day, probably to the other girl he said he had. The first time I saw his gun, it was laying on the car console, a .38 snub nose revolver. He told me he carried it for protection when he brought large sums of cash from the club to the drop box at the bank. He said he had a license to carry. That was a relief. At least he wasn't the type to play sex games with a gun, like Luca, who nearly scared me to death.

Rio was so jealous that I could never speak with men, or women for that matter. I hadn't looked at another man since the black eye, and my sugar daddy didn't get to see me that much anymore, even on the side, which was a problem because he wanted me full-time. I only took the chance to hook up him when he had a hotel room of his own, and I could sneak up for some quick cash—boy, did it come in handy. I heard rumors that Rio was going with a square, but I didn't believe it. I also heard he was married with babies. I doubted it. I thought about asking him, but I knew his reply would be that I was hanging out gossiping too much and that meant I wasn't working. It wasn't necessary for me to talk to the girls—they made a point of speaking loudly enough for me to overhear them anyway. I figured I'd keep the information to myself. Everything seemed to be running smoothly with us, and I was comfortable with him. He never caught on about me seeing the sugar daddy. The sugar daddy proposed, and said he would take care of me, that he was getting a divorce in a month or two. I never believed him.

I was frequenting the 663 Lounge on Washington Street. Rio knew the bartenders there, and he was well respected. Robin and Katie would come in at different times to work with me. We were all really close. I was learning so much every day. Katie would sit with her cigarette in one hand, her Miller beer in the other, sipping daintily like a lady. She was a bar girl, never on the streets; she didn't like picking up men that way. Many guys were interested in participating in threesomes, and we would have ménages à trois with the customers for large sums of money. Katie constantly tried to pull me home with her to freak later with her man, Will, and his buddy. I never agreed because it seemed unnatural to me to do that with a friend and her man. She and Will had been fighting lately and we chatted about it one cold night. Katie and I had been friends since the moment the bartender at Enrico's introduced us. As it turned out, Will became part of her past and she ended up going with his friend. She said she was tired of paying Will and that the friend would chip in money for her rent and bills instead of taking her money. He was a big sucker for her. She was done with pimps and their bullshit, as she put it. She was tight with her money and stashed it away. She always enjoyed people waiting on her, and he was perfect for her. As Will said of himself, he was a homey.

Each day was getting progressively colder. One slow night I had to hit the streets because not many guys were in the bar. Katie wouldn't go out on the street. I went alone. One of my steady guys would come around in his Volkswagen because he loved looking at my hot pink lips as I slowly went down on him in his car in the Back Bay alleys. I moved smoothly and erotically, back and forth over the condom until he was totally aroused. He would cum within seconds and then back away, like I repulsed him; but he was just hypersensitive. He always parked the car in the alleyways behind Newbury Street. Another steady client was a crazy, young guy recently home from active duty in Vietnam because of an injury. His family had money. He obsessed about my back and neck, touching—almost worshipping—those parts of me. That really freaked me out. I kept an eye on him because he was so strange, and he'd always stick around for hours after he was done, peeling money out. He was always staring at me when I was walking on the street or went into a bar—like a stalker.

One night at the bar, after seeing my soldier boy, a guy named Reggie introduced himself to me before I hit the streets again, and as I was walking to the door he called out that he wanted to talk to me. I kept moving. How did he know my name? I told him I couldn't, but he was relentless, following me all the way to the Park Square cabstands. I walked faster, trying to lose him. He was so persistent that I stopped even though my fear of Rio giving me a beating hung over my head. I was headed for the Sugar Shack, the place for pimps, hoes, and hip squares. It was around the time that lots of groups were in town: the Parliaments, Funkadelic, Al Green…so many. As I was walking, Reggie told me he was relaying a message for J.N., who had met me and thought I was pretty and qualified: he wanted to hook up. I was quick to shoot him down. "Who is this J.N.? Give him a message. You tell him, whoever he is, that I'm not interested in his lame invitation." Reggie was urging me to stop and listen. "I can listen to you while I'm walking. I'm not getting caught over whoever he is, or you for that matter." "He's the guy you chewed out in Chinatown, the guy sitting with his blonde chick, Lindsay."

"That's who you're talking about? He has a square bitch he can't control and I have a man, so don't come back again. I don't need any admirers without cash." Reggie snickered.

"I hear ya, baby," he said, "and I know who you are. Everyone knows you are a moneymaker."

"And, furthermore," I asked, "why the fuck did he send you? Are you his messenger boy?"

"Hell no, we're just friends from West Medford, and he thought you would call him all sorts of names so he stayed away."

"What? He's so right. If he can't take it then he's not worth it." I wondered who this young blood was and why he wanted to talk to me. I shook my head in disbelief that this J.N. person had the gall to try elbowing his way into my life through his buddy.

I walked with a quick step back around to Tremont Street, caught a date, and left Reggie in a trail of dust downtown. When I came back to the bar, Katie was perched on her stool with her cheery Miller's beer face, happy with the couple of hundred she had made that day. She didn't have a man, or should I say didn't have a pimp, but had a square man, even though everyone thought she was still with Will. She let them think that, easier to be protected on the street because she was mouthy, but he had left Katie without any hard feelings between them, even though she was pregnant with his child. I told her about Reggie and what was going on with this J.N. guy wanting to hook up. After I told her, she wanted to know, "Well, is he a fine young blood?"

"I guess," I said, "but I don't care—he looked too square." I wasn't bothered about Reggie and his friend anymore. I was apathetic, but Katie was interested and ready to take him on. She loved to freak.

"Come on, let me have him and I'll tell you if he's worth it. Send him to me," she said. Funny, I knew she would say that, and that she would do it too. I fluffed it off and left.

CHAPTER THIRTY-EIGHT

On the Streets

A lot of girls on the street looked after me because I was always sure to make them money, and I had their backs. I could defend myself just fine now after getting in some fights with bitches about simple stuff like territory, who had what corner. I wasn't afraid because I simply didn't care. When I was a child my father read the Farmer's Almanac, and now I would recite to the girls what the weather was supposed to be on any given day. They all thought I was nuts to be predicting the weather according to a book. Even though most of these bitches were backstabbers, I tried to help them out. I didn't care; it didn't cost me. I'd hustle the guys into doing doubles and the girls liked that…they didn't have to walk a lot. Early on, I had a good rapport on the street with all the sister hoes who knew that I was down. Most of the white girls weren't good hustlers—they were so stupid and fickle they would constantly flat-back the customers, lying down like a straight girl. They had no game. At least I made good conversation and learned the rap from the black girls I worked with. Only a handful of whites had natural hustle. The black girls' problem was that they had an excessive amount of game and were too aggressive. And they were robbing, which created a bad reputation for the good ones. The white men who only wanted a good session got robbed and ended up backing away. It was difficult for them to get dates, particularly if they had dark skin because the white tricks only wanted light-skinned girls. So instead, they stole from clients to make up the difference. I'd go where the money was and wouldn't peel a trick, that is, rob a client. I would never pull a twenty out of some man's wallet—too small, chump change. I didn't want to do that. I aimed at pleasing my clients so they would come back as regulars and tip me, unlike the other girls who didn't care for repeats. The police would come down on a girl more if she stole or if she did drugs. I could fend for myself on the street. I learned the hard way from my experiences, particularly when they involved fighting. After that Russian trick messed me up, I got tougher.

Once, when I was first turned out, I had my ass kicked by a girl. I had no idea what her problem was. There was a date that pulled up in a car on Mass. Ave. where there was a whole string of us on the road. The girl who was standing in the hoe line ahead of me talked to the trick. He took off and came back around again, stopping in front of me. He asked me to get in. It was obvious he didn't want the other girl, so I jumped at it. When I got back, she was pissed and spat at me, "Bitch, you need to pay me that money because that was my trick!"

I answered, "That wasn't your trick. He wanted to see me, not you. You just…" That did it. She didn't want to hear.

She was screaming at me. "You don't own tricks, and the guy wanted me instead of you!" I yelled out in my own defense. And the next thing I knew, I was on the ground. That was stupid of me because she caught me off guard. I hadn't been schooled yet to pay attention, but she taught me. I got my ass kicked—royally—and then I was going to get it kicked again when I got home for losing the customer's money to this girl when she took it from me; so, getting my ass kicked twice and learning the hard way. It never happened again, but it hurt, and it was a hell of a lesson. The other hoes laughed and said, "Better toughen up, baby girl!" From then on, I wouldn't fight somebody if I knew that person could take me on, rather, I would manipulate the shit out of them and come out on top. But if I had to, I would fight. I didn't want to go to jail for assault. Sometimes fleeing the area was the best alternative, especially in New York or Philly. The turn-outs were clueless and were tossed out to the wolves just like I had been. But I did get into other scraps and was able to fight and handle them—just glad they weren't with knives.

When I was first turned out it was on Tremont Street in that dark, abandoned building. Now I could control how many men I saw and where I saw them. I learned to love all the old hotels, like the LaSalle, the Broadway Hotel, and the Chandler, the most popular though the sleaziest, with beds that had bad springs. The Essex was way better than all of those. I had a fight at the Chandler when one of the clients attempted to take back his money. I pulled out my knife. He backed off and didn't touch the money. I knew I wouldn't use the knife unless I was in a life or death situation, but he didn't know that. There were a lot of incidents at the Chandler Hotel—girls, tricks, pimps, and hoes all getting into it. The Chandler Hotel has since been renovated and is now the exclusive Chandler Inn. Hmmm, if those old walls could speak they'd probably say, "Hoe! Hoe! Hoe!"

****

The female federal officer just came in to tell me I would be getting lunch soon. I thanked her. I already knew I wouldn't be touching that food, but I was thirsty. I went back to my thoughts, envisioning myself going up and down hotel elevators all day long and crossing the thresholds of many hotel room doors, risking my life yet determined to keep on going. The rush gave me confidence to make more money.

****

Once I figured out how to deal with the girls on the street, I always tried to get them to double to avoid having a trick inside me. The street girls preferred fucking their dates, whereas I would rather give head any day. I tried to save myself as much as I could. I considered having sex repugnant because of the way I learned about it, so I would try to get customers off by giving blowjobs, first talking dirty to them, and continuing to do so intermittently as I sucked away. I was unusual, the girls told me. "Oh, honey, save your jaw and let them fuck you," they'd tell me. No thanks! The other girls would spread their legs willingly and as often as they could. Many of them enjoyed it. They said giving head was too much pressure on their jaws. They didn't want to work, just flat-back. Why would I want their sweaty bodies on top of mine? Most of them didn't shower first. I was a talker and loved using dominance as a strategy to get them to go along with me. I found that with giving head I got them off without any problems. And I had more clients than I could handle, coming back for me week after week. My technique was becoming more sophisticated with every stroke. It was stories, sexual fantasies, and fetishes that intrigued the customers. I was more than just a screw and a suck. Sometimes I would study the facial expressions of these girls while we were in threesomes, and I could tell they were having a great time. What was left for their men? They definitely weren't saving themselves for them. I never could figure how they went home to their men and jumped into bed. What the hell… That made their man nothing special. Why not screw the clients exclusively? Why were these girls choosing to be with a pimp and get off on every client who came along? They weren't taught, the way I had learned from W.D., that this was a business. I just kept my opinions to myself and worked according to the rules, doing my job the best way possible.

I didn't like customers going down on me. I was self-conscious enough with my man and never let them do it, even though they asked. Rio tried, but I couldn't relax and faked having an orgasm. He never even noticed. When I was sent to a madam's house, it wasn't easy to work because I couldn't getting into it the way the other girls did. I could satisfy the clients, but they were all so insistent on getting the girls off. I learned how to fake coming so expertly that the clients truly believed I was into it—my inner muscles pulsated according to their rhythm and expectations. The madams loved me, said I was truly a gem in the room. Later, when I had to sleep over with the sugar daddies, I would think of every reason not to get in the bed with them. If they put their arms around me to hold me, it was disconcerting because I lacked any kind of love or caring for them. I hated the way it felt. What I did experience was a feeling of nausea. I could sexually tease to satisfy someone as long as they understood that's all they were getting from me. They got everything except for an intimate situation. Although many men tried to please me, I didn't come. There have been relatively few men with whom I've shared a mutual connection. The street was the right place for me. I didn't have to feel anything.

CHAPTER THIRTY-NINE

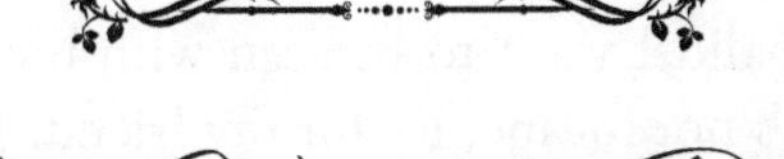

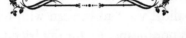

Who Wants to Die for Eighty Dollars?

My thoughts are racing. What if I get time? Who will take care of my house and my bills? What will happen to my life? What if my son needs me? He has no one. His father never gave him a thing. No support. And he lied to R. Lee about seeing him all the time! I am his only family! Will I lose my home, my only sanctuary? My clients will be alarmed when they can't reach me! I can feel myself panicking the longer I stay in this white porcelain room. I go back to my long and often unsettling past, knowing—no matter what happens—how lucky I am.

****

My regulars knew my hours, and like clockwork, they would be there waiting in the Combat Zone outside Enrico's, the 663 Lounge, the Garden of Eden, and in the parking lots. I walked down to my other hangout in Park Square to see the early birds at Hayes-Bickford's. I had seen the young blood J.N. there several nights, and I assumed he was waiting for his little girlfriend. I knew who he was now but stayed clear of him. It seemed strange that he was popping up at the places I was catching my tricks, locations I had never seen him at before. I had no fear of him because he just seemed to look lost.

I could feel it was going to be a good day. I broke luck with a man on his way to the office, then another and another. I got great tips. I was on a roll until I stepped back into Hayes-Bickford's and saw that guy Reggie again. I turned on my heel and headed out the door. He followed me. I didn't want to talk to him again. I didn't have the time nor did I want to be seen with him. "Wait, please! I need your help! It's not for me; it's for my friend, J.N.! Stop! He's in big trouble, and I don't have the money to help him!"

I stopped and turned around. "So, what do I look like, a bank? Tell his girl to help him. She's more than capable. I can't help anyone except my man, who'll beat my ass if he ever finds out I've been talking to you. Leave me alone!"

"Listen, please! He's in big trouble," he said, "Moses is going to kill him for real! He said he would shoot him if he doesn't give him eighty dollars for the pistol he lost!"

"Lost? Pistol? Why did he need it? How did he lose a piece? Is he stupid?"

"Somebody took it, a chick he met after his girl ran back home. She's taken off and he's broke—nowhere to stay, no money for food, especially the money owed, nothing." Man, why did he have to tell me all this? It's cold out. Where is he sleeping? That touched my heart. I hated to hear about anyone going hungry or not having a bed to sleep in. I felt badly. I knew what it was like to be without. But I did not need anything to touch my heart. "I know Moses. I'll leave the eighty on the tray with my milk. I'd better get it back!" I told him. "I can't be seen out here, I *gotta* go. And after this don't talk to me, neither of you. Hear?" "Okay, okay, I'll tell him. Check you later…"

After leaving the money, I didn't expect to see it again, although I found out Reggie was telling the truth when he told me that Moses was after J.N. I saw Moses; he was looking for him and appeared very pissed off! His two girls told me the story. Late that night, J.N. came to thank me. He appeared pale and skinny. Because the other working girls were watching me, I told him to leave me alone. I dropped twenty dollars down for him to buy food, and he could hang out at Hayes-Bickford's all night. When he saw it on the table, he grabbed it. I realized that Moses might have killed him over the eighty dollars for the stolen pistol, or maybe just beat his ass.

Moses heard about the story from J.N., who said he had borrowed the money from me, and he came down to tell me to be cool. "That boy told me you gave it to him. If your man gets wind you loaned that punk money to pay me, your ass is done," he said. "I told him to keep his mouth shut. So stay away from that fool. I won't tell. I have your back, the same way you watch out for my people. You've always been straight with me."

I thanked him. He owed me that favor for all the times I helped his girls from catching a case. And once, when one of his girls was getting dragged by a bunch of crazy young white tricks, I caught up with them in Sess's car and, after cutting them off, pulled her away. The white boys didn't like black girls and made it a point to call me a coon lover and spit out fucked up names at both of us. Moses knew me when I was a turn-out and then with Sess. Since then, he had always been cool with me. I was respectful and stayed to myself.

I couldn't be cool about J.N., who still showed up everywhere I went, like he knew where I would be. It was obvious he liked me. He didn't seem the type to be on the streets—a real square. He spoke to me in passing and told me he had been a foster kid and was adopted. *Wow,* I thought. Knowing we had that in common, I became comfortable with him, letting my personal stuff start to spew out. I helped him with a few bucks from time to time for food and to get a hotel to sleep in until he found a new girl. It was costing me money helping him, and I was still giving money to Rio. But then, I pulled back from him, afraid that our relationship was becoming too close. He was attached to me, and in a strange way, I felt responsible for him. I made an effort to stay clear, but I did find that hard to do because I was starting to like him. I heard that he might have gotten a girl. I was happy for him. Then he appeared on the street again a week or so later, and he looked so sick I handed him money to sleep at the Bradford rather than the Essex and told him to get some cold medicine. It was enough to pay for the whole week in advance and food money. I worried that Rio would catch on. Even though I was uneasy about something happening to me, I was more concerned about J.N. and worried that he was hungry or sleeping on the streets. I never believed he was playing me because he was for real every time I saw him. He wasn't that streetwise, and by no means was he a bona fide pimp or even a Pepsi-Cola pimp. I was becoming fond of this square, more and more every day. I would actually look at him and feel some sort of spiritual connection, like two kindred spirits. I didn't realize what that meant until years later.

CHAPTER FORTY

Finally Eighteen

November 10th, 1968, was my eighteenth birthday. It seems like a lifetime ago, but back then it was a milestone I had been anticipating for years. Being eighteen meant that I was totally free, and I could confide in Jennifer about what I was doing and perhaps even see her baby daughter. I was thrilled. Growing up, I never had gifts like other kids, only when my mother Rose was alive. I couldn't wait to go out, and Rio told me he had presents for me: something to wear, and a special gift. He seemed to be as eager as I was. I was deeply touched, and the excitement was almost too much to bear. My father didn't acknowledge the day at all—I never received as much as a card from him, just letters telling me to be good with a five dollar bill slipped into the envelope like an afterthought of happy birthday wishes. At least Esti's family celebrated my birthday with a cake served after supper.

I had recently found out from the girls that I indeed had a wife-in-law somewhere, and that she was a lesbian. Really, that puzzled me. Rio never mentioned it at first. He didn't approve of lesbians, and he didn't want us working together. Now I knew why he didn't want us to get close. Lesbianism wasn't an issue for me. The girls who were closest to me were all lesbians, or bisexuals like Pam. And I never told Rio about those friends; he only knew Katie. When I was with Rio, he told me I wasn't allowed to go inside the gay bars. I snuck out anyway to pop into the tough bar on Essex Street above Izzy Ort's. All the gay girls I knew hung out there. I was comfortable there, and sometimes the queens would do doubles with me—that was a trip. Some of them looked better than women and even appeared to be more feminine. But they were men, and because they were men, they knew how to pleasure a man. They taught me loads of new tricks!

The night of my birthday, Rio told me to meet him at the 663 Lounge on Washington Street. He would be there talking to his good friend Johnny, the owner. I put on my long false lashes and drew wings with black liner around the corners of my eyes to give the impression of cats' eyes. The look was considered sexy then. And, of course, I'd never go out anywhere without my hot pink lips. Nowadays, a woman doesn't have to be a hooker to wear whorish clothes and makeup—it's a common everyday look for lots of girls and women. The fashion industry seems to adore it. My transformation from plain to street was extreme then, and to think that look is considered high fashion now! No, I like the elegant, movie-style clothing. Audrey Hepburn and my favorite, Liz Taylor, dressed in a classy and sexy way.

I imagined Rio would be drinking already, but I never saw him doing drugs like the other men. He wasn't inclined to because of his brother, Bunny—a big-time drug user who affected Rio in the same way W.D. was turned off by his mother. Both were polar opposites from their family members. I walked as fast as I could down to Boylston Street, then onto Washington, because I didn't want to lose any time getting there. Rio didn't like tardiness. I was wearing black from head to toe, with high heel boots and leather gloves. I was dressed up much classier than I would ordinarily be, and when I passed the King of Pizza, the girls sitting by the windows waved and winked with thumbs up. The doorman at the entrance to the Downtown Lounge whistled when I walked by. As I approached the door of the 663 Lounge, my stomach was performing acrobatics. I felt like a little girl meeting up with her daddy while wearing a party dress for the first time. But once I went inside the small, smoke-filled bar I felt grown up. Apparently, Rio told Johnny and our Boston-nicknamed Legs Diamond that it was my birthday because they quietly congratulated me on turning eighteen. I felt normal for the first time in years, the way I might feel if I were a straight woman going out on a date. I didn't catch a glimpse of any of my clients, although later they told me they were there and saw me. They said they wanted a date, but it was a good thing that they didn't dare approach me because I was with my man. There was someone at the end of the bar I recognized, a close friend of J.N.'s, who would glance at me from time to time. I quickly turned my attention back to Rio, avoiding the stares of J.N.'s friend. Rio had given me change to play songs on the jukebox. I sauntered over to where it was located near the front door. I put on Lou Rawls, one of Rio's favorite singers: "You'll never find, as long as you live, someone who loves you tender like I do." It was his favorite song. Rio had a different kind of intelligence and was unusually perceptive. He controlled his women with his mind, not strictly by the fist, and he certainly didn't control me by using sex… that was out of the question. Even though I hadn't finished picking out the songs, when Rio signaled for me to return, I went back to my barstool. He was talking to Johnny, and he turned to me and told me to wait, not to head back to the jukebox yet. Legs pointed at me with his walking stick as if to say, "Good job—a man who gives a shit." Rio handed me a small, square box, urging me to open it. He said, "You deserve it, baby," and softly kissed my face. His cologne was mesmerizing. It was as much of a turn-on as his soft skin touching mine. He whispered, "I love you and always will."

I melted. I said, "I love you too," and in a strange way I did. I opened the box and inside was a gold ring with a large topaz, my birthstone. It was beautiful and made from solid gold. He said he had one more gift and would give it to me before we left, first we were going out for dinner and then to a club. "How are you feeling, baby?" he asked.

Beaming, I told him I was fine, just fine, and with tears of happiness streaming down my face, I kissed him.

Rio handed me some more change and asked me to keep playing songs on the jukebox. I knew every Motown record and the words to all the songs. I listened to music constantly and sang my heart out whenever I was alone. I became self-conscious about singing or dancing in front of people after my mother Rose died. The times I had enough confidence to perform were few and far between. I stood there flipping through various artists and songs, put the change into the slot, and pushed the buttons for "Lonely Girl." Not only was that one of Rio's other favorites, but it was one of J.N.'s favorites too; I knew this because he had told me during one of our more personal exchanges that it reminded him of me. As I stood there, J.N.'s friend Ted walked up to me, towering over me with his six foot two frame. Even in heels, I was short, and I nervously tried not to look up at him. I hoped he wouldn't speak to me because Rio might be watching from the bar. The panic I was in nearly froze me in place. When I looked over at Rio he was in the middle of a conversation with Johnny and Legs. Maybe he didn't see. As he pushed the buttons for his song, Ted spoke to me. Trying to ignore him, I was just about to walk away when he mentioned J.N.'s name. "I have to give you a message," he said. "Go to his room at the Bradford when you can. He wants to talk to you…"

Interrupting him, I said softly, "I can't talk to you; I'll get in trouble," and I walked past him as briskly as I could. When I reached the bar, Rio turned and said, "Thanks, baby." I would melt every time he called me his baby. "Everything okay?" he asked.

"Yes." I was relieved to think that he hadn't seen me with J.N.'s friend, but I could feel that friend's eyes staring at me. And Rio's vibe changed. The friend should have known better, but he was too square. I didn't turn. After downing a couple of Harveys Bristol Creams on the rocks, a drink Rio said would be easy for me, I became more relaxed. Rio and I were laughing and joking, and I spoke with Legs D. and Johnny. I loved hearing all the gangster gossip from Legs in his sexy voice. He sounded just like Melvin Franklin from the Temptations. It was time to leave, and Rio handed me my next present, a baby blue corduroy coat. Oddly enough, I had never worn anything blue before. I pulled it out of the big Filene's box and put it on over my thin jacket. Guiding me with his arm, we began making our way out; he was always so protective and gentlemanly. I could never go back to the hard-core pimps. Johnny said goodbye from behind the bar. Legs threw a kiss. I was so eager to go out and be seen with Rio. I had to make lots more money before I got a real fur coat—every pimp said that—or they bought a coat from a booster, the next best way to get a fur coat cheaper than in the stores. We kissed. His lips were as soft as butter. "Wait, baby. It's cold out here." He buttoned the coat and tightened the belt, then pulled my body to his. I felt a stimulating force inside. I could smell the vodka on his breath, and again he said, "I love you, my baby. Do you understand?" I told him yes and that I loved him too. Strange, he asked me if I understood. Of course, I understood, but he had knocked back quite a few and was kind of fucked up. Rio was all over me. We kissed again. We waved goodnight to the others and walked outside into the cold air. It was November 10th, 1968. I had made it to the date I had looked forward to for so long, my eighteenth birthday. Yes! This was a date I would never forget…

We walked across the street to get his car out of the Chinatown lot on Stuart Street. There was light snow on the sidewalk before I had gone inside the bar, and there seemed to be a few more inches now. As we stepped onto the curb there wasn't any warning—BOOM! I was on the ground with blood flowing onto my new coat and the pristine, white snow. My new baby blue corduroy coat was ruined! I didn't know what hit me! I squinted at the blinding street light above me as I looked up from the ground, trying to focus. Rio came into view. The blood wouldn't stop draining through my nostrils; I could taste it. He had sucker-punched me! I felt nothing at first because of the shock. *Why?* I wondered. He helped me up onto my feet. I was shaking. "Why, Rio, what did I do?" He tried wiping my face, ever so gently, with his handkerchief. It was red, saturated with my blood. I took the hanky he handed to me and held it to my nose, trying to understand.

"You think about it," Rio said. "You know the reason why. Now get a cab and go to the room. Here's a twenty. I'll see you later. Happy Birthday, baby."

I remained in shock, numb, and barely able to see or speak. *Never mind,* I told myself, *just walk away.* I headed back toward the corner of Washington Street to catch a cab. I didn't know how badly I was hurt. I held the hanky to my nose and clutched the twenty dollars he gave me for the cab. I had walked away after he kissed my forehead, and I knew I would never go back to him. Never! And I would never wear blue again, that was for sure! He had hit me three times altogether since I'd been with him: once a black eye, then a slap for asking too many questions, and now this. If he knew about me helping J.N., then I deserved it because I had broken the rules, but I couldn't deal with the beatings from my men anymore. Anita had been enough. I certainly didn't want to get them forever. I remembered what J.N.'s friend told me about J.N. wanting to see me at the Bradford. I had been the one to give him the money for the room. Going back to Rio wasn't even a consideration. I had to go to J.N. at the Bradford; I thought for a moment and recalled his full name so that I could ask for the room number. I couldn't go anywhere else because Katie was working and Robin was dancing. I was running from one man to another man I had been supporting behind his back. I had never been with this guy before in any intimate way, so I didn't feel guilty about going to him, but I felt remorse that my life had turned out this way, barren, like a garden where no roses would grow.

Waiting for the cab, I envisioned my mother. I recalled the expression on her face, that look of love I never saw again after she passed away. She always looked at me with such devotion when I was hurt. Now I wished she could be here for me. In my imagination, I smelled the sweet fragrance of her American Beauty roses whenever I wanted to escape reality. I questioned whether I would ever see that look on the face of a man I loved or if I could give a child the kind of love my mom gave me. Was I capable? Street girls are underestimated. Sure, they may be rough cuts, but some are intelligent and just caught up in the life. Others never advance beyond the life. I wondered how many of them had experienced real love in their lives. I hoped that someday I would be in a position to experience life beyond the streets, and then, with my streetwise knowledge, take what I've learned to help others. My face was numb, the blood was still draining from my nostrils, and I could feel some pain now. I had to get there fast. As soon as I sat in the cab, the driver asked, "What hospital, lady?"

"No, no, driver. Go to the Bradford Hotel." It was only around the corner, but I had him circle around the block just in case.

"Are you sure?" he asked. "Girl, you need a doctor."

"Yes, I know. Please drive, I'm okay."

"Yeah, sure you are," he said.

The cab driver felt sorry for me and tried to persuade me to go to a hospital, but that was out of the question. Cardinal rule for hoes, never tell on your man—so I certainly couldn't show up like this at a hospital. In thinking of Rio right then, there were aspects that I liked. For instance, my confidence grew because when he said he would be somewhere he was always there, not like the others in my life who never kept their word. He brought me orange juice for breakfast and always had my clothes cleaned for me. I felt important and would have stayed with him if he hadn't struck me that one last time. Why couldn't he have asked me? Would I have told him the truth? No, I could not. The cab pulled up to the Bradford, and I got out, giving the driver a twenty-dollar bill and telling him to keep it for the one-dollar-and-seventy-five-cent trip. I wasn't thinking clearly. "Be careful," he said. "And take your money."

"No, no. I don't want it."

"Here, take it back, you'll need it." The cabby extended his arm toward the open window, trying to hand the bill back to me. "No charge," he said flatly. I didn't want the twenty back, but I took it. Good thing I did!

I ran to the front door and, with all the people staring at me, pushed myself by the doorman. I knew the manager. He wasn't there, but in his place was a desk clerk who rudely told me to get out because I was causing a scene. I refused and told him I had a room. I asked him for the number of the room I had paid for, reciting J.N.'s first and last names. "It's mine," I growled at him. "I paid for it."

"Then you should know the number," he replied. My head was beginning to hurt. "Look," I said, "I don't fucking know the number of the room. I just got here, okay? My husband came earlier, and I was in an accident." I grabbed him by his collar, and he was freaking out because the blood was dripping on his counter. The next thing I knew, he was calling the doorman. Luckily, I remembered the manager's name, a nickname his friends used for him, and the desk clerk relented, saying, "Okay, okay." He could see I was desperate. The doorman recognized me and calmed everyone down, especially me…I had threatened to beat up the poor desk clerk. He gave me the room number and the extra key, and as I walked to the elevator, people stood back, forming a path for me like I was some sort of monster. It reminded me of my childhood when the kids at school made fun of me, saying I had cooties. Everyone was backing away from me like they did then. Maybe if I didn't look like a beaten-up hooker they would have helped, but I wasn't dressed any more radically than some women with heavy makeup and high heels, who went to nightclubs. Nowadays, square girls look like hookers and hookers look like square girls—it's crazy! I was finally in the elevator, and my head was pounding. My eyes were throbbing, and they were nearly swollen shut. I was terribly thirsty. Even though I had the key, I didn't use it. But I knocked hard and kicked at the door. I would have to wait if he had a girl in there. Even though it was my money that paid for the room, I had no rights. I certainly never anticipated meeting him here this way. I banged at the door again. "It's Libbe!" I called out. He opened the door the moment I said it was me. At first he was surprised and then his expression turned into shock. The room was small and darkly lit. I sat on the double bed, feeling dizzy. The TV was on, and it made my eyes hurt terribly! I looked around, no girl here. It was a typical room in an old hotel, with well-worn furniture. He helped me take off the bloody blue coat. "Oh my god! What happened?" I didn't feel the horrific pain until I was in the room and relaxed; the fear, shock, and adrenalin had totally numbed me. I was woozy. J.N. was upset and angry. "I'm going to kill whoever did this to you!" He walked me into the bathroom and threw my coat into the bathtub, running the cold water over it. I had no idea what my face looked like until I saw my reflection in the mirror. Oh shit! My face! Although my vision was blurry, I could see that my nose was twisted and pushed to the side of my face. I was panicking. "Oh god, my nose! Will it go back in place?" I asked. My face was swollen and my eyes were bruised and misshapen. J.N. insisted that I see a doctor.

"Your nose is broken," he said.

"No," I said. "If we go to the hospital they'll think you broke it. I'll push it back. Help me."

"No, we can't! We could make it worse!" When I touched my face the pain was excruciating. My black eye was really bad. I had been beaten with hot wire hangers and Anita's belts, but this was a different kind of pain. J.N. washed my face with cold water and told me to tilt my head back a little to stop the bleeding. He told me he had to fill a bucket with ice from the hallway to freeze my nose and then he would push it back into place with my help. He said that it would hurt like hell. It hurt like hell now! J.N. brought me water to drink. He acted like he was gravely worried and really cared. He left to get the ice. I wasn't his woman, but I was his ticket. I wondered if I was more to him than that since our exchanges of confidences. He came rushing back into the room and was gentle as he touched my face. Although my sweater wasn't soaked with blood because he had placed a towel over me after he removed my jacket, he suggested that I take off my clothes so he could try to get the smaller stains out. I'd be more comfortable with looser clothes on. He gave me one of his shirts to wear. He propped up the pillows on the bed and covered me. I jumped out when I noticed the white sheets. "I don't lie on white sheets," I told him as I wrapped the bedspread around me and held it tightly under my chin. I had the chills. I said that white sheets reminded me of my stepmother.

"Why?" he asked.

"Well, after her beatings, when I peed on the sheets she would force me to sleep on them as a punishment." I let him know that white sheets always triggered those awful memories, and that my mother, Rose, had been lying on them in the hospital Room of Death. J.N. listened without commenting. "Sorry," I said. "I needed to vent. I never told anyone about that."

"Well you can tell me," he replied. I thought back to how I graduated to sleeping on the floor in the locked boiler room. I didn't explain about Anita or the boiler room to J.N. then because my face hurt when I spoke. As I lay there with my body changing from fever to chills to intense pain, I told him what had happened with Rio. He applied the ice to my nose and eyes. My nose was frozen and still hurt like hell. J.N. warned me that what he was about to do would be more painful. "All right, just hurry. But if it gets worse or doesn't go back, we have to go to a hospital, okay?"

"Okay." Then, with the ice and cloth, he pushed my nose until I heard it snap. The pain was so extreme I lost my breath and almost blacked out! I cried out and nearly fell off the bed. I stayed conscious, my head resting on propped-up pillows. J.N. pulled me a bit upright to keep me from bleeding more, and from choking on it. Shit, my nose hurt like hell! He held the ice packs on and off for a while. When I could get up, we looked in the mirror. It was impossible to see whether my nose was still twisted or if it was deformed because of the swelling. It was clogged and even more swollen than before. I breathed through my mouth, holding the ice on and off. J.N. handed me some aspirin tablets to help with the pain. He told me it was okay to take them because two hours had already passed since I had taken the hit. J.N. held the ice there so that my nose would stay frozen. I was totally limp. What next… I could not make money until the pain and swelling went down some.

J.N. wanted to get a gun to shoot Rio. I told him to stay away from Rio because if anyone was going to be shot it was J.N. "He has a gun and will shoot you," I told him. "And if you hurt him his brother Bunny will get you." J.N. appeared to have little fear, although when he owed the money for the gun to Moses he was obviously shaken. He should be scared now, I thought, but he wasn't. It was his manhood expressing itself; he thought as a man that he needed to protect and avenge me.

I had been taking bombers days before, and now I was hungry because the pills were wearing off. I was so tired and needed to sleep, but J.N. was adamant about not sleeping for at least three more hours. He gave me peanut butter and Marshmallow Fluff on Wonder Bread, which was painful to chew even when taking small bites. He said he would get me milkshakes with the money he had left over after paying for the room. J.N. told me he planned to find Rio to settle my situation—one way or another. I told him I had twenty dollars he could get food with. We were lucky the hotel was paid up for the next five days. I also had a few bucks in my boot because I had walked to meet Rio earlier, never spending my cab money to get to the bar, so that was extra money too. This was the closest I'd ever been to J.N., and I liked his sympathetic attitude toward me and the way he told me he never wanted me to work again. Although it was a nice sentiment, I knew that would never happen. He had no one, and neither did I. I told him again that I was a foster kid and adopted as well. That brought us closer together. So many of the relationships I'd had with men never possessed the quality I needed at the time. We had so much in common, and I accepted every inch of his caring, even more so when he held me to soothe the pain. But I was cautious about taking it to heart. He told me he was going out to get some more money. How was that possible? I wondered where he'd get it from when I seemed to be his only source. I was in too much pain to worry about it. I had thirty dollars in my boot, plus the twenty dollars, and it had to last; I gave it all to him for whatever else we might need.

He started talking about himself, explaining that he had been adopted by his foster parents and came from West Medford. I already knew he was adopted because of our conversations when we first met, but now he was explaining the story. He was smart, unlike anyone I'd met in the life, whether it was W.D., Rio, or any of the other pimps I knew. He was not slick. He reminded me of Huckie in the way he expressed affection and respect for me. He had a heart. Even in my condition, I was checking him out. He was extremely good-looking, tall, and slender. All in all, he was attractive except for his processed hair, which I hated because it was too straight.

The hours were passing, and I still hadn't fallen asleep. The aspirin wasn't strong enough for the intensity of my pain. I lay on the bed in a fetal position, moaning; crying silently to mask any weakness—tough street hoes don't cry! The cold ice on my sore face was becoming uncomfortable, like needles. I would place the ice on for fifteen minutes, then off for fifteen minutes. J.N. rubbed my upper back to relax me. His warmth and sincerity made me feel like a queen. The experience was intense but not the least bit sexual yet, loving was more like it. After he finished, he went out. While he was gone, I nervously looked in the mirror several times, worrying that my face would never heal, and I would look disfigured for the rest of my life. How would I be able to work looking so swollen and abnormal? No one would ever pick me! I couldn't wait for J.N. to get back. I actually missed his company.

When J.N. came back later, he rolled a joint out of a nickel bag and told me to have some so the pain would go away, then I could fall sleep. I inhaled and felt like I was floating. With all the opportunities there were to smoke marijuana, I had never wanted to try it. Surprisingly, I liked it and it helped with the pain. I went to sleep next to J.N., who held me in his arms like we had been together for years. I was so heavy with sleep that I never asked him where he had gone. I was comforted and knew I was in a safe place for the time being—a warm bed, no hassles, some food, and a caring man.

Hours passed. I awoke to the low hum of the TV and J.N. pacing the room, smoking. When I tried to stand, I was a bit dizzy and couldn't get up right away. I could hear the TV in the background; The Dating Game was on. I told him I could go to work in the early morning at the Essex Deli or before the bars closed, and a couple of my regulars would pay me despite how I appeared. He was insistent, saying, "You can't go to work today or for the next few days!"

"Oh, yes I can. We have money to buy sunglasses."

"No," he countered, "you're not going out there. If we have money you can stay in!"

"No, I don't have that much!"

"Look at yourself, Libbe. Your face is too swollen, and you're still in pain. You still stagger. You could pass out somewhere." I got out of bed and stood in front of the bathroom mirror, wobbling. My nose was even more swollen after snapping the bone back in place. My whole face was black and blue. "Just stay here and I'll get some food for you, and a pair of sunglasses. I have your money, remember? I only spent ten bucks. And I can double or triple it if I buy a bigger bag of weed and sell some joints. You need more days to rest. I'll find your ex-man and tell him not to bother you anymore, that you are not going back to him!" J.N. seemed confident that was my choice. He wanted me to stay with him.

He sat on the bed and asked, "Do you want to be with me?" I wasn't sure. With the pain I was in, this wasn't the type of choice I wanted to be making at the moment. Was I ready to leave Rio or was I just upset because I got caught and he beat me to set me straight? "I don't know you, and you're not really in the life," I told him.

"I know, but I'm trying," he replied. "I want to be, but only with you, not the others. Give me a chance, and I'll prove it. I'm a good man, and I can help you out." I could hardly believe it when he told me, "I could even get a job." He said, "You chose your other men without knowing them." He was right—I did. "So you know *me* better. We've talked quite a bit." Maybe what I needed was a square-type man who could learn the ropes from me. Right then and there, I decided to be with J.N. He told me I wouldn't be sorry and that he would take care of me. The truth was that I was capable of taking better care of him than he could of me, just not at that very moment. I told him where Rio would be at one a.m. The discussion with Rio was about to be on. J.N. dressed in a gray leather jacket and wore his eyeglasses as he usually did, never taking them off. When he was changing his clothes, I wondered what being with him sexually might be like, but of course, I had to wait until I was totally sure of him. Because he wasn't a pimp, the ball was in my court. I needed to wait a bit for the swelling to go down so I could look more appealing and make money again. I wanted this time to be different than the other times, when I paid my man for having sex with me. Hopefully, everything with Rio would be resolved and J.N. could get my things from my room. I held the ice to my face so it would heal faster and took more aspirin for the pain. J.N. went to the store with my money (plus twenty more that, as I later learned, he had gotten from selling the joints he'd made). He was about to get the other bag of weed to make even more money.

He leaned over me, tall and slender, and left after kissing me gently on my forehead. I had visions of J.N. lying in a pool of blood, shot by Rio at the bar. *Oh god,* I thought, *please, let this go smoothly!* I was so hyper, I smoked a little of the joint that was left in the ash-tray. Two puffs...and that calmed me down and made waiting for J.N.'s call easier. The pain had eased, and I felt hungry. I ate some applesauce as I waited, and then the phone rang. It was him. "Are you okay?" I asked, my voice strained and tense.

"Yes, I'm okay. Are you okay? I'm just going in now to speak to him. I wanted to check on you first." His thoughtfulness impressed me. He said, "I'll see you soon. Stop worrying, we are two grown men." And just when I expected it to be over, my panic returned and I was breathing rapidly, listening to the beat of my heart pounding in my chest. I was actually scared for this man. Leaning back against the pillows, I felt my nose and head throbbing to the beat of my vibrating heart. More time passed. I had missed the Honeymooners earlier. I stared at the TV, not paying much attention. I waited and waited, opening the jar of Marshmallow Fluff and slowly letting it melt in my mouth as I ate spoonful after spoonful. It was now almost three a.m. I was about to take off J.N.'s shirt to get dressed to go out and find him when a key turned in the lock. My heart skipped a beat. There he was, alive and well—with a delicious milkshake, soup, soft bread, applesauce, and the sunglasses—and my happiness showed in my painful grin! J.N. hugged me and told me Rio wanted five hundred to let me go, saying that was a bargain price for me. He said we had a week to give it to him to get my clothes back. J.N. said he told Rio my facial swelling had to go down first, and we would need a few more days. He allowed for the extra time. I couldn't believe that Rio let me go that easily—he seemed so attached to me, still, it was only right that he do it. Maybe he felt so badly about punching me that letting me go was his way of apologizing, or it was a game to get me back. Also, I guessed that he suspected I had someone else. I never had the chance to ask if he was married. I did get all the information once I wasn't with him anymore; it poured in like front page news in the Globe. He was married with kids and had a lesbian girl for cash on the side. I was his main gig to bring lots of extra cash home to his honey. He was so smooth. I had been so engrossed in my work that I chose to ignore what was right under my nose. I couldn't believe I fell for all that, but as time went on, I realized he would always have a place in my heart, and I had a place in his, always. Others, from the bartenders to the steadies in the bar, assured me that he actually loved me. I respected him despite the broken nose, and we remain friends to this day. I would miss going to the clubs with him—he knew all the owners—like Wally's on Mass Ave. and the Pioneer Club, which he loved.

J.N. and I lived in the room at the Bradford for a full week, plus he paid for two extra days. It gave me time to allow my face to heal. I needed to make money for another room to work out of, maybe in the LaSalle, where I could get a good deal. Until then, I worked for two days out of the room at the Bradford with my steadies. My face improved every day. The bone had gone back into place when it snapped, but it stuck out on the side slightly, and without a doctor's care, it has stayed that way. The bruising and swelling around my eyes took longer to fade, and despite my dislike for face makeup, I covered the black and blue with a thick coating and rehearsed what I would tell the street clients. J.N. and I still hadn't had sex; we slept with our clothes on in each other's arms, feeling the click of electric current running through our veins. He was truly comforting, yet it was impossible to deny the sexual tension brewing ever more forcefully with each passing day. Rio and I were supposed to go to New York for New Year's Eve to Tommy Smalls, better known as Small's Paradise. He had taken me there one time before, and to some clubs in Harlem that were tiny, but packed. I would not be going now…

CHAPTER FORTY-ONE

The 1200 Beacon Street Hotel

I was planning to move us to the 1200 Beacon Street Hotel in Brookline, where everyone was—the new cool place to stay for all the working girls. There was easy access in and out. I made Rio's five hundred in one day; my clients were happy to see me no matter how I looked. The deal was done…although I still thought about him and wore the ring he gave me as a token. He kept his promise and gave me back my belongings. Some of the club owners told me Rio was really hurt about my leaving, but that he understood; even the underworld guys at the lounges would tell me this. This choosing wasn't done exactly the way I would have liked because, considering the circumstances, the decision was made so quickly. I was becoming fond of J.N. We clicked because our backgrounds and values were similar. I could leave him anytime, now or later, because he was square and it wouldn't be hard, but I was getting used to him, more so with each passing day. He didn't have to leave me to go to someone else, and I liked that. He got me a warm jacket to work in, always paid for the hotel, and bought food—yes, with my money, but he would hustle, and buy and sell herb for small cash. He never squandered the money I gave him. J.N. was set. He had one of the best working girls in Boston and money pouring in. I pushed him to buy nicer clothes, and with some street style, he appeared even more attractive. Slowly, I was turning *him* out so he would be more respected on the hoe stroll. J.N. looked healthier now that he was eating more, and better, food. I could see that girls were taking notice, and they wanted to choose him. My friend Katie was looking. He was up my ass everywhere I went, and I liked that because he wasn't interested in anyone else besides me—that was a new experience. I gave him money for a separate room at the 1200 Beacon Street, and he took the one next door to his buddy Junior from his hometown. I couldn't picture them as friends. He was more down because he was already in the game; I thought he could manipulate J.N. far too easily, and I was right, he did. I called New York and steadily talked to Charlie, a blonde madam from Sweden. She was sexy, big-boned like Mae West, but a bitch for sure, tough as nails. I was booked to go there soon. I had met her when I went to other madam's places and had been at her place only one time.

I was in the Park Square building catching clients when J.N. came in holding a puppy in his arms. "For you," he said.

"Hell no, I can't have a puppy! I work all the time and hotels don't allow them." He was so cute, but there was no way I could take care of him. "Give him away to someone. Don't bring him to the hotel!" I knew that wasn't nice of me, I was being cold; I didn't mean to sound harsh, but now wasn't the right time. He was surprised, if not somewhat hurt, but I was firm—no puppy! I didn't want to get soggy, so I averted my eyes. J.N. took the dog away. He had gotten his first knockdown. He was disappointed because I'd told him how much I loved dogs, and he only bought the puppy to please me. I had no idea he would actually buy one for me when we didn't have a home for it. Later, in a lighter tone, I explained the reason I turned away the puppy and apologized to J.N. for hurting his feelings. He understood, or I thought he did. Plus, I went out of town frequently and we moved around a lot, so it wouldn't work.

Unlike the other pimps who pick a day to sleep with their girls, J.N. and I were kissing and becoming closer day by day, like boyfriend and girlfriend, spending all our free time together. I suppose it was comparable to what squares do when they are dating. We were supposed to hook up after work with Gidge and Junior at the 1200 Beacon Street. I was falling into a routine of work then meeting up with J.N. and his friends. I hadn't seen Rio since he broke my nose. Katie told me she had run into him and that he wanted to talk to me at her apartment when I could. I didn't think it was a good idea, bouncing back and forth from one man to another, but I wanted closure too. Even though I missed him and wanted to see him and explain, I wasn't ready just yet. It was the end of November and freezing cold outside, but I didn't have time to feel the cold—I was working. The hotel was a step back financially, costing more money than I wanted to spend. I needed to rent another room or get an apartment. I didn't have a big-time pimp now, so I had to move into a more tenable situation. We both were ready. He said he liked to cook…while I, of course, loved to eat. Getting an apartment seemed to be the best solution. Charlie kept calling. She asked me to come early. I said I had to just keep my regular bookings for now.

J.N. had friends from his hometown on the street, but only Junior and Davey J. hung with the bigger-name pimps. They got respect because they hustled and had connections. J.N. was becoming known on account of my reputation. His friends were wild and immature, and I kept on thinking about Rio and his maturity. Rio was not young and restless. At the time, I didn't care anymore if he was married or not—now I do. Had I stayed with him, it might have weighed on me eventually, and leaving sooner was the better and wiser decision. I was socializing with my friends, going to Katie's house parties, and enjoying myself like people outside of the life do. This was a switch—having the best of both worlds.

Drugs never interested me before. Now, on top of smoking my cigarettes, I was smoking weed. It relaxed me, and I felt more sexual. Even the tricks were coming to me like magnets when I was high. We were hanging out in the room; Junior handed around some blow. After a couple of drinks, we did a few lines. I got so high! The lights were out, and Junior and his girl were going at it. The mood was set. It was time for my new man and I to get it on. And we did, hot and heavy! I was melting, my heart raced with anticipation!

J.N. hovered over my tiny frame. He lowered his head to my face, never touching his body to mine as he kissed my lips. Then he softly lay down on top of me. I felt his large, hard penis against my pelvis. I wanted to feel him inside me but he took his time, a long time, until the moment was ripe. He stood and stripped off his pants and then slowly mounted me again. He pushed my legs apart with his legs, his erection never touching me except for the tip of his penis against my leg. As his finger gently entered inside my wet lips, I knew I wanted him. I squirmed according to his touch, the drugs enhancing the pleasure I felt. I was ready. I yearned to have his penis penetrate me. I had been prepped for weeks now, and my nose was healed. He pulled out his finger and tasted it, and directed his penis with his hand right to the lips of my wet vagina, entering smoothly and ever so slowly. I felt so full, and there was a twinge of pain followed by an intense sensual sensation. I was in a total floating moment. Whispering, he said, "Just the head. I'm putting in just the head."

"Yes, yes," I replied breathlessly, begging for more.

"Okay," he said. I felt intense pleasure in response to the pressure of his body against my pelvic bones. He inched his way in slowly, like a worm, and I opened up. I was moaning as he softly plunged farther inside me, now more than halfway. It began to hurt when I felt he was deep in my stomach. I felt like I was splitting in half. I felt the secretions inside me burst and flow. I was feeling high, not fully conscious of reality at that moment, but acutely aware of how deeply erotic our coupling was. J.N. continued moving, gyrating inside me. My stomach was cramping a bit, and I could feel his member way up inside my abdomen. It began to burn down there. I was trying to catch my breath and came up under his arm. I pushed against him, telling him to stop. "Please, for a moment!" He was coming, so he thrust deeper! I moaned at the moment he slightly pulled back. My squirming must have triggered his climax and, with sounds of pure pleasure, he kept on coming. I could feel that the sheets were soaked underneath my backside. Junior's girlfriend quietly asked, "You okay over there? You want a cloth?" I was shaking from the climax I'd had when he came. I held my hands down there to stop the flow of cum as he pulled all the way out, inch by inch—I could feel how long he was. Now that I was somewhat sober, I could feel how huge and wide he was. It was incredible that he had been inside me. I lay there perfectly still, trying to compose myself. Junior asked if I was all right. I was relieved once his penis was outside of me. His size was way larger than average, thicker, and much longer—twelve inches, for sure. The soreness inside was becoming worse as the intensity of the moment subsided.

When J.N. first lay down on top of me, I felt pins and needles throughout my body. He was not a pimp or a show, rather, he was a man I wanted deeply and who wanted me. It was such a different experience from any of my other men. His friend said we turned them on by listening to the sounds we were making. J.N. didn't let me touch him before he entered me, unlike so many other men who wanted head. I enjoyed every minute of being with him. This was something different—I was connecting with J.N. in a more profound way. The sex I had with him was great because he knew what to do, and how to do it, even though his size could have been an impediment. He did everything perfectly. I just couldn't understand why I was in pain.

Junior sent Gidge over to me because, as he told her, J.N. was hung like a horse and he wanted her to check on me. A small lamp in the corner of the room went on. As I pulled the covers over me, I saw the blood all over the white sheets. "Oh shit!" I screamed. It was everywhere. Did J.N. have sickle cell too? Like W.D.? Was it me, my period? I wasn't due. Gidge ran into the bathroom to wet some white facecloths with cold water. J.N. was frantic. "Oh baby, I'm sorry!" Both of us had been in the moment and neither of us realized I was bleeding. Cum was floating in the blood. Gidge said she'd looked and that there was a tear at the mouth of my vagina. I had never experienced anyone that big inside me—no one. There were other pimps who were big but not even close to J.N. Why didn't I realize that when it was happening? I asked J.N. if he had sickle cell. "No, of course not. It's your blood, baby." I spent the rest of the night in and out of an ice-cold tub to lower the swelling. I told him Vicks would help too. I knew that from my turn-out. I slept like I hadn't done since my bout with pneumonia in W.D.'s house. I was relieved that I had made enough money to stay in for a couple of days. It was my call how long I needed to rest, but I felt guilty about taking the two days because I retained my "good hoe" mentality.

The only days off in the life were when your man decided to take you out. J.N. and I went out on the town the next day, spending money and having a good time. I was just too sore and swollen to have intercourse, but blowjobs were okay. I forgot about work, wanting to be with J.N. exclusively. After our interlude, he said he didn't want me out working, that he wanted me sleeping with him every night and doing things with him during the day. I didn't want to get lazy. I missed Rio, I admit, but J.N. was intriguing because of the way he treated me, always waiting for me and sleeping next to me for companionship, with or without having sex. This relationship was better than others I'd had. I was becoming attached. I didn't pay attention to his friends because they were annoying, the young pimps and their half-assed girls. I couldn't be bothered with them when they would say hello on the streets just because I was with their friend. I walked past them—this wasn't elementary school. We stayed at the 1200 Beacon Street Hotel for a few more days. The maid who cleaned up the bloody sheets was cool about it, and J.N. gave her a generous tip. We had to find an apartment fast. Because of the chemistry between us, I wished I had met him earlier in my life. Being comfortable in an intimate relationship was still a challenge for me, and something I wanted to achieve. I was happy with my new man and comfortable because I didn't fear him. He even made it possible to relax and cum with oral sex; he was great at it for sure. I called and talked to Charlie a few times. She needed new girls. I told her I would see if any mine would go—that is, if they were good enough to work in her place and take her orders.

CHAPTER FORTY-TWO

Freaked

The surge of energy I experienced drove me to work even harder so I could make more cash and finish earlier to see J.N. He looked forward to spending time with me, and I felt the same way. We loved to go food shopping. Still, Rio was on my mind. I missed his fatherly ways and how he would call me "baby." Without my consent, Katie set up a time for us to meet in her apartment before the holidays. J.N. invited me to go to his family's house for Christmas. I told him I had to work and couldn't go. I felt no need to explain that I was not fond of family gatherings. Going to visit his family was something he resumed doing after running away to be on the streets. I didn't want to go anywhere for the holidays; it was never a great time for me. I wouldn't have gone to Jennifer's even if she asked me because her family was always there, and I couldn't bear to be around them. I could see through their phony friendliness toward me, and it would only bring up negative memories. J.N. assumed he and I would always be together and we talked about it constantly. Marriage! No, no, no… Everything he said referred to "us" as a unit. His confidence in the two of us as a couple frightened me. How could he know what the future would bring? I wasn't that certain how our relationship would end up—despite the attraction we had for one another and how we clicked sexually. I had never been in a relationship before, so how would I know my future? Could it be that I felt sorry for him and obligated to take care of him on the street…or was I falling in love? I was torn between Rio and J.N., just like I was when I was with Michael and W.D. How would I know how to feel without having any guidance? I hadn't seen Rio since early November and now it was the first week of December. I loved Rio for the mature image he portrayed and the sweet smell of his cologne, but that's not real love. J.N. and I were getting along well, and he asked me to square up and marry him several times. I felt as though I loved him enough, but I stayed disconnected because of my business. He never asked me about what I did at Katie's house. Of course, I wasn't going to tell him about meeting Rio. I talked to Katie about Rio and J.N., and she let me know she thought Rio was more for me. But I told her that J.N. was younger and better in bed, and he loved me. She was judgmental but hypocritical: even though *she* was always juggling men, she said what I was doing between the two guys was far too dangerous because they both loved me. But I assured her I did not want to go back to Rio, that I had fallen hard for J.N.

I felt like the life was right for me. I could never square up. It was almost as if I had done the same thing in a previous incarnation. Katie told me to let J.N. get a job. No way! I was making between three and five hundred dollars a day, and starving from paycheck to paycheck didn't appeal to me. What could anyone offer to a girl to get her off the street with that kind of earning capacity? McDonald's, Burger King, maybe three hundred a week, if that. How could anyone talk someone out of this job? Money keeps girls in the life, and society doesn't offer them alternatives that pay as well. And the state has no clue how to change that! Finding an occupation that interests them more than the money they earn does happen, although it's rare. (I know the system and what it would take to get working girls off the streets, and someday, I hope to have the chance to do just that.) I kept thinking about J.N.'s offer to marry me, and then shut it out of my mind—it was totally out of the question. No, I didn't need a piece of paper that essentially said that somebody owned me and took care of me. I want to be able to care for myself and others.

I bought presents for J.N. with my own stashed money at Brodney Antiques and Jewelry, gold with diamonds, and put them away until Christmas. I thought that by buying gold—it was always a great investment—I could sell it if that ever became necessary. I had learned about that from my clients. I dreamed that if I had children, I would provide for them and give them only the best whether I was married or not. Then, once I had enough money to pay for it, I would search for my baby girl. J.N and I talked about her lots of times.

When Katie had arranged the meeting between Rio and me, I thought that I would finally settle the question of which man I wanted to be with. J.N. always told me he was afraid I would leave him because it seemed like I missed Rio and was always comparing them. I never meant for him to feel insecure. The apartment Katie used to live in before she moved to Acton was up by the Franklin Park Zoo, off Blue Hill Ave. Normally, I never would have chanced going there to meet him. I felt both fear that Rio would claim me back and excitement about seeing him. I was turned on. If he held me, I was certain that I'd melt like a little girl—the little girl I felt I was whenever he was near me. When I arrived at her place I went into the kitchen, where Katie and Rio were sitting and having a drink. She excused herself and quietly left, leaving the two of us face to face. Even though I chose J.N., it was then I was sure I missed Rio. The freak was on. I gave in to my desire like a kid in a candy store. He was sober! Wow! Katie had already told Rio we could use her bedroom. The plans had been made ahead of time…again, leave it to my friend to arrange things without telling me. She had done lots of surprises I'd walked away from; this one I didn't. My attraction to Rio wasn't sexual, it was mental. There wasn't a physical connection. It was like being with a client for sex and—emotionally—with a dad for stability. It was how he spoke to me, telling me I was beautiful and how he missed sleeping next to me. "Oh, baby, I want you," he said, and I was putty in his hands. He began touching me all over, sucking on my breasts, and kissing my stomach until his mouth was on me. The pleasure was intense, more so than it had been in the past when he had too much vodka and passed out when he aimed to please. I couldn't come at all from oral sex because of my past when I had been molested. I held back from coming in any way with men, even with J.N., who swore every time we had sex he would break me of that problem. I lifted up Rio's head to my chest saying, "Just go inside, please. I want you inside me," which for him was the consummate turn-on. He came inside me. Oh god, I tried to pull him back but I just couldn't. I hadn't felt anything sexually and told myself that it had been a mistake again, although I wouldn't have been certain that something was missing if he hadn't been sober when I had sex with him this last time. I satisfied him but had cheated myself, and cheated on J.N. I hadn't brought a douche with me and cleaned up the best I could until I could get out to buy one before I worked. I'd had sex with many men; now I knew there was only one who could satisfy me and wouldn't give up, and that was J.N. He was the same age as me, smart, and nice-looking, and he never stopped telling me how much he loved me. I hoped he meant it. Even though I tried suppressing them as much as I could, my feelings for him were becoming stronger and stronger. I cared for him deep within my soul. I was never with Rio again in that way. He understood that I'd already moved on, but he wanted to be in touch with me always. At the time, I never told J.N. about what happened that day with Rio, and I prayed that it would never come to light. Many years later, I did tell him. He was happy that I opened up to him about it, but said that he wasn't surprised; he knew in his heart.

It was bitter cold, and it felt even colder wearing short skirts, hot pants, and high heels. My reliable Farmer's Almanac had informed me that it would be an arctic winter. A pimp had once replied to me when I mentioned the Farmer's Almanac, "Farmer's what? We don't do farmer's anything, you hear?" I always laughed when I thought of that because I was usually accurate when I predicted snow, sleet, or cold weather, with the men saying, "Bitch, you aren't the weatherman." I was working hard, saving for an apartment in Mattapan. We had already looked for apartments and found one we both liked. This would be my first real place—no more rooms or hotels to contend with. J.N. was so happy we were together, and according to his plans, we would be together long after Christmas and New Year's. J.N. and L.S. forever… And Christmas in our new place would be so special. I was happy.

I had to go to Charlie's place to work for five days. I was not pleased about it, but I knew I could make good money and stay off the streets. So I went, for four days instead, and it was a tough call. She wanted girls to do everything, took their tips, and she got a fifty percent cut. Shit! But I went and did a short week with regulars. She said the next run would be with special clients who pay more.

CHAPTER FORTY-THREE

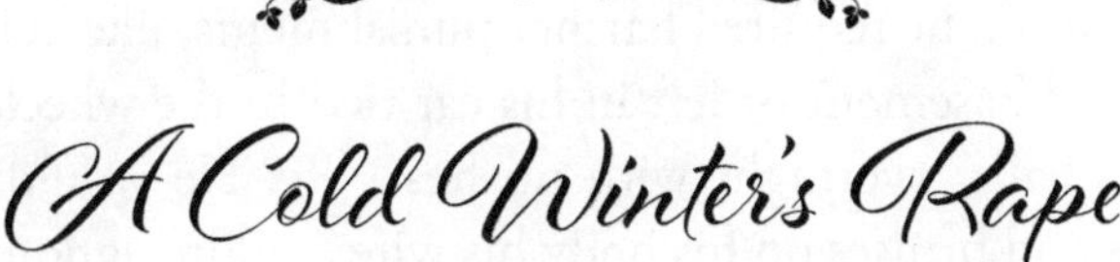

A Cold Winter's Rape

J.N. missed me terribly, and was so happy when I came back. Rio's name was seldom mentioned. J.N. and I were signing a lease for a two-bedroom apartment in a three-story house on Goodale Road. I had all the money to pay for the apartment. Katie was getting to know J.N. better, and occasionally, they would have beers and laughs together. She was very flirtatious, and I could see she wanted a piece of him. I worked every day except Sundays, when we went out. We had been approved for credit at Summerfield Furniture. J.N. looked for the furniture while I worked. He told me that I could pick out the small things for the apartment but not to use our entire credit line. Little by little, we were collecting furniture. But we also needed a car. We were conventional in the sense that we were like any other young couple trying to establish a home. Things were going well. J.N. was establishing his own credit with my earnings, but I wanted nothing in my name because of what I did. And, once again, I had allowed man to take control.

I had my regulars, and new clients came in daily. "Harry the Whip" was one of my more notable dominance customers, a stockbroker who was a great guy but had many sexual issues. I loved tying him up and putting a collar around his neck, attaching a leash that encircled his scrotum, and leading him around the room while I spanked his ass until it was red. Harry couldn't get enough. I constantly made up new sexual fantasies to tell him. I wish I had published them back then, I probably could have made a good living out of it. Who knew? He enjoyed himself, especially begging me ("his mistress," as he put it) to shave him, torture his penis, and lock him up. I asked him how he could have the area around his balls shaved without arousing his wife's suspicions, and he said that he told her he sweat so much he didn't have a choice, he needed to shave them. As time went on, he required harsher punishments, like being locked in an ice-cold basement or left in his car tied to the wheel, from his neck to his balls, overnight with no heat, etc. He would go home with marks and bruises on his body his wife couldn't ignore—he had to tell her. That was his downfall, and he wound up divorced. I knew Harry for many years, and he would come to see me all the time.

Even though it was in an older house, J.N. and I loved our apartment. I set up a Christmas tree and strung it with popcorn, and we exchanged gifts for our first winter holiday together. He went to his family's place by himself for Christmas Day, but we spent New Year's out on the town, at clubs and after-hours. It was a new life for me. My thoughts for the future I was slowly creating were, *I've got to get girls to send to New York. In addition to what I was already making with the locals, I could make two hundred on each girl I sent.*

I kept the room at the LaSalle. The manager knew me, and he always cut me a good deal. As far as I knew, the hotel was safe. I never had any problems. I would go to the room with tricks or they would meet me there. Harry, unlike other customers, flaunted his money on the street. He was constantly drunk, always repeating himself, and would deliberately annoy me by yelling while standing outside the hotel to get my attention. Most of the domination clients also attempted to goad me, but they wouldn't call attention to themselves outside the hotel rooms because they were financial bigwigs, prestigious lawyers, and prominent doctors. Harry was big too, a successful stockbroker, but he didn't give a shit.

Like all the working girls, I was familiar with the street thugs, and we gave some of them a few dollars to help them out. In exchange, they watched out for the police and other thugs. The dancers used them as errand boys. Sometimes there would be conflict between the girls and the dancers, who considered themselves superior to the streetwalkers. There wasn't really much difference between them because the dancers gave blowjobs in the clubs and hand jobs at the bar and tables, sometimes taking one or two clients home for extra cash. "Dancing hoes." Their favorite saying was, "He's my sugar daddy—that's all!" Yeah, right! They were all hoes, although they would never admit it. It was the working girls who kept the flow of customers coming back to all the bars and hotels, and they weren't inferior to anyone. The dancers would tease and, while they stayed on stage, the clients ran to the hoes to get taken care of. The voyeurs stayed and just watched, hungry. The Combat Zone, and its clubs and hotels, was a place to find drugs and a like-minded congregation of prostitutes, pimps, dancers, gangsters, and thieves. Chinatown gambling houses were also the settings of all sorts of corrupt enterprises. The local thieves and street thugs knew who to hit and who to leave alone. The stragglers from out of town hit and ran; they would get their thrills and leave. And if they were businessmen from out of state, they would return to the same spot.

The working day had almost ended for me, and things had gone smoothly. It was late, and I had already seen five tricks and Harry, my slave. After Harry left, I pulled in several more. It had been a good day, and I was on my way back to the LaSalle to change clothes. J.N. encouraged me to eat breakfast late at night with him, so I was meeting him later, at two a.m., on Boylston Street, next to the Jazz Workshop and Paul's Mall. Everyone ate there after working or just to drop in someplace for a break and to hang out. I couldn't wait to see him. I passed through the lobby, climbed the steps, and walked down the narrow hallway to my room on the left, thinking about J.N. the entire way. I fished in my small purse for the keys. As I was putting the key into the lock, I turned the nob an inch to open the door. That's when a hand from above me opened the door all the way and pushed me inside, holding me by the neck so I couldn't turn. I panicked! The door shut with a slam! I looked at the bed in front of me as he told me not to be a crazy bitch or he would kill me! I needed something to grab onto, but what? I didn't scream because it was too early to tell if he was lying or not. Would he really kill me?

I felt his strength in the grip around my neck; he was choking me from behind. I knew by his voice that he was serious. I had to fight or die! My body went limp and I dropped, screaming, "Help! Help!" He leaned down and picked me up, throwing my body over, and cupped his hand across my mouth, cutting off my breath. I looked at his face. His pupils were dilated and his eyes were menacing. His face was unfamiliar to me. I twisted and turned, fighting him as best I could while I moved across the floor trying to reach the telephone in the corner. We were struggling, and occasionally his grip loosened enough for me to breathe. Just a few more inches and I would be able to pull the phone cord or table leg. I had to get to the phone! He was on his knees straddling me and leaned forward as he unzipped his pants with one hand, giving me another moment to catch my breath. He told me he was going to fuck me then kill me, and I believed him! His strength overpowered me. I grabbed at him, scratching his skin with my short nails in an effort to get loose. It wasn't working, and the phone was still on the receiver. He held my mouth tightly shut and I couldn't get out a scream, but I saw his mind wander for a brief moment as he was thinking about entering me and managed to wriggle my arm free with enough strength to get to the side table with the black rotary phone. I held onto the leg with all my strength. He ripped my top and the bottom of my skirt. I reached for the phone cord and pulled hard on it until the heavy phone fell off the hook to the floor with a loud bang. He took the cord, choking me as he mounted my body. "You bitch!" he hissed. My skirt was pushed up. I was losing air flow. My stockings and garter belt were ripped and hanging loosely around my hips. My panties were made of silk and lace, easy to tear apart. He was concentrating on pushing his penis inside me and wasn't using his hands to choke me, so the phone cord loosened. I coughed and coughed. He was like a crazed animal, desperate to get off. When I tried to scream for help, barely a sound came out and I panicked even more. He took his hands and was about to stretch the cord around my neck again when the unlocked door opened and the manager and doorman burst into the room. The rapist pulled out. He was obviously panicked that he would be recognized and caught, and ran past the manager, shoving the doorman aside, and hobbling out of the room with most of my money in his hand. He had taken it when he ripped my stockings, snatching it from where it was rolled up and hidden underneath my garter belt straps. A few bills slipped out. The manager was concerned about me and went to me first without trying to stop the thug. He told the doorman to call the police.

I hadn't noticed the stranger watching me in the lobby or anywhere at all. He must have been lurking somewhere in the shadows. I was extremely upset as if I was a virgin having sex for the first time. I had always felt confident on the streets and in the hotels because I was sure that no one would ever attempt raping or robbing me. I wondered how it could have happened. As it turned out, the thug—a tall, medium-complexioned black man I assumed at the time was a pimp—was, I found out, new to the streets of Boston, fresh out of Philly. The incident took me back to my childhood experience of sexual assaults. At that point in my life, I didn't like to dwell on my past, but I couldn't help it. I thought that as an adult the memories of my childhood abuse would disappear and that the rapes wouldn't happen anymore. I was wrong—almost literally dead wrong! Sexual abuse was still part of my life. In fact, it was my life, the difference being I was not coerced and I was paid for my services. But I never asked to be raped or kidnapped; those were clearly acts of aggression against my person.

I was half-naked and thoroughly shaken when the staff from the hotel came in. Despite my profession, I felt all the same emotions any women who has been raped feels. The police came into the room, asking questions. At first I refused to be checked at the hospital. They told me I had to go down to the station to look at pictures but should be checked after that to be sure I was okay. Okay? No, I wasn't! I was shaken and needed help to put pants and a jacket on. They drove me to the hospital, then to the station to view mug shots. They did not have a choice; they had to take me because I was an assaulted rape victim. After that, the officer took me back to the hotel, where the manager had locked my belongings inside the room. There were bills scattered on the floor that no one had taken, money the thug had missed. The manager had promised to keep the door locked, and he kept his word. My next thought was that I could have contracted a disease. The clothes that I left behind were rags, and my hair was still knotted and disheveled. The tenderness of my scalp made it impossible for me to touch my head. The officer who had stayed at the hotel to take a report in the room, to reenact what had happened, asked the hotel maid to help me change my clothes. She wiped the streaks of black mascara from my cheeks. Tears rolled out. I was grateful. I'd been defenseless against this man who had caught me off-guard. He had cracked my tough, street-girl exterior, leaving me broken and vulnerable.

I had enough money for cab fare home. I got in touch with the waitress at the restaurant to find J.N. for me. He met up with me and told me he didn't want me working anymore. He was furious and wanted to hunt the guy down. He was still sympathetic, not ruined by the streets yet. I had escaped death again. My life was spared because the switchboard at the front desk lit up when the phone receiver dropped to the floor, alerting the manager, and the doorman had heard suspicious noises coming from the room. I viewed the switchboard as my hero; the hotels should have never let that service go.

It took me one day to get back to work. I refused to let a fear of the streets incapacitate me. The thought of going back to living in one room brought out my claustrophobic fears. We needed the money to pay the rent to the landlord, a nice man who lived in the Goodale Road building on the first floor. I had only one hundred twenty dollars left after the thug stole my rent money. Our new apartment was spacious compared to the rooms we had been living in, and I was able to bring a few of my steady clients there when J.N. was out. It was comfortable. The apartment had hardwood floors and linoleum in the large kitchen. In the bathroom there was a vintage medicine cabinet and aged tiles. I felt safer in the apartment than living in hotel rooms. We didn't have all our furniture yet. We had a bedroom set, and the kitchen set that J.N. bought was fifties-style metal and vinyl. Neither of us had extensive wardrobes. Material things were becoming important to me because I never had them. Although I wasn't in a position to buy large items yet, I started collecting jewelry—a small, but wise, investment. I bought silver and gold with my extra money, along with a good share of glamorous rhinestone jewelry, and put it in a box to hide it all.

There was a booming market for marijuana. And whenever J.N. bought some, I told him there were girls on the street who always wanted to buy a joint or a nickel bag. So he would make up a bunch of nickel bags, and we made a considerable profit on them. The dealers selling kilos and cocaine were making the big money in enterprises far too risky for my taste. Being locked up didn't appeal to me. Making a small margin of profit was enough for me, and I learned from the smart ones, the bartenders and club owners, to be cool, not greedy. My education certainly wasn't conventional. I would often wonder what use it might have later in my life. No one was about to award me with a diploma for what I was doing, and what kind of job could I ever get based on my skills and street references? Thinking back, I should have been more selfish and married Huckie, or finished hairdressing school. But I thought about him first, not wanting to involve him in my life, and me doing hair like Anita, nah…

I understood the foster care system and its shortfalls because of experience. The extent of my knowledge about the court was limited. I learned what I could from the other girls and their cases. I was about to learn even more about the court system, and not from the lawyers who were my clients. J.N. said don't worry, they will lock him up just because you are white and he is black. Well, *that* was proved wrong this time. After being beaten, raped, and nearly killed, I had to bring charges against my rapist and stand before a jury. I met with the attorneys in the Public Defender's Office, a room that was a clear reminder of the system: a room with hardwood floors and white clinical walls decorated with lackluster pictures. While I was there I received a piece of news I wasn't anticipating—I was pregnant. Pregnant! Shit…I could hardly believe it. I was far enough along so that the baby couldn't have been the rapist's child, thank god, but whose baby was it? It could only have been Rio's or J.N.'s, and I wasn't sure which, so when the social worker at the hospital asked me, I didn't say anything. When formally questioned, I said the father was unknown. I was immediately worried about the baby and, despite the bad timing of the pregnancy, happy that I could conceive another child. I worried that the baby could have been injured in some way during the rape, and I prayed every day that my child was all right. The social worker was worried about the court case because, even though the rapist was a thug, I was a prostitute and the system was weighted against me. I thought, *How dare they!* An attorney from the court was appointed to my case because I didn't have enough money to hire one after I paid my bills. J.N. had told me not to worry because I was female, and that according to the police, the thug had a long criminal history. "That's in your favor, Lib. Don't worry." Knowing of the rape, I had a hard time telling J.N. I was pregnant. I wrote down his name after seeing him in court several times and put the piece of paper away. I didn't want to ever forget him or his name. Thinking back, I realize I did forget it, but I know the piece of paper is hidden somewhere along with the rest of my memorabilia.

As soon as I could, I went to see Mrs. Easterday. I didn't fully trust the doctors who examined me and preferred someone I knew. She tested me extensively. I was pregnant and the baby was fine. I was about two and a half to three months along and healthy. No one would take this baby away from me, no one! J.N. was elated when I gave him the news, although I added that I wasn't certain it was his because of the timing when I was first with him. Rio insisted it was his baby, which irked J.N. I was confused about the time of the conception because the doctor hadn't given me a delivery date. J.N. was still happy but wanted to know. I figured it was the last week of August or the first week in September. I could have found out definitely who the father was with a test that neither of them was willing to take. So I had to wait and hoped the relationship between baby and father wouldn't be harmed. All I could think about was the movie *Rosemary's Baby*. I wanted the baby to be happy with me and whoever his father was—J.N. or Rio—and the suspense was killing me. Mrs. Easterday said she would help me get through the ordeal of telling J.N. and Rio if I wanted her to. I was grateful to her. Her infectious smile always cheered me up. I knew she was a good mom and woman. We would have to wait until the baby was born to be able to judge by his features who the father was, but I did believe it was J.N.'s because of the time of month. Next, I faced the trial with the rapist being present, and I was feeling confused and violated. I would be out of my element in court, and so my usual confidence was lacking.

The court date dragged on. The court-appointed lawyer told me the thug had a prominent criminal attorney. I assumed he must have money. He also had a record a mile long. His friends threatened me to drop the case on several occasions. One night, as I was coming out of the Downtown Lounge (where I had given my friend Ruthie some herb), he was there waiting for me. He crept up from behind me and said, "I will kill you, bitch, if you go ahead with the charges, and don't even think about yelling for help!" There wasn't any way I would drop the charges now! Rage coursed through me like when he was on top of me attempting to kill me, but I just walked away from him. There was no doubt in my mind that I intended to go through with the case, no matter what. He wasn't from Boston, and in town I knew too many gangsters who could run him out. I knew he wouldn't do anything in the Zone because I knew too many people, and the bouncer was standing right there at the door watching. I didn't panic or cause a scene. He disappeared. I never told J.N. about the threats because I didn't want him to confront these dangerous street thugs from Philly who were up here robbing folks; I knew they were tougher than he was. The pregnancy was on my mind, and I was certain that neither the foster care system nor my father's lies would prevent me from keeping my baby this time. I just prayed for the baby to be healthy.

I worked in the bars now rather than on corners because of the pregnancy, and had even more customers than before. I never realized that so many men were turned on by pregnant women and breast milk. Refusing to do straight up sex, I used other techniques, like golden showers and pandering to foot fetishes. I even did small bondage clients, who only wanted lightweight stuff. There were men like Harry the Whip, who got off on acting as my house boys and loved pampering me, a pregnant woman. Imagine, a pregnant woman getting as much, if not more, attention as a woman who was not pregnant! I was a pregnant dominatrix, and wonder to this day how I managed to pull it off. I still had control over my clients and didn't allow the pregnancy to affect my work. My gay and straight friends looked out for me. I started speaking to Kathy again, but only for a short time—it was the life and what happened was part of it. I had to accept that, but I did not forget. The taste in my mouth remained bitter since the time of my turn-out, when she set me up without saying a word beforehand. She said that she did whatever her girlfriend told her to do, and W.D. was her girlfriend's brother. Yeah, sure… I had come to understand the nature of these kinds of relationships; you did what your pimp said, no questions asked. Although I worked in my own circle, I was closer to the whole clan, more than I had been when I was with W.D. The group of them hung out in every inch of the Zone and Park Square. There was a lesbian bar upstairs from the Golden Nugget, known for its brawls, and another one in an alleyway off Tremont Street. We also hung out at other gay clubs, like Jacques Cabaret and The Other Side. Mojo the Dyke's Jewish girlfriend, Marle, was one tough bitch and knew the gangsters. She was a hellraiser on the lesbian track throughout the city. When the police came into the club above Izzy's place during one of her outrageous fights, she was on top of the bar brandishing a shattered bottle. She jumped on one policeman's back and began punching him. She and the others were arrested and escorted out. Every one of the cops knew each other, and they knew Marle really well from her frequent fights. It was easy to get out of trouble if you knew the right people or names to drop in Boston, and she knew them all. There were favors done constantly. Boston was well connected then. In any city, for that matter, it's all about who you know, whether in business or politics, and it's no different on the streets. Things are tougher now because of the internet letting everyone's business out. No more rules. Kids can see smut, and singers say "fuck" and "bitch," etc.

I will never forget the other bad fight that took place in Mojo's apartment when her daughter was there. Marle went crazy about something and she and Mojo got into it. Marle was so infuriated she thrust her arm through the glass fish tank, pulled it out, and continued fighting with deep gashes bleeding out everywhere. I felt badly for Mojo's daughter because she had to see fights like that fairly often. If I ever needed a tough girl on my side, Marle would be the one to call, or Alice T., a huge black dyke, a big motherfucker over six feet tall and at least three hundred pounds, who didn't take shit from anyone. She pimped out a good number of white girls—they loved working for her, although at the time I couldn't figure out why. She looked rugged and hardcore, certainly *not* a pretty woman, but everyone on the streets of Boston knew her. She had done time and had a reputation with the male pimps not only because she was tough, but also because she sold black beauties, a black market pill that was an amphetamine used for dieting and speeding, to all the bitches downtown. Looks never assured success on the streets—it was the game, and if someone had a good game they could get whatever they wanted. That was street sense. It's called "marketing" in the square world, a legal con, making convincing sales to people in the same way religion can do in the wrong hands. Even in square life, attractiveness is not as important an asset as knowing what to say or do, or having better persuasion skills than other people. Just like politicians, it's the game they have that wins elections. Then do they keep their word? Not often, and more and more it becomes a backward, high school he-said, she-said game.

It was the time when Martin Luther King Jr. had just been assassinated on the balcony of his motel. This was momentous for black people, as earth-shattering as John Kennedy's death was for the generation of young people who witnessed the tape and the aftermath on TV. It shook the black community, as well as the fellas on the street and the girls in the life. So much was happening in the world during my case. I hated watching the news because it was always negative. It still is, it's full of lies that are hyped-up reporter's versions.

The roundness of my belly was getting pronounced on my slight frame, and my boobs were large. I had my first dates at six a.m. on Essex and Washington Streets as usual; they were my "good morning guys." I nibbled on saltine crackers between giving blowjobs so I wouldn't feel nauseous and vomit on clients—the crackers always worked. The newspaper truck drivers would circle around, waiting for me to come back from each trip, beeping and waving when they saw me. After breaking luck with my first date, I would eat my usual bowl of mashed potatoes and Land O'Lakes butter. My waitress gave me double helpings now, along with my spaghetti and apple pie with vanilla ice cream in the evening. I was going back for more servings of the mashed potatoes as my pregnancy progressed, and devoured lemon meringue pie when it was available. I didn't drink alcohol and smoked fewer cigarettes and joints now. I was so nervous about the court date, and when it finally arrived, the public defender tried to relax me by telling me that the thug would never bother me again and most likely would go to jail because of his prior convictions. I was happy that he wouldn't have the opportunity to go after other girls. The first time I had been in court for this case I didn't look pregnant, but I was showing this time and the jury had to be told about the pregnancy. I later learned that being pregnant wasn't in my favor. I couldn't fathom the reason for people being put off by seeing me pregnant, other than the usual prejudice the straight world holds against working girls, period.

I was advised to "dress like a lady" for court. I knew that, and I would have dressed properly without the attorney feeling as though he needed to instruct me. If I had learned anything from past experiences standing before a judge, it was to dress with respect for the court. I assumed that because I didn't look like a street hooker, the jury would be on my side—at least that's what I thought. He had the record, after all, not me; I had only a juvenile record. When we went into the courtroom the jury stared at me, and I lowered my head, feeling ashamed, as though they were stripping me down with their eyes. I hated being stared at. My reaction to their stares was to feel embarrassed by the work I was involved in. And I did feel that way. This wasn't the street corner, where I felt proud because I was someone in the life, but a place of judgment in the square world. I lost my confidence again. At the same time, I was belligerent. Who were they to judge me? Were their backgrounds so superior to mine? Were they all purebred with no skeletons? I doubted that.

The court was in session, and other cases were tried ahead of mine. My eyes were fixed on the ivory walls and mahogany woodwork. By the time we were called, I felt like I wanted to die. Instead of smoking during the long wait, I had bitten my nails. The lawyers argued back and forth. The manager of the LaSalle testified, saying he came into the room but didn't see what had really happened, neither did the doorman, only that the man charged was holding me down. He testified that he didn't know me well and was in the room only briefly with the doorman when the man ran right by them. When both he and the doorman were questioned, they said they weren't sure if I was just having sex with the guy or if there was a fight going on. He obviously didn't want to get involved, and no one else was there for me because I was a whore. I never liked the word "whore," it was much more insulting than "known prostitute," which was the term the police used at the initial court hearing. I didn't like that word either—it reminded me of calling Jews "kikes" and blacks "niggers." I heard these words used often enough and hated them all. I felt persecuted. By belonging to a group whose profession had been vilified throughout history, I was considered less of a person, not a part of the human race. I thought of prostitution as a profession that filled a need: keeping rapists and child molesters and men seeking extra sexual fulfillment from committing crimes against women and children. Why couldn't we just have brothels like they had during the Old West era? But this time, with better management of drug control, health issues, and prevention of underage recruitment and abuse.

I could see the looks of disgust on the faces of the men in the jury, and I wondered how many of them had been tricks at one time or another. What was running through their brains? I knew many lawyers who begged to be tied up and spanked and some judges who were coke dates. There was one judge from Roxbury Court who, at my friend's apartment in Brookline, had a leash put on him, barked like a dog, and sniffed coke from a dog's dish on the floor. As I returned the stares of some of the jurors, it reminded me of the squares I passed by every day in town. I knew who they really were beneath their normal, respectable appearances, the deep urges hidden by their judgmental exteriors. It made me uneasy, yet satisfied that I could see through them.

****

Sitting in the cell room, my back straight up against the wall, I gave much thought to the fact that I am busted. I would prefer going to jail rather than give up the names of my clients or co-existing madams (the girls won't matter to the law). My clients would never want my identity to be known either, and getting my name in the newspaper could be detrimental to me and stressed them out so much that they would pull away. This was a private business. The older madams taught me to be silent and never reveal the secret lives of the tricks. And I never would. They couldn't be exposed, no matter what the circumstances. They were my business and I had to "keep them happy" and protect their privacy—always. Nowadays, the madams and girls don't uphold that standard of respect. No one would believe half of what I've seen out there and who my clients were, but I would never implicate them. I am afraid of the justice system, which may put me in jail not just for one day, but for a considerable length of time for making a living from my personal services. But it was my choice. I have to face the music! One mini-madam caused the Circuit to be shut off and exposed. Returning in my mind to the past, I wished I'd never spoken to that girl!

****

I was being called up to hear the jury's verdict and to find out what punishment this bad guy was about to get. I heard, "We find the defendant 'not guilty' of the charges against him." What? I glared at the judge and then the jurors. I was shocked! How dare they find him not guilty? Not guilty! Did they not know what a crime was? He beat me up, raped me, and took my money. *He tried to kill me!* But because I was a "known prostitute" (the term used once again in the final verdict by the jury), they said that I couldn't be raped. The jury questioned the legitimacy of the rape of a prostitute. How dare they! I was still a woman, a human being! Not only was I shocked and outraged, even the judge was taken aback by the verdict and said that the jury did not evaluate the facts fairly, and they should never be jurors again. Well, great! What about now? My court-appointed lawyer was blown away too. I held in my tears out of respect for myself. I looked my attacker directly in the face, and he had the nerve to smile at me.

I wanted him dead! The only positive outcome was that this thief had to leave Boston and not return, and so chances were I'd never see him again. Court was adjourned. Our justice system? What the hell! My faith in the justice system was obliterated by the jury's decision and from when I was put in the Home For Little Wanderers and the Youth Service Board. These squares really didn't know how to judge anything beyond a PTA meeting. The system didn't—and still doesn't—know how to weigh out when a criminal is telling the truth or lying. They do not live lives of crime, so there still is no inner core of understanding.

****

And here I am facing a big charge in a court with the same justice system. Where will this take me now? In this federal jail cell, I know that not much has changed since then. I am more than outraged by a system that has judged me unfairly since the time I was a child. Although I connected with them later, it's too bad that the Coyote group, which started in 1973, wasn't around at the time of that rape trial. They believed they were fighting the system by taking political action. They supported the fair treatment of working girls and the decriminalization of prostitution. That rape verdict loomed large and impressed upon me that there was no justice for prostitutes in the legal system. We were dirt! What kind of reasoning was it that said a working girl couldn't accuse someone of rape and find justice? Whores, like blacks because of color and Jews because of faith, are not accepted as human beings subject to the same protections that exist for other women and people in society. We get murdered and no one cares. We are a stereotype to the square world. We are considered "sluts," while other women—housewives, college students, even high school girls—who do the same sexual acts as prostitutes are somehow acceptable. Is it more acceptable for a college student to put herself through school by selling herself? So all we need is a degree? Although it is considered passé among younger people for the man to pay for a date, traditionally, it is accepted. And a man anticipates having sex with the woman at least by the third date. These women prostitute themselves for the sake of dinner, gifts, and money in the same way we do, the crucial difference being that hoes openly make it their profession. No games! Girls who search for rich boyfriends or husbands to marry are more acceptable. Prostitution could be legalized, or decriminalized, and controlled like in Nevada, except with intelligent and fair madams running it—no men! And not squares who have money and clout. Its enormous revenues from taxation could be put toward the public good. Even long-established madams in Las Vegas aren't allowed to run brothels. If they are good businesswomen, and clean of drugs and alcohol, then why aren't they allowed to manage and own their own operations? The trick businessmen own the services and have experienced ex-madams or working girls running them or working there. They are the big money men who invest in the sex industry and receive all the glory while the madams and girls aren't acknowledged for their skill running these businesses. All over the world madams have run brothels. Why put these places only in Nevada? Madams are businesswomen who deserve recognition for their achievements. I would like to see that in my lifetime. And to see the girls who have worked and achieved be recognized as well! Escorts came long after brothels. When we die, others write about us and get all the credits. The system needs to know the true stories of these people who live among them. The sex industry will never die, but white slavery and the exploitation of young girls need to be stopped!

CHAPTER FORTY-FOUR

Woodstock

A bitter taste remained in my mouth following my experience with the judicial system, but I had a new focus. I was almost due. It was August, 1969, and burning hot outside. My due date was approximately the twenty-fifth of August. The heat was unbearable, and I longed for the winter. I was so big now that it was impossible to conceal my baby bump with large tops. The doctor had given me my due date, and Marcie gave me advanced warning that she wanted to go to Woodstock with me. She already had the tickets. "Oh man, that's five hours away, is there a hospital out there?" I asked.

"Of course there is!" she replied. "I know the distance because I've been to upstate New York before." Although I was due any day, I wanted to go so badly. The festival was to take place August 15th–18th. Being so far along, could I bear it? And what would I tell J.N.? I could say I was going to be working for a few days.

I wanted to get away from my crazy client who followed me everywhere. He had recently been let out of military service because of an injury. He was so obsessed…he would wait day and night for me, always offering me rides and money. I would have preferred waiting in the blazing sun than drive with my crazy-in-love client for hours. He was a steady customer, and I had to do very little to satisfy him, but he was getting on my nerves. He had a fetish for my back and neck. I was careful, and watched him out of the corner of my eye every damn session to make sure that he wasn't going to choke me from behind. I didn't trust anyone. He was always hovering somewhere nearby me. He was devoted to me and even asked me to marry him and adopt my baby. No way in the world was that ever going to happen!

Still, I was going to let the customer give me a lift to visit the doctor one last time before I was due to give birth. It could be anytime within a matter of days or a couple of weeks. The baby was becoming restless and constantly kicking, probably because I never was still for long; my hyper personality never let either of us rest. The indigestion and heartburn never let up, and the girls who had kids told me that meant my baby would have a full head of hair. I was a believer of wives' tales because so many were true, like don't walk under ladders or let black cats cross your path—I did none of them.

Woodstock—yes! I decided that I was going! Knowing J.N. wouldn't approve, I planned to put away some cash from the day before and get more money from my client for being with Marcie and I. He would be my cover if J.N. wondered where I had gone all those nights. I just had to go. I was irritable and tired from working and from the heat. Guys were paying me to touch my belly. My poor baby was getting all sorts of attention from strangers. The girls would rub my round bump for luck before they hit the street. I hoped it would work for them. Everyone was touching me. I felt like my privacy was being invaded. I had to put a stop to the men touching my bump; it was annoying. I was becoming protective of my unborn child. My clients were cool and they understood. I had to slow down my mistress role-playing, and so I sent those clients to Marcie, who was also talented in that department, plus, she gave me a cut. I worked for a couple of local madams doing doubles in domination when they needed help. I would put lacy panties and blindfolds on my cross-dressers and tell them an erotic fantasy that lit their imaginations from the time they left for work until the time they disposed of the sexy underwear before they went home to their wives. There was a demand for my soiled underwear, which I sold, often telling the clients some fantastical stories that most likely stuck in their heads while they were in bed with their partners. Because of the pregnancy, I did not allow any oral contact with the customers' mouths on any part of my body because it felt like an invasion. Along with my round bump, my boobs were a full C cup—almost like Elizabeth Taylor's boobs, which pleased me. I wore a push-up bra and pressed them close together. My admiration for Liz was still alive after so many years, and I would draw a beauty mark on my face like hers every day before I went out. My blue-black hair, big eyelashes, and hot pink lips were a signature I could not step out the door without. At Woodstock, all that would be off!

Although I had seen many musicians at Paul's Mall, the Sugar Shack, the Jazz Workshop, and in other cities and towns, I wanted to see Janis Joplin and Jimi Hendrix outside in the open air, not in a club. J.N. was built like Hendrix, and actually resembled him when he smoked hash and got high. He would lose his inhibitions and do an imitation, playing the guitar and singing in Hendrix's style when he got together with his boys from West Medford, who smoked hash in the big bong pipes. It was possible that J.N. might have wanted to go to Woodstock with his friends and did go, but I never asked or knew for sure if he went—he wouldn't have seen us anyway given the extraordinarily vast number of folks who found their way there and were spread out over thirty-eight plus acres. Marcie borrowed one of her sugar daddy's cars, and we were off to the festival!

We dressed like tie-dye hippies, Marcie more so than me. I wore a colorful, cotton empire waist dress that emphasized my cleavage, with elasticized-waist pregnancy short shorts underneath, and comfortable flat shoes I had bought. I had no flats because I always wore heels. I brought a pillow from my couch, a blanket, some joints to share, and plenty of drinks. We arrived at the field on the first day, and it was packed. We were well-equipped with all the gear we needed: joints, some blow for Marcie, homemade cookies she'd made loaded with crushed buds, a baggie of hashish (which I did love because it was pure with no chemicals), and her brass pipe, which was better than mine. She stopped on the way to buy bags of food to have extra—it was a long drive up and back, so we especially needed my candy bars and Hostess Cupcakes. I had made peanut butter and jelly sandwiches and my specialty tuna fish salad sandwich (the 3 Diamonds brand in the black can that's off the market now) with celery, onions, Hellmann's mayo, and cut veggies. I also brought along bags of Fritos and potato chips, all of which we kept in Marcie's small cooler. My crazy client followed us up the whole way, and when we made stops he bought me whatever I wanted. The ride was so refreshing. I was away from the streets and free! When we finally got there, we parked next to each other in case anyone got separated or lost, as we had discussed on the drive up. My client said he would stay with us so that if I had to go to the hospital he would be there to help, but we let him know we wanted our space. "Just park where we can find you," I told him. He was such a puppy dog he probably went right back and stayed near his car for as long as we were there. I knew he would sleep in his car, not on the field. There were so many Volkswagens there, all painted different colors, and my favorite Volkswagen buses. Maybe one day I can get one!

We mingled in the crowd, intentionally trying to separate from my obsessed client, but he hung in there. Everyone was high on something, doing whatever drug they could, and although they were mellow, there weren't enough police to manage the groups of people and so they were partying out in the open—big time, but fairly calm. We found a good spot, not too far from the edge, and before we had a chance to settle, a girl started to draw on my arms while others were lying on me and kissing my stomach. The baby was attracting so much attention that, finally, I just lifted my dress to expose my bump because that was what they were going to do anyway. I was glad I was wearing shorts underneath, but because the heat was so oppressive at times, I removed my shorts to cool off. I had worn the bottom part of a bathing suit as underwear and didn't care if my bathing suit bottom showed underneath my big baby belly. I had stopped smoking cigarettes, and even though I wasn't smoking anything else, I was experiencing a huge contact high from the people around me. They were blowing reefer and hash smoke in my face. So many were tripping on acid. The girl next to us was passed out from taking orange sunshine like candy drops. These were people I had just met for the first time, and yet I didn't feel threatened. I felt like a free spirit for the first time in my life. The people there were spiritual, something I wished

I could be one day. The feeling of being totally free was new to me, liberating and exciting, not like the everyday frustrated folks in the working world. I wanted to stay there. No one cared who or what I was, and if I had told them it wouldn't have mattered. The whole experience of Woodstock and the people there were way ahead of their time in their acceptance of all different kinds of people. I didn't need the mask of makeup I painted on my face every day to play the part. I did not need to hide! I was so happy to be there as part of the scene, unburdened, and free from pressure. These people were not like the regular squares—they were different. I wished that I could have remained a hippie like them for more than a weekend. I liked their tie-dyed clothes and peace signs, their rejection of the senseless war in Vietnam, their lack of pretension, and their openness. I hoped to experience that kind of life again sometime in my future! People shared great music, exotic food, poetry, and deep conversation. There was Janis Joplin, Jimi Hendrix, Santana, etc.—all unbelievable! Still, I had to go back to my world and face my life: "the life." One weekend of mud, wet rain, and peace. Good thing Marcie brought the big plastic sheet she used for her golden shower clients. Only the streets knew who I was. But did I want to go back there? Could I quit? The streets gave me my identity, the money to survive, and confidence. I couldn't quit. And what would that do to J.N.? Would he have joined me in this free-spirited adventure? I never found that out.

At Woodstock, I pondered what kind of person I was, and would be in the future. Was I capable of leaving the money, becoming a hippie and living in a commune? No, but close. Growing vegetables wasn't appealing to me; I liked the action of city life too much, but living in peace, yes. The question wasn't even arguable with the baby coming and considering how much I loved J.N. and could never leave him. Lying on the grass before the rain started, I watched the smoke floating in the air and everyone kissing. All the girls in the audience cheered and roared when Joan Baez went onstage. And what can I say about the Grateful Dead? Mind-blowing! Marcie was stoned and I volunteered to drive her car back when we left. I would have to let my crazy client know, but I had no idea where he was. As it turned out, he was waiting for me in the field by our car, like a lost puppy, and he had slept in his car. Getting out of the parking area was such turmoil that we couldn't see, but we did hear a backdrop of loud yelling and music. He totally irritated me on the day we left, clinging like a leech as he trailed behind to help out, saying that he had spent his time looking for me at the concert and waiting for me here in the lot at our car so he would not miss us. It was time to return, and he followed; I needed him as an excuse for my absence anyway.

The show, as much as I could see of it, had exceeded my expectations. It was unforgettable. Jimi and Janis were so fucked up onstage that you didn't have to be able to see them to hear it—but their performances were amazing. We stayed, like so many others who lingered afterward, and considered crashing on our blankets, but I had to get home. I was thoroughly tired by the time we arrived back in Boston. After we got out of the cars, what I heard from J.N. was, "Where the hell were you! I couldn't find you! I looked and called everywhere, I even called the hospital!" I said that I was with Marcie (who was really fucked up and went directly home to sleep it off) and my client. He was upset for a few days, but then got over it. J.N. didn't question me about the small amount of money I brought in because I was pregnant, and he knew my sugar daddy only paid me five hundred a night since we couldn't have sex. I went to work the next night, but I didn't stay out on the streets past three a.m. When I got home, I was so tired that I slept through the next day. J.N. was worried and said to stay in, but I could not. Out again…

I kept on working. Time flew by and I passed my due date. It was set for approximately the twentieth of the month, and it was already August thirtieth, so there obviously was some discrepancy about when I became pregnant that made it pretty clear it was J.N.'s baby. A cab brought me home, where J.N. was waiting for me. The steps leading to the front porch were steep enough, and I slowly made my way up three more flights to the apartment. Wow, that did it…I was feeling weaker than I usually did. I never should have hit the streets this particular evening, but going to work was ingrained in me. I just had to go in town; it was like a magnet to me. As I climbed to the top of the stairway, I was out of breath and felt heavy and slow. My back ached, and I was a little hungry, but J.N. wanted sex as usual, though we couldn't do much because of the size of his dick. We didn't kiss and there was hardly any foreplay. I straddled him, hovering just above the head of his penis so that he entered me slightly, only an inch or so inside, maybe less. He came fast, knowing that I couldn't tolerate any pressure. I was soaked from his cum, and I could feel the liquid oozing between my thighs. I quickly went into the bathroom and sat on the toilet to clean up, and suddenly realized that I was leaking water. "Oh my god! J.N., come quickly!" I called out. "I think we caused my water to break!" He saw what had happened and told me to stay put and to take it easy…breathe. He skipped down the stairs to the first floor in his underwear. He banged at the door and asked the landlord for a ride to Beth Israel Hospital because our car wasn't there. It was five thirty-one a.m. when my water broke and precisely six thirty-one a.m., August 30, 1969, when my baby boy was born. Thank god, safely! We had gotten to the B.I. on time, and the birth was totally natural. Even though the baby was breached coming out, Dr. Suda repositioned him, and he was born fairly easily without a C-section, which I was against having unless the baby was in danger. She was so happy to know that this time I would be keeping my baby—and so was I—but as they took him away I got scared, even though they were only taking him to suction the mucous from his mouth so that he could breathe. It occurred to me that he could have swallowed the secretion in my vagina from his dad as it traveled up the birth canal. My baby was so far down in the birth canal he didn't have far to travel to come out. He was healthy and so beautiful, with a head of thick, black hair just as the girls predicted, and smooth, light tan skin. He had a powerful set of lungs, and his cries resounded in the room. I kept asking them if they would bring him right back to me; I was getting panicky. The doctor assured me one more time that they were just suctioning out the mucous and told me not to worry. "Your baby isn't going anywhere," she told me. I thought about the day at Woodstock and what could have happened had he been born there. I was relieved that the birth had gone so well and that the baby had been born safely at the B.I.

Still, it would have been totally interesting if he'd entered into the world at Woodstock.

J.N. was there waiting in the hospital while the baby was being born, and he went home afterward to see about the car and because I would be resting for a couple of days at the hospital. This was a joyful time for both of us, but it was also upsetting: J.N. would not be picking me up with the new baby—something I later regretted. I told him not to waste money on a cab and that I had a ride. J.N. was not pleased when he learned I had a ride with a person other than him, especially my ex Rio. That mistake I will not forget or forgive myself for.

I wished my first baby, my daughter, were with me to share in my joy and to have a little brother. I would have liked my son to have had a sister. Rio had a car to drive me home from Beth Israel, and he was insistent about taking me so he could see the baby he believed belonged to him. I couldn't be certain whose baby it was by hearsay, but the dates were accurate. Neither of them would take the paternity test, and according to the birth date, it was so close that it could have been either of them. Despite the baby looking like all newborn infants, his features looked like he was J.N.'s—the shape of their eyes, noses, and hands were the same. Rio was thrilled by the baby and was happy for me, but he yearned to be the child's father. We spoke about what I was going to do now that the baby had arrived and if I planned on staying with J.N. "Yes, I am. I love him. We're good together," was my reply. Just the thought of having to raise my baby without the man I loved frightened me beyond words. I wasn't about to leave, certainly not now. Rio didn't pressure me to leave for a very good reason: he was married and had kids. Oh, yes…he was! And I would not go. I told him, "You have other women and J.N. wants only me. I don't want to share anymore." From the earliest time in my life I believed that marriage was forever, whether it was good or bad. I could never accept a married man, not even in the life. I would not make that mistake again. I wouldn't cheat if I were married, unlike Rio who lied to me and to his wife. I couldn't trust him the way I did before. He walked me up the stairway to the apartment, where J.N. was waiting for his precious bundle. Rio said goodbye, although this wasn't the last time we would speak. J.N. would never admit it, but he was still threatened by Rio. He was possessive and jealous of whatever I did and became more so with every day that passed. He didn't realize that I truly loved him and didn't have any intention of leaving him. J.N. loved our baby. We were a family! I had a man and a baby to love, and they would love me back and never leave me. What could be better?

In the Jewish tradition, I named the baby after a deceased relative, my Mommy Rose, using the "R" to guide me. I didn't want a common name and chose the perfect name. His middle name was to be Lee. J.N. helped me pick the name, and we didn't consider the confusion people might have pronouncing his Spanish-sounding name in school and that they might make fun of him. He was precious, with large brown eyes and a ready smile. His appetite was like mine, and he was always moving, never wanting to sleep. Every day his resemblance to J.N. was more pronounced, and J.N. loved him from the moment he first saw him. He responded to our son's every need, and I hated leaving them to go to work. I wanted to share in those moments with them, but I had to provide. With more expenses, there wasn't any question that I had to work to pay for the three of us.

The day I brought the baby home from the hospital was bittersweet because two days after I gave birth I was back at work. J.N. again asked me to quit working and told me he'd get a job. Whatever job he could get would pay him in one week what I made in half a day. I refused. I wanted to make enough to buy a home. I was tough and hard-headed. The money I was making was more than enough to cover the usual expenses of rent, a car, clothing, and a baby's needs, so he never tried looking for work after that. Unfortunately, he just collected the money and became slicker by the day. I continued working with my dates, trying to come home earlier when I could. During that time, I was close with Katie, Kayen, and Linda, as well as other girls from town. We all hung out with each other, having get-togethers and cookouts with our kids. Most of my work involved dominance—spitting in the faces of my clients, role-playing, tying them up by their balls, humiliating them at their request—and ménages à trois with husbands and wives looking for a new kick.

There were men who asked if they could drink J.N.'s semen. I would bottle it and bring it into town, and they paid fifty dollars a pop. I learned that they preferred drinking it at room temperature so it wasn't as difficult to swallow. Yeah, guess so! I was attempting to get away from the straight sex clients as much as I possibly could for the bigger money to be made in perversions. Learning the intricacies of various fetishes rather than having sex was more interesting, and I felt better about myself. It wasn't long before I was expert at talking and telling erotic stories with props that tickled my customers' fancies. My conscience was always troubling me now that I had a child and was so much in love.

Throughout the day, I was thinking about going home to my baby. I couldn't wait to see his face—he made me so happy! It seemed as though I was living a double life: one domestic and the other as a sex professional. I cringed at the thought of him someday finding out what his mother did for a living. Oh god, what will he think of me? He was the only piece of my existence that was true and real, an actual being who loved me unconditionally and filled the void inside. He would be in my life always. I had a reason to live. My self-esteem grew. I was balancing motherhood and work, and felt good about myself. Not only was I able to support him, he was given all the nurturing I didn't have after my mother passed away. My ambition to succeed grew, and I knew I had to get somewhere other than the streets. In the early morning, I would take care of my baby, then J.N. took over while I worked. R. Lee was fed the best food and dressed in the best clothing. He saw Dr. Bloom on Blue Hill Ave. regularly, and we followed Dr. Bloom when he moved his practice to Canton, miles away, once our car had been fixed. He was a great doctor.

We decided to move into a better apartment, especially one with fewer steps, and after our lease was up, there was an empty apartment on Morton Street just waiting for us. It was a three-bedroom apartment on the third floor, but not as steep, which was an improvement in comparison to where we were. The walls and kitchen were so nice. One of our friends, Byron, was planning to take the extra bedroom to help out with rent. He had a girlfriend, and she offered to babysit if we ever needed her. She was straight and sweet, a college student who worked three days a week and now babysat for me nights so J.N. could go out more. That, as it turned out, was a mistake: easy money, easy lifestyle. Our son was eating great and growing. We had stayed on Goodale Road long enough for the landlord to get another tenant. He was happy with us. We were more than ready to move on in our lives. With R. Lee we formed a unit, and belonging to our small family made me feel secure and complete as a woman.

We went out on a special shopping spree. Me, I had to go to the House of Nine (I think that was the name) for my size 1 and 2 clothes. And J.N. went to Crystal's for some new shoes. All the players and entertainers went there, like a daytime after-hours. It was my man's favorite shoe store. It was like a boutique and had amazing shoes and accessories. We then went to Jack and Marion's Deli in Brookline for Kosher food that I loved. We went there at least twice a month.

CHAPTER FORTY-FIVE

Disappointment

We had hardly anything to take to the new place (crib, bed, kitchen set), so the packing was easy, and the move went smoothly. Byron settled in after the first three months, and we were glad to have the additional money. Lots of his friends visited at first, giving us hashish. I loved the mellower high than with marijuana and that there was no paranoia. His girlfriend was cute, with blonde, curly hair that was styled like Annie in the musical. She was a real doll and great with R. Lee, who smiled and giggled whenever he saw her. Usually, he would shake the crib by holding onto the railing and jumping up and down. He spent most of his time bouncing in his Jolly Jumper, never lying down in his crib to sleep. He was rugged and energetic, a healthy and happy baby boy. I wondered if he would slow down when he got older or have the same amount of energy—he was always up at night babbling on. My guess was he was as hyper as I was. J.N. was slower than me, but he was running the streets with his West Medford crowd, getting into the life, always wearing a new leather jacket or outfit I bought him. He was becoming more and more confident in his fashionable facade, even abandoning the square way he had been processing his hair, going for a more radical appearance. It was a time when Afros were in style, and he let his hair grow out and left it natural. He even became more radical. Because he was both black and white mixed, his hair was soft to the touch, no tight curls, no hair relaxers needed. He was crossed between the street life now and his upbringing of piano lessons and private school with his conservative, educated adoptive black family of college graduates, teachers, and doctors.

Everything was going so well that I wanted to see my father. I prayed he would give me another chance. Esti had Freddy's number; I was still not allowed to have it. She had spoken with him a few times, so I asked her to get in touch with him for me or to give me his number. I called her only once in a while since I'd left, never wanting to get too close. They arranged a time for he and Anita to visit their convenience, either at the end of the fall or in the spring of the following year, whenever Anita decided to come back to Boston to see her relatives and Dad's family. Esti advised me not to tell him I'd had a baby, just to say that I was babysitting. She thought that once my father saw the baby he would be happy, but not to rush, let him come up to Boston first before telling him the truth…or maybe after a few times. When my dad and I spoke, we decided that spring would be best. R. Lee would be older than a year by then. He was already reaching milestones. I loved kissing his pudgy cheeks and holding his small, delicate fingers. My world revolved around him. Any baby bottle he was given was gone within a few minutes, and when he was ready for food, his appetite was equally as healthy. He loved the baby food veggies, except for the peas; his face would twist up every time a spoonful entered. I was so careful. I made sure that he was watched at every moment. Perhaps I was overly careful. Yes, too much. Whenever I was separated from him, I feared for him. I knew that when I was in town I had to be more cautious and take fewer chances so I would always be there to care for him—that meant fewer car dates and more dates in the room. My fear that without me he wouldn't have food or shelter was intense. Every day I lived with stress, worrying that my baby would be taken away from me. I was overly protective and anxious that he might hurt himself or become ill. One night when he was only two weeks old and we were living on Goodale Road, R. Lee choked in his sleep and turned blue! Screaming, I picked him up out of the crib and J.N. took him and gently turned him upside-down while he gave his back a few light pats. Within a few seconds, R. Lee started breathing again. It was an odd and terrifying occurrence, and when we explained what had happened to the doctor, he said R. Lee was fine and that some babies even choke on their own saliva. I was so afraid after that I hated going to work. I would call home frequently throughout the night. The baby always came first. I couldn't buy enough toys, clothes, or food for him, and I wanted to always keep my promises—even if I had to stay on the streets forever to do that. He wouldn't lack for anything, not the way I did. I worked even harder to earn more money to buy him things when we moved to the new apartment, taking as many hour dates as I could. We even put our couch on hold so we could buy more for him. Christmas was quite a celebration, with many gifts for R. Lee. He was the best thing that ever happened to me.

The months flew by, and before long it was March. The time for Freddy to visit had arrived, and I told everyone to stay away from the apartment and to come back late at night. We still didn't have enough furniture for the living room, just one chair standing amid a sea of toys. My father wasn't aware that I was with a black man, and I didn't plan on breaking the news to him until after he met the baby, and, hopefully, accepted him. I bathed R. Lee, washed his hair, put powder on him, and dressed him in one of his many outfits. The apartment was sparkling clean and neat. The hardwood floors gleamed. My son was cooing and babbling a few words; he was always in a happy mood. Our apartment was on the top floor—my dad was strong and could handle the climb up the stairs. The TV was on in the background, showing the latest news about the war in Vietnam dragging on. Why the countries had to fight was beyond me. I did not get into the world of politics then. Now I do. I voted once for a president I believed in but haven't before or since. And if I don't watch the news, that's fine with me. I wasn't ever able to watch TV with the other pimps I was with because I was working every minute. J.N. didn't care if I watched or not, or if I took days off. We bought the TV and cabinet at Sozio's in Revere, the same place where we ended up buying the kitchen set; the unit was beautiful. We had ordered all our other pieces of furniture from Summerfield's and it would be arriving soon.

The baby was in his usual good humor. I wished the furniture for the living room had been in place so my dad could have seen it, although it really didn't matter because it was impossible to impress him. The front room looked bare except for the crib I had rolled in—and the baby in his Jolly Jumper in front of the TV. He moved his feet back and forth as though he was going somewhere, but he always bounced back. Whenever the Red Rose Tea commercials with the monkeys flashed across the screen he would say, "Ra-ra rose," without fail. We ended up calling him that as a nickname because he said it so often. He was excited about everything, my happy baby, my lucky charm. He was something great to look forward to everyday.

The doorbell rang. I buzzed him in, and then listened to the echo of my father's footsteps as he came up the set of stairs. I couldn't have been more nervous, scared of being reprimanded and ridiculed even though Anita wasn't with him. His acceptance was important to me. There he was, standing in the threshold of the open door. We didn't hug each other. When I made a move toward him, he stepped aside and walked down the hall…I was heartbroken. I had been feeling nauseous up until the time he came, and I chalked it up to nerves. I hadn't seen him for quite some time, although I had written letters to him. He told me he didn't keep them and had a difficult time answering because Anita was always around. His excuse was a poor attempt to mask how he really felt about me. He easily could have gone somewhere else to answer my letters if he truly wanted to. Trying one more time, smiling from ear to ear, I leaned in to give him a hug as he turned to go into the kitchen, but he held his hands to his sides and stood back, cautiously, saying, "Hello, how are you?" He returned my smile with a slight upturn of his mouth, an uncomfortable half-smile to break the ice. He withheld everything—money, love, even a smile. There was no change in him. He was the same icy, skeptical man, as if I were a stranger making an unwelcome overture to him. I had set myself up again, hoping he would be fatherly and tell me he missed and loved me with a hug. My expectations were based on what I wished for, not reality. It was confusing for me to deal with my dad. I moved the baby from the Jolly Jumper in the living room doorway to his crib for some quiet time so we could talk for a short period before I introduced him as my son. "Is someone here?" he wanted to know.

"It's my friend's baby. I just watch him." When I asked if he wanted to see the little boy, he told me he had come to see me and find out what I was doing. He stressed the point that he couldn't help me and I shouldn't ask for anything…not that I had ever asked him for anything before. He assumed that I might ask for money, but why? He wouldn't give it! He said he would give me ten dollars to buy clothes when he left. *Ten dollars?* I thought to myself. I didn't know how to respond to him, so I was silent for a moment as I wondered if the Great Depression still held such sway over him. I told him I didn't need any of his money and that I was fine, thanks. "How do you survive, then?" he wanted to know. Why would he even care! Even during the times I was starving, I didn't ask him for money. "I work, Dad," I flatly stated. For some reason, it was vitally important to me to have this man treat me like a real daughter, even though he had proven time and time again that he couldn't and that I didn't belong. I shouldn't have spoken to him after he broke my heart when I gave away my baby girl. I should hate him, but I had prayed that he would take this visit as an opportunity to make amends and maybe see my baby in a positive light. The echo of his silence always left me feeling stranded and alone. I couldn't think of anything to say.

I brought R. Lee into the kitchen to sit with me, comforted by the overwhelming love that bonded us together. I calmed down as I cuddled him. He is my heart. My dad went on asking me questions about my work and, of course, I lied about my jobs. He said he hoped I'd changed and was behaving myself and that what he did was for my own good. *Oh, for god's sake,* I thought, *he never stops.* I could feel the anger building up inside of me, but I didn't raise my voice. He said he didn't want to discuss it more because I was upsetting him. He filled me in about the traveling and the trips he and Anita had taken together to Israel, etc. *Lovely,* I sarcastically thought to myself. I could see that there was nothing we shared or could discuss in a straightforward way. Still, I felt as though I had to try. I mustered up enough nerve to ask him if he wanted to play with the baby. And he did, enjoying himself as he jounced the baby on his knee thinking, of course, that the baby belonged to my friend, not me. During those few moments, he was almost human with me. I told him the baby was a good child, and he said that if I behaved myself and some man wanted me after all that I'd done, and we married, then I could have and keep a baby of my own. How endearing of him… That was it! I was fuming, and I dropped the ball. I couldn't maintain my composure for a moment longer, especially when I had to listen to him speak the way he did about me and praise Anita for how good she was when she was so evil inside. I heard her hateful voice in the tenor of his words and pictured the demonic squint of her eyes. I announced, "I have something to tell you, Dad, and please try to understand." I could see he was puzzled. Silence filled the kitchen; even R. Lee was quiet. I took the baby from my dad and put him down, watching as he wobbled into the dining room where his toys were. "What is it, Anita?" he asked at first, and then immediately corrected himself, saying, "I mean, Libbe." Sure, thanks. It was as if he didn't want to acknowledge me or that he was so used to speaking to Anita he didn't even see me. I cleared my throat and said, "Dad, that's not my friend's baby and this is not her apartment. The apartment is mine, and that's my baby boy. *He is my son and I'm proud of him!*"

He was stunned—no, shocked. He stood, yelling "How could you do this to me? You shame us! You are a tramp! Are you married?" "No, Dad, not yet, and I don't want to be. The last thing I want is to be in a marriage like yours!" He was offended to such a degree that his face was flushed deep red. He began screaming, "I don't want to see you ever again! You're a no-good tramp and will always be a tramp, just like your mother! Anita was always right about you!"

"That's right, Dad. Think what you want. I can never change you. It always comes down to Anita, not me. And what about my son? He is a good boy! You have no reason to hate him." My dad handed down his judgment there and then as he gripped the chest pocket of his sports jacket and tore it completely off as a sign I was dead to him. He disowned me, and told me in a threatening way that I shouldn't call him anymore. It was lucky R. Lee was so young that he would never remember any of this. I was crushed and felt the tears rolling down my face. "Dad, please! Try to understand! All I want is for you to understand!" He never turned back as I called to him, pleading, "Please Daddy, Daddy, please! Come back! I'm sorry!"

How could I still love this man? My life was an endless attempt to have my so-called dad love me back, not as much as I loved him, but...something. He wasn't going to change. Why did I continue trying when the outcome was always the same? At least my son will know I love him and that I would die for him. I would starve so that he could eat and would never let him go without. I wasn't the only one in the world who had a hard life. I knew this from the stories I heard all the time from other girls out there who had tough lives too. Their parents were often addicts, alcoholics, and hustlers. Although there were some from great families who just wanted to be in the life. I would never allow myself the luxury of becoming a victim and feeling sorry for myself, or as many of the girls did, use drugs to mask the pain. I refused to do that—I couldn't and I wouldn't. I had to keep going. My heart was broken again, but I would make it by trying harder. I have a child now who needs me! I had an urge to run down the stairs to stop him from leaving, even though I knew there was no stopping him and I would be more disappointed as he drove away without giving me a second thought.

****

Coming back to the present for a moment, I wonder how my dad and Anita would have dealt with me being in a federal jail. The name-calling would be endless, beyond my imagination. It's all hypothetical anyway. I am a mature woman and their opinions ceased to matter a long time ago. The only opinion that matters to me is that of my son.

****

It took some time after my father left to stop crying and to feel calm again. Holding my son took the edge off. I felt sick after my dad left and went to the doctor. My eating habits were erratic. R. Lee was getting bigger. Every time I took the baby to see them, J.N.'s family were thrilled with him. We were spending a good deal of time in West Medford on the weekends. I wasn't big on family events, but I did the best I could to get by. Because Byron's girlfriend had moved in, she was there more often to help me out with R. Lee. Still, in my opinion, there were far too many of his friends wandering around the apartment. J.N. disagreed, but he finally came around and saw things my way, and together we told Byron that we didn't want his friends around our son. J.N. told him that he had until the beginning of the winter and then he had to move. The baby was so active that we wanted the entire space to ourselves. He was always into something, and I was anticipating that he would be even harder to control running from one end of the apartment to the other. He needed plenty of space to explore. Plus, to my complete shock, I learned that I was pregnant again! Shit! I was four months along and never knew it! Even though I didn't show yet, I should have known because my breasts were growing larger. They told me I would be giving birth in August or September, just like I did with R. Lee. He would now have a sister or brother!

I went to work even more determined than before. I wanted to make it, and to be financially well off to prove to my child and J.N. that I was somebody. My client list had to get longer now. I felt pressured to make more money for the new baby, but R. Lee—my savior—gave me the greatest motivation to succeed. He would look at me with his big brown eyes and warm, innocent smile, and I knew I had to make a better life for him no matter how I did it. I filed to get my GED and failed the first go-around, but I was proud that I had tried again and passed the test, even though it was by a narrow margin. J.N. had a different kind of intelligence than I did, more intellectual and academic, and he talked about going back to college. He grew up in an environment that was much more stable than mine, where studying and music were encouraged. My education was foster care and pure street. After graduating from private school, he hit the streets, but getting into college was the logical step for him to take now. We were making a life together, and I dreamed about owning a home, even perhaps marrying J.N. someday. Then bad news came.

Rio had a big case in May, before the baby's first birthday, and was sentenced to jail. I sent him inspirational cards and wrote letters.

He had been working at a bar called The Place on Dudley Street, and was holding drugs for a friend. Another man, an undercover agent, had befriended Rio and busted him at the bar. After that went down, the bar never reopened. Rio was sentenced to eighteen months; he was old-school and took the rap. I respected that. J.N. didn't stop me from getting in touch with him while he was in jail—he knew Rio needed a friend, and the letters helped pass the time. Had I been with a real pimp, he never would have allowed that. I was glad I wasn't. I knew there was never going to be any connection to Rio except as a friend.

I was going home earlier now, before the bars closed, to be with my boy. The summer had passed so quickly, and it was already the end of August—time for the baby to be born. On August 31, 1970, after a long labor, I gave birth to a healthy baby boy, but his arrival was fraught with problems. Mrs. Easterday was there with me in the birthing room, and as soon as the baby made his appearance, she expressed alarm: the baby was white and had red hair! We quickly concluded that the child couldn't possibly be J.N.'s, so she immediately had a hospital social worker come up to the room, and then called Jewish Family Services for me to make arrangements for a permanent adoption. I wanted him so much, but I wanted the baby to be raised in a happy atmosphere, where his origins wouldn't always be an issue. Because I did not know for certain what characteristics ran in our families, with loads of regret, I gave the baby away. J.N. had been gone for days, hanging out with his buddies, while this was happening. He never saw the child and was not pleased with me at all. I could only hope that time would heal us. Years later, J.N. found his real mom and dad. And to our surprise, she was white Irish with reddish hair and he was black Jamaican. Oh my god! I made another mistake!

I had been watching more TV lately. And I realized how clueless Dr. Ruth was about the real sexual behavior of men and women. Her cookie-cutter, book-learned views didn't include a whole range of behaviors I observed in my experience with clients and couples—reality being broader and deeper than her "normal" permitted. Each sexual encounter in my business taught me more about real life, and the differences between people, than Dr. Ruth ever examined from her limited viewpoint. How many men did she go to bed with—thousands? Experience is the best teacher.

Marcie and I became closer friends. We started to have other girls see our personal clients for a cut. R. Lee was so smart! We had celebrated his first birthday is a grand way, with many friends and gifts galore. Good thing we had his party before the new baby was born. R. Lee was at an age when he could make his need to be with me at home known. His hysterical crying whenever I had to leave him to go to work made leave-taking difficult for both of us. His love for me was unwavering, and I felt a pang in my chest each time I walked out the door. I still feel sad when I don't hear from him or see him, even more so now that I am getting older. J.N. still could not get over me giving the baby boy up without discussing it with him first. It was good that he was away with his so-called friends when I gave birth and missed it all. It took a long time for me to heal from having given up that baby.

CHAPTER FORTY-SIX

Busted on Morton Street

Life had fallen into a certain rhythm: money was good, R. Lee was healthy, and we were happy again. I was trying to see the birth of the baby boy as a positive thing, as what was best for him. The agency assured me that my baby was in a great home, and I was satisfied. I did feel confident in their placements. But later, I wished I had kept both he and my daughter.

It was election time, and the heat was on. Many girls were getting busted on the streets. I went to Marcie's and worked inside, bringing along my black bag containing rope, handcuffs, a riding crop, dildos, stockings, and toys galore—which no one would have guessed unless they opened it like door number three on *The Price is Right* and got the surprise of their lives! For more money, I would go to New York as much as possible. J.N. hated it when I left to go out of town, but it was great to mingle with the older madams on what was a close-knit circuit.

J.N. and I always took the time to go out. Byron's girlfriend took great care of R. Lee. It was almost November, and they would be leaving soon. I was making enough money to pay bills, buy things, and even have a night or two off. I was essentially working for myself, without pressure. J.N. was learning the game, but he still couldn't control me. His pockets were lined with cash. We had met under unusual circumstances, and despite his jealousy and acting out all the time, our relationship had lasted longer than any other arrangement I'd had thus far. I stopped coaching him and never took him to the big after-hours anymore, even after I had introduced him around. He wasn't slick enough to play with the big players. Marcie and I would go together on the Q.T. We were respected and well known in the life in Boston, where we never encountered flak from anyone. When I went to the Sugar Shack, I'd meet Katie and tell J.N. to come down later. In the beginning, I wasn't sure how he would be received by the big pimps, but time healed that. All the pimps respected me because of the way I handled myself when I left them, so they gave him respect too. But the downside to having a good reputation was that many other pimps would rap to me to come work for them, slinking up behind me and whispering in my ear, talking shit, "Come on, baby, you need a true man to handle you." They messed with me because they knew I chose a square. But they saw me respect him, and, finally, they stopped harassing me. It's life on any scale: when you earn respect you get it back. J.N. began dressing the part, and time healed his questionable standing in their eyes. He was looking really good now, and bitches were checking him out.

The streets were always jam-packed with traffic from all the pimps pulling up and double-parking outside the Sugar Shack on Boylston Street, across from the famous Boston Commons. They hung outside the clubs to be noticed by all the hoes working the stroll. The squares would drive by and gawk. And how could they not, when the area was where well-off people came to see plays performed next door at the Colonial Theatre, where I met Judy Garland at the front doors one night. She smiled a sad smile and gave a quick wave. I smiled and said, "Hi!" Her face looked lonely. The pimps would be decked out, studded with diamonds and gold bling, strutting their stuff for all the girls to see. J.N. had nothing on these fellas yet when it came to glitter. But he had a better education. Their jewelry wasn't quality but quantity, although some looked fine, like Sess—he was sharp. It was a fashion show of styles before their time, with the pimps looking like rappers do now, and the hoes dressed like fashionistas, with their come-on skirts and high, spiked heels that said, "Come fuck me." Conversely, it was said that "A lady on the outside and a whore in bed" was what men wanted, not a whore on the outside and a refined lady in bed. They should take that into consideration now. That was true then and still is the truth today.

J.N. and I were both dressed to the nines! He wasn't ready to wear fur quite yet, and the truth was he really wasn't the type, not for minks… I had to look the part all the time because it was my job, and I wanted the attention to make money. I never would leave the house without my false eyelashes heavily mascaraed in black and wearing my high heels. I wore a new black and white lamb fur coat over a sleek Ava Gardner-style slinky black dress. I was told I had sexy legs, legs like 1930's women. My lipstick was pink; it had to be pink. Still is! I had long blue-black hair, permanently now, no more childhood chestnut brown. I appeared to be exactly what I was—if you look the part, then you probably are. After being out for a few hours, we listened to the group that played at the Sugar Shack; it was background music to all the pimps talking shit.

We had a great time that night, and I could tell that the other fellas were beginning to talk to J.N., nodding their heads at him or raising a triumphant fist in his direction, letting him know I was a good catch. For some reason, that night I felt as though I needed to go home, so we left to go back to Morton Street earlier than usual without going to the after-hours. It was meant to be. When J.N. drove down Morton Street from Blue Hill Ave., as we got closer to the house, I sensed something wasn't right. I mentioned it to him, "I feel funny. My stomach is nervous."

But he said, "Nah, it's nothing." He pulled down the side street to park, and I when I got out of the car I paused. Something was causing me to feel anxious, and again I told J.N., "Something is wrong, I know it!" He didn't say anything in reply. As we were approaching the front door of the house, he was following behind me. I opened the door—and a white man was facing me holding a gun, aiming it at me! He asked for my name. And then, two other men came out of nowhere, grabbing J.N. as he was running toward me to help. They said they had a warrant for my arrest. "For what?" I asked. "We weren't doing anything wrong."

"Go up!" they ordered. We went upstairs. My stomach sank. I knew there was something up. There, at the door of the apartment, were more detectives milling around, waiting, and searching. The head detective of drug control was directing the group of officers. They circled me as if I were a drug dealer or murderer. I was worried about my baby; although they were guarding me, they allowed me to stay near him. They asked who the guy and girl were. I told them he was a roommate, and she was the babysitter, and they believed me because she looked like a student straight out of Harvard University. Her name was Bridget, I said. The head detective was tough and ordered his men to decimate the apartment. He showed me the warrant. After the search, I found out that Byron had been selling enormous quantities of hashish out of his room. They found packages and packages of hash piled in his bed, stashed. There was one joint in our bedroom, but it was my house so I was responsible. They tore apart the baby's crib, thinking that drugs were stashed in his mattress. I was just sick that R. Lee was involved in all of this. I didn't want them near my baby, and it was upsetting to me to have them take off his diaper to check there too. They wouldn't let me hold him, and I thought how fortunate I was that he was a good-natured baby. When they took off his diaper to check for drugs, he giggled and jumped around, feeling free. He thought they were playing when they took his things apart. He laughed through all of it, bopping up and down as if he were watching the Red Rose Tea commercial. The whole scene was confusing, and I didn't know whether to laugh or cry at that moment. R. Lee kept calling out, "Mama, Mama…"

The cops were bigots, and mean. "Is your baby a mixed breed?" one of them asked. One glance would have told them. Funny, my father never noticed. I felt asking me was rude, an indication of their prejudice. Then, you couldn't say anything back to them. I held my streetwise tongue. I wanted to lash out so bad, but J.N. was calmer, so I held back. It wasn't considered incorrect in those days for officials to use that kind of language. Another one called me a "nigger lover" when they had J.N. in the kitchen. They had radioed my name in to the station and discovered that I had idle and disorderly charges on my record, plus juvenile. They were taking me to Station Ten on Morton Street, where Leonard's friends hung. But no need to be afraid of them knowing about me in any way. They took J.N. and Byron separately. We all were in handcuffs. Bridget stayed to be with my baby. I prayed he was young enough not to remember what he saw that night. It was lucky that Byron and Bridget were awake and not in bed together. They never guessed she was Byron's girlfriend or they would have taken her too. I spent the rest of the night standing in the cell at Station Ten, without water and holding in my urine. I asked to use the bathroom, but they told me to pee on the floor if I had to go, that I was used to the streets and could squat. How fucked up was that? They didn't stop making cheap comments about my record and about being a nigger lover with a nigger baby. I hated all of them. How dare they! I could have murdered them then and there. When I was taken before the judge, he gave me probation because the drugs weren't mine; J.N. was also given probation. Whew…that could have been much worse. Byron took the blame, as he should have, admitting that the drugs in his room belonged to him. The lawyer handled the rest, and we paid a fine. I was a white girl with a black man and a mixed baby, and I was looked upon as trash—even worse than trash because I was Jewish and a working girl in addition to that, so I was really the dregs of society. If some well-known millionaire and his daughter did that, it would have been covered up by saying that she just made some mistakes.

After court, I made the decision to move out of Mattapan. That was a horrific night. I thought about my son the entire time. I didn't care about anything else. My heart was heavy with fear for him even more now. I wondered what my daughter would have thought if she were with me because she would be old enough to understand. I was thankful I had some friends in real estate. One of my clients knew of a house that was available to rent somewhere in Somerville or Medford. I needed to be out of this area now. I was certain Leonard's friends would pass on the information about me, and they did. We wanted to wait until our lease was up, and we packed and were ready to go to the first house he could find for us.

I wondered what my life would be like had I kept all three kids. I recalled how after my second baby boy was born the hospital phoned my dad, Mr. Wonderful, and asked for his consent, because I was under twenty-one years old, to have my tubes cut and tied. He gave that consent in the blink of an eye. "Make it permanent, please!" Nice man. I can't help thinking about my last baby. What if his father was one of my customers and I had conceived during one of those rare occasions when the condom broke? J.N. was still extremely angry at the hasty decision I made, and I wasn't entirely convinced that the baby was the result of a mishap with a client, but I didn't want to raise a child in a bad environment where J.N. would always question whether that child belonged to him. I wanted the baby to be loved, not resented. I was heartbroken, yet I felt as if this time I made the right decision—I had to let him go. Oh, my god, what if? I can't think about that. I knew J.N. was never happy with my choice. I told R. Lee the baby was with a family that didn't have children of their own. He was very young and soon forgot the pregnancy. I hoped I had told him the right thing. I continued to tell him he had a brother and sister; I would remind him often.

I had given up two infants for adoption: one by choice and the other against my will. I had faith that they both would be safe, but sometimes I couldn't help wondering. It weighed on me heavily. Later, I learned that my red-haired baby went to a loving home with a college-educated mother and a father who was a successful businessman. I still wonder about him from time to time, and pray that my mistakes and decisions have given others health and happiness. When I checked on how my baby girl was faring, I received reports that she was thriving in a loving home, not well off financially at all, but with caring parents. Had the circumstances been different, R. Lee would have had the good fortune to be brought up with a sister and brother to love; however, it was not meant to be.

J.N. was staying out a lot and in general was screwing up. I caught wind of him being in West Medford fucking square girls, not for money the way I did, but for fun. This was clearly a slap in my face. I was in love with him, so now what?

CHAPTER FORTY-SEVEN

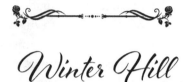

Winter Hill

We moved in mid-September, and I had no time to sit and feel the void of another baby gone. I was always busy, and J.N.'s actions kept me distracted. The house was in a white, blue-collar community in Somerville known as the Winter Hill area. I wasn't familiar with this town like I was the others on the North Shore, but I asked Johnny and his brother about the gangs. And then the guys in Enrico's Bar started talking about the Winter Hill gangs. I had many old and new clients come from the North Shore to the house when J.N. and our son were out. They loved the convenience of the location. We had bought a 1965 Mustang convertible for me by that time—a sports car that would have been a great classic had I kept it. I loved it. The house was a single-family on a dead-end street with trees, a yard, and a large basement I rented out to clients who wanted it for bachelor parties. The parties were great fun, with all my friends working for me, along with a couple of out of town girls from Mary's low-end house in Philly. The money flowed in. The guys were cool, and there was always a bodyguard from their bunch to make sure everything stayed under control. Katie did a few parties with me, performing girl-on-girl sex; and, of course, she wanted it to be real. Then we hired other girls to do the shows and see the guys afterward, and that took the weight off me. Ruthie did her sexy strip show, and she would get the men all riled up for two girls kissing. Almost all the men preferred watching two girls together going down on each other, and they would get up into our faces to make sure we weren't faking it.

J.N. found another babysitter for R. Lee in Medford because it was too far from Bridget's school to come all the way there. He was hanging out much more, talking shit just like his buddies. I should have known better than to let him hire girls from his West Medford hometown because he was taking advantage of my money and hanging out there. The babysitter came from J.N.'s neighborhood, and her name was Patsy. She was young, fresh meat for J.N. It wasn't long before I came home and found them both pulling up their pants from a hot session. I went off, throwing her out of the bedroom to the living room and freaking out on him. After discovering J.N.'s true colors, it was only logical to suspect there were other squares he had been entertaining from way back, even though I wasn't able to prove it. I busted him this time. He denied it, of course, and went upstairs, laughing...yeah, big joke. I cornered her, questioning her until she was in tears. She confessed and promised never to do it again, although her word wasn't worth shit so I didn't believe her. I just knew they were meeting up everywhere. I was right about that. Later, I found a photograph of the two of them with R. Lee, in the Bonneville I bought him, by the beach. The pieces fit together. They were all going to the beach, riding around in the car I bought while I was out there on the stroll working to pay the bills. They were lounging in the sun and spending my money. I should have been the one having a good time! I ought to have known better than to trust a square man with a square girl. And then to top it off, I learned J.N. had known her—been fucking her—for quite some time, then let her come into our home to be R. Lee's babysitter. It infuriated me so much that I regretted ever having helped him out in the first place. Marriage was out of the question! Ever! Then he gave that bitch Patsy a ring that he took from me. That did it! But I had my plans to get it back. No square was going to get away with that! I was better off hanging downtown on my own rather than hooking up with this cheating man I fell in love with somewhere along the line and had a child with. He was no different than my customers, who were always on the hunt for a blowjob or some pussy. The fellas from West Medford all had a rep in town, why didn't I listen? Why?

I began finding out all sorts of unusual things about J.N., especially from Narky, who had grown up with him. He revealed a secret I'm sure J.N. would have preferred remain private. He had sucked J.N.'s dick on several occasions. Surprised, I asked Narky the reason he did that with J.N., and he explained that he liked him. Okay, so did that make my man bisexual? Or what? I never let J.N. know I heard about it from Narky; it kept him from getting his ass kicked by J.N. and saved J.N. from total embarrassment. I was learning more about the man I was with than I needed to know.

J.N., Katie, and I were doing threesomes now. I figured it would flip things around and keep J.N. preoccupied with something other than his straight girlfriends. I shouldn't have done the threesomes, but I thought I might as well try it because J.N. seemed to have a need for other girls. When we started experimenting with having ménages à trois, Katie would lose all her inhibitions and get carried away with J.N., like he was her man, like I did not exist. Boy, that was fucked up. I was falling too deep in love with J.N., more every day, despite how unhealthy it was for me. I didn't appreciate sharing him in sexual arrangements anymore. This square man didn't appreciate me at all. Yeah, he loved me, but not as much as I wanted to be loved, and not enough to not screw up.

The last and final experience I had partying privately at the house was when they convinced me to take a hit of orange sunshine. We were sitting in the basement, and I was feeling adventuresome so I took a small piece. Everyone was doing it, and they seemed to be okay. Shit! I thought I was going to die! Immediately, I felt horrible and frightened—the mattress was sinking into the concrete and enfolding my body… As J.N. began having sex with me in front of Katie and her man, I felt like I was melting away. On one hand, it was frightening, although, on the other hand, the sensation was pleasant and so sexual I could not find words to explain how it felt. I lost all my inhibitions. Katie was telling me to go with the flow. Whatever I looked at became three-dimensional. I diverted my attention from the effects of the drug by getting into the sex more, and reached one climax after another until I had had so many in a row I felt faint. Once the drug's effects wore off, I was never so happy as I was to feel normal again. I didn't enjoy feeling so high or being in any kind of altered state. Katie laughed at me. They all did, although Katie's new man from the South felt badly for me. I wasn't able to do drugs the way she or J.N. could. These mind-enhancing substances didn't agreed with me, and I should have known better than to try another one, ever. I vowed never to do it again, for anyone or for any reason.

I liked the house we were renting. It was secluded and safe. We spoke to the landlord about doing a "rent to own," and he agreed on the condition that we pay more money each month. My dream of owning a home was coming to fruition. Having a house for R. Lee to grow up in was my dream. He was getting older, and I would have to stop using the house for my dates soon. I had talked to madams about trading more girls. I still went to work in town, looking forward to making enough cash to buy the house. I had another couple of bachelor parties lined up, and on one of those nights, the house was packed with Somerville, Cambridge, and Medford guys. It wasn't particularly late when the phone rang. I ran upstairs to get it. I answered the call and heard a man's muffled voice on the other end. He told me he ran the Winter Hill area and had considerable interest in the part of Medford where we lived. I listened intently without speaking. "So you can continue your business here if you pay me five hundred dollars a month gratuities and every party two hundred extra," he said. I wasn't sure that the call was for real. How did he get my number? He spoke with confidence, like he was sure of what was going on. Then he mentioned Mafioso names, and I believed this was not a prank call! All the names were familiar. Even the way he spoke convinced me the call was serious. I knew once I started giving money I would always have to pay, whether I worked or not, and that there would be no end. Just when I was about to have a real home the rug gets pulled out from under me. J.N. said the call was bullshit. He had education, but no knowledge of the real world or the life. He didn't how these things work. I did, I learned that really quick.

The entire situation was nightmarish, and I decided it was time to move back to my comfort zone in Mattapan, where I felt more secure and liked living in an urban atmosphere. At least we wouldn't be a magnet for the police or mobsters—or so I thought. We packed up again, this time with more baggage. I had found a great two-family house on Tennis Road in Mattapan, where there were plenty of kids on the street for R. Lee to play with. The neighborhood had more black families now than when I first lived there, and I was very comfortable with that for both J.N. and R. Lee. Simco's was one of my favorite places to stop and eat, and now it was only a couple of streets away. Still, I was upset about losing my chance to have the house in Medford for my son, and I comforted myself my doubling the determination I had to buy another house someday. I needed to work even harder. The house was nice, but there was no rental on the first floor.

I loved this apartment; it had French doors, hardwood floors, and lots of room. A few weeks after we moved in, I woke up at six a.m. to go to the bathroom. I had worked until three a.m., and I was partially asleep. R. Lee's room was directly across from the bathroom, and when I looked in as I usually did to check on him, I saw that the blankets were bunched up in a corner. I couldn't see his head, and when I came out of the bathroom, I went right to his crib to straighten out the blankets. We still had him in a crib even though he was two years old because he was so hyperactive. We had ordered bunk beds for him, and they were due to arrive soon. It wasn't as safe in the crib anymore because he was a wild child, curious and into everything. He had been climbing out of the crib since he was nine months old, but he would get freaked out hanging from the side railing to get down, so he stopped doing that. But not this time…

That morning when I lifted the covers, he was gone! I screamed his name out, looking in every room, every closet, anyplace where he might be hiding! J.N. came running to me, asking what was going on. R. Lee was really gone from the apartment! Should I call the police? Just as J.N. and I were dressing to go outside, the doorbell rang. Images and possible scenarios went flashing through my mind. Oh, my god…has someone taken him? I ran down the steep stairs of our apartment, almost falling. I was hysterical, totally out of my mind. Just as I opened the front door, there was my baby boy with the oil burner man, laughing and talking silly, with his cheeks bright red. The wave of horror I had been experiencing passed, and my heart sang out! J.N. scooped R. Lee into his arms, saying, "Boy, don't you know you can't go outside? It's freezing!" The oil man said he had been talking up a storm, saying, "Truck, truck, house," and all kinds of words. He said R. Lee started whining for his mommy and pointed. Finally, he got R. Lee to point to the house where his mommy was. The house was new to R. Lee—it was amazing he recognized it. I grabbed him from J.N., cuddling him into my neck, and felt that he was freezing even though the man's coat had been wrapped around his partially nude body. I gave the oil burner man his coat back and thanked him profusely, tears of joy rolling my cheeks. "You're welcome," he said. "I know where he lives now. Don't worry!"

"Well, I hope he will never do that again!" I answered. R. Lee was wearing only his training pants, and his skin was red and blotchy from the extreme cold. J.N. wrapped him in blankets until he was mummified while I made him hot soup for his breakfast. Afterward, he fell asleep in my arms, tired from his early morning ordeal, and I thanked God he was okay. He never even got a cold. The next day, two sets of top locks were installed on the front and back doors, and we put screws on the windows that limited how much they could be opened. Although no one had taken him, as I imagined, I became even more cautious than before. I knew that I would never be able to deal with life if anything ever happened to him. My son was so curious that he could get into anything. That was my fear, and still is to this day.

It was the dead of winter. We kept a close eye on R. Lee, whose twin beds had arrived. He loved his new beds, and was up on the top bunk one night and down on the bottom the next. He changed somewhat after the incident with the oil man, and I realized just how frightened and cold he must have been. The move back to Mattapan was uneventful except for R. Lee and the oil man, and then the unannounced visit of the area detectives, who must have been tipped off by the Somerville police, who in turn were tipped off by the detectives from Winter Hill, and so on… That was the next surprise. The apartment on Tennis Road was spacious, and both of us were satisfied with its location until that day. Early one morning the doorbell rang, and when I went downstairs to open the front door, I was met by two Dragnet types, dressed in plain clothes. It was not difficult to see that they were detectives. They told me not to even think about working in their district. One was playing good cop, and the other was playing bad cop. I told them both that I had no intention of doing that. Keeping my own trick house was the better choice anyway, not "shitting where I ate" as they say. The detectives had given me their sternest warning, and I took heed. J.N. overheard all this and said no sweat, that's bullshit, but I told him that it was serious and no surprise to me that word had spread. Somebody always knew somebody. I was not crossing this line…or maybe only for a regular once in a while.

I had used all our cash for some new furniture and other things for the apartment. We sold the Mustang. J.N. said we didn't need two cars, and besides, he was looking at a Grand Prix to replace the Bonneville. I always regretted selling that Mustang. He thought I was crazy for believing that mobsters or anyone connected existed, and that I shouldn't worry about them. I knew there were mobsters and that was all that mattered. I was aware of who they were, and I paid attention. It was naive of him to think things couldn't go wrong. I paid no attention to J.N.; I did what I thought was right, and minded my own business. I knew that the visit from the detectives was serious. I expected them to watch the house for a while. My steady dates sometimes came to the apartment but not often enough to draw attention. I knew them as well as they knew me, and there was never a problem. I was truthful with them too. So if they ever got stopped or asked what they were doing, we already knew the answers to give.

In the winter, I was out all night in the freezing cold, and occasionally waited for Robin to finish her last dance so we could make some extra money together. She didn't like going out to work alone, and we would sometimes work together after she finished dancing at the Downtown Lounge. On New Year's Eve, Eric, Robin, J.N., and I all went out to party for the night while our neighbors, Reverend D. (a minister) and his wife, watched R. Lee—that became his second home. Robin had steady customers who enjoyed being teased by her nude body. Because other dancers felt superior, they would always make remarks about the street girls, but Robin never did. The truth was that off stage, in regular lighting, many of them had average if not unattractive bodies. Loads of makeup and red lights made them look better than they actually were, and when a girl had a spectacular build, it was obvious to the naked eye. The dancers put out just like street girls but the cops treated them as if they were princesses, and their high opinion of the dancers never wavered when essentially most of these girls were hoes too. The Zone was an entity created by the bars and prostitution, not the dancers, yet the dancers were the subject of a much-hyped book about Boston's Combat Zone. The tricks and girls on the street and in the bars weren't mentioned, even though we truly were in large part what the Zone was about. The customers primarily came to the Zone for the hookers. They would booze it up, watch the dancers and become aroused, then hit the streets for the raw sex they were really interested in.

Robin was Jewish, and from the start we had a connection. People thought we were sisters. Robin's real name was Ruthie, and she came from Revere, living there with her old-fashioned mother who was harsh with her, always yelling and screaming—a real browbeater. She didn't speak about her private life much, and I learned the reason later on when we became better friends. Her insecurity made her easy prey for pimps and hustlers; if anyone told her she was beautiful, she would melt and follow him. She was well known downtown as a dancer and had her costumes made by the lady who created all the outfits for the showgirls, both dancers and strippers (I can't remember her name). From the first day we met, I was certain we would have a lasting friendship; the same sense I had when I met Katie. They were my two best friends for life who were from the life. When I hung at the lounge where Robin worked, the guys would ask me to dance with them, and my answer was always a flatout no. I would tell them that they didn't have enough money to be that friendly. Mostly, these guys were the pill poppers, cokeheads, and beer drinkers with breath that could knock you out. Robin and I had a good time together wherever we went, particularly when we went to Revere Beach. Although we were at the beach often, she refused to get her hair wet or have her perfectly applied makeup even slightly smudged by the elements. Her habit of looking in mirrors was extreme. She knew it annoyed me, but she couldn't help herself and did it anyway. She couldn't go by a window without looking at her reflection, and when she was walking through a parking lot, she looked in every car window. She positioned herself at an angle when there was a mirror so she could see her face, and she constantly looked at her reflection while she sat at bars. Socializing or working, she could usually be found in the ladies' lounge, fixing her hair and face, and pouting back at her own reflection. And don't ever give her fingernail polish because she never had a steady hand and it would be on the table or on her skin—a total mess. She could be a trip, but I loved my dear friend. She was special, then and always. Ruthie/ Robin…

CHAPTER FORTY-EIGHT

Mr. Seafood

We only needed one car at that time, to save money, but I had to get a new car. Junior had borrowed the Grand Prix we had bought to replace the Bonneville, and after having the car for only a couple of weeks, he ran into a bridge, totaling it, and we found ourselves without any car at all. Although J.N. chased him down, Junior never paid for the loss of the car, and J.N. didn't want me to confront his so-called buddy. Sure, it only cost *me* money. It was a good thing I had customers at Clair Buick, on Route 1 in Dedham. I could get any car I wanted, brand new and without credit, just a push through with a little money down and, of course, GMAC payments. Our credit was good, and with the loan, we could build even better credit. J.N. had everything put in his name, of course... When I walked into Clair Buick for the first time it was like a dream come true; the salesman was so respectful and accommodating that I thought to myself how money—and sex—talk. And this was powerful knowledge. Not only did I have the cash, but I also had the girls they liked. My customer told the other salesmen who I was, and they were all over me, trying to help me in any way they could. I got the new car I wanted: a 1971 Buick Riviera Grand Sport, fully loaded.

I talked to my friend Katie about taking the car to Florida on a test drive for a few days. I told J.N. that I was leaving and would see him when I got back. We went to Florida, and in Miami I caught up with a few of my Jewish clients, made some money, went to the beach—where we both got a tan—spent all our money, and headed home. I bought candy and some fresh fruits for Nana while we were on the road. As I was driving through South Carolina at about a hundred miles an hour—loving that fast and beautiful car—I saw a state trooper and, trying to hide, I sandwiched between two tractor trailers. I heard the siren and pulled over. The trooper was white, and I didn't want to have to open my wallet for identification and have him see J.N. and R. Lee's mixed-race pictures. I thought he would just give me a ticket but instead he said, in a deep Southern drawl, "Miz Lady, follow me. We're going to see the magistrate."

We drove down a side road off the highway. That made me nervous. We finally reached a spot where there was an old colonial-style house with a big wide porch that looked like a haunted house in a horror movie, and we pulled in there. The trooper said to bring my identification. I had to bring the entire wallet because he was watching me. We followed him up a ramp, and inside was a large, old-style desk with a man sitting behind it and a wheelchair off to one side. The magistrate was a heavy-set, older white man with a serious Southern accent. He asked for identification from both of us and, after seeing my name and that I came from Boston, asked about my nationality. Katie and I assured him that we went to church every Sunday. He hassled us back and forth about what we were doing there in the South and about how fast we'd been going. Then he said, "I normally would fine you two hundred dollars, but this time, I'm going to allow you to pay one hundred dollars cash. Otherwise, y'all will have to spend five to six days in our county jail." We paid up! "I suggest that you stay in accordance with the speed limit. Have a good trip, now. Y'hear?" We stayed in accordance as long as necessary, "Y'hear," then I put my foot to the pedal and proceeded home at my regular ninety-five miles an hour. I didn't want to ever appear before a Southern magistrate again.

At that time, one of my big money customers was Mr. Seafood. He was wild and crazy, constantly high on black beauties. He was one tough bastard with an ego as tall as the Empire State Building. He showed off his wealth by hanging around poorer people, or hookers who loved doing him service for cash as he humiliated them. But even those girls took him for a one shot deal—they couldn't hang. I read him like a book, and knew what to say and do. Not only was Mr. Seafood too much to handle, he was not particularly liked or respected because of his arrogance. He behaved as though he was a king, and I rarely accepted that kind of difficult behavior just because of money, but he was an exception. I gave it my all. He had girls rubbing him down with Noxema for an entire night, and attempting to give him a blowjob, non-stop, for hours at a time. They hated him and never came back. The black beauties he swallowed made him so speedy he couldn't get an erection, and he would grunt and groan trying to get off. But I had the right technique: a soft, easy touch with a feather around his nipples and, slowly, down around his lower back and the cheeks of his butt. He responded so well. He had a host of frustrations and ample cash. I talked dirty to him—he loved that. When he didn't get his way, he became angry, pacing the floor as he swore. I had the patience to deal with him most of the time, but it was easy to see why others didn't. The money was great, and between Mr. Seafood and my regulars, and the extra cash the side girls were bring in, I was earning enough to pay off my car. What I loved about that car was the speed, and I wanted more speed, so I took it to my friends in Lynn to soup it up—and did they ever! They took off the air pollution device and pumped it up. Mr. Seafood requested that I become his full-time patsy, like so many others he had asked who refused because they couldn't come through and handle his shit. I demanded far more money than the other girls. I was paid because he was out of control, calling me twenty-four hours a day. He liked me and the way I handled him. I stuck in there, responding to his every whim. My life consisted of the streets and Mr. Seafood with hardly any time left for my family. I was more stressed from him than I ever was on the streets.

The new car was exciting, and I would speed around in it whenever I could to keep my mind off Mr. Seafood. Everything in my life was going well again. My son was as much a challenge as he was fulfilling. Spoiled rotten—my fault! I began collecting Liz Taylor memorabilia, small things that had anything to do with her. J.N.

and I and R. Lee went out regularly to Fontaine's Chicken in West Roxbury. I loved it there; we all did. Southern fried chicken, mashed potatoes, gravy, biscuits...oh my. I drool when I think of it now. We went there one night, and J.N. told me he was getting ready to enroll at Brandeis in addition to his main occupation, which was screwing the various young chicks he had in West Medford and the neighborhood. I found out most of the time. And, as usual, when I confronted him, he denied everything. I was afraid school would provide him with even more opportunities to cheat on me, but I didn't say anything—to him I was out of sight and out of mind. The difficulties of being monogamous and in my profession were enormous. I was forewarned about him being a square, still, my heart told me to go for it. Our son was growing up, and as he grew, I regretted the degree to which he was exposed to heated arguments between his father and me. J.N. was exceedingly possessive; at the same time, he was in the habit of taking off with his friends for the weekends, always with girls accompanying them...at my expense. But if I went to the corner or to Simco's for food, he would be so jealous, thinking I was meeting someone.

We finally bought all the rest of our new furniture at Summerfield's. Our credit was great now. The car was in J.N.'s name too. Having a credit account at a store didn't carry much merit, but the car did. I gave J.N. my cash willingly to start school, but at the same time, I felt resentment because I was getting him a new car soon. Helping everyone but myself seemed to be a way of life for me. His endless lying weighed on me, increasing the irritation I already felt. I should have left him in Park Square and kept going. Too late! I was in the quicksand of love, or what felt like love—my heart hurt.

Mr. Seafood was a constant challenge, high stress, and J.N. only added to it. Now Mr. Seafood was aroused by watching black men fuck white women in pornographic movies. But that was not enough for him—he wanted to watch actual people engaged in black on white sex. He was only fascinated by black men with huge dicks, and I sometimes wondered if he was more into the men than the women because he loved a finger or two up his ass when he was getting blown, the harder the better. I was relieved not to participate in these sessions beyond arranging them. Although he pressured me relentlessly, I simply said no. But J.N. wanted to participate, and he did. He had no issues. During the time the sex acts were taking place, Mister Seafood would begin speaking gibberish, often prodding the men on to fuck harder. Many times, the men lost their erections and he would pay them less, degrading everyone involved by name-calling—fucker, you black motherfucker. I did not like this at all. I put up with this ugly behavior because of the money. I still wonder how I got through it. Then he wanted young girls. I lied to him and found twenty-year-old's to dress as if they were fifteen; that was young enough for my taste. I hated men who liked little girls. I'd had enough of that when I was younger. It was easy to dislike this man, who had a wife and children at home. I detested the way he thought because I was raped as a child. He went too far, and when he asked for twelve-year-old's, it triggered dark memories, but it was better to play roles than to have him participate in this kind of thing in real life. He revealed that one of his fantasies was to rape the babysitter. This was a sick, utterly deranged man. At least while I was still keeping him as my client, the various scenarios I created for him kept him from acting on his impulses and actually hurting young girls in real life.

The outlet prostitution provides for men to act out their anti-social impulses gives my profession a purpose beyond sex. These feelings are not gotten rid of with counseling, and I have the ability to do so with no degree; you have to know how to direct these thoughts and teach these men other outlets. Mr. Seafood's pedophilia stayed within the realm of fantasy as long as I was there in the room controlling things, and I felt that I was contributing in my own way to the protection of the vulnerable and the betterment of society. There were clients who had me act like a little girl after I was first turned out. Although the simulation sickened me, I handled it. I did it because I knew just what they needed. My mind did not happily travel back to the time I was raped as a young child. I blocked out these feelings and concentrated on making money off the pedophiles, keeping these men satisfied in their dream worlds—and away from young children! If only society understood what good prostitution does when it is controlled.

It was 1972. I had known Mr. Seafood for about a year when he became a fixture in my routine, someone I would keep until he ran out of money or I became sick of him. His last-minute plans had me running around here and there at all hours, and interfered with my time with R. Lee. One bright, sunny day Mr. Seafood asked me to meet him at an upscale hotel he frequented as a guest, to eat at the restaurant, where he would always show off and be ignorant—he was an egotistical son of a bitch, grunting out his commands. It was early in the afternoon, and he wanted me to bring another girl. It was going to be a surprise, he said, and he would pay me ten thousand dollars. Knowing him, this was going to be outrageous. He was in the suite, pacing back and forth like a mad dog, as he always did. This time he was even more agitated. Noxema filled the air. My working girl, Jill, who was in her early twenties, asked for money for her time waiting, and he told her she had to wait longer; he never liked a pushy girl. Once, he told me to get ready to go to Florida and to bring J.N. and "the kid too," as he put it. The plan was that I would see Disney while I was there with him. "But don't ask for any money," he said. "I'll pay you when we get there." That's usually a sure way to get fucked. That's how he felt about paying upfront. He did pay, and dearly, but I sweated it because J.N. and R. Lee were involved. Mr. Seafood's anxiety was getting worse than I had ever seen before. His forehead beaded with perspiration; as he dropped down into a chair, he demanded that I take a seat. Checking his watch, he told me his guest would arrive any minute. *His guest?* I thought. I asked him who the guest was, and he told me he was giving his wife a gift for their anniversary—a threesome! I was mildly shocked that Mrs. Seafood wanted a threesome, although several times while I was giving him head he said that his wife wanted to be with a woman. I wasn't sure he was being straightforward because clients will often suggest a threesome to hype up their fantasies with their wives. At that time, I passed it off as another one of his fantasies, but this time, it was for real. Jill asked for more money when she heard the date involved a threesome. Once again, he told her to be quiet, that he would tell her to leave if she continued pestering him. She should have let me handle it. She was getting top dollar anyway, three hundred an hour. Normally, my cut would be sixty percent, but I was giving her a break on the out call because I was there with her. So my cut was only fifty dollars an hour, but that was way more than fair.

There was a knock on the door, and Mr. Seafood answered. His pretty wife came in the room. Mr. Seafood was hyped up, bouncing on his feet. She was Italian and classy, and she appeared utterly puzzled, although she must have had an inkling of what was going on because of the strange expression on her face. She was somewhat shocked, but she was controlling her reaction until she was certain. He was pacing and grunting, and signaled me to approach her, waving his hand so I would go up to her and gently get her in the mood. She wasn't pleased, and I realized this was not going to happen. She never even knew… As I walked away, she flipped out, screaming in both English and Italian like a crazy woman. I retreated a few more steps as she screamed. She was angry, and said, "You set me up, you prick! This is the last time! And you, you stay the fuck away from me!" I backed even farther away, apologizing. I told her I was under the impression she had asked to be part of the arrangement. "No," she said, "that was my sick husband!" She began crying hysterically and asked me to walk her out. Reluctantly, I said okay. I told the other girl I'd be right back, but Mr. Seafood threw money at her and ordered her out of the room, saying, "Get the fuck out!" He was pissed off. She bent down and gathered the bills from the plush carpet. I was totally humiliated. His face was red with anger and embarrassment, but he didn't direct any of his venom toward me because he was aware that he needed me. His wife and I went to the lobby bathroom to give her a chance to pull herself together; cold water and someone to vent to. She said how fucked up her husband was, and that after years of abuse, she could not take it anymore and was going to file for divorce. She said that there was someone else in her life. I told her how sorry I was for the misunderstanding. I said that she was doing the right thing; her husband needed help. I felt for her and would never tell him what his wife revealed to me. That was the last time I saw her. Her exit was as classy as her entrance. I went back to the suite, where I calmed Mr. Seafood down by replacing fantasies about his wife with new fantasies I created on the spot so that in the end he would pay me after he forgot about the tense scene he had created. He kept calling her a cunt and saying, "fuck her!" It seemed to me that the richer the men were, the greater their sexual hang-ups. Money can't buy sanity, nor can it buy happiness. And sex to the limit just escalates the next step up. Then what?

I had enough of living on the edge. I had to get a little calmer. No amount of money was enough for me to continue with this kind of torment. The streets were much better. I weaned him away, seeing him only a couple of times a week. He was threatening and aggressive. He offered me thousands to go out with him, and then he would pay only one thousand. Now he was getting back at me for not acting out his fantasies about his babysitter and sixteen-year-olds. He mentioned Florida again, and I knew he was playing games with me. It was becoming a chore to think of new sex stories every time I saw him because he was so unpleasant. I was wearing down, tired from turning tricks on the streets and having to deal with Mr. Seafood at all hours of the day and night. I wasn't paying attention to what my body was telling me. I didn't listen to J.N. or the crying of my son. I was happily servicing my clients, but Mr. Seafood was slowly draining my good nature. I was taking care of everyone except myself. Psychologically, I needed a break from this sicko.

The role prostitutes play in preventing men from acting out their fantasies on women and children is enormous. There is a need for us to be out there. Society doesn't acknowledge this and probably never will. We curb aberrant behavior! When will it learn? Prostitution should be allowed by society, and maybe it would be if society were more educated about the business of prostitution. The internet makes protecting children from sexual predators all the more difficult for parents. Technology has made it worse. Certain sites should not only be policed, but also controlled by tighter restrictions. Sex is free for everyone to view, including children. The predators should be jailed forever for the crimes they commit—why aren't they? Men and women like Mr. Seafood are around every corner. I have never hurt anyone, and my liaisons are between consenting adults. A shift in perspective is necessary to change people's attitudes about prostitution. According to existing laws, what I've done is criminal. But the laws governing the system should be changed to reflect current reality. And the same politicians who make the laws break them! All the time!

We did go to Florida, but only after I demanded that Mr. Seafood give J.N. money upfront when we arrived so that he could go out with our son without playing games later. I needed one last bout of big money! Out of desperation to be in my company, he agreed. We went, and he had reserved a penthouse suite at the King's Inn where Bob Hope was staying. When we went down to dinner one night we saw Mr. Hope and his guests sitting at a large table, and the comedian didn't even crack a smile the whole time. It was the same with me: always smile for the audience, but not when I wasn't performing. Despite our excitement experiencing Disneyworld, my dislike for Mr. Seafood had become so bad that was obvious to him. I simply could not, and did not, give in to all his demands. The trip couldn't be over fast enough for me. J.N. had the money first, so I didn't care. When we arrived back in Boston, I changed my telephone number so I wouldn't have any contact with that maniacal, sexually-crazed man again; doing so caused me to lose some of my client contacts. I didn't want to be associated with his abusiveness and problems anymore. What stayed in my mind and clinched it for me were the fantasies about his babysitter and the time we went back to the very ritzy Colonnade Hotel and he showed up in shorts and a tee shirt, shouting obscenities and put-downs at the staff at the top of his lungs, all while we were in a classy restaurant getting ready to have wine and food.

My life was back on track with Mr. Seafood out of the picture. He left me messages with girls he knew worked for me, but after a while, he stopped. Time flew by. J.N. was happier once I was not as frazzled, but the pressure of him being in school stressed both of us. The money was so good for so long that I had enough to buy a Chrome Yellow 1973 Riviera GS demo off the showroom floor with not too many years of pay-off. We had two cars again: the 1971 souped-up one was mine, and J.N. drove the new 1973; it suited him better. I participated in races, and the car won every time. I won some extra money on hundred dollar bets. She was a pretty fast car.

My son was developing a stubborn streak. He was maturing and could understand situations between his dad and I, but I was careful not to expose him to anything that might be upsetting. The only advantage to being molested as a child and being in this business was that I could sense who was a pedophile simply by observing his face and actions. There were so many out there. My experiences honed this keen sense, making sure that no one like that went near my son. This was something I could never learn by reading a book. I was sensitive to men's needs, including J.N.'s, but he seemed to be drifting away from me, partying constantly. And girls, girls, girls. He was changing, needing other things, not just new women. I didn't have a clear sense of what the difference in him was yet. His moods and conversation were not the same.

I was getting ready to go with Candice, nicknamed Candy, to work in Florida and the Bahamas. It was an ideal time to take a break away from Boston without Seafood Man trailing me. It was 1974, and the police were cleaning up the streets. It was time to disappear for a while. Candy, a great worker, was a ditsy blonde with lily-white skin. We had traveled together to New York and Philadelphia but never to Florida before. When we were driving through the Carolinas, we saw a young black boy hitching on the side of the road. It was very late at night, dark, the weather was very cool and he was not dressed warmly enough. He seemed to be in a hurry and too young to be out so late. As I was pulling over, Candy was screaming in my ear, "Don't pick him up! No way!"

I fired back, "Shut the fuck up, Candy, I can handle this!" He was reluctant at first and backed off. I finally was able to coax him, but he was seriously scared as he got into the back seat. He ducked down in the seat, not wanting to be spotted with two white women. "Miss," he said, "I don't want to be seen, and your lady friend is blonde!" I let him know that I would assume all the responsibility if we were stopped. How dare anyone tell me who I can and cannot be with! The boy just needed a ride home. We were in the South, but I wasn't frightened at all, motivated by the unfair way blacks were treated as a result of white prejudice. We drove into a small town and slowed to a stop. It was very dark, full of shadows, and the faint glow from the old street lights was just enough for us to see by. The boy hunched down and slipped out of the car, said "Thanks, ma'am," and ran. I wasn't concerned about myself getting caught, but I was touched by this young boy who ran so he wouldn't get himself or us in trouble. It was heartbreaking.

How can we live in a world such as this and say we are free? I had been to race rallies and heard the derogatory comments spewed out by the KKK, and shuddered. I had experienced prejudice as a child when I was called a "kike." The KKK hated Jews too. It seemed to me that the only reason white extremists lived was to hate, and I knew black people whose main preoccupation was to hate whites, the difference being that the blacks did not hang with whites because of the color of their skin. Lynchings of whites by any blacks were, to my knowledge, unheard of! Looking back, when my son was only two years old, some white kids at a pizza place called him a "nigger kid mixed breed," and I was so glad he was too young to understand. I wanted to go after them, but the owner came out and chased them off. "Don't get yourself involved," he said with his heavy Italian accent. "They're just punks." There were incidents, too numerous to count, when people stared at me for being with a black man and a mixed child. I didn't care; it was the others who were bothered because of their small, narrow minds, not me. They were ignorant! Race was still an issue, whether in the North or South. Today, racial profiling continues to ignite confrontations in the streets between police and those people who object to their unwarranted aggression. There are good and bad in every race. Blacks referring to another black sometimes use the "N" word, but when used by a white man it's insulting. Neither side should use the "N" word—ever, not even in music! It's not a good word to pass down. My stomach knotted when Mr. Seafood called the black men he hired "niggers." They didn't protest even when I spoke up vehemently in their defense because they wanted the money. Money makes people do things against their self-worth.

CHAPTER FORTY-NINE

Kidnapped

Downtown was really hot. Police were cleaning up the streets. I left for a while to work for some madams. When I went to Charlie's place for the second time, the woman was crazed and filled to the brim with her own ego, much worse than when we had first met. She was in a nice apartment; her desk was in the hallway by the entrance door. She was Swedish, with blonde hair, a real dom-looking woman, wearing leather from head to toe. She made the better part of her money herself for her first years in business. Before this business, she worked for the airlines. Her list of rules was long. I could tell I would never come back to her place again, but doing business with her for girls, like we had done before, would be fine. She cracked the whip as if the girls were B and D clients and she was the dominatrix, expecting her girls to have anal sex with the customers for the same cut of money, no extras, all hours of the day and night, and cum as many times as they could in one hour. Later, we found out she even tapped into the tips, that she was pocketing the extra cash that should have gone to the girls. I mean, how fucked up was that? Throughout all the years I did business with her, she never changed. She wasn't the only bad madam either—there were plenty of them who skimmed off the top and supplied their girls with drugs to make themselves more money and keep the girls constantly in need of them.

I was going to another lady not far from Charlie's. I had only heard about her and not met her yet. We had talked on the phone and discussed the subject of me going up there and trading girls prior to my trip. Leaving Boston was the best strategy for me. I loved to travel. I was at ease about R. Lee, who stayed with the reverend and his wife—they were the best! I was okay despite the fact that I missed my son.

I needed more money now because we had spent the money I earned from Mr. Seafood on cars and tuition at Brandeis University. I always made money on the road, going from state to state and city to city. I went to Florida, Georgia, the Carolinas, and to the Bahamas whenever I could, but it was more complicated now because of my son. I tried to make these trips short so he wouldn't have to suffer any prolonged anxiety while I was away. R. Lee was well cared for by a family who loved him and he loved back. The madams I met and would be doing business with all had odd characteristics, except a few good ones, and there were only a handful of those that I knew of. It was time for me to trade girls and stay home more. Every time I called, R. Lee would cry for me to come home. I swore I would make up for the time I spent away from him before life passed by. I still work on that to this day.

New York City never failed to be lucrative. Key money poured in from every inch of Manhattan, bigger money than Boston. There were hordes of madams, but only a few on the Circuit, a closely-knit group. At this time, I would be the only Boston Circuit one. These madams belonged to a national network of brothels who exchanged girls on the basis of how good they were "in the room," a phrase that was used to describe their ability to perform sexually, and is still used today. The girls were judged by their attractiveness, personality, the shape of their bodies, and—of course—how they were in the room. And the madams' conversations among themselves about each girl determined whether a madam recommended her to another in a different state. If a girl wasn't good, she would be blacklisted and couldn't get into another house. Those were the rules that were enforced by true madams. The Circuit, which began in the late 40's and 50's, flourished in the 1960's, spreading connections throughout the U.S. and Europe. I had joined that circle, but Marcie didn't want to work with out-of-state girls. I was more geared up to make money at the new house, sending dates to my selected girls while I still worked. I wanted to bring back names of girls to work in Boston and trade my Boston girls to them. I had already channeled quite a few, and Charlie sent me more as long as I sent her the best of the Boston hoes, as she put it. She charged her girls three hundred for the referral numbers. They were tough M's. The madam I was going to see wanted all my girls to come to her. The trade-offs made the Circuit what it was. We did not need a computer to keep track of the girls; all we went by was trust in the word of the madams that a girl was good in the room. And the added volume of clients confidentially referred from madam to madam in every state made us more money.

It was cold in the city, with tall buildings creating wind tunnels that chilled to the bone, and skyscrapers that blocked any sunlight on my way to the apartment of one of the Manhattan madams; a good one, I was told. It was located on 57th Street, a nice building with a cool doorman who was expecting me. In our conversation on the phone, she told me that her hours were from twelve to twelve, including occasional overnights, but if there were big-money special clients, she would wake me at any hour. Oh, how I hated overnights! I could sleep until eleven a.m. some days, others I was up at the crack of dawn. After she got to know me, she said I could do her phones if I stayed longer. Nah…had to go to my son. She told me in advance that, depending on the businessmen's schedules, late nights until three in the morning were sometimes required. I introduced myself as Libbe to the doorman, but as he buzzed the madam's unit, I told him my stage name was Ramie. "Okay, my lady." We went up several floors. He was congenial and told me to call him if I needed anything. He was staring at me with a big smile on his face. I thought it must be what I was wearing that caught his eye: a sleek black dress, black stockings, shoes with a sexy strap on my ankle, and fur—I loved my mink! Her apartment faced the front of the building, and had she been looking, she would have seen me coming in. The doorman knocked, and I could hear her talking to somebody. As the door opened, I saw that she was an older woman, classy, and dressed in a long, kimono-style, silk housecoat like the ones Marcie and I owned. She was deep in conversation on the phone, and she signaled me with her hand as she slipped ten dollars to the doorman. The room was eclectic with Chinese and vintage furniture from all eras scattered around, long, heavy curtains, and oriental rugs with deep rich colors and various patterns. Everything looked expensive, including the art on the walls. I watched her red lips as she spoke. Her appearance fit the stereotype of a madam. I wanted to be different so that people would not be able to tell who or what I was according to my appearance. I wondered why we all wore the same kind of kimonos and loved ornate fixtures. I thought of my Victorian fixtures and decided that they had to be changed!

She pointed for me to put down my bag and sit in the living room. Sinking into the plush cushions of her sofa, I loved the feeling. I could overhear her from the kitchen describing me: she said I was skinny, young, and sweet, with long black hair and big brown eyes—a "sexy, young look."

"Oh yes," she said, "and she's great in the room." She hung up. That was her description. I wondered how she knew, who had told her. Maybe Charlie? Or maybe that's what she said about every new girl who came along. I didn't realize that all the madams communicated with one another about me ahead of time. The only difference was that others said my eyes were big, black, and sexy, and I was Jewish. As she walked with her phone, it didn't stop ringing, not for a second, like my phone at home. "Lots of Chinese clients," she managed to tell me, aside, as she spoke on the phone, "and Jewish men." "Oh shit, Chinese men," I said under my breath.

I was a mother, a part-time madam working my way up, setting up my clients with girls, working the streets and houses, trying to be as domestic as I could to fulfill my responsibilities at home. I had matured, absorbing each new experience like a sponge. The two names I used outside of Boston were Ramie and Leah, and rarely did I use Libbe. The madam knew me as Ramie, although she knew that I was called Libbe in Boston. Finally, she stopped talking on the phone for ten minutes. She explained what her rules were as she walked me to my room, the one in which I'd work and live during my stay. The madams had their girls stay in their apartments with them to be near the money in case a girl ran off. The madam collected all the money. I noted that there were two mirrors in the room, one was an old vintage mirror in front of the bed, and the other was narrow and took the place of a headboard. It was common to have one or two extra bedroom mirrors so the clients could watch themselves in the act—they loved that. Charlie's place had a bedroom with a mirror on the ceiling like they had at Caesar's Palace in Vegas. On top of the tall dresser there was a tray with a wash basin, soap, and facecloth, and inside the drawers were condoms, every size of rubber dildo, handcuffs with fur sewn around the inside of them so they wouldn't leave marks, nipple pinchers, gag balls, whips, ropes, and vibrators—virtually every toy imaginable. She made it clear that she would count these toys before a girl left. If you didn't bring your own condoms, she would charge three dollars apiece for them. *Wow,* I thought, *she made a large profit there.* The madam told me that when girls stayed with her they were sworn not to steal and their bags would be checked before they were allowed to leave. This didn't unsettle me at all. Her bedroom door was locked with a deadbolt for security.

The girls who worked for the madams were predominantly American white girls, although there were some French and Italian. There weren't any Spanish girls, and only the top light-skinned American black girls worked in the houses. They had lower-end houses for other ethnic groups. Asians were considered less desirable, while the Spanish were the bottom of the barrel. Asian girls carried lots of disease then. She finished telling me the rules: no smoking cigarettes in the room (only on the terrace or in the living room), no drinking until after work, and no drugs! I could go out only after one or two a.m., and if it was slow, by twelve midnight. I followed the rules. With the clients, I had to behave the way a guy's girlfriend would behave with him, doing anything and everything he wanted except anal, which was extra and only if I consented—and I did not! It was called GFE, a girlfriend experience. As much as I hated it, I did it when the madam said it was necessary. It's funny that I ended up telling my girls later on the same thing. Even though I had just taken a long bus ride and was hungry, she cracked the whip. I jumped in the shower, put on a young girl's dress and knee socks, and removed all my makeup in five minutes. She told me three Chinese men were coming back to back. They were expecting a sixteen-year-old girl to be in the room. Great. That's just what I need on an empty stomach. Oddly, I had a craving for Chinese food… This was not going to be pleasant, but I had overcome my issues. It was like riding a bike and falling off: you get right back on. They came into the room, one trick at a time, and left tips from two dollars to five dollars, which was not very much at all, but I knew they weren't big tippers, only the Japanese men were (some would tip fifty dollars, and they were polite too). They all fucked me hard and fast, and when each one climbed on top of me, I somehow quelled my feelings of disgust.

After three in the afternoon, the Jewish garment district owners paraded in and were served their favorite drinks. They would bring her small (sizes 1-3) sample clothes. The madam had a local girl working in another room, and we were humping away. If they paid for an hour, the madam would give me only half if the john left early, and pocketed the rest—something I vowed I would never do. She was slick, very slick, and unfair, as they all were. I got the other girl's number to come to Boston later. She was happy to hear I would not take tip money. I was busy for the next three days; I had quite a few repeats. The madam was pleased, and my money grew to over two thousand dollars in a short time. I was happy. She gave me some more local numbers she did not use that much because they steal her clients. It was comfortable there, and the madam didn't have much time to speak to me because she was so busy with the clients and her boyfriend/sugar daddy.

Madam liked my ability to work, and I even answered the phone for her at times when she ate lunch or was taking one of her baths in giant-sized-bubbles while nibbling on chocolate and sipping her wine. There were two days left to go. I had three-thousand-plus dollars. At midday, a visitor came into the room. It was one of the madam's local black girls, who was supposedly there to see a client. I was in the room with a trick when she came in. She didn't disturb us. When I was done, I washed up, and waited in the living room for the next one. I hadn't seen the other girl yet. On Thursdays and Fridays, there was a constant flow of customers, but we worked only until six p.m. on Fridays because the Jewish clients went home for the Sabbath at sundown. Madam customarily went out to dinner, and it took her two hours to get ready. On Saturdays, the Jewish clients from the garment district hardly came in at all. Sunday was their good day, as were lunch hours during the week and afternoons before they went home.

I could hear the girl speaking in the bathroom. Her voice was familiar, and when she came out I saw it was a girl I knew pretty well. We hugged. "Hey girl, what's up?" she asked.

"Damn, of all the places to meet up. I didn't know you worked here," I replied.

"No I don't," she answered, "I come up here when it's slow, every couple of months. I bring girls to her. I've got some regulars here too!" "Well, bring them to me in Boston. I'm recruiting here."

She said, "Yeah, no problem. I know some cute white girls here in the city. I'll pass your number around. Hey, how 'bout you hangin' out with me? When do you go home?" I told her I was leaving early this coming Saturday, around ten a.m. "Okay then," she said, "come on out to the after-hours tonight. It's a big night and my man's in town."

"No, can't do it. I've got to work, and I can't go without my man, and he's in Boston." Rule number one. "You'll be with us. Madam won't care because it's after midnight. She's out on Friday nights usually! I'll get you, okay?" she coaxed.

"I told you, I can't go!"

"I'm telling you," she countered reassuringly, "you're in good hands. You know my man, he's got your back." I knew the rules. What was I thinking? Rule number two: There are no friends on the streets. "Okay, I'll go. See you later." After I said yes, she left, saying, "And dress sharp. Those other bitches can't outdo us." It was tough being inside every day. I needed some air. Once I made the decision, I was excited to go out. I always liked the profile (posing) of the pimps and hoes at the after-hours. They were dressed to the max, so it was a good thing I had my best clothes and jewelry for when we went on the rich out-calls. I had some tip money to take with me. I watched the clock. I was nervous and had a premonition that I shouldn't go. I wasn't going to tell J.N. He did so many things behind my back. Why should I care? I felt justified because he lied and cheated all the time. It was about twelve-thirty a.m. The madam wanted me back by five a.m. to get a few hours of sleep so I would look rested before I started at eleven. I assured her not to worry, and that nothing could keep me away from working.

When I went down, the doorman was impressed that I was dressed to the nines. He said, "Girl, be careful out there. You look too good to be going out unchaperoned by a man."

"Well, you can be my escort," I flirted.

"I wish… In a heartbeat I would, but I gotta work the door. I'll take a rain check!"

"Okay," I said. My girl pulled in the cab and I waved goodbye to the handsome black doorman as we drove off into the city lights. On the ride over, I told her I had to be back by five a.m. "Sure thing," she said. Her man was waiting there at the glass doors of the after-hours entrance when we arrived. It was on the West Side of 6th Ave. The lights in the building were dim. We walked down an unusually long corridor. Her man complimented me. "Hey girl, you're beaming. Don't mind having you to sport tonight," he said as he pulled me to his side to front me, to show me off, like I was his other woman. I thanked him for the compliment. "Don't want the wolves messin' with ya," he said. I had no comment. Unlike Boston, where the pimps were easy-going, New York and other larger cities had harder breeds, especially Philly, Chicago, and Detroit. The place was packed wall-to-wall with people wearing minks, diamonds, and gold. The light reflecting off the jewelry was blinding. This was a party for one of the richer, bigger pimps. One of his friends at the bar stood so the two of us could sit. J.N. was always jealous when I went anywhere. I made sure to call him before I left to ease his mind. R. Lee was asleep. I lied to him and said I was going to bed early. I had worked hard that day. He took good care of our son when I worked, and that eased my mind somewhat.

Her man ordered drinks and paid for them, telling me not to reach for my money. A sense of paranoia came over me. She was talking about how great her man was, but I knew better because of all the times she had gotten her ass kicked and bragged about it. I listened anyway. I was feeling uncomfortable, bothered by one of the big-time pimps who was staring at me like I was his meal ticket. He wore a full-length mink coat, and his white diamonds glistened in the light. My diamonds shone as well, and I turned one around so it wouldn't reflect the light; the diamonds he was wearing sparkled endlessly, no matter how or where he stood. He was fine, and he knew it. J.N. wasn't big time like the fellas here. Some big-time musicians would hang out with the players, especially Marvin Gaye, who went to Tommy Small's place on 7th Ave. in Harlem, where I had gone in the past. J.N. would never fit in with this crowd. He was still small and unknown on the streets of any city outside of Boston. The reputations of the pimps at the party were known in every city. I was wearing my gold and diamond eternity ring, a diamond bracelet, wedding bands with large stones, a pair of one-carat diamond earrings, and a one-carat diamond necklace hidden beneath the neckline of my dress. I had on my full-length fur coat that I had gotten from a booster, and underneath was a sexy, black outfit that clung to the curves of my slim body.

The after-hours was enveloped in a cloud of smoke, and the smell of cheap perfume and cocaine burning in the cigarettes wafted in the air around the bar. I had no business being there with my so-called friend and her man, and I could tell it showed. The icy stare of the pimp across the room frightened me. Somehow, I sensed that he knew I wasn't with my friend's man. I wasn't choosing, and I realized I had to get out of there. Her man shouldn't have fronted me as my pimp either; plus, I knew better. Why did I agree to come here? He knew better. Was he planning to snatch me later? I had to go. I knew the rules. These pimps pack guns—they don't play here. As I turned to tell my working friend I had to leave, her man stood up. He was going to find some blow. I should have left with him. I was freaking out. "Is he going to be gone long?" I asked.

"Hey," she said, "it's cool. Just hang tight. You're too tense! You're with me. Everybody here knows me and my man." That was enough of a reason to leave; everyone knew I wasn't with her man. I didn't see anyone I knew at the party. "Yeah, but they don't know me, and he's not my man," I told her. "I'm going back to the house. I never should have left."

She could see I meant what I said, and replied, "Girl, you need to stay put. Please?" Even though J.N. had too much square in him to be a full-fledged pimp, I didn't want to break the rules I was taught. And I definitely didn't want him to know I had been out. I had to get back in case he called. I regretted that I'd lied. He trusted that I was only going to work, and upsetting him wasn't something I wanted to do. He was showing more of a temper from being on the streets lately, and that was not comforting. I said goodbye and avoided any stares from the fellas there watching. I turned my back and walked as fast as I could in the direction of the entrance doors. The dark, gloomy hallway seemed longer on the way out than it did on the way in.

I made it down the hallway and went up two steps to go out the door. I put my hand on the handle. It was one of those doors that you pull. It was in the basement of an apartment building, so you had to go out through the lengthy corridor and then to an outer hall to get outside. Just as I put my hand on the door, another hand went "katoomph" on my hand. It was a black hand. It was the pimp with all the jewelry. Oh, shit! I knew who it was—that decked-out fella. I didn't have to turn around; I stood still. I didn't want to see his face. He pulled my hand off the door, turned my face to him, and went "whoom!"—right in my jaw. I went straight down on the floor. He had sucker-punched me for no reason. I didn't feel anything break like when my nose was broken, but I ended up with a swollen welt underneath my chin that grew instantly; it was becoming huge and it throbbed. I was lying on the floor, startled, and as I looked up he said, "Now get the fuck up, bitch. You're on your way out to the cab with me. Solo at a party? You should know better. No man, huh? I know everyone's woman in there." I was shocked.

"Look, can we talk?" I said. "I have a man. He's waiting for me. Let me get my friend."

"Fuck that," he replied, "fuck your man, and fuck your friend! Where is your man right now? Your friend, she let you go out alone. She's not a friend I would want on my side. Bad move, baby. Let's go. Bitch, you just chose. I don't give a fuck who your man is or who your friends are. No bitch fucks with me! There are no friends in the life."

"Look," I said, pleading, "I have to go!"

"Open your mouth one more time…" he threatened. "Now get the fuck up off the floor so we can get a cab. We're leaving." I had no choice but to say okay. I hadn't anticipated any of this. When we went out the door, he had me by the arm. I thought I could get loose outside, but his grip was so tight I couldn't get away. He hailed a cab.

"Please," I begged, "I can't! I have to go back! I have some money. You take what you want but I'm outta' here. I'm not going with you!" I pulled and tugged to get loose. He warned me again, "You open your mouth one more time and I'll lay you on the street for dead." I just looked at him and knew this man wasn't playing. I stiffened with fear and became as quiet as a church mouse.

"I'm gonna tell you my name once, just once, and you will remember it forever because you're gonna be with me, understand?" I looked up at him with a deliberately alert expression on my face. I wanted to say something, but I couldn't—I knew better. I looked into his eyes, and I saw myself dead. For some reason I knew not to play with this man. The cab dropped us off. We went to his hotel. I don't even remember the name of it. I knew it was around 8th and something. He was familiar with the guy at the door, and the guy at the desk nodded at him, saying nothing as he tossed each of them a fifty-dollar bill. He walked right past them as the door was opened for him. I was silently freaking out and felt that way all during the ride in the elevator. This was a set-up. He wasn't doing this for the first time. He must do it all the time, racking up bitches. He opened the door, and when we went into the room, I saw he had all sorts of leather ties there on the bed in the dark, musty atmosphere. My stomach was in knots. I stood in one spot. The way the room was set up it was obvious he pulled girls here. He took off his mink coat and said, "You stand in the middle of the room, and don't move an inch." The tears were flooding my eyes and were rolling down my face. I was actually trembling with fear; the boldness the street always gave me was crumbling away. He grasped my hair, and was turning me around by pulling it like a cord. He looked and looked. "Baby, I like that, you look good." And every time he'd say that, I wouldn't let myself cry because that seemed to turn him on. But I didn't know if that was the way to go with it, what would happen next. It reminded me of when Anita made me stand still, not moving one inch, only to beat me the next moment for breathing.

He took his custom suede jacket off and I saw the shoulder holster with his gun in it. *I'm dead. I'm fucking dead,* I thought. I envisioned my lifeless body sprawled on the floor in a pool of blood, found in this room like a scene in a murder mystery. "Please," I begged, "I'll be with you! I have no problem with that. I'm a money-maker. Just let me go out and prove it!"

"Did I tell you to open your mouth?" he snarled. Then he stared at me and said, "Do you think I'm stupid? Do you? Do you think I'm a chump? Bitch, don't play me…"

"No, no," I said. I had to figure out what this man was about. If he wanted me to choose and make him money I'd play the game, but he knew I was toying with him. "You think I don't know what you're fucking doing? You're scared, bitch. Your so-called man's not here. I thought you were tougher than that since you took your trim white ass out to the after-hours." That annoyed me, so I stood there and self-assuredly said, "I've been in the life too long to be scared about working."

"Oh really? You're not working now. Are ya? Well, by the time this day ends, you're gonna be so scared of me that you won't walk out of this hotel without calling my name fifty times out of your mouth."

"Okay," I answered, with a twist of sarcasm in my voice that I immediately regretted. He stared at me—if looks could kill!

And then he began in earnest. Still standing in the middle of the room, he took my coat off me and dropped it to the floor. He said, "Bitch, strip the jewelry down and hand it to me!" He kept grabbing my hair just to emphasize that he was hardcore and could easily snap my neck. I could feel the strands ripping from my scalp. He pulled out his knife, held it to my throat, and said, "Bitch, if you don't do what the fuck I tell you, I'm gonna cut your fuckin' throat!" I didn't say anything, thinking it was better to stay silent. Slightly, I tried to shake my head. "You gonna speak? I'm giving you one last chance to say something." Scared to death, I was acutely aware that the wrong move could leave me dead, so I said nothing. "Take your dress off, baby, *now*!" he ordered. He put his other hand around my scrawny neck and squeezed hard. I had to remind myself that he was no trick. I could not fight him. Then I was stripping, taking it off. He retreated to sit on the edge of the bed to watch. He took out his bottle of cocaine and sniffed it from the end of his knife. That's all his intentions were? He just wanted to scare me? What am I, a turn-out? Well, can't take any chances… He used the knife for the coke, repeatedly cutting it into fine powder. He was sitting there, sniffing, laying across the bed watching me get undressed to my bare skin. I had taken everything off and dropped it to the floor. He put my jewelry on the table, closer to him. "That's some nice jewelry," he said. "You must be a good worker to afford shit like this. My baby, Daddy's got it now—this is just a portion of your choosing money." One of the rings had sentimental value. J.N. bought it for me, and I knew I was going to be in trouble if he noticed the ring was gone. The other pieces had the E.B. Horn insignia and my initials etched in them, and none of the jewelry was insured. I looked at him. "Please, that jewelry belonged to my mother! I can make more money than they're worth. Give me a chance!" "Don't think so," he replied. "You walked into the wrong place, your bad!" Sentimentality had no place on the street. "Here's the deal: you stay with me for one year and you can have one piece back at a time." I had nothing to say. Would those pieces be worn one year with this man or did my love for my son and J.N. mean more? I knew that answer.

I could see that his body was perfect. Emotionally, he was cold-blooded. If I moved an inch, he would reprimand me. He had me standing there for the longest time, arms out, looking straight ahead without moving. He was trying to break me down. "I'll tell you when to let your arms down, just keep them up. Let's see just how strong you are!" I was so tired, but I wanted to stay strong. I gazed at the picture on the wall, a house with trees and flowers, a simple scene in an overly ornate gold frame with dust particles on it—a country setting in a diamond-studded horror scene, totally mismatched, like the old-fashioned nightstand and modern lamp. I wished I were in that scene on the wall. My arms were killing me, but my will was tough enough to keep my arms up as long as I had to. He took off his silk boxers and began stroking himself, gently and sensually. I tried not to look directly at him, but my eyes glanced in his direction. Watching him was erotic, and he knew that. He put some coke on the tip of his knife, sauntered over, and told me, "Open wide!" He blew it to the back of my mouth. I swallowed the bitter-tasting powder and felt my mouth and throat going numb. "I'm gonna fuck you to death." He was talking shit from the cocaine, going on and on. I was high, barely listening to what he was saying, in a fog. He did love it when I cried, he told me so, and I held back my tears as much as I could. Every time he thought he could wrench another tear, he'd go "boom" right across my face to get me to feel the sting, and then he'd say, "That's not enough? Let's do the other side, see just how tough you really are." The smarting of each successive slap across my hot and inflamed cheeks was getting to me. I wanted to break and fall to my knees…but I held tough.

The situation was intense—he had me there for what felt like hours already. He didn't even attempt to fuck me, just talked about it. He talked on and on, and was torturing me mentally and physically until my legs were like Jello. Watching him drink his booze, my thirst was unbearable. I was drained, my body and mind weak beyond imagination. Beads of sweat covered my skin. My will and my body were broken. I was inert, a malleable piece of flesh, putty in anyone's hands. I was numb after standing in awkward positions. He decided to tie me up in the corner of the room so he could feel more powerful. He ran the shower then came to get me, placing me in the tub. The water was freezing on my back. It didn't faze me. He didn't know about the cold showers Anita had subjected me to, and the Youth Service Board, where the water was always cold. It felt good because I was so hot. I twisted my neck to drink some of the water. When he caught me with my neck craned, he jolted my head forward. Then, like Anita, he pushed me down in the tub. The way this man used the rope to tie me up was sensual. When he touched my body, I could feel the sexual electricity.

He had worn down my resistance to such a degree that when he took me to the bed the only thing I could do was weep. This man wanted my soul as well as my body. He buried his nose in my long mane of hair, smelling it as he ran his hands over my chest, pinching my nipples ever so lightly with his fingers, and caressing my thighs so that I twitched to his touch. The tears were flowing. And the more I cried, he commanded me to cry more, "Cry, bitch, cry! That's my baby…you know who your daddy is now, don't you?"

"Yes," I replied meekly, in a sexy whisper as he entered me. And although he ripped my insides because he was so rough and large, it felt good. I was soaking wet inside. I was under his power as he flipped my body around, front to back, back to front—again and again—breaking me down further until I was his ragdoll. Some blood stained the sheet from his being so rough.

Even though I was sore and tender from working all week, and he was extremely large, I took it. He exuded confidence as if he knew his penis was powerful. He didn't even want me to suck him, he said, "You ain't biting my dick, bitch, 'cause I'll beat you to an inch of your life." He was clever. He saw that I was so weak he could do whatever he wanted, and when I would enjoy it, he stayed clear of me, tormenting me sexually even more. He told me, "You got a fuckin' weak-ass man, baby, someone who can't handle you. I can tell because your body's crying out for a real man. He ain't no pimp! If you had a real man, your ass wouldn't have been in the after-hours." He knew every inch of me, and I didn't have to open my mouth, ever. "I don't want you to talk to me at all. You will never be satisfied by him, remember that. By the time I get through with you, you'll be begging me for more. You know me now, bitch, I'm Diamond, and you won't ever forget that! Diamond is a girl's best friend, baby, that's me." He had pushed me to the breaking point, and he had me. That was hard to do, but because I was so street, he knew what my weaknesses were. Breaking me down to such a low level where I could relax enough to have sex and enjoy it had taken all this time. He didn't want me to be hardcore with him; he wanted someone he could fuck like a man but pimp like a whore. He had to take me back to the most basic level, the level of a young turn-out, to manipulate my response to him, like a virgin's outpouring of love for her man after her first time. He now knew that I couldn't function, that I was like jelly, that he could just throw and toss me around and I would keep cumming. I couldn't help it. I had never done that in any relationship, whether it was loving or professional. The stimulation had been so intense I was taken to a place I had never been before. Even with all the pimps I'd been with, it never went this far. Never. I could tell this man was a good lover before he ever pimped. Diamond was etched in my memory, but I knew his power over me would last only until I was out of this dismal hotel room and away from him. I had a son waiting for me, and no amount of sexual desire could keep me away from home.

When he put his penis back inside me, his words vibrated in my brain, "I know that you want this now, don't you?" As he stroked me with his penis, pulling his member out slowly, then in slowly, he whispered, "Come to Daddy, baby. Come on." He looked in my face, right into my eyes, and I answered yes as my back arched. "Yes, you do want your daddy, I can tell you do, I'm gonna give you some, baby." He was playing this back and forth verbal iceberg game, drawing his dick across my turn-on points, my belly, my breasts, saying, "I'm gonna stick this knife so far inside you I'm gonna cut your pussy to shreds if you're not mine!" Fear overcame me, and I didn't know whether to believe him or not, especially because he had tied me to the bed and it was difficult to see what was in his hands. Beads of perspiration on my forehead ran down my face. I could feel that my body was drenched. He planted a sexually violent thought in my head—that I was going to be cut; I was frightened, yet aroused at the same time. It was impossible to gauge how serious he was. I didn't know what level I was on. It was just like a rape scene. Then he entered me ever so gently, and he stayed still, with his penis inside me. I didn't think I was going to make it out without a severe beating or some other punishment he had planned, but in some kind of perverse way, the situation was highly intoxicating for us both. I came while he remained still inside my wet walls. No fabricated scene could be as erotic as what was happening. He was so good at what he did that when he finally took the knife away from my side, I no longer felt threatened. He became a man, or what I thought was a man. Still, he hadn't cum. I could tell he wanted to, but he'd stop, and pull back and say, "You want Daddy's cum, baby girl? Not until you are all mine!" He put my ass up in the air while my wrists were tied. My pussy was soaked, and all I knew was that he was slapping me and my body was accepting whatever he did. The pain was exquisite, and as he upped the pain, the more pain I wanted. He'd get to the point where he was about to cum, and he'd pull out again. The very last time he withdrew his dick, he squeezed it and said, "See that, you know what that is?" His cum was squirting, and he rubbed it on my face and lips, turning me on even more, putting his fingers with the taste of him in my mouth. I did not bite. He wanted me to want him, and I did. He wanted to reduce me to my lowest level so I would desire him. He had such control over me that he had full confidence if he left the room I would be his whore. Little did he know me. He touched his lips, dusted with coke, to my tongue to freeze it again, then balanced a rock on his tongue and stuck it inside my pussy to tease me and freeze me there. I felt as though if I wasn't already with someone I loved, I would choose him in a heartbeat. Even though I knew this wasn't reality, it was only a game he was playing, I was still vulnerable, too vulnerable for my own good. Was sex my weakness or was his control that powerful?

He controlled the situation totally, and I was restrained, both physically and mentally. When he had anal sex with me, that's when he was proving his point, that he was a badass. He was into me, yet gentle at the same time, rapping softly in one ear then the other. The sheets were soaked with both of our sweat. He gave just enough pain and pleasure. If I moved my hips toward his penis, he'd pull out and, holding my head, he'd violently pull my hair and jaw open, sticking his tongue deep inside my mouth, taking my breath away. He was all over me. He was good, and I knew and understood the reason women chose him. If I didn't love J.N. and adore my son, I might have chosen him. But then again, I had already decided that being back in the pimp game was out of the question. And this man could fuck me up. The smoothness of his brown skin, the size and shape of his eyes, and the texture of his shiny hair attracted me. His mouth and teeth were perfect. He was a diamond as far as I was concerned, and he knew he was the total package. He even smelled good. If I got away, I'd never want to run into him again. Diamond put me in a place I had never been, stirring up a mixture of fear, sexual excitement, and erotic pleasure that I had not known before, and have not known since.

He didn't leave until he was sure that I wasn't going to do anything else but be with him, and he said he always got his women. "No bitch ever leaves after she's been with me, baby," were his words as he shoved more coke up his nose and mine. He was so sure of himself. He took all my clothes, every piece of clothing, and my shoes as he was leaving. "You won't need these until I get back. When Daddy gets back I'm gonna get you some new threads." He turned my makeup case upside-down and let the cosmetics drop onto the bed. That was the extent of what was left of my things. "Go take a shower and be ready." He got dressed and went through the door. I breathed easier once he'd left, taking a minute to regroup. I couldn't wait to get out of there. I went into the bathroom, washed off my face and body, and even soaked my hair, scrubbing wildly with soap to take away the sex smell. The sudsy water splashed everywhere, forming puddles on the floor. I hurt all over. I covered myself with the big bath towel and stood by the door, listening. After a short time, 15-20 minutes or so, I booked. Looking around, petrified, I kept going; I was terrified and panicking that the man was waiting around the corner in the hallway. *He's downstairs at the elevator—I know it!* I thought. I was wearing a towel, a fucking towel! I was so scared I didn't know what to do next. It was approximately twelve floors down to the lobby. I hadn't paid attention to the numbers. All I knew was that I had to get back to where I had been because Madam would've called J.N. by now. I had been gone for the entire night and part of the morning. It was just before ten a.m. My ass was dead. I was black and blue everywhere, ripped to shit, and weak. My jaw hurt from the punch and had a lump. I was free! I ran past the doorman! I was putty, but I got the nerve and hailed a cab, towel and all. I was in the middle of traffic, cars everywhere in New York City, and I didn't give a shit. I stood in front of a cab, wouldn't let him move, and said, "You *have* to pick me up! My doorman has money, please!" Seeing the desperation on my face, he let me in and turned the heat up. I gave him the address, and he took off. When I arrived at Madam's place, I had the doorman pay for the cab. He recognized me and was concerned. "Oh, baby! What happened?" He was blown away. I went out all dressed up, looking so sharp, and came back with a knot on my jaw, naked, wearing only a towel in the cold. "Baby, I told you, be careful out there!" I gave a short smile, he was so right! As I ran by, I told him I'd catch him later. I went upstairs, shivering, frightened by the possibility of Madam fining me for missing the workday, and a stiff fine at that. Maybe she would just fine me for the clients I missed after I told her…

When I got to the door, madam stopped me at the threshold. I asked, "Please, I have to get some clothes on. I'm freezing. I'll explain…it's not what you think. I hope you didn't call J.N." She was gesturing to me, trying to keep me from saying more. But I continued, "Look, you'll never believe what happened to me…" As I rambled on, I noticed she was suddenly stiffening and pulling back. She herself was afraid. What? "Oh, are there clients in the room?" I politely asked. Maybe there were a couple of girls in the room with dates. No, that wasn't it, I was wrong—it was J.N., in the kitchen, listening to every word. "Ramie," Madam spoke, "I'm sorry. I called him because I was worried about you, and I couldn't get your pal on the phone all night." I walked into the kitchen and J.N. was standing there. I was in shock. My heart fell to the floor. He ripped the towel off me and was looking at my body until I saw his eyes stop at the knot under my jaw, and it was then he slapped me right across the eye. Boom! "But you don't understand…" I begged as I fell down into the cabinet. "Don't even try to explain yourself," he said.

"You have a Chinese date waiting in the bedroom, and there isn't a girl for him. Go to him. Make up the money you've lost."

"No please, I can't!" I begged. "Please, you have to hear me out J.N.! I can't do him, I can't!"

"You did whomever all night so you will do it again, now!"

There I was, buck naked, beat up, feeling really awful, and he was telling me to work. The madam wiped off my face with a cold cloth and rubbed some cream on me. "Get in the shower quick—two minutes. Go," she said, "you can do it." Sure, what choice did I have? I had no choice. All they cared about was the money, not my well-being. I went in the room and was crying the whole time the Asian guy was on top of me, fucking like a rabbit; he loved every bit of it. He was screaming, "Oh, oh, oh yes! I cum, I cum!" He must have thought that I was underage without any makeup on. He never asked me about my bruises. The scene was horrible. I felt so degraded having to do this trick that I was taken back in memory again, feeling sick to my stomach, the smell of Chinese food seeping from his pores onto me. Now I had to walk back to the kitchen to face J.N. But Madam was the only one in the kitchen now, and she nodded for me to go to the living room. "He wants you in there right now."

"I have to wash," I told her.

"He wants you right in there. Wash later." I went and stood in front of him.

"You have fun?" he snarled.

"No!" I shrieked.

"Go wash and get your clothes on. We're going back to Boston. This is your last time in the city." J.N. looked and acted just like a real pimp—a new role for him. He had learned the game and was using it now. I was the one who facilitated it, turning the tables on myself. It was obvious he didn't believe me; he thought I freaked with some man willingly, but if I did why would I give up my things and get my ass kicked? He didn't want to hear that I had been kidnapped, and I couldn't convince him, even though I had walked through the door wearing nothing but a towel wrapped around my naked body. I was relieved to hear that the madam didn't fine me for the entire day, just three hundred dollars. J.N. told me she said I was her best in the room, but then he added, "You fucked up, you won't be coming back! You better tell me everything that happened because I'm going to find that man who was with you, and I'm going to kill him after he gives back your stuff!" The madam gave J.N. all my money. "No please!" I pleaded. "This guy is crazy! He packs… You can't go find him, just leave him alone, J.N., please!"

"Now you're protecting this motherfucker?"

"No, no!" I cried.

"So, Libbe," he said sarcastically, "Madam just told me what you were wearing when you left, and now, obviously, he has all your jewelry and your fur. Because you came in with nothing, fucking naked!" Madam went into another room with J.N. to speak privately, and when they came out he was calmer. She told me to be cool, to stop talking because it was making the shit worse. She intended to dig up what she could about Diamond on her own and then pass on the information to me later. She told me not to forget to call her. The trip home with J.N. was tense and unpleasant despite Madam speaking to him about the likelihood of my story being true, and had she not discussed the kidnapping with him his reaction would have been worse than it was. After getting home, I was back on track working; the heat on the streets had let up.

Diamond did come to Boston looking for me, with all my ID's, my license, and credit cards. He showed them around. No one said anything to him, but they gave me the heads up. I cancelled everything and got a new license. He was looking for me, but he never found me—thanks to wigs, etc., and everything was listed under an old address. Thank God J.N. never knew who he was and couldn't find him. I remember the words Diamond told me, that "Cum is thicker than blood," an old saying I had heard from other pimps. Even though the saying is true in all walks of life, it is particularly driven home in the sexuality of women in the life.

J.N. was slow in trusting me after that incident; he had issues about me working out of town now. His new threat was that he was going to pimp me out. His tone became exceedingly domineering. Hanging out with so many players wasn't helping him—he was getting high often, and that only complicated our issues. I wore a wig for a while to camouflage my identity from Diamond, and he didn't have my address in Mattapan, only the Medford address, where if he went he might have gotten into big trouble. He must have given up; he left town. After being with Diamond, I couldn't help thinking about Anita's total control over me when I was a child. So many of my issues came to light during that night and day with him. The reason I chose to have men controlling me became clear. I realized that a man had to have ultimate control over me for me to respond sexually. Would that ever change?

CHAPTER FIFTY

At Home

The episode with Diamond passed. He was no longer trying to locate me, and I stopped wearing the wig to disguise myself. J.N. had enrolled in his second year of school and was busy registering for his courses. I brought the best take-out chicken to him from Fontaine's in West Roxbury. I had to do my trips before school began. I managed my trips to the South and to the Bahamas with Candy, and even another New York booking with a different madam. I had to calculate there because J.N. was monitoring me carefully. I was able to do some out-calls for the madam I was working for when I left New York with him. I was careful not to run into Diamond. J.N. bothered me about Diamond for several months after the kidnapping, and I knew it was best to say nothing or he would go crazy. I never told him the whole truth about the man. The memory of the relentless mental and physical stimulation I experienced with Diamond stayed with me like a good movie. J.N. had to go down on me for me to reach a climax, which was always inferior to the sensation I had when he was inside me. He overfilled the space inside me, and although the sensation was spectacular, it was almost too much and the experience was not as intense as it was with Diamond. J.N. pressured me for information about him, particularly when I went back to New York. I reassured him I'd never go out at night like that again, not to worry! And I didn't.

Our money situation was good. R. Lee would be in school soon. J.N. was adjusting to Brandeis University and socializing a lot more. Our son was spending time at the reverend's house, loving every minute of it. He was coming home with stories about what he did while he was there. He loved Nana's home cooking; her lemon cakes were his favorite. R. Lee went to the Methodist Church with the reverend and his wife on Sundays. They were like family to my R. Lee, the grandparents he never had. J.N. drove the '73 Riviera GS and I drove the '71—I loved those cars! I want to get a few more. We acquired a new addition to the household, a dog we named Muggsey, who was a cocker spaniel and basset hound mix. The name fit him. He was precious. He was a rescue, black, with long ears, stocky legs, and a long tail, an ideal and affectionate companion for my son. We were a family.

My relationship with J.N. was the longest I'd ever had, and I wanted it to continue forever. I just hoped being at school would soften his attitude back to normal. He asked me to marry him on numerous occasions and I always refused, not only because of my fears of being married, given the profession I was in, but also my hang-ups from the past…plus his forever cheating. It was becoming harder and harder to be in the life and to be in love. Sometimes when I came home from work, I felt dirty and didn't want to be touched. I distanced myself. Smoking reefer alleviated my guilt at those times, but it was just a crutch, a temporary fix. I was getting in touch with my feelings of love, although I pushed him away in other areas. This shift cracked my armor and often caused me to cringe whenever a client touched me—definitely not a good thing for business, so I smoked more joints to feel more relaxed. I knew I had to get the girls working, but I made more money when I did the clients myself because they always chose me. I still made great money from sending the dates to the girls working for me. I had plenty of customers.

J.N. was enthusiastic about school, and he was doing well. Getting away from his street friends helped him get used to student life and back to his square lifestyle, but at the same time, he was becoming increasingly jealous of where I went and with whom. The influence of his street friends was always negative when he talked to them on weekends. Some days were worse than others. I didn't visit him at school. I didn't belong there; I was too street to fit in. He was on the fringes himself, torn between his friends and the life. Plus, he wanted to know where I was every minute.

I had to work to pay for everything; J.N. was using up lots of money. When Christmastime came, I lavished my son and J.N. with gifts. I gave R. Lee things I couldn't have imagined when I was a child, and J.N. was given jewelry to fit into the nightlife. R. Lee was spoiled by the amount of material things he received, but he lacked what he truly wanted, which was more attention from J.N. and I. We were so busy, and did not realize the harm we were doing. I didn't know how to give him what he needed all the time. We were always occupied with work and school, and he became more aggressive; he had always been hyper, but now he was acting out. The reverend and his wife calmed R. Lee somewhat by providing more of the nurturance he needed, but there were times J.N. had to swaddle him in a blanket to keep him still and relax him. He would squirm until he had tired himself out, and then I would rub his head, my hand gently petting his hair until he immediately fell asleep—it was Mommy's touch he yearned for. I now regret having lost so many loving moments we could have shared, but at the time I didn't realize what was missing. Because I lacked affection as a child, I didn't understand what he was feeling. I tried to hug him and tell him every day that I loved him. It was easy when he was a baby. I thought my perpetual excessive energy contributed to his hyperactivity because when I was pregnant, I was always moving, never stopping to rest. And R. Lee, to this very day, never stops.

I had developed a close friendship with Mendy, from Simco's hot dog place, who was right down the street from Tennis Road. He and his brothers owned the business. I confided in him, and he was like a father to me. He said he would rent the empty store on the side of his restaurant to me if I wanted it, in part because he was trying to help me get out of the business I was in. I suggested taking it after Christmas, at the beginning of the New Year. I always liked trying new things, so why not this idea? I had the money to start up a venture for us. J.N. was good at building and woodworking and could make things. He did odd stuff around the house when needed, and I had always wanted to design…still do. We would primarily be creating frames for waterbeds. I could see myself in this business and felt confident that I could make it work. J.N. said that he had a friend from Africa who was a master carpenter, and he could help. With the two of them building the furniture, and my crazy designs, the idea might pan out. Although I had the money to invest, we needed to save a few more dollars to cover both J.N.'s school money and the bills from the store. J.N. could work when he was not in class, and his friend said he could work more regular hours. We had a plan, and a good one. The spot where the store was located couldn't have been better, Blue Hill Ave. at Simco's. So may people stopped there.

Jennifer and I were talking more often, like grownups—not like me as a kid, her as a grownup. I still avoided her house on holidays and went to J.N.'s family instead. Sometimes she would come with her friend to visit me at the apartment in Mattapan, and they were always entertained by R. Lee and his antics. Her daughter was the cutest child, but she had severe asthma and Jennifer was always on guard, continually bringing her to the hospital in a panic, fearing that she might stop breathing. Jennifer's panic was a factor most of the time, but she had no idea that it escalated from her worrying. Although Christmas had gone by, I was overindulging my son by giving him things almost daily; I felt guilty and insecure in my role as a mother. There were wonderful people taking care of him, yet when I left him to go to work and he was awake, tears would roll down his cheeks as he said, "Mommy, Mommy, please don't go! I want to play with you. Stay home with me!" I can feel his hurt even today, how could I leave my boy? I was the only source of income for the family—what else could I do? When J.N. and I first met, I rejected marriage and the norm of having a man support me. Damn, I was stupid. I hoped next year would be better once the store took off, bringing in an income so I could be home more often. I spoke to Mendy, and he said not to worry, people would come into the store and buy because it was the first of its kind in the area to sell waterbeds and custom-made furniture. And they did come in, and it got really busy. But at the same time as J.N. was taking orders, he was screwing as many of the single women customers as he could. Who knows how many? Maybe he was screwing the married ones as well.

J.N. enjoyed hunting with his West Medford friends on his days off. More time away… He liked guns, all sorts of guns, and all of them legal. He had a permit to carry. I even had a black and silver .22 automatic anniversary issue rifle for myself. R. Lee was into everything, and, of course, we hid the guns where he couldn't possibly reach them: on a tall shelf in a closet, pushed way to the rear so that he could never get to it without a ladder (which we did not have). He never saw them. I believed that guns were not the problem, but who had them and what they did with them always would be. The more violence shown to children—initially only on TV, then video games, and now also on their phones, computers, and pads—the greater their chance of copying it. They don't see how death really is, and the older you get, most of the time you feel it. Young people are braver. We screened what R. Lee was allowed to watch on TV. The only violence he could see was karate with Bruce Lee, which his dad liked too.

J.N. would bring the rabbit carcasses back home after hunting to clean and cook, and although I wasn't enthusiastic about it, our son didn't really make the connection between J.N.'s hunting and the dead rabbits. I chose not to tell R. Lee about his dad's hunting because I believed that killing animals should only be done as a means of survival and not solely for sport. The whole culture of hunting and guns was foreign to me. And, as I learned later from the West Medford girlfriends of his friends, the sport of hunting was more an opportunity for J.N. to be out with his buddies and square girls for a night or two. Sex parties. It figures. All kinds of information surfaced, but I didn't dwell on who he was screwing anymore; it made me too crazy. I kept busy with our most important projects: building the waterbed store into a success and raising our son. And hopefully, J.N. would achieve his goal of becoming a doctor.

Taking care of J.N., R. Lee, and our wild and crazy dog, Muggsey, was a job in itself. I was working constantly, and despite the fact that I was spreading myself thin, it was a liberating feeling to have a business apart from the life that made money on its own. I designed several beds and was actually proud of myself, but I never got any recognition for my designs, only J.N. got the praise. One was a special heart-shaped bed that was sold to a fella from the life. He had lots of girls and wanted it for his Marlborough Street basement apartment, a prestigious place to live in Boston's Back Bay, then and now. The weight of the waterbeds made it necessary to put them on solid floors, and the basement was perfect. J.N. was making the beds fairly fast with his friend, the master carpenter, and Muggsey stayed with them at the waterbed store while they were working, always getting into mischief—dragging things about, chewing on electrical cords, and getting totally covered with sawdust. But he was such a cool dog!

I was hopelessly in love with J.N., and my son was growing by leaps and bounds. It was almost time for him to go to first grade, and I wanted to enroll him in a Hebrew school to learn about the Jewish faith because my mother Rose was religious, and she would have wanted it. I wasn't overly religious and shunned certain aspects of organized religion, like having to contribute money to a church or temple to be able to pray there. Why? I believed in prayer but resented the politics. For my son's sake, I enrolled him in an Orthodox religious school in Milton, and he was set to go. For the past year, R. Lee had been attending a Methodist Church in Roxbury with the reverend and his family, a place he loved. Even though he couldn't carry a tune, he was enthusiastic about singing the hymns, and would sing them at home, as well as the popular song "Mrs. Jones," screeching it as loud as he could, off-key every time. Every time I hear that song I can hear him and see his face and big brown eyes trying to sing his heart out.

The largest detriment to our happiness as a family was my working in town every day. J.N. had acquired a taste for what my money could buy and didn't try to stop me like he used to do at the beginning of our relationship. I paid for everything, including gifts for everyone in both of our families, especially Jennifer, who got lavish ones. Our lives were still shifting, though, and I sensed something wasn't quite right. J.N. was becoming friendly with Jaff, the neighbor across the street, whom I already knew. Jaff's cousin, a kind of cute, young, light-skinned girl, visited him fairly often, which raised my suspicions about J.N. I was relieved when my friend Coco moved into one of the apartments across the street, next to the reverend's house with her younger sister because then I had someone in the neighborhood to hang with after work when I was alone. Coco and I were tight. She was a pretty, dark-skinned black girl, a hard worker, and great with kids. R. Lee adored her. We would go into work together at night. She loved R. Lee and called him her baby; her brother's son used to play with him. He had light skin and a huge, blondish-brown, floppy, curly afro. He was so handsome. One night, Coco told me that J.N. was across the street at Jaff's. I wasn't surprised when she said he was there all the time. My eyes were open, but I was never at home to catch him. By the time I found out he was there, he had left. J.N. approached me one night, asking me for extra cash to go to Canada for business, something to do with the waterbeds, a trip to get new ideas and possibly order some mattresses. I agreed. I didn't follow the business closely enough and didn't know the number of orders we had. I believed him and gave the trip a nod without a problem, and with plenty of cash, a few thousand...still trying to trust him.

I enrolled R. Lee in Hebrew school at that time, and not long after, I received a call to come to the school. It was an emergency. I panicked, thinking something awful had happened to my son. I arrived there in a flash, and the rabbi greeted me. He reassured me R. Lee was okay and invited me into his office, explaining that the children were asked to sing a song they knew. My outgoing son's hand was first to go up, saying, "I know a song!" He filled his lungs with air, getting ready to burst into song, and as loudly as he could, and in front of an Orthodox rabbi and the class, shouted out, "Jesus loves me, this I know!" The rabbi and the students were shocked. He was immediately taken out of the class. The offense was so serious in the rabbi's eyes that R. Lee was forbidden to continue at the school. Before we left, the rabbi asked me how my son had learned the song. I told him about R. Lee and the reverend and his wife, that he called them Grampy and Nana, and they took care of him while I was at work. That song put an end to his education at the Milton Jewish school. My understanding was that they could not have R. Lee there because having a non-Jewish influence was contrary to their religious teachings. Later, we went to Temple Israel, a Reform temple that was far more liberal. I told him he was not allowed to sing any more church songs, especially ones with Jesus in it. R. Lee saw the new Hebrew school, and he liked it much better, so after discussing why he could never sing that song again, my son's religious training resumed…with no more "For the Bible tells me so."

J.N. went on his excursion to Canada with his pockets full. I checked on his partner, who was assembling the bed, and kept Muggsey with me until J.N. came back. He was supposed to be gone a couple of days. Two days turned into five days, and he never gave me a reason he was staying. But he asked me to send him more money for expenses via Western Union. I sent the money and later kicked myself for not making a phone call to find out if there actually was a waterbed convention.

Usually, I worked during the week and sometimes took off Saturdays and Sundays to be with my son. This weekend, I decided to work Saturday night because of the extra money I'd sent J.N. And instead of working with me, Coco took care of R. Lee and her nephew. Katie walked with me to Boylston Street to stand by the Sugar Shack before going to the bar—she was flirtatious and loved talking shit to the players who were hanging outside. I had no time for that because I had to catch a date. She left me to go back to the 663 Lounge, her comfort zone, with her Miller beer, and I stayed on. The early play was getting ready to start soon and the people were lining up out front, moving slowly to go inside the Wilbur Theater. I looked at the cars to my left to watch for some potential dates—and there was J.N., in our '73 Riviera GS, driving leisurely down Boylston Street with Jaff's square cousin beside him in the front seat! "Holy shit! What the fuck?" I shrieked. And I went ballistic, with all the players and girls watching me as I ran up to the car and kicked her window as hard as I could with my high heels. I wanted to break the glass. The traffic had stopped; he couldn't go anywhere. I went to his side to try to break that window, and I saw his suitcase and hers in the back seat. She had been with him in Canada, using my money to have a good time! Oh shit! This bitch was spending my hard-earned money! I should have known better. J.N. was seeing her all this time, and I didn't know it. Jaff never mentioned it, not even one word, and he was my so-called friend. Jaff was hinting that I should go out with him, so why would he do that? Hmmm… It was his cousin J.N. was with while he was always flirting with me. Now it all made perfect sense. J.N. had too much play in him. I knew he was still seeing that bitch Patsy too—David J., Mark's brother, had let that one drop one night when he came to the bar drunk. I wondered how many more there were. I knew he would go to the house because I had threatened them, saying I was going back to get a gun and shoot them both. By the time I went to Chinatown to get my car and found Katie to tell her I was leaving, he had already gone back to the house and taken his guns and my rifle to the waterbed store. Even Muggsey was gone.

I went to the store stark raving mad and broke the front glass window to get in. I felt as though I could have killed him. He hid in the back room, behind a closed door, telling me to calm the fuck down. Instead, I told him to stay away from me. He swore it would never happen again. Liar! I knew in my heart he was lying. I should have known better, but my love for him was so blind. It was apparent I had to keep an even more watchful eye on him, but what kind of a relationship would that be? I knew it would be difficult because he had freedom to go wherever he wished while I was stuck making money, stuck in the room, stuck in my house answering phones, stuck in jail. It always came down to my stuck lifestyle. J.N. continued screwing girls behind my back; all of them were squares. It was easier now with the business, and the girls at Brandeis, plus the West Medford chicks—he was having a ball and I was working as hard as ever. Why didn't I leave sooner? The pattern was so ingrained it was impossible for me to break. And I was afraid to raise R. Lee without a father. After suffering not having parents of my own, I didn't want the same for my son.

The whole scene went out of control. The police were involved because they had to answer the call for the alarm going off, and J.N. told them that he had broken the window himself moving some lumber. I left before they arrived. I spoke with Mendy, who had heard about my wild attempts to shatter all the windows from his brother, and he calmed me down. I needed a break. I had to get out of town. I decided to go away to Atlantic City with Bobby Jo, another working buddy. She reminded me of Mae West. Bobby Jo was tall and busty; she was a Double D redhead. R. Lee was safe, and J.N. was staying clear of me. James Brown was playing in Atlantic City. I knew his manager, Walter, and he asked us over, so we all met up there after work. The cocaine was flowing in the room. I told Bobby Jo I didn't want to stay for any of the after parties. I needed cash not parties, and besides, I was still upset about J.N.'s trip to Canada, so I wasn't in the mood. My primary issue with partying was that we weren't with our men and it could be a problem. Bobby Jo was wild and wanted to party anyway. I wasn't up for hanging with the crew. It took a lot of coaxing to get Bobby Jo's ass outa there. Finally, we left and walked up and down the streets, catching dates. Bobby Jo's boobs were humongous, and with her flaming red hair she attracted men like flies on sweet paper—they stopped short in traffic to find out how much we wanted. She caught most of the tricks. I made some good money too. We talked about working the Bahamas. We ended up going back to Boston so she could pay her man and I could see R. Lee and pay Nana, and from there we decided to go to the Bahamas.

Two weeks later, we were on our way to a hotel on the beach. The men at the hotel watched us from the first day we were there. The sun was so strong that it burned my skin to almost third-degree burns the first day out. And, on top of that, the piggish manager of the hotel took every opportunity he could to try to corner me in my room every night. Eventually, the manager succeeded in getting a feel. He grabbed me, but I refused to give in to anything else. It reminded me of a night when both of us were in Atlantic City and two cops had their minds set on getting blowjobs. I refused, and they threatened us with jail. I couldn't have cared less but Bobby Jo took care of them—her choice. She probably saved our necks. The hotel manager in the Bahamas watched us work the bars, so he knew we made money; he just wanted a free ride. He had his front desk clerk accuse me of not paying my bill during our stay when, in fact, I had paid it in full, in cash. His plan was to detain me in the Bahamas until he got what he wanted, and so I told him to meet me in the room. Meanwhile, Bobby Jo got caught buying herb from some islanders, and the police took her off to jail. I never saw her after that, not in the Bahamas or back in Boston. I had to leave or I would be next. They threatened me. I did not need to be set up, and it seemed they were trying to pin me. I had to service the asshole manager to get off the island. I also offered to do it hoping it might help get Bobby Jo out of trouble. The manager had observed us bringing our tricks back to the rooms our whole stay. On top of not leaving with my friend, I had to pay that fucking asshole extra money. And even after giving him extra sex, Bobby Jo did not get out. I had no rights in the secret life I was living, and certainly no rights on that island. I never did find out what happened to Bobby Jo, no one seemed to know. When I got back I spoke to Bobby Jo's man and gave him all the information I knew, and he took it from there. I hoped that her man would be able to get her out, and to this day I still wonder what happened to her. Not only was that a tough time, leaving a friend, coming back to Boston to face J.N. was another problem.

CHAPTER FIFTY-ONE

A Shocking Crime on Tennis Road

After sharing back and forth with Coco about my trip and J.N.'s cheating, he and I reconciled—even though I knew his affairs wouldn't end. I lost trust in him. I wondered if that was what love was all about, the constant worry that someone was going to cheat on you. Are there any great relationships out there? I want one…

Wood, metal, and stone fascinated me, and I felt as though I wanted to create things out of these materials. Every time I went to the waterbed store, I would play with the discarded pieces of wood and make geometrical designs with them. I loved to repurpose things. The urge to design was buried somewhere deep inside me. I fought to find expression. There were so many things I wanted to do but suppressed for lack of time and confidence in my ability. All the men I chose only wanted me for money and sex—nothing more, or so I believed. Robin and Eric, and my clients, told me I was talented, yet if I were so clever why didn't any of the tricks offer to help me find a good job? The clients wanted me under their desks giving them blowjobs. I would always have to pay a high price.

I had worked with Coco the entire week. We were home late every night. She was always up really early to take care of her nephew. R. Lee usually slept in until eight a.m. I didn't have anything planned this particular day. I was sleeping in when the phone rang and rang. I finally got up and answered it. It was about five-thirty a.m. "Shit." J.N. hadn't gotten up to go to the store or school yet. "Hello?" I said, in a tired, raspy voice. At the other end of the line was a terrified voice, whispering, "Libbe! Libbe!" That jarred me.

"Speak up! Who is this?" I asked.

"It's me," she said, using her real name. It was Coco, the name she used for her in-town job. "What's wrong?" I was slowly waking, just not fully conscious yet. "Libbe, you have to come over here right away! It's important!" She was hysterical.

"I'll be right there!" I threw on whatever was handy and shook J.N.'s shoulder to let him know where I was going, then I booked out the front door, running across the street.

I knew by the panic in her voice that it had to be something serious. Maybe someone got arrested or had broken into her apartment. I couldn't imagine what it was. Coco lived on the first floor, and as I approached her door, she opened it immediately, like she was watching for me, and pulled me in as if she were on the lookout, hiding from someone. As she shut the door, I noticed her eyes were bloodshot. It was obvious she had been crying. She appeared to be frightened of something, and said, "Come, come with me, you have to see this! I can't believe it!" I didn't know what I was getting into. Baffled by her strange behavior, I followed. "What's wrong?" I asked, "Tell me, where are we going?" We walked through the kitchen to her back door.

"Be prepared," she warned me. We pushed the door with all our strength, but could only move it enough to peer out, and there on the floor of the back hallway was a large body with a plastic bag tied tightly over its head. "Oh shit!" I said. "Who is it? Did you check for a pulse?" She shook her head no. We had to push harder, the feet were pinned against Coco's kitchen door.

I told Coco we had to go out there to check if the woman was still alive and remove the bag if she was. "I can't touch her," she said, "I'm too scared." I told her I would do it and to call the police immediately. "Coco, go! Hurry!" She didn't want to get into trouble, and I assured her she wouldn't as long as she had nothing to do with it. 'We have to get help!" She wasn't even sure that the body belonged to a woman because she was too frantic to really look closely and the face was turned to the floor, the body laid almost on its side and stomach. I could see that it was a woman's body. I went to her side and felt for a pulse—there wasn't any! Her hand was cold, and I assumed she must have been dead for some time. The corpse didn't frighten me as much as the police did. Like Coco, I was nervous about what they would think if they ran our names; it would be obvious what we did for a living, and they might view us as suspects, criminals because of what we were, not as human beings.

When the police and the homicide division arrived, they asked question after question: our names, addresses, and places of work. Coco said she worked for her uncle. I felt liberated to be able to say that I owned a business, a legitimate business, even if I had a record in town, a business I could be proud of in the eyes of society. Finally, I was accepted as a human being, they addressed me as "Miss"; funny, but I felt as though I had clout because of the way they said that. "Oh, I know your landlord," one of the officers said. "Mendy, what a great guy!" "Yes, he is, we're friends." Unless they checked further, no one would know that I had a record, and they didn't catch on to Coco either. We had to go to the apartment upstairs when the police discovered that the woman was a relative of the occupants there, and I had to call J.N. to tell him I wouldn't be back anytime soon and that he should dress R. Lee and take him to Nana's house. We spent hours there, and at the end were instructed by the detectives not to discuss the case until it had been resolved. Coco wasn't comfortable staying in her apartment while the murderer was still loose. I offered for her to stay with me, but instead, she went to her brother's house, where she could watch his son and her younger sister. It wasn't too long before the truth came out: it was the woman's brother-in-law who killed her. What a nightmare—a member of her own family killed her because of an affair. I thought these kinds of things happened only in the life or the movies. Coco came back to live in her apartment despite the creeps she got whenever she opened the door to the back hallway, thinking that the dead woman's spirit lingered there. Life went on as usual, with our frequent get-togethers.

J.N. was partying at Brandeis with his new friends. He was staying in his dorm room and wouldn't be coming home. "I have to study late," was his reason. I went back to my grueling schedule of work and more work, giving out money left and right. I could tell J.N. didn't want my type at his school. I stayed away so there was no conflict. He was taking drives to Cape Cod with his friends on weekends, and I was paying for it all. At the time, I didn't know he was meeting Patsy there. Muggsey would come with me just about everywhere. We had to take him because when we left him alone at the shop, he would chew on the electric cords dangling from the walls when they were still plugged into the sockets. I had a crazy life, a crazy dog that liked to be zapped, a daredevil son, and a cheating man.

I don't think there was a single day before I went out to the Zone when I didn't feel afraid, especially as R. Lee got older. I had been extremely uptight of late. Whether it was the man I was with, the possibility that I wouldn't make enough money to get by, the fear that the wrong trick might get hold of me and I'd end up dead and my son would have no one, or that the cops would pick me up and arrest me—there have always been fears, big and small. Even now I have fears. I want some peace of mind. From childhood on, throughout my entire life, I've had worries and fears, but when I got out there on the street and started my day, my fears would disappear the more I got into it, same as later. The money healed over any wound. Being able to earn more money, much more than the average worker, made me feel like I was a hero in my world. I set my goals high and was living on the edge every day. Even though my life has been full of disappointments and tragedies, I am grateful.

While I was pregnant with R. Lee, I bumped into my first man in the life, W.D., at the 663 Lounge. Then I saw him again. J.N. was at school and R. Lee was playing with his friends in the street on Tennis Road. Muggsey was about to give birth to her puppies. There, in front of our house one fall day, was W.D. He told me he knew someone who lived on Tennis Road. He appeared different than before. I was surprised. We talked, and he confided in me that when we were together he was putting himself through school. He offered to pay me back the money—I had put him through college! Oh, my god! During the short time I was with him he had used the street money to pay for his education. Well, what the…! When I first saw him that day in the lounge, he said he wanted to marry me and take care of both my baby and I. I told him I didn't know him in that way and it would never work, although I appreciated the gesture. He let me know he really did care about me when I chose him. I remembered his monstrous indifference to my turn-out gang rape and how he brutally attacked me with the wire hanger, and I told him I could not go backward, only forward. He understood. I told him I didn't want his money. It was so long ago, and I was happy that he had put the money to such good use, even though I had gone through hell to earn it. I was also happy he was well, and not as bothered by his sickle cell anemia as when we were together. He told me he had gotten married since I last saw him. After I explained to R. Lee that I had known W.D. a long time ago, they played together. He came around from time to time for a while. I lost contact with him because I was too busy paying attention to J.N., chasing him down the streets of West Medford. I was so in love, and I couldn't imagine being with anyone else besides him. I lived my life for everyone I loved.

Lately, when J.N. would come home, he would walk around the house like he was lost. I had been aware of some subtle differences in his behavior, but now he was getting overtly paranoid and weird. Perhaps he was using drugs. I had no idea what the problem was. He asked me to drive behind him to school one night because he believed someone was following him. I tried to assure him that no one was watching him, but he insisted it was true. I stayed in back of him until we reached the school. He asked me to wait until he went through the door. I had no problem with that, although it seemed strange. I started telling him about my day before he went to his dorm room, catching him up on R. Lee, but his face was blank and he didn't respond, he just walked away. Maybe he had been smoking weed, so I didn't panic at that point. I walked him to the door of his dorm room and stood there. After a moment, he said he was okay and told me to leave. When I went to kiss him goodbye, he pulled back as if he were scared of me. He slipped into his room, closing the door behind him. I stood there, puzzled. I got his roommate on the phone later when I was back at home, and he said that J.N. was sleeping. "Is he okay?" I asked. "Do you know if he's planning to come home later tonight or in the morning?" He didn't know if J.N. was going to be staying at the dorm or not. This was the beginning of my perilous ride through hell with J.N. What I was about to encounter was totally unexpected.

When we spoke on the phone the next day he jabbered, mentioning the names of people I didn't know and refusing to talk about R. Lee at all, as if he never existed. That topped it off. "Are you all right?" I asked. "Did you smoke a joint or take some acid?" He didn't answer, and his lack of emotion was beginning to concern me. R. Lee and I decided to go to J.N.'s basketball game, and even that was uncomfortable, although I toughed it out. R. Lee enjoyed watching his dad, and his odd behavior didn't seem to affect him. Whenever I went to his dorm to drop off food and money, J.N. would say he was busy, and I'd just leave his things with his roommates. And when I called, his roommates would say he wasn't in. He was better off in the life than in school if this is what's happening to him; he was completely unresponsive, with a blank look on his face all the time now. I wasn't sure how to approach it yet, but if it kept going on like this, I knew I had to see what was up.

CHAPTER FIFTY-TWO

Bay State Road

J.N. finally called and told me he would be home sometime in the evening. He sounded normal. But for the present, he said, he had to stay at school almost all the time because of the amount of studying he needed to do. He encouraged me to go to the games on Fridays with our son, which made R. Lee enormously happy. I was relieved that he asked about his son. Maybe it was just a fluke that he was acting the way he was, or exhaustion. I asked him if he had any tests, and he said he did and was pressed to do them all on time. Well, that must have been the reason for his odd behavior. When R. Lee and I had gone to his dad's games in the past, R. Lee loved watching his father play and would mimic him.

I was getting ready to go to work and had plans to meet Robin and Eric. He was playing with the Charmers at the time and was going to meet us later when he was done playing his gig. Eric was similar to J.N. in character, although Eric was more street from hanging with all the fellas in the clubs, plus, he had relatives out in the life. One of his relatives was Don K., who always hung out on Boylston Street. All in all, though, both Eric and J.N. were square at heart. Eric liked getting extra money from Robin because it allowed him to practice additional hours with the band, buy suits for performances, and make more recordings.

Robin's real name was Ruthie, and no one knew that except for Eric, J.N., and me. She was brought up in the Jewish faith and lived in Revere, near the beach, where there was a large population of Jews. I met her mother once, and it appeared to me that she wasn't the nurturing kind, and she seemed to have mixed feelings about her own daughter. She was bitter and lonely. Her many opinions were voiced loudly. It was obvious that she was an overly strict woman. I thought she would have wanted her daughter around to visit but not by the way she acted. Her low, scratchy, smoker's voice reminded me of Mrs. Taffee. She was an older, lower-to-middle-class Jewish woman who dressed terribly and had mostly used furniture and old-fashioned decorations in her dark, dreary apartment. Robin's mother, like Mrs. Taffee, was abrupt with me from the moment I stepped into her place, and I felt insulted by her manners and the abusive way she spoke to her daughter. Both Mrs. Taffee and Robin's mom never cracked a smile. Robin was a stripper most of the time at her spot, the Downtown Lounge, where she felt at home. She could not wait to hit the stage, high as a kite to show off. She was insecure about herself and didn't have confidence, even after she swallowed her diet of five Valiums per day along with three or four other pills. After a couple of drinks she strutted her wares, and never passed her reflection without having to look at herself. She loved men's attention. She went to the bathroom every ten minutes to sniff a line of coke and put more makeup on top of the ten layers she had already applied, as did many of the girls. She was wild, and I loved her.

Eric had a deep, sexy voice, like Otis from the Temptations. He was as flirtatious as Robin, and they were a perfect match. J.N. clicked with both of them, and we often got together for barbecues at parks or in our backyards with Katie and her friends. I then met Sherri through Katie, and we all got along. Robin enjoyed our parties, particularly when Sherri came because both of them danced. I loved to cook for summer barbeques, and also for the holidays.

It was real busy in town, and Ruthie and I were catching doubles in the bars. I went out singly to catch dates before the end of the evening for us. Robin had a crown on one of her teeth, and it would drive me to distraction when she glued it in her mouth instead of getting up in the daytime to go to a dentist—she was one lazy girl in the daylight. One night, we were standing in the doorway of Enrico's when two nice-looking young guys pulled up, enticing us to get into their car to go to our place. I had a bad feeling about them; when I looked closer, I could see how young they were and didn't want to drive with them in their car. "Nah, no way," I told Rob, but she smiled, soaking up the attention, and purred, "He's so cute."

I retorted, "Cute is not money!" I should have relied on my instincts. As she fluttered about, Robin was insistent that we go with them, seeming to take a real fancy to one of them. We told them how much it would cost and they agreed, saying, "Hop in!" "Not yet. Show me your money," I said, and one of them did. Still, I refused to get into their car, and I told them to follow us in our car, which didn't seem to please either of them. They tried hard to coax Robin into their car, telling her they would drive us back, and arguing that it didn't make sense to take two cars. "No, Robin, come on…I'll drive with her thanks…" Again, I told them to follow us, and as we walked over to the parking lot on LaGrange Street, I told Robin I was leery of these two and thought they were trouble. She disagreed with me, insisting they were so nice, and suggesting that we go to her place on Bay State Road. Once we were off LaGrange Street, I drove in front of them. I told Robin to take down their plate number and leave it in the car. She wrote down the number on a piece of paper, all the while looking at herself in the mirror. I knew in my gut there was something wrong and should never have agreed to it, but I didn't want to leave Robin alone with them.

Arriving at the apartment, I told them to park in front of the building while we parked slightly down the street. The feeling that I shouldn't go persisted. As we walked back to the entrance, the trees were still and the air was chilly. I loved Boston's brownstone buildings. We gossiped until we were in front her apartment. "Hey guys, all set. Do you have your money?" I asked again. Both said that they did, and Robin opened the door. I calmed down a little as we went into her living room, having scoped out other apartments in the building where I could go if I needed help. There was a lot of old, cheap furniture in the room that Robin had acquired. Just like her mom, she was a second-hand queen. Her mid-century couch was upholstered with brown material and had reddish-brown stained wooden arms. A lamp was perched on an end table. There was a chair off to the side, where I headed to lay my jacket down with my small purse that contained lipstick, rubbers, and mascara. I glanced at Robin, who was standing outside her bedroom door, which was to the side of the front entrance. The guys were just hanging there, still wearing their jackets. That was not the norm. I asked who wanted to go in first. One guy stood next to Robin, pawing her, and the other approached me in front of her couch. Her coffee table was pushed back far enough to make a passage between the couch and table. My nerves were heightened, on edge, and I suddenly tensed—I knew there was something wrong here. A lump formed in my throat. I had to think fast. Shit, I had forgotten my knife in the car. One guy was touching Robin without having paid, so I told both of them to put the money on the table or we couldn't go any further and they would have to leave. "Well, *we* want to stay," one said as he grabbed and pulled Robin along by the hair. "Stop! Right now! And get the fuck out!" I was pissed. I lunged forward to help Robin but was stopped by the guy in front of me, who was trying to block me and held me back with his extended arm. I screamed again at the one with Robin to let her go, and when I started to walk around the coffee table to get to her, the other guy near me moved toward me again. As I popped off the top part of the couch's wooden arm and turned to hit him, he sucker punched me in the eye before I had a chance—blam! Although I lost my balance momentarily, I remained on my feet, knowing this was no time to fall to the floor. Robin was panicking and screaming, and the guys were yelling, "Give us your money!" I held the arm of the couch and swung, whacking him hard on his arm and side. He looked at Robin and his friend. I meant business, and as I reached behind I said, "I will shoot you both!" playing like I had a gun to bluff our way out of the situation. When they saw me reaching, they booked, not sure of whether I did have a gun. He bought it! Phew, that was close… During the commotion, Robin had given the guy the money that was in her bra. Oh, man, how stupid! "Why did you do that?" I asked her. She told me she was scared. She was intimidated and didn't know how to fight. I hardly ever carried any money with me, usually leaving it in my car.

It was a nightmare in Back Bay. The neighbors had called the police, assuming a murder was underway. Fortunately, it never came close to that. Robin was hysterical, and I told her to calm herself. "Oh, my god!" she gasped. "Libbe, look in the mirror!" I was angry I had gotten hit and that Robin's money was stolen, not to mention the arm of the couch I had wrenched off to use as a weapon. I knew these punks were no good from the start. Robin handed me one of her many mirrors just as the doorbell rang. "I'm sorry," she told me, "I should have listened to you." The police were at the door. As they introduced themselves, I was looking at the mirror in horror—my eye was swollen and nearly shut! I wondered how I would explain the eye to J.N. and what Eric would say. The officer was taking a report. The neighbor told him that two men had fled the apartment. I stopped Robin from talking with good reason: she would have said something stupid. I wasn't going to mention that she was a dancer unless I absolutely had to. I told him they had followed us home, and when we came to the door they stormed inside and held us up. One of them, I explained, had hit me. "In self-defense, I hit him back with the couch arm and clipped his arm and side. They ran fast, officer."

"Is that all?"

"No, Robin ran to the door as they left so she could get their plate number." The officers told us they were going to follow up and contact us when they located them. Yeah, sure. They did not seem thrilled.

Once the police left, I knew that was it, there would be no follow-up. They could read the situation, and why bother? The worst nightmare was having to call our men to explain. Eric was first to see me, and he called Robin stupid and screamed at her for giving up her money. It was the money that always came first. I told Eric it was my fault, that we had gone even though I wasn't totally sure it was safe. He knew I was covering up for his girl. I should have acted on my gut at the beginning. When J.N. found out, he told Eric that Robin and I were most probably fucking around. His mentality was part pimp and part square, and he wasn't able to distinguish one from the other. He was so wrong. I didn't hear the end of it. Robin and I had to be on our guard. We couldn't hang out together for a month as a "punishment," which is what would have happened anyway since she was dancing most of the time, so no big deal. Robin became even more timid after the two men strong-armed us, although Eric didn't carry on about it the way J.N. did. Eric just didn't want Robin to go with customers we didn't know.

I was saving money for a trip to see my dad. I cherished the letters he wrote, even though all of them basically said the same thing. Thanks to Hilde, one of my cousins on my father's side of the family who I was in touch with, we were speaking. She pushed Freddy to write me at her house, and he could visit me there too. She was close to my dad and knew things about him that nobody else knew. I had also been speaking to her husband. We all really liked each other and became good friends. As it turned out, they were among the few family members I talked to over the years, but I was thrilled to have someone out there. J.N.'s partying took up the major part of his life. And every day now, he was so different. He was running around even more, and because we had sex all the time, I was nervous that I would catch something from him. I was always careful, he wasn't.

I didn't know them as Melodie Stankiewicz, 26, or Holly Davidson, 22, or Kathy Williams, 17, but all three worked the Combat Zone at the same time as I did, and all three ended up dead, their bodies found north of Boston. Williams turned up first, in December 1974, off Rte. 495; she was strangled. Holly was found next, in Methuen in March 1975; she was also strangled. In June of 1975, Melodie's body, stabbed repeatedly, was discovered in a pond in Salem, NH. After her body was found, I received a call from one of my clients, telling me to be careful. The client's tone aroused my suspicions and put me on edge, and I wondered if he could be involved. I told one of my cop friends about my suspicions, and the client was checked out and not considered a suspect. Good news. The Boston homicide detectives wanted to talk to me, so I went in town. I was told that a cop in New Hampshire wanted to meet with me and show me crime photos and the place where Melodie was found. This homicide detective thought my insight might help the investigation.

I went to New Hampshire to meet with the officer, and he showed me Melodie's photo—how she was gutted in a precise and efficient manner. He and I went alone into the woods to see the pond where her body had been located. This spooked me, going alone with him into the woods. That he was a cop meant nothing. He was a stranger, and the fact that he was the law didn't mean that he couldn't still be a killer himself. I tried to keep him in front of me as we walked to the pond. He knew I was watching him. We left the pond...that was a relief. When I returned to Boston, I thought and thought about the haunting photo of her body. There was no evidence that I could see that any of the three fought back. Perhaps they went into those woods willingly, which would suggest that they may have felt secure with the killer right up to the moment they died. I wondered if, just possibly, someone in uniform, maybe a minister, a steady customer, or a friend could be involved. It might have been any number of different kinds of people. I had my suspicions. Time to leave. I called the Boston detectives and ran into a wall: no response. They acted like they knew nothing about me or the casework. No one was listening or returning calls. Even my cop friend acted dumb, and he knew the case. Maybe I was right. The cases went cold.

The deaths of the girls occurred at about the same time as Mama Cass Elliot from the Mamas and Papas group passed away. That was a very unexpected and deeply felt loss for all of her fans. Although the girls' deaths were a tragedy, I continued working and taking chances with my life. Many years later, in 2008, I found out about a newly-published book from a friend who knew the story of the unsolved murders from me. Further investigations had led to the publication of *The Paradiso Files: Boston's Unknown Serial Killer.* In the book, author Timothy M. Burke, a former county prosecutor in Massachusetts, makes the argument that Boston area fisherman Leonard "The Quahog" Paradiso, a convicted killer and rapist, murdered Stankiewicz, Davidson, and Williams. Paradiso died in prison shortly after the book came out. I wasn't so sure about his guilt in the crimes against the girls, but I'm no detective. Burke also made the case that Paradiso killed Harvard University graduate Joan Webster, who was last seen at Logan Airport on Thanksgiving weekend 1981, after getting off a flight back from her family's home in New Jersey. Her body was found in 1990 in an unmarked grave in Hamilton, a town north of Boston. This was disturbing, especially in light of my thinking that the three murdered working girls may have felt secure with their killer, and that he was a either a client of theirs or an official person. Those who doubted that Paradiso killed Joan Webster said she was far too cautious and aware to go off with anyone other than someone she trusted. The story accounting for these deaths is murky, although it is perfectly possible that my suspicions were wrong.

Going from 1990 into the 21st century, things are still not good for vulnerable females. I will tell you a story that transcends timelines. It is Saturday, October 5th, 2013, and I am writing about the emptiness I felt when I was younger, a constant sense of loneliness and the wish to die that often accompanied it. A woman came through the entrance of my store. Timing, they say, is everything. A wave of anxiety washed over me as she headed directly toward me. It was seven-fifteen in the evening, and although I usually closed the store at seven, I was writing furiously and didn't want to stop to lock the door. She was shuddering and there were tears in her eyes. She told me I knew her daughter, who loved coming in my store to shop and chat with me. She looked as if she were about to break down, but pulled herself together enough to explain that her daughter had been missing since Thursday. She pulled a flyer from her purse and handed it to me. It was a picture of a pretty, dark-haired girl, smiling. Yes, I knew her. My heart felt heavy as if the mom's pain entered my body. I hugged her and told her not to worry, that her daughter was smart, and prayed that I was right even though my spirit felt hollow. From the mother's perspective, it sounded as though her daughter was missing because she had run away and wasn't planning on coming back. I felt her profound loss and imagined myself in her place—I would want to die if my child went missing. In fact, I had just finished writing a short novel about a missing girl that explored the emotional experience of her mother. I was working on that book in tandem with this one.

The mother talked to me as I stared at her daughter's beautiful face, trying to remember the last time I saw her in the store and what we spoke about. I remembered the times she had come in looking for retro clothes, particularly around Halloween every year. I was stunned. And the hurt the mother carried seemed to be unbearable. I remembered that her daughter had once bought a vintage dress that fit her perfectly, and she looked like a young woman born in that era. She was wearing Converse sneakers that day. She told me she loved coming in my store to dress up because it made her happy. I glanced at the clock. It was seven-thirty. Two customers came into the store. One was just browsing around, and the other had come in to pick up a vintage table she'd bought and was so relieved when she found I was still open. I didn't want to leave the mom and felt torn. So, rather than give my full attention to the others, I spoke very little, giving them each a flyer about the missing girl and telling them to look out for her. I remembered the last time she was in the store and that she wanted to come back for a sterling necklace. The mom continued speaking, saying that her daughter had a problem with bulimia for a while and that there were secrets she couldn't share. She was frightened for her daughter, who had been seeing a social worker. I understood what she was trying to say, having experienced sexual abuse as a child, and immediately thought of suicide. She told me that her daughter might have taken oxycodone, and that she left a note with her friend saying that she was leaving and wouldn't be coming back. The queasiness in my stomach lingered as she spoke. I identified with the emptiness her daughter must have felt. There were many times in my life when I felt that emptiness, even now as an adult. It dwelled in my core, perpetually there, and although I wasn't aware of it at all times, it crept up. This girl came from what appeared to be a great home. You don't have to undergo an extremely abusive childhood to feel lonely and desperate in the same way I did. Her mother mentioned she was suicidal. I promised her I would help in any way I could—all she had to do was let me know, anytime, day or night. I told her the protocols social workers and psychiatrists follow make it impossible for them to reach these lost children on an emotional level. Repeatedly discussing sorrows doesn't allow the sadness to heal over. Professionals do not experience the same depth of pain that prompts a child or an adult to wish for death. They dwell on the same subjects in therapy, constantly opening wounds, and write prescriptions to numb the children's feelings, making them worse. The chemicals they prescribe sometimes induce a suicide attempt. Having walked in the same shoes, it was more likely for me to succeed with them; I hope I can have the chance to help one day. The vacant look on the mother's face told me that there was nothing I could say to comfort her except to hope that her daughter was safe somewhere. She left, and I put one flyer in the window and one in my purse. I got her phone number. I had to drive the customer with the table she bought to her house because she didn't have a car, and it was late. We discussed the missing girl on the way, and we told one another that we would pray. The daughter was due to come into the store the same as she did every few months, but especially now before Halloween. By the time I arrived home, my heart was racing. I couldn't get this girl off my mind. When I took out the flyer and looked at the photograph again, I realized there was another girl who resembled this girl so closely that they could have been sisters. I recalled in sharp detail when the other girl shared with me—after she read my first book, *A Thorn in Rose's Garden* (the story of my early childhood)—her secret about having an incestuous relationship with her father. The missing girl, by the smile she wore for others, gave the impression of being happy all the time, and whenever she was in my store, she relaxed and had fun dressing up in a funky way, getting my sincere compliments. I emailed the mother to continue our communication. I prayed for her daughter. We spoke once more on the telephone; her despairing voice was intense. If her daughter needed me, I would go to her and speak with her, regardless of the hour. I thought about all my friends who had suffered from some sort of problem or another, and where they ended up. Girls run away when they want to escape, when the pain of their existence becomes intolerable, and they resort to drink or do drugs, or to the streets as I did. Everyone has considered suicide at some point in their lives, felt the absence of hope and the acute pain of the moment, but doing it is something else entirely. The loneliness this girl must have felt put my problems into perspective.

When I woke the next day, I felt the urge to call her mom but didn't. I turned on my computer and read October 6th, 2013. I called her mother—no answer. I never talked to her mother again. I found out that they had found her body the night before. She was dead! Oh god, she had so much to live for! That could have been me as a young woman. What was it that drove me to push through? The pressure on girls to appear a certain way is enormous. To be skinny and to dress according to fashion, to be sexy, is overwhelming, and parents' expectations weigh heavily too. Drugs are easily available. Kids are inundated by images on TV, computer sites, and billboards. Even by members of their own families they are pressured to attain some ideal. The competition to be successful has negative as well as positive aspects. The pressure is greater and growing with each passing year. Computers make the problems worse. There was so much this girl had to live for, yet she cut her life short because she couldn't withstand the pain of her existence. There are so many levels of hell that exist in life that no social worker or psychiatrist can ever learn in a book. I hope she is in a peaceful place and her family can recall her in all her complexity. The girls in the straight world and the ones in the life share the same emotional problems even though their lifestyles differ. Everything happens for a reason, and the synchronicity of meeting the mother of this missing girl wasn't just a coincidence. The concurrence of the girl's disappearance and death with writing about my loneliness in life meant something to me. Thinking about this girl interrupted my writing and took me back to that empty place beyond the jail cell. I look forward to good days when the roses in my garden open to the sun as I watch them and accept the days when my roses bend and wilt until the next regrowth. I pray for the mom and dad and sister to remember every smile she wore. Getting back to my story, feeling the sadness of a life cut short…

CHAPTER FIFTY-THREE

A Trip to See Dad in Florida

I decided I had to go to Florida soon. My 1971 Riviera GS was over five years old and riding rough. The valves needed work, and in my last letter to my dad, I explained the problem and he advised me to come to him. We never spoke much about me, but he did ask about "the boy"—his *grandson*, R. Lee. Dad told me what to add to the gas and which oil to use. He told me that when I brought the car down to him, he would fix it like it was brand new. I was flattered that he would take the time to do this, and I jumped at the offer. I could get to see him, if only for a short time. I tried to see him the first time I went to Florida with J.N., but he stood at the screen door and yelled that he couldn't come out. Another time, when I stayed at the Fontainebleau Hotel, he stood me up again because Anita wouldn't let him go out. He always made excuses. Except for the sunshine, the trips were a waste of time.

My black eye from the young guy at Robin's apartment healed with the help of red meat compresses and ice packs, followed by gobs of my lemon Pond's cream, which I have always used for my skin. I healed completely. J.N. didn't mind my taking the trip to Florida; he was busy with school and who knew what else. I gave him money beyond what he made from the waterbed store. Nana agreed to watch R. Lee while I was gone. I was free, unfettered by work, to drive where I pleased. I loved long trips, and once I was behind the wheel I didn't want to stop. I swore to myself that I would have the leisure to jump in the car and go all day and all night without worries…one of these days…in a convertible…

My bag was packed, and off I went! On the way, I made a couple of stops to see two madams, and even had several fast dates in Hartford, Connecticut, where I didn't stay long, just a couple of hours. The madam told me she would tell her girls I had extra customers in Boston and to come up to see me. My next stop was New York, two to three hours max, in and out. The madam there was a young Chinese woman who worked special clients and had other girls working for her. I had been there before and remembered her beautiful apartment that was decorated with Japanese furniture, black lacquer carved statues, sexy room dividers, colored lights, and lotus flower paintings adorning her walls. Her tables were made from carved wood. She soothed her customers by burning candles and fragrant incense and serving them a cup of jasmine or black tea before they entered the room, which was all black lacquer, Oriental bed, and nightstands with soft lighting. I saw one rich client before I hit the road, and I told her I would be back to work soon. I felt so mellow. She also said that if one or two of her workers ever came to Boston, she would give them my number. Great! I knew that within the next year or two I would have a full-swing apartment going for other girls, not just the local ones.

I was at my best driving down the highway, listening to my tapes of Bobby Womack, Marvin Gaye, and the Temptations. I floated along without feeling pressured by the constraints of time, stopping only to call my son. I checked on him constantly, and when I spoke with him I felt safe. "Mommy, I miss you," he'd say, and I'd reply, "I miss you more."

"When are you coming home?"

"Soon. I'm going to visit your grandpa in Florida, and I'll bring some goodies home for you."

"Come home soon," he said, "I love you!"

"Yes, I love you too! And give Muggsey a kiss for me."

"Okay, Mom…"

I would call him two to three times a day—I had to hear his voice, and an occasional woof from our dog. R. Lee was my anchor and my hope for the future. J.N. didn't seem like he was in the mood to talk. His buddy at the shop did all the furniture crafting and was at the store six days a week, while J.N. did the drop-offs. As seen through other people's eyes, it appeared to be a normal existence. Our being in the life was invisible to them.

****

Now, as I sit in my cell, I think to myself how I hid behind the protective walls of my straight life, and I wonder who it was that squealed. It was someone, but who and where? Why? They asked me about New Orleans, but I haven't been able to put the pieces of this arrest together yet. Baby and her friend warned me to close down two months ago, and I took them seriously and did so. They said something was going on, and I didn't want to take any risks. Apparently, that wasn't enough because I have been sitting on my butt in this cell for so long that it hurts. I need to get out of this room! What happened? Oh, please, someone come and release me! My thoughts are traveling back and forth, from past to present, and I cannot stop thinking. I'm getting a headache. Ah, yes, my dad…

****

So many years had gone by without having a relationship with my adoptive dad. I felt like it would be now or never. My life went on, as did his, and although I missed him, I can't say he ever missed me. Those years were wasted because of Anita. I wanted to have one person I could call family for my son, a real grandpa, even though he wasn't related by blood. I assumed he would always have his dad. I'd been driving straight through for many hours, and bypassed the houses in Washington and Philly, trying to make better time. The madam in Philly, who I was constantly in touch with, was disappointed that I wasn't dropping by, but she understood that I couldn't make a stop. Uncharacteristically for the business, she was Jewish, a savvy lady with a low-end house. I always wanted to meet her but never did have the chance. If I stopped, it would have taken me a lot longer to get to Florida. I felt stressed about the time. Maybe I would stop and see the madams in the Carolinas and Georgia on the way back. Usually, it took me twenty-eight straight hours to make the trip, but I stopped too many times on this run and I was way off. In Charlotte, I filled the car with gas, checked the oil, wiped my windows, grill, and bumpers clean of the splattered bugs. And after a quick bite to eat—food in the South is *so* good—I was back on the road again. I was getting closer, and decided to make a stop at the orange grove stand to send a box of them home.

I was North Miami bound. The smell of the air changed as I drove deeper south, over the Florida line. I could smell citrus and some sort of blossoms. The palm trees and flowers always pleased me; they were so warm and inviting. If Boston weren't my home and I had no ties there, I would move to Florida one day to retire or, preferably, to my dream place at the French Riviera, where there are cypress trees and the climate is balmy. Someday? Well, I am a dreamer.

I was singing along to the blasting music, with my windows wide open. The fragrance of the orange groves was intoxicating. I stopped again to buy some chocolate-covered coconut patties, which were only available in Florida as far as I knew. I loved them. I was so glad to be over the Florida line. After finishing every single patty in one package, I continued on, still tired but thoroughly determined to reach my destination of North Miami Beach. I was so excited. I stopped at a payphone and called the telephone number of the gas station that Dad had given me, and the man who answered said my dad would be there soon. It was only seven-thirty in the morning. He told me he would call Freddy and tell him I was in Florida and on my way to the gas station. With the address and directions clutched in my hand, I headed over. I was weary, but relieved my car had made it. As I pulled into the station, the man let me know that my dad would be there soon, and he offered me the use of his bathroom. I washed up, brushed my teeth, changed into cooler clothing, and wet my hair to refresh the style—and myself. I had booked a room at an average hotel near my dad's house, not the Fontainebleau this time. I waited impatiently.

Dad pulled up. Teary-eyed, I waited until he stepped out of the car, then I walked over to him. I could smell the sweet tobacco from the pipe he held in his hand, a scent I had always associated with happiness and safety as a child. He came closer and gave my back a pat. He *seemed* a bit happy to see me. Even so, I was thrilled. We exchanged greetings. He said, "Anita wanted to know where I was going so early in the morning, and I had to tell her."

"Why?" I asked.

"I didn't want to lie to her—that would be worse."

I thought to myself, *How would she ever know if you didn't tell her? You're a grown man, for god's sake!* "Your car may take a couple of days to do," he said.

"Dad, can we go to lunch or supper?"

"I'll see. I can't be gone too long or she'll be upset if she can't reach me here at the station."

I felt let down once again. It was one disappointment after another, but a short time with him was at least better than no time at all. Anita, Anita, Anita—it was always Anita! It was her then, when I was a child, and now as an adult. Anita, Anita, Anita! There would be no end to it as long as she was there. My dad was the ostrich his sister Eva said he was, his head always buried whenever he had to confront something or someone, especially me.

Watching my dad beneath the hood of a car when I was younger was always a pleasure because he loved what he was doing and was expert at it. We strolled over to the Riviera. He opened the hood and told me to start the car while he examined the motor. "Libbe, turn it on now." As usual, I felt warmed whenever he said my name. I loved it when he called me "Libbe." He lit his pipe again and stood there thinking. I watched dad wondering where to begin. The familiar smell of the tobacco burning brought me back to when my mother Rose was alive. My mom and dad loved me then—every day I keep that memory close to my heart. Looking over his glasses, which had slid slightly down his nose, he told me that he could smoke only when he was out because Anita didn't allow him to smoke his pipe when he was near her or in the house. "Gee, Dad," I said, "at least you can go out and have some happy time to yourself." He shook his head at my answer.

"Let's go drop you off..."

He drove me to the hotel, making sure to tell me to stay there and not to go out as if I were a child. "Sure, Dad, I'll be here," I assured him. He told me he would talk to me in the morning and maybe we would go out to lunch, which was encouraging. I entered the hotel lobby alone. I got the key and couldn't wait to get to my room, shower, change, and call my son. I was overtired, and looked forward to going to sleep after the long jaunt. Seeing my dad the following day couldn't come quickly enough. I could have worked if I went to Miami, but I chose not to.

The next day, I went to lunch with my dad. He brought me to a deli he told me he had been coming to since he moved to Florida years ago. He knew the owner and all the waitresses. I tried not to smoke cigarettes in front of him; he still believed I was not old enough yet. Freddy just couldn't come out of the past. We ordered our corned beef sandwiches, and he told the waitress extra kosher pickles and some to take home. "Yes, Freddy, I know." The conversation was mostly about him, Anita, and their friends. I was like a stranger to him. He asked me how my child was, not remembering his name. He didn't let me finish speaking when I was telling him about R. Lee, and I let it pass, seeing that his train of thought didn't include my son or me. When the waitress brought the check, I tried to pay but he refused, and then put a twenty-five-cent tip for the waitress on the table. Whoa! What was that? I asked him what the quarter was all about, and he replied that it was the tip, and that the waitress knew that whenever he came in she would get a good tip. I told him he should leave more, and he put another quarter on the table. *Oh, my god,* I thought, *fifty cents!* I couldn't believe it. What did he think she was, a slot machine? Freddy told me he used to give her five cents when he first started coming in so she wouldn't get spoiled. His thinking hadn't changed; he remained in the era of the Great Depression. As we stood up to leave, the waitress dropped off the leftovers and a bag of pickles as she gave old Freddy a kiss. I caught her attention and handed her a twenty-dollar tip, and she thanked me. "You don't have to do that, honey," she told me. I apologized for Dad, the big tipper. "Oh, I'm used to Freddy," she said. "The more they have the less they give." So true… That was the miser in him: save every penny but complain when you don't get precisely what you ask for. That was his response to having grown up during the Depression.

We left the restaurant, both happy about how well lunch had gone. I was particularly pleased about giving the waitress what she deserved for her service, although still not anywhere near enough for all the years he had been coming there. Dad fixed my car, and it ran like a charm, better and faster than when it was brand new. We said goodbye to one another cordially, and I cried as I took off, cherishing my bittersweet memories of the visit.

Back on the road again! My car had been fixed by a man I loved, and I had those few stolen moments, among far too few, to fondly recall. I wondered how many more I could steal in his lifetime. I had to get back home—J.N. sounded strange when I talked to him, and my son wanted me back. I left the state of Florida with tears running down my cheeks. I wished my father and I were closer, but I knew that would never happen. All the windows of the car were wide open, so the wind swept my hair. The music was cranked up as I bid farewell to the palm trees and the sunshine, vowing I would return soon. I drove straight back without any breaks except for gas and food.

CHAPTER FIFTY-FOUR

Breakdown at Home

J.N. stopped attending most of his classes at Brandeis. The store was about to close. He didn't go out to the customers' houses to install the beds anymore. All this was happening so fast. His actions and speech were bizarre. He was behaving as if he were having a breakdown of sorts. Much to my displeasure, he informed me he was planning to drop out a year before graduation. He and his friends at school were experimenting with mescaline and acid, smoking weed, and perhaps more, I wasn't certain. His friends explained that they were testing how much they could take and not to worry because J.N. could handle it. I asked myself how they could possibly know that. I knew the signs of drug-induced behavior: the pupils of his eyes were fully dilated, and he was paranoid. Every day, he demanded to know where I was going and with whom. He constantly had me write down the names and telephone numbers of people I was in contact with. And then his paranoia escalated to the food I cooked. I was so afraid of him that I had R. Lee stay at the reverend's house more often. Every day was an adventure of unknown craziness. If he came home after me, he would force me to eat dinner first so he could be certain I wasn't poisoning his meals. He would follow me and watch me in town. Fortunately, most of this occurred when R. Lee wasn't at home.

I spoke to the reverend about J.N.'s behavior, and he told me to watch him carefully, and to be on my guard. J.N.'s family, especially his Aunt C., wasn't able to accept that her favorite nephew was anything but perfect. He was schizoid, changing from moment to moment, and becoming worse with each passing day. I didn't know what to do or who could help him. It was particularly difficult because he was at home all the time now, and R. Lee was frightened. He was coming in town regularly to pick me up and insisted that I had no car and that I go with him—even though my car was parked on LaGrange Street. He was adrift in his mind and wasn't listening to me when I spoke to him. When we arrived at the house, he said I put poison in the food because he felt sick, even though he watched me cook it earlier. Then he had me eat the entire amount of food I made, enough for four people. I felt sick, but held it in. As I spoke to him, his pupils were dilating, and he would just sit there and watch me until he was convinced we weren't going to die from poisoning. After that, J.N. would go back to sitting in front of the TV, like nothing unusual had just happened. "I have to get my car," I told him.

"Well, go get it."

"When? It's in town and I need a ride, okay?"

He just sat there! I ended up having to go there on my own, without his help, which was fine. He never even knew I left. What happened to this organized man and his love? Did I do this? No, he went to school and took all those drugs.

When I returned, he was still sitting in the same spot, blankly staring at the TV. He showed little interest in going back to school. I begged him to go back, thinking that the atmosphere at school might be better for him—without the drugs—and maybe a counselor. I realized he was beyond having his friends straighten him out. Katie and Robin suggested that I tell his family, but I had already done that and they didn't respond well, denying that what I was telling them was true, and suggesting that I was "the problem." Eric couldn't reach him and neither could Katie's man. His friends at school passed his strange behavior off by saying he was a little crazy from getting high too much and he'd be okay, to leave him alone. Alone. What did they care if he took too many trips. He took an absence from school but decided to give it another try and lived on campus with his friends once again. When he didn't call or come home for over a week, I decided to go there one evening. The suspense was killing me. I drove to the school to bring J.N. money and some pastries he liked. I went to his room, and his roommate told me he was in the cafeteria. Well, there he was, just sitting there like a mummy, and he didn't recognize me. "He knows me. Why is he like this?" I asked.

His friends' answers ranged from somewhat informative, "He won't know who you are, and he won't talk to you either," to being very vague, "Oh," and, "He's in a state…" Really? No one said what kind of state J.N. was in because they were all in a similar one. I was angry and concerned when I sat down across from him and the group of people, his so-called friends. I put the pastry box on the table. "Hey, J.N." Nothing. I nudged him, "J.N.!" The others told me that he wouldn't answer, and he'd been like that for a while. "A while?" I questioned. "Oh, about two days, he'll come out of it soon," I was assured. "Well, shouldn't we call the doctor to take a look at him?" I asked. They were waiting for J.N. to come back, they said. "Come back?" I retorted. "Back from where?"

"He's trippin'," someone explained. "Trippin'. That's all. Let him have a good trip, okay!"

Really? "Oh shit! What if he doesn't come back at all?" I cried out, and heard, casually, "Don't worry, he will. We all did." I tried calling his name, repeatedly, and then I changed seats and pushed myself directly across from him to be in his line of vision. He was in another zone altogether, tripping out, with his pupils fully dilated. I could see that now. He stared straight ahead, never blinking or acknowledging me, even when I waved. I was scared and wanted to take him to the hospital, but his friend reassured me that it would wear off. And they could all get in big trouble too, even J.N. "What did he do?" I asked. They told me they didn't know all of what he took, although some of them had taken several types of acid, and eventually it wears off. What the fuck? I was pissed… "You are all so intelligent in college, yet so stupid that none of you have any answers? I find that hard to believe!"

They were academically adept, but had limited worldly awareness. They thought I was rude. I didn't care what they thought! I wondered why men like J.N. and the rest of these guys would experiment on themselves? I was afraid J.N. would never be the same again. When I tried to discuss it with his friends, they made no sense either, like real educated airheads. And they said J.N. had given them instructions that he didn't want to be disturbed by anyone, under any circumstances. "So don't try to take him home," one of them said. "He doesn't want to go."

I was clearly out of place at the school, and did not want a fight or hassle that might get me arrested—not them, of course. I had to protect R. Lee. It was bad enough that the girls and men in the life were hooked on cocaine and drinking, it was also bad on campus, worse than I ever knew. One thing was for sure—I didn't want J.N. to be a basket case because of drugs. He was the father of my son and I loved him. I left him sitting there like a zombie. And after that, life turned into something worse than any horror story.

The first time I saw him when he finally came home from school, I had just gotten back from work, and he was standing in the hallway of the top floor of our apartment. The reverend's grandson and R. Lee were sitting on the floor and J.N. had a .30-30 rifle aimed at our son's head, saying he was going to kill him and his friend! I arrived home to this! I immediately tried to defuse the situation by calming J.N. and distracting his attention to me long enough for the boys to get the hell out. This took some time and careful thinking. The boys were freaked out! R. Lee didn't want to leave me; I had to signal twice for them to go. I had gotten J.N.'s attention by making it sound like I wanted to talk to him in private, but how long could I hold his interest? The expressions of horror on the boys' faces… Those looks have never left my memory. That was so close! They walked quickly down the stairs and out the front door. They got away!

It took the rest of the evening talking to J.N. until he chilled out and put aside the gun. I made a call to Nana, who said she had calmed the boys down and put them to bed. I stayed with J.N., who watched me with a wary expression on his face. We were both tired from the ordeal and had fallen asleep, but I awakened to him standing over me with the same blank eyes as I had seen before. This happened again the next night. He was looming over me, not saying a word, but he seemed calmer. I was afraid of having our son come back, but he returned to a semblance of his normal self after a few days, and I relaxed somewhat and had R. Lee return home. J.N. would not leave the house at night, or any other night. When the phone rang, he would not allow anyone to answer it. The atmosphere in the house was infused with his bad energy. R. Lee was afraid of him, and I was too. At first, I did not leave R. Lee with him when I went to work, but he argued about that until I gave in. J.N. seemed like he was normal again.

One night, R. Lee was home when I came into the house after work and J.N. began beating me in front of him. He choked me with so much force that foam was oozing out of the side of my mouth. R. Lee jumped on him, trying to stop him. J.N. shoved R. Lee aside into the dresser, hurting him. He wanted to kill me; his rage was uncontrolled. I couldn't think why he was doing this. Something must have clicked in his brain—our son was hysterical, yelling and crying for him to stop, and he did for a moment, looking strange. I was coughing, gasping to draw air into my lungs as I stood and grabbed R. Lee by the hand and ran outside with him. There was snow on the ground, and it was freezing. I was wearing only a short, black dress. I drank in the cold air and my breathing eased. I swooped R. Lee up into my arms to calm both him and myself, hoping I would keep him warm. Tears of sorrow flowed from his big brown eyes. He was still wearing his Hebrew school clothes: corduroy pants, a white shirt, and a sweater vest. I had brought my small, handsome son into this unstable, volatile life.

I hugged him as he patted my back, asking me if I was all right. "Mommy, are you okay? I'm afraid! Please don't go back inside, okay?"

I replied, "Yes, baby, I'm afraid too. Daddy is sick." I told him we had to go back inside, and that he was to go directly to his room no matter how he felt about leaving me alone with his father. "Just until Mommy figures things out," I explained. I felt I could handle it. He pleaded for me to stay in his room with him, but I told him I had to see his dad, then I would. My dress was stuck to the mound of snow and ice where we were sitting. R. Lee pulled the fabric with me to loosen it from the ice as I stood up. "Trust Mommy, we have to get out of here," I told him, "but we have to wait until it's safe to go, okay? And we need clothes. I'm going back to keep your father calm and then we'll get away afterward."

"Okay, Mom. It's our secret." He looked up at me, sadly, tears still streaming down his cheeks, "I love you, Mommy!"

"I love you too! So much!"

We went back inside. I had some money put away where no one would think of looking for it in case of emergencies, and it was a good thing I did. I was terrified, but I had to deal with the situation, just as I dealt with situations on the street. I went to R. Lee's room and instructed him to run to the reverend's house instead of staying home with me. I could feel the bad energy. He wasn't happy, "Please, I don't want you to go!"

I tried to reassure him, saying that I would bring his things later. I wrapped him in his thick winter jacket that hung in the hallway and scooted him away! I could feel the swelling bruises around my neck, and swallowing was uncomfortable. I had to call the police if his father came near me again. I prayed that it wouldn't be necessary to go that route, but in my heart I knew it was going there. The man I loved had become a monster, and I didn't know what to say to him. There was a time I would have done anything for him, and even now I would try to get help for him—but not with R. Lee and I living in the same house. He had to be put somewhere to withdraw from whatever it was he was putting into his body, or deal with his flight from reality in some other way. I knew it was time for R. Lee and I to escape from his father. I couldn't bear it anymore. My son's life was at risk, and so was mine.

I kissed R. Lee and pulled his clenched hands away from me to go. He turned and looked at me before he left. He obediently went to the reverend's house to wait, turning around to see me disappear in the front doorway. J.N. was in the kitchen and Muggsey was lying in his bed. I never thought about the dog during the episodes with J.N., but J.N. had never done any harm to him, except for once when Muggsey had been hit by a car on Blue Hill Ave. The veterinarian at Angel Memorial told me that Muggsey may never walk again and needed a pin in his hip, and that the operation would cost a thousand dollars plus. I asked the hospital to give me a day to consider it, and when I presented J.N. with the dog's predicament, he said he would take care of it. When he came home from the animal hospital, he told me Muggsey had gotten worse and they had to put him to sleep. I cried, and then thought about how I would break this to R. Lee, who was young and loved his dog. But something told me to go to the hospital to see what they did with Muggsey, so I went without telling J.N. I hurried down to the Angel Memorial, and they informed me that they were waiting forty-eight hours for an answer and then they would put the dog down. I had time.

My so-called partner, my common-law husband, had lied! He told them we were married, and they thought that he had the authority to make the decision about putting Muggsey down. "No, don't put him to sleep, he is mine! Please do the operation," I told them. I had five hundred dollars stash money with me to make at least half the payment. I specified to the doctors that I was the sole owner and no one else could sign him away. They put Muggsey in my name only. When I confronted J.N. later, he brushed it off, saying Muggsey was just a dog and the operation probably wouldn't have helped anyway. I didn't care what J.N.'s opinion was—the dog was part of the family, and I would gladly pay whatever it cost to save him. I didn't trust J.N. with Muggsey anymore, but I couldn't take him with me if we left town. I had no choice. Muggsey would be the only company he would have at the house, and he had already healed so no one had to carry him to the bathroom. Muggsey was a tough mutt and was able walk again. He was like me, determined. Perhaps having to care for him would help J.N. I loved the dog, but my son came before anyone or anything—he was first, so we had to go by ourselves.

There was a faint knock at the door downstairs. It was R. Lee. J.N. yelled to me to let him in, and I opened the door for him as he cried, "Mommy, I was worried about you!" Uh oh. "Go right to your room and no noise!"

"Okay…okay…I will…" He scrambled up those stairs as fast as he could to his bedroom, shutting the door. Oh god, why did he come back? I prayed he would stay in his room. Entering the kitchen, I saw J.N. sitting with a thick phone book on the table and his shotgun resting behind the book close to his chest. Shit! Why did R. Lee have to walk back into an unsafe environment? How can I get him out of here now? "Lib, sit down," J.N. told me. I sat as frozen as an icicle, my spine straight, with a shiver passing through me, making me tremble. The oven door was open, and the oven was on because he said he was cold. He didn't say anything about R. Lee as if nothing had just occurred. "Pick out the names of all the people you have coming after me and write them down. Do it!" he ordered.

"Who J.N.? What people?"

"The ones you hired!"

"I didn't hire anyone!" I replied.

"Yes you did! You have one hour to write down their names and numbers or I will kill you! You understand? Write!"

"J.N., I'm not sure I understand?"

"Write!" His pupils were so dilated that his eyes looked black and distended, a visual reflection of the darkness within him. I could hardly think and asked for the phonebook. He turned the phonebook so it was facing me, and I picked up the pen. I didn't know what to do, perhaps choose names at random? Then he would go after them and possibly hurt them. "Okay," I told him, "I'll write all of them down, but first I have to get R. Lee to Nana's so she can give him supper. Okay? I will be right back." I stood without hesitation so he wouldn't have any time to think about it. J.N. was loading the gun and looked up at me as I walked out of the kitchen…expecting a bullet in my back. I walked with confidence, and he did not make a move. I made it to R. Lee's room, where I handed him some clothes and pajamas to hold in a bag. "Come on. I'll take you back to Nana's and come to you later. I promise, but stay put! I have to stay with your dad." We hustled out the door, R. Lee in front of me. We went down the steep steps and I unlocked the latches, all the while expecting the worst to happen. I kept my son in front of me for his protection. If J.N. shot, I would be the one to take the bullet. "If you hear a loud gunshot, then run fast to Nana's house," I told him. "Do *not* look back for me, just go!"

"No, Mommy. I want to stay!"

"No!" I ordered him. J.N. was watching us from the porch above, I just knew it, and when I turned there he was, with the gun directed squarely at me. I waved and said I'd be right back, like it was normal.

When we were at the reverend's door, Nana opened it and hugged R. Lee. "Don't let him go out, okay? Be sure of that!"

"Yes, I understand." We both went inside and it was then I broke down and cried. I asked to see Reverend D., and placing R. Lee's small bag with his clothes on the floor, she led me to the living room, which was decorated with dark, old furniture and lit by a dim lamp—a perfect setting for how I felt. When the reverend came in to join me, I told him the story of my relationship with J.N., speaking openly and quickly. He said his feeling was that I shouldn't go back to the house and to stay away from R. Lee's dad. "Let him get help from his family and heal," the reverend advised. I felt a calmness come over me after speaking to him. I told him I had to go back to the house for my clothes and identification, plus the money to get away. He said I shouldn't go unless I was escorted by the police. He was right. "Stay here until the police come," the reverend said. When the police arrived, I told them my story. "Does he have a loaded gun?" they asked, and I told them yes, that as far as I knew it was loaded when I left. We crossed the street, not knowing what to expect.

Silently, we crept up the stairway, and when we reached the top, I stepped into the entryway first. There were hardwood floors and an area rug, the same place where J.N. stood when he threatened his son and the reverend's grandson. The floor creaked as I stood there. J.N. was sitting at the table in the kitchen with his gun open. The police went in, guns in hand, surrounding J.N. They asked him if he had a license for the gun and if it was loaded. J.N. denied it was loaded and added that he was just cleaning it. "Yes, sir, I do have a license."

"Step away from the table, sir," one of the officers said, "nice and easy."

"Okay," J.N. said, and moved away. After they checked, they saw there were no bullets in the gun. "Show me where the bullets are," one of the officers asked. J.N. showed them the box of bullets on the shelf, and they saw the bullets that were lying on the table beside his gun. "Do you intend to do something with these bullets?"

"I left them out accidentally, sir," J.N. replied. "I just removed them."

"Well, put them away in the box while we are here," the officer said, "and put the gun on the floor." The other officer told me to gather my belongings.

I did. I went in R. Lee's room first and took as many of my son's things as I could and the money I had hidden in there. In my room, I gathered up clothes, I.D.'s, and some precious jewelry I'd been collecting. One of the policemen had been speaking to J.N. in the kitchen; he seemed to have mellowed out. Muggsey had to stay with J.N. I had made sure there was plenty of dog food for him, 2-3 big bags. I didn't know what the fate of the dog would be with J.N. taking care of him, and I felt a twinge of sadness. The officers spoke with me, and said that it was obvious J.N. needed help with his mental condition and that I should call his family to tell them about the incident. Even though I knew that his aunt and uncle would never listen to me, I told the officers I would get in touch with them. They walked me to the reverend's house. I took a cab with R. Lee to Logan Airport to buy two tickets on the next flight out to California. One of my friends lived there, a guy who told me he would always help me anytime I needed it. After sleeping in the airport, we left on an early flight out in the morning. I left feeling sorry for J.N., but I couldn't help him; someone else would have to. I felt even worse for R. Lee, who slept curled up in my lap the entire trip, sad and holding onto me. We were safe now, and my small son was comforted as I held him in my arms, never letting him go. He would be my primary concern always, until the end of my life.

CHAPTER FIFTY-FIVE

Safe in Inglewood, California

California was not new to me. I had traveled there before to work Hollywood and Vine, and had met a great madam who had big clients. She would be a good connection for girl trading. And on one occasion, I went to deal with J.N. and his episode with Marop, the sex-changed girlfriend he almost left me for in California. She was pretty, and I was floored. Memories… Another one of his waterbed trips! This trip was entirely different. I learned more and more each time I went there. I wanted the break from J.N. to be clean, and I avoided making any phone calls. I didn't want anyone making me feel guilty or trying to talk me out of it. Boarding the plane, R. Lee had what seemed like a thousand questions: about his daddy, would he be going to school in California, and would I be going to work at night like in Boston. "Yes, I'll get a job there," I told him, "but not at night." My son thought I was a bartender in downtown Boston. I even took him to the bar, and I had the bartender ask me what time I was coming in to work just so he believed me. *Now is my chance,* I thought. *Nobody knows me here.* My friend Octave, a black man who was a professional in the corporate world, was looking forward to my visit. I knew him from before I met J.N. He liked me, and even though he was a square, he had always wished there could be a relationship between us without the complication of the life I was in. All the right opportunities and I took the other side. He was another in a line of good men I hadn't given a chance to along the way. But no one has a crystal ball to predict the future. We stumble through life, following paths we think are right for us at the present time.

When Octave came to the airport to pick us up, R. Lee was timid at first, but then warmed up to him within a couple of hours. As we drove to his house, Octave was open to R. Lee and welcomed him to California. My son was so excited about being in the sunshine without any snow. His two-bedroom apartment was small, so R. Lee would sleep in one bedroom and I would be on the couch. We were so tired from the trauma from J.N. and the flight that we stayed in the first two days. Then I was out with my son looking for jobs, but without success. I wasn't going to give up and resort to the streets—no way. The six hundred I had saved in addition to R. Lee's one hundred wouldn't last long out here, although Octave didn't expect me to pay him anything, not even for food. The weather was perfect, and Octave showed us around town, treating us to movies and restaurants. We took long walks together, and R. Lee enjoyed himself, no stress. It was so nice to relax that I had to crack the whip on myself to get moving. I hadn't called Jennifer yet because I wanted to settle in first, but I had to do it soon because she would wonder where I went.

Going from place to place looking for a job all day long was discouraging, and then I saw the Ramada Inn's "Help Wanted" sign. I went inside to the desk clerk, who told me there was a daytime bartending spot available by the pool. R. Lee said, "Mommy, that's what you do for work!" After hearing that, the clerk simply asked if I wanted it, and I said, "Yes, I'll take it if my son can sit by the pool until I arrange a babysitter."

"Then it's yours if you can start right away," he told me.

"Sure I can," I said. Oh man, can I do this? There were no questions about my experience as a bartender at all, and that was it—I had freedom from my past, and I felt elated and clear-headed but had a lot to learn.

R. Lee was happy he could be with me. I was going to attempt to do the job, learning as I went along. I was already familiar with some drinks I had seen bartenders make when I sat at the bars, and from watching Rio long ago. I figured I'd finagle the rest. I started the next day and people seemed to like me, especially the men. I got along with them right off the bat, and they even coached me through each mixed drink I wasn't familiar with. R. Lee was having fun in the pool. The waitresses adored him and would bring him whatever he wanted to eat. We were content in our small world. We had a roof over our heads and money for food and clothes. We didn't miss anything in Boston except for Muggsey. R. Lee wanted me to call his dad to see if he was feeding Muggsey. I told him I was sure he was, but we shouldn't call.

Around the third week, I made the mistake of phoning Jennifer to tell her I was in California, had a good job, and was going to stay. I didn't have any plans to return. Unfortunately, what she told me changed my mind. How stupid I was. My son and I were both thriving and I should have stayed, but the distress in my foster sister's voice compelled me to go back. She told me that J.N. had threatened to kill her family. Not thinking about our own welfare, I made the arrangements. Our life in California was cut short by that one phone call. Octave was disappointed and hoped I would return someday to resume life there. The sunshine was a sure draw. I wish I had stayed, but J.N. caused trouble and we had to return to Boston. I liked California and left the possibility open with Octave, but I tried not to encourage him—he was sweet, but I wasn't attracted to him in that way, at that time. I promised him I'd call to let him know I was all right and we said goodbye. When he dropped us off at the airport, R. Lee said he wanted to stay, although he admitted he missed Grampy and Nana. I lost contact with Octave over time, misplaced his number…another one left behind. As the plane took off, I wondered what life might have been like had I stayed. I was certain R. Lee would have fond memories of playing in the sun and water, and fun times. As an adult, he moved from the Northeast to live in California, a place he loves. And he's still there.

CHAPTER FIFTY-SIX

Oatmeal Man

Once again, I felt like I didn't have control over my life, and the choice I had made to return wasn't mine. Concerned for everyone but myself, I had to decide between protecting one and helping another…just when everything seemed to be going so well. I was straight and adored being around my son every day. In California, we were connected in a way that was unlike at home, where I was in and out of bars and brothels, working at places my son couldn't go. He could see me at this job and was happy. I was proud of myself for taking the chance to step into an unfamiliar world. I promised my son that someday I would have a business that would be all my own, and we would have a home somewhere, not to worry.

Jennifer was terrified of J.N.; he threatened her and her family. He would sit in the car outside her home, watching to catch a glimpse of me, suspecting that she was hiding me. She wondered why I never told her ahead of time I was leaving. I said that now was not the time to discuss it. I tried calling J.N., but he didn't answer. He had an aunt and uncle who we sometimes played cards with, and when I contacted them to find J.N., they told me he had threatened to kill them too. That was another reason I was going back. He had so many people scared because of me that if something happened to them I wouldn't ever live that down. Octave continued to beg me to stay, but I couldn't—worrying about what J.N. might do was too much for me to bear. R. Lee wanted to stay in California because of the pool and the fruit tray he loved to eat. He thought every crack in the ground meant there was going to be an earthquake; that was his only worry. My son was scared about going back. Frightened, he asked, "Mummy, is Daddy going to hurt you again?" I tried reassuring him that no, Daddy won't, that I was only going to talk to his dad, and we wouldn't be living with him quite yet. I told R. Lee he was going to stay at Grampy's because he was far better off with Nana taking care of him now until we figured things out.

Then it occurred to me that I should have called the reverend's house to warn them before we landed in Boston. I had to phone them right away because we were about to board our flight. When I called Nana, she told me to hurry and bring her baby back. I tried to reach J.N. one last time. He answered, and upon hearing my voice, said how he missed us both and launched into what sounded like a sincere plea for me to come back. "Tell me, J.N., what about the threats you made to my foster sister and your family?"

"Lib, I was trying to find you. I was desperate. I'm sorry, I wasn't being rational."

"J.N., are you telling me the truth?"

"We'll talk when you get home. Where are you?"

I told him I was on my way and the time the plane would be landing. "I'll be at Logan. I'll pick you both up."

"I have to go. My plane has almost finished boarding."

"I love you," he said. I did not say it back. "Say hello to R. Lee for me." For a moment, I was relieved that he sounded like his old self. But what would I tell him when he asked where I had been staying? I experienced an unsettling feeling in my gut—it was fear. I couldn't tell if he was being honest or not on the phone. My love for him blinded me to the truth. His voice was hypnotizing. Despite my fear, in my heart I wanted to believe him. "C'mon Mom, our plane is leaving!" R. Lee exclaimed as he pulled my hand away from the phone. He didn't say anything when I told him his father had said hello. Safely onboard, we were on our way back to the freezing weather in Boston. I told R. Lee not to tell his dad where we had been staying but, instead, to say that we stayed at the hotel where I worked. Would he remember that? While he napped, I held my son close as if I wouldn't be seeing him after we landed. I had already told the reverend to call the police if J.N. ever made an attempt to take R. Lee; my name was on the birth certificate—not his. I lost my baby daughter and my infant son, and I couldn't lose the only child I had now. Because the circumstances of the birth of my other son were questionable, I made the decision to put him up for adoption quickly, perhaps too hastily. I second-guessed myself throughout my life for making that decision, and it haunted me. Maybe he *was* J.N.'s son. I was so nervous during the flight, I couldn't nap.

The stewardess was preparing us for landing. R. Lee stretched and asked if we were home. "Your dad is picking us up. Nana made a lemon cake for you, your favorite!" I could tell R. Lee was uneasy, but I didn't want to say anything else about his dad. I knew there would be plenty of home-cooked food waiting for my son, and that's all that mattered to me at the moment because he had slept through lunch. By the time we found our luggage, J.N. was outside waiting for us, sitting in his yellow Riviera. He got out and came over and greeted us like we were coming back from a family vacation. He was behaving normally, and I wondered if the drugs he had been taking had worn off completely without leaving any after-effects. J.N. scooped R. Lee up in his arms, and by the delight on his face it was obvious R. Lee loved his father...he was also afraid of him, and those conflicting feelings confused him and became an issue for R. Lee during his childhood, and even as an adult. J.N. could be great, and then the next moment, like Jekyll and Hyde, he would become monstrous. I prayed that this time he would be the way he was when I first met him.

Once J.N. asked where we had been, R. Lee told him everything; he didn't understand that what he said would get me in trouble. I wasn't able to interrupt him because when I tried, his father said to let his son speak freely. R. Lee was just so excited to tell him all of it and was, of course, too young to grasp that there would be consequences to what he revealed. He had forgotten all about our white lie, to tell his father what I said about staying at the hotel when he asked him questions. My stomach sank. J.N. was encouraging him to talk more. Then his smile disappeared and his face changed into a solemn mask—the lack of expression that suggested he had a mental disorder coming on. R. Lee's mentioning the nice man we had stayed with didn't help the situation. I was feeling claustrophobic, closed in. Taking shallow breaths, I stared through the window at the trees and buildings so I would be distracted by the familiar brick architecture of Boston. I tried not to show my fear. Immediately I regretted coming back; I should have known better. I wanted to jump out of the car with my son and run, but I felt frozen in place.

We pulled up to the reverend's house. R. Lee was anxious to see them and to eat Nana's cooking! I carried his bags to the door and could smell the aroma of the food. My stomach growled. I should have gone in the house and not come out. She hugged R. Lee, and he ran inside his second home. "Where's Muggsey?" he asked as he turned to me.

"Oh, I don't know, probably at our house. I'll let you know and bring him over in the morning, okay? See you tomorrow." He ran to me. "Mom, you come back, okay?"

"Yes, I will, but not tonight. Your dad and I have to talk. Nana is here with you, and she will call if you need me." I looked into his big, brown eyes and saw his uncertainty. I did not want to leave him. I put all the money I had left, along with my personal stuff, in the bottom of his bag. I told Nana it was there. I had to go, but I told myself that this would be the last time I leave my child—our bond had become much stronger during the time we were away. I fully realized how important simply "being there" was to a child. It was his security.

J.N. was already at the house, and had brought my bags upstairs. I walked in the front door and it felt so cold, almost colder inside than outside. It was dark as I climbed the steps, and the apartment was eerie and still, a scene out of a murder mystery. I stood on the top landing. It was clear the heat wasn't on. I continued standing there, freezing, looking through the French doors at my plants in the living room—all dead, except for some green left on one that J.N. had given me. I walked into the den, a room that should have been a dining room, and saw the slick film of ice that covered the walls. The black leather couch had icy dew on it. I asked him why it was so cold. I entered the kitchen and saw the walls. I was taken aback by the scope of it. The walls! My God! He had written all over the four walls—from ceiling to floor—with black marker! I stood there and read, among the words of others, the lyrics written by black poet/musician Gil Scott-Heron in "We Beg Your Pardon (Pardon Our Analysis)" about "Oatmeal Man," a radical interpretation of the sound of the ghetto. The words were huge and vivid. What stood out most was, "**WE BEG YOUR PARDON AMERICA**."

I felt ill at ease. J.N. was in a schizophrenic state of mind. I glanced over at Muggsey's bed and he wasn't there. When I asked J.N. where Mugs was, he didn't answer. The expression on his face was cold and twisted with hate. "J.N., please explain. Why isn't there any heat and where is the dog?" "The dog is gone, Lib." "Gone? Gone where? Please!" "Houghton's Pond. That's where." "Houghton's Pond? It's freezing there! Why?" I begged. "Why?" "I gave him to a man there. I couldn't keep him." I knew he was lying, but there was nothing I could do. I was sick inside. He had played games with me to get us back. He was angry and demanded that I go to work that night and get some money for him. "That's all, just go make up what I've lost," he said. I was tired and didn't want to argue. "The waterbed is warm. You stay here." "But J.N., there's no heat." "Well, you can fix that. Make money. Isn't that what you're good for?"

Shit! This was the final curtain call. I had to prepare to get away. The waterbed store was closed, and he had dropped out of school with just one more year to go. Why? I was disenchanted with him as it was, but then he acted heartless, cold-blooded pimp style, like he hated me. He explained nothing and did not care about anything. He told me I had to earn the money to get my car back and make things right. "I'll be back after the bars close to get my money," he snarled. The truth was, he couldn't hold things together. It was obvious when he said, "Call Grime's Oil. I'll give you the money for that, and have them put oil in the tank. The pipes may have burst so let them know that there's been no heat for two weeks. Get yourself together, you left me, remember! You didn't care. Here's ten to get you in town." I didn't question him. My plan was to work enough to be able to get away, and soon. He didn't search me, a relief because I had fifty dollars stashed in the lining of my shoe. To this day, I beat myself up for the mistake of coming back to him and for the many other mistakes I've made over the years, and still to come.

At times, I was happy that my baby girl and other son were placed in good homes and weren't exposed to the kind of life I was living. It was enough that R. Lee was going through hell now, two more would have added to the worry and financial responsibility, in addition to the question of who would watch all three. I prayed they were safe, and that R. Lee could be in a stable home with me where he wouldn't have to go through the hell of J.N.'s bizarre behavior and my lifestyle.

CHAPTER FIFTY-SEVEN

Frozen

The love I felt for J.N. was wearing me down. I was heartbroken. Octave seemed to have had my best interests at heart. Still, at that time, I thought he was like all the men who just wanted to go to bed with me. I could have been wrong, he never attempted anything, but I'll never know for certain what he might done if I had stayed. J.N. left to go out, and I felt a great weight lifted from me. I had the house key, and found, to my astonishment, that nothing had been touched since I left. My clothes, my bags, and my shoes were all there in the same spot. The house was so bitterly cold, I couldn't shake the chill in my bones. No heat. I ran the hot water and stood in the steamy shower for a time, thinking that raising my body temperature would make getting out of the shower more tolerable, but I was wrong. It ran out, no more hot water. After I dressed in layers, I walked around the house looking at my belongings, thinking that the apartment used to be a collection of memories. Now it was a tortuous place to be.

I gathered some pictures and personal things, then hid them in R. Lee's closet. I packed up more of his stuff so he would be ready to go when it was time to raise up. I wanted to drop it off at Nana's as soon as possible. I turned on the stove to have heat while I was there. I walked outside, leaving the hallway light on. I scurried across the street to check on R. Lee and bring him the clothes, some toys, and his Hebrew books to take when we go. Getting all his things out of his room would have to be done gradually. Where will I go if I leave here? Where can I run to? Somewhere safe, where there are good schools. My plan was to find a place and pay for it in advance, then work out the details by making a list of what needed to be done. R. Lee came running to the door calling, "Mommy, Mommy! You came for me!"

"No, baby, I have to go to work to have money for a new apartment."

"Where's Daddy?"

"He had to leave, but I'll see you tomorrow. I love you."

"I love you too. You promise?"

"Of course I do." Nana told me not to worry and that he would be fine. "I will not let J.N. inside at all," she told me. Great! I was fortunate to have the reverend and his wife. She said she and her grandson would keep a close watch on R. Lee when he went outside so he didn't go anywhere with J.N. I told her to take the money in the bag that she already had for whatever she needed. I thanked Nana and said, "Here's another bag of R. Lee's things." While he was playing, I quietly left. The haunting thought of J.N. coming to get me or get crazy on R. Lee was like a knife in my heart.

I went to work, unable to shake the chills I had. Everyone was happy to see that I was back; that welcome was needed after my bad encounter with J.N. The bartenders had lots of messages, and the girls gossiped about who was choosing whom. I was comfortable with it, but I missed the feeling I had in California. I liked working in the bar with R. Lee there. I did well, my steady clients were overjoyed to see me, but my jet lag and chills were slowing me down. A girl in town gave me a joint; she said it was some new shit. I decided to save it until I went back home, where I would really need it. J.N. wanted me back when the bars closed, and I knew that I'd better do that. I walked out as the bar was closing and there he was, looking cruel and heartless, without a smile on his face. "Get in," he said, "I'll take you home."

I felt like I was getting into the car with a stranger. Quietly, he asked how much money I made, and I told him it was around four hundred. He took the money, gave me forty dollars back, and told me to use twenty dollars for Nana and another twenty dollars for food. "What about the oil? I need the money!" I begged.

"You can get the fuel in a couple of days," he said, icy cold—like it felt in the apartment. I had already stashed a twenty-dollar bill in my shoe, and that gave me another twenty dollars to give to Nana for taking care of R. Lee. He never took me to buy food. We went straight back to the icebox of a house. No kiss goodbye...no hint of tenderness at all. He drove off. I was crying as I walked up to the cold, lonely place. The waterbed was warm, and I layered covers and towels on top of me to retain the heat once I lay down. My stomach was growling, and I got up in the cold and looked inside the kitchen cabinets. They were moist from the little bit of heat the oven gave off. I found a package of crackers and boxes of Prince Spaghetti in the pantry cabinet, but no sauce. There was a full bottle of ketchup in the refrigerator, which was gourmet to me at this point. After preparing the pasta, while getting whatever warmth I could from the stove, I had a huge, warm bowl that tasted better than I could even imagine—a million dollar supper. I saved some to eat for breakfast. I was warm in the bed and made it through the night, falling off to sleep without a thought in my head about J.N., just about R. Lee and moving. I never did smoke that joint.

The night passed quickly, and when I woke, it was ten a.m., later than usual. I dreaded having to take a shower, my nude body in the frigid air and cold ice water. The conditions were so poor that I began planning how to free myself from the situation. I couldn't tolerate it much more unless I had an ideal place for my son to go before he started the first grade in September. I needed to get the keys to my car back so I could get around faster. After showering—ugh—and getting dressed, I scarfed down a bowl of spaghetti without heating it, feeling pressured to accomplish a number of things. I wanted to spend some time with R. Lee and give Nana her money. Then I wanted to talk to my friend Mendy at Simco's. I wanted one of those great hot dogs—that would tide me over for the day. Mendy was glad to see me. We spoke for a while about things in general. He gave me two foot-long hot dogs, fries, and a Coke, all for free. I told him my plans. He was aware that J.N. and I had been going through a bad time and that it was about a year of torment since he began acting strangely. I told him I was thinking of moving to Brookline or Newton, and he told me that Brookline was the better of the two, more liberal, and great schools and commute. J.N. was staying in Lynn, most probably with a girl. I sensed something was up. And to top it off, he was still seeing the babysitter, Patsy. I always knew, because I went from club to club chasing him down, that he was seeing other girls at the Jazz Workshop and Paul's Mall, and about all his crazy dealings. He would never change. After my talk with Mendy, I called to see who was at the bar before I went in. Mendy had given me sound advice, and I knew just what I had to do.

I walked down Blue Hill Ave. to Morton Street, and from there I caught a cab to downtown. I told Johnny M., at the 663 Lounge, to hold some money for me until I had saved enough to get away. I knew J.N. would come looking for me when I wasn't at home, and I certainly didn't want to have a stash of money on me. There weren't any places to stay, although Katie offered her apartment to us. I said no because I knew he was safe with his Nana and Grampy. My friend had an apartment I had sometimes used as a trick house before, she told me I could stay there temporarily but not with R. Lee. J.N. had already visited her, making threats when I first took off, and had hit her. That came as a shock to me. I had to try to convince her to drop the charges she had filed against him. She called her parents to go to court with her for backup. Another night passed, and I stashed four hundred again. I had to be in court the next morning and give money to my lawyer for J.N., in case. J.N. said he would be back to get me. The only thing he said was for me to get my friend to drop the charges. We went inside the courtroom, and when the judge saw me, he immediately dismissed the case because I knew him personally—the judge was my cokehead customer. J.N. was aware of this, and that was the reason he had me go to court with him—so the judge would clear the case and there would be no charges. That was slick. My friend and her parents were upset, but I had to do it. If I didn't show up, J.N. would have been found guilty and put in jail.

That friend and I never spoke to each other again. And, of course, the offer to say with her was gone too.

I worked hard and was able to give Johnny M. two hundred dollars more. If I continued working like this, it wouldn't be long until I would have enough for a small apartment. My steadies were reliable, and there were lots of stag parties going on. Marcie had a big party date, and I made great money there—over eleven hundred dollars. Six hundred dollars was all I gave J.N. I'd given him plenty of money already, and I couldn't imagine any reason he wouldn't have the heat turned back on…but he didn't. When J.N. picked me up, he seemed to be distant. His mind was in some other world. He told me I was out to get him and other horrible thoughts. Again, he picked me up precisely at two-thirty a.m. He persisted in asking me insane questions and declaring that he knew I was planning to have someone kill him. I swore that it wasn't true. As his paranoia grew, his driving became more erratic because he thought someone was following him.

When we arrived at the house, he went upstairs and took some of his clothes. He gave me fifty dollars and told me he would be back once the heat was turned back on, and that in the meantime, I should learn to live with the cold. "J.N.," I pleaded, "you took all the money, and I can't get the heat turned on." He didn't return my car and he didn't give me money for cab fare.

"Go to work and make your man happy," he said. I was flabbergasted, totally blown away. I could tell the street guys were coaching him, and that his unbalanced mental state made him even worse. He left. I had cupcakes in my bag, and there was one box of spaghetti remaining. I decided to put off eating until the morning, just smoke the joint to try to relax, and go to bed. I was so glad I left money at the bar. I didn't care about the heat anymore—I just wanted to get out and put all this craziness behind me.

CHAPTER FIFTY-EIGHT

Trip to Beth Israel Hospital and the Escape

When J.N. took off, I couldn't have been more upset. I was pacing the cold floor, and then I lit the joint. Now was my time to relax and smoke it. My friend who gave me the weed said it was the bomb. I liked smoking herb, but it gave me the munchies, and there was only uncooked spaghetti and a pack of cupcakes left for me to eat. The clothes I was wearing were layered, and as I puffed away, I put on more. I thought of the time I got the call from J.N. when he was in California. He told me he was not coming home. He had met a girl and fallen in love! But…the girl was really a man, Marop. I fell to the kitchen floor. Why? How could he! I did not want to think anymore. I went to California and rescued him, brought him back. *Big* mistake. The friend never warned me that all I needed was one hit, it was that strong, and—what the hell—I smoked the entire joint thinking that everything was okay, trying not to envision J.N.'s antics. Good thing it was a super-skinny joint.

I was wishing Harry the Whip was there with me; he loved the cold, and during my last romp with him, it was sub-zero weather. He wasn't dressed, having taken off his pants and shirt, and I tied him to the steering wheel of his car with his necktie and draped his coat over him. I was sure he would be calling this week. I fired up the roach, and inhaled again as I thought about different tortures to perform on him. While he was doing whatever I chose for him, he would cry out, "Oh, Mistress, please Mistress, more, more!" A queasy rush was building up in me. I was feeling funny, kind of paranoid, and I became concerned. Something wasn't right. My heartbeat was racing, and I didn't know what was happening to me. I was in the moment, listening to and feeling the beat, beat, beat of my heart. I stopped thinking about Harry the Whip and tried walking it off. I experienced a wave of a combination of anxiety, nausea, and panic. I couldn't speak. I had to get a cab and go to the hospital. Shit, the words barely came out! I took my coat and scraped some change together, leaving on my pajamas. My heart rate wasn't slowing, and I knew something was wrong—really wrong. I began to feel faint. I barely made it down the stairs.

I was terrified when I got in the cab, and when the cabby spoke to me his words sounded jumbled. "Please hurry! Beth Israel Hospital Emergency!" He took me there in record speed: up Blue Hill Ave. to Egleston Street by way of Seaver Street and Columbus Ave., then he cut over by Parker Hill Ave. and *boom,* I was there. I wasn't talking, just holding my chest. The driver helped me inside. A doctor rushed to my side, and after telling them I smoked a joint, they took me right in. "It was probably angel dust," he told me, "and a panic attack." The nurse gave me a shot of Valium or a combination of Valium and something else, and I finally calmed down and felt sleepy. My heart rate was back to normal. That was a frightening trip, and it made me feel that I never wanted to smoke weed again. After they released me hours later, I walked half of the way to save on cab fare. Exhausted, I went home to get ready for the morning. I had to see my son, then go to work. The night had passed quickly, and if there wasn't enough excitement already, I had to shower in my cold house and get dressed to go out to be in many rooms making my money, once again.

I had been back for almost two weeks and was almost set to make my exit from the apartment. Johnny at the bar was holding a good deal of my money. The heat was still not on and, finally, I called Grimes to tell him about the situation, but as Mr. Grimes told me when he came to look at the house, the problem was not just an empty oil tank but the pipes now, too. They had frozen, and it would cost us a lot of money to fix them. J.N. would never spend the cash on it, and neither would I unless he and I were back together again—and that was not happening. I was leaving! J.N. was still acting weird, although he did finally give back the keys to my car because I told him about the trip to the hospital. I couldn't get to the car until later in the day. He would drop the key off. The reverend's daughter enrolled R. Lee in a program at Tufts daycare (where she worked) until school began, and I promised to drive him there and pick him up. Afterward, he would be ready to enroll in first grade at either the Devotion or Pierce School in Brookline for the coming September, where I was planning to move. I figured R. Lee would have plenty of time to spend with Nana and Grampy until the moment came when he had to leave their house.

I put the money down for a studio apartment in Brookline. The landlord would call me as soon as it was ready. Meanwhile, I was stuck in the freezing apartment on Tennis Road, and concentrated on reading once again some of J.N.'s scribbling that covered the kitchen walls, trying to see what his mind was doing. J.N. had added in his own references to being in the life with me. The black marker that extended from the floor to the ceiling began to run once the oven heated up, and the frozen water cascaded down the walls in shallow pools of melting ice. It looked like black blood dripping, a gloomy sight. Truly, I was living a nightmare. J.N. did not care, he still left me in the apartment by myself to suffer the cold, but he collected the money everyday like clockwork. Each time I saw him, he was more haggard and disheveled than before, skinny and unshaven. J.N. needed serious help! I didn't want to look at his vacant eyes—they reminded me of his cruelty and insanity, and I'd had enough of feeling bad. Knowing I would be moving kept me going; I was working all the time, sometimes staying up all night to go through my things.

One day, just as I was going to see R. Lee and then head to work, the call that I had been waiting for finally came. I told the landlord not to speak to anyone except me when he called and to say he was an insurance salesman and hang up if a man's voice answered the phone.

I told him why and he understood. Fortunately, he reached me and I was relieved. He asked me to come over to sign the lease and put down the remaining money. It was late morning, and I had to pick up the money Johnny had been holding for me to pay for the new apartment. First, I had to see R. Lee and Nana to tell them I would be back later and not to worry if I picked him up while he was outside, and to tell her to please have our things ready just in case. When I called the 663 Lounge, Johnny told me he would run out when I pulled up. Then I would be Brookline bound!

I paid all the money plus one month extra, received the keys, and was on my way back to get R. Lee. I had to get him quickly before J.N. came looking for me! March was blustery but not freezing. I sped around Blue Hill Ave. to Tennis Road. I saw R. Lee playing outside. I gathered him up and hurried back into the car. I would have to come back for our things at a later time. I was about to put the car in drive...and there he was—J.N., in his car, directly behind me! He had a crazy look about him. I peeled off, up Tennis Road onto Walk Hill Street, driving as fast as I could through the neighborhood and Forest Hills into Brookline. R. Lee was horrified and crying. "Mommy, please stop! You're going too fast! Please..." My car was made to be much faster than J.N.'s, the pollution pipe was off and the car was souped-up, so I stayed ahead, but he was still on my tail. The police spotted us speeding and put on the siren for us to stop as we entered Brookline. I was relieved; it was better that they stop me now rather than me having to call them later. I was so close to the apartment that I kept on going until I pulled onto the street at the corner. Two cruisers pulled us both over, and one officer approached R. Lee—"Are you okay, son?"—and asked us to get out of the car. I was sorry I had to put my son through that chase—he was too young to understand the depth of why I had to escape from his dad. The other officer told J.N. to step out too. We were briefed, and because it was clearly domestic, one of the officers left. Then J.N. called to R. Lee, and he refused to go to him, holding onto me. The officer asked R. Lee who he wanted to be with, and R. Lee, who was confused and hadn't stopped crying, said, "I want to stay with my mommy!" I didn't want to take out a restraining order because

I knew J.N. would be disturbed even further by having to deal with the police. R. Lee was in my name anyway. The officer gave J.N. a warning to stay out of Brookline, a stern warning, and said that if he persisted they would arrest him. He understood and left, the officer following behind him in his cruiser. R. Lee and I had escaped his father and the apartment with some clothes and personal items I had in the trunk, as much as I could fit. I would go to Nana's for what I had left there. I didn't care about R. Lee's furniture because I knew I'd be able to go back later and take the living room furniture and other belongings once J.N. was out and back in West Medford. But if not, I would buy more. I knew he couldn't stay there without an income and no heat. That's why he took his clothes out. There would be no more freaked-out nights, lying there sleepless, worrying about what J.N. might do to me and his son.

Still, the move was traumatic. I loved J.N., and R. Lee missed his father, but I had to be strong and stay away from him. Eventually, we exchanged letters back and forth. He hadn't gone back home to live in West Medford. In my heart, I felt I had done the right thing. R. Lee was registered at the school in Brookline. He was all set to go! He was attending Tufts daycare, where Nana's daughter was, and he met a new friend, a teacher named Hario. He would come home and tell me what activities he did during the day with Hario, and after a while, I met him. He was so good with my son. We started to date. I was getting all sorts of flak in town from pimps because I was solo. And because J.N. was checking on me, I was afraid to be by myself at home. Hario was a square. I wasn't entirely sure of him, but it seemed like he would be able to handle J.N. He was streetwise. I was highly emotional and wanted J.N. back, but I couldn't give in to that wish. He was watching me when I was in town and in Brookline. I could only let J.N. speak with R. Lee on the phone. My fear of him was greater than my love. I got in touch with the madams, and once I got a bigger place, I would trade girls again.

Marcie was in full bloom running her in-call service, and she wanted to include me in the business. We were becoming closer now that I was back. I met Kara, a girl from New Bedford, and she and I were working together along with Kay, a pretty Jewish girl from

Brookline. I never understood the reason she wanted to be part of the life. She had everything—great parents, a sister she loved, good looks, and on and on. Along with Linda, all of us were on a roll. They worked the bars and streets, unlike Katie and Robin. There was an older guy in town from Ohio, Vin, who was with a classy black girl. She was trying to pull me, and he was getting another white girl at that time too. He had a tough reputation and, like J.N., was a Taurus. I put off choosing because Hario was coming around more. His wild personality attracted me, but, clearly, I was not ready for intimacy, and my lifestyle was not what he wanted. The more I enjoyed his company, the more he came around the apartment. He would watch R. Lee and take him out with him. He was so good to my son, and my son took to him. Between Grampy and Hario, I felt secure, but still not safe from J.N.

The place in Brookline was too small; it was a studio apartment, and I needed much more space. The landlord understood it was temporary and that we had to move. Hario and I were becoming closer everyday, but I wouldn't have sex with him yet; he was so frustrated from desire that he got blue balls and had to go to the hospital. I felt terrible, and it wasn't long before we were together. The sex was powerful—he knew how to please a woman, and his voice was magnetic. Even though he had street smarts and street friends from growing up in the hood, Hario was a square by choice. He hated the fact that I was rooted in the life. But above all else, my son was attached to him and they had fun together.

The new place I found was in a brick apartment building on Harvard Ave., off Harvard Street in Brookline. It was a basement apartment with a front and back door, so when I worked with my regulars they could enter through the back door and leave that way too, directly into the parking lot and straight to their cars. We moved in. Hario and his friends helped me go to Mattapan to get my things. I took my couch and my stereo system with my reel-to-reel over to the new apartment. R. Lee had all his furniture and things. He was doing well at the Pierce School, making new friends, and did not act out. I took up playing backgammon again, just as I had played with

J.N., and with his brother and sister-in-law, and I was getting even better at it.

I had a new place, a peaceful one with space for us all, and yet I was uneasy because I missed J.N. Still…I loved him so much. Kara was messing around with this guy behind her man D.G.'s back. I warned her to be careful bringing that man up to their apartment and having sex with him. She was so careless, I was afraid she would be caught someday. I told her that even though I wasn't with J.N., I wouldn't want him to see me with another man. Of course, it would upset him. How dumb could she be? Just a matter of time! I was worried for her. R. Lee was getting lots of attention from all my girls, but I worried about him too. I was too controlling, not realizing that I was smothering him with my overly concerned love. Without good models to guide me, learning how to bring up R. Lee was a matter of trial and error that progressed with time. I look back and see all the messed-up things I did. I also look forward at all the things I did good.

CHAPTER FIFTY-NINE

Another Father Figure

J.N. was still a problem. He didn't know the address of the new place we moved to, so he called constantly. Kara and Kay were over all the time, hanging out in the kitchen and seeing some of my regulars. Hario was becoming possessive and wanted me home more often. I didn't want to be that close. I slowly edged away from him, hitting the streets even more. He wanted me to stop working. Like J.N., he wasn't able to handle it. I didn't want to have deep emotional attachments. And even before I entered the life, I chose not to become attached after my experiences with Anita and Freddy. I asked myself why I couldn't stop, and the simple answer was that I was driven to succeed "on my own." I didn't want to be dependent on anyone, ever. I wanted to have a man in my life, but I kept my distance.

It finally happened. Kara got caught fucking around on her man. I knew it; I had tried to warn her. The drug dealer she was with, D.G., was no joke. She played the wrong one this time. It was early in the day, Hario was at work, and there was a knock at the back door. It was D.G., and he had blood on his hands and clothes! Oh shit! I was reluctant to let him in, but it was better to have him inside than out back where someone could see him. I signaled him to come to the kitchen sink. The first thing he asked me was if I had seen my buddy Kara, and I told him no, not since last night when she had been with us. "Oh, well, your friend is probably in the hospital along the Jamaicaway by now. I tried to kill her."

"What! Why?"

"I caught that bitch in my bed fucking some nigger I knew! That motherfucker! He was on top until I came into the room. I told them both to get the fuck out! I'm gonna bust a cap in his ass next time I see him! And I jacked her up in the house this morning, then I took her to Franklin Park and whupped her ass! I woulda killed her if some kid hadn't come along."

I gave him towels and ran the cold water. I told him I was going to the hospital. "Stay here and shower, cool down if you want, at least until you've washed the blood off and changed." I gave him a white tee shirt of Hario's.

"You tell her to stay away from me—she really fucked up!" And he was right. He loved her and would have done anything for her, but she had bad-girl habits. He was wrong to beat her; he should have just let her go. I got dressed and left, speeding in my Riviera the entire way to the hospital. The nurses in Emergency told me where she was. When I went to see her, detectives were there asking questions, so I stepped back. They hadn't taken her to an in-patient room, she was still in Emergency and in danger, and they were all over her. She had been there for two hours, and it was an hour before they let me in. Oh, my god…when I saw her she was so swollen, cut, and bruised that her eyes and face were nearly twice their normal size and her legs and arms had indentations that were blue and red from the crowbar he used to beat her. How lucky she was to be alive! A young kid had witnessed what happened and brought the police, saving her life. From my own experience with Rio and J.N., I realized that messing with love, from anyone and especially with players, wasn't the right way to go. I planned to seek out Vin, a pimp from Ohio, to watch my back. But I resolved not to get too involved sexually or to fall in love again while I was in the life. I had to get a father figure for R. Lee; that was all I needed. Kara was in the hospital for more than a week, and when she was released, she didn't go anywhere near D.G.—a good thing! It wasn't too long before we were hanging out again with Kay B., and the money was pouring in. Hario and I had decided to part friends, and we remain so to this day. The life was too much for him. We were fighting about my working; he became so jealous that he came close to hitting me. I was talking to J.N. on a regular basis now. And I was looking for another place to live that had even more space. When I find another apartment, I will not be giving my address to anyone!

Word was out that I was looking to have a discussion with Vin. It took a relatively short time to find him; there he was in the parking lot, looking handsome and conservative, a well-built, black male at least fifteen or twenty years my senior, who drove a silver Cadillac. He told me he was from Cleveland, his hometown, and that he was planning to go back within the next six months. His long-time girl worked only part-time and was going to take a straight job once she was back in Ohio. My guess was that they were married or he had known her for a number of years. Vin wasn't a hardcore pimp. He would have my back, and that's what mattered to me. I told him briefly what I wanted, and I let him know that I didn't want sex or anyone living with me because my son had enough confusion in his life. We came to an understanding, and I chose.

Another apartment came along, this one bigger than the last, with a basement included! It was a three-bedroom in a two-family Philadelphia-style house on Atherton Road in Brookline, with an eccentric, but cool, landlord. She was like a hippie biker chick, a real free spirit. When I moved, all my furniture from Mattapan fit into the new apartment. I did my best to arrange the apartment nicely, and it looked pretty good. I kept Vin happy by making money, and he kept the pimps away and J.N. off my back. Although Vin disciplined my son a few times, it didn't bother me because R. Lee was getting mouthy and was extremely protective, crying and screaming if Vin came close to me. I understood R. Lee had seen his father abuse me and he was hyper-sensitive, but he couldn't take any man being near me and was now like a guard dog. I wasn't into Vin the way I was with other men, I only wanted an arrangement. But two weeks later, the moment Vin took his nightly money he wanted to go to bed with me. We got together—his choice, not mine. J.N. was doing irrational things like leaving a car in a garage with only two GMAC payments left, and then for no apparent reason, running off to Canada. When he got back, he called and told me he had gotten a great job as a plant manager and met someone he wanted to marry. Marry! What the hell! J.N. wanted to see me. "When I get an apartment," he said as he spoke, sounding loopy and disoriented. It was impossible for him to conceal his craziness, and I knew we would not be getting back together no matter how much I cared about him. R. Lee loved his new school and made friends fast, but he was bratty at times, hoarding his toys and not wanting to share. I didn't know how to control his behavior and told him he would lose his friends if he kept it up.

I started to have two girls at the new apartment for daytime dates, and worked the bars at night. The madams I worked with sent girls to me one week at a time, only two weeks at most per month right now. They stayed at hotels most of the time, where I sent them late clients after one p.m. They only came to the house when R. Lee went to school. Telling Vin about them wasn't an option because I didn't want to involve him in a larger scale operation. R. Lee was having learning difficulties at school. Because I wasn't at all academic, I blamed myself for not being able to help him. I didn't know what to do. Vin and I decided to go our separate ways; he would leave after his new white girl was settled out in Ohio. She was having his baby, and after the birth, he planned to join her there, which was a relief to me because we weren't well matched at all. Then there was J.N.'s so-called planned wedding!

Things became calmer. I had my apartment all hooked up, and Eric and Robin were always over. We were all close, going to the clubs together and eating out after we went to the Jazz Workshop. There were lots of barbecues with Katie and her kids. J.N. called to talk frequently. R. Lee always asked for his dad, but I maintained a distance between them. J.N. was staying at his foster home in West Medford, and I didn't want to be alone with him yet, not until the air cleared completely. We wrote letters to one another, and I kept R. Lee busy as much as I could, hoping that one day soon his father would be back to his normal self and R. Lee would be able to spend time with him. Vin. told me he would watch out for me until he left and stayed over at my apartment only when it was convenient for me.

CHAPTER SIXTY

Looking for Mr. Goodbar

I was still working, sometimes at the apartment of a lesbian named Pala, who rented out one of her bedrooms for a trick house; it was easier than getting my own. I put off most of the girls from New York until I had a larger and better place for them to see clients. I was getting calls from girls all over the U.S. and Europe to book in. Hotels were okay, but you had to pay off staff. And using Marcie's wasn't working out because she was too messy for my taste and busy doing drugs. Her apartment was nasty and smelled of sex, and I was a clean freak. She never encouraged the girls to be neat, and she was always so high she didn't have the energy to do anything but have sex and drink. The girls would be coming to my new place soon enough, where the clients were used to having clean towels, sheets, a shower, and empty wastebaskets with no piles of condoms in them. On Thanksgiving, I made my choice clients homemade apple pie from scratch.

I parked my car and walked near the bar. I needed to catch at least two more clients and then head home. I spent longer amounts of time with R. Lee in the early morning before he left for school, and I was only working at night in town. I knew I had to be more responsible than I had been before. R. Lee had homework now, and because I couldn't help him, I would become frustrated when I told him I didn't know the answers, fearing that my lack of education would have a lifelong effect on him. The streets were quiet. My antenna for danger was finely tuned, more so than many street girls. I felt sad and lonely, wanting to be home with my son like everyday moms. Maybe someday I would be a more conventional mother, but for the time being, I had to go out to make money.

Around closing time at Enrico's, the crowd was not a collection of the most balanced and stable types in society. Mixed in among the working girls and their dates were the misfits, the drunks, and the drug addicts—all soon to shuffle out the door onto LaGrange Street, in the heart of the Zone. Inside, the walls of the place were sweating smoke and stale alcohol, the floor was grimy and sticky, and adhered to the soles of your shoes. All of it filtered through your clothes and soaked into your pores. Money and sex blinded these people to the reality around them. Almost all of them were miserable, beaten down, and chemically hooked. There were men and women who were poor, others middle class, and some wealthy. Not a few of the rich ones were looking for excitement, showing off the money in their pockets to tease girls to get extra then tip them little or nothing. Cheapos! They were there to get their quick nut (get off) and return to their princess wives, all satisfied and calm so that if their spouses refused them they didn't care. They were just trophies. The hard-working men were scruffy and cheap, but were always willing to pay for a good blowjob. The alcoholics were gaunt and chain-smoked, and it was tougher to get them off; the cokeheads…forget it. So many of them hated their life and their wives, and it amazed me that a bit of affection and romance sometimes eked out of these people, but it did.

Some of the tricks, unlike the ones in a hurry to connect, came to see the strippers and would approach us afterward…or, if they were too cheap, would go home and jerk off. At closing time at Enrico's, there were lonely and bored guys purchasing last minute bargains and company: a date for fifteen minutes, or maybe an hour if they weren't married and had the cash. For the hoes, Enrico's was guaranteed business, especially after two a.m. I figured on walking outside the bar to the street to see what business could be had before I went home. I stepped out, and when I opened the door and stepped into the cool, starlit night I relaxed for a moment—then a honk and the whirl and lights of the city brought me back to the street scene. I almost bumped into this guy standing on the sidewalk. He was facing the entrance to Enrico's. His hands in his pockets, his shoulders slumped low, he had a kind of sheepish air about him. Strangely, he was right in front of me and not moving.

"Oh, hi, honey, do you want a date tonight?" I asked him, thinking he'd had too much to drink.

No answer. He just stared at me.

"Honey, is there anything I can do for you? Are you looking for company?" I was apprehensive but not afraid.

Not smiling, not frowning, he just continued to look at me with those eyes—soulless eyes that were not mean, yet unfeeling.

"My name is Bob," he said, enunciating each letter.

"Okay. Sorry. It's a habit. I am used to saying 'honey' when I don't know a name."

He was about 5'8" or 5'9", thin, with a babyish face and short hair with wispy bangs. He didn't seem to be looking for anyone in particular or to want anything.

I said, "Well, okay, that's cool." I stepped around him and was leaving. "Have a good night," I said softly.

"Yeah, wait, I do want something." His voice was low, the rhythm unsteady.

I spun around to face him. He had seemed timid!

"We can do something," I said. "Do you know what you want?" I needed to chat because his silence bothered me.

"Not really," he said. He seemed slightly irritated.

"Did you want a drink? Well, we have a few minutes," I said. "I know the owner, he's cool. I can get you a last one if you like. Have you been here all night?"

"No," he answered.

I asked him if he lived nearby, and he said "no" again. Even though he wasn't wearing a band on his finger, maybe he was married. He stated that he didn't usually do this kind of thing, hire a prostitute. I thought to myself how they all say that, expecting to get the ultimate screw at a discount price.

I knew, while talking and trying to figure him out, that this was one of those times I felt more uneasy than usual. It as if he were expecting some sort of strange and unusual sexual encounter, but I decided I would go with it anyway. I felt that something was okay in a weird sort of way.

"How much is it for a half-hour?" Bob asked.

"Honey, that's a hundred bucks. Does that work for you?"

Bob didn't have a problem with the money. But he said, in a somber tone, that he wanted the bed and the room to be clean. "Well, honey, that's just what I have!"

"Sorry. I keep calling you 'honey.' I mean Bob." Bob wanted to drive us in his car to the place with the clean bed. But that wasn't going to happen. It was important to me to drive my customer; I didn't like being in their cars. It was too easy for them to just take off with me, creating a vulnerable, captive situation.

"No, honey. Oops...I mean Bob, sorry. I'll drive," I said. "My car is right outside in that parking lot." I pointed to it. "It's easier. We'll go to my place, which is a short drive from here."

"I really want to drive," he said—unsmiling, unemotional, almost mechanically.

"Well, Bob, that's not the way I do it. Trust me, I'm a good driver. If not, I'll just say goodnight."

Bob was now overtly irritated and nervous; his eyes glanced to the left and right, and over my shoulder. He shook his head slightly and said, "Yeah, sure...okay. Let's just go."

"C'mon, Bob, this way. Follow me," I chirped as I stepped past him.

On the street and to the left, about a hundred feet from Enrico's, was my beige Buick Riviera with a big heart of a motor, a 455 that could get me away fast if I needed to. I had raced and beaten Corvettes in my powerful baby. I walked toward the car, my heels clattering on the pavement. Looking over my shoulder, I saw Bob sauntering along after me, about ten feet back, hands in his pockets. I got to the car and opened the driver's side door. I said to him, "Just go over to the passenger's side and I'll let you in." I slid into the driver's seat and tucked my purse between my hip and the door. Leaning over to unlock the passenger door for him, I got that little squirrel of unease again. Bob wasn't just standing upright outside the car waiting for me to open it, but instead he was bent over, his face close to the door window, staring at me—an intense stare. Then he opened his door and got in.

"I'm not far from here," I said, "just a couple of minutes." I was careful not to call him "honey" again.

Only seconds down the street, and we were beyond the smoke and rancid air of Enrico's, and LaGrange Street, loaded with late night traffic on the hunt. Sitting next to each other, I smelled a medley of scents wafting through my car: my Shalimar perfume, the pine essence of my car freshener, and the familiar odor of the client—a mix of drink and an overly sweet, bargain-priced aftershave.

Dead silence, no conversation. I could feel a nervous cough rising in my chest. We were moving past my urban business and battle zone. One more intersection, and then a right turn at the stretch of brick buildings, off onto a narrow street. Pala's place was four doorways up on the left, and I had a parking spot directly in front of it. Great!

"This is it, right here." I could hardly wait to get out into the fresh air and breathe easy. Again, no word from Bob. He was out of my car as soon as I turned off the ignition. I grabbed my purse, knowing my knife was in there, and stepped outside. Experience had taught me to carry. I hardly ever left home without it. I looked over the roof of the car and there was Bob, facing the brownstone, his back to me, hands in his pockets once again. He looked to his left and right, and then back at the building. I asked Bob, "What do you have in your pockets?"

"Oh nothing. Just a bad habit," he said. He pulled his hands out to show me, and I could see his pockets were empty.

Not a soul on the block, just the shadow of the buildings against the streetlights. I walked around the car, past Bob, and up the walkway to the brownstone, waving for him to follow me. "Come on up!" As I put the key in the lock of the front door, I had that high-intensity feeling of what was over my shoulder and directly behind me. As I turned the key slightly, I heard the clicking sound of the lock.

He stepped in front of me, pushing the door open. "Whoa…hey… wait…I'll open the door, thanks. This is my friend's apartment, so we have to respect that. It's cool here. I pay her, it's all business." Bob scowled and looked hesitant. He stood there for a couple of seconds then, stiffly, stepped all the way inside. I could tell he was not happy.

The hallway, which ran from the front door to the back of the apartment, was dark, illuminated only by a nightlight in a socket low on the wall. But at the end of the hall, kind of angled off to the right, was Pala's front door. The door was unlocked and open now. I closed it behind us and locked it. A dim light was on down the hall. Pala must have been reading. She was a bit feral herself, and she was also good and efficient. I needed her there tonight—normally, no. The door to the left, the room that I rented from her, was her bedroom. I opened it wide and stepped into the room. When I snapped a light switch on the wall, a ceiling lamp dropped a warm, orangey-yellow-ish glow on a place where your grandma could have slept ten hours a day. It was a furnished room, everything in it owned by Pala's landlady. There was an overstuffed chair to one side and a heavy oak bureau against a chipped wall. The wood matched that of the frame and large headboard of a big old bed that had a thick box spring and double mattress. It looked like furniture from the forties. I hadn't used the room in more than a day, and the bed had fresh linen and a clean quilt tossed over it.

As I shut the door of the room, I got that really intense, queasy feeling in my stomach. And I felt claustrophobic. Bob was standing a few feet away, staring at me.

"Okay, first things first," I said. "We have to square up the money, okay?"

"Yeah, sure," Bob replied, and he pulled some folded bills out of his front pocket. I think that's what he had been holding onto. He handed me two fifties, which I put in my purse, and then I went over to the bureau and placed the purse on it, within easy reach; I checked, yet again, the inside of the purse. All was there, and as I was snapping it shut…cold branched from the bottom of my feet up my body, into my heart, and out to my fingertips.

Although I didn't know why, I froze.

Bob was behind me, against me now, his left hand on my shoulder, his right hand moving lightly from my jaw up to my cheekbone and into my hair. His touch gave me an eerie chill; he scared the shit out of me. I smelled it again, the mix of booze and the alcohol-laced sweetness of bad fragrance. His face and his nose were nuzzling along the back of my neck. Like a dog, he was sniffing my scent.

I stayed still for several seconds. I had to think fast. I was getting creeped out and didn't want him behind me. I was sure of that, and I shifted my body slowly so that I wouldn't startle him or show my fear. "Hey, hey, you know what?" I said with a tense voice while turning to face him. His hands, no longer on me, were open, fingers spread in front of my face. It was a tight fit for me between Bob and the armoire. A semblance of frustration was in his gaze. I took his hand in mine. Facing him, I started to pull him toward the bed, saying, "Why don't we just go over here, get comfortable and have some fun?"

Bob didn't object. He shuffled forward along with me, his eyes vacant again. He was standing facing me, his back to the bed headboard. Suddenly, he was aroused. I could tell by his dilating pupils and the erection showing beneath his pants, pulling the fabric taut across the area of his crotch.

I said, "Why don't I just loosen your belt here, and put my mouth on you so you can feel better. Just lie back. Sound good?"

"Sure," he said. His body felt cold.

Damn, that stare. I'd seen it before. This guy had some problems. He reminded me of that crazy sugar daddy from the service who followed me everywhere, until one day when I drove him to the police station in the South End and told the cops he would not get out of my car. When they asked him to leave he refused and was arrested. After that, he knew I was serious and stopped following me.

I was on my knees as I pulled on his belt buckle. I undid the zipper, then I pulled his underwear and pants down all the way to his ankles, slowly and sensually. I watched his face for any changes as I attempted to remove his pants, the hard-on he had before decreased and disappeared. Apparently, he wasn't expecting much, or I wasn't doing it for him. Bob was totally flaccid. I looked up again, and he was looking right into me—with intensity and no emotion. It was not sexual. He was tough to figure.

"Just lie back and try to relax. I'll give you a body rub."

Bob didn't lie back on the bed. He just sat up, his back arched against the pillows, like he didn't want me to touch him. He was tense. I was about to get up and lie down next to him on the bed.

"Stay there…on your knees…can you try again?" he said, finally speaking up, asking me directly to put my mouth on him.

"Of course, I can," I replied sweetly. I looked at his face, and his eyes were now telling me yes. I was sure that something had livened up in them. He was thinking and getting turned on, almost as though he wanted to mount me. I began to lick and purr and coo and stroke. The tip of my tongue danced on his member from the head down to the shaft, and then the underside. I tongued at the base and then licked and kissed back to the head, my fingertips using a tickling motion across his balls. I was gentle, trying to relax him, all the while touching his body sensually. Amazingly, there was only a very slight awakening from Bob. Not much was happening at all—then nothing! I was calm and stroked his legs with my hands. His face softened. I did not speak the way I would with other clients to arouse them but held back, sensing he would not go for it, almost as if he were the type who didn't like women.

"Do you think this is funny?" he asked. The question wasn't right. Why would he think that, I wasn't even smiling? And there was a change in the tone of his voice, it sounded edgy and psychotic—perhaps related to what I was now seeing, the evil which had started to dance in his eyes. I pulled back and looked at him closely; his eyes were focused on me and there was an urgency in them. I got nervous. I thought fast and said, "Maybe I'm not doing it the way you like. Let's try a bit more." I went down again, doing my best to coax a rise and response for another few minutes without success.

And then he said it again, "Are you sure you don't think this is funny?"

"No, why would I?"

A smart working girl appreciates how things can turn on a dime, and how quickly the situation can arrive at the point of no return.

Something had just changed in a hurry. I didn't like his calmness and lack of sexual drive turning into something different. Bob's question, in its tone and cadence, had me altering my strategy, reworking the game plan so that I could ward off what I was beginning to think could become a big problem. My antenna had honed in on danger. I sensed he was about to grab me.

I stood up and blurted, "You know what? I messed up. I pushed you to go out, and maybe you weren't ready. I'll be glad to give you your cash back. I would never accept your money when I haven't fulfilled my end of the bargain." Bob looked stunned by what I had just said. He was now leaning on the bed, propping himself up with his elbows, his pants off and lying on the floor. He couldn't maintain an arousal, but the look of anger on his face was dissolving into curiosity; he was studying me.

"I never take money if you're not pleased," I repeated. "It happens often, and I understand." It didn't really happen that often, but I wanted keep him calm. I went to the bureau, took the hundred bucks out of my purse, and tried to hand it to Bob. He was sitting up straight now, but kept his hands at his sides, palms flat on the bed, skepticism and doubt on his face.

"No, please, I'm serious," I said with my arm outstretched toward him, gently waving the cash in my hand. "I want to give your money back to you and drive you to your car—no hard feelings. Neither of us was in the proper mood." He wanted to say something but stopped himself. He just stared, no movement…one second… two…three…four seconds…still staring, still no movement. *Not good.* Then, finally, he reached up slowly and took the money, all the while looking at me as though trying to figure me out.

"It's cool," I said, still nervous but relieved because that usually means that the contract between us is cancelled. "Come on, I'll give you a ride back now, okay?"

"Sure," he mumbled as he stood and bent down to pick up his pants. I did not laugh or say another word, but he still asked if I thought he was funny. Bob handed me the money back, saying, "This is yours, you earned it." I refused, but he just put it on the dresser. I took it so he wouldn't be insulted, but I was still on edge. "I *am* pleased that you were truthful about the room being clean! I was going to get on top and fuck you to death," he said boldly and in a manner that was totally out of character from his previous behavior, "but I decided not to." Wow, I was floored! Now I felt more than just concerned about what could have possibly happened. And he kept repeating that he was surprised about my not thinking he was funny.

When we got out of Pala's place and went to my car, I realized that my quick and smart thinking had saved my ass. He could have just fucked me and taken his money back. I had enough experience to know how things like that could go very wrong. If Bob wanted to hurt me he would have done it inside the apartment, but not without a good fight from Pala and me. On our way back to Enrico's, I didn't say anything and turned on the radio to have music in the background. It was about three a.m. Bob asked, "Is that your real name, Leah?" And because Leah was my middle name I told him yes, it is!

We were only a couple of hundred feet from the bar, its sign still lit and visible ahead, when in a wry voice, Bob said, "You don't know how lucky you are that you didn't think I was funny." I was puzzled and frightened. Why did he keep on mentioning that? I kept a straight face. Bob didn't just make me feel nervous, he scared the piss out of me, but I stayed quiet. It was about being alert.

In front of Enrico's, I put the car in park but kept the engine running. I turned to him and once again said, "I'm sorry things weren't better for you." He sat still, looking out the front windshield. For a moment or two, he just sat there. Then, again, he said, "You sure are lucky that you didn't think I was funny." I was speechless.

Bob opened the car door, put one foot on the pavement, and then turned and looked at me. My heart was pounding and banging up a racket. I put a hand in my purse to grab hold of the knife. I met his eyes—his dark, empty eyes. "Have you seen the movie, *Looking for Mr. Goodbar*?" he asked.

"I've heard about it. Diane Keaton is in it, right?"

Bob giggled. "Yeah, Diane Keaton is in it. She got what she deserved. You should see the movie. It was a good thing you didn't think anything was funny. Be sure to go see it. In fact, I insist you go see it, and once you do, you'll understand. I may be back one day to quiz you…"

Those were his departing words. I will never forget his expression. I felt as though I had been spared. I had to see this movie, or it would haunt me. So as soon as I could, I caught an early matinee of the film at the cinema near Massachusetts General Hospital. I sat and watched the movie that was based on a Judith Rossner novel of the same name, which was inspired by the true-life story of Roseann Quinn, a young woman who taught at a Catholic school for the deaf in New York City in the early 1970's. Quinn was a beloved teacher who enjoyed hanging out at night and picking up men at bars not far from her apartment in the Upper West Side of Manhattan. She preferred hard-edged types, not her social or mental equal. She brought them home to engage in rough sex. Some of the men beat her. Bob seemed to be so conservative, I couldn't fathom why he wanted me to see the movie. He wasn't that type…or was he? In my business, I should have known better than to make assumptions.

Quinn searched for abuse and torment. On New Year's night, 1973, she scored all of that, big time. She picked up a guy named John Wayne Wilson at a bar across the street from her place and brought him back home. As this sicko later described, he and Quinn smoked marijuana and then tried to fuck, but he couldn't get it up. He said the two got into an argument, and that Quinn told him to leave. When it got physical, Wayne grabbed a knife, and—according to him—Quinn said, "Kill me, kill me please!" Wayne did just that, stabbing her eighteen times, and then, now excited and erect, he screwed the corpse. Before he left the apartment, he shoved a candle up Quinn's joy canal and then took a bust of Quinn (I guess one of her students lovingly made it) and smashed in her skull with it. Wayne covered Quinn with a bathrobe, took a shower, and left. A cold-blooded killer. John Wayne Wilson was caught; he hanged himself in jail before he got to trial.

Imagine how disturbed I was watching *Looking for Mr. Goodbar.*

The memory of that night with Bob spooked me—in the movie, Quinn laughed at Wilson when he couldn't get it up.

None of us girls ever saw Bob in the Zone again. I described him and told them to be wary. Where did he go? Had he ever harmed anyone before? Would he have killed me! Did he go from city to city, possibly throughout the country, looking for prey? I wondered for a long time if he would come back to ask if I saw the movie.

Going over this in my mind now, I ask myself how I kept going—one slip with the wrong person and you're dead. Surviving the streets is work that demands focus, and so many girls have not been sufficiently alert to the dangers of their profession. The worst part is that when street girls are murdered, no one cares unless her family happens to come from money. People cared about Quinn, a woman who picked up many men because she was first of all a teacher, not a woman "in the life."

If I were one of those girls who lacked awareness I could have been killed, but with greater psychological insight, you don't go with just anyone with money, and you learn that with time. What I did went deeper than just sex. I dealt with the feelings and emotions of my clients. People's emotions are more profound than any textbook can teach you, and they are spontaneous. Watching *Mr. Goodbar* affected my future dealings with clients. I never told Pala the story. She would have shut down her place. I thought about the movie often. I've told it to the girls who have worked for me. The important and instructive message of it strikes a chord even today and stays fresh in my mind. Young girls with no training need to be educated about such things, in regular life as well as on the street!

CHAPTER SIXTY-ONE

A True Tragedy

I didn't go back to Pala's apartment for some time. The vibe was not good anymore. I was working out of Marcie's apartment, and often booked my regulars at home during the time R. Lee was in school because Marcie was so high. All the while, I was thinking of ways to leave the life behind, trying to hone in on things I liked doing and did well. It was definite that Vin and I would stay together only until his new girl and the other girl were set up in Cleveland; we had an understanding he'd leave once that happened. I was relieved that J.N. was faring better. It was even evident by the sound of his voice when we spoke. Vin helped out with disciplining my son. In the end, R. Lee developed respect for him because he knew Vin meant business but also showed affection. J.N. was still in my thoughts and would always be. I wanted to go back to him *so* bad. Slowly, I was breaking away from being on the streets seven days a week. My girls were doing good, but I still wanted and needed more.

Running my own business was something I could do with my eyes closed. It was necessary to write down rules for the girls to follow because most of them were scatter-brained, and rules were a necessary means of maintaining order and a certain quality of service. Among other things, that meant no girls under the age of twenty-one could work for me. Occasionally, an underage girl with a fake ID would slip through and I would fire her; these girls were cute but immature and silly. My best Boston working girls were Kara, Kay B., Katie, and Robin; they serviced my clients well. I sat at my kitchen table one night and wrote down a separate list of rules for my steady girls. Katie had already broken them all: no drugs, no cigarettes, no alcohol during a session, practice etiquette, wear dresses, makeup, stockings, and nice shoes—and above all, be attentive and seductive. I put the list in a drawer, intending to have it typewritten for them to read and follow. When I got it typed up, I sent it to a few close madams, along with my comical newsletter. My friends, particularly Katie, did as they pleased and were always talking shit. I was set on having them respect the rules if they were going to be working with my customers. If they didn't follow them I wouldn't call them to work as frequently…and I didn't! She would get pissy, but what the hell, it was my apartment.

Kara was beautiful and classy. She came from a wealthy family in Brookline and really didn't need the money that came from working. She liked the life. She had a way with the clients, treating them like human beings rather than sex-crazed animals, the way that most street girls did. She was friendly and pleasant to the other girls and was well liked by all of them. She was a nice Jewish girl from a lovely Jewish family, who should have stayed home!

I had some dates lined up for the early evening and planned to go to the bars afterward. I had gotten a late start getting out that night and missed one of my steady guys. Vin was going to the after-hours and said he'd call around four a.m. to make sure I had made it home. R. Lee wanted to stay awake as long as possible, which was his normal routine. His sitter, a college girl, would be coming later. One of the neighbors had recommended her. We struggled about his bedtime. He was asking me questions, and I was sure that he would be asking a lot more as he got older. Finally, he settled down to go to bed. The sitter was expected any minute now. As always, I couldn't wait to get out of the house to make money, yet felt drawn back because of my son's needs.

When I arrived in town, I immediately lit a cigarette, inhaled deeply, and hit the bars looking for Kara. I was supposed to work with her that night. My clients who saw her, loved her. She had the keys to

Linda's place, a studio apartment in the Back Bay area of Boston, so she could take her bar dates there. Although I had sworn off weed, I still had a joint from time to time and would take a puff or two at the max. But no angel dust, that's what the chick gave me and never said what it was that time. I asked now! I saved a joint for Kara to share, but since she hadn't shown yet, I went to hang out with my friends at the gay clubs between clients. I pulled a couple of customers. One of those was a guy in a black trench coat, who I didn't know was a priest until we got back to my place and he took it off and there was his collar! It didn't bother him or me…normal trick without his collar on. It was only later that I questioned the sacrilegious aspects of the situation. After that, I was back within an hour, and then I saw her. She said she had been busy. We both pulled a date, so we separated again. The clubs were about to close, two a.m. I saw Kara waiting on LaGrange Street. I parked in the lot and we stood outside the car to smoke some of the joint. A man hailed her over and she approached the car, trying to get us a double. He refused the double. I told Kara that I was going to take my gay friend to her car, and from there, I would meet her back on LaGrange to smoke the rest of the joint and maybe catch a couple more. As I put the joint in the ashtray, I suddenly looked up—something told me to get the man's license plate, which we did from time to time. To be safe, I tried to get the plate of the man's car, but he sped away and I could only get the first couple of numbers. He took off rather fast.

I dropped Suzanne back at her car and went back to meet Kara. I waited and waited, catching two car quickies in the dark lot. She hadn't come back; I assumed that when she didn't see me, she'd gotten another date. The darkness of the area struck me. There were shadows from the few sparse streetlights along the way. Cars were creeping, men driving up and down to catch the late night sex romps they knew they wouldn't get from their wives and girlfriends at home, especially because of the late hour. I felt worried; it was odd that Kara never came back, she loved weed. LaGrange was deserted that night. Usually, girls and clients would be straggling along the street, but there was almost no one. I got a couple more quick dates, cheap ones, and it was four a.m. I didn't smoke the rest of the joint but left it in the ashtray of my car for the two of us to smoke the next time I saw her. She must have gone home. Glancing at my clock, I saw it was nearly five a.m.—shit! I had to go. I didn't see Lynn either. Weird. I knew I was going to miss Vin's phone call, and the sitter would be upset.

Traffic on the way home was zero. I got back in no time. The sitter was asleep, and I woke her and let her go, calling her a cab. She had another job later that day. Tired and hungry, I dozed off into a deep sleep. Vin came in from the after-hours. Usually, he stayed until seven a.m. or later. He called for me to come into the living room with him. Stumbling out, I asked him, "You're back already?"

"I have something to ask you, baby. Where were you tonight?"

"Working," I told him.

"Why didn't you answer my calls?" he anxiously replied.

I was curious why he was asking so many questions. If I wasn't home, why did he expect me to answer the phone? "What were you doing, and who were you with?" Vin asked. And before I could answer, he asked, "When was the last time you saw Kara?" At first I thought he was asking because he thought I was with another man.

"After the bars closed," I explained, "I was supposed to wait for her, but it was so late. And we kept missing each other. I put our joint in my car ashtray. It's still there."

"Listen, baby, Lynn's man was at the after-hours and said Lynn found Kara's body at the trick house and called the police. She was dead."

"Dead? Oh no, no, no—it can't be! It has to be a mistake! No, no way!" I was *so* freaked out. "I saw her! I did get the first few numbers of the car she took off in! She was fine! It can't be! You can give the plate numbers to her man! I swear she was okay!" Vin tried to calm me. "What should I do? Where is she? I don't believe it!"

"Did you know the guy she was with?"

"No."

"You know a cop from town. Call him, and ask him to check," Vin said.

"Okay, I'll call him now." I was shaking as I tried to remember the cop's number. I didn't want to call him, but I needed to. It had to be a mistake! No, not her… When I called Lynn she didn't answer her home phone, and Vin said she was probably with the police. "You're for real?" I asked him. "Yes, baby, I am. Now call."

Both of us were shocked. I left my number for my cop friend to call me back. Silence filled the room. The phone rang. I was hyper, biting my short nails even shorter, and smoking cigarette after cigarette inside the house.

"You called the station and left a message. Are you in trouble?" "No, not me. It's Kara. Did you hear about anything on St. Botolph Street? Did something happen there?"

My officer friend wasn't forthcoming and asked me if I knew what happened. So something did happen? I told him what I heard. There was a pause, and then he told me he knew, that he was on duty when the call came in.

"Yes, it's true I'm sorry to say. That's all I can tell you. Your friend Lynn found her and called it in. She was identified—it was her. Let me know if you have any more information. I can't really discuss it yet."

"I do have information! I have the first couple of numbers of the plate and the color of the car she got in. That was the last time I saw her." Oh, my god, I don't believe it!

"All right, give them to me but not to anyone else." *Here we go again,* I thought. I have to trust him, even though I had tried to help him before, and I also helped him solve a big gun sting chase out of Park Square to the Expressway—risked my life and got no credit for it. We were sitting in my car, having coffee in a back alley, when I saw a man getting robbed. We followed the robber, I drove while he called it in. Big chase, big catch—a load of contraband weapons in the trunk! I stayed anonymous, and he got all the recognition…

"Okay, but I'm not sure that he was the last customer she saw."

"It's okay, we can check it anyway," he told me. Tears were trickling down my face. This was actually happening! It was for real.

He was on duty and had to go. "Goodbye," he said, "and be careful."

I broke down in a flood of tears. "No, no, no!" I cried. Vin held me and comforted me. He understood how close we had been. The girls didn't even know she used to come to my house and hang out when she wasn't working. We lived only two streets away from each other in Brookline. Vin told me he would understand if I didn't want to work anymore. He was going away in any event—what did it matter to him? With all the murders and beatings in town, I had never considered quitting because I had to make a living. I was concerned with being more careful because the business was as risky as it was, then and now. We talked for hours. The sun had risen in the sky, and I couldn't go back to sleep. I had to call someone to vent. Finally, I got ahold of Lynn, who had been with the police all morning. She said she had talked to Kara before the date she caught, and she said it was her last date of the night. Her voice was shaky, and she was crying as she spoke. She already knew that I was supposed to meet Kara on LaGrange when she came back. I thought that if I had been with her, she might have had a chance, but the man didn't want two girls, I explained to Lynn. If she had been somewhere else, perhaps if she went with me, she wouldn't have met him. I thought of all the reasons she died, but excuses would not bring her back.

Lynn said that when she went up the steps to her trick house, she paused at the landing in front of her door and it was slightly ajar. She didn't have a good feeling about it—she felt a cold sensation that sent chills down her spine. She entered the room, and Kara was floating in a pool of blood on the floor, her breasts cut up and her face unrecognizable. Her stomach was full of blood. The sight was brutal. She backed away, never turning, hoping against all hope that she was alive but too afraid of approaching her body. It was a fortunate thing she didn't search the apartment because, as we later learned, the guy was still in the room when Lynn came through the door! He heard her and hid until she left. She swore she would never go back to work again, and she didn't. Never.

So many of the girls out there die and are forgotten. This murder was a headline because Kara came from a well-off, Jewish family in Brookline. They found the guy, but I didn't go to watch the trial in court because I didn't think I could bear seeing the photos of her dead and mangled body, and seeing the killer would have made it impossible to keep my composure. I wanted to always remember her beautiful face. I felt so bad for her parents and sister. A huge Jewish funeral was held, then a burial. All the players she knew were invited to the burial ground and the family's home to sit shiva. She was a girl who had advantages other girls did not, yet she was a working girl. She was in the wrong place at the wrong time. We come from different walks of life but we are all human. No one should judge us as stereotypes based on our backgrounds. Some of us come from good families and some from worse homes, some without homes. We are women with the same emotions and feelings that all women share. After Kara's death, I had to take a deep breath before going forward in the life, discretely looking at clients and gauging their potential to be murderers.

During the aftermath of the murder, J.N. called me to express his regrets about Kara and to introduce me to a new friend of his, a girl he was dating. I went to Dugger Park in West Medford to meet them, and to say the least, I was shocked by what I saw—a girl with gold teeth, grinning as she stood beside J.N. Gold teeth? Where was she from? What could he be thinking? He said he was going to have them fixed…yeah, sure. He liked her because, supposedly, she had been a virgin when he met her; he could mold her to suit his needs and wishes. She was Puerto Rican and some of them had gold teeth, he said it was their signature. Wow, classy… She was a square who knew nothing. Sarcastically, I thought to myself that was just what he needed. She really had no idea of what she had to look forward to. He told me they had been dating for a while. Later, he called me and gave me an ultimatum: either to marry him or he would marry her. I asked him if he was serious, and he maintained that he was. I was stunned. He needed someone, anyone, to be there for him—all the wrong reasons to get married. He said he was not in love with her at all. And then there was his propensity to be unfaithful; she was in for a run. We both loved each other, but I couldn't accept getting married for the convenience of having someone to be with. He was prepared to marry whichever one of us said yes. I could never do that, and I didn't believe he would go through with marrying her. What he said in our conversations was that all he wanted was someone barefoot and pregnant.

CHAPTER SIXTY-TWO

The Wedding

Vin was packed to return to Ohio, the place where he felt at home. J.N. was serious when he told me about getting married to the girl with the golden teeth he'd met at work, and he called to tell me the date of their wedding. He said he wanted to see me first, to talk. I didn't want to go to the wedding, but at the same time I didn't want to appear as though I was afraid to face him and his new girl. My friend Dana was going with me, and Vin was accompanying us. She was strong and great to have as a friend. We were becoming best friends in the straight life. She was a square I had met a few years earlier when she was seeing an old schoolmate of mine from Mattapan, R.G. She lived in Brookline, and we began hanging out together, tanning up on her roof deck. She was extremely talented artistically. When I confided in her, telling her what I did for a living, she didn't flinch. I was amazed—I had a friend who wasn't in the life, and she couldn't have cared less about my profession! She appreciated me, and I loved her! This was a new experience for me. She was a good friend, and to this day remains close to my heart. Even though she moved to Florida and we lost touch for a time, the distance making our relationship difficult, she was always a presence in my mind. We are back in touch now. She has been a tough cookie, fighting off cancer. And, believe me, she will conquer her illness and travel the world as far as her adventurous heart will take her. She always said that once we grew old, we would sit together on a beautiful, sunny beach drinking cocktails. I hope to do that one day.

I went to see J.N. at his apartment in a brick building on the waterway in West Medford. Still in disbelief about him going through with his marriage, and frightened to see him after all this time, I went nonetheless. It was easy for him to break down my defenses. I melted, and we eagerly climbed into bed for a hot and intimate session. Sometime during the sex, when I was positioned on top, he asked me to marry him—last chance. Tears dropped down my cheeks. I made it clear that I couldn't, especially since he had another woman and had already asked her. I knew he would break her heart, and mine had already been broken numerous times. I was used to experiencing heartbreak with him, but she would be more fragile. Plus, I was sure he would cheat on me and still see her anyway. I let him know that collecting the money he owed me was the reason I came to see him in the first place, but then I told him to forget about the money and took off, confused and conflicted. All those years with J.N. were gone, and I was left with an empty heart. He said that he would wait until midnight for a final answer. I wanted to accept in the worst way but controlled myself. I had to think about what was right for my son and me.

I spoke with Dana, who said that if he really wanted a marriage just to have someone there for his own sake then he should do it, and for me to let him go. Dana was right. After considering his proposal, I called him at twelve midnight. He said that he already knew my answer. The disappointment he felt was apparent in his voice. He told me that he wanted me and truly loved me, and always would, and that I would regret it later. Yes, maybe he was right, but I was willing to risk that. As it turned out, I did regret it for a long time because of the love I felt for him. I just couldn't accept his proposal, not only because I wasn't ready for marriage, but because there was no way for me to be sure he wouldn't hurt R. Lee and I again. The damage had been done, and there was no way to reverse it. It would take his new wife years before she caught on to what he was capable of doing behind her back. She was a square. I asked him if he needed anything, and because he knew I could get it from one of my clients, he answered that he wanted liquor for the wedding. J.N. had a new and larger apartment in the Somerville/Medford area, where he and his new wife would be living, and it was there that I delivered the liquor, feeling vulnerable once again. My head and my heart weren't together on the same page.

It was a highly emotional roller coaster ride, and we ended up christening his new bedroom one day before his wedding. In my heart I believed he belonged to me forever, and that if he cared for and respected his new wife-to-be, he wouldn't have done it. I was his bachelor party, performing only for him, without compensation. What I got in return was a broken heart for giving away my love to J.N. for the last time, or so I thought. His wife would never have the kind of love we had shared—we loved each other to the core. I regretted that I was in the life. Perhaps things would have turned out differently had I not been involved in working the streets. But as fate had it, that was how J.N. and I met. I'll never know the person I might have become if we had stayed together. Perhaps it would have worked out with J.N., R. Lee, and me...something I would never know. It was going to be a mess tomorrow; I felt it. R. Lee was already upset about losing his dad, and Dana and I tried to console him. His heart was broken—he had believed his mom and dad would be back together someday. He cried and cried and was so angry with me. He said it was my fault because I let his dad go. I had to live with his heartbreak. The reasons I left his father were too complicated for him to know. Involving R. Lee in his parents' business would have been a mistake. He had to understand in his own way and time. Encouraging my son to hate his dad was something I would never do, and so he believed his father was the better parent and I received the brunt of his anger. And it only got worse.

Vin went to the wedding with me, and Dana took R. Lee to meet us at the church. We made a brief stop at a bar in Chelsea for a well-needed drink. Although I didn't drink as a rule, I was such a wreck I drank one down fast and then another. Vin's advice to me was to pull it together like a trooper and act like a lady, and as though I was happy, so that I wouldn't make a spectacle of myself and put the focus of the spotlight on me. We left the bar. I sat through the ceremony. That was really tough. My son was the ring bearer, and he was so upset that it showed. I gave my gift to J.N. and his wife while they greeted their guests in a line, and walked away. Vin had said to act happy, and I did. I acted my way through life, why not J.N.'s wedding day? I was the leading actress in the drama I had created for myself. Because I had given J.N. his wedding gift the night before, I handed them a card with a check, smiling all the time. But deep in my soul it hurt. I had truly loved J.N. and would miss all the great days and nights we spent together. We had been through a lot in our young lives. I pushed aside the darker times and resentment I felt toward him because of his cheating and abuse and remembered only the good times.

When we first met Dana and R. Lee in the chapel, Dana stood with Vin while R. Lee and I joined the wedding party. There R. Lee was, handsome in his white suit, walking in procession with his dad and his soon-to-be wife. I could see that it was taking a toll on him; he didn't hold his head up but gazed down at the floor, tears rolling down his face. When the ceremony was over, R. Lee had to stand by and watch his father leave in the limo with his wife; he broke down crying hysterically because he had to stay behind. He shouted, "Dad, Dad, Daddy, don't go! Please don't go!" like this was the last time he'd ever see his father again. He cried so much, he lost his breath. It tore me apart, and Dana too. There was nothing I could do but hold him. I felt his anger as I held him in my arms with my friend Dana by our side. I loved J.N. and let him go—I realized that marrying him for the wrong reasons was something I wasn't capable of doing, not even for my son, whom I would die for.

CHAPTER SIXTY-THREE

Damsel in Distress

Vin and I were still living together after J.N.'s wedding, but the agreement between us was that I was on my own. I was so happy to be working without a man. After Kara's murder and my son's meltdown at the wedding, things shifted. It was time for me to stop taking chances. I was the mother of a child growing up without any other family—it was just the two of us. If something were to happen to me, what would happen to my boy? The last thing I wanted was for my son to be with J.N.'s wife, and my adoptive father's family never did, nor wanted to do, anything for me. Aunt Rose on my mom's side talked with me on the phone, and I visited her a few times, but not with her family. She showed some interest in knowing how I was, and I had taken R. Lee with me to meet her once when he was a baby and then another time when he was older. She didn't extend any invitations to me to come over after that but said to always stay in touch, the same as Aunt Fanny, who had little interest in me beyond curiosity. They were not my real family. I sensed that they felt no connection, and so I didn't initiate any close contact. As far as J.N. was concerned, he never contributed anything toward R. Lee's support and, in this respect, he wasn't much of a father. His family accepted me only because of J.N., but otherwise thought of me as white trash and didn't accept me into their bourgeois black family, believing that without their precious adopted son, I would be nothing. One of his foster brothers and his wife, who were the black sheep of the family, were friendlier to me, and continued to be even after J.N. had threatened them when I went to California with R. Lee. I didn't like their excessive drinking, but at least they were real people. I worried that if something happened to me, my son would be by himself. My foster family wouldn't take him in either unless I left a will with plenty of money for them. They would only offer because money talks, but to feed and care for my child—no way. Funny, I would if the situation were reversed.

Money makes a difference. It bought me respect, and the more money I made, the more everyone wanted to be my friend. And not just people in the life, these were regular people. I thought how perverse that was. I will always remember that Woodstock was like heaven because the people there didn't care about society's values; they were free spirits. It's not what you have that gives meaning to life, but who you are, the mark you have left of yourself, and who you've helped.

My son was growing so fast. It was the right time to bring girls onboard full-time and see only the clients who wouldn't go with anyone else. I still kept my business within the time frame of R. Lee's day at school. Those were the clients with whom I had developed an attachment; they were friends, and came to see me not only to have me meet their physical needs but to talk. Some would just call to say hello now and then without money being an issue. All my clients respected my need for privacy. I was so careful not to expose R. Lee to my work. My clients had children of their own, and so it was easy to understand why I was so protective of my son. Katie had daughters, but she lived too far away now, so she worked at my place and the bars only. She ended up getting a part-time job and seeing clients on the side. I was glad about what she did, that she had a square side. I learned and was moving up, looking at what else I could do for my future. That was my goal from the start: getting ahead. I'd had enough abuse in my life and didn't need to torture myself with a lifelong trip of dependencies—there was enough of that in town. I wanted my son to have a good life and become a good man, no matter what he chose to do when he grew up. R. Lee's father and his wife trashed me all the time, which only made me stronger and even more determined. Sure, J.N. was smarter in school and had potential to go farther in the work world, but I was not only more determined, I was wiser. I cared about people's feelings and didn't want to step on any toes to get ahead.

I went in town to give my personal phone number to all my steady clients who did not have it so they could see new girls. I had to convince them to become regulars at my house, to get use to other girls, not just me. I was slowing down on the bar scene and doing less and less on the streets. I called New York, California, Philadelphia, Connecticut, Chicago, Florida, and many states down South. I reached the houses where I had been or knew of and told them to have their girls call me when they came to Boston, and I would trade my girls for them. Now it was for three weeks in the month. My clients were excited about the idea—they didn't want to pick up girls in town; they wanted to get off the streets because it was getting a little too hot there. I sent my regulars to Marcie's girls temporarily when I had no one in, and she sent hers to me. Things were rolling along.

I was dressed and ready to go out. It was one of those days I wanted to get in town for an early start. I had on my hot pants, a tank top, and a pair of heels—not too high, just a little lift—my long blue-black hair down my back, eyelashes, and makeup. I was wearing my outer costume to go to my second home, the bars in the Combat Zone. I went out the door, down the stairs into the hot summer daylight, and to my car. Just as I was starting to drive off, I heard a rough rumbling, and then the sound of my muffler falling to the road below. I pulled to the curb. Great. I had to go back upstairs. Vin was off playing golf somewhere—his favorite pastime. What I thought was even more out of character was that he was going to a straight job when he got to Ohio. I guessed maybe that's what others do when the life and its glory come to an end, or you stay in it and die…or just get old and worthless, and never get a Social Security check. His going straight put my not paying him anymore into the realm of possibility for me someday. He once told me the story of catching his wife in bed with another man when he came home early from work, and that was what caused him to be in the life. It was quite a story. I couldn't imagine the sense of betrayal I would feel finding my husband in bed with another woman in my house. At least he didn't try to hurt her, like what happened to Kara.

I went up the stairs and into the house to get a wire hanger to tie the muffler back in place. I always had a blanket in the trunk for when I would meet Robin to tan down at Revere Beach; I thought how handy it would be for lying on my back while I secured the faulty muffler. As I crossed the street, I saw him standing at the rear of my car: a caramel-skinned guy with taut muscles, prepared to rescue me—a damsel in distress. Who and where did he come from?

He had reddish-blond hair slicked straight back, big blue eyes, and wore a pair of denim shorts split open at the sides with shredded threads hanging down that showed his muscular legs. He wasn't really tall, but powerfully built, a type that wasn't particularly attractive to me. I preferred a cut, toned body, slender and tall, although this man was interesting. It was our first meeting; I had never seen him on the street before. He introduced himself as David and asked for my name. He said that he and his partner Mack were working on a house he pointed out directly across the street, but I could not see it because of the thick branches of leaves on the tree-lined road. It was an unusual meeting for me, one that took place on the street where I lived. As I looked more closely, I could see the ladders leaning against the house—he was telling the truth. Funny, I was used to observing any place where I found myself, but I went out every day and had never paid attention to that house.

With everything happening at once, it wasn't the best time for me to be meeting someone new. He was young, or at least he acted that way, and I had to admit that he was handsome. He had beautiful skin and was mixed, but I didn't know what kind of mix. His eyes were a bedroom-blue, and his smile was beyond charming. He was a knight in torn painting armor. "I can help you tie your muffler," he said sincerely as he positioned himself underneath the car. He asked me to hand him the hanger and described where the pipe had broken. "I'll take it to Midas from here," I told him. His legs were exposed while he was underneath the car and it was a nice sight. "Do you paint for a living?" I asked him. Then I thought how stupid a question that was since he was covered with splatters of paint. He replied that he was a general contractor and the business belonged to him and his partner. "And what do you do?"

"Housewife," I quickly said.

"All set," he said as he pulled his body up and brushed off, his muscles flexing. I looked at him, and he smiled at me with a genuine, pleased smile. "If there's anything else you need, let me know. Glad to help you."

I thanked him. "Listen," I said, "do you smoke? You know. I can bring you a joint." I wanted to give him something like a tip, and he looked like he smoked weed.

"Sure," he said, "I'd love it." Later, I found out that he was actually carrying an ounce of weed himself in his back pocket. "I'll catch you later and bring one back," I told him.

"Great. Can't wait. Hey, maybe you'd like to go out sometime?"

"Sorry, not right now. I'm with someone, but thanks." Although I wasn't really with anybody, I didn't want any other relationships, especially with somebody straight (like J.N. and Hario had been) who would find it difficult to deal with the life, who wouldn't understand it or be able to live with the jealousy that naturally comes from my seeing clients. Besides, I was getting ready to expand the business, having other girls work for me, and it would be an obstacle if anyone came by. This man was square and immature, although I had to admit his sweetness was appealing. I just wasn't in the frame of mind to trust men. I couldn't get involved only to be hurt again; love was too much for me now. My son needed my love and time more than ever.

He mentioned that he had a friend on the street that I knew. "Oh yes. I know him, he lives two doors down." The project across the street would take him another few weeks, he said. And as he waved goodbye, he repeated that his name was Dave. After that, he had lots of opportunities to intercept me, and he took advantage of every one of them. The next night, he rang the bell and I handed him the joint I had forgotten to give him during the day. He thanked me over and over again every time he saw me. I kept putting him off, but he was persistent and continued trying. Every time I looked, he was there. When he asked where I went at night, I told him I was a part-time bartender. He wanted to stop in where I worked and have a drink—I nixed that idea. Finally, about two weeks after we met, I agreed to go out with David, but just to have a drink. I told him about Vin, and he let me know that the neighbors thought I was married to the black guy they saw going in and out of the apartment. I said they were wrong, and David was even *more* encouraged. He admitted that he had been watching me even before the muffler fell off. He revealed to me that he thought I was beautiful and sexy, and that he was distracted by me and had a hard time working whenever he saw me. I explained that Vin was about to go back to his hometown and that, although we were never married during the short time we were together, we had a live-in arrangement. He asked me if I had ever been married, and I told him no. He almost danced for joy. He was likable, and so different from all the other men I had been involved with in my life. He was very immature, but he had personality plus!

Dave was Portuguese, light-skinned Portuguese and mixed, as far as I could tell, yet all his mannerisms were white. When I mentioned it to him he said he was white and that was what he was brought up to believe. His mom had died of cancer, and his father was an alcoholic. He had a sister and three brothers. Dave could down some beers; he liked to have fun and party on a daily basis. When he told me he had fallen in love with me the day we met, I backed up and thought, *Oh no. Shit, this is way too fast and he's way too square.* Was he in search of someone to fall in love with, and I just appeared at the right place at the right time? Or did he fall for every girl? I would have to tell him the truth about myself one of these nights so that he would be able to move on. Just when someone sweet showed up again, I wasn't ready. My Prince Charming comes along, and I'm in the life—that's what I told myself over and over again, and yet there was an attraction. It may have been too soon or perhaps I was confused, but we liked each other, and he made me laugh. The only men I had ever chosen were pimps, and the others had always found me. I had turned out J.N., which was the worst mistake I could have made.

David was single. I did not want him hurt. He told me he had loved a girl he went to school with, but her family had come between them because he wasn't white, they said. He tried persuading them that he wasn't "colored," as he put it. He couldn't accept that he was mixed black and white because his father had been so adamant about his white color when he was growing up. His mother was medium-dark Portuguese, but her side of the family was considered black, whereas his father's side were light-skinned Portuguese who considered themselves white. I told him my son was bi-racial, but on his birth certificate he was black. His father was black and I was white. It wouldn't help him down the road if I did not put the correct color on the certificate. I told him that if my son had children, they would be black and white mixed. It wouldn't be easy for him to fit into society with lies. It is better to simply accept yourself for who you are. Sure, it's tough, but so are many things in life. Although David had been rejected and hurt because of his color by his first love's family, he didn't have as many problems about it as his sister and brothers. His dad, who knew what the deal was, never told the truth to his children, that they were not white. The father was concerned about his children's getting over in the white world. Dave claimed he never saw his birth certificate. He showed me photographs of his family, and anyone looking at them would say that the family was mixed with black roots. His mother resembled Coretta Scott King, an attractive black woman whose color could not be mistaken. David's characteristics were not black but his look was, and having been brought up in the vanilla world, he was taught to act and think one way to fit in. If he stayed around me he would have to deal with it, not straightening his hair and putting in blond streaks to look white—be natural. I didn't know if I would stay with him long enough to get that far. Or would I? I had to pick a night to tell him about myself. I didn't want to burst his bubble, but not telling him would have been unfair. It would shatter him to hear it from someone else.

We went out quite a few times—bowling, dinner, bike rides, and going to Larz Anderson Park for picnics. He loved them, and so did I. We were getting too close, and R. Lee was a bit jealous. I told him I would meet him at his house to talk because he had started looking for me in town to see where I worked. David was out of bounds. I parked out in front of his apartment, a two-family house in Brighton. I beeped the horn and he got into the car. His sister and brother were there, so I didn't go in. I had to tell him about myself. He was floored. I waited for the silence to end. He just sat, staring at me. And then he decided. He still wanted to hang out with me. I said that he had to deal with it because this was the way it was going to be, I wouldn't change for him or anyone. It was my life. I could see him struggling with the dilemma. If he couldn't handle it, then we wouldn't be doing anything together. David chose to deal with it, but he didn't deal with it totally. Just before Vin left to go to Ohio, David developed a serious case of hives while he was in my apartment; Vin was there at the same time. His jealousy about Vin living in the same apartment with me was affecting him physically. Vin and I soaked him in a cold tub, and he stayed at my house that night, sleeping on the couch to be near me. More likely than not, he wanted to make sure I wasn't sleeping with Vin. R. Lee thought David was like a kid and joked about him. In a strange way, he seemed to like him. One of the biggest things Vin did that I hated—and never knew until he told me when was ready to leave—was having David upstairs in R. Lee's room (while he was away at school) and able to listen to me in my bedroom, fifteen steps down from there with the door open, perform with a date. Vin was in the room with David, making sure he knew what was going on! I hated him for that! David was so hurt.

Things got a bit out of hand. David was showing up in the Combat Zone while I was working, and he would tell me to leave with him. A few times he offered me money not to work, which I found insulting and let him know it. I threw the money back in his truck and told him to leave. "Never ask me again!" I said. He was desperate to change me. His interference had been going on for a couple of weeks, and I told David that he would be given his walking papers if he continued. He backed down. "Okay, Lib. I won't go downtown anymore, but call me so I know you're all right," he asked. As I looked into his big blue eyes, I told him I would call.

Vin was finally homeward bound, and David and I spent more time together. R. Lee was not taken with him once Vin left. He thought David was a fool, as he put it. My son didn't like change, and he was truly upset with me. He was just getting used to Vin, and then a new man appeared. I saw that David didn't take too many things seriously and could be silly, not the best role model for a growing boy. But his lighter side took me to another level and relaxed me. It was a new experience for me, but because of my background, I was putting up red flags constantly. I couldn't understand how this man never frowned, was never unhappy, and smiled from morning to night. His good heart won me over. Even my son started laughing. David didn't have a mean bone in his body, and looking at him you would think he was a big bad guy. He never had a fight in his life, but he took up karate, he said, to protect his loved ones. His childish demeanor was what carried him through life. I was concerned that if I ever slept with David, R. Lee would have another meltdown like he did when he saw Vin sitting next to me in the den one night; he ran back to his room, crying that he wanted his dad to come back home.

I told David about J.N. and that I still loved him, though slowly I was separating myself completely. At first, he didn't care, and said that if he had come into my life on the rebound then he would wait for me no matter how long it took, and that I would fall in love with him one day. Amazingly, he became friends with Vin before he left, and went to the golfing range with him—David's first time. Then he met J.N. and got along with him. David stuck to me like glue and was there with me every possible minute, like my shadow. This was a wholly new kind of situation for me. It seemed like a rare occurrence for a man to come down from a ladder behind a tree to rescue a girl with a bad muffler and bad lifestyle. I could hardly believe it happened; the angels were there for me. If this was another piece of my puzzle, I didn't know where it fit or how long the piece would stay intact.

CHAPTER SIXTY-FOUR

The Blizzard of '78 and a New Beginning

"The Storm of the Century," came to Boston on February 6, 1978. It would be a gigantic storm, but the meteorologists predicted it was just another Nor'easter that would dump maybe ten to twelve inches on the ground, nothing more. "We are going to get hit hard," was one of many similar statements made early that morning by Harvey Leonard at CBS. Still, without a real clue as to the potential magnitude, Bostonians went about their business. Few people were listening anyway because the weather watchers of the time were cynical and often did faulty predictions. The maps were sliding blackboards, not rotating satellite images or zooming 3-D maps and precise ten-day forecasts. David and R. Lee were home with me when the snow started in earnest. The atmospheric conditions made for the perfect storm, lasting for over thirty-six hours. Road conditions began to worsen in the late afternoon. Those people who were fortunate enough to be at home were banned from driving and even told to stay in. Traffic stopped, and drivers on the highways were left stranded in their cars without options. Winds were howling upward of fifty-plus miles an hour. Phones lines were affected, as was the power for many areas, and drivers faced the choice of fleeing to some unknown safety in the awful blizzard or waiting for rescue as snow piled up around their cars.

We had shelter and were safe in Brookline on the first floor of the two-family home I rented, so the storm was not as dangerous as it was for others with homes out in the farther suburbs. In fact, it was fun. As nightfall came, we huddled together, looking out the window at a world of all white. And by the morning of February seventh, nothing much had changed except for the height of the snow piled up against the windows and doors, making it nearly impossible to see out or get out! The snow was still falling at an incredible rate, and the winds had pushed what had already fallen into mammoth drifts. We were pinned inside the house by snow barricading the doors. Dave climbed out one of the side windows to shovel us out. Although the headlines were horrific, there were as many stories of neighbor helping neighbor, a spirit among people who lived on our street. I met new neighbors and mingled for the first time. David fit right in with everyone, as usual; Brookline was his hometown, and he had gone to school here. Young people were cross-country skiing on Beacon Street, enjoying what turned out to be days of no classes or work. Finally, after a record thirty-three hours of continuous snowfall, the skies cleared, and President Jimmy Carter declared parts of New England as federal disaster areas.

We were together throughout all of it: R. Lee, David, and me. We shared meals, played endless games of Monopoly and cards, and had fun—no streets or phones for me when I was with my family. The girls were taking up my clients, so I had more time. J.N. and David had contracting in common and were supposed to meet up after the famous blizzard. David was getting along well with J.N. and his wife; everyone seemed to like one another. With David at the apartment, I wasn't feeling as vulnerable as I did before, and my fear of J.N. losing control, and me being weak around him, disappeared. R. Lee was happy to see his father more often, although J.N. found it difficult to get time away from the new family he married into to spend time alone with his son and was always making excuses. I could sense his wife was jealous of me from the beginning. She kept it quiet, but as time passed, it showed itself in various ways, the most obvious being the instance when she came over to my apartment and let me know that I should allow R. Lee to live with her and J.N. in order to give him a better way of life and education. I didn't slap her from across the table; I held myself in check. But how dare she say that I couldn't give my son a good life! I was insulted by her comment, which went way over the line. She never knew who was crazy here—J.N., not me! David had a calming effect on me, and I gathered myself together enough to tell her I loved my son and wouldn't allow her, or anyone, to take him—ever. I asked her what made her a superior mother, she hadn't even experienced motherhood yet. I told her that I was doing everything for my son with unconditional love. He would always have the best of everything: food, shelter, the best school system…and his mom! His real mom. I admitted it was true that I couldn't help him with his homework. I didn't tell her that attending PTA meetings was something I did only grudgingly because the dads were flirtatious (and some of them were my "clients") and the moms seemed to be semi-conscious. I socialized with his buddies as much as possible, and R. Lee had some great friends. I told J.N.'s wife I loved my son with all my heart, and there was no one who could ever replace me in his life—it doesn't get any better than that—and, if anything, let your husband, his father, do a better job! Well, that will never happen. She suggested that I think about it, and the subject was dropped. J.N. didn't interfere; he knew me too well. She never brought it up again. From what I saw when I looked at her, she was in no position to think she was better than anyone as her outer look was hardly the epitome of class and refinement.

We had a Lhasa Apso I adopted by the name of Panda, and whenever J.N.'s wife came to visit the apartment, he would bark and snap at her. He knew… R. Lee spent time at his father's house, hanging out, but the last thing I wanted to happen was for him to be influenced by them. Not only was his wife tasteless and old-fashioned, she came on far too strong. David and J.N. took on some small projects together, some of them on the street where we lived. Eric and Robin were our closest friends and were over at my apartment all the time, either having supper or going out for a bite to eat and a movie with us. They had an apartment in Allston, close to the border of Brookline. Lately, they had been discussing doing some traveling for Eric's new job, and he continued singing in clubs on the side, drinking like always and doing big party shit. Many times, David would sing along with him, and it was obvious that they were both talented. Eric became a salesman on the side, selling pots and pans on the road; he was excited about his new prospects. Travel would be ideal because he could take Robin with him, away from her popping pills and stripping. He was drinking like a fish and snorting coke, so it was good for them both to get away.

My business had taken off, and the money was rolling in. I was also still taking my big cash clients myself while R. Lee was at school and David worked. But what I really loved to do was physical labor, and David took me with him on the late night jobs. I learned a lot more about contracting. And I picked up far more knowledge than Esti could ever teach me about decorating at the foster home. I enjoyed it so much I wanted to do it all the time, but I made better money at what I did with less wear and tear. I wore overalls David had bought me—pink, white, and baby blue ones—and I loved them! He really enjoyed having me there to help him with his work, but wearing false eyelashes didn't go with the outfit, so I lost the cat eyes. Wow, stripped down. I hadn't been feeling as naked without my mask when I was with David, and it occurred to me that someday I could be happy feeling natural with him. He liked my face the way it was without makeup. He would tell me all the time, "Lib don't wear anything but cream on your face, I love it." But I still needed my shield in public.

One night, before I went to see David, I'd gone out with Katie and two guys she knew. The black guy I was with was tall and had a medium complexion. He was extremely fine. He wanted to go out with me exclusively, and I explained that I was out with my friend to have some fun and not to be with a man. David and I had only partially committed to each other. He still lived in his own separate place, although he left some of his things and slept over quite often. I went with Katie and the guys to Walden Pond, way out in Concord, and had some drinks. It was a beautiful night. I was finished working and still had on all my makeup. When I went in the water with them the guy said, "Your beauty is masked by your makeup. Take it off."

"No, sorry, I like my makeup!"

He tried washing it off, using his hand and some water, rubbing it until it was gone as he kissed me on the forehead. "Don't you feel better?" he asked me.

It surprised me that I felt as good as I did without my mask on, but I did feel very self-conscious. He expressed the same sentiment as David, that I didn't need the makeup to be beautiful, but I didn't want to get involved with another man. I was into David too much now. Possibly both of them were right, and maybe I didn't need to wear my war paint anymore. I was older and didn't hang with the players. But *never* would I remove my hot pink lipstick. I would encounter another argument against wearing eye makeup later, but for the time being, I kept my face on when I worked—my eyes were like magnets to men.

I was beginning to fall for David. He loved me for myself. We shared many things in common, things I had never been exposed to and didn't even know I liked until I experienced them with him. Every day was another adventure: like feeding the ducks at the pond and going to the circus with R. Lee. When Dave spoke to me, I could see his pain beneath the smiles—the heartache from his mom's tragic death and the neglect he suffered as a result of his father's alcoholism. And now me, someone in my line of work. His mother believed she had foreknowledge of events that hadn't yet occurred but would happen after she passed on, such as the end of the world from disease and war in 2025, the early deaths of two of her sons, and the serious accident of a third son. David said he knew he would be one of the sons to die young. I told him his mother had been dying a long and painful death, and her pessimism was understandable. I didn't want to believe her predictions, but I couldn't put them out of my mind because of my own premonitions that later came true.

David entertained fairytale dreams about life much in the same way I did, wanting to live in a faraway place that was beautiful and peaceful, growing our own food and living free of society's issues. But given the harsh realities of my life, I couldn't go there except in my imagination. One day, Dave and I were driving down a street in Brookline Village where a squirrel had been hit by a car and was lying on the road. David made me stop the car in the middle of the street and he ran over to the animal, picked it up, and placed it near a tree. He didn't have any fear that the squirrel would bite him, nor did he care. I watched him as he gently pet the animal and talked to it as it lay there dying. David was a hero on both a small scale and a grander one. His quests involved helping people at any time, no matter who they were. He reminded me of my dad when he was with my mother Rose, looking at neighbors' car engines and lawn mowers, fixing them without expecting or wanting anything in return. David dug up worms to feed baby birds abandoned in their nests. When he fished, he threw the fish back in the water. He loved animals. But with people, Dave made jokes both good and bad. Facing life in an adult manner was beyond him. He didn't take life or death seriously. Looking back at when we first met, he wore his father's old, unstylish suits. I had to change all that. He became more stylish once I was through revamping his wardrobe; everyone who met David loved him, but now he was standing out in a crowd. He acted in a more mature way as his appearance improved. His temperament remained as happy as ever. I just hoped I wasn't ruining him.

Sex was great with David—he aimed to please. He always wanted to make love, and he was gentle, whereas I was used to rough play. No matter how hard I tried to elicit another response, he was still gentle. He just didn't have it in him to be any other way but tender. The tender touch or saying I love you all the time was difficult for me. I maintained an exterior that was stern because I was afraid to show any vulnerability, so I would back away. I didn't want to put love before work. I was a sexy bitch in the bedroom, but I kept my heart hidden to protect myself. My generosity extended to David in the same way I bought R. Lee the best of things. But still, there was something missing. I hadn't learned to give my heart away and be vulnerable without backing away for fear of being hurt. I didn't allow myself to experience love fully, in all its facets and reciprocity. The closer I became to Dave, the more I pushed him away, ignoring that part of myself that wanted him. He would give me his paychecks and shared himself in all ways. I felt safe with him in my life in that he would protect me, but I produced my own financial security. What if he left? I shared with him by giving him money and things, but that wasn't what he wanted. He just wanted to love me, and I had no frame of reference for that. R. Lee had become comfortable with David. He had already been hanging out for months now, and the time had come for him to move into the house with us. He offered to pay the rent and all the household expenses.

Dave had abundant common sense and communicated using the simplest of words, unlike the pimps and their preacher-type psychology. He recited Murphy's Law constantly. I was renting another separate apartment for the girls because R. Lee was older, and I didn't want to disrupt our normal home. I found a place in the Brighton/Allston area. It seemed to be the best business solution I could've come up with. My life was good, whereas Marcie wasn't faring that well, and her girls would call me to complain. She was getting way too high. I hired a driver to take my girls on out-calls, using out-of-town girls so the guys wouldn't have any embarrassing moments being with somebody they knew. Plus, the local girls would always give out their numbers to the men, even though they knew they weren't supposed to, and if one of the men got caught with a number it would fall back in my lap, not theirs. In New York, they would be fined and blacklisted. David was relieved he could come in from work at any hour knowing he wouldn't be disrupting anything at home. He was happy he moved out of his hellhole of an apartment in Brighton, where he had been living unhappily with his brother and sister. We were a family: David, myself, R. Lee, and Panda, the Lhasa Apso.

CHAPTER SIXTY-FIVE

Decisions

That first year with David passed by like a flash. Everything was light-hearted and spontaneous, like when we woke up one morning at five a.m. and said, "Let's go to Florida," and we all went, R. Lee included because he was on February school vacation and business was slow. And my girls covered, making the money and answering my trick phone. Ever since J.N. and I broke up, traveling to Florida during the winter had almost become a bi-yearly ritual. My various Rivieras made all the trips in the early seventies. Neither of us showed a care in the world, and we left reality behind. R. Lee was still going to the Hebrew school at a Reform temple in Brookline to study for his bar mitzvah. Traditionally, the ceremony would coordinate around the date of his thirteenth birthday. But because he was having difficulties, I was considering doing it later, closer to his fourteenth birthday, to give him more time to learn his portion of the Torah.

One of David's passions was singing, and he was good at it. His voice just needed some training, and he could use more practice in developing a style. I introduced him to soul music when we first met, and then he was hooked: the Whispers, the Temptations, the harmony of the O'Jays, and Peabo Bryson. His singing excelled, and he soon developed a soulful sound much like Peabo's, and the Whispers, his favorite. He was singing every minute. When he and Eric sang duets together, I would sometimes sing along with them. We provided our own entertainment at our many cookouts and parties at Canobie Lake Park and Lake Winnipesaukee in New Hampshire. R. Lee's adjustment to David took a while. He had gotten better with time, asking Dave to help him with his homework and having private talks with him. David made a point of talking to him and paid attention to all his needs—they were buddies. He was constantly helping my son with his homework. I promised Dave that one day we'd have a studio where he could record. I believed he was talented.

I was bored with the girls and the phones, and wanted to open a business in another field. I even tried to get some of the madams to all pitch in together to do properties, buy and sell. But no, they were all afraid to put their cash in. I didn't go in town as often as I used to, so helping David paint and do small jobs was my favorite thing to do. There were evenings when I felt edgy, and I would go in town out of habit and just drive around to soak in the atmosphere. David watched R. Lee when I just had to go out. It was at those times I could see that he was jealous and upset, like when he broke out in hives before Vin left. David controlled himself, understanding what I was telling him when I said I wasn't going to change after we first met. Even love could not prevent me from going in town or continuing my work. I still held back, afraid that David would turn out like J.N., and he would be unable to deal with the life.

Suddenly, R. Lee was becoming rebellious, not listening to either David or me and acting up in general. He missed his dad and insisted on living with him. The grass on the other side looked greener to R. Lee. David and I made the decision together, letting him go for one school year to get it out of his system. This was the best time to try because R. Lee was young, and David was relatively new to our household. I fought with my feelings, but in the end, I had to let him go. In September of 1979, R. Lee went to live in his father's home. My heart was torn after we made the decision. I hated for him to go, but he would have hated me if I stopped him. Even though the thought of having him with J.N.'s wife was upsetting, it was better that he go now, before he got any older.

David told me about Eva, a fortune-teller who was famous in the Waltham area. Both he and his mother had gone to see her, and he swore by her. She was Russian, an older woman. When David saw her, she told him he was going to meet the love of his life. I told him I would go later, maybe before New Year's, but Dave said to go before my birthday in November. I wanted to wait, but maybe he was right. He thought I wouldn't worry so much about R. Lee if I spoke with her.

Right before R. Lee went to J.N.'s place, he went for a short stay at a summer camp. Dave and I went to New York and New Jersey while he was gone and hung out at Charlie's lavish apartments, with all of her four girls running naked in and out of the bedrooms between customers. We went to Jersey too, and hung out even more with some new girls. And we had a great time finding R. Lee gifts and discussing future plans for when he got back from his trial run at his dad's. I was planning on driving him to his new school in Somerville to take a look at it. The school system was very different than in Brookline. I prayed I hadn't made the wrong decision, but the choice wasn't mine alone. It broke my heart to see him go. I made an appointment to see that reader, Eva, at the beginning of October because my son's absence was so excruciating. The house felt empty, especially during the evenings. I wanted to go in town, and David tried to keep us busy because he knew I was bored and missed R. Lee so much. We decided to divert my attention by taking a quick trip to South Carolina and hunting for another '71 Grand Sport Riviera so we would be driving twin cars, much the same as I had done with J.N. We couldn't find one there and drove back home. On the way, near Washington, D.C., I stopped in on one madam, very briefly, but she was too low end. When I got home, I phoned junkyards. One of the them called me back with a '73 that had everything I wanted, except the windows had been broken out, and with some work it could be perfect. Yes, I wanted it. We had gone all the way down South only to find the car in Malden, Massachusetts. My '71 was all done up, and I had it ready to enter into a show. I had put twenty thousand dollars into it, and she was sweet—soundproofed, the best stereo system, custom interior paint job, and special tires—the car was a showpiece, and I couldn't wait for the competition. For some reason, I was extremely attached to this model car, and I wanted to have at least two or three more custom made. The car was invincible, and I knew I would have them forever. I had many races with her and won every time. We went down to pay for the Riviera and to have it towed to the lot in Lynn where I had my cars worked on. I was so enthusiastic about the car that my mind was preoccupied with thoughts about the project. I put off Eva's reading until the end of October. I wanted to be sure Lonnie was around to get my car. But his plan was to wait until the lot was empty in November to store my car and work on it when it was slow in the winter.

I had gotten lots of presents for R. Lee for Christmas. J.N. took him to his family and his wife's family, but he hated it. The weather was bitter cold; this winter was brutal. R. Lee was unhappy and calling every day to come home, but he had already committed to stay for a year, and I told him he had to stay there until school ended and then he could come home in June. I couldn't wait—I was excited about him coming back home; without him there, my soul was missing. I was glad he got to see what living with his father was like so he wouldn't harp on going there anymore. It was apparent that R. Lee already figured that out, and quickly. David advised me to go get him because he was so unhappy, but an inner voice was telling me no, to leave him there so that his education wouldn't be disrupted mid-year. R. Lee hated his father's wife, who was totally different from me and the other mothers he was used to from Brookline, and he dearly missed his friends. Christmas and New Year's would not be the same without him. We had lost Panda, who passed away from a car hitting his hip the summer just before R. Lee went to J.N.'s. His leash got entangled and pulled him underneath the car. His injuries were so severe we had to put him to sleep. We replaced him with Reece, another Lhasa Apso, who was extremely intelligent, and we took to him even more. Both dogs had the good sense to snap at J.N.'s wife, who didn't like dogs in general. R. Lee missed his new dog, Reece. I couldn't wait until my son came home!

For my reading, I went to see Eva by myself in Waltham, where she lived. The first time I went I was with David, and he got a reading. I had lingered outside, memorized the address, but never met her. He said she was right on the mark with all her predictions, and she could tell me things from the past, present, and future. He said his mother had been born with a veil and was a close friend of Eva's. I was skeptical at first. I had a keen sixth sense myself and could read all people. Sometimes I would know things before they happened. I dreamt about people who had died passing over me, people I didn't know, and as a child I would have dreams that later happened in real life. I could see through my friends, and knew when they were about to lie even before they'd opened their mouths. I could tell when something was wrong with strangers. If I touched them, I could feel if they were going to be ill, that something was going to happen to them. I could sense their energy. I often tried not to get too close to people because of the nature of my vision. I believed the origin of my intuition had to do with my background and my horrific stepmother: I tried to be one step ahead of her, anticipating her next hateful move to hurt me. My sixth sense was finely tuned. It was much later in life that I found out what powers I truly had. Funny, but I could sense exactly where J.N. was when he was with somebody and could easily find him. I felt it when he lied and knew it in my soul. I experienced a feeling of distrust with David, but it wasn't clear yet. He hadn't done anything I could prove, and I wondered why I was suspicious and experiencing nervous feelings in my gut. He was always asking me to marry him, but something held me back. There were times we were holding each other and I felt a distance, like I was losing him, but to whom? Or what?

I had an hour-long appointment with Eva. Her daughter answered the door and led me inside. Eva would be coming out soon, she said. I was to sit at the table and shuffle tarot cards. I owned a deck of my own tarot cards, and a Ouija board that frightened me because it would move all over the place when it answered my many questions…and accurately. Lots of energy went into that board. I had dabbled for a while with some girls who had gatherings on Newbury Street, testing each other's powers to move objects like a glass or dishes. Given enough time, it worked. I had a talent for reading people just by being close to them in the same space. If this woman was gifted she wouldn't have to rely on the cards to read my future.

Eva appeared. She was a mature woman, short, with dark hair and a simple dress. She pulled out the chair to sit. She didn't say a word. She peered at me, trying to engage my eyes. We were in her kitchen, and the room was darkened. Looking straight up at me, she said hello. She nodded, her face pleasant, but I could tell she felt something. She asked only for my first name—telling me to please say nothing else—and for the cards I had shuffled, which she then spread out. She reached for my hands and, as she held them, she went into a trance. I could feel Eva's energy. I knew she was the real thing, not some phony character taking me for my money. I felt a tightness in the pit of my stomach. And then I felt concern, perhaps because R. Lee was so much on my mind, begging me daily if he could come home. I wondered if she felt my sorrow. No, it was this dark-haired mystical lady who was causing me to feel that way. As Eva stayed in her trance, I studied her face. I felt more at ease, though queasy. I knew she sensed something intense. I could hear the faint sounds of a TV in the background and voices, maybe her family or friends. I was waiting patiently, and after what seemed to be an awfully long time, she looked up at me, no smile, just her softened face staring right through me. She asked me if I had any questions. Even though David was in my life, I wanted to know if I would be involved in any new ventures, either personally or in business, and if there was anything she could tell me about children. I asked her about my present and future. She said I wouldn't be having any more children and that she had mixed visions about existing children. She said there was someone close to me in my personal life, a fair-skinned, younger man whom I loved and who loved me. There would be no marriage, but some sad and troubling news in the future. She told me that something major would happen in my life in the very near future, but she wasn't clear about what it was. She was vague about any of my children. "You have sadness now, but it will pass. You make money and are successful in all avenues of your life. In business, you are successful and live comfortably, but there is something…" She spread out the cards, touched them, and put them back into a pile. She looked straight at me, her eyes meeting mine, and said, "I cannot tell you your future. You will not able to handle it, and of this I am sure. It would alter your decisions. You would spend all your money if I told you, and you would not be in the right place in life." She had unsettled me.

"Why? Please tell me!"

"No," she replied, "your life and its timing would not fall as it should. If you live through this, you will be dealing with the illness of a loved one, and also with many lawyers throughout your lifetime. You will have a home and a business and will be a rich woman, but richer in much later years, very rich, not only rich in money but rich in happiness."

"Please, tell me what's going to happen!"

"No, I can't. Your fate is already in motion, and you will be foolish if you know. I'm sorry." She stood, telling me she couldn't say any more.

"Please, I have to know!"

"No, and there is no charge."

"Oh no, I have to give you something." She left the room, and I put twenty-five dollars on the table. The girl I assumed was her daughter came into the kitchen to show me out, but I had already seen myself to the door. I walked out because I was freaked out—I could tell it was something bad that was going to happen, but what? My son was foremost on my mind, then myself. What's going to happen?

I was tense. I knew from her energy that this was no joke. My head was so tight I was getting a severe headache, and I was surprised because getting a headache was a rare occurrence for me. I felt as though I had to put my head in cold water; I didn't care if my hair froze from the cold. I was in the habit of going out with wet hair all the time anyway. I drove to Waltham center and stopped at the first beauty parlor I saw—a place that looked like it catered to white-haired ladies from the fifties. I parked at the far end of the center and ran in. "Please, can I get a wash? Please? Right now! I don't need a cape, and no shampoo. Just cold water."

"Yes, of course. Please, sit down. Are you okay?" she asked me.

"In a minute I will be." She wet my hair with cold water from the sprayer and massaged my scalp. I felt some relief. "You will catch your death of cold. Are you certain you don't want warm water?" "Please, more, more cold!" She kept on spraying and rubbing my head. I felt numb, and the tension was dissipating as I calmed down. She turned off the water when I told her I'd had enough. I sat up and towel-dried my hair while I explained what had happened in the fortune-teller's kitchen. "No charge," she said. She told me that she was the owner, and had heard about Eva's reputation but had never gone there herself. I gave her twenty dollars for a tip anyway, both for the water and her kind ear. She wished me well. I went back out into the cold, but I felt nothing. I was anxious. Walking back to my car, I felt like I was in a slow-motion movie. My hair was stiff, like icicles. I wanted to get home and tell David about what Eva had said and to call my son to see if he was all right. What was it she couldn't tell me that was so disconcerting she refused to tell me at all? I felt as though something awful was dangling above my head and was about to drop. But when? And what?

CHAPTER SIXTY-SIX

Police Chase

I obsessed about Eva's reading for about a week or two, and then I let it go. Everything was okay. Dave calmed me down. My new Buick had been sitting in the lot at the junkyard, still waiting to be towed over to Lynn. I had them wait a bit more until Lonnie was ready for them in the lot; he was going away and closing down over the Christmas season into mid-January. The holidays were desolate without R. Lee there, even though we celebrated with him on Christmas Day. New Year's Eve was truly sad and lonely. R. Lee was carrying on, begging to come home. I tried to placate him by answering, "Soon, soon" and telling him how much I loved and missed him.

The weathermen were predicting either snow or possibly freezing rain to fall. The car was going to be exposed when they brought it over from the junkyard to Lonnie's because it didn't have windows to protect the interior from the elements. I wanted to go to Lynn and cover it with a tarp to be sure it wouldn't get drenched. I had been busy all day managing clients and sending them to see the two girls. I was ready to go to the car and put a cover over it, but then David called and suggested we go together later when he got home. When he came in, I was in the den talking on the phone to Robin. I told her how excited I was to get working on the car, and she told me about her and Eric's day, and that she was going to see him sing that at a club later that night. I had cooked David's favorite tuna melts for supper, adding a small amount of mushroom soup to the tuna for flavor, and then putting the tuna on toasted English muffins with melted cheese. Both of us ate and were satisfied and relaxed. I had forgotten about the car until the weather forecast came on TV. "Shit!" I realized that the car was exposed. I called my son to say goodnight. He had eaten his supper and complained to me about the cooking—another reminder of how much he hated living there. After the news and weather, Dave and I started watching a TV show. "Maybe we should go to cover the car before it gets too late," I suggested. Then I changed my mind. "Maybe we can go tomorrow, how bad could it be? But, then, the interior was so nice..."

"Lib, are you sure, because it's getting late?" It was around eight p.m.

"Yeah, I guess we should go now," I said, finally making up my mind, but something was pulling me to stay home. My stomach was in twists. My intuition should have kicked me.

We put on our coats and headed out. As usual, I took the back roads for the city atmosphere I loved so much. We were bound for downtown, with Reece in his spot, perched on my lap looking out the window, and Dave in the passenger seat. The music was on, and Dave was singing his heart out. The car was airtight except for my slightly cracked window, which was opened for Reece to get some air. I usually drove with my window open, even in winter—halfway with the heat on—but it was bitter cold out, the temperature was zero. I never passed up a drive through the theater district or the Combat Zone. Those places were magnetic, and I never missed an opportunity to see what was going on there. Old habits... I was pulling up Boylston Street, headed for the corner of the Tremont Street intersection, where I would cut through and drive directly to Lynn on the highway. Traveling east on Boylston Street, I stopped for a red light at the Tremont Street intersection. The lights turned green. I always turned my head both ways and waited a few seconds before stepping on the gas. I could hear a siren only faintly because my car was purposefully soundproofed. Not knowing it was a police chase, I proceeded slowly after looking to the left and the right once more. No cars. It was January 29, 1980, eight-fifty p.m. And then, a terrible sound—BOOM—and blackness! I never knew what hit me! I blacked out from the impact. I never asked if Dave went out too.

Because of my impact reaction, I forgot to ask.

Time stopped during impact of the '78 Oldsmobile that collided into my door at an incredibly high speed. Later, we found out the car clocked in at ninety-five miles an hour. I had no idea of what happened. No realization of the hit at all until, maybe seconds later, I heard the sound of Dave's voice saying, "Oh, my god! Libbe! Libbe!" I couldn't answer, I could not do anything, but I was conscious enough to hear that. It was like I was suspended. My car door was open, and David was standing there to the left, reaching in for me. I couldn't feel or speak. Everything went still—time stopped. I was told later that Reece had fallen out and was lying on the ground below, knocked out. David must have thought he was dead and kicked him aside. His arms were reaching in to pick me up. In the distance, I heard a man shouting. A voice yelled, "Put her down! Put her down!" David had lifted me and was placing me on the sidewalk. I had no air and felt nothing, like I was adrift. It was zero degrees and I didn't feel cold, nor did I feel pain. Where was I? What kind of space was I in? Later, I was told that I wasn't breathing. I had died. I could see and hear people talking to me, I could see myself, but I didn't see David. I heard him in the distance screaming my name.

The police were in pursuit of the car that hit me. And because they could see that an accident was about to happen, they called ahead for an ambulance. It arrived as I lay on the pavement. I could see and hear them talking to me. I answered in my mind, but they did not hear me, and I was listening when they said, "She has no pulse, no pulse at all, and she may be bleeding internally! We may be losing her…" They did not hear me. *I'm here, I'm okay! Please, God, I have to live to get home for my son! Please! I have to live long enough to leave him something—don't take me away! Please!* I was begging God as the paramedics worked on me, first cutting my clothes off at the side of my body. I could hear David's voice in the background but couldn't see him or hear his words. I was above the people looking at me on the ground. I had separated from my body, though at the time I wasn't aware of it. As my clothes were being cut open I felt no pain, only peace and calmness amid the chaos. Then they found a pulse. "We've got one!" they said. "Barely, but we've got a pulse!" They said my name, "Libbe, Libbe, can you hear me?" Then they asked me my name over and over again. I was only able to inhale shallow breaths. I felt cold, very cold. My head and chest hurt, and when I breathed it was painful—I could hardly take a breath. Oh, the pain now! Sharp, and chill! "Breathe," they said, "breathe as deeply as you can." "What's your name?"

I whispered, barely breathing, "Libbe," but they hardly heard me. I prayed to God, *Please let me live. My son has no one...please, let me live.* "Her name is Libbe!" Dave shouted. I was in severe pain and my head was bleeding—it was cut on impact, although I didn't know it at the time. I couldn't move at all, but now I could look up at the faces peering above me, groups of paramedics all around me, working on my stationary body with my clothes cut and hanging.

They said, "We can move her now!" and they lifted me onto a stretcher. Intense pain surged through me as I shook uncontrollably from the cold. Someone was talking on a phone or walkie-talkie, saying I was stable and they needed to move me immediately to the trauma unit at Tufts to save me. They weren't sure I was going to make it to the hospital. I kept praying, and they kept asking me my name and what day it was. I was lucky enough to barely get out my name, never mind the day. *God, please, don't take me yet! I have to see my son!* I repeated over and over. I heard David calling out my name. "Libbe, stay with me, please stay...Libbe! Libbe! I love you! I need you...please..." They told him to ride in the ambulance up front while they worked on me to keep me alive. I remember them asking me questions, and though I tried, not being able to answer. I was so cold—only a white sheet covered me. I don't even know if they put a blanket on. I hurt *so* bad. Every part of me hurt, and the only times I made a sound was when they were touching or moving me. We were at the hospital in a matter of minutes. Tufts was right around the corner, and they said they had to go to the closest hospital to make sure I made it there. I was happy to go to Tufts or Mass General, both good places.

They had called the trauma unit to be prepared, and once I was under the bright lights beaming from the ceiling, I could see David standing above me, looking distraught. I heard his sobbing voice saying, "Lib, you're going to be okay! I love you, Lib! Please, don't leave me! I love you!" I tried moving my fingers to respond. They asked him if he wanted to call family members, just in case. Although I could see he didn't want to, Dave went with the nurse. I didn't want to be left alone, but it wasn't up to me now. I could not talk at all. David made calls first to J.N. and R. Lee, then my dad, my foster sister, and my friends. He was angry and went looking for the kids who had been driving the other car, but they wouldn't allow him to see them—he was way too emotional and wanted to kill them. David, with his Gentle Ben personality and manner, was insanely pissed off. If I died, he might try to bust their young butts. It wasn't normal to be experiencing such trauma at such an early stage of our relationship. January 29, 1980, eight-fifty p.m. But it was happening…

David was okay, just a cut on his forehead where he hit the windshield. God had spared him, and I was relieved. My injuries were life threatening, and they performed many tests. My heartbeat was rapid. "We have to slow it down," they were saying. They gave me heavy doses of morphine for the pain and to slow my heart. I did *not* want the morphine but didn't have a choice. The cut on the left side of my head was deep. I was in Emergency for hours, and then I was going to be moved to the ICU for them to monitor me until it was clear I was out of the woods. Because I had been so close to death, David was permitted to stay with me in Emergency and in the ICU all night. They checked for internal bleeding, and the x-rays indicated that all sorts of things were going on. There was a lesion on my lung, eight front-to-back broken ribs, but no internal bleeding as far as they could see. I had a fractured clavicle, and it was difficult for them to see more because of the swelling of my entire body. They were going to do a lot more tests once I was out of danger. David told me my son was on his way. Thank God! He would bolster my strength to live.

My foster sister couldn't come because she didn't have anyone to watch her kids. What a blow that was at the time and for a long time afterward. But Jennifer did say that she wanted to be notified if anything changed. Okay…well, I am a foster kid and no relation. A nurse took the call from my dad who said to let him know if I passed away. That response didn't, and still doesn't, deserve comment. This was a test of true love and friendship—seeing who would visit me at the hospital when I was in dire shape. If the situation with Jennifer were reversed, I would have dropped everything to see a person I cared about, left my kids with someone or taken them with me. J.N. and my son came immediately, and that was what mattered most to me. Seeing R. Lee could pull me through anything. I had to live for him. I couldn't let him stay with his dad, and that gave me the will and strength to go on. J.N. told me not to worry, and if something were to happen to me, our son would be cared for. R. Lee hated hospitals, but he was so brave for me he even watched as they stitched my head. He told me I would be okay and how much he loved me. He was my lifeline. "Mom, I can't wait to come home! Please be okay, you have to be okay!" As he took my hand and held it, I nodded just enough for a yes, thinking, *I will make it, just for you!* David and J.N. cared; I could see it in their faces. J.N. said, "Anything you need, okay?" He meant it.

Just as the doctor was finishing up, unexpected visitors came rushing in. Apparently the accident was all over the news, and Eric and Robin saw my gray suede boots on TV in the shot at the scene. Eric knew those boots! He said to me, "Poor baby, you'll be fine." I could tell he wanted to cry, and Robin too. She was teary-eyed and extremely upset. I was happy to see them. Then Kay S. came in. She was hysterical, out of control, which for her was entirely in character. Perhaps she was still affected by Kara's death and was worried I would be next. I was going to intensive care and everyone had to leave. Katie, my Miller beer friend, never came! I wanted my son to stay, but, of course, he couldn't; that was an emotional moment for me, seeing him leave, but it was best for him to go. The doctors and nurses insisted that I rest. I felt helpless, like when I lost my mom. My son's terrified eyes were heartbreaking to look at. What if I die and never see him again? *Please, God!* I prayed. And I prayed to my mother for her help. *Please, let me live!*

I was scared to death and my heart rate was skyrocketing. They said they had to slow it down or I could possibly have a heart attack. I whispered, "No, no drugs. I want to be alert." The doctor said, and David agreed, that I had to relax. "You have to get the medicine." All I could hear was the rapid rhythm of my heart beating on the monitor: beep, beep, beep, beep… David said he wasn't going to leave until I was out of danger. "Please, go home," I said, slurring. I could barely talk it hurt so much, even when I whispered. David was so worried that it made me nervous. The intensive care nurse came in and sat next to me, emphasizing as best she could that I had to relax. "Try to sleep," she said. Sleep? I may not wake up…there was no way. I had to remain awake and pray. One thing I regretted was not putting my affairs in order in case I passed. Who ever knows… All I had in R. Lee's name was my small insurance policy. I was about to get another before this happened. *Please,* I prayed, *let me live so I can secure a home for my son!* My brain was working overtime as I half-listened to the intensive care nurse tell me about her boyfriend, who had been in an accident similar to mine and unfortunately didn't make it. Great! That was exactly what I didn't need to hear. I turned my head to feign sleep. I was sure she meant well, but I wasn't in any frame of mind to listen to her. David left as I started to doze from the morphine. The dose of morphine they had given me was so strong I was in a state of suspense. It numbed the pain, which would otherwise be far too much for me to bear. Doctors were checking me around the clock. Even if I had wanted to sleep, it would have been impossible. I dozed, always staying semi-conscious and frightened.

David came back very early the next morning. The staff was there probing me and checking my eyes too. I was so happy to see him. Eric and Robin came back but stayed for only a short time. I had to rest… They were good friends. Even Kay S. came back, but David told her I needed to rest; because of her non-stop chatter and high emotions, she had to go. Jennifer didn't visit at all or call in. I felt slighted by Katie, who had been my friend for so long and didn't show up either. Eventually, Jennifer's husband showed up carrying a dozen red roses before he went to work at *The Globe*. That was after the intensive care unit, but he came.

Finally, I was out of danger. The rhythm of my heart was back to normal thanks to the morphine. David told me my son had called several times, and he had talked to him two times this morning already. I told David to tell him that I was going to be okay and not to worry anymore. I prayed to myself that I would make it and see R. Lee soon. I still could not talk above a whisper, and they gave me a breathing contraption that would help me fill my lungs and lessen my chances of getting pneumonia. It was plastic tubing that would be going with me when I was brought to my new hospital room. The realization that I had made it was slowly dawning on me. I wanted to leave the hospital and go home, but I wasn't capable of sitting, walking, or doing much of anything yet besides lying in the hospital bed surrounded by white walls, white sheets, white everything—which I hated. The doctors told me I had multiple rib fractures, eight in the front and eight in the back, a fractured clavicle, acute cervical strain, lacerations on my head, scoliosis, a concussion, severe contusions, a sprained left shoulder with tendonitis, a large hematoma on my left lung, and a fractured pelvis that they were monitoring. The doctor told me it was lucky that I had stopped smoking two years ago; it gave my lungs a fighting chance. Had I been a smoker, it would have killed me. It was a miracle! I was a miracle, and I believed I was meant to be spared for a reason: to help my son and to help others. The doctors knew how hard I was fighting to be well again, and I was relieved to be out of intensive care. They were moving me to a new room with new nurses, and I had a renewed sense of the meaning of my life.

CHAPTER SIXTY-SEVEN

Hospital Discharge

David was by my side every minute; his terrible fear of losing me was so obvious. Because it was difficult for me to speak, I would write notes to my doctors insisting that I be allowed to go home to rest as soon as possible, which, of course, was highly unrealistic of me given my condition. Their answers were, "You're still not out of the woods yet." David told R. Lee that I was going to be home real soon and that I would see him when I was out of the hospital. We weren't totally sure that would be the case, but he told him anyway so that my son wouldn't worry. It was too much pain for R. Lee to see me every day, and J.N. did not let him come back after that one time. I could not fight him. I had such a hard time dealing with my foster sister not coming to the hospital to see me. Her story about the babysitter blew me away. I loved her so much! Why? My dad's response was cold, but that didn't surprise me—he didn't care one way or the other because of Anita, and if I had died it would have been one less thing for him to worry about. There wasn't anything I wouldn't have done for Jennifer, and still would to this day. But as years went by, I did distance myself because it was too hard not to fit in, so I thought it best to stay back some. When her husband came with a dozen red roses, by himself, it touched me. He didn't have to; that was cool. At least *he* cared enough to come to the hospital. He had spoken with David, who said to come back once I was out of intensive care, and he did. The remainder of my stay was as short as I could possibly make it. I hated hospitals and was antsy. I was hoping to go back to work soon. As crazy as that sounds, I had a lot to do now…if I lived.

My gold elephant necklace had somehow disappeared during the accident, and because I wore the necklace for good luck, it bothered me that I didn't know what happened to it. The strangest part had to do with the chain. I asked David where it was, and he told me there was something odd about the elephant's disappearance. The gold chain was around my neck, but the elephant, which was soldered on and never should have come off unless the chain broke, was gone. He searched the car, and it wasn't there. I didn't understand the significance of the missing elephant; I wondered if there was any message. Even though I wasn't particularly religious, I was clearly superstitious. I later whispered to David that I believed God had given me another chance when I spoke to him. When I died, I felt like air was being blown into my lungs from a higher being. I was driven to get my life in order so that everything would be in place when the time came for me to go. I would use this chance. I told David, and he understood. I would live every moment as if I could die the next day, and I would try to make as many people around me as happy as I possibly could. I finally got a room because my heart was strong enough to be out of intensive care.

I'd had enough of the hospital, and of the new nurse from Jamaica pulling me up by the arm to go to the bathroom and then nonchalantly apologizing for never checking my chart for my broken ribs after causing me excruciating pain that took my breath away! I asked the doctor to release me, and I assured him I could manage on my own at home. He was reluctant but knew I might leave anyway. "I don't want to die in here," I said.

"Okay, Libbe. But rest and be careful." After a week, he let me go. David brought my black and white lamb fur coat for me to wear and soft clothing that would be easy to slip on. But none of it was easy; every movement was painful, and I was weak and cold. It was snowy out the day we left. The body shop had pulled my other car together fast so it could go on the road. David used it to pick me up. It was by far a show car like the one that was hit. But not quite yet; even though it wasn't totally done, it was clean and had heat, windows, and a plate. I told David to drive to the place where my car was in Lynn. "No, Lib," he said, "the doctor said home and bed rest." I argued with all my breath, "I have to see my car! Please take me..." I was in tears, barely able to talk. David gave in, and we were on our way to Lynn. At the lot, we pulled around to the back of the auto body building and I saw it—crushed, the axel up into the middle of the car, my door smashed in, and the front middle pushed up. David's seat was intact. *Oh, my god,* I thought, *If my son had been with us he would have been killed!* It was fate that kept him away, and my gut that left him there. For the first time, I was glad he was with his dad. With David's help, I walked closer to see my car. And I wept, not for the car, but for my son who was spared as were David and I, and how lucky we had been. Lucky! That was the significance of the missing elephant! And then it hit me like an epiphany—Eva! "Eva... Eva," I said.

"Yes, Lib? Eva what?" He helped me into the car, where I sat still, in excruciating pain.

"Eva told me all this, Dave," I whispered. "She knew my destiny."

"Yes, Lib, you said she scared you. It makes sense." Dave thought about Eva's predictions as we sat there. He remembered how freaked out I was after her reading. And to think it actually had happened as she said it would! But I had lived through it. How long have I been granted? That was the real question. I couldn't help but wonder when I would be taken away. It haunted me for some time; I had trouble falling asleep out of a fear of not waking up. I wanted my son home earlier than June, and I asked Dave to speak to J.N.

We drove slowly on the way home. Speaking with some effort, I asked David, "Do you remember when the car was first towed to Lynn, and we said we had to go back and cover it? Do you recall when we drove down Green Street at the corner, and you turned right by the little store—going past the black cat—and I told you to back up? I said something was going to happen because a black cat had crossed our path. You didn't turn around... Eva said something would happen, and I felt that cat was an omen that something *was* going to happen. I knew, and begged you to turn, but you said we had already gone by and added, 'Don't worry, Lib.' You didn't take my premonition seriously."

"Yes, I remember," he answered. "I understood, from what you and she had discussed, that something bad was going to go down, but not like this!"

"I knew something bad was going to happen that night, and it did!" I declared. I was slowly getting it all out, but with every breath it hurt. David told me to rest my voice and my lungs since I was breathing heavily, but I continued whispering because it was helpful; it kept my lungs open so I would heal faster. I was in so much pain—but I was alive!

I knew the doctor said bed rest, but to sleep, eat, speak, or do anything, I had to sit up. I hadn't laid down since the accident, and I thought how nice it would be to lie down again. My clients had been calling David, and brought by money for me only because they felt badly about the accident. I couldn't book my girls until I could speak, but they were loyal. They said I owed them nothing in return. They actually cared about me, much more than I ever could have imagined. Robin and Eric, my two best friends, and J.N. offered to help me out with money right from the beginning. Funny how no one else did—and not one get well card from all the other people who knew me! J.N. called every day to check on me, and Robin and Eric were the only ones who came to visit me when I got home, bringing me food and anything else I needed. I learned who my friends were, and I decided that in the future I would act accordingly. Get rid of the baggage, non-reciprocal friendships, and freeloaders in my life. I now saw who stood by me.

At the time of the accident, our dog Reece lay on the ground and appeared lifeless. David just assumed he was dead and kicked him to the side of the road. But the man who had yelled to Dave at the time of the accident to put me down picked Reece up and took him to the animal hospital. He hadn't died. He had been in shock, knocked out, and only suffered an injury to his kidney. Dave knew because the man phoned him. He had given the man his number to let him know where he took Reece. On the day I returned home, I had no idea Reece had survived and that he would be there. David had to go back to work so his sister had come to the house to help me, which was not what I wanted. I knew I would recuperate fast and that the arrangement with his sister would be short-lived. I didn't like anyone fussing over me, and I was glad I was sitting up on the couch in the den in a position that allowed me to tolerate both the pain and the houseguest. I detested taking pain medication or, for that matter, any meds! Dave had closed the den door after we came home so I could rest without being disturbed by noise in the house. And then I smelled an awful odor! It was becoming more and more noxious. I could hear two voices yelling at each other. David was obviously upset with his sister. What the hell was going on, I wondered? Not even home a couple of days yet, and I was exhausted from straining my voice; whispering to clients on the trick phone line to explain what had happened took a lot out of me. It sapped my energy. When I rang my bell for someone to come to me, they couldn't hear it and no one responded. Painfully hoisting myself up and rolling off the couch, I held onto the wall as I walked from the den couch to the door and opened it wide. The stink wafted into the room all at once, and I coughed and coughed and could not catch my breath. My hand was covering my mouth, and then I looked up and saw our dog—he had survived! Oh, my god, Reece! Tears rolled across my dry skin. I was shocked and delighted, but I had to hold in all my emotion in my condition because my chest hurt so badly. Dave ran in and saw how happy I was. As I learned later that evening, the guy who had picked him up and taken him to the hospital had brought Reece to his own house to help him out after the doctor saw him. He even paid the bill. Dave gave him the money back. Reece lived, and here he was! But he had just been sprayed—skunked when he went out to do his business in front of our house. Skunked big time! "Oh, my god, Reece, you're alive!" I whispered with great joy. I was so happy to see him, wanting to hold him even though I wasn't able to because of my injuries. And, as Dave warned me, he stunk to high heaven! It was so wonderful he had lived, but boy, did he smell! David washed Reece so many times and used my good powders and perfumes, but not much helped.

After the ordeal with the skunk passed, I demanded of David, "Send your sister home." I was confident I could make it with just him. My son was calling constantly. I wanted him home, so plans were made for him to come back to Brookline in mid-May, weeks before school let out. I was so happy that my outlook improved. Even if I was in pain, I wanted to go on my annual trip. February had rolled around, the time of year when I would drive to Florida and stay for two weeks of vacation, escaping from the cold of the Northeast. I decided that this year wouldn't be an exception. Broken bones and all, against doctors' orders, I would go to Florida. *Yes*. I had to—I was driven to prove to myself that I could do it, pain or no pain. The other '73 Riviera GS was fixed up and ready to make the trip. I planned to do the driving, all propped up with pillows, despite the pain and the warnings. I understood the risks, but living on the edge was, at least in part, how I went through life. The doctors said that if I got into another accident, it would probably kill me. I wanted to go for it. Life was short, and there is no chance that anyone knows when their time is up. I had pain pills with me just in case.

It was a painful drive, made with great determination, lots of water, and Tylenol. Dave and I made the trip together, only the two of us, without R. Lee this time. I made it to Jacksonville, over the Florida line, in twenty-eight hours. I did it, but then Dave took the wheel. I could not endure anymore. We were going farther south to Fort Lauderdale and Miami Beach, and even riding in the car as a passenger was a challenge in itself. Although the trip had taken longer than usual, my goal was to make it across the Florida border; I accomplished what I set out to do and then some. I was alive thanks to all my angels guiding me. There wasn't a doubt in my mind that I would continue as long as I was willing to fight for my life—the doctors had told me that the severity of the accident injuries could still cause my death. I maintained my determination to stay here for my son and David.

CHAPTER SIXTY-EIGHT

Challenges Ahead

Vacations in Florida were never disappointing. The skies were blue instead of a wintry gray, and warm sunshine beat down from the heavens above. Even if it rained, sunshine came right behind the sky tears. Sun and salt water were the best antidotes for broken bones and tender flesh—and I was all for it. I loved watching the sway of the palm trees in the breeze. I couldn't wait to lie on the hot sand. The money my clients had given me covered the entire two weeks, and David had money from his construction jobs, so we were set. He had contacted my insurance company before we left about the accident and given them the information they needed, paperwork, and all my receipts. They said they would pay me twenty thousand dollars for what I had put into the car, which had been about twenty-eight thousand; their coverage for injuries took care of all the hospital bills from the accident. We had gotten an attorney to sue the city but found out that back then it was not happening because there were no laws to cover police chases. That was a hardship considering I could have died and did sustain life-long consequences from the injuries. Spring would come soon enough to Boston, a time when the sun begins to get stronger by the day. I told myself that I would heal faster as the weather improved.

I had no fear of driving once I was behind the wheel. After our stay, I drove half the distance back to Boston, and David drove the last half. That was the best way to conquer fear—just jump right back in. I took the wheel the way I approached life: without any apprehension at all. I thought about the truck stops we passed while we were on the road back, and how I used to jump in and out of the cabs of trucks when I was first turned out, how many cities I traveled to making money for pimps, not for myself. None of my past seemed real at the moment. I thought about my life during the time I spent healing in bed. I wanted to leave the life altogether and have a one hundred percent legitimate business soon. The timing of such an extreme move was a question mark.

The trip to Florida and back was meaningful to me. I realized that I could die at any time, and by traveling, I was distancing myself away from my trauma so that I could heal, returning to a future full of changes for the better in my life. I had plans, lots of them. David and I discussed some of them before the car accident, like flea market sales, which we had done already using stuff that he had collected from the attics of people he worked for. I wanted to buy real estate, fix up the structures, and sell them for a profit. I was thinking about opening up a strudel place in Faneuil Hall with my foster sister, if she wanted to. She had a great strudel recipe and was always saying that she needed money. Why I would even want to do that after her not coming to see me was beyond my understanding, but that's love. Opening a business with her would give her the opportunity to do something with her life, but for me, it was just business. Faneuil Hall had some places outside in the open air meant for tourists, shopping, business lunches, or a Sunday afternoon stroll. And it had a huge hall inside, lined with food vendors. I told Jennifer I may open it for her, but I had to look into it first. Her place in my heart had never shifted. If I were some other person in her life, perhaps one of her close friends or her real sister, she wouldn't have thought twice, she would have come to the hospital with her kids in tow. And it still bothers me. I had even given her my favorite topaz ring, the one Rio had given me on my eighteenth birthday. I hope it's a reminder of my love for her. I should have kept it; it had sentimental value. Regardless, I had to go for everything without holding back. I needed a business. I considered myself fortunate to have this second chance.

And from a wider perspective, I felt I had good fortune other times in my life, escaping death and thriving physically and mentally despite my horrible past—like a cat with nine lives. I was excited because R. Lee would be coming home! His room was ready for his return. He had missed a year of Hebrew school and had to continue studying for his bar mitzvah.

A few months passed, and the doctors expressed amazement at the speed of my recovery. The damage to my lung had healed, and the hematoma bruise there was gone! The doctor was shocked at that. He could not find the bruise. He advised me to keep up what I was doing. I had lost my taste for refurbishing old classic cars for the time being, but I kept the one car as it was in case I changed my mind…and I suspected that much later I would. I do now, never too late. Once R. Lee returned, our family was complete and we were back on track. He made me happy and alive! Reece lost his anxiety about riding in cars, and his kidneys slowly improved. The perplexed look on his face every time he squatted and I had to wipe up his pee from the floor made me think that he was sorry for having accidents in the house. I was a neat freak, no shoes worn in the house, and I washed my dogs paws when they came in from outdoors. The vet said he would be back to normal in no time, but his kidneys would remain weak so don't be upset if he has accidents. No, I did not give a damn—because he was alive!

My son was so relieved to be home. His tension was gone. Our whole family was looking forward to a better year. My business with the girls was flourishing and back on track. I had meetings set up to look at different properties to buy, or just rent, for apartments for work. We held flea markets on weekends. My clients were pleased to be seeing me again. But I was different, I could tell. David wasn't as enthusiastic about it—we had a few spats. There was a house at the end of our street that I wanted, and he and I talked about buying it. It had been empty for a while, and people in the neighborhood were superstitious, saying that the home was haunted. It was a mess. But I was not afraid of ghosts! They wanted one hundred fifty thousand dollars for the old two-family Victorian, and it would need over two hundred fifty thousand dollars worth of work just to start. There were major issues. It would have to be gutted right down to the studs that held it together, and the sills had to be jacked up and redone. Structurally, it was an awkward, ugly duckling, but I saw beauty in its frame and wanted it. I had money saved, and when I called about it, the owner said I could have first option on it once the estate cleared toward the end of the year. The house was made for me, haunted or not. It was a two-family, and the rent from the other unit could be put toward the cost of fixing it up or the mortgage. I had more than enough to keep me occupied—no more thinking about my aches, or death. I had a goal…my son. I was on my way to fulfilling my dream of making a home for R. Lee and myself. I was granted life to proceed to a home for us that I had always prayed for. Eva had been right. I believed that my determination and Eva's predictions would make the project work.

This summer would be the last we would be having barbeques and get-togethers at the same old address or parks. All the girls I trusted, and even clients like Harry the Whip, attended these events, as well as Marcie, who once showed up half-naked in a see-through top to shock all my Christmas guests. I wasn't pleased, and she was so wasted she didn't even realize it. I couldn't let her stay in her state of mind. I felt badly for her, but she did understand that she had to leave because my son was there and it made me uncomfortable. Dave was fine with her, of course, and so were all the male friends there, but no way—she had to go. That was our last apartment get-together; we had to move on.

The madams from all over the South, low-end and high houses, were calling for Boston girls after they got a taste of the few that they got from the Circuit who came from me. They were recommending their clients to my place in exchange for my traveling clients to their cities all over, especially Chicago. Things were really picking up.

CHAPTER SIXTY-NINE

Overdose

Marcie had everything going for her: a huge, multi-unit building on Marlborough Street that she bought (one of the classiest streets in Back Bay) and tons of money. Also, she had graduated Northeastern University with a major in mathematics. However, she had been on a collision course with death for many years. It was amazing how she could be disciplined and organized enough to be able to run a brothel and own property but couldn't overcome her alcohol and cocaine habits. She never listened to me. I begged her to only party on weekends, but she could not stop. Her freebasing was consuming her life. Each time I saw her, it was obvious to me that she was becoming worse. I did not understand that level of self-abuse; I cherished life. When I dropped off money or picked it up from sharing clients or girls, she was messed up. She was half-bald from plucking out her hair strand by strand, and her two Dobermans, Say and What, ran her apartment, jumping across the furniture, totally out of control, pissing and shitting. She was in bad shape, and talking to her about it was a waste of time. She couldn't wait for me to leave so she could go out to get her next hit, or have her drug boy deliver it. She was killing herself, and it weighed heavily on me. When she came to that final party at my apartment she was at least able to speak, even though her speech was slurred. Some people took offense and spoke about it. And, needless to say, I certainly didn't want my son to have a full view of her on drugs. It bothers me to this day that I had her leave early. It wasn't too long after one of her last visits that Marcie was found dead in her bathroom, sitting on the toilet—her heart frozen from freebasing. This was the demise of another good girl who was pretty, bright, and had everything to live for. She left behind a daughter her mother had always taken care of. Marcie never appreciated the importance of making smart life decisions; she was brilliant, yet foolish at the same time. Despite how stressful my life was, I made the decision day after day to stay away from drugs and booze, except for minimal use on holidays or during sex. Keep your body and mind clear and honest and you will always be on top of your game. My phones were flooded with calls from her customers wanting to see my girls instead, but I refused the fucked-up ones. They cared only about their own needs and didn't even give a second thought to Marcie's tragic death, too bad they said… Money and sex seems to override all emotions and friendships.

After being in correspondence for a while with Faneuil Hall, I was in full swing, going to a meeting at the Wharf about the strudel shop. I wanted to pursue that. I had a design in mind for a small spot in their food court. I was dressed up as usual, but even more professionally, as if I had a rich out-call: black business suit, heels, expensive jewelry, and tanned. I was early for my appointment and sat on the couch in an outer waiting room, and the longer I waited the more anxious I became. Then the door opened and a good-looking, older man with salt and pepper hair stepped out. He smiled flirtatiously and asked me if I was waiting for Mr. Kirk. I told him yes, I was there to speak with him. "Are you friends or partners?" I inquired. He told me he was Mr. C., a business associate at Faneuil Hall Marketplace with the man I was about to speak to. "Well," I said, "that's the reason I'm here…to get a business in Faneuil Hall."

"And what are you selling or promoting if I may ask," he said as he looked at me, up and down, waiting for an answer. I still hadn't been called in, so I thought, *Why not? I'll tell him.* And I flirted back, a natural habit. I got into it, as I always did when I believed in something, excitedly and convincingly! As I spoke to Mr. C., he was impressed as well as intrigued by me and my enthusiasm, and we discussed different people he knew and I knew, and all the names he mentioned were my clients, although I didn't tell him that right away. *Small world,* I thought. It didn't matter where I went—Clair Buick, ticket agencies, banks, law offices, courts, any place in Boston—there were clients from all walks of life, everywhere. After talking a while, I gave Mr. C. a personal business card with my numbers and he gave me his card. I had a feeling he'd been around…girls, etc. He told me how he had been a simple toy salesman who moved up the ranks and was now a rich businessman. The one question he asked that struck me was, "Do you really want to do this with your money?"

And my answer was, "No, but it's a stepping stone for me into a different world, and my foster sister does make an exceptional strudel."

The time for me to see Mr. Kirk arrived, and he asked me to come in. Before Mr. C. left, he put in a good word for me, saying, "Take good care of her. Give her a spot, but she is to call me first before taking it." He turned to look at me, and I said that I would definitely call him—and the rest, as they say, is history. I called Mr. C. before I accepted the spot and we met for dinner. I made sure that I was appealing. My beeper rang constantly. By the time we had finished our meals, he knew too much about me, and I knew quite a bit about him, and with that information, he made a deal with me on a handshake. I knew he was a trick; little did he know he'd be paying me three-hundred-dollars-plus an hour very soon. Mr. C. paid for dinner and tipped the waiter, and we went into business together shortly after that. I had money put away, but not for the strudel business; it was for what I wanted to do. This was the beginning of a great friendship, business venture, and sexual agreement.

1982 was a big year for investments. I was getting what I wanted: to secure my future with R. Lee and David and to purchase my own house. The lawyers contacted us about the house in Brookline I was waiting for, and we were ready to go into some more properties. Mr. C. had most of the cash for other investments, and David had the brawn. I gave him my savings, which had accumulated over the years, putting the money in his hands to purchase our first property. It was a large, beautiful home in Brockton, a foreclosure that was a cash deal and cheap. David and I did the work on the house. Mr. C. knew someone who wanted it, and we made a quick thirty thousand dollars on the deal. Then we bought buildings in the South End and finally closed on my home in Brookline. The lawyers had all the finished papers from the estate, and we bought the Victorian house in Brookline for eighty-five thousand in cash. Mr. C. and I were co-owners. The house needed to be gutted to its core to restore, not destroy, its beauty. We wanted to bring it back to its original state or even better than it was, using only the best materials, from the copper and brass screws to the plaster coated sheetrock that was meant to last. And believe me, it did!

We had also purchased and renovated two buildings in the South End. One was on Pembroke Street and the other was on Mass. Ave. We fixed them up, and the first one sold quickly, but the second one, which was on Mass. Ave., was a challenge. At first we kept it as rentals. The salesman from Betty Gibson Realty was a jerk and an asshole who took off on vacation and left a black, elderly couple without any heat at Christmastime. It was a good thing we checked out the building. We saw lights on and went up the long staircase, knocked on apartment doors, and didn't get any responses until the top floor, the last apartment.

A frail voice answered the door, saying, "He…llo…Hello…" Oh shit! I waved to Mr. C. to come up. "Hello, can you open the door, please?"

"Okay, one minute. Who are you?" she replied.

I said, "We're the new owners." I could hear a man's voice grumbling in the background. Mr. C. stood beside me. "It's supposed to be empty, right?" I asked.

"Yes, of course," he said. The door opened and a petite black woman stood nervously in the doorway. I peered around her and saw that the oven door was open, and roaches were scurrying across the floor. I reassuringly told the elderly woman that we were the new owners. She then appeared to become more relaxed.

"Who is it?" the man asked angrily in the background.

"It's our new landlords," she said.

"Oh you are, are you?" the man said gruffly. "When we gonna get some heat?"

"You don't have any heat?" I asked, startled by the question.

"No," she said sweetly, "that's why the oven door is open, to warm up the apartment. Our old landlord said that you would take care of it."

"Oh, really?" I replied. I could see that Mr. C. was fuming, as I was too. "We will, but first we have to figure out why he left you here without any heat." I turned to Mr. C. and whispered, "That fucking landlord said that?"

The woman said, "Miss Lady, I'm on dialysis and I sure could use some heat." We both were outraged.

"Oh, I am so sorry, ma'am." What the fuck! How could anyone leave to go on vacation and let two elderly folks freeze? They must have been in their eighties. And the place was roach infested—they were crawling everywhere, even across my boots. We asked them if they had blankets and enough to eat. "Do you have family that would take you in?" I asked.

"We ain't goin' anywhere!" the old man shouted. "This is mah home, this is mah home, and we want heat!" Then he said, "We've been here for over twenty years, and I can't go out…got no shoes. I need my shoes."

"Shoes? We can buy you shoes," I told him.

"No, you can't. I want only my shoes! Do you hear?" With their permission, we looked around the apartment, following the sound of his voice to the combined bedroom and sitting room, where all over the floor were dozens of shoes. He had plenty of shoes. "But they don't fit him," his wife said. She apologized for her husband and added that he loved his shoes and clothes, and was *always* in a bad humor. I told them that we'd be back, and that we were going to get some things for them.

"We were told that you had gotten another apartment."

"No ma'am," she replied. "We never did. The old landlord said you would. We don't know what to do."

"Okay, you just stay in there."

"Yes, ma'am, we'll be here." This surely was an unexpected twist. Both of us were furious, and Mr. C. said, "You mark my words, they'll have heat by morning!" We went on the phones ASAP.

Having to care for these folks was a nightmare, especially because celebrating the holiday at home would be interrupted, but to think of them sitting there in that hell hole made us both sick. We had to take care of them and get them a new place to stay, but first we had to call Kennedy Heating to get the mammoth octopus burner downstairs fixed or replaced so they would have heat, no matter the cost! The rest was an adventure. Mr. C. and I went shopping right away and spent five hundred dollars for food, clothes, blankets, slippers, anything warm and comfortable. We included a small Christmas tree, with decorations.

We returned to the apartment with our arms full. The woman cried when she saw the gifts, although her husband didn't share in her joy—he was too set in his ways and focused on his shoes. The heat was temporarily turned on that night and it cost plenty, fifteen hundred dollars, to have that done on the day before Christmas Eve. Mr. C. left insulting messages for the bastard landlord, and we told him he would be in trouble. They couldn't live with relatives, and when we finally took them to visit, David had to carry him through the snow, up and down stairs, all the while listening to him rant about his shoes. He stayed barefoot and wouldn't even wear the slippers we bought him—one stubborn man. I banged and bitched and threatened to call the media if the social services for the elderly didn't help me find them a place. I had called everywhere. I wanted them to arrange alternate housing for the old couple, but they never responded and I took care of it myself. After many threats to the caseworkers about the media, a home was found. David had to carry the man again, down the stairs to the car, and then into the new apartment. All he said was, "My shoes! My shoes! Don't forget my shoes!" We bought them new dishes, a few lamps, small appliances, clothing, and gifts for their new apartment on Tremont Street, which came to over fifteen hundred dollars. The woman exuded happiness, and the old man finally said thank you under his breath, but only to David for carrying him and bringing up his shoes. Their place was new, with all the amenities elderly people require. It was our good deed for that Christmas and the New Year. It felt good. We were giving people with nothing a new start in life, and we expected nothing in return. They deserved it. Mr. C. dealt with the asshole landlord later. And there was some money back for the furnace and a small portion of the realty fee. I had a great New Year's Eve knowing they were safe and warm.

CHAPTER SEVENTY

Construction and Changes

Mr. C. was falling in love and lust with me. He became my sugar daddy and didn't want me to see any clients other than him. We were compatible in so many ways and got along well, and if he weren't married, he might have proposed. He would always say, "If only I were single…" He loved his wife, but it was a different kind of love for her and me. We had a great crew of guys working on the buildings: my son's dad, David, and some laborers. Mr. C. was working out some deals with the man I met with about the strudel shop, his buddy, even though I begged him not to; I didn't like his manners and hustle from my first meeting. I said no to Faneuil Hall for my own reasons. "Let's just flip buildings," I said, and we did. It felt so natural to me, I loved construction. It was going great and I enjoyed it. I was running crews, learning as much as I could on every project. It was a passion, and I wanted to do construction or house design full-time if and when I ever quit my other business. David was getting more jealous of me going out with Mr. C. while he worked. Mr. C. gave me anything I needed and paid all the bills for the price of my body. But David wanted me all the time and was becoming more possessive, even R. Lee noticed it. Dave was giving rides to my girls, taking them grocery shopping and driving them on calls. He was acting out, staying out later, and becoming a different person at times. I didn't pick up on it at first that a change like J.N.'s might be occurring. The girls were trying to lure him in, and they did. It took me a while to catch on because I was so busy and because I trusted him. My son was feeling left out, and Reece was moving slower, chewing on my shoes, and developing more bad habits. I was so into work and making money that I had blinders on. As it turned out, that was a big mistake. I asked for a second chance in life, not business. Blinded by the determination to make it, I didn't see that I was neglecting to give the love that was needed from me to the people I loved. How could I be so blind…I am sorry to this day for that!

I was possessed by business and working, even more of a workaholic than I had been before. David decided to put me to the test, saying that if I didn't give up my madam business and my sugar daddy, he would leave. Most of his anger came from my relationship with Mr. C., not the business. Mr. C. even upped the ante so that I would stop seeing my personal clients, drop that business entirely, in order to have more time with him. That scared me—the same as marriage did. They were both gaining control now. I didn't like the situation, but I felt secure because of the money the business made. I could see fifty men without having attachments to any of them and be happy. It was harder to handle one man with thousands of dollars seeing me. It was stressful to the point where the scent of his sexual organs would make me gag; I liked Mr. C. but not in a sexual way. He would never go for a lack of physical encounters. But I had to make a choice.

I stopped for David's sake. I cut off my number. I made one call to Ma Bell, and that was the end of my 5209 phone connection. It felt like I was letting go of a lifeline. The business was my anchor. I was living in a bubble with two men who loved me and wanted to possess me, but that wasn't what I needed to be happy. The construction kept me occupied all day every day with decorating, planning, painting, and working physical construction too. My foster sister volunteered to help me strip the woodwork of my house in the first floor apartment. We made a party of it. I was into every inch of my home; it possessed me as much as I possessed it. It was mine. It belonged as much to Dave, who put his soul into it, and R. Lee—it would be his home someday, all of it! *I did it! I made it! I had a real home!* But the life was still in me, and I had to drive in town from time to time to look. I felt empty without my clients and the girls. I knew I had to let it go, but how long could I continue without it? I didn't feel as though I was myself anymore; I had lost my identity. The madams would call for girls and to chat. I missed my business and I told them I could tell I was going to come back soon. I gained weight after the accident, and being unhappy wasn't helping me take it off. The gain was only from a size 2 to a size 6...then to an 8!

I thought about the last out-call I made before I closed down, a memorable encounter for a number of reasons. One of my clients referred me to a politician from New Hampshire who would be staying at the Parker House Hotel on Tremont Street. To protect his political career, his encounters had to be kept safe and quiet. His wife would be involved—her first experience with a woman—and they wanted someone classy, someone who could be totally discreet and knew how to handle a couple. They requested that I go because I had been with couples before and understood how to make their experience memorable without jealousies.

I met them for a cordial drink in the grand Parker House Hotel lounge, and then we proceeded upstairs to their suite. As I normally did in these encounters, I felt out the situation to make certain the woman was, first of all, comfortable with me. The husband would inevitably be aroused by that rather than feeling jealous. When we went into the room she was timid, but became flirtatious after a couple of drinks. I could tell her husband loved her and wanted her to be more satisfied than she was able to be with him. I told him he should join us when I thought it was an appropriate time and, if not, he would be there for her and be the voyeur. He was the first truly unselfish man I had ever met in this kind of arrangement. Slowly, he and I got undressed, and I carefully and gently helped her disrobe. Piece by piece, while I touched her body, I removed her clothes. She seemed to be very turned on. While I was telling her we could lie down and talk to relax, I caressed her neck and strands of her hair, slowly rubbing her sides and bottom. Within a few minutes of my caressing her arms, speaking sexually and touching her hair, she was fully aroused and moaned and whimpered. She was putty, her body arched like a cat's back. She was slender and plain-looking, with no makeup, a real country girl, but powerful in the magnitude of her response—it was intensely sexual. The vibe between us clicked and we were locked, kissing each other sensually with our lips as I caressed her back and put my body across hers to connect. When our breasts touched, she lifted her pelvis toward me. I'd never had a connection with a woman like this. No female ever turned me on to that degree, before or since.

She had orgasm after orgasm, each tripping the next, and when I lowered my body on top of hers and our breasts and stomachs pressed tightly, I could feel her wanting me. I caressed her lips and eyes with my tongue. Had I been a man, I would have penetrated her ever so gently. I didn't have a thought about her husband who was waiting, but knew I had to break away from the intimacy she and I both shared to be fair to him. I realized that she was a customer and not a fling, and it was time to direct that sexual magnetism back toward her husband for them to make a connection. I knew he was thoroughly aroused and ready to take his wife for the best time they ever had. I waved for him to come over. I pushed their bodies together and held them like that for a few moments, then I gently pulled away. After the session was finished, the wife wanted more of me, but I stood firm. When she followed me into the bathroom and told me she wanted to meet sometime alone, just the two of us, I let her know that it wasn't a good idea. Although she gave me her telephone number, I did not give her mine. She asked me to consider it, and I told her it was best to remember the moments we shared as a fantasy for her and her husband to help intensify their own sexual responses to one another. I knew she wanted a woman for fun, and perhaps she did it again with someone else…who knows? I tossed out her number but never forgot her. I didn't want sex to be responsible for the breakup of such a long, loving marriage; they were so into each other again by the time I left. The experience of intimacy was memorable for them and for me, and I have to say I always wondered about what happened to them and what would have happened had I pursued her.

Eric and Robin had been making plans for their trip to Mexico to sell pots and pans, and I was planning to open a shoe store in

Mattapan and establish it while they were away. The work was piling up. Mr. C. was involved in establishing shoe franchises with Mr. Kirk, whom I felt could not be trusted. Mr. C. was taking out bank loans, and when I told him I wanted the store name to be my choice, he agreed—no franchise with that guy, thanks. I had the connections to get the larger size shoes for the store in Mattapan. We had finished up the Pembroke Street South End building to put on the market and it sold. We wanted to keep the larger four-unit Mass. Ave. property to rent for a while.

I wasn't only investing in the real estate projects, but was also giving money to a musical group, Eric and his friends, to make demos. My hands were in all these ongoing projects. The group was fairly good and had potential. However, they needed practice and some hard work, and their drug use was interfering with their progress and personal relationships. I realized the drugs had to go and did my best to get them under control. I should have been more skeptical because, as it turned out, they needed a babysitter more than an investor. One of the musicians had his mother move into the unit I had rented to them, and they began screwing us on the rent. They were supposed to be working for the cleaning company I started, and they couldn't even show up on time, and when they did it was a fuck-up. I was up all night cleaning every store they had supposedly already cleaned. Three months passed without their paying rent, so I gave them notice and stopped paying their music-related expenses; they were taking the money and instead of using it for studio time to keep the group going, they were partying with it. They were a waste of money. Then one of them said he burned his hand because of a faulty stove and brought a case against Mr. C. and me, also alleging that we stole their furniture—furniture that was mine and I had given them to use in the first place! The judge fined us fourteen hundred dollars, even though I had receipts. Talk about our judicial system… It took two more months to have him evicted by a sheriff. Even though I had caught him with the supposedly injured hand (no bandage) wrapped around the stair railing—and in a fit of anger almost threw him over the rail into the stairwell—the court wouldn't re-open the case. Then he got another tenant on the top floor to buddy up with him, and we had to evict her too. They were causing too many headaches. Mr. C. and I made a quick decision to sell and put the money toward the store and my son's bar mitzvah, which was already scheduled to take place. We followed through with our plan to sell. I thought it was a great idea at the time. No more headaches from vindictive tenants. I wouldn't have to deal with them anymore. In retrospect, I wish I had held onto the buildings. I would have been a rich woman. But going through the ordeal with the musicians left a bad taste in my mouth. There would be more musicians to come, with a whole lot less stress.

Robin and Eric had been sending postcards from Albuquerque and were on their way home. They came back from their pots and pans sales trip with no apartment to live in but lots of cash, so we put them up until they could get one. Of course, I would never charge them, but Eric tried to give me money for their expenses all the time. It was fun except that all of us were sharing one bathroom, and Robin hogged it for two hours at a time. She looked the best she had for ages—no drugs or alcohol and plenty of fresh food and sunshine. They thrived in that business, but she missed the club and her pills, she said, and so she resumed her downtown life. I wished she hadn't. I called a few of the numbers in my old book so she could make some cash on the side for their new apartment. Eric was saving the money they made from his sales to buy a new car. I told Robin I had been away from my business for almost a year, way too long, and I couldn't deal with that anymore, so I was ready. I got in touch with some clients, and without saying anything about it to David, I put an ad in the Phoenix and called my girls to see customers. It caused some issues with Mr. C., but many more with David—more than I bargained for. David's smiling face changed into a scowl. I had never seen him that angry and out of control before, but I felt more secure running my old business again.

It seemed as though I was taking the good with the bad lately in a conflict between the various businesses and my personal life. I was not paying enough attention to R. Lee at all, and compensated for my neglect by buying him things. I was driven by acquiring things I never had while growing up. I was greedy, earning more money to get ahead. And though I was grateful for what I had and shared with others, I was often pulled in diverse directions. I was good in real estate and wanted to stay with it, but I didn't want to listen to David telling me I shouldn't go back into my business with the girls. And I was hardheaded about it. I told him he could leave or stay and let me be. I was frightened to be without my phones and clients—I needed and wanted that security. It was not that I didn't trust David to put food on the table and contribute to the expenses, he always did, but I didn't want to be controlled by him in the same way Mr. C. attempted to with his money. That sickened me, I would never marry for money! The arrangement with Mr. C. wasn't as threatening as my relationship with David primarily because Mr. C. had a wife and children, but the combination of his financial power and his sexual needs caused me stress and unhappiness. I consoled myself by eating cakes and candy, my drugs of choice. I had grown at least another size, into a 10.

David was always getting high with Eric and J.N. They were snorting coke while working with the crew through most of the night on the first floor apartment in my home in Brookline so that it could be finished and rented. The building on Mass. Ave. sold, and it couldn't have been soon enough. I didn't want to be bothered by the renters anymore. David believed and trusted in all people, and I tried as much as possible to be the same way. But by being exposed to my lifestyle, David had changed into a person who was no longer totally naive. He had become skeptical of some people too, but only a couple: Mr. C. and another steady client. I didn't consider his evolution into a more cynical person necessarily a bad thing, and so I pushed on. We were making arrangements with Mr. C. for our excursion to Israel, packing, and preparing R. Lee. He was so nervous that he might not remember his studies and be unable to read the Torah completely. David accepted that I was working again, but at the same time he had plans of his own, which he had already put into motion. I was just unaware of what he was doing.

Things with Robin and Eric were not going well. Robin wanted to work at the ranch in Springfield all the time, and Eric was pissed off because she was never home. After their trip, he changed the way he felt about Robin working—he wanted her for himself, for them to get married. But, like me, she didn't want to give up her freedom or stripping at the clubs. Our business was not a good thing for relationships, and this year proved that. Then a call came in to me from Robin saying that she was leaving Eric and staying in Springfield. *Oh, shit,* I thought. She said she was going to talk to him later about breaking up. I tried without success to talk her out of it, begging her not to leave him because it was a mistake. I told her how much Eric loved her. She said she'd found some guy up there. When she spoke to him before I had a chance to go to her or see him, he went off the deep end; he couldn't believe that she would ever leave him. The result was disastrous. He was screaming and crying on the phone. David had to go to Eric's apartment to watch him after he threatened to commit suicide; he refused to see anyone except David, including me. I went to the ranch—I had to go—and tried my best to make Robin see that the new man in her life was just using her, he was selling drugs and would not able to be there for her, but the attention he gave her was more powerful than me or Eric—proving once again that cum is thicker than blood or friends.

I had enough experience in life to realize that money was not a cure-all, particularly for emotional issues, but I still put it first, like a drug to an addict. I sat with David and told him how badly I felt for Eric and Robin, and what a great couple they were and could possibly be again. It occurred to me that the same thing could happen to us, and I didn't want that to happen. How could I prevent it? I wanted them to be together for my own selfish reasons, so we would always be close friends, hanging out for the rest of our lives. But I had issues of my own now too.

David was partying too much, and I realized I had to curb his getting high behind my back when he was away from the house. I would have asked Eric to speak to him, but Eric was having a difficult time taking care of himself, and he too was indulging in freebasing and snorting, and drinking way too much. He was the one who introduced David to smoking coke. I had to keep David away from things and people that would lead him down a bad path.

CHAPTER SEVENTY-ONE

Coma

I was deeply in love with David more and more every day, but I hid the fact from him, trying to protect my deepest feelings so I wouldn't get hurt if he left. I thought the pain would be too overwhelming, so I missed out on experiencing a closer intimacy with him; my mistake, for sure. If only I could turn back the clock… I thought it was crucial for me to maintain a tough exterior. It took effort to keep those walls up, and I did so as if my life depended on it. As usual, I was setting myself up for possible failures, although I didn't realize that at the time. I caught him lying to me about the girls several times. I became jealous, suspicious, and possessive—three negatives that are enough to kill any relationship. The result was that I pushed him farther away from me. I couldn't help asking him where he was going whenever he went out the door, like I had to know every move he made! I knew something was up. I wanted to trust him, but I couldn't. People were innately dishonest, and David wasn't an exception. However, I made it easy for him because I backed away. And him picking up my girls and taking them on calls did not help us at all; too much exposure.

Whether it was coincidence or fate, in business I was succeeding beyond my dreams. And as time went on, I continued buying material things and selling valuable vintage items, spending the profits on trips, jewelry to put away for a rainy day, collectible furniture, and animated art—many of the things I bought had triggered my memory of my mother Rose or had great value. Once a streetwalker, I wasn't following the script at all: no drugs, no bottle, no slavish devotion to some pimp anymore, and I wasn't in the grave. I was on my way to being a bona fide success. I thought of myself as skillful, straddling the worlds of the illegal sex trade and the everyday life of the straight world too. But I was failing with David and my son. I felt that I had been failing on a personal emotional level. What can I do to get back on track? I was not sure. My son and I were not as close as we once were, at least in part because he was at the age when his friends took precedence over me. As difficult as it was to accept that he was no longer a young child, I gave him his freedom. He was beginning to see the world with adult eyes now. There were days I didn't feel smart or successful, and my thoughts were rebounding to incidents in my past. I felt vulnerable and insecure. R. Lee needed love from me for him to know what love is one day, but I was not always capable of expressing the true connection of love with my child.

I had been trying to connect with Robin again at the ranch in Springfield ever since she came to see me and bumped into Eric. She was always out with her son or with her crazy new druggie boyfriend, who I tried to talk her out of seeing. She never came to Brookline for my barbecues or parties anymore. We were all used to having her and many others in the life, as friends, and she had ample opportunity to come to my house and visit. My arms were always open. Part of the problem was that she knew Eric would be at these occasions. He had suffered an emotional breakdown and came close to killing himself because she had left him. Robin wanted to avoid seeing him because of her new man and Eric's new girlfriends. She hadn't called for a while because of a petty disagreement that festered as the result of her bumping into Eric and Tanya, his new girlfriend, at my house. When they ran into each other that day there was a huge argument in my kitchen that almost ended in a fist fight. Robin got pissed and stormed out, saying that if Eric was coming to my house with his bitches she would never come again. I ran after her to tell her that if she came with her man that would be fine with me. I begged her to understand and to stay. That was the last time I saw her until the day of the call—a call I will never, ever forget.

I'd been helping my manager at my retail shoe business, and David was on a job. I had a phone girl taking calls at the apartment to book the two working girls there. By the look on my store manager's face when she handed me the receiver, I knew the call brought bad news. It was Ruthie's (Robin's) mother. "I have no car, and it's Ruthie—she's in the hospital in Springfield! Please, can you help? I know you're best friends, you're the only one! Please, can you go to the hospital!" Hospital? "The doctors say it's an emergency! She's in intensive care!"

I was stunned and didn't give it a second thought, "Of course I'll go!" I told her I'd call when I got there. I gave her my beeper number. Then I took a few dollars out of the register, called home to leave a message for my son, and beeped David so that he would call the store and the manager could explain that I was on my way up to Springfield, Massachusetts. I called Eric and left him a message.

Frantic, I drove over a hundred miles an hour, and didn't care if I got stopped. First Kara, then Marcie, and now Robin is sick? It was unbelievable. But was Robin just sick? Her mother said she was in an accident, and didn't delve into it beyond that because she didn't know anything more. I was speeding, but it certainly wasn't a joy ride. Who next? I prayed the entire drive that she was okay. My beeper went off non-stop, but I didn't have time to pull over. My friend was in trouble—it was an emergency, and I didn't give a shit about anything else in the world. I was rehashing all the times I drove to Springfield to talk Robin into coming back to Boston, even trying to force her, but that never worked. She loved dancing at the ranch, her second home. The influence of the guy she was with was bad. I felt myself panicking. All my friends were having difficult times, except for Dana, who was smart and straight and had good sense, and whose only hang-up was dating young guys, like Mae West did. She was my tanning buddy, and she was a great connection to the straight world. We hung out, tanning on her rooftop, watching the helicopters overhead fly low to get a view of our topless bodies lying out in the sun, unable to touch us. We had fun talking, eating, and drinking. She had the softest skin and a great body. And now she is Florida, by her pool every day. We talked about our retirements to a tropical climate where we would lounge, have drinks, and live life. Can't wait for that day! I often return to thinking about that dream life. I thought about Katie, who drank like a fish and was so carefree about life; sex, drugs, booze…all of it good, but not something I wanted in my life. She was who she was—wild—but I loved her. Just like Robin, she was a flirt and would drop her drawers for a hung man and a compliment. I never understood why Robin couldn't stop pumping script pills from morning 'til night; but she never felt that good about herself. The pills didn't help and gave her face a tired appearance. I began to think that the reason she loved looking at herself was because she needed constant reassurance that she looked pretty and was sexy, not because she was so enamored of herself. Why was Robin in intensive care? Did her man beat her? I thought about calling her mom when I got there, but she didn't have any more information than I did when she first called. I would have to wait to speak to the doctors and nurses.

I finally reached Springfield and had to locate the hospital. I knew it was downtown. I had believed that Ruthie would never commit suicide because she loved herself so much, but then again, there was the possibility she really didn't love herself and she took an accidental overdose of Valium. No, not Ruthie…not my vain friend! My mind was going a mile a minute. I saw a small group of people walking, and I pulled over and asked one of them where the hospital was. "Turn around. Proceed through two stoplights, take a left, and go straight. You can't miss it." I put my foot on the pedal, followed the directions, and yes, there it was. They were right. I seamlessly pulled into a parking spot, grabbed my bag, and rushed through the Emergency entrance doors. I went directly to the woman sitting alone behind the desk and asked where Ruthie was. They told me. Oh, yes, I recalled, intensive care. Why didn't I say that! "Take that elevator to the second floor and when you get to the nurses' station, ask for her room." My heart was pounding as I ran down the hall to the elevator. I hoped and prayed that Eric had gotten my message. My beeper was still going off incessantly, and I turned it to silent.

Everyone would have to wait. My son was fine and with his friends, and I doubted he would mind if I wasn't home because Dave would be there to get his dinner on the table.

When I asked for Ruthie's room, the nurse wanted to know if I was a relative, and I explained that her mother had sent me and I had been her best friend for years. We were like sisters. The nurse informed me that Ruthie's mother had given authority over to me, and I could sign any papers that were required. I hoped I was a good candidate and up to the job! The nurse told me how Ruthie had been brought in the day before, in late morning, by a neighbor. "Her little boy tried to wake his mommy up for breakfast, and when she wouldn't get up he became upset. He ran to a neighbor to have them wake his mom. When they got there she was not responsive, so they called the police and an ambulance. She was in a deep coma and her body was failing. Her kidneys shut down, and she was put on life support. The police found pills and cocaine on a table by the couch where she was lying, and it was clear she had overdosed." "Oh, my god! Will she be all right?" My heart pounded from fear! "We don't know. I'll have the doctor paged for you. Is there anything you need?"

"No, no."

"We have to contact her mother again for her to give permission for you to sign now that you are here." The neighbor had given the paramedics Ruthie's mother's telephone number from the address book they found in her house.

"May I see her?" She told me I could sit by her, but that Ruthie wouldn't know who I was. The nurse led me into the room, and I prayed every step of the way for her to be okay. I never imagined she would be this bad! I loved her crazy ass, and I was so sorry for the fight we had the last time I saw her. *Oh, please forgive me,* I said to myself. Oh, God, don't take her away! The details of that last day I saw her at my house are etched in my mind forever.

As I mentioned earlier, Robin had come to my house when Eric and his new girlfriend, Tanya, were already there. Robin was belligerent when she saw Tanya, and Tanya wanted Robin to get out of her face. Eric and I intervened, telling her that she had a new man and Eric had the same right as she did to have a new friend. I thought I was being reasonable and adult-like, but as her best friend I should have given more consideration to what was going on in Robin's mind. She wanted me to herself. The visit turned hellish. Robin had come home that weekend to get some of her costumes for stripping at the Ranch Club and came by my house unexpectedly. I was so happy to see her, and then Eric dropped by; it was the weekend, and he was used to showing up because I would always cook for everyone. I wished I had known he was coming over, but who knew? She was jealous and enraged when they came in, but I sided with Eric, saying it was all right that he had come and that everyone could stay. They had broken up, but were both still my best friends. No matter who they were with, they still did love each other. No favorites—we could all get along. "How could you have him at your house with that bitch?" she screamed. She couldn't deal with it and stormed out of the house, with me chasing after her, begging her to come back. "Wait, Rob! I love you, but I love Eric too. Let's be reasonable." She said she wasn't in the mood to talk about it, and then she yelled at Eric. He was on the porch calling to her as well, to have a talk just with him. That was the last time I spoke with her. It broke my heart to see her this way, and my rehashing of our last encounter was soul-wrenching.

Walking into a cold, white hospital room made me uneasy. It always triggered memories of my mother Rose in her room with the white cotton drapes, white bedding, and white walls—and me almost dead at the hospital in the same atmosphere. When my mom was dying, I could smell sickness in the air. In one sense, I love the color white because it reminds me of my final moments with her, but in another, it brings back terrible memories of the way I felt seeing her in bed for the last time, almost unable to sit up. I was traumatized by that long-ago visit to the sanitarium. Now, I found myself looking at my friend Robin, her long black hair cascading down the white pillow case. She was pale, with tubes and fluid lines attached to her. Her eyes were shut, and I noticed they were fluttering beneath her eyelids as if she were trying to open them. Otherwise, she was totally unresponsive. I told the nurse she was a dancer and had been taking Valium for years, along with some uppers and downers. I didn't know what else she might have been taking, and the nurse said the doctor would be coming in soon to answer any questions I might have. "If you need anything, just ring," she offered, and I asked her if I could use the phone in Ruthie's room. "Of course you can," she said. I put my bag, keys, and jacket on the chair and sat next to Robin on the bed, taking her lifeless hand in mine. "What did you take?" I asked her as if she could answer. It took a moment for me to compose myself. I couldn't believe my eyes. Praying silently was all I could do to help her. I wiped away my tears with my sleeve, touched every finger on her hand, and rubbed her frail arm. I leaned over to speak in her ear, "Robin, wake up! Robin, it's me! I'm so sorry! Please forgive me! I don't want us to argue anymore. We never should have fought. I shouldn't have let you leave! I never chose anyone over you, and if you can hear me, please understand! I love you and I love Eric. Both of you are my best friends, and I want to keep your friendship. I'll tell Eric to call before he comes to the house from now on and not to bring anyone with him ever again. You can visit anytime you want without calling me. Please, I love you and I want you to get better! Please talk to me! Come back! Do something—can you wiggle your toes? Anything? Keep listening, please, Robin! You can do it! I'm going to call your mother. I know you don't get along, but she's worried sick about you and loves you so. Rob, talk to me, please!" Tears rolling down my face, I held her cool, limp fingers in my hand, feeling death knocking at her door. She just has to be okay! I kept on calling her name and talking to her as I massaged her legs. "Please, Robin, move!" The tears were now running down my face nonstop. I had to believe she would wake up, and even if she called me an asshole I would take every bit of it.

I made calls, first to David to let him know I was fine, to find out how R. Lee was, and if everything was all right at the store. R. Lee was okay, eating his supper late after doing his homework. He got on the phone to say he loved me and then wished me goodnight. David told me that he had called Eric and was waiting for him to call back. I told him I wouldn't be home until Robin was out of danger, and then I'd come back to get a change of clothes. I had my credit cards so I could get a hotel to shower and go right back to Robin's side until she snapped out of it. He told me to be careful and asked if I wanted him to come to Springfield. "No, watch R. Lee. He needs you there."

"I will," he said. "I love you and miss your face."

"Miss your face, too," I told him. I had given him Robin's room number in case he had to call me in an emergency. I tried Eric time after time, but there wasn't any answer. The call I dreaded was the one to Ruthie's mom…I couldn't put if off any longer.

"Libbe?"

"Yes, I'm Libbe," I said. The doctor came in and introduced himself. "We have permission from Ruthie's mom to talk to you, and permission for you to sign for your friend in case an emergency surgery is necessary. I'm sorry your friend is this state."

"Will she be okay?" I asked, in a pleading voice.

"I'm afraid not. If she survives, it will be a miracle. Her body is unresponsive, and there is a likelihood of permanent brain damage if she lives through this. She won't be able to do things for herself. She had huge quantities of drugs in her bloodstream. Although we don't know what combination of drugs she took, her coma was caused by an overdose, and it was hours before she was found. That's why the situation is deadly."

"Where is her son?" I asked.

"He's with her neighbor. We have the address at the desk for you."

"I don't want to leave her side. Is there anything at all that can be done to save her?" "We will continue doing what we're doing now. The life support is what's keeping her alive. Her condition is stable, and we'll know if there are any changes the next time we take her vitals. It's good for her to hear familiar voices. Often people in comas do miraculous things. Let me know if you have further questions."

"Yes, doctor, I will. I'll be here talking to her all night. Could she possibly take a good turn?" The doctor just shrugged his shoulders, shook his head in doubt, and left the room. The sorrow I felt was unfathomable. I broke down crying while I held her hand, and then spoke to her some more, without taking a break. "You can't leave me, Robin! You have to come out of this! You were there for me when I had my accident, and we've been through so much. Think of your son, little Eric he needs his mom! Think, Robin!" I talked about all the places we had gone together and how much fun we had. "Remember, Robin, you were floating on my silver blow-up raft while I rowed you, Princess Robin, around the waterways of Revere Beach, the beach you loved going to with all your male admirers whistling at you as you got tanned. Remember the time the raft collapsed and you were freaking out, saying, 'My makeup! My hair! I can't get my face wet!' And your face got wet and your hair was a tangled mess… You were so pissed off, and you screamed at me for laughing; it was so funny to me but, needless to say, not funny to you. Please forgive me, Robin, but you were beautiful without any makeup. And then we laughed about it at the bar the next day, when you were all made up again and we had a drink to relax." As I told her the story, I fought back my tears for her sake, but my voice did sometimes crack. I couldn't control my emotions like I did when I was working the Zone—tough and immune to feelings. This wasn't the Combat Zone; this zone was real life, and my feelings were overwhelming me. The situation was life and death, and neither of us had any control.

It was time to call her mom. I glanced at the phone, not wanting to be the one to call, but I had to. I dialed the number, and her mother answered in a harsh, deep voice. "I'm sorry, but it's not good news." I paused, waiting for a reaction. "The doctor said she was bad off. I'll stay with her, I promise. All we can do is pray."

"I can't come up there," she said, "and I can't take her little boy. I'm too old."

"Don't worry, let's get her better, then we can figure that out, okay?"

"Will you call me back?" she asked in a concerned tone.

"Yes, I promise."

"I will say a prayer for her," she said. Although Ruthie's mother was stern, her heart hurt because of her daughter. She had a response even though her love for Ruthie had been buried for years. I could tell she loved her daughter deeply. Whatever issues had caused a rift between them didn't exist anymore. I stayed by her all night. There wasn't any change in Ruthie's condition, just a reflex in her finger and no other activity. I had stopped calling my friend by her stage name, Robin, and only used her real name now. The intimacy between us during the night seemed to erase that part of her identity from my mind and she became Ruthie—just plain Ruthie. The nurse told me she would get me a toothbrush and hairbrush for when I went back to the hotel, which was what I was about to do. The stores near the hotel wouldn't be open yet. I called the nurse in when I saw a different pattern in her eye movements, as if she were straining to open them. The nurse said that was normal, and that Ruthie might even open her eyes and keep them that way. I believed Ruthie knew I was there!

I left about five a.m., exhausted and hoarse from talking for such a long time. I never made it to the convenience store to buy snacks. The hotel was nice and clean, and I jumped into the shower and stood there like a mannequin, crying my eyes out while I let the water pour down over me. I felt like I was in a rain forest, nude. So much ran through my mind. I imagined a home with a rose garden, a peaceful place like my mom's rose garden, away from the streets and the daily chaos and drugs and the life. Roses in my garden; roses cut and placed in vases inside my home for me to enjoy the natural, small things in life. There were so many good things happening in my life—why this? David's cheating was insignificant in comparison to the seriousness of Ruthie's condition. This was beyond my dreams of a rose garden in life.

After showering and having some tea and a bagel at the hotel, I went directly back to Ruthie's room without sleeping. Before I could go inside her room, the nurse saw me and announced that they had discontinued life support. There had been improvements since I left. Ruthie had started breathing on her own around six a.m., and her kidneys were functioning. Such great news! She was taking a turn for the better! Thank God! I took a big sigh of relief. I had to see her, perhaps that would help even more. I peeked into her room. "Hey, you beautiful creature!" Her eyes were open. "Hey there," I called out, "my pretty girl's awake! Shit, can you see me?" Her stare was vacant even though she was holding her own with only one needle in her arm. It was a big improvement. She was cleaned up nicely and looked like a new person, but that stare…it was empty and soul-wrenching.

I had been there about an hour when Eric came bouncing into the room as caustic as ever. He had been drinking all night, even after David told him what was happening, and was not in a state of mind to handle the situation well. "Hey, baby," he said in a deep voice to Ruthie, "come on, get the fuck up and stop playing games!" He grabbed her hand and started shaking it.

"Easy Eric, she's in a coma…she's not fucking with you! You need to go, Eric, you're drunk! Sober up then come back." He leaned over to Ruthie as if he were about to kiss her, but instead he took her by the shoulders, pulled her up, and shook her saying, "Wake up, damn it, get up! We're going home! Stop playing with me!"

"Eric, enough! Leave! Get out of here! I can't deal with you now. I'll talk to you later." He stayed a short time more, swaying from side to side, speaking nonsense while I stood between them to block his crazy moves. I knew he couldn't cope and that he would leave and get high somewhere, either snorting or basing. He was known to go on binges right up until the after-hours closed, or sometimes later if he wasn't working a gig or job. This was no time for him to be getting macho on her. And her new man? Where was he? What the hell! I hadn't even thought of him yet.

Eric left in a tizzy. I stayed with Ruthie, speaking to her until three a.m. When I touched her, she moved her hands and feet, and when I waved in front of her face, her eyes moved. The doctors and nurses seemed pleased, but they still insisted that the movement was probably a reflex. I felt it was okay to go back to the hotel to get a couple of hours of sleep before returning. I needed it desperately. None of her so-called friends came to the hospital, and her boyfriend, who had left her, never showed up either. What was his issue? Did he know? I wondered if he was there now?

Ruthie was stable, and that was the best news. I called her mother and then David and R. Lee. I told Dave about Eric's bad behavior at the hospital and that he was probably somewhere getting high at the after-hours—I wasn't sure. "I'm going to shower and sleep for at least two to three hours." I told him, "Miss your face."

"Miss your face too," he replied.

"Give R. Lee a kiss and hug for me." We hung up. I had stayed at the hospital all day until the wee hours of the morning, then said goodbye and left. I kissed Ruthie. She seemed to know and was calm. When I got back to the hotel, I took a shower and used the hotel's mini shampoo to wash my hair, which smelled of hospital. The toothbrush, toothpaste, and comb were my only supplies. I was ready to get some sleep before the sun came up when there was a knock on my door. It was four-thirty a.m., and I was just dozing off. What the fuck? "Hello?"

"Hey, baby, it's me, Eric…and my friend."

Friend? "Eric, what the hell? It's four-thirty! Meet me at the hospital in the morning. I'm tired." "I can't. I need to see you now. I have to get some sleep too. I have to go back to Boston soon.

"Come on."

"For what?"

"Just open the door, please?"

"Okay, I will, but no acting up." It didn't occur to me to be suspicious of my friend Eric, especially because of Ruthie's condition, even though he was messed up. I let them both in. I had never seen this other guy before. "So, who's your friend, Eric?"

"Oh, baby, this is my boy…from here. Yeah, we hooked up," he stuttered.

"Yeah, when? Tonight, when you copped drugs? Eric, you don't know who the fuck he is!"

"Oh, yes, I do. He's from Springfield. When I come here to hang, we hook up. For real! Robin knows him too."

"Whatever, you both can't stay." It was possible that Eric could know him because Robin had been working at the Ranch in Springfield for years. "Well, what do you want? When do you plan on seeing your girl? When you're sober, I hope."

"I'll stay here for a couple of hours, then I'll go with you in the morning, okay?"

"No, Eric, you can't stay over to sleep, and your friend needs to leave now. I don't know him, and I definitely can't sleep with him in my room."

Eric sat on the bed beside me and said, "Oh, c'mon baby, you know me." Eric could always sweet-talk, but when he was drunk he was uncouth as hell, clumsy and obnoxious. "Lemme give you a hug." I hugged him back but he pulled too close.

"Okay, Eric, enough!"

"You look like my baby girl—you both always looked like sisters. My baby's all fucked up…" He was melancholy. "She's okay, you know. She's just acting," he said.

"Eric, she is better tonight but not okay! Her vital signs have all improved, but she's not out of the woods yet."

"Great, baby. Great," he responded in a fucked-up slur. "Lemme sleep next to you…I won't bother you. I just wanna hold you close. Look, you're my baby too. You're best friends—she won't mind."

"Well guess what, Eric? I do mind. I mind a lot. You need to go! My friend is lying in the hospital fighting for her life." I tried to get up and wrench myself away from him, but he got hold of me and dragged me from the end of the bed all the way across it. My leg got caught on the frame and cut open; as I pulled it free, I yelled for him to stop. Blood was dripping down my leg to my foot—the gash was deep. I let him have it! I took all my anger out on him. "Ruthie's lying in the fucking hospital, possibly dying, and you're fucking around with your get-high buddy and trying to score me? You should be with her, not here hitting on me! Get the fuck out! Both of you get the fuck out now!" I screamed.

"Oh baby, I'm sorry. Let me see."

"No, Eric, get out of here! I don't want you to touch me. Sober up, and think about what you're doing. You're no good to anyone high."

Eric did feel badly, but in his state I was not going to deal with him, and I was so wound up that sleeping was going to be impossible unless I calmed down. I went into the bathroom to run the cold water over the cut so it would stop bleeding. The skin had torn off and the gash was oozing blood. I didn't appreciate that Eric was trying to hit on me. He knew better, and I had to stay away from him. I debated whether to tell David, but in the end, I decided not to; this wasn't the time for bad feelings. When I had calmed down, I slept for two, maybe three, hours and was awakened by the sunshine coming through the partially opened curtains. I felt drained and just wanted to go back to sleep when the phone rang—it was David, calling before he went off to work. That was a welcome call, even R. Lee said good morning, and hearing his voice helped me wake up and, even with no sleep, feel energized. I told Dave I had overslept but would be back at the hospital in an hour. Robin looked so much better, I told him, and he said that everything at home was okay and not to worry, that Charlie had called from New York and needed a girl to come there in two weeks. I said I would handle it. He had picked up the money at the store and made deposits for me. Mr. C. passed a message on through David that he would talk to me when I got back. He had met Ruthie a few times, and I knew he would come to Springfield if I asked, but in no way did I want to have any other hands pawing at me. Would I ever make an attempt to escape the pain of my life like Ruthie, or would I be able to walk away from the money, the mental and physical abuse, and move toward freedom? Her overdose had me thinking more about my own future.

Once I was dressed, the first thing I wanted to do was to see Ruthie. I would get tea and a bite at the hospital. I got my tea and a muffin, then ran up to see her. I asked the nurse if Eric had visited Robin earlier in the morning, and she told me that I had been the only one to visit. He hadn't gone back to the hospital, and that was fucked up. "How is she?"

"Well, go and see for yourself."

I walked briskly to her room and stood at the threshold of the doorway without speaking a word, and I swore she sensed me coming into the room. She turned and looked straight at me, her eyes staring. "Hey, Robin, it's me, Libbe. Do you see me? You do! Did you miss me? I missed you."

Her eyes followed me over to the side of the bed. I was certain she was aware of me and knew who I was. I held her hand and squeezed, and she squeezed back. "Robin, if you know me squeeze my hand!" and she did. "Oh, my god, you're okay!" I called for the nurse, who already knew she had improved, and I showed her what Ruthie was able to do. She said she would tell the doctor. I sat there talking to my friend, holding her hands, rubbing her feet, and putting lotion on her legs. I was smiling, and in my heart believed that Ruthie had turned a corner and had undergone a true breakthrough. As I was about to go and get something else to eat, Eric came in. "Hey, baby…" "Well Eric, I see you've come."

He went to Ruthie's bedside, and rather than bullying and browbeating her, he cried. "I love you! I'll take care of you! I don't want anyone besides you…you're my baby," he promised her, and then he hugged her frail body and told her he'd be back. I could see he had sobered up. The emotion of that real moment erased the bad issues from earlier, but I still had to keep some space between us.

He asked me to go to Ruthie's apartment with him. Early in the morning, he had gotten the key from the neighbor, who told Eric she was getting high every night with her new man—uppers, downers, drinking, freebasing. Eric was pissed off to the point where he wanted to kill him. The neighbor told Eric where he thought he could find the man. He asked me to go with him, and I let Ruthie know that I would be back shortly, that we were going to check on little Eric. I drove Eric to her townhouse, and we went in to find her man's number and take anything valuable for Eric to hold for her until she got out of the hospital. We couldn't find the man's number, and Eric took her phonebook and some random numbers scattered around on pieces of paper in a drawer. Ruthie was a scatterbrain. I took the gold ring with the flower Eric had given her. She cherished that ring. He said for me to hold it for her and that if anything happened, for me to keep it always. I knew where the ring should go, back on Ruthie's finger. We took a quick ride by the ranch, and Eric got her new man's address, but they told us he stayed with Ruthie most of the time. Eric said he would handle her man. I didn't care about him and wasn't going to involve myself any more than I already was, I cared only about Ruthie getting better, and where her son would go. I could tell he had given his behavior that night some thought because he slyly said, "David doesn't know I came by last night, right?"

"No, I didn't tell him."

We parted in the parking lot without saying much more. Eric was silent except for the few words he had said and his usual "See you later, baby," spoken in his deep, sexy voice. No hug this time.

I went back inside the hospital room and drank my cold tea with my muffin. I could see and feel the tranquility emanating from her, a kind of contentment that I was there. I could feel and hear her soul. She was fighting. I just hoped that what I felt was true. I rang for the nurse and asked her if she thought I could go to get a change of clothes later in the day since Ruthie was doing so well and was out of danger. She said that Ruthie was doing well, that in her opinion, I could go. She told me the doctors were amazed by her progress and thought it was due to the positive feedback she was receiving. I asked her to watch Ruthie and explained that she had some quirks, like about people not touching her hair. No one, not even I, could touch her hair. "Watch," I told her. I softly touched her long hair and she squinted. Then I said, "Watch this, if she understands, she'll respond." I said, "Ruthie, I'm going to cut your hair." She was agitated, waving her hands in the air, contorting her face into a mean expression, and making an "Mmm" sound. The nurse was shocked by what Ruthie had done and said that was not a reflex, and she must tell the doctor that she was expressing her feelings. I was so happy! I sat and told her stories, recalling so many things. This day was really positive. I stayed until after midnight. I told Ruthie I was going home to get some clothes and that I would be back in the morning, about ten or eleven a.m. "I promise, okay? When I come back, I will stay until they release you from the hospital." She frowned. "I promise…you're getting better…just keep it up. I'll be back—it's just a half-day so I can get some clothes. Get some sleep, please. I promise, I love you!" I left the room but stayed just outside the door, peeking in a few times before departing to make sure she was okay. I could tell she was aware of what I was doing. She stared. "Love you…see you soon." I threw her a kiss. "Don't you worry," I told her. "I will be right back when you wake in the morning." I felt horrible leaving her, but I comforted myself knowing they said she was holding her own. More than anything, I wanted her to recover. I wanted to help her and to be a good friend. Maybe when she leaves the hospital she and little

Eric could come live with me until she recovers. I didn't want her to stay up here near that guy and the ranch. Not one of her friends from there came to the hospital, and they all knew.

I sped back to Boston, went by the store to pick up the paperwork that had piled up in my office, and then drove straight home. David was up waiting and had supper ready for me; he was good that way. He was so domestic—he cleaned the house and always cooked great food—he did everything he could to help me. R. Lee was in bed sleeping, and I adjusted his blanket and kissed his forehead as I whispered, "I love you." I was ravenous and couldn't wait to eat. I had to be up by seven a.m. to see my son off to school before I made the drive back to Springfield. Excited by her progress, I told David everything about what Ruthie was able to do. And, as always, he supported me in my bedside vigil. I was desperate to sleep so I could return to the hospital. Dave and I lay side by side, and all our problems seemed to vanish. We passed out talking to one another. When he tried to wake me, I was in a deep sleep. It was a telephone call from Ruthie's mother. As Dave roused me, I understood. I shook off my sleepiness and grabbed the phone. She was hysterical. "Ruthie died, Libbe! She's gone…she's gone! My Ruthie passed!" What? Both of us were crying. I did not understand this…no way! What the fuck? We were in shock, particularly after the turn-around she had made. I hung up the phone. "I never should have left!" I cried out. "It's my fault!" There was no reason for it to happen. I didn't want to believe she was really gone, even though the nurse had repeatedly warned me that patients sometimes die after an initial improvement. All I could think of was that she died alone. I wasn't there for my friend…

My friend, my sister in the life, was gone. Now at peace, she was buried at a cemetery in Revere. I convinced her mother to take little Eric. I thought, and believed, that he would be better off with her than with big Eric. I just did not want the little boy to be in the kind of atmosphere big Eric and his new family would create with his drinking and drugs. He wasn't the child's biological father, and Ruthie's mother was related by blood. She would have a more fulfilled life bringing up her grandchild; it would keep her vital and alive. I hoped she was the better choice. Still, I wasn't entirely sure that staying with his grandmother was best for the child either, and I second-guessed myself more than a few times, not wanting to make a grave mistake. As years went by, I checked on him often. Eric was a total mess at the cemetery and for a long time afterward. We all cried, endlessly—Eric was sobbing hysterically, and R. Lee and David broke down too. After the ceremony, I spoke briefly, one friend to another, with Eric. It was so emotion-filled that we both promised to always remain friends, no matter what happened or happens.

Robin's death was a profound loss for me. I kept the depth of my sorrow hidden, although I couldn't control my tears at the graveside as her body was lowered into the ground. *My poor friend. There won't be any mirrors where you are going.* But Robin (Ruthie) would always be with me; every time I looked in a mirror I would think about her. She was close to my heart. I called her mom to check on her and little Eric and told her if she needed me to call anytime, but she never did. Unlike the deaths of Kara and Marcie, Robin's took a toll on me. It was impossible to imagine my future without her in it. The antidote to my grief was to keep busy, as I always did. I moved on to my next venture in life.

CHAPTER SEVENTY-TWO

Store Open

Eric was partying way too much and using Ruthie's death as an excuse for bad behavior. Whenever he was in that state of mind, I kept my distance from him. I was into my real estate and being a mom. I too had a terrible healing time, but drugs were not the answer. Secretly, I was going back to my old habits, including the Circuit; this time really heavy, and trading more and more girls now. During the time I closed my madam business, I felt like I had lost a friend. That business was me. I had started it from scratch and built it up over the years, first seeing clients myself to get it to the level where I had it, and then letting it go because of David's resentment and my financial involvements with Mr. C. That was not what I wanted; it took away an important part of me. The relationship with Mr. C. held firm despite my going back into business. He didn't care as long as his needs were met—a true client. I wasn't attracted to him at all, but he was a friend, and I bartered my body for his help, a trade that never comes without side effects. His wife was in love with him, and she went along with all his shenanigans; that was her security, not only with me, someone she knew about, but also with other swingers. Sex and pleasure came first for Mr. C., as it did for so many men I knew and dealt with.

Despite my past, I wanted a monogamous relationship. The reality that so many people cheated and couldn't be trusted in everyday life stunned me. I had been with hundreds of men and some women, yet what I wanted was to be with a man I could trust, never questioning if he was cheating on me. That's a peaceful lifestyle. Yes, temptation is out there if you're weak. It was a given I was having sex, but it was for money. David's point of view was that having sex for money was being unfaithful, so why couldn't he have sex with other women? That was a good point, but for me it was just business, it was how I made a living. I was never jealous when I was with pimps whose lifestyle was up front about having other working women. But there is a different mindset when a man promises to be with you and only you. You commit your heart to him, and you're accountable to him, as he is to you. If bodies and beauty are more important, stay single! I watched David's metamorphosis into a Lothario. From his exposure to women he worked for in his contracting business to the dressed-to-kill all-American white girls who worked for me, David had his pick of women. Essentially, with this relationship, I was stuck in the middle of love and my sex business. I had to accept his womanizing. I was in love with a square again, and never guessed he was as weak as he was when it came to women.

I wanted to be with a strong man I could trust, who would not weaken over a quick attraction. Someone who was not led by his dick. The probability of having an exclusive relationship built on mutual trust while I was in the life was nil. There would have been fewer problems in the beginning if we knew we were going to have to accept and maintain love in an open arrangement in which both of us were allowed to cheat. I wanted to be with David as one, and for him to be with me as one. I was catching wind from girls, madams, and even clients, that David was not being faithful. Even his contracting partner let his lips spill out shit about him. I sensed it too, and I had to deal with that while at the same time working the store and phones and properties. He used my business as an excuse to stray even more. The worst part was he was having affairs with squares—his customers, and girls from his hang-out bars in Brookline and Brighton. I was about to reclaim my independence. He did what twenty-five percent of men do: cheat on their girlfriends and wives. I am sure it's more than that considering the lists of prostitution clients in the USA! Of course there are those who don't, but the statistics are not in their favor. There is so much more to living beyond sex. Society—especially television and movies—is a tease that tempts you to believe that it's all sex, sex, sex and money, money, money. Ultimately, the quality of people's relationships is so much more important than the trappings of just sex and money. Who in the hell teaches us that? No values…no discipline… But it goes way back, and can never be stopped. It's the animal instinct.

The store was looking great. Kay S. and I were talking and hanging out at night seeing customers, missing our friends. She learned a lesson about cheating when her former man beat her within an inch of her life. She had a new man, who was chummy with David. He was a bad influence on Dave, talking shit to him about how to treat women from a street point of view. He was fine to look at, and women loved the look, but I knew it was not good. David was changing like J.N., only—thank god—without J.N.'s coldness and cruelty. The shoe store was looking great, and I was back in full swing, having girls seeing customers again six days a week. I saw only a select few, and kept that hidden from everyone, including Mr. C. He was still giving me money from his company, and I went to New York with him on occasional weekends that combined business and sex. I hated spending nights with him in New York because he would put his arms around me as if I were his girlfriend. That was a bad scene. My sugar daddy's feigned affection was unsettling. I never could get past sleeping overnight with a customer. I even did a small amount of coke in front of him so that he would think that was the reason I stayed awake. I was a good actress, but I wasn't that good a performer when it came to bedtime togetherness. However, these trips were often necessary for buying shoes for my store, and Mr. C. would take full advantage of it. He enjoyed taking me to the shoe vendors and franchises to show me off. I wore a small, size six shoe, and he loved my legs in heels; all the men I knew said I had great legs. Mr. C. trusted his franchise partner, Mr. Kirk, but I didn't. He never listened to me and I knew he was going to be a thorn in Mr. C.'s side.

The house in Brookline required my full attention. I felt love for my house from the first day, like Scarlett O'Hara in *Gone with the*

Wind. It was my home, a place to call my own and to have always, until I died...or so I thought at the time. I wanted the structure to be solid, both the interior and exterior. As the months of construction passed, we had continuous arguments over what and how to proceed, but I loved it, every inch. It was like *War of the Roses*, but with no divorce. It was permanent; a home in my life of wandering and roaming from place to place, and it would belong to my son someday.

I got instant gratification from turning over the residential buildings we worked on—my creations—and the store belonged to, and was also, another piece of me. I was eagerly awaiting the new store's opening, especially after the sadness of Robin's passing. My first store was so good that I knew a second one would be great. All of us were working day and night. David was able to pull the all-nighters by sniffing his fifty dollars' worth of coke. I was being a mom (no drugs or drink, except on holidays), and I was handling the phones for setting up clients with new girls every week. They came into Boston from all over the United States. The girls from Europe would call for their bookings when they got here. They let us know they had arrived in town, and David would go pick them up. The second store opened, and it was a success on a grand scale—a hit! I never imagined my shoe business could be as profitable as it was. There was no way I was going to give up my other business again. The girl I hired to manage the Mattapan store was the girlfriend of a guy I knew in the life. Originally from Barbados, she was the best in sales and managing, and I would help on the weekends, when the pace was frenetic. There was money coming in from everywhere. There were three stores: the little handbag and jewelry store next to the River Street shoe store, and now the Dudley Street shoe store. After that opened I proceeded to my next one, a rundown dump of a store in Revere for small-sized women's discount shoes. It never occurred to me that David was going to use this store as his personal space for having sex with my cute employee, but I would soon find that out. Four stores, and all doing great!

The hustle of life and money took over, and I was known—and proud to be known—as a businesswoman. I embraced that, but there was a price to pay for my reputation, and that was the cost of the time spent away from my son and David again. After Ruthie's death, I hadn't been seeing my friends as often as I used to. It bothered me that Ruthie gave Eric the impression that little Eric was his child when she knew he wasn't, making him feel responsible for the boy…and he did. I did not want that on Eric, no matter what he did. When she was alive, she unfairly said that she wanted him to pay. That was the only thing I felt should have been set straight, and later, I did speak to Eric, and he said that he already knew, that he would always take the responsibility for little Eric. I was so sorry she never got to see her son again.

Katie made it over quite a few times to shop without paying. It was too much, and I felt she was taking advantage of my good nature. Once, twice, okay, but five-ten-fifteen times—no! And not one or two pairs, but six or seven pairs now! The last time she came to the store she said to bill *me* for the shoes and bags she was taking without my knowledge or a call! She had never paid what she owed. I had to stop her the next time, so I had my manager call me when she tried to take bags of free merchandise again. She was asked to pay, with a huge fifty percent discount—no profit for me—but she was insulted and angry like I had a nerve to charge her at all. I couldn't conceive of doing the same thing if I shopped at a store that belonged to her, or any one of my friends. I would always pay!

Eric had stopped by the new store, still broken-hearted over Ruthie's death. He wanted to see if I was okay. He missed us. He said he was dating a new girl besides Tanya. This one was bisexual and had a good job. He was still drinking all the time and didn't care. I had eventually told David about what went down in the hotel room in Springfield. I could never keep a secret like that for too long. He spoke to Eric, and we all got past it. To this day, I still have the scar on my leg.

I loved my store. It was a huge place with many styles to choose from, and the customers were always happy with their purchases. I had given permission to a group of musicians, who I worked with and thought were great, to use the two thousand square foot basement to practice in without having to pay rent. They were all good, and I knew that one day they would get somewhere. They appreciated the space, and came to practice all the time. They were truly dedicated to the music industry, then and now; they forged ahead and eventually became very well known, and still are today. David was inspired by them and swore that he would make his own record someday, and I knew he would because I was planning to help him turn his dream into a reality.

I had one wild, Jewish client who was partying for two to three days at a time. I had to tell David. He was a regular, and spent piles of money. But this client was so needy I had to have David babysit him as he peered outside the windows, paranoid that someone was going to come to the hotel he was staying at to take him away. I questioned why anyone would want to get high if that was what happened. He was one of many of the big businessmen who needed release through extreme sex and drugs.

V cxThere was an important event coming up soon that both my son and I were waiting for. I even told my dad about it, and he finally said he was proud of my son and what was going to take place. Wow! He was proud of my son, who was part of me, he just never was proud of me. Mr. C. made a call to talk to him about me, and being a "landsman" (fellow Jew), it gave Freddy a sense of security. However, he still didn't express any pride on my behalf. Mr. C. spoke on the phone to my father for a while so that he would know how well I was doing. But, as usual, his attitude toward me hadn't changed. "She'll be back to her old tricks one day," he said. Well, that was true, I went back to my old tricks for sure… Anita told him on numerous occasions that I would never change and my dad stuck to that. I was succeeding in the world, and I wished my mother Rose could see it, not just in spirit, but also in the flesh. *She* would be proud of me, and what I'd accomplished, no matter what.

****

In my present jail cell, with the white walls and hard bench, I feel an overwhelming urge to cry, but I am choking it down, refusing to allow the tears to crush me. I do not want to become a spectacle for everyone to gawk at, especially these law enforcement officers. As I cup my hand underneath my chin to rest my head for a moment, I am thinking about my reality, and how reality to me has always seemed to be a matter of life and death, not something in between. How I kept my life intact often amazes me.

CHAPTER SEVENTY-THREE

Israel, Egypt, Greece, and Rome

My life has been a roller coaster ride. I make my way to the top then dive downward, at incredibly high speed, to the bottom. It has been that way since I was a child, and I don't expect it to be any different now or in my future. Things would seem wonderful on the surface, but then unforeseen circumstances always pulled me down; like now—in a glass cage and, even worse, a federal one—when I find myself uncertain about my present situation and beyond. Everything is surreal.

****

Plans for my son's bar mitzvah at the Wailing Wall in Jerusalem were underway. I felt proud that I had arranged the event by myself, with Mr. C.'s additional help in finding Jacob, our driver, and covering the travel costs of the plane fare. Our flights were booked, and R. Lee was more than ready to get the bar mitzvah over with, but taking the trip to Israel was really cool; he couldn't wait to go. He was so nervous about reading the Hebrew that it affected him physically. My understanding was that a bar mitzvah could take place whatever the age of the person. We were joyful—it was going to be an adventure! David would be accompanying me, and Mr. and Mrs. C. were coming, along with their daughter. Mr. C. planned to stand with R. Lee when he read from the Torah because my father, of course, would not. I left a girl to answer the client phones, ensuring that it would run smoothly. And my stores would be fine, with the manager from Mattapan taking charge of them for me. I felt as though my life was expanding, I was spreading my wings and taking flight. Having a business in the straight world and my behind-the-scenes one was a lot more of a secure feeling now.

We had moved into our house despite the ongoing construction. The first floor was finished and could be rented for the income. The work on the rest of the house was done piece by piece and built with only the best materials: copper brass nails, oak woodwork, custom oak doors, and milled moldings, plus Italian tiles. Building this home was a labor of love. My son had his own room *in his own house* for the first time, and I had the house I had dreamed about and prayed for from the time I was a young child; I believed all of this had come to fruition because of faith and hard work. Eva's predictions were coming true. My gift to see inside people was like her ability to predict the future, and neither of us needed cards. I was great at sales in both worlds.

My son was so nervous his stomach bothered him. He was afraid of the Orthodox and Hassidic rabbis. He thought that he would get one of them for his bar mitzvah, and he didn't want to fumble his lines. One thing about R. Lee's bar mitzvah that bothered me was that my son never received cards or gifts to commemorate the day from anyone except Mr. C., myself, and David. Even my dad, who said he would have gone to stand up for R. Lee if it weren't for Anita, didn't send a thing, not even a card. Well, what did I really expect? Nothing! And how could my so-called friends and entire foster family be that inconsiderate? I certainly wasn't that way with them. I didn't believe my dad anyway—he wouldn't have come even of his own accord. I made a point of trying to make everyone happy in life and would share my last cent with anyone. I was insulted by the lack of acknowledgement my son received. I stored that information deep inside, even more than Anita's beatings.

The day of the flight arrived, and R. Lee was sick from the time he stepped onto the plane until after it landed. We didn't get any sleep at all. And David had a little bottle of coke in a pendant around his neck and took a few toots here and there. The religious Jews were davening, praying in loud voices as they swayed back and forth, back and forth, standing by everyone's seats. The other passengers were animated and talking, even shouting. It was not peaceful by any measure, and we didn't sleep for the entire eleven hours and twenty-five minutes of the flight to Israel. It was chaos, but we survived—and later, we saw tee shirts and memorabilia saying that!

Mr. C. went over our itinerary. We were going to be at a kibbutz for a couple of days, then go on to Tel Aviv, and then Jerusalem for the bar mitzvah. Afterward, we were going on tour for a week to the usual places: the Dead Sea, Masada, the Arab market, and then to the jewelry district to buy a mezuzah for R. Lee. After the long, noisy flight, we disembarked into the burning, hot sun. There were soldiers spread around. We met Jacob, the driver of the Mercedes we had hired to take us for a private tour of the country; he was there to pick us up and take us from the airport to our first stop. Poor R. Lee wasn't talking at all, and this trip was all for him. He was sick and pale, but David spoke to him and got him to talk a little bit. He told us he was too nervous to eat. We checked into the hotel, and we had a day more to prepare for the kibbutz. Jacob had a meeting in the lobby with all of us except R. Lee, who was too sick to come down because he was in the bathroom so much. David went to get him because he was the subject of the discussion and Jacob had to speak to him. My sick son appeared and sat down, frightened to death. I hugged him and explained he would be just fine. Jacob calmed him when he said that the rabbi performing the ceremony with him was Reform, not Orthodox. The color returned to his face immediately as he listened. I knew he would be back to his usual self when he felt comfortable—wild, always getting into something—when his big day was over. I knew that then he would want to do everything.

Originally, we were supposed to go the kibbutz first, but because of my son's queasiness, Jacob changed the plans and he put off going to the kibbutz until after we went to the Wall, when R. Lee could enjoy it more. For the time being, we would be staying in Tel Aviv. We all ate a light dinner, even R. Lee ate some, and we went to sleep very early because of the jet lag; all of us desperately needed to sleep.

We were still exhausted when we got up the next day, and took most of the morning to regroup before the next big event. We walked around and did some shopping. We went to the beach, making sure we weren't far from a toilet for R. Lee, whose time was mainly spent running into and out of bathrooms. But I must say that it was a lot less now.

The next day, we were up bright and early to dress in our finest. R. Lee was nervous, but his stomach had settled down. All the plans for the day were arranged at the hotel: a party with cake to celebrate and his certificates from the bar mitzvah to cherish. We had no family for a function at home, and since we were just with Mr. C.'s family, what better place than Israel to celebrate my son's bar mitzvah! I was so proud of R. Lee and thankful to be in Israel—away from the humdrum of Boston and the phony people I dealt with so much. I was surprised to see so many people praying at the Wailing Wall, praying and pushing small pieces of paper into the crevices of the ancient stones. I crushed small pieces of paper—that I had written prayers for my son, David, my mom, and myself on—into the wall. It was so stuffed with hundreds upon hundreds of paper scraps that the pieces of paper could have been the mortar that held the stones together. I was in awe of the holiness of the site and felt it was a blessing to be standing there. Mrs. C., her daughter, and a gentleman her daughter had met on this trip, stood with me on the upper wall where women were segregated. They were banned from standing with the men who were in the areas below and inside, where David and Mr. C. stood up to get the Torah with R. Lee. I filmed the ceremony and took picture after picture of this momentous occasion. I don't know what happened to the video film. Mr. C. said he was going to have it developed when we got home, but he never gave it to me. I felt a great deal of pride as a mother. In this space and time, I was no longer the person I was in Boston, and although I had to stand apart from the men, I was a free spirit. I cried, as did my son, as he read from the Torah along with Mr. C. My heart was full, and I prayed to my mother Rose, hoping she could see her grandson and me at that moment. The date was August 18, 1983. It was the greatest day that I'd ever had, and especially because I shared it with my son, R. Lee, and my soul mate, David.

David had all he could do to hold the yarmulke on his head. He was comical to watch. I felt pride in him because he was there for R. Lee and me. My son finished reading his portion of the Torah, thank god. R. Lee was more comfortable with this rabbi, who could perform mixed marriages, and bar mitzvahs for single moms, who would otherwise not be allowed up on the bimah (podium). The next part of the ceremony was walking through the iron gates to the cave where the Torah was kept. When he was walking, holding the Torah, R. Lee had the widest of smiles across his face because he had made it through the big ceremony. He was proud of himself, as I was proud for him and of him. I thought, *Yes, my son, you made it!* And who would ever believe that I had a son whose bar mitzvah took place at the Wailing Wall…me, an adopted child, foster kid, street girl, prostitute, madam, and now an entrepreneur. I realized that I had to be more than careful, not for my sake, but for my son's—I did not want him tainted by the things I'd done, not then and not now, not ever. I have worried about him every day of my life. I worry about him today and will worry about him tomorrow. I will worry until the day I die. And even when I have expired, I hope that what I've done will never hurt him or his future. I'm sure that R. Lee will love me despite it all.

We went back to the hotel to eat cake and celebrate. Then Jacob drove us to do and get anything we needed. We had to cover our arms and legs to visit the jewelry stores in the religious district, searching for just the right mezuzah. We found one made in Israel from solid gold. Even though the driver said none were allowed, I took pictures very discreetly as we drove out of the district, and they were incredible. We then went to the Arab sector, where I picked out a beautiful pink Persian rug on sale for seven hundred dollars. Although Mr. C. bought it for me, he said that I would have to carry it back on the plane. I knew that David would carry it for me, and he did. R. Lee bought some small things and was so happy now that his fear of reading the Torah had passed! He had the formal documents, written in script on gold-edged parchment paper, to show that he had done it! R. Lee's energy was boundless now that this trip was no longer plagued by his anxiety. He chattered enthusiastically and was in a great mood. At the Dead Sea he had no fear, and floated away for miles until he was a dot on the white water. I screamed for him to come back, waving my arms frantically in the air, worried that he would float out of sight or that the salt would eat him up! When he finally got out of the hot water, the salt had turned his tanned skin chalky white. We put mud on him to bake in the sun—the minerals were supposed to have healing properties and smooth his skin. I still kept the mud I bought there, unused. We then visited Masada, the place where the Jews battled the Greeks almost two hundred years before Christ was born. David ran to the top of the mountain in one-hundred-ten-degree heat to prove to us that he could do it, and R. Lee followed him, making it only halfway because of the relentless sun. The rest of us went up the easy way, and at the top of the plateau Jacob explained every bit of the history of the fortress. We went to sit in European-style cafes as the Israelis do. There was even enough time before retiring for the night for me to stop into a dress shop in the hotel, where I had them make me a beautiful outfit out of soft suede in a lovely sea green color, which I still have today. I no longer fit into it, I will never be a size five again…

We went to the Holocaust Museum. It had the aura of an unworldly place, deeply moving and sorrowful. Visitors were sobbing as they viewed the photos all over the walls that told the history of the concentration camp victims who were starved and tortured. I snapped as many photographs of the exhibitions as I could—undercover because taking them was forbidden—the victims pictured in the exhibitions were haunting. These people were killed out of hate for their religion, just as the blacks were enslaved and killed because of the color of their skin. It was an eerie experience, like the time I visited the slave plantations in the South. I could never get over that, and still can't, and when I went down South in the seventies, I hated the signs that said "Whites Only, Niggers Not Allowed." Although while I was there I didn't see photos of the black slaves hanging from trees, I sensed the same feeling of horror while looking at these pictures. Anti-Semitism and the profiling of blacks existed then and still exists today. The plight of the Jews and blacks is what I am familiar with in my life. Sadly, the world hasn't changed much. Perhaps someday the human race will evolve to the point where we see that we all bleed the same red; and if blindfolded, we would never see color.

We explored the caves, traveling on a lift down a mountain, below us was water, which was exhilarating. When we rode on camels in the desert, the camel I was riding hissed and dropped me to the ground… I guessed that I was not his favorite tourist! I stayed on long enough to get my photo. R. Lee was fine on his camel. We took a photograph of R. Lee standing with a group of soldiers who were guarding the border. He was thrilled when they let him hold one of their rifles. Great picture.

R. Lee's experiences on the kibbutz were so positive that he wanted to stay there. I was tempted, but I wanted him at home with me—I would be lost without him, and I felt he was still too young to be on his own so far away from me. I told him if he chose to go back later, then I would consider sending him. It was new and exciting, and although he would have been assigned a surrogate family, I didn't think I could bear the separation, not then. I did not want him to go away again. I often wonder how the experience of staying and living on the kibbutz might have affected R. Lee's character, and future.

We had so much fun! I soaked it all in, and actually forgot about my own world. My son, David, and Mr. C. were going back to Boston, and Mrs. C., her daughter, and I would be staying on. R. Lee had school, and David said he would be fine taking care of him and also all the businesses. I was skeptical about how well David would do overseeing my phone business, particularly because of his fooling around with my girls behind my back. I was sure he would have a ball! It didn't stop me from having a good time, though. I refused to dwell on his cheating. I wanted to see everything I could.

Israel was an unforgettable experience. It was impossible not to feel the magic of the land. It is truly God's country. R. Lee and I had an opportunity to bond without the hustle of my work world and him being involved in school with his friends. It was a special time in our lives. We hugged, kissed, laughed, and stayed happy! On the morning of his bar mitzvah, when I took pictures from the top of the dividing wall, I saw him look up at me and smile—a moment I will take to my last day on earth. I threw him a kiss and thought how lucky I was.

****

Today, here in this place, gazing at walls of glass instead of steel bars, my heart is weeping not out of joy, but sadness because I will have to explain to R. Lee about my arrest. I know he is being informed about it as I sit here. Can I handle someone else telling him first? How I have always dreaded this day! He has already gone through so much in his life because of J.N. and me. I hate for this to happen, but knowing how good a person he is (even his temperament as a baby was sweet) he will eventually accept me. I have to think good thoughts, like how he thanked me when he was leaving Israel, saying, "I love you, Mom. You're the best."

"I love you too. See you in three weeks." I knew in my heart then that he loved me—my baby, my boy. Together, we had experienced as much good as bad. I remember how I kissed and hugged him, and watched him walk away with David and Mr. C. as they left for home, and we girls went back to the hotel to prepare for our further travels. Recalling the trip at such a low point in my life makes me realize just how fortunate I have been and still am. I will keep my spirits up no matter what, or where I am. Even if I am stripped of all my worldly possessions, I will still have R. Lee.

****

The cruise on the Nile would be another experience, but just cruising without having any adventures lacked excitement. I wanted to see more than Egyptians bathing and washing their clothes in the Nile River. The tour guide, Jamal, took a liking to me, and told me he had friends in Aswan. We were scheduled to stop there, but weren't permitted to get off the boat. Oh, really, what fun is that? With everything we were told to do, I always asked why. I knew my next move, my plan: I was all for sneaking off the boat without being seen. Mrs. C. wasn't, until I talked her into being bolder and having some fun. "C'mon," I said, "we're in Egypt. We have to check it out—just floating down the Nile isn't exploring!"

"But they don't permit us to go off the boat!" she pleaded. "Oh...well, I'm taking over, and I permit you."

She decided to go but left her daughter on the boat with family and friends. Her son and daughter-in-law were there as well as another couple from Mr. C.'s office, who met us in Egypt. It was a special trip set up for Mr. C., and he let me go with them in his place.

It took some doing, but I managed to get the guard out front away from the dock entrance. Mrs. C. and I slipped away to meet Jamal and his friend, who had a home in the town of Aswan. We were both all dressed up, but to be safe, we left our money and jewelry onboard. As we left the unarmed gate, we hurried up the boat ramp and carefully made our exit through the outer gate to the road, where we saw men sitting on the ground in front of what looked like a store. They were wearing their long, white cotton garb with turbans on their heads. However, what struck me most was that they were carrying rifles, automatic machine guns just like the guards in Israel had, and that made me wary and a bit frightened. Mrs. C. was scared shitless! Jamal and his buddy showed up a few minutes later. Whew! The friend was not bad looking. Jamal was sweet, and now that he was not acting in his role as our tour guide, I could tell he was more attracted to me—it was obvious, although he was nothing other than polite. I certainly wasn't interested in a sexual affair in Egypt...not with them.

The car was small, and his friend let us in; we were squeezed tight, like sardines. He put his foot to the gas pedal and sped away like a New York cabbie, driving so crazy fast that even I was shaken. The road was pitch black, lit only by the headlights of the car. Mrs. C. had been damn near holding her breath throughout the ride, holding onto the seat, and if she wasn't nervous enough already, she certainly was now. We pulled into the yard of a stone house. The house wasn't locked, and we walked into a den with candles burning and soft Egyptian music playing in the background. The ambience was sensual—I could tell it had been staged for us. They offered us some kind of Egyptian spirits. Sipping the drinks slowly, we tried our best to converse with them for about an hour. They were gentlemen, although when they slow-danced with us their closeness suggested an intimacy that wasn't innocent. We made sure not to behave in any way that might be encouraging. They saw we had no interest in being there and recommended that we go to another place, which was like a club. So again, we got into the car with our manic driver and took a short ride while I gazed at the amazing, star-filled sky. Because the streets weren't lit at all and it was so dark, it was impossible to gauge what kind of area we were in. The car stopped short in front of a rather plain stone building where a group of men were standing and smoking. The smoke drifted over their heads like clouds in a stormy sky.

It was a small underground club, and a man with a gun greeted us at the entrance. Jamal assured us that it was normal for men to have guns in this part of the world, particularly guards. Yeah, I gathered that. We descended a curved, stone stairway. There was music playing and two rows of long, high tables and benches inside the stone walls below ground. The underground room was crowded with people, lots of good-looking women and handsome, tan-skinned Egyptian men. Mrs. C. was nervous, but I was overjoyed—I was out, and at a club in Egypt! As I looked around the room more closely, I saw that there were only Egyptian men, and women with black hair and dark olive-toned skin who appeared to be Spanish-American. When I asked Jamal what was going on, he explained that the men were, in fact, Egyptian and the women were either Italian or other tourists looking for a night or two of fun with the men. He said it was common here. "Well, if you brought us here because you think..." "No, no, Libbe," he said accentuating each syllable. "You said you wanted to see some excitement, well then, here it is." I thought to myself, *Nothing for nothing.* I told him not to get any ideas. He totally understood. My paranoia kicked in.

"Of course," he said, "we are gentlemen. I am the tour guide for you and your friend, and you can ask me any questions you wish. I will answer." They *were* gentlemen. They hadn't made any rude advances, but did look at us with suggestive side-glances. The driver, who spoke broken English, didn't say much, and Mrs. C. just chilled out with her glass of Egyptian cheer.

Watching everybody, I was entertained. I told Jamal there was something about this club that was familiar to me, but I couldn't quite put my finger on it yet. As we were waiting for our next round of drinks, a man at the front of the room began playing his flute-like instrument. There was a large basket on the floor, and I assumed it was for tips. Jamal and I kept talking and I asked him, "What's up with these women?" He leaned over and whispered in my ear that the women want the Egyptian men to sleep with them, and they shower these men with money and expensive gifts. Oh, shit, I had a feeling. "So, tell me, where do they come from?"

"Well, the Italian women catch a flight here and spend two to three days, and the tourist women sneak away from their boring husbands and pay the men to sleep with them for a short period of time. There are many that come over from Italy, and their husbands never know what they do. It goes on all the time." Sex is the same everywhere. I wanted more answers, but Jamal was pretty straight and said he didn't know much more than he'd already told me. Mrs. C. wasn't entirely innocent, but she expressed shock, perhaps because we were in a foreign atmosphere. She knew about me and my past, and had quite a few skeletons in her own closet with Mr. C.

The music sounded odd to my Western ears, but I liked it. I was not as unexpected as what happened next. Mrs. C. and I were holding our drinks, fixated on the head and neck of a cobra that stretched straight up out of the open basket! Oh, shit… Mrs. C. was in shock! The melody must have enchanted the snake. Mrs. C. and I drew our legs up off the floor onto our seats as it slithered out of the basket between the tables. This was not the Pied Piper, but a grizzled old man wearing a turban hypnotizing a huge poisonous snake with a flute. I'd seen enough and told Jamal we were ready to leave. Snakes and insects never thrilled me. Mrs. C. grabbed her bag off the bench, and we made our way out. Jamal and his friend tried talking us into staying longer or going to another club, but Mrs. C. insisted on going back. It was five a.m., and I was satisfied with our adventure—it was time to go back to the boat before breakfast. Jamal agreed. Even with a few drinks in her, having had quite enough, Mrs. C. was happy to leave the cobra behind. Me too! Our driver got us to the docked boat in record time and let us off before we had reached the gate. Safe and sound, we walked right past the guard at the door like nothing happened. He was trying to talk to us, obviously stressed, and speaking in Egyptian. We couldn't understand a word of what he was saying, and we smiled and waved. The next day, we received a stern lecture for going off the ship. The captain said it was far too dangerous and never to do it again. We were sweet as sugar, apologizing for our excursion. I took the blame. "Sorry…" When he asked where we went, I shrugged my shoulders and told him we had gone to sit somewhere. I guessed from his disapproving look that he didn't believe me. Oh well!

During the day, I wrote in my journal and sunbathed. I loved the last highlights of the trip down the Nile: dancing on the ship and the buffet. It was quite a spread, and Jamal saw to it that I had whatever I wanted. He was at my feet, smitten by me. I was a bit drunk at the dinner party they held a few days later. My clothes and shoes were expensive; my tan and jewelry all glowed, and lent me a certain amount of class. At home, I had at least two hundred of the best designer shoes imaginable, and I had brought five pairs with me on the trip: three to wear when I went out, and two pairs of flats to go on our tours. Tonight, I was wearing silver evening shoes that had cost four hundred dollars, and I wanted to dance out on the floor. Mildly drunk, I didn't want to trip or scuff the shoes so I decided to take them off, and asked a few nice, Egyptian gentlemen to watch my shoes. They looked at me without answering, and I sat the shoes on top of the end of their table. They had no food in front of them, just drinks. I went out on the dance floor, exhilarated and tipsy, and was dancing when Jamal rushed over to me. "Please come now! Please, hurry!" He kept bowing. He brought me over to the table where the kind men were watching my shoes. Jamal was arguing back and forth, with some desperation in his voice, sounding as though he was trying to reason with them. I wondered if they wanted my shoes or to dance. Jamal told me to apologize to the men. "Do what? Why?" I asked. "I didn't do anything."

"Please, please, you could die over this! You've insulted them."

"Die? Die because of what? My shoes?" I asked as he pointed to them.

"Yes, you put them on their table. These are very important men having a meeting on the ship, and your gesture insulted them." Everyone was watching me. "It's an insult in our country."

I bowed and said, "Please forgive me." I went to take my shoes off the table and Jamal stopped me, nearly slapping my hand. "I will get them. Do not touch their table." I followed Jamal's lead. I could see by their expressions that they were serious. Jamal motioned for me to say that I was sorry again, and I did. "I am terribly sorry. I never meant to do any harm." The alcohol had worn off, and I was sobering up fast. I could feel the evening was coming to an abrupt end. One of them bowed his head and signaled for me to leave, and Jamal took me by the arm with the shoes in his other hand, which he said he was told to throw away. Jamal ended up saving them as well as my ass. He said he would give them back before I left Egypt. Good thing, I almost blew a gasket! That was a big learning curve.

Jamal walked me out to the deck. The moon shone brightly on the still waters of the Nile. I was feeling warm and fuzzy, like I was beginning to fall for Jamal—or maybe it was just a quick attraction, and the mood of the moment. There was a cosmic attraction. He handed me a cup of water he'd retrieved from the river and told me to drink it. The expression on my face clearly said no. "It is said that if you drink from the Nile, you will always be youthful." I paused, thinking about how by day the Egyptians bathed and washed their laundry in the Nile, and who knew what in the evening? I would be drinking their dirt and sweat, and what else I dared not imagine. I looked out on the beautiful, mystical waters of the Nile, flowing gently beneath the star-filled sky, thinking it was only the beginning of our trip and anything else that followed had to be even more exciting. I prepared myself and drank the whole cup of smooth, sweet water without fear, never thinking that I could become deathly sick later. I had learned my lesson about not putting my shoes on a table in Egypt no matter how expensive they might be! Mrs. C. and her daughter commented on how I managed to put myself in these situations, not so much adventuresome as they were crazy. We had no trouble during the rest of the Egypt trip. Jamal and I exchanged numbers. There *was* an attraction, but neither one of us made any advances. I had my bags packed, and I was ready to move on to Rome for my next adventure.

After checking into our small, double-bed hotel room—of course, I got the roller cot, very uncomfortable—we slept late because of our jet lag. We were in Rome, and ready to shop for the beautiful leather in the famous designer stores. Even though we hadn't slept enough, we didn't want to miss out on anything. By the time we'd finished taking our showers it was twelve noon. We had a quick cup of tea and went out to do our shopping, but as we walked around, all we saw were people sitting and relaxing, and every store we tried to shop in was closed; we didn't know that they closed at one p.m. Oh, shit… We asked the locals about restaurants, and a man from one of the storefronts said, with a thick Italian accent, "Come, sit down and eat, please," and we couldn't refuse such a cordial invitation. We went into the small stone building, its picture windows open to a view of other buildings. It had wrought iron grilling and was on a cobblestone street, much like a restaurant I would imagine in an Italian movie, and it wouldn't have surprised me if Sophia Loren had strolled right in. We stayed from one p.m. until four, tasting plate after plate of food, sipping one glass of wine after another, until we just sat like everyone else—stuffed, satisfied, and plump. That was Italian food… Although we wanted to shop, the wine made us lethargic and we figured we'd shop the next day. We had only five or six days left, Rome first, and then we'd be heading to the sandy beaches of Greece, where I looked forward to tanning on one of the many topless beaches there. Rome was beautiful, and feeding the pigeons in the courtyard of the Vatican was like being in a movie. The Vatican was breathtaking, inside and outside, and seeing the exhibition where baby Jesus lay was really interesting. There was barely enough time left to do a little shopping. Our trip to Rome seemed far too short, and before we knew it we were back on the plane, going to Greece.

The view of Greece from the plane as it landed was truly spectacular, coming in over the beautiful blue-green water. Our cab driver at the airport, on the other hand, was a mean-spirited bastard who was so rude that he abandoned us on the sandy road that led to our hotel. I was going to yell at him but Mrs. C. stopped me, and I resigned myself to walking in the hot sun, dragging my heavy bags behind me. It was then that I experienced what was a true catastrophe—I broke off one of my fancy sculptured fingernails! "Damn it!" I screamed. "Oh shit!" Then another "Shit!" Alarmed, Mrs. C. and her daughter came to a halt. I dropped my bags. I just had to find the nail and glue it back on myself because, I impulsively rationalized, there probably weren't any nail salons in Greece where we were staying. I went down on all fours in the sand, wearing designer shorts and high-heel sandals, sifting through the fine, white Greek sand and stones for my nail. Hot and tired, we all searched for over an hour. And, finally, there it was! "Hallelujah!" I screamed. We laughed so hard we nearly peed ourselves, and as we walked to the hotel with our luggage in tow, we were practically in tears from laughing so hard. Mrs. C. shook her head, saying, "Only you, Libbe. Only you!"

At the front desk, the man gave us the keys to our room, which consisted of two queen-size beds and nothing else. That was it…certainly not ultra-luxurious accommodations. There weren't any shower doors or curtains for the shower, only a drain in the floor. Our room was below ground level, and the sand had, of course, blown in and was everywhere—just another added trip feature! We sat down to catch our breath and cracked up, laughing again. This was our final stop before returning to Boston. As far as I was concerned, sleeping with all the sand was not going to do, and I marched to the front desk and asked for our room to be changed to a higher ground level! The desk clerk said he would try to put us on the other side, where it was less windy and the sand wouldn't blow in through the slats of the window blinds as much, but the lower one was the only level available now, and he couldn't move us until the next day. We resigned ourselves to staying in our uncomfortable, gritty room for the night. There was sand in our beds and scalps, so much fun…we were up at the crack of dawn, having lost sleep because of it. All was forgotten once we switched rooms, *way* less sand. And I glued my nail back on! We went to check out the shopping and the restaurants; everything was so clean, so beautiful. I liked it here a lot and would definitely want to come back.

I rented mopeds for all of us in Mykonos. I drove with Mrs. C. on the back behind me, and her daughter drove her own. Mrs. C. was screaming as we went on hairline turns, convinced that I was going to drive us off the edge of a mountain. During the remaining few days, we went to Santorini and then Athens to eat and shop, then I went to the beach, lying topless among all the women who routinely sunbathed totally nude. My breasts got badly burned, but it was worth it. The azure color of the Mediterranean was breathtaking, and the calm water was soothing; I lay in it to heal. The fine, smooth sand was as soft as silk. I watched men dive for sea urchins then carefully open and eat them. The shops that we went to were quaint, and the pastries were sweet delicacies. I had some clothes made for me in one day—the tailor measured and fit me that quick—loved it! The ancient ruins in Athens had such history, and the time I spent in the mountains and the cliffs on the edge of the sea at Mykonos was etched in my memory. If I was single and had no maternal ties I would have stayed in Europe.

I returned to my world of Circuit girls and endless phone calls, managing retail stores, and going to rather boring PTA meetings. Two more stores were still under some construction, one at Dudley Street and the other at Revere Beach on Shirley Ave. Things were moving along. There was one glitch. Mr. C. wasn't aware of it, although I had warned him about Mr. Kirk. I did not feel secure about his deal with a new shoe franchise. Mr. C.'s name was on all my dealings with him, including the house and the three shoe stores. I trusted him, but not his new partners. I was happy to be home with R. Lee and David. However, I had been bitten by the travel bug and longed to see new places. Traveling was my dream, and the more I was exposed to the serenity of peaceful places, the more I longed to leave the life and Boston one day.

CHAPTER SEVENTY-FOUR

My Son, My Home, and My Soul Mate

When David returned from Israel, he immersed himself in projects at the house and was working crazy hours to bring in extra income so that (even though I had it covered) he could contribute toward paying our expenses. We spent lots of money on that trip. He never shirked his responsibilities and was always there to help me. R. Lee's studies were off somewhat again. So Dave kicked in to make R. Lee's studies easier, spending hours helping him with his homework. I was no help there. And I was smothering him, always worrying about where he was, and obsessing over him when he got the smallest cut or bruise. I was paranoid when it came to my only child. Too much love wasn't good. I was overbearing with him, making up for what I had lacked in my childhood, or so I thought. I felt guilty when I was working and not home with him. I put him into counseling soon after I got back; he went to a well-known psychology professor from Harvard. The psychologist suggested putting my son in a private school for the coming year, one that was a good distance from home—and from *me*. From me? I suffered from anxiety, worrying day and night, when he went to his father's house to live, which was only twenty minutes from Brookline, and when he went away to summer camp to have fun. His suggestion, the doctor said, would improve our relationship and help R. Lee gain some independence. He was to go to Maine, three hours away, to the Oak Grove Coburn School. He said the way I smothered R. Lee was hindering him and that it was possible to love him and let him go. For me, it had been all or nothing, and I needed to learn the happy medium in expressing my love. This was the first time I ever had accepted help, and it was sound advice. Now the challenge would be to implement the doctor's counsel. And David was a huge support—he loved R. Lee like a father, and R. Lee loved him back. Dave understood how difficult this was for me and how frightened I was, and so he repeated over and over again how great it would be for R. Lee. "Come on, give him a chance," he urged, "he'll be okay. And you too!"

When I packed for R. Lee, I put in extras of everything—lots of clothes, money for going out, first aid supplies, and snacks. It was an expensive school, but I would give any amount for my son. He was anxious too, and I could tell that the change was difficult for him; I tried not to break down in front of him, I didn't want to make matters worse than they already were. Both of us had a hard time with separation. There was the bar mitzvah last year in Israel, and now he was off to Maine, and I wondered whether a year on the kibbutz wouldn't have accomplished the same thing. The professor wished us luck and said to call if I needed him again. I listened to his wise advice.

Now that he was old enough to be hanging around with girls and dating, I needed to tell R. Lee something important. I said to him that when you go out with girls, ask them when their birthday is. If it is September 16th, 1967, it's okay to be friends, but be very careful to not date them because they might be your birth sister (as I wrote earlier, at the time, I confused the date she was born with the day I signed the adoption papers, so the actual date had been two days earlier). And also ask them if they were adopted. He said that it was weird to ask that stuff, but I cautioned him that it was important. I had no way of knowing what she looked like now, so I couldn't tell him anything about that.

The drive to R. Lee's new school in Maine was long, with everyone packed in the car, including the dog. When we arrived, I was struck by how much land the school was on; although Dave and I had seen it on an earlier trip, we were much more aware of details now that we had R. Lee with us. We parked on the stone-paved driveway and went into the main building, where a staff member greeted us. He was there to show R. Lee to his room and then help him sign in. Together, we took a tour of the grounds, cafeteria, offices, and classrooms. R. Lee was excited, but obviously scared of being separated from me, of being left there alone. Time flew by, and we had to leave so that he could set up his schedule. Both R. Lee and I cried when David and I were getting into the car. Hugs and kisses were overkill, but so needed! I thought to myself that he would be gone for a year, maybe more, but I was doubtful about that because in the next year or two his friends would be starting high school, and he wouldn't want to miss the whole high school experience in Brookline. We said our good-byes and drove off. Dave and I held hands and, with Reece on my lap, I talked all the way home because I was so nervous. Several times I wanted to turn back to get him, but no, I can't!

****

Ever since losing Mommy Rose so early in my childhood, separation had always been a particularly sensitive issue for me. I learned to cope with it over the years, but not without difficulty. Once I am accustomed to someone or something, I do not part with it easily—like my home, for example. I don't want to leave my only home! Sitting here with this federal case dangling over my head, I know I would never sell it unless I had no other choice—and I pray I never have to make that decision.

****

I devoted my time to pulling things together and was making the stores busier than they already were by placing ads on the radio station W.I.L.D. R. Lee wrote and called frequently at first, then less and less after he settled in and made friends. One day, I received a call from the school that R. Lee was terribly sick. They said his throat had closed up and his airways were obstructed by a particularly bad case of strep throat. Oh, my god, I was so scared! After I rushed up to be with him the next morning, I saw that the doctor and nurses had taken excellent care of him. But I stayed there just to make sure his fever broke. Still, I worried the rest of the time he was up in Maine. He told me much later he was scared and wanted to be home, but once he could breathe he felt okay.

David and I were happy together. We loved each other and our sex life was wonderful and back on track, or so I thought. He wasn't going out as much with his buddies to the bars. Hmmm… When he went out at night to get my money from the girls, he would stay out longer and longer each time. That was becoming an issue. I noticed, but I was trying not to let myself be overwhelmed by jealousy. I wanted to trust him, but instinctively I knew better. Emotionally I would go back and forth, forgetting how we first started—that's where I went wrong.

A new year had begun, which meant that my son would be coming home that much sooner. I called Ruthie's mom to make sure everything was okay, and she sounded happy, better than I had ever heard her. She told me her grandson was getting big, and growing up to be a wonderful boy. I knew I had made the right choice for little Eric at that time. I had my own boy to focus on, so I did not keep close enough tabs on little Eric. I was stocking the house with food and fixed up R. Lee's room for when he came home. I bought him new clothes and planned on cooking his favorite meals. The Jewish holidays and a new school year were coming up. We took the long ride up to Maine to collect *my* favorite, my son.

R. Lee was back at home to stay. There would be no more boarding schools. I controlled my tendency to overdo my mothering to the point of stifling him, and he was so much calmer, not anxious anymore. He had learned how to deal with his anxiety about his dad and school and was even more polite. I just hoped I could find the right balance and didn't pull away from him too much. His schoolwork had improved. He wasn't an A student, even B's were hard, but it was the effort he put into his schoolwork that I cared about. During the time he was away he had matured.

The apartment on my first floor had the same tenants for years now; they loved it. The upstairs where we lived and the basement unit were both under construction—construction that would go on for years. The intricacy of the details took time. Restoration of a house required more thought and money than renovation. I helped paint the house and did the yard work myself. I chose a raspberry color by Kyanize Paint for the house, with ivory and khaki-green trim. The house was a true painted lady, and I was so attached to it that I thought if I ever let it go, I would die. I felt that, strongly, for years but that was because when I was in the car accident I wanted to live long enough to have a house for my son, and I did. I wanted my house to be special, with original Elizabeth Taylor posters and animated art on the walls, toys, and memorabilia from the past; I put my stamp on my surroundings. My extensive collection of Disney art and movies would be going in my office, a spacious room with built-in cabinets, and a large walk-in closet. The house was alive. Every room was wired for sound with a Bose system, and we played music constantly. We lived on a great street. All the neighbors were friendly with us, and we were well liked. Our house was referred to by everyone as either "the pink house" or "the Pink Lady." The only negative thing about fixing the Pink Lady was that we found bats in the walls when we gutted my apartment upstairs. I detested them, and David reassured me that he would get rid of the ugly creatures, but they came back without fail every year, even after every hole was closed up. They would fly by us in the hallway, in the office, everywhere.

I loved my 535i BMW. It was a fast car. No more Cadillacs or Rivieras. (I sold the last one to an old friend who loved it; he still owns it and I wish he would sell it back to me now.) That was a positive, but my partnership with Mr. C. was becoming very problematic. He was being demanding, requiring servicing far more often than I wanted to give it. He was clingy. It turned me off, and I was extremely stressed by the pressure he put on me. I finally told him that I was on the phones almost full-time, and I didn't want his money for work anymore. I would take care of all the bills I had. That pissed him off, and we had an argument in his office. He slapped me as if I were his bitch! That did it—a client had hit me! Although he apologized, I took it to heart; once a customer or a friend does that, I am done. One time, Clarence, a past client, dared to get violent with me, and that was his last time too. I had been put through enough physical and sexual abuse. I didn't have the tolerance for abuse anymore and had withstood more than enough of it. That part of my life was in the past, and I wanted it to stay there. I didn't want to trick and then be tricked.

If I pass on any knowledge gained by experience, it is this: never sell yourself short to pay your way. Do it if you must to get yourself to the next step, but then get out...run out! Think twice before selling yourself as a lifetime venture. Don't wait until you get so old that you look in the mirror and say, "Why do they want me?" or "Why do I still have to do this?" or "Look at me now, I'm old and have to settle for less money." And then start asking about how to keep it going, like "How can I look good enough to make a buck, or to be noticed to satisfy my ego?" or "Which red light bulb makes me look sexy?" and "Do I shut off the light so my lover doesn't see the real me?" Taking it further, the final question might be, "How many surgeries do I have to do?" These procedures are common in most actresses trying to maintain their careers and the wives of the rich and famous to keep their men. And working girls have to keep their faces and bodies up to snuff. I'd rather be with someone I love for no money, someone who accepts me for who I am, someone I can grow old with and have a fulfilling life together—wrinkles or not! A little tuck here and there to maintain your looks is okay, but changing yourself is not. Your face is your signature.

I had to go with Mr. C. to pick up my car because of extras that were added. He apologized again and again, saying he was sorry, and that married or not, as a real man he should never hit a woman. He agreed that I had a right to my personal life. I questioned whether the money, cars, and things were worth what had to happen to get them. As I received more money, more was demanded of me. We talked about that on the way back in my car. We left the Cadillac I had leased there last year; even though it was comfortable, the BMW was more my speed! And two cars for me made no sense. Mr. C. wanted me to go on the road to do some more locations for his shoe stores again. I had already done some for him in great areas, and he wanted me to find some more. I told him I had other plans but would do it for him on the weekends. I loved the speed of my Beemer and looked forward to driving to New York, Philadelphia, and New Jersey again. The Caddy had been too much luxury and not enough sport. Once I'd dropped off Mr. C., I was itching to drive. I never showed off my car or jewelry to the girls and kept a low profile. What I owned was mainly for my own enjoyment. To go unnoticed, David would always drive the girls in his Ford pickup. I thought the situation was comical, a high-priced girl in a pickup—like Jed and Granny in the old TV sitcom the Beverly Hillbillies!

I had spoken with David about his partying; of course, he denied it. But the madams from New York were calling and telling me that the girls were talking to all the madams on the Circuit about him. I told them I would watch him more closely, but in my heart I really didn't want to know. I did not want my new home, the rose garden, and our love to die off because of all this interference from the life. But what seemed to be a good life was about to take another turn. It was something I was not in the least prepared for.

David's younger brother was furious when he found out that Dave had slept with his girlfriend. I was furious too, but then he took out his anger on my son and I, as if we were somehow responsible. I was in the living room doing some early decorating for the holidays, and R. Lee was in his room upstairs. Our front door was usually unlocked during the day, and he stormed up the stairs, screaming at me that it was my fault because "I was a fucking hooker and was no fucking good," and that was the reason David had slept with his girl. What? I couldn't believe it! How dare this boy come into my home and chastise me! He accused me of being a no-good streetwalker, that I took men for their money, and I used his brother. Actually, it had nothing to do with me! David was a flirt long before I ever met him and fucked girls whenever he could. Years later, David's painting partner told me Dave's brother's girlfriend was a big slut, that she slept with lots of other guys and his brother never knew about it. His brother went on and on, driving the dagger in deeper, and I screamed at him to leave! R. Lee heard all of it from the top of the staircase. My nightmare…

My son believed I was a bartender at night, and that I was a mom like all the other moms, working on the house during the day. R. Lee approached me and asked me if what he heard was true. As he was saying this to me, Dave's brother was still screaming as he slammed the door behind him, yelling that my son was also no good, like me. I fell silent. I felt naked in front of my own son. I answered that yes, it was the truth—mainly because I was afraid that if I didn't, he might hear it from someone else. "You're one of those girls me and my friends make fun of when we drive to Boston? I can't believe it! My mom is a hooker?" He was profoundly hurt, shocked, and bewildered! His eyes reflected a distance, like he didn't know who I was. He didn't want me to touch him. It felt as though my heart was being ripped from my chest! I didn't know how to explain or where to begin. My son told me that he no longer trusted me, that I had lied to him, and he didn't want me to be near him. When he finally stopped questioning me, I told him I knew that one day I would have to tell him. I had wanted to wait until he was old enough to handle the truth—but, prematurely, that day had arrived. He said, "So that's what you had to tell me!" It was an injury so great that there would be no tenderness between us. He told me he wanted me to leave him alone. I questioned his love for me, when would it return… I hated myself now, and the self-torturer that lived inside my heart cursed me over and over.

This torture lasted for years. He would ask me where I was going and what was I doing, and when the house phone rang, the caller would get the third degree. From time to time he asked me, "Are you sure you stopped?" and I had to lie.

"Yes, I did," I would tell him, my stomach tied in knots. In a way it was true, I hardly went to the Zone anymore. But my grand moment of truth had come, and I had to admit to myself that I was living a lie. My secret life, what went on behind closed doors, had been revealed to the one person in my life I cared about most, my son. Will he forgive and forget this or will it scar him? What would this do to his future relationships? Could he love me again one day, when he could swallow this knowledge of his mother? His mother, a working girl of the Combat Zone.

CHAPTER SEVENTY-FIVE

Long Overdue Meeting

At first, when R. Lee found out what I did to make a living, I stayed away from him. And it took him over a year to get past knowing the truth and accept me for who I was, although he still kept his distance from me. He was at an age, fifteen years old, when I should have been discussing relationships between men and women with him, but I wasn't presumptuous enough to even give it a try because I was afraid of how he would take it. At least R. Lee was talking to me more often, but he vented to David all the time. It was upsetting to watch him, because many times he would come home drunk or stoned. What could I do! I did not want my son to go down that road. I dealt with my pain, and his, while he never knew.

In the meantime, Mr. C. and I had been searching, along with private investigators, for my biological mother and father. I had also tried for years to find my kids, but nothing came up. I wanted to meet my mom, and it took two years of private investigator services to finally get information about where she was. One morning, Mr. C. called me into his company's office and told me they had dropped off the information about my birth mother and father. I was anxious to know about them. He told me my mother's name was Goldie and my father's name was Joseph, they were having an affair and were not married at the time I was born. But later, after divorcing their spouses, they went to Florida, where they were wed. Unfortunately, by the time I found them it was too late—she had died in the hospital after a freak car accident in which her only injury was caused by hitting her leg against the door. When she was brought to Emergency to check her leg, she died on the emergency room bed of an aneurysm. Besides an occasional headache, she had never been sick. One of my sisters, who resembled me so closely she could have been my twin, had also passed from a car accident. There was another who lived on the South Shore in Massachusetts, was married, and had two kids, a girl and a boy. We called a family member listed in the phone book, and when I questioned her about her relationship to Goldie, she stated that she was indeed a part of the family and knew her daughter. When I identified myself as another daughter, she was in shock. She said she never knew I existed, and neither did anyone else in the family. She said she would tell M. and ask her to call me. The day I had waited so long for had come, but would she want to speak to me? Pieces of the past were fitting together. I waited for the call to come. Then, late one evening when I was not thinking about it, the phone rang.

That night, David and I had been working on the top floor of our house, closing up all the openings we could after our most recent bat incident. On that night, our mattress was on the floor, and we were having great sex. The room was unfinished and the tall, angled attic ceiling gave the room an open feel. I was on top and moaning, totally into it, focused on the sex and nothing else, when David said, "Lib…Lib… Stop! Stop!" Dave pulled me down on top of him, and covered me with the blanket as he carefully maneuvered himself out from under me. I was left wet and wanting to finish, but…"What? What are you doing? I was in the moment…"

"Stay down, okay?" he said.

"What's wrong?" I asked.

"It's a bat." "A what? Another bat! Again? Oh, shit! I thought they were gone!" I pulled the covers over my head, and when I peeked out I saw David. There he was—naked—chasing a big bat, tennis racket in hand. I screamed out for him to be careful. There was a thud—he got him! "It's okay, you can come out now."

"Are you sure?" I looked over the edge of the covers and watched Dave as he was putting the bat in a shoebox of mine, wearing just his robe and a pair of Timberland construction boots he had slipped on. It was just like that scene in the Steve Martin movie *The Jerk*, when he was walking out of his house with his dog, Shithead, chair in hand and wearing his boots and bathrobe. My laughter was choking me as David, who was clueless, asked what was wrong, "You find this funny, do you, huh?" I couldn't speak. He left, Steve Martin style, into the cold to dispose of the dead bat in its box, wearing nothing but his bathrobe and boots. The only things missing were the chair and Shithead the dog. When David came in from the cold, at approximately nine p.m., the phone rang and he answered it. I stayed under the covers.

It was M. on the phone! "It's her!" David cried out.

"Who?" I asked.

"Your sister!" he replied. I couldn't believe that she was really on the phone!

"Yes, this is Libbe," I answered. We greeted each other and went right into our questions, for over an hour, as I lay on the floor in my room, eyes darting from corner to corner to make sure there were no more bats. It dawned on me that I was speaking to a blood relative, a real sister. She knew all about me, but she checked to be sure of my identity, asking questions to which only I would know the answers. We set a time for us to meet at her house. I was petrified, but I had to find out about my background, who I really was and where I came from, anticipating that the loneliness I felt throughout my life would suddenly disappear. I had to face whatever I was about to learn about myself. Another weighty confrontation...

The weather was nice the day that we planned for our meeting, a blue sky and brisk, but milder than it had been recently. Because I was so familiar with the town, finding her house was easy. It was a small, single family home. I had called her from a payphone just before I got to her street, and as I pulled up, driving my shiny, black BMW, I spotted her looking through the glass door. She was pretty, but unlike me, had short, reddish hair. She was nicely built and had beautiful eyes. We were staring at one another as I walked up. We said hello, and as I entered her house, I noticed all the elephants. "You collect elephants?" I asked.

"I do, and my mother did too." That was the first coincidence, but not the last—I collected elephants too, and had been doing so for quite some time. Her house was well taken care of, neat and clean just like mine, everything in its place. She showed me around, and on the wall there was a picture of her when she was young. Oh, my god…we looked like twins!

We sat in the kitchen, it was early morning; she drank coffee and I had a cup of tea. Then we spoke about our mother, and she told me she'd hated her. She told me about her death first, and then I told her about the phone call her mom made to me at the foster home, when she tried to get me to work for her. It was then she knew for certain that I was her sister. "Yes," she said, "I know she called you. She wanted you to see men for money." What! Hearing that, I was in shock. Then I asked, point blank, "Why did you hate her?"

"Everyone loved my mother, and you would have loved her too. I can tell you would have done everything she wanted."

"Why do you say that?"

"When my mother was with Joe, your father, she would have done anything for him, but what she wanted me to do was work for her, seeing men for money."

My heart sank. "You too?"

"Yes, just like she tried to get you to work for her. Your dad was a bookie, and he had a shoe store on Columbus Ave. that was a front for his business. He would send men to my mom to see girls. That's what she wanted you back for, to work for her because you were of age. I hated her and what she was doing to me, and I wanted out."

I was stunned, not only because of the coincidence of being in the same business, but that my real mother was going to prostitute me out, and I would have ended up the same way, or possibly even worse than that. And my sister, too! That's the reason my dad said she was a tramp. I understood now. "I hated her because she forced me to work," M. said. "She called herself Stella. After our drive to Florida and my sister died in the car crash, we came back to Boston. She was run out of the city because she called your adoptive dad and blackmailed him after she had photographed you at the Robin Hood School in the parking lot. I ran away with a man, a drugged-out musician, and never went back. I didn't want anything to do with my mother. I never saw her again. I was on my own, I had a job and got married. Do you see why I hated my mother now?"

"Yes, I can see, but I don't think I could hate her the way you do. I would hate what she made me do, not her."

"You turned out differently than me. You would have done anything she said," she confidently stated.

"Well, I have to tell you the entire truth about me," I replied, and then took a deep breath. I told her A to Z. She didn't flinch. I was the same age as my sister when I started on the street and she worked for my birth mother. Both of us had strikingly similar things happen as teenagers that I will always keep confidential out of respect for her privacy. It was uncanny how closely her life shadowed mine. She told me she had a grown son and daughter from her marriage, and that although she was sure they would love me, she wasn't going to allow them to meet me. "I'm sorry," she said. "And it's not because I'm shocked by what you do. I'm certainly not one to judge. I have movies of you from the times my mother stalked you at school in Stoneham and in Canton. Our mother was born with a veil, and all of us have a sixth sense—we can feel and see things others can't. We have insights into people others don't have. You've done much the same as your mother did, and she collected the same objects that we collect. I've changed my name and appearance, and I don't talk to my family. I want no part of my past. It's sad that things have to be this way, but I have my own life now."

"I know all about your life," she continued. "I knew your biological dad. You also have another sister who wants to meet you, your father Joe's daughter. Her brother was really bad, in and out of reform schools and jail. Your father came from Dorchester, and besides his bookie business, was a boxer. I have pictures. I'll give you a few if I'm able to find them." "What do you do for work?" I asked her. She said she worked in an office as a secretary. "My husband and I do all right. We have our house and a vacation home up north." I could see she had a chip on her shoulder, and I wished that someday she would let go of it. She told me that when she got the call her mom had passed away in Florida; it was from Joseph, my father. They had an issue with the hospital about her dying without having her checked thoroughly by the doctors for signs of the aneurysm or trauma. She said that when she flew to Florida, she didn't cry and wasn't grief-stricken by her mother's death, she simply helped with the arrangements. Joseph died later on. My birth parents must have loved each other deeply. I had missed the chance to meet either one of them. I still wonder about them and only wish that one day my half-sister will call and tell me more.

We spoke for eight hours, and I thought we might have made a connection. She took me into her bedroom, the guest room, and her children's old rooms. There were photos of her and her husband scattered throughout the house, and others of her son and daughter, both with blondish-red hair. We both had given birth to boys and girls, and we'd both had one miscarriage—another coincidence. At sixteen, we still looked so much alike we could have been twins. M. gave me photos to take home of everyone except her husband. I also got pictures of my other sister, the one who had died in the automobile accident. She said she would send more later, but she never did. Although we had never met, we were alike. It must have been in the blood. She told me I was just like her mom, who loved gold and diamonds, nice clothes, and cars. People loved her, she said. She could tell from meeting me that, like my mother, I had a kind of magnetism that attracted people to me. Seeing my sister and speaking with her filled my heart and exceeded any dream I had ever imagined of what it would be like. My sorrow was that I never met my birth parents.

I wanted some connection with M. and wanted it desperately. I couldn't wait to see or talk to her again; there was so much more to say, so many questions I wanted to ask. When we said goodbye and separated I felt a longing. I went home, replaying the day over and over in my mind, as if the hours we had spent together weren't enough. David was excited for me and wanted to meet M. I assumed the reason R. Lee showed relatively little interest was because at his age he didn't yet appreciate having ties to family, but the importance was not lost on me: my child had blood relatives. I hoped they would meet one day. And there was yet one more coincidence—a real shocker! Mr. C. called two days later, saying he would like to see me at my house in a few hours. He said it was important. We met, and he asked me if I remembered his best friend, the engineer, who had come by my house in Brookline to check the soundness of the structure when the walls were torn out. "Sure I do," I told him. "You talk about him all the time." "Well, sit down because you're not going to believe this one…" Mr. C. knew my sister! He said he met with his friend at his office the day I went to meet M. at her home. The office secretary, M., who Mr. C. had known for years, was not in that day. As coincidence would have it, M. had told her boss the story about me. M., the secretary, was one and the same as M., my half-sister. "My best friend's secretary is your sister," he said.

I couldn't believe it when he told me! "You're kidding!"

"No, I found out the day you met her for the first time."

The interconnections of the people in my life floored me. I was so excited and couldn't wait until the next time I saw her! Every day I waited for M. to contact me. I wrote her cards. No response… Mr. C. was floored that he knew her for years and now that she was related to me!

A few months later, I received a letter from M., a lengthy letter, telling me in a gentle way that we can never see each other again. My heart was crushed. She wanted nothing in her life to remind her of her past and her mother. I was devastated, both hurt and confused. It was yet another loss in my life. But I was glad it came now and not later, after I'd gotten to know her better. That day we met I felt like she was part of me, and now it felt like she had been suddenly ripped away. Because of all we shared in common, I connected with her and wanted her to be a part of my life—we came from the same blood. I tried to understand her need for privacy, but her pulling away from me hurt for a long time, and I have to say it still does; I often wish I had a sister to talk to. She withdrew from my life just like my dad when he disowned me, tearing the chest pocket from his jacket. I wonder where M. is now, and what her life is like. I wish I knew, but I guess it was not meant to be. If only I'd had an opportunity to meet my birth parents—once would have lasted a lifetime, just as those eight hours did with M. I cherish the letter she wrote to me. She wrote, in part, "I want to be honest with you Libbe, so I am going to tell you how I feel. I am still very confused about all of this, and I am not really sure what I want to do or should do about it. I believe you're who you say you are and that there is some blood relationship between us. I just don't feel anything. Our meeting was like something out of the past and it brought back a lot of memories, mostly sad, not good ones. [...] It's not that I don't want to know you, it's more like I don't know what to do about you. I have a family now, and for the first time in my life I am really happy and content. I never thought I would be able to say that, but I can now. My past is dead as far as I'm concerned, and I don't want reminders of it. What our mother did to both of us was wrong, but we made our own lives, good or bad. [...] I hope you won't hate me for this, [...] I want you to know that I wish the very best of everything for you, and I am not sorry that you got in touch with me. [...] Take care, M."

It took years to get over the hurt I felt, but finally I understood. We met, and that piece of my life was solved. It was the end of a long search, and the beginning of whatever was to follow.

CHAPTER SEVENTY-SIX

Store Changes

The situation with my sister was heart-wrenching, and I tried not to talk about it. Fortunately, I had so much going on in my life—at home, my business, the stores—that I was able to keep it in a quiet place inside of me.

Mattapan was a comfortable location for me to have a store. I had lived there and knew all the streets and many people. My shoe stores were doing well, but it was tough buying closeouts and large-size designer shoes for the Mattapan and Dudley Street locations. The Revere store was okay, I had all the small size shoes go there. David was getting stupid—he had a crush on the young sales girl that was so overwhelming he wasn't even hiding it. I knew it from the first day the girl was in training. It was out in the open now. I had a big fight with him over her. David was bringing her lunch and gifts. He just could not keep his dick in his pants! I closed down that store within one year to get rid of the problem. She kept in touch with him for a while, and then, to my knowledge, stopped; after I spoke with her, she got the message. But who really knew, David had been caught lying too much. Our lease for the Mattapan store was going to be renewed, and I wanted to do more with handbags and jewelry, but not there. My friend, Mendy, at Simco's, kept urging me to go into hot dogs. He said it was a great business, and I told him maybe one day I would. He advised me to save my money so I could buy the business when he and his brothers retired. I later regretted not taking him up on the opportunity he offered me. I was good at what I was doing and already familiar with the businesses. If I had made the change it would have been life-altering. I treated my girls well, never exploiting them or stealing from them the way other madams would so often do. I enjoyed retail—the sales and the people—and I loved working with handbags and jewelry. Decorating the stores and selling were profitable hobbies. I knew how to make the women feel good about themselves when they purchased something beautiful from me. But it was time for a change, and that meant having one store instead of three. Rather than relying on employees, I thought it was better to make sure the customers were happy, gift wrapping their purchases and catering to them myself, one on one. Answering phones and having three businesses was becoming too stressful, And I could not keep up with the personal problem of David. Because of his screwing around I was fed up, hanging around in the Provincetown gay bars, considering switching sides because men were just too much work and heartache. I responded to the stress by overeating. I gained too much weight and hated my appearance. I had to change things up and I knew it. My customers did not seem to care because it was the performance, not the weight.

Mr. C. was getting sued by one of his franchises. A woman was suing him and Mr. Kirk, and I thought it best to get away from being part of his business ventures, and he agreed. We had a gigantic closing sale advertised on W.I.L.D. radio and sold out the total inventory of our shoes and bags. I was in and out of the store during the closeout, and discovered that my manager, whom I had trusted for so long, was stealing cash from the sale to put wall-to-wall carpeting in her apartment at the urging of her hustler of a man. I suppose I should have expected that an employee might steal, but not that particular person. I had trusted her so much. I fired her instantly, handling the rest of the sales myself. Getting away from shoes was best because Mr. C.'s partner was involved in so much fraud. And it also helped me pull away from Mr. C. a bit more, because traveling for shoes and handbags meant he came to New York with me.

I moved to an area closer to the heart of Boston's Back Bay, in the St. James Building on St. James Street. It was a small but sweet store in a prime location, with Liberty Mutual and countless offices upstairs, and lots of traffic through the first floor hallway, where there were many kinds of stores—from furniture stores, to a Brighams's ice cream shop, and a hat store. Mr. C. and I talked about it; needing a straw because of the lawsuit he and his partner were in, he put his half in his daughter's name with me. He still wanted that attachment. I customized the small store, decorating it in two different tones of purple. As in the designs that we'd had drawn up, the shop was beautiful, and even more so when all the jewelry was hanging or encased. We got the lease without any problem, as well as a license. There were purple custom cabinets along the walls with specialized lighting effects. The space wasn't more than four hundred square feet, with plush plum purple and gray rugs. There were four custom earring trees that held one thousand pairs of earrings per tree. We lit up the store and cabinets, and then we opened—the effect was stunning! I loved the small space. I even had a small window for displays. My all-leather handbags were outrageous and studded with rhinestones and tassels. I had high-end jewelry; Thelma Deutsch was one of my favorites.

Owning and managing one store was easier than three, and I was calmer running only that store and answering phones for my other business. R. Lee's many friends kept him occupied, as did playing sports. He saw that I was involved in legitimate businesses, and he stopped drinking as much. I had a full plate with my responsibilities of being a mother and role model, keeping David in check was full-time, and Mr. C. happy. I was eating on the run and gaining more weight. Dave was present everywhere I went, except when he worked or went with the girls. He was spending time with my girls, taking them to shop and out to eat. Nice. I told him several times not to linger with them, but he never listened. I loved him, but it was tough going. If he wasn't up my ass he was fucking around with my girls—all of them. He wasn't ever refused; they all wanted him. We fought, and it was upsetting to R. Lee and our entire existence. I did not want another J.N., a total cheat, no way.

David's patience with me wore as thin as mine with him, and he finally put his foot down about my arrangement with Mr. C. Keeping Mr. C. as a sugar daddy became problematic. My unwavering love for Dave interfered with my business dealings with Mr. C., and seeing my regular clients was already out of the question—the girls had to handle them. I was used to being ultra-skinny most of my life. Now I was the heaviest I had ever been, size eleven!

Business on St. James Street was booming. We were constantly busy from Monday through Saturday, and on Sundays I took a day off from the store. I hired the girl who sang with the other musicians in the basement of my old shoe store, a pretty black girl with a sweet personality, who fit right in as sales help when she dressed up and put on makeup. She was a hit. I was working every day, committed by necessity to the phones at home or on my beeper. My help handled sales during the daytime in the store. David was playing with my girls and having sex with them at pick-up times, in addition to sleeping with his female contracting customers and the squares he met from the local bars. I began to see clearly what he was doing. I was anxious and continued chowing down to soothe myself. I even hung out at the gay bars more and more. I almost crossed over with two close friends but held back. First Sandy, then Mindy—I loved them, but I could not do it. I hadn't caught Dave with his pants down yet, but I didn't doubt that would eventually happen because he was so careless and believed that I didn't notice. The business was profitable, and I banked lots of money. I should have been happy, like some housewives who take the check and turn the other cheek. But I wasn't like those women. I had my own money, and I didn't need his. In large part, my unhappiness was my own fault. I took the business too much to heart, continually wanting to achieve more, and allotted virtually no time to the ones I loved, to the detriment of my son and David. I was planning to leap into another store next year, a flower shop in another space in the hallway of the St. James Building. I was moving up again and would be even busier. Inside, though, I was lonely and angry; I didn't feel good about myself. I flirted with a young man who worked at the Brigham's ice cream store, and he was flirtatious back, always smiling and talking to me. I was sure he did that to all the women. I wanted to get back at David—not a bright move! I learned the hard way every time, so now was no different.

Things were moving along at a fast pace. I met a woman from Liberty Mutual who had a handicap. Liza's arms were shorter than average, and very noticeable because of her cold exterior—until it finally melted, then she lost her handicap in my eyes, and others also, I'm sure. She was beautiful, sexy, and smart, but hadn't blossomed until she came into my jewelry boutique. After a few visits, we clicked. Thanks to my boutique, we became friends. The flower shop, Très Jolie, opened directly across from Brigham's, where I had a constant view of the young man who was drawing my attention. His sexy voice was the appealing part. He dressed Brooks Brothers square…I don't know how I got past that.

As time went by, my son and I spoke more in depth. He was maturing and had learned to accept me after we both pulled away. It had given him time and space to work things through, with David's help. He was far more understanding of me than he had ever been. But I still could not find it in my heart to have sex talks with him at all because of my profession. Knowing the truth about who I was and my business had its effect on both of us, particularly because he found out about me during his adolescent years. We both wanted to be closer, but neither of us could find a way. So, once again, I reverted to spoiling him with material things to ease my guilt. I prayed every day that my son would not be scarred from my life, but I could see there wasn't any chance he could not be affected in some way or another. There were many nights when R. Lee was a teen that David found him asleep on the floor in the bathroom or his room, drunk and passed out. David told me to let him handle it, and I did. I was happy he grew out of all that and about the changes he made on his own.

****

I knew it would always bother R. Lee to some degree. But, like me, he eventually chose a path of success instead of escape. Now I worry that my arrest will hurt his reputation or that he will become the target of ignorant, hateful people who will say that his mother was a whore. At times it amazes me how cold, cruel, and ignorant society can be given their own skeletons. That's what keeps the bad people being bad; others never give them a fair chance or offer their honest help. I pray that one day my son will be able to love and be loved, and not wait until it's too late to find it.

CHAPTER SEVENTY-SEVEN

New Girlfriends and Boyfriends

Liza and my friend Lady were hanging out with me more often at the gay clubs while David was seeing girls from the local bars in Brookline, Allston, and Brighton. I was having a drink or two here and there. We had been fighting, and agreed that we should take a break from one other, but separating only made things between us worse, not better. I was overly possessive and jealous, paying far too much attention to him, putting my focus on David and where he was rather than on my son and myself. I almost liked it better the way it was at first, before I fell so deeply in love with him. He lived with his sister and brother, where he should have stayed. Liza, who became a close friend, was there through it all. She had been in a bad marriage to a drug-addicted husband who did love her, but hardly ever took her out, used her for money and sex, and never said or did anything that would support her or improve her self-esteem. We leaned on one another. There were many nights I cried on her shoulder and she cried on mine. She was the first friend I ever broke down in front of, letting out my true feelings. I was the one with the real handicap—not her. She had a good job and was such a beautiful person, although she didn't feel that way. Sometimes we would hop the trolley and go out just for fun. The first time Liza took the trolley, she was worried that other people would stare at her, but I told her to stare right back at them if they did. She and I helped each other get by and move on. I know now that we should have remained close after she moved; I wish I had taken the time to go see her then. It was a mistake I regretted, and I have recently reconnected with her. She has moved back to her old town after having a promising relationship take a bad turn and fail. She was devastated.

I had to stop running after David, making myself appear stupid and childish. I needed to let go of him. But letting go of my soul mate wasn't easy, and I struggled; I didn't know how to do it. I brought men into my life to spite Dave during the time we were arguing about his cheating. It was a mistake that turned around and bit me in the ass, and I became the fool. The guy at Brigham's Ice Cream was way too young for me, but his attention was flattering. Even though I saw him flirting with customers, people passing by, and the girl who worked for me in my store, I lowered myself to sleep with him and became just another notch among the many in his belt. He didn't respect me and would make fun of me in a backhanded sort of way. Soon after I slept with him, he humiliated me by trying to get me to sleep with one of his buddies. That was nasty, and I should have slapped the shit out of him and split, but the feeling of being mentally abused as a child still haunted me and was all too familiar and comfortable. I put myself in his bed many times. The sex we had together was great, without any hint of affection. I was his toy and a teacher because of what I did for a living. He became more knowledgeable about sex from my street education and was always asking me about other men or women I had been with for his own arousal—he was immature, and pushed sex to the limit. He loved that, asking for ménages à trois (either way, two guys and a girl or two girls and a guy) while he watched porn videos or looked at pornographic magazines, trying to get me to look at them with him while we were having sex. He could fuck, I'll give him that, like a machine with Energizer batteries. He did aim to please and was very romantic, but lacked maturity. I was running a sex business, why would I need or want a man that just wants me for that! He constantly asked me about what my girls did in bed. He was like a client, not a man I wanted to be in a relationship with! No matter how many times he asked me to be with him, I knew in my heart that this could never be a real relationship. He was motivated by his lust and his fantasy of big tits and he and I together with other women; after all, I was a madam with many girls and many stories. I told him that I planned to write a book someday, but I'm sure it never occurred to him that he would have a role in that book, or that I might take the opportunity to say what I really thought about him in print. He humiliated me, and although I enjoyed going out with him because he had a romantic side—flowers, rose petals, and spur of the moment sex—I still resent the way he treated me. I understood that this young man and I were having sex and nothing more meaningful than that, and I wanted more. When he took pictures and videos of me, because of comments that he made, I worried he might hold them over me at some point in my life. He would joke about having a disease, like AIDS, to get an arousal; he had some bad habits. In my heart, I never really trusted him, and it went on until the day he told me he couldn't wait to read my book but only the smutty parts. I'd had enough! He couldn't get beyond the fact that my business was based on sex, and never understood what I was really about. Sometimes in life we learn the hard way. I did...reluctantly, I cut him loose, and did not call. I'm sure he will be interested in the sex parts in my book; nothing else will matter.

During this period that David and I were fucking around with other people, we lost precious moments together for no reason that either of us could figure out. We hurt each other so many times, and to such an extent that even R. Lee, on top of all he knew already, was aware of it. He tried to side with both of us, but he shouldn't have been involved at all. Bad move on my part. What kind of understanding of love was I passing on to him for his future? He was the last one I wanted to know about what was happening with me and men—he was carrying enough of a burden on his shoulders, and he didn't need more. I still had my clients call when he was at school or after he went to bed; although the fighting between David and I was loud, at least that aspect of my business was kept quiet. It was a good thing he had sports and lots of extracurricular activities, not only for him personally, but because it gave me time to manage both him and my phone business. I had told him the first white lie when

I said I would never do it again. Shame on me. For the time being, I had to lie about Mr. C. because he still gave me money. I kept that promise to him for as long as I could. And with David, enough was enough. Girls, girls, girls… It must have appeared to my son that I had nothing better to do than delve into what Dave was doing. I felt weak and ugly chasing after the girls I thought he was with. We were so upset with each other that David would come home and play The Whispers and Peabo Bryson on the guitar to get a message across to me. I never heard; I shut him down. He even wrote and sang his own love songs for me, but I was stubborn, and he wasn't changing. Why didn't I know then what I know now? And him too, why didn't he stop?

****

As I sit in this hellhole, knowing that R. Lee has to be told everything about my business, not just pieces, I am relieved I explained to him about what I did long ago when it came out that time because of David's brother. Will he wonder if I am still working? He has been suspicious of me for a long time and leery of my friends, especially the classier girls, who were flirtatious by nature, that I would have over to the house on holidays when they weren't working. They were dressed in a come-on manner, with fancy clothes like all the rich, flamboyant housewives on TV now—jewelry, furs, and sexy gear. They were not typical conservative Boston girls. He never asked me about them, not even once, but I would see him frown. He would leave the room when they came around, explaining to me that he wasn't being rude but preferred not to socialize with my friends. That indicated that he had an inkling about the girls. I was once one of those girls. And now his mom is sitting in a federal jail waiting for an attorney, and then to go home to an unsettling atmosphere. I am intensely unhappy, but I have to make the best of my next choices. So here I sit, thinking, and wishing that I could have changed certain things a lot earlier. I should have gone with my instincts and followed the voice inside my head and heart. But still, no regrets.

****

I had been happy about my stores, but now Mr. C. and Mr. Kirk were being sued. My house was in both his name and mine. I was bummed out by the prospect of another loss. We had to work fast to get his name off my house; this lady attached it because of Mr. C.'s bad partnership. She was going after him and attaching all their properties to get her money back for the franchise. I had saved some money, and I paid off Mr. C. in cash as he requested. It was a great relief once the house was in my name only. We sold my St. James Street store and closed T. Jol., the flower shop. It was fortunate that I had gone back into my phone business. Even though David and I were suffering through our disagreements, he was always there for me, and I was there for him.

Time seemed to be moving fast. Before I realized it, R. Lee had grown up and was graduating from high school. His first apartment was in the South End, and then he and his roommate moved into the first floor apartment of our house. He took some time off after graduation, and then went to college in Virginia where he studied psychology. R. Lee wasn't a stellar student academically, but he was adept socially, and that was where his intelligence showed. Except for his gullibility—he trusted too easily, still does—he was quick in his dealings with people and is to this day. After a year, he left school and said he didn't want to go back. He had some issues in Virginia with some badass guys he did errands for so he wouldn't have to ask for money from me. They jacked him up and left him for dead in his car. When I learned about it, I was horrified! He was bad off, with an injured eardrum, and rather than call me when it happened, he told his dad, who was living in Florida. He assumed J.N. would understand better, having been in the life with me when he was younger and probably experienced similar situations to the one he was in; but no—he was judgmental! When I got R. Lee's call, the first thing I wanted to do was go get him, but he said no, he would talk to me later.

When he was able to drive again, R. Lee took the six hundred dollar car J.N. had given him for attending college and drove to his father's house in Florida (where he had moved). Although it was a junky car, it was the first gift J.N. had ever given his son. R. Lee didn't want to worry me by telling me what really happened to him at first because I would have been out of my mind and gone to find those guys. But despite his promise to R. Lee that he wouldn't tell me, his dad couldn't keep a secret. R. Lee was already on the road from Virginia to Florida when J.N. called. It couldn't have been worse timing. David was smoking cocaine, and I spent my time watching him freak out every night. He said he was on bat watch! He could not help. Things were pretty fucked up. When I finally spoke with R. Lee directly, he told me he had been beaten badly by some Jamaican drug dealers who offered him money to drive to New York to drop off a package. He thought he was delivering cash. It was good money he was making, R. Lee thought, and he made the trip twice. A girl who knew these men told R. Lee what he had been transporting, and he wanted no part of it—he knew if he got caught it was his ass, not theirs. What he didn't understand was that he knew too much. Because he knew the address where he had dropped off the packages, the gang wanted to kill him. They weren't familiar enough with my son to know that he never would have told anyone. He was out of danger at his father's house, but J.N. turned on him like a rattlesnake, and instead of sympathizing with his son, J.N. treated him terribly. He'd had enough of his dad browbeating him and of his wife agreeing with her husband. She made my son feel small, like he was a nobody. R. Lee left, leaving a note behind for his father, and drove to Boston. He was home for his twenty-first birthday, and I was so happy and relieved to see him in a better space. We put on a big bash in our basement, and everyone had a great time. It was special having him around, and what had gone on wasn't discussed. Not yet. It was a mistake, and it was done. But what his father wrote in a letter to him that arrived at the house was unforgiveable; I didn't see it until later. R. Lee wanted to go to Atlanta to make a new start for himself, and I thought it was a good idea.

The six hundred dollar car was the first and last gift R. Lee ever got from his father. I could not believe that J.N. and his wife had the nerve to ask for the car back. I was glad that he was getting rid of that piece of shit, which had made me nervous from the start because I was afraid it wasn't safe to drive. J.N.'s selfishness left me speechless, as it usually did. R. Lee had made an effort to reach out to his dad and what he got in return was vicious criticism. Both J.N. and his wife badmouthed R. Lee to his face, but later on had to deal with their own demons, as they did when they first left West Medford and now in Florida. We left the car in front of the house for them to pick up. I was glad R. Lee would be home while he was healing. Now, more than ever, I was afraid for my son. What if the gang members came looking for him?

I took a short break in 1990 while I searched for a new location for the store. I finally found a spot. It needed some work before I opened. It was in a totally different area of Boston, Brighton, a middle-class, predominantly Irish and Greek neighborhood. The store was in Brighton center. The size of the store was ideal. I loved the customers there; they were down-to-earth people. The basement needed work, but Dave could do that. He was a master when it came to construction, and he and I could easily do the work by ourselves. There was no need for Mr. C. to go into any more stores with me.

Time was flying by, and my son had grown into a man. He liked his freedom. College was not for him; he wanted to find his way outside of an academic setting. He wanted to be in a business and chart out his own future. He was so good with the customers when he worked in the store, especially with the ladies. I had a hard time forgetting about him stopping at his dad's, thinking that J.N. could help him but never did. It was a mistake. When he went to college, J.N. thought he was being generous—imagine—by buying R. Lee a cheap car. In hindsight, it would have turned out much better had I gotten R. Lee a car, as I had planned. When he went to Florida to see his dad with his problem, J.N. bullied him, making him feel uncomfortable and low, as if he and his wife were superior. This man, who partied, free-based, snorted, smoked, and sold herb, and screwed any girl who crossed his path, considered himself better than his own son. I finally got to read the letter from J.N., R. Lee almost didn't let me see it. I couldn't believe that his father had written such poison. He wrote, "Your mother is nothing but an uneducated whore," and called his own son a "fag" because he had long hair and trendy clothes. He wasn't able to see himself at the same age, nor did he recall actual experiences he had with men. He fell in love with a person from California—a transvestite who had a complete sex change—and yet he was insulting to his own son! He had never, ever, paid anything for his boy's upbringing. R. Lee needed a dad, someone who would care, but J.N. didn't take the time. I had paid all the expenses, bringing up R. Lee from infancy until he became an adult. In my estimation, his father had gotten off too easily. I told my son, whose feelings had been so hurt, that he had understandably gone to Florida expecting help from his dad, and instead found an angry man who wanted R. Lee to be an Uncle Tom, to say "Yes, sir," and "No, sir," while wearing a white, button-down shirt, sporting a short haircut, and looking preppy. His wife wanted to belittle R. Lee because of me. She, too, was emotionally abusive toward him. That hypocrite! Not only had she called me to their home and accused me of sleeping with her husband, I then watched her crawling on the floor—while their baby slept upstairs in his crib—freebasing with J.N. in the house in West Medford he had inherited from his aunt. That was the house he sold to be able to move to Florida. It was a chilling and freaky experience! I was the bad one, huh!

I knew this was the beginning of the end of any relationship between R. Lee and his father, and that R. Lee would be bitter and sorrowed for years to come. I was glad to spend time with my son before his big move to Atlanta, to help him clear the air. He felt better since he was about to have a new start in a new place. He had weathered visiting his father. Now it was his time to fly, to determine his own direction, and it was my time to open a new store.

CHAPTER SEVENTY-EIGHT

Trouble Brewing

Brighton opened its arms for the grand opening of my new store, and crowded the beautiful interior that David had constructed with built-in cabinetry and slat walls. This was a new kind of location for me; the jewelry was no longer high-end Newbury Street prices, but styles that fit the tastes of my customers in Brighton and surrounding areas. Just earrings would not do for the new store, so there were dolls—my topline—plus collectibles, gifts items, cards, fun merchandise, and all sorts of fashion jewelry. It had come out so well I was more than happy about it. David made a funky commercial, and my friend did shout-outs on Kiss 108 radio. New customers came in every day. I had a full-time girl who was young, sweet, and great with customers. Even R. Lee worked there when he came home for the holidays. Things between Dave and I had calmed down; however, he was getting high on cocaine too often and was constantly paranoid at night. Eric had introduced him to freebasing—that was such a mistake. I tried to curb or stop him countless times, the first time with Eric, then when he freebased with J.N. and his wife, and then with Eric again, several times. That was messed up, but I couldn't tell a grown man what to do. I should have kept my friends away from him but he was an adult and knew better. Of course, I couldn't see what he was doing when I was working or he was at work, but I knew, just like I knew when he was with another woman—my instincts would kick in. We would argue and then talk about it, and make up again and again…

Katie and I were speaking on the phone again, but only briefly and not often; I was always working, and she had her job. We had gotten beyond her taking merchandise without paying for it, a betrayal of our friendship. She realized she had been over the top, coming and going when she felt like it. After Ruthie's death, my point of view changed and I didn't want to separate from a true friend over money. Liza, who moved out to Dover when Liberty Mutual left the St. James Building, talked on the phone with me. I had introduced her to a cab driver she ended up seeing in a relationship, or half a relationship—a man who unfortunately turned out to be a pig and wanted her only for sex. He was another one who loved behind closed doors and never took her out in public. That was so fucked up. They barely left the bedroom, and that was fucked up too. She had so much more to offer, and I hated that I introduced him to her.

Because I was having a hard time getting my soul mate back on track, I continued doing things just as damaging as he did, hanging out at gay clubs, and still seeing other men during our so-called separation. I found one man, with a big ego, who was attentive to me, but incapable of loving only me. He, as David did, liked women too much—as they all did—and again I was taken down a step by sleeping with him. I fired the girls who had gone to bed with David, but I couldn't fire them all. It was about to get nasty. Unable to control my temper any longer, I left the house to him and went to live with the girls, cooking and cleaning in their apartment for them, making sure they looked pretty, with not a lot of makeup but dressed *so* sexy. By leaving David to live in the house alone, I thought he would miss the two of us being together and work on us getting back on track, but no, instead he got worse. I could have expanded to four girls any time, but that would have been too crazy.

I did have standards for those living and or working in the apartment. Here are the rules I set:

If you are rude and swear or are disrespectful…
If you have a bad attitude…

If you shoptalk and gossip…

If you talk badly of others…

If you volunteer information heard around about me or others…

If you act like this you should not expect to stay here!! I will not make an effort for people like this. Don't expect me to be your mother and treat you like a child!! You're a grown-up person and you must take responsibility for your own actions, like we all have to do.

Consideration, cooperation, sincerity, and kindness will earn respect. We believe in rewarding the people who deserve it.

Please set the alarm clock to wake yourself up. Be responsible!!

HYGIENE

You must have proof of having an AIDS test within 4 months of being hired!!

Wash, shower, and brush your teeth before each friend's visit. Keep your hair clean! Your breath should always be fresh and clean. Manicure nails and feet and have them polished ALWAYS. Also, clean your feet and apply baby powder for odors.

If you smoke, check yourself thoroughly to make sure YOU DO NOT SMELL OF CIGARETTE SMOKE!

THE RADIO

The radio is set at a soft jazz station or set at soft music. Do not put on the TV or, especially, any movies when a client is here. Play only the radio or special porn movies!!

CLEANLINESS

DO NOT COOK FISH. EVER!!

DO NOT USE baby oil or creams for massages. Baby oil leaves yellow stains on the sheets. Baby powder only, please! If you have to use cream, please put a towel down!

Keep your room clean and odor-free. Never leave food lying around.

IMPORTANT: Do not throw anything in the toilet other than toilet paper!

Try not to wear perfume please.

I hope your stay here will be a pleasant one. If you have any questions, do not hesitate to ask us, anytime!

David came to the apartment where I was staying, saying he was sorry and wanted to work things out for good. I told him I was going on a trip to Panama with my friend soon, and that if he didn't lie to me, we could talk about getting back together when I returned. He vowed things would be different. After breast surgery to repair a burst saline implant with silicone, I took the trip to Panama and had a great time without him, going to barbecues, festivals, and sightseeing. I was really sore, but it was worth it. Except for an incident with a man my friend knew well, a lawyer, when we went to a country festival and while hanging out I went for a ride with him. Turned out we went to buy cocaine from a guy he knew, big bags to choose from—I didn't need to get busted in Panama with a cokehead attorney! Back at the festival party, I did a couple of lines with him; but I got away, no sex, although he kept after me until we left for home. I was not attracted to him at all! Panama…a lawyer, doing coke…what a getaway from my man doing drugs…

When I came back, David said he had something to ask me. He told me that he was planning for us to go out for Valentine's Day together—I was thrilled! During the separation, when I was with the girls, I missed him but held back from expressing my love. He was staying in the house alone, except for my crazy houseboy, who took care of cleaning and errands, and any other work I needed done. I also tried helping my houseboy get straight during the time he worked for me on the condition that he not do any drugs or drink, and he almost always respected my wishes. He had bad habits when I met him at another Boston working girl's place; she aided his drug addictions to manipulate him. And it worked, he kept slipping back there.

The separation between David and I was supposed to give us time off from each other. Despite my skepticism, I believed, naively, that was his intention. When talking with him he always sounded high. I prayed I was wrong! Valentine's Day arrived, I waited at the girls' apartment all day, but there was no call and he never came by.

How fucked up I felt! I had made numerous calls to him on the home phone and his beeper, and they all went unanswered. By late evening, I was furious. That was it! I charged out of the apartment and took my ass over to the house. I hadn't gone to the house for about a month—when I said it was a separation, I meant it, and told him that until we were back together completely I would stay away. I had kept my word until then. I went in the house and yelled upstairs for David. *No David.* The main floor, where the living and dining rooms were, seemed fine. The kitchen needed cleaning, but that was about it. All the lights were off. When I climbed the stairs to the bedrooms and turned on the lights, I had a bad feeling… My stomach turned, like from food poisoning. As I walked through the doorway of our room I saw that the bed was unmade, and there was a distinct smell of sex in the air. There on the bed were a pair of panties that didn't belong to me, and in the full waste basket next to my bed were two rubbers, each with cum on the inside and blood on the outside. To top it off, there were makeup pads. I was boiling mad—I didn't wear makeup, nor did we use condoms! Not only had he blown off meeting me, but he had someone else *in our bed, in my house! My house!* The stuff in the basket was still warm, so whatever had taken place had happened not that long ago. I searched carefully in every room, especially in my closet, where all my personal belongings were. One of my jewelry boxes was out, and as I rummaged through it, I could tell that certain pieces were missing! I hit the roof! And to think one of my clients, Bilber, had cut a check for a sound studio for David and his brother! I wished I had known about David's screwing around in my bed before the studio was built; I never would have allowed Bilber to invest. For him to fuck outside my house was one thing, but inside my house was something altogether different—it showed no respect for me! Not to mention that it was Valentine's Day, an important celebration as far as I was concerned. I loved cherubs and pink pretty things. How could he do it when he promised me he would change and everything would be all right? I concluded that he was never going to change and made a phone call right then and there to the twenty-four hour locksmith to have all the house locks changed. I refused to take any more of his shit, and then to have my jewelry stolen on top it…I didn't get this far in my life to be subjected to such disrespectful shit. He would be coming home to the surprise of his life. I started packing up his stuff, all the while listening to the pounding rhythm of my heart. My head hurt, and I hated to do this.

I was totally irrational. I wanted to kill him with his own gun. I paced the floor and had a couple of drinks. I even called R. Lee in Atlanta, dragging him into my personal affairs because I couldn't think of anyone else I could vent to. I told him I wanted to kill David, and he said he was on his way back home and for me to be cool. He would be on the next flight out. I was awake all night, pacing like a caged animal. I wanted to escape, but this was my own home. I had to wait and confront this man who had fucked up for the last time. Girl after girl after girl—I could not be with enough men to avenge him, and I hated myself for trying. Having sex to retaliate was free sex and not love, and it was humiliating that I got nothing out of it except for a bad feeling about myself. What I was left with was a low sense of my own worth. Why did I love him so much? I swore I would never accept that kind of treatment again. Hours passed.

Then he came home. The doorbell rang; he had no key anymore. During the night, I had put all his things out and lined up his packed suitcases downstairs by the door in the hallway and anywhere else I could pile it. I said hello through the door when the bell kept ringing. "Lib, let me in! What's wrong, Lib? Are you there?"

When I opened the door and saw him, I wanted to pounce on him like a cougar, but I held back, savoring my revenge. He saw his bags and his things scattered everywhere. "What's going on, Lib? What's up? Why was the door locked?"

"You don't know, Dave?" I asked. "C'mon, don't be coy. You know you fucked up and this was your last time. You had me thinking you had changed, and then you didn't show up for Valentine's Day when I planned on being with you. You lied! And then lied again! You brought some bitch into my house and into our bed! The panties on the bed weren't mine and then there were bloody rubbers in the fucking basket! What the fuck, Dave? You fucked her with her period! And to add to the insult, my jewelry is gone! No more, David. No fucking more! Get the hell out of here and don't come back!" It was morning, and I was hoarse from a lack of sleep and screaming. David denied it and begged me, making a fool of himself. I was on the edge, and had his gun—threatening to shoot him—when the doorbell rang. My son came through the door and broke up the fight. R. Lee wrenched the gun out of my hand, and when David asked for it, I told R. Lee not to give it to him, and he held onto it instead. R. Lee helped calm me. David knew he had messed up; he couldn't keep his dick in his pants, ever. R. Lee and David spoke for a while. Reluctantly, my son told him he had to go, and asked him before he left, "What the fuck, Dave? You should have had more respect for my mother! Take a girl to a hotel, not home." David grabbed some of his clothes and as many of his belongings as he could fit in his Ford 150 and drove off like a dog with his tail between his legs.

My once happy home had become the scene of a nightmare, but my love, the insane love I had for Dave, continued. He was truly my soul mate. Deep inside, I knew that he loved me too but couldn't overcome his weakness for women and his use of drugs. David's construction partner told me Dave was sex-crazed and needed help, he knew that way before our relationship started. I refused to do anything more for David, though at the same time, I couldn't envision my life without him. I could only pray he would change someday, before we both died. My son stayed for two days and returned to Atlanta, where he eventually bought his own home. That was a blessing. Time proved to be healing, and R. Lee and I became closer than ever. We were bound by the ties of mother and son, yet we also became friends, even after all the ups and downs. We spoke constantly and confided in each other. David inched back. And, for the time being, I accepted staying in contact if we needed each other, allowing him to come over to do work in the house but not allowing any physical contact.

CHAPTER SEVENTY-NINE

Doom and Gloom

It wasn't long before my son opened a business in downtown Atlanta. R. Lee's detailing enterprise was successful—he had his own garage and shop, and it was doing exceptionally well. I was working on the house to keep my mind distracted from thinking about David and when we may get back together. He called the house all the time, and we would speak, but only about the house and the studio, never personal stuff. I missed him. He had moved his things into the Allston recording studio I had set up with my friend Bilber. I was happy Dave was in the studio, singing and taking advantage of it to work on the music he wrote. Even though I was still angry with him, I wanted him to succeed at his singing and songwriting. Both of us were dating other people. I was getting close to one of my clients, an affectionate Jewish man, who was interested in me and asked me on dates. Wary of womanizers after my last experience, I kept my distance from him. Mr. C. and I had stopped the pace of our arrangement; he was way too much for me to handle. He had invested in some big stores whose owners went bankrupt, leaving him and his family in a messy situation. He moved and sold some of his property, and was still in debt for millions of dollars. We talked and concluded that remaining friends was a better idea than continuing as we had before, when sexual favors were exchanged for monetary gain.

My store was bustling with business every day. It was mine and mine only; Mr. C. was not involved, and that was a relief. And we were not involved sexually anymore. David was more like a friend since he moved out of the house, but we loved each other still and expressed it often. I knew that going back with him wasn't anything that was about to happen soon. He had to get all his desire for other women out of his system first, and no more drugs. I liked my Jewish client, and we were talking to each other more often, but I hadn't allowed him to get closer to me yet. If he were able to control his clinginess, we might have had a chance. He was an extremely affectionate man, a touchy-feely type, and I wasn't ready for that kind of intimacy. I still loved David and hung on to the hope that we would get back together someday. He started coming around to visit more often and helped with construction issues at the store and the house when I called him. I knew there would always be a connection between us because I still had part of the recording studio with Bilber. I was concerned for Bilber. He was using drugs, and his personal life was out of control, but I made sure he was straight when it came to our business. I was starting to get out of control in my own life, but not with drugs—my feelings for David since he left were torturing me. Staying busy didn't always work. My son had to talk me down on more than one occasion, and I had spoken with Liza on the phone about him several times. Based on my behavior, any psychologist would have diagnosed me with some disorder and prescribed drugs to meet their protocols, but that's not what I needed to work through my obsession with David. There are far too many people who rely on medicine to cope. Everyone, including myself, has issues that can trigger emotional reactions, but then emotions subside and, hopefully, we move on.

With everything that was happening in my life, I certainly didn't need any more doom and gloom at my doorstep, but that's exactly what I got. Katie's daughter called me and said her mom was in the hospital. "For what? Is she okay?" I asked. Her voice cracked and there was a pause. I was glad that Rio and his new girl, who was so sweet, were getting along, and that Eric, though drunk all the time, had married his bisexual girlfriend. Tanya and I remained friends nonetheless, and she and her daughter were doing well. But Katie, one of my oldest and dearest friends, as close to me as Ruthie had been, was in the hospital. My mind was racing. "Mom has AIDS," she said between her sobs. "Libbe, she's very sick!"

In '93, when the disease was rampant, and treatments were not as sophisticated, AIDS was viewed like the plague, and many people were dying from the disease because there weren't any medications yet to keep the virus in check. She hadn't been hoeing for years, and had a good man and a straight job at a bank. How could this happen? I was in such shock I couldn't think! I couldn't imagine how she had gotten the virus, and I asked her daughter. She told me that her mother had shot drugs with Roger, a man she went with for a while during a period of time we hadn't been hanging out with each other. She used with him a few times, and later, after she left him and was with Dern, she repeatedly caught colds and was sick. Finally, after a year, she had some tests done and they told her she had the virus and probably had it for over a year. Now she was sick with pneumonia, and the hospital was keeping her there and wouldn't allow her to go home. I felt ill. *Katie is so young,* I thought. *I shouldn't let small issues with David affect me when there are so many more serious things in life, things far worse than feeling resentment and arguing.* I told Katie's daughter I would be up to see her right away, and she said to wait until the next day because her mother was extremely tired from seeing visitors. Once she gave me Katie's information, I wrote it down. I was stunned. Oh, God, please help my friend… No matter what I had planned to do the next day, I would drop it for her, she was someone I loved. God, is this really happening?

I needed someone to talk to, and I called David. He offered to come to the hospital with me, and I told him I'd call him back when I was ready to go there, sometime in the mid-afternoon. I talked to Katie that evening. As her daughter had told me, she said that she was too tired to have guests, but tomorrow would be fine. Her voice was sad and weak. "I love you and miss you," I said. She said the same. I didn't want anything to happen to another friend. Too much time had passed since we had gotten together. Phone calls were never enough; we should have seen one another. But after the run-in we had at the shoe store my feelings were hurt, and then, when she had slept with a man I was dating, and thought it was okay, that was it. Like with Ruthie, the gaps of time between seeing each other were too long. I had to see people more often than once a year, make the time to share life with friends and loved ones. I had loved and lost too many. I said that to David when I called him back. "Oh David, I feel so bad about Katie. You see how things happen? We never know from day to day."

"Yeah, Lib, I know."

"I don't want something like this to happen to us, getting together after it's too late."

"Yeah, me either."

"We have to think about our future sooner than later," I told him.

He agreed…

I wondered what I could do to help Katie. I could just be there for her, but I thought I would do some research about AIDS to find out what medicines were out there. I called several of my doctor clients for answers. Among the many things I loved about Elizabeth Taylor was her activism on behalf of the disease. Because of Katie, I was even more impressed by Liz's dedication to finding a cure. In my mother's memory, I always donated to the St. Jude's Organization for children with cancer. Since he had grown up with her daughters, I reminded myself to call R. Lee to tell him about Katie. The news took him by surprise, and he asked me to wish her well. I dreaded going to see Katie sick. She just had to come through this!

David and I went to the hospital, and there she was in the bed, looking frail and jaundiced. She had always looked so healthy despite her beer drinking and cigarettes; the hue of her skin was yellow. But David started joking, and I had to get down on his case, asking him how he would feel if he were sick and someone visiting made light of his condition by making jokes. "Lib, I'm just trying to make her smile and have some fun."

"Not now, David. She has a severe headache." It was difficult for him to remain serious, not something he did well, and because he had smoked a joint it was even harder. We stayed and spoke with

Katie. I told her I would make it there every other day, or every day if I could. She asked us to speak more softly because of her headache, and I shot David a sharp glance. I asked her for a list of things she needed, and—of all things—she wanted a porcelain rabbit, or a few of them made from different materials, and a Forrest Gump video. Okay, strange request, but I would do whatever she wanted! I looked at her lying there and recalled the last time I saw her. We were in bed together with E.F. for a three-way at my Beacon Hill Condo, where she routinely saw my dates after we talked again. I got up and left when she and the man I was dating were getting into some heavy sex. That's what I remembered. I clearly never wanted to be with his ass again, he too just wanted to be with other women.

I brought her the things she asked for and was there every day as I promised. The doctors said Katie was terminal and determined that Youville, a hospital in Cambridge for end-stage patients, was the best place for her and arranged for her to be transferred there. She wouldn't try any of the new medicines and continued smoking until the end. I tried to convince her to take the meds, but she refused—she was one stubborn woman! There was nothing they could do for her. It was sad watching her waste away. Her daughters were with her on most days, and she had some friends who dropped in for very brief visits. I continued visiting every day, and we talked about hospice, a subject she didn't want to discuss. But before she was supposed to enter hospice, I received a phone call telling me that my foster dad had just passed away. I didn't tell Katie; that was the last thing she needed to hear. I planned to go to the funeral, which was on that day, in accordance with the Jewish tradition of holding the funeral as soon as possible from the time of death. Katie resisted the idea of going to hospice, but the doctors said it was necessary. The next day she reluctantly agreed to go because there was no one at home to take care of her. I told her I would come either late in the evening or early the next morning to go there with her so she wouldn't be alone, and if she wanted to leave I would take her out. She really didn't want to go, and we planned to discuss it in the morning one more time. We said goodbye late in the afternoon. "I love you, Katie," I said.

"I love you too," she replied, with a half-smile and a wave of her fingers. I hoped she would decide to go to hospice. Leaning over her, I kissed her face and I could feel her fear…a feeling of death surged through my body.

After Leonard's funeral, I went back to Esti's house to pay my respects. I felt nauseous, probably because of the funeral and Katie being so close to death. I had to leave. When I came home about twelve a.m. to change my clothes, Bry, my houseboy, told me that the hospital had called and said it was very important. I quickly called the telephone number, but there wasn't any answer. I was still wearing my black dress, stockings, and heels as I ran out the door in a panic and drove through every red light along the way to Cambridge! After parking the car, I ran to the front door. It was locked! I banged hard on it until the security guard came to let me in. I ran to her room, right by the nurses' station, and when I got there I saw her lying on her back with her eyes wide open—she was dead! *Oh, God!* I thought. *How can this be?* It was surreal, I broke down crying… Then I rang the bell for the nurse; she had been dead for hours, and they had never come in to close her eyes! What the fuck! Where were they? I called out to the nurse that entered her room! "Why wasn't anyone here with her?" I asked.

"We are so sorry, she passed suddenly!"

She died alone, like all my friends. The nurses left the room, and I sat there weeping, tears pouring out of my eyes. Her eyelids wouldn't close. I went into the bathroom and wet a cloth with hot water to soften them, all the while talking to her as if she were alive. "You knew you weren't going to hospice. You knew you were going to die, didn't you? Deep down inside, I knew it too. I should have known better than to leave you, I think in my heart I knew all along. Oh, Katie, I am so sorry I wasn't here to hold you!" I felt like I was floating in another space and time. It was morbid, being in the darkened room with Katie's lifeless body, the friend I loved. With both best friends, I had missed the cues and wasn't with them in their last moments, but why weren't their kids here every minute, or her sister? How horrible to die like that! I will never leave anyone's side again, I thought. I cried and lay across Katie's chest. I said I was sorry.

"Forgive me!" I begged over and over again. We separated because of a man who wasn't worth the time we lost.

I called David and he came right away, sitting with me, holding me in his arms until six a.m. when her family finally arrived. They had been notified when she first passed away, and it had taken them all this time to get to the hospital! I would have broken my neck to get to her! There were no words to say. They should have been by her side. One of her daughters was screaming. The scene was chaotic, and Dave and I left. She never wanted the new treatments and had given up when she found out she had the disease. It was her conclusion that she was going to die, and she took it as if she didn't care. She gave up on life, and so the others around her came only when they felt like it. Dying was easier than fighting, and she wanted her smokes more than anything else. Poor Katie had no fight in her to live. I've wondered why since the time she passed. She died in 1994, my friend who loved gladiolas and her Miller beers.

CHAPTER EIGHTY

Mt. Auburn Hospital Phone Call

Katie's death took its toll on me, and brought me back in time to when we were friends and all the things we went through together. She had asked me to watch over her kids. She left them with a good deal of money from an insurance policy, and they went through it in no time, so I ended up buying one daughter's twelve hundred dollar wedding dress for her. When I attended the wedding, it was as if I weren't there, and I left early, feeling unappreciated; but I already knew that, this just confirmed it. As always, I was only about the money. I shouldn't have expected more from Katie's daughters—they couldn't even make it to their mother's bedside. It was time to separate from them. They were adults with their own lives, and I had to let go.

Bilber, David, and David's oldest brother were all making decisions about the studio, and Dave and I called them to have a meeting at my house one day in the early afternoon. Dave's brother and a guy from Connecticut were working on a painting job, so they had a limited amount of time. I ordered Chinese food from the Golden Temple on Beacon Street, in Washington Square, for a quick lunch for everyone. They all came on time, but were rushed to get somewhere else; they picked at small portions of food on their plates. We talked and set our business plan forward. I divided up the food, giving each of them something to take for later. The meeting went very well, and everyone was elated by what was happening, Dave was singing, we laughed and joked. Bilber brought a check to invest in equipment and advertising. Dave had just finished recording his song, "Ecstasy," which was written for me. It was beautiful, and someone at a record company in Atlanta, Georgia had heard the demo and was interested in it. David had to polish the demo, and then he planned on sending it. I felt as though things were back on track, that I was healing from Katie's death and my separation from Dave, but it was also a trying time and not easy to endure since he was still dating one of my girls. She was a Portuguese woman who was in the relationship for the chase, a spiteful bitch who was more into fucking a man and taking him away from some other woman—especially me, a madam—just because she could. She was less interested in the relationship with Dave; she just wanted money and to score. There were several occasions when I warned him that these kinds of women were money hungry, slick, and played with a man until a better one came along. It was rare to find a girl in the life who was sincere, and the girl he had chosen certainly wasn't true blue. She was using him, and he fell for it hook, line, and sinker. I came to the conclusion that it was not my concern unless it affected my business or personal space. Then I realized that it did affect me. I had to admit that I was angry, but I never lost complete control over my emotions; not yet, I figured I had too much to lose. One day, though, she pushed me—she was at the recording studio! I told Dave to get the hoes out of there, and screamed at her point blank, "Get the fuck out of here, and never walk on the same side of the street as me!"

I stayed home after the meeting. I had enough to do answering the phones and overseeing Bry, who was cleaning the house, dusting, and shining the leaves on all the plants and being obnoxious; I knew that he wanted to get paid tonight to go get high. Dave told me his playmate was going out of town, and he was dropping her at the airport. I spent the rest of the afternoon in my office upstairs, writing in my diary and catching up on some bills and bookings. A couple of my gay male friends came over, and we talked about their move to

New York. The phones were somewhat quiet until thehouse phone rang and Bry answered it—it was not the line I used for the girls. He handed me the receiver.

"Mrs. B?"

"Yes, this is she." I had used David's last name, and my first name, to list the number. Why not? We believed that one day we'd be married. "This is Mt. Auburn Hospital calling. Are you a relative of—?"

"Yes, my husband's brother. Why?"

"I'm sorry, but there's been an accident and his condition is critical. We would like his family to come to Emergency immediately." This took my breath away! "How could this be?" I said to her. "Are you sure of his name?"

"Yes, we are."

"Of course, I'll be right there! What kind of accident?"

"Please, we will explain when you get here." It must have been too terrible to discuss over the phone. I had just seen him a few hours ago! What could have possibly happened? Critical? Bry told me to go and that he would continue beeping Dave and answering the phones. My friends hugged me and left. All my clients knew Bry, and he was more than capable when it came to booking appointments. I asked him to also call Dave's sister too. I had tried reaching her, but she didn't answer. I told him to tell David where I went and what happened and for him to meet me at the hospital as soon as possible.

David and his other, younger, brother had been on the outs ever since he had screamed out details of my past and ruined my relationship with my son for several years, so I surely was not the one to call him. That rant, as I have written about previously, was because Dave had screwed his brother's slut of a girlfriend—while we were living together! She had also gone, on her own, with a friend of mine who was a pimp she met at my house one New Year's Eve, and I knew nothing until the pimp told me about it. Even though the incident took place years ago, Dave hadn't gotten back together with his brother. But he was a member of the family, and at such times, family squabbles needed to be put aside. Dave was closer with his brother in California and the older brother who was in the hospital.

I was sweating, completely freaking out! I was also praying. When I got there, I went straight to the person behind the front desk, who took me to a small room and closed the door. I had never been in a private waiting room before. There was a knock, and the doctor and a nurse came in. "Can I see him?" I asked.

"I'm afraid we have bad news..."

I felt weak, like my blood was drained. "Oh, no! No! No!"

"He has passed on. I'm terribly sorry. We did everything for him and his friend, but the impact of the crash crushed them."

"This can't be! Are you sure it's them?" I lost my balance and sat down for a moment; the nurse helped me. "May I see him?" The tears poured out of me.

"I don't recommend that," the doctor said. "We had to break his ribs to massage his heart. He looks pretty bad, his chest is still open."

"No, I don't want to see him like that! I just saw them earlier... they were so happy! We ate Chinese food! No, no, no, no!" I dropped my head into my hands and sobbed. "I don't believe this! I can't believe this! David is going to be so messed up." I stayed in the room weeping and in shock. *What happened to them,* I thought, *Weren't they on their way back to their job? Why them?* I was hyper, trying to catch a breath...all alone in this room of doom, waiting for someone to come. Where is everyone? Finally, David was escorted into the waiting room, and the first thing he wanted to know was where his brother was. "Bry said he was in an accident! Where's my brother, Lib?"

The tears were streaming down my face as I said, "I'm sorry, David. I'm so sorry."

"What the fuck!" he said. "What the fuck are you saying?" Then he opened the door and screamed, "Where's my brother?" The nurse came running, and she helped as I held him up, bracing him, preventing him from collapsing on the floor. David screamed out and punched the wall, crying in horror! I could hear his younger brother coming down the hallway toward the sitting room with his sister, and the moment he entered the doorway to the room, he charged at David, kicking him and spewing out, "It should have been you—not him—you should've died!" He shouted at David some more and then accused *me* of being at fault! I tried calming him down by saying that it was no one's fault; it was an accident, a collision between a car and a truck. David spoke up in my defense, repeating that it wasn't my fault, "Leave her alone, it's got nothing to do with her!" His sister was crying, and trying to control her younger brother. "He's your brother and you need to forgive each other." He was still angry and spiteful, raising the specter of an old situation. They all went to see their brother while I waited; I didn't want to see him that way. The other brother was not in Boston and would have to fly in. The bad luck didn't seem to end, and I felt cursed like the Kennedys, who suffered one tragedy after another. Year after year, and last year Katie, and now David's brother. *Please, God, no more!* I prayed. I felt as though I couldn't deal with another tragedy. About the only good thing happening at that time was that my son now had a home and business.

David came home with me to process what happened and to make phone calls. He was ragged, and cried inconsolably for hours with his head nestled in my lap. "I'm so sorry,' he repeated as he wept, "I'm so sorry for the things I have done." The scene at the hospital had been an ordeal, and he was sad and humbled by it. The accident was reported all over the news. Apparently, an Iraqi student driving a Mercedes was speeding and ploughed head-on into the Toyota truck. The driver who caused the accident was saved by an air bag. His car pushed through the center of the smaller Toyota and crushed the front end so that they were pinned. The driver of the Mercedes was taken to Massachusetts General Hospital and wasn't badly injured, while David's brother and his friend went to Mt. Auburn in Cambridge, a hospital closer to the site of the accident but, unfortunately, less equipped and trained to deal with most traumas than Mass. General. Although they tried everything they could to save them, they died because of the driver's recklessness. A case was brought to court after the accident, but there wasn't any hope of compensation when the driver of the Mercedes went back to his country. He had gotten away with murder with not so much as a slap on the wrist! Despite their brother's death, David and his younger brother were still not on good terms, which made the atmosphere tense at the funeral.

Dave's brother had broken up with the girl who had caused their rift, yet even tragedy hadn't brought them back together. This made his brother's death even sadder.

David wasn't in good shape. He was drinking and wearing himself down, and I was worried about him. He was dating another weird chick, one who fed him pills she took for lupus, and that Portuguese bitch from Providence, who he shacked up with off and on when he didn't stay at the studio. She was an ass, and I knew she treated him terribly, without the least regard for his well-being, and he tolerated it. He had been sick with colds ever since his brother's death, and when I finally saw him, he looked like he wasn't eating or getting much sleep. My foster sister's daughter and her husband were selling their home in Brockton, a small house, and they offered it to David, who accepted and put some cash down on it. They took back the mortgage until he got one from the bank. I told him his situation would be better instead of sleeping everywhere. It was—he moved in with the furniture I had given him and was working hard on his recordings. I saw him about twice a week, either at the studio or the house. We were mellow with each other now. The lowlife hoe from Providence still saw him and visited him at his new home in Brockton, but he was coming around to my house more often. We were getting along well, and I was more accepting of him seeing other women, we just weren't intimate. He had a gig coming up singing at a bar in Somerville in a month or so, and things seemed to be back on track. He was anxious to get a deal with his demo. He said he was straining his vocal chords because of a cold he had gotten recently that wouldn't go away. A few weeks back, he had called to tell me that he had the flu and wasn't well at all, and the cold-hearted bitch in Providence wouldn't even buy juice, aspirin, or food for him because, she said, she didn't have the money. She was a working girl—that was bullshit! I encouraged him to come over to the house and I would nurse him back to health, but he said he didn't want to burden me and it was just a cold. He said he could fight it and would be over to see me as soon as he was better, "I don't want you to get sick Lib, okay?"

"Okay, Dave…" Later, I regretted not calling the doctor to schedule an appointment for him to get a check-up.

David had his birthday on March 2nd, and was happy! I could see that our relationship was healing and on track. He was going to come over to the house and finally put the beams in my office ceiling. The future was looking good for us, although Dave seemed to be working too hard. He was losing weight and had circles underneath his eyes. I was concerned, and told him to come to the house and I would cook for him. I questioned him about the dark circles under his eyes, and he claimed he was just tired. He refused to eat any food I cooked for him when he came, giving the excuse that he wasn't hungry. I sensed something was really wrong, and the day he came to install the beams I cooked his favorite barbeque ribs, mashed potatoes, and sautéed green beans, but he said that he was not really hungry! The long, heavy beams were loaded on a truck, and Bry had to help him come up the back of the house to push them through a window. One of the beams smacked the side of his head, and he got a bump and a massive headache. When he sat down to try to eat again, he couldn't even taste the food. Since I was a child, I had developed a sense of knowing when someone was sick simply by touching that person, and when I touched David, I felt sick myself and knew that he was ill, but with what? When I asked him about it, he said he just had a headache. I answered, "No, David, your eyes are red and you need to put ice on your head." And we did. That hit caused more than his headache. He told me not to worry, and that the beam had struck a soft spot on his skull and that's why his head hurt so much. But I felt his sickness through my body—like a wave of poison!

CHAPTER EIGHTY-ONE

March 13, 1995, Wake-Up Call

Murphy's Law, David's favorite, was that if something can go wrong, it will. Although he missed his brother being at the studio with him, he was smiling and happy again, singing the songs he had written in the studio before the beam hit him. I was still worried. Dave was always tired lately and getting colds regularly, and they lingered without going away. I told him to take vitamin C two times a day and to rest. It was strange for David, who loved my cooking, to not want any food. He told me his first gig to sing at a bar was coming up. I went to see him perform with a group called Chance and the Band on Saturday, March 11th, at a club in Somerville called Ollie's. He greeted me with a big hug and a kiss. "Lib I am so happy you came!"

"Me too!" He was good on stage, but didn't seem to feel very well that night. He was straining to sing, and his clothes were covered in sweat. He had been like this off and on for months, and I was becoming alarmed, especially watching him sing. He said he was tired again. We left Ollie's for the Bugaboo Creek restaurant in Watertown. Even though it was cold outside, he was still sweating when we walked to the cars. "You must have a fever," I told him. We ordered steak, but Dave wasn't hungry and didn't eat his meal; he pushed it around on his plate and left just about all of it, only having two forkfuls of potatoes. I thought that he must be catching another cold, but that never stopped him from eating in the past, and I asked him if his stomach was upset. He denied it, and then was very soft-spoken and humble when he told me he wanted to be serious, and to talk to me. "Now?"

"Yes, tonight…"

We drank and had a heart-to-heart talk over dinner and, as usual, we touched base about the possibility of us getting back together again. But this time was different; I could feel his sincerity. David asked me to marry him and swore in all honesty that he was through with everyone else. "I've got it out of my system, Lib. I promise you." He was dead serious. *He was ready.* I looked into his blue eyes, and for the first time I saw that he was being truthful.

"Yes, Dave," I said, "I will marry you. I miss you. I love you and always will." I had never said those words to anyone in my life. A smile crossed his face. We had a good evening even though he did not seem well to me, he looked drained and pale. He held my hands across the table, and after we left the restaurant, we kissed goodnight in the parking lot, a kiss with meaning—like when we first met. He told me how much he had always loved me and that we belonged together. "Yes, David, I know that. I promise to dig deeper this time, to be more in touch with my feelings too." This was the moment I had waited for. We parted, me going to Brookline and Dave to Brockton. We both wanted to be together that Saturday night, but it seemed better to wait until Dave had rented or sold his small house and moved back in with me. We would begin our lives again where we had left off. Soon! David called me the minute he got home, telling me he was so tired.

When we spoke in the morning, on Sunday, Dave said he had a cough and was going to rest—he wouldn't be coming by. I offered to go to him, but he said no. By Monday, early in the morning, he called and said he was not going to be coming to work because he felt even worse and was coughing a lot. He said he would try to see me later. David expressed that he even had a hard time taking Perrii and Oscar out to go to the bathroom. Now I was really worried! I insisted that he go to the hospital right away to be checked by a doctor in case he had the flu or pneumonia. I told him that when he got back home to call me! He went at eleven a.m., and was back by one p.m. with erythromycin, an antibiotic. He called and told me that he took two pills about twenty minutes ago and was feeling worse after taking the medicine. David never complained for any reason, ever. He asked me to keep checking on him because he had an excruciating headache that wouldn't let up. I told him I was coming out now! He said to wait to see if the pills would work, that he'd call me back. Something felt wrong... On his next call he could barely speak, and said he felt very ill, like he wasn't going to make it. "I feel like I'm dying, Lib!"

"I'm leaving now," I said. "I'm on my way! Call the house and talk to Bry if you feel worse. I'm on my way!" Bry took over my phones, and I ran out the door in a frenzy! I was so scared that I was driving at over one hundred miles an hour to get to him, but there had been an accident on Route 24, the road into Brockton, and the traffic was stopped. I freaked out and drove down the narrow breakdown lane of the two-lane highway. I did not give a shit if I got stopped! Before I left the house, I told Bry to call 911 and the fire department to explain the situation, and to get someone over to Dave immediately because he was having trouble breathing, possibly an allergic reaction. I finally made my way through the traffic, breaking every rule of the road there was, and drove as fast as I could to his house. Amazingly, no one stopped me.

The dogs heard me as I drove up, and were whining at the door and jumping up and down. My cocker spaniel was out of his mind. Oscar was just whimpering. Dave must not have taken them out, but I didn't care if they peed in the house at this point. The door was open. When I went in, I was totally unprepared for what I saw! Dave was lying across the bed on a pile of clothes, holding his head in extreme pain. His eyes were beet red, his ears were blue, and his hands were a gray color! "Oh, my god, what did they give you?" He was hyperventilating, and it was obvious that the medication the hospital had given him resulted in some kind of allergic reaction. Where were the police? I had gotten there before the ambulance and firemen. When they came charging in a few moments later, they immediately gave him oxygen, and thank God they did because he needed it, he wasn't getting any. Perrii, our cocker spaniel, was going crazy, biting at the firemen's boots, scratching and howling, and Oscar, our dachshund, was crying out and running in circles. I called Bart, one of the guys I had recently dated, who lived in Brockton with his family to come by to watch the dogs. He knew David, and we were all friends. We still are friends. I was in a sheer panic because of the medicine Dave took, which made him sicker!

I took the medicine they had prescribed and kept the bottle even though one of the firemen asked for it. They put David on a stretcher. He was screaming out in pain! I called one of my doctor clients at Mass. General Hospital and asked him to meet me at the Brockton Good Samaritan Hospital. After I explained Dave's symptoms, he told me it wasn't a problem and that he'd meet me there. He was put in the ambulance, and I asked Bart to close up David's house so I could follow him to the hospital; I trusted him.

When we arrived at the hospital, I had to give them David's information because he wasn't able to speak. I knew that he must have been in overwhelming pain because he did not talk. When Dave fell off a thirty-foot ladder and landed in a bush, he never complained; when he hit his head on the windshield of my car at the time of my accident, he didn't complain; when he was stung by a bee, his throat constricted and he was within three minutes of death, and he never complained. He had almost lost his hand once when he cut open his finger shooting paint from a sprayer, and he joked with the doctors. But now he couldn't see, talk, or listen to the nurses who were telling him not to scream out even though he was experiencing intense pain. How dare they! What kind of hospital was this? I would never recommend anyone to go there! They wouldn't give him any painkillers or aspirin because they had to wait for doctor's orders, but to let him lie there like scum, without so much as a sympathetic word, that's inexcusable! Then the doctors came in and asked questions. They said they were going to do blood tests and to bear with them. I regretted that Dave had ever been taken to this hospital. They asked what medicine he had taken, and I told them, suggesting that he was allergic to it. They said he might have had a reaction to the medication, but that it was unlikely that the problem was the medication because of the severity of the headache. My doctor friend arrived and asked what Dave's symptoms were. "Sounds like cancer," he said. That was certainly not what I expected or wanted to hear! "Are you sure?"

"Almost positive by your description, but not a hundred percent."

No way, not my David!

I tried to soothe Dave by rubbing his side and putting cold cloths on his head. After more than two hours of waiting the blood tests came back. His headache wasn't as severe as it had been. The doctor called over the nurse who was holding the results. My doctor friend from Boston stood by. "David, your white cell count is extremely high. And, to be honest, most people wouldn't be alive with your level of 100,000. Your red cell count is extremely low. You have either of two conditions." David's pain showed on his face as he attempted to concentrate on what the doctor was saying. "AIDS or cancer," he pronounced. "David, do you hear me?"

"Yes, I do. If I have AIDS then kill me Doc, but if it's cancer, I can beat it."

Oh, my god, I was shocked and scared! My doctor friend was right! I felt as though I was wading through deep water or caught in a bad dream. I wanted to scream out loud but held it in. Everyone fell silent. "Dave, don't worry; we will beat whatever it is together."

I filled out the papers and they admitted him into the hospital of hell. They planned on testing his bone marrow early the next morning. The nurse made it clear that I had to go at eight p.m.—no exceptions. What the fuck? "What if I never see him again!" I begged the nurse. Spouses were not allowed to stay, or anyone else. How could the hospital have such a policy when the patient may be in a life or death situation? She was getting him something mild for his headache, and I kissed him and held him, then told him I would be right back. How could a hospital be so heartless? I hated leaving him in such an atmosphere. Out in the hallway, my doctor friend told me it was definitely cancer, not AIDS, because of the headache and his painful, red eyes. He wouldn't know more until the results from the bone marrow test were back and that the hospital would know first. I thought, *Oh, my god, this can't be happening! Shit, I can't deal with this—no way! I just saw him, and, yes, he looked sick, like with the flu, not cancer!* My friend said goodbye to David and told me to call him any time, day or night. "Take care," he added, "he'll be okay," and then left. I wanted to go up to David's room with him and stay in the hospital overnight in the worst way, but the nurse said again that everyone had to leave, without exception. I was petrified something would happen to him overnight, and I wouldn't be there! *God, please don't take my David from me!* I prayed. Dave tried talking to me, saying, "Lib, I'm okay. I can beat it, whatever it is." What was wrong with him? He was always so healthy. "Okay, David. I'm scared."

"So am I, but I'll be fine."

"I love you."

"I love you too," he said.

We sat together on the bed without speaking, waiting for eight p.m. I rubbed his back and held him tightly. I could feel his energy—he was scared! He seemed to relax in my arms. The nurse gave him more medicine for his headache. The doctor explained that the antibiotic he took earlier triggered the headache because of his high white cell count. I told the doctor he had also hit his head while he was carrying the solid beams up the stairs on Friday afternoon before he sang at the club. The lump might have started the whole process of decline during the weekend, the doctor informed me. I didn't want to leave, and he didn't want me to go. No matter what happened in our lives, we loved each other deeply. And now, when I had finally said yes to marriage, a ton of rocks rained down on me, blocking me from going any further! When I left, I felt that a part of me stayed in the room with David. I wanted him to cling to my life as much as I wanted to cling to his, forever. On the ride home, I envisioned all the things we would do together once the tests had ruled out AIDS or cancer. I prayed… We wouldn't know anything for sure until the results were in from the bone marrow test early the next morning. Now it was a waiting game, a torture of my heart.

I had to believe that what David had was curable! I went into the house, where his sister was waiting with Bry; she'd called her other brothers. After I told them what had happened, I called my son. He helped me get through the night by telling me that Dave was tough, and he'd be okay. R. Lee was totally stunned by David being sick. Everyone who knew Dave thought of him as a powerful picture of health. Katie was the most recent friend of mine to go, then David's brother, and now David was going to be put through the test of his life—number three. I was going to be put through the test of my life as well. I couldn't sleep, thinking of him alone in the hospital. My son was very upset and told me to call him the minute I heard anything. After talking to Bry and David's sister until the wee hours of the morning, I was able to get a couple of hours sleep, with the phone close by my side. I got up early, at six a.m., and washed up. I stood in the hot shower, the water trickling down my body, penetrating my pores like a healing treatment. I didn't care if my business closed. I felt my life was at a standstill. The crazy ringing of my business phones started at seven a.m., from men wanting their morning sex to get them through the day. I was the only one who was thinking of life and death right then, not pussy for sale. But the show must go on…

I had to go to the bank in the morning before driving to the hospital. Bry was in tow, riding in the car with me. I pulled into the bank's parking lot in Brighton at nine a.m. sharp. They hadn't called me yet from the hospital. They were supposed to right after the test so I could be there in his room when David received the results. Just as I was about to go into the bank, the phone rang. It was David, thank god! "Hey," I said, "how are you feeling?"

"I'm all right. Here, the doctor will tell you." My stomach dropped! David handed the receiver to the doctor.

"Mrs. B, sorry to have to tell you this but David has a serious illness—a matter of life or death. He must undergo treatment immediately and has be moved to another facility that can service him in his present condition."

I asked, with a swallow, "What illness?"

"David has been diagnosed with acute myelogenous leukemia, or AML. His white blood count is unusually high, and he needs to be admitted for aggressive chemotherapy right away. I have to be honest with you, Mrs. B., David is going to die if he doesn't undergo treatment *now.*" I took a breath and, holding back the tears, I kicked the car door! The doctor named off a list of hospitals for me to choose from; David said he wanted me to pick one out. There are many outstanding hospitals in Boston, and I chose Tufts Medical Center. To me, everything about Tufts was positive. I had survived my accident with their care, and I trusted them. I spoke to David and told him my decision, and he agreed. I'd see him after dropping off Bry at home. "I love you—miss your face."

"I love you too," he said, "Miss your face."

"Lib, don't worry. I'll be fine," Dave assured me. He was putting on a jolly persona, but I knew that inside he was frightened to death. I didn't give a second thought to my business and told Bry to handle it. I had to go. My world consisted of my son and David—nothing else mattered. Nothing. I drove like a race car driver to be by his side! Bart brought the boys, Perrii and Oscar, to my house in Brookline for Bry to watch.

Once in the hospital, I went directly to his room. There were all sorts of papers scattered around. They had already made arrangements for him to be transferred to Tufts. I believed I had made the right decision; I was putting my trust in the doctors there until I could research other avenues. I was living proof of the excellent care they provided for trauma, but cancer? The ambulance arrived to transport him, and the transfer was painful because he was seriously ill. Why hadn't I seen or felt the seriousness of his illness before it came to this point? He was at death's door! I had felt a weird butterfly feeling. Perhaps I did know deep inside that something was wrong but couldn't face it.

I thought about many things as I followed Dave in the ambulance, among them the nature of death and love. Before my car accident, I never feared death, and even afterward, when I had died and come back, I remained calm in the face of it, but that was my fate not my soul mate's. I had been around it enough over the years and feared it more so for others than I did for myself. We all have our public lives and our private lives. The self that I showed to others masked my real, deep emotional feelings. Before I matured, I used to fear love, but David taught me I was capable of true love for a man—as intense and profound in it's own way as the love I have for my son. It was something I hadn't known until after I'd met David.

Unexpected things happen in life. Not so long ago, I was hard, not showing myself, always in control, worried what others thought about me because of my hidden secrets. I am able to love because of David. Love in a real sense, not like Rio or J.N. David loved all of me, both good and bad, and I loved him, good and bad. What was deep in our hearts was more important than all the trivial things in life. We always wait until the last moment before we accept. I don't care what he has done, just let him live, God! Just let him live! Both of us have our faults. And now, this diagnosis... Are we supposed to prepare ourselves for him to die? Oh, no, not without a major battle! There will be arguments with the doctors, with each other, and with God. David has been my soul mate, lover, my best friend, and a great father in spirit to my son for all these years. I never reflected as much as now, but the word cancer and the threat of death makes you think about your life with your loved ones. Why can't we all see that, every waking moment? I am not the only one who has ever gone through this and won't be the last.

Nothing in my dramatic and sometimes tragic life meets the intensity of the present moment. It is March 14, 1995 at three p.m., and my partner for over fifteen years is going to be admitted into Tufts Medical Center, and then brought to his room for chemotherapy. As they hooked him up to the reddish-orange chemical, all I could think of was the possibility of the chemo killing him first. He was scared, I was scared, R. Lee was scared—all of us behaving hyper, edgy, and nervous! Perhaps that was an expression of our consciousness of death. David was too proud to admit any fear, and in a light-hearted way, joked about cancer with his new doctors. "Is this all it is?" he asked. "I can handle this." He told Dr. Miller, "Today is March 14th. If by next March 14th, I'm here, I'll make it. If not, I'll be dead."

"Okay, David," the doctor replied in a patronizing way, not knowing us yet. Dave recognized that he was making an attempt to control his future—something not even Dr. Miller could do.

This was the same year Madam Alex from California had passed away, 1995. I had spoken to her a few times in the late 80's, 1989, and 1990 and 1991. We exchanged a few girls. Our conversations were short but cool. Everyone on the Circuit knew her or knew of her.

CHAPTER EIGHTY-TWO

Admitted to Tufts Medical Center

I shed many tears for my love, watching his strong, beautiful body be pumped up with poison. David and R. Lee were close. He had been a father to my son and stood by him in every way. R. Lee was devastated by David's illness. The man I loved and treasured—possibly my future husband—was in a fight for his life, but by no means was he alone. I took notes every minute, jotting down the medicines he took, questions I had, and research I'd looked up every single day. I lay beside him on the bed, feeling his pain and watching him endure the chemo fluid pumping into his body to kill the cancer. It was traveling through his veins, but there was no indication it had affected him yet other than an improvement in the severity of his headaches. We were told that it would take time. He didn't have an appetite, and the nurses told him that the large doses they were administering could make him feel sick and nauseous, and that food would have a metallic taste. He still joked and flirted, more out of nervousness than anything else. They explained the protocol for every step they took. And then they said he could die within one to three months! I emphasized that not everyone responded in the same way. They then told me all the typical things they knew would happen and that he would most likely lose his hair.

Because David didn't have health insurance anymore, the doctor suggested that he participate in a new study program for his leukemia at no cost to him, and David accepted. He would be receiving the most advanced treatments that existed for his AML. The doctors said that only he and I could make decisions, and that as his wife, I was his proxy. Social workers would drop by occasionally to discuss how we felt about David's illness and care. I thought it was the patient who suffered the most in these circumstances, but caregivers suffer watching their loved ones go through the pain that they always want transferred to them instead. Not only do we suffer along with them, but we also go through the frustration of not knowing how to help. I was terrified, not having enough knowledge to help Dave. This wasn't your average cold or virus, deadly cancers have become like a plague in the world. Cancer is a powerful disease that continues to have treatment advances restricted because our government has control of pills and the medical industry has the money.

I swore that I would do everything within my power to keep him alive and provide a good quality of life for him, with his choice of medication and my choice of holistic care and Chinese herbs. Although Tufts was doing a great job, I wanted him home with me and out of the hospital atmosphere. I trusted the doctors, he had two great ones, with the best medical knowledge and experience, yet at the same time they were not well versed in the spiritual aspects of healing. Knowing that his immune system was compromised and he could contract a staph infection in the hospital worried me. And, to add to my fears, they gave him antibiotics, which could suppress his immune system even more!

Tufts was conducting a study on an experimental medicine that was more advanced than other treatments and could possibly help David without him having to undergo a bone marrow transplant. At the very least, it might hold it off until we had to. The transplant could be done only if a match was found. Who would that be? Siblings are often the closest match, but anonymous matches are sometimes found through donor registries. Now it was up to the strength of David's will and the new medicine, luck, and prayers. They said that if he didn't spike a high fever or experience other complications, they would release him from the hospital as soon as the first round of chemotherapy ended. David's cancer struck me with such force that I had difficulty concentrating on my business. His illness jolted me, putting me into a state of overwhelming apprehension that he would no longer be there for R. Lee and me. How would I go on living without my love, my friend, someone I could trust with my life and my son's life?

The doctors respected my wish for David to convalesce at home. I understood that he had to undergo the chemo to control his white cells, and in case anything went wrong, he could not be too far from Tufts. Going back to Brockton was out of the question—it was not even an option. Living with me in Brookline was the best situation for David until he felt better. I had the bedroom all set up for him, clean and bleached, with vases of non-toxic fresh flowers and eucalyptus. We were happy to leave the hospital, but on our way home we hadn't driven very far when I had to pull over for Dave because he was so sick from vomiting and dry heaves, and he looked pale and drained. I would drive another few feet and he would be carsick again. The chemo seemed to be taking control of his body.

David had canceled his health and term insurance, and I never knew that until he got sick. He told me it was a good thing he was in the study because his expenses would be paid for, with the exception of some costly medications, which I could pay. I found that out when we had made it home, after making four or five stops for Dave to throw up. When I called the hospital and asked if there was something they could prescribe to curb the nausea, they said yes. Then why didn't he already have a script for it? What the hell, why let him feel sick! They told me his study didn't include some meds, and I told them to call it in, that I would pay for it. Someone should have at least told me that! I didn't care that the expensive medications weren't covered, it was fine, but why not give the option? I wanted only the best for David. I sent Bry to pick up the prescription at the pharmacy, and I put Dave to bed. He was suffering, spiking a fever.

My phones were ringing nonstop. Because I couldn't easily respond to my beeper when I was in the hospital, Bry had taken the calls. I was relieved to be home and able to cover the phones again so I would make more money. I took over all Dave's bills and his mortgage, and although I felt stressed about making enough money, it kept me busy. Doing homecare, I reluctantly closed my store and was relying on just my girls and clients to pull me through for the duration of his illness. I thought it was the right time to add another girl, to have two or three all the time, to pay for Dave's bills and meds, anything he wanted. Before closing my store, I had huge sales and could pay my own bills from that income. I sold a lot of my jewelry, a few designer handbags, and some of my furs and jewelry on the side to bring in even more. The money that came in went right out again just for David—all of it.

I began looking into acupuncture and homeopathic remedies more, from Chinese herbs to Reiki, anything to help cure his cancer. I considered the X drug from Canada I had researched—I wanted him to try whatever it took—and when I spoke to the X people, they told me his cancer might be too far advanced, they could not tell. I was on the phone with libraries about the Asiatic and Indian herb drinks I was studying; I put him on Essiac herbal liquid, a Canadian Ojibway Indian formula. I made sure that anyone who had a cold stayed away, and I sterilized my house daily.

Whenever I could get out of the house for the short walk to Coolidge Corner, I bought David new clothes at the Gap and small gifts at Party Favors to make him feel better. But March through May was a tough time. It was agonizing to see him so sick from the ongoing high doses of chemo. The doctors told David that he would have to have a line in his chest soon because the number of meds going into his system by injection might damage his veins; more poison…I would have to learn how to clean the Hickman line. They told me he would develop thrush in his throat from his inability to swallow, and that was what happened—the chemo was poisonous, and was destroying so many parts of his body. His hemorrhoids had grown in just a few months, and were so large that he couldn't sit without discomfort. He was a mess, alive, but at what quality of life? I prayed that I could switch places with Dave so that I would be the sick one rather than him. I was his full-time nurse, a lover who became a friend, a madam constantly on the phones, and a mom to my son, who was always there for David as he was there for me. R. Lee was miles away but he was with me, giving me pep talks whenever I needed them. He was rooting for his stepdad to pull it off and improve.

April and May were rougher than the previous months. I was doing a daily chart for David whenever I could. The doctors said that because his reaction to his first chemotherapy was so extreme, his next treatment wouldn't be until April. He was sick off and on during the two weeks before his next appointment in May. Watching him and other cancer patients in the hospital made me see that curing cancer was, in a way, like a business; it was financial as well as medical. And because money was involved, some were cured for a time (even though there was a chance the cancer might return) because they could afford treatment, and some were not as fortunate, depending not only on their cancer, but also on their financial means.

David was tired. Advil stopped his headaches most of the time. He would become nauseous and have a fever off and on. When that happened, I recognized that his immune system needed more fuel. I gave him Compazine to help him sleep. Watching David go through hell was one of the worst things I have ever endured in my life. My pain was nothing compared to his merciless suffering, and as I watched him, I would sometimes have to turn my head away and stare out the window so I would not run to his arms and cry all over him.

May was the tougher of the two months because Dave's next treatment was scheduled to take place. He laughed and joked, but nervously, out of fear; he did not want to be sick like that again. One day we were in the waiting room, and we talked about chemotherapy and his anxiety. The doctors were checking for a change because of the chemo, and also from the prescription meds that they gave him: for nausea, and an anti-anxiety drug to relax. Fearing the chemo would make him sick again, he was very tense, and so was I. The hospital finally ordered and paid for Zofran to coat his stomach. I decided to take a walk to the bank while he was having his chemo treatment so I could breathe in the fresh polluted air of the city traffic. He was okay by then because of the meds, and I figured he would be comforted by the company of the other people in the room with him, who were having the same treatments. The doctors were keeping a close eye on David. They were reassuring him that the reaction he had to the drugs the first time wouldn't happen again. Everything went according to plan. David came home, slept great, and ate a big meal that consisted of two Ensures, chicken, rice, wheat bread, sugar-free cookies, and water. I found out years later that Ensure was not good for him—and that's what the doctors said to give him! I was relieved that his appetite had returned, and he was getting used to his treatments. David felt so well that he even wanted to go back to Brockton to organize his things and have a few friends over. He had all the extra medicines money could buy, and I started him on a regimen of black Chinese tea (a tea with the most foul-smelling odor imaginable, but the best thing for him), loads of vitamin C, and lots of vitamins for his immune system.

On the day after his treatment, Dave was still feeling well. I got up and, as usual when all is well, cleaned the house. I called in for a refill of his Zofran prescription. I'd had him take his regular meds an hour ago. The nurse came and checked his vitals. After she left, Dave ate half of a bagel with no-salt butter, a half-glass of milk, and an Ensure. He was nauseous before the pill, but nothing major. He was okay to go to back his house. Bry cleaned the hallways and bathrooms with bleach, and I left to go food shopping while his sister sat with him. He told me later that she got under his skin. Had I known beforehand how irritating she was to him, I wouldn't have allowed her to sit with him or be in the house as much when he was there. At least she was a backup for Bry.

A few days later, Dave went back to his house in Brockton to organize and to go fishing with a friend. It was a cloudy day and they had no luck, but he was happy, and that was lucky enough! He was feeling better and wanted to go out more often. The doctors said it wouldn't be a problem but to be careful because his cells were up from zero. He had his girlfriends over to his house, and though we had a verbal commitment and spoke on the phone day and night, I couldn't deny him his right to see them if that was what he chose to do. I brought flowers to Katie's grave while he was out in Brockton. I remembered how much she used to love gladiolas, and I sat by her gravesite, talking to her. I cried for her, but mostly my tears were falling because of David and the emotion I was trying to hold inside. I told her I didn't want to lose David and for her to please guide him. I prayed to my mom for her help too, and asked Ruthie to join in! It was hectic booking new girls while David was so sick. I had to keep a level head.

The next day, David said he wanted to come to Brookline to talk, and he let me know that he felt he could be on his own now. We would hang out together, he said, on the weekends; this way, I could get some things done I needed to do. He was right…and he obviously still wanted his freedom. I was not about to remind him of his marriage proposal. We packed the car and bought flowers for the neighbors who had visited Dave and sent cards. I stayed over so we could drive to his mom's cemetery in Rhode Island first thing the next morning, dropping off a bouquet of flowers as he sobbed at her grave. He needed that moment, just as I needed time with my mother in Sharon on the way back.

Bry had come with us, and cleaned Dave's house while we were out that day. By the time we got back it was three p.m., and I could tell Dave was tired and needed to eat and sleep. He was in the backyard, walking slowly with the dogs and looking around with a sad expression on his face, like he was lost. He said he wanted to smoke a joint and that it would help his appetite, but I warned him against it because it could cause fungal spores in his lungs. He said, "I'll just smoke a little." I agreed to it, despite my reservations. David was becoming more tired; his mood was even lower than it had been before he smoked. I often wondered whether getting high using a copper pipe had contributed to his cancer, or perhaps it was the time the lead paint had gotten into his bloodstream that caused his illness. I wondered whether he had contracted a blood disorder from his girlfriend who fed him pills for lupus. Every day, I racked my brain for the cause of Dave's illness.

David was super hungry, and I made pasta without sauce for supper. The sauce had too much acid for his stomach, so I cooked ground hamburger, from Bread and Circus, with a little garlic, salt-free butter, and vegetable seasoning. He ate most of it—wow, that was great to see! I had to go and bring groceries to the girls. I waited until ten-thirty p.m. to pick up my money in town, and then I drove to Brockton in the pouring rain because Dave wanted me back. Perrii and Oscar were with me; they loved being in the car. When I got back, I lay down next to him with the dogs. He was comfortably asleep with his head on my chest in his bed, the bed that was our old bed in Brookline. I watched his movements as he slept. His body was jumpy. Placing my hand on his arm, I concentrated on his body, trying to think his cancer away, believing that any positive energy was better than none. I cherished every moment I spent with David and couldn't conceive of ever losing him, no, not ever!

By the end of June, things were going well, a bit up and down, but his spirit had picked up and that helped so much! Dave stayed at his home, and he made it through the blind study. I hadn't been taking care of myself, not even getting a simple manicure or going for acupuncture, eating bad fast food: cookies, cereal, quick stuff. I was totally focused on David, and I believed that there would be a miracle. But after the study, they checked his white cells and they were high again. He got the news that his leukemia was back—that was a shock, and I got sick to my stomach. I didn't want him to go through chemo again. He had made it past their three months of treatment only for his life to end! Why now? It all seemed so unfair! We were planning to go to New Jersey the next day. "Let's just go, okay? Why not?" I said. Maybe not New Jersey, I wasn't sure where. He was game for anything. We went to Coney Island and the New Jersey shore, good decision…I refused to allow any negativity in our lives. Life did not seem like much when I wasn't with him; and when he was sick, I got sick. I cherished my time with him, and I let him have his own time. He was my heart. My son and Dave were the only two people I would die for. I would give all I had to them. *Please, God,* I prayed. *I want David to be happy and healthy. Please help Dave!* He survived the car crash that I was severely injured in with a forehead scratch. Why was this happening? When we returned, we packed Dave up to stay in Brookline for treatments. He would be going back into the hospital. I thought of the quote by Ralph Waldo Emerson: "What we all call results are beginnings."

David insisted on going out before his treatments. We ate Chinese food at the Golden Temple on Beacon Street, requesting no sodium, and after Dave drank three Mai Tais, the combination of his meds with the alcohol resulted in some goofy behavior at the table. He could see I was upset with him, and said, "Would you deprive me of a drink if I were going to die tomorrow?"

I quickly replied, "No, but you're not going to die tomorrow." David laughed and laughed.

"Okay, Lib. You've got me there!"

Before heading home, we went to the park where we had gone when we first met. We made love on the ground in the field back then. We didn't care who saw us. I had lifted up my sundress and sat on him, under the stars. Since our breakup and Dave's illness, making love had turned into something altogether different. It didn't involve sex; it was friendship. We just kissed and held each other, lying on a blanket, counting the stars, silently dreaming. When we got back at one-thirty a.m., David went to sleep the moment we got into the house. He had been so strong before he became ill. His cancer was relentless.

I talked to Dave the next morning and could tell he was depressed. We picked up his check from the state and went shopping for some personal items for him. I bought him a guitar and a CD holder he wanted. That brightened his face, and he played the guitar. Late in the day, we began packing for the trip to the hospital for his treatment, and I planned on driving Bry after that to the Brockton house to clean, rake, and take care of the boys (the dogs) while he was there. Dave suggested that we take another trip after his chemo. He said, "Just fuck it, I don't care if I get sick." I didn't know where we were going, just that we wanted to get away to some place where Dave could play his guitar and sing. R. Lee was coming in on Saturday. I spoke with Dr. Sprague, and she explained that David was in the midst of a clinical depression. I already knew he was down and that his depression could make his illness worse. More than ever, I encouraged him to speak about how he felt, to vent his emotional pain. Because he was out of remission, I was afraid he would get a cold or a fever after the chemo, but we still left for the Cape right after, not going out of state this time, staying close to his doctors in Boston.

We had a room at the Sheraton Tara in Hyannis and were expecting an eight a.m. wake-up call to take the ferry to Woods Hole and Martha's Vineyard the next day. I worried that his stomach wouldn't tolerate the ocean trip, so I packed lots of saltine crackers. Dave was in better spirits after having a beer onboard and did fine on the ferry ride. I didn't…I ate the crackers. While we were eating lobster for dinner, I thought about how someday I'd like to eat as many lobsters as I could just to find out how many it would take before I'd had enough. Six? Eight? The most I'd ever done was five. Dave was better now and had two beers with dinner. The doctors had given their approval but stipulated not to overdo it. David didn't listen. He didn't care. His attitude was, "You only live once." He said that he was feeling fine except for his skin, which felt uncomfortably sensitive to touch. He relaxed after I gently massaged cream over his silky, soft skin. I was very tired and wasn't sure that I would be able to hang for the movie we were waiting to watch at one a.m. He said he was going to stay up. We held each other, but I fell out. During the night, the lobster and beer caused Dave some digestive problems; it was too rich for him, and I should have known better. I gave him some Tums out of the over-the-counter arsenal I kept in my bag. Small things like indigestion frightened him. He would exaggerate his symptoms, turning them into more than they actually were, while he had a devil-may-care attitude toward his far more serious cancer. Through all his aches and suffering, we were happy together on the Cape and wished that time could stop right then and there, but we had to go back to reality—and my phones, to make money for the ongoing bills.

We drove back from the Cape after we took the ferry early in the morning. David couldn't tolerate the movement of the ocean, and on the way back, he became seasick. We left Falmouth and hit Route 28 North. We were both quiet after my rant on the boat, getting on him for drinking before his treatment. "Getting better's the goal," I told him, "not getting worse and putting yourself in jeopardy. Please, Dave…" I begged. We got into it, arguing for some time. I couldn't bear the thought of not being able to see, hear, or touch him. I had to learn to shut up, but if I let him do whatever he wanted, I could lose him sooner. Yes, I was selfish and wanted him to live so that he would be mine forever. I was being overly protective, like when R. Lee was young. David was quiet on the drive back, and I kept trying to break the ice. After staring out the window for some time, he began talking, and at one point asked if I thought he was inconsiderate. I told him no, he had never been inconsiderate; he was just scared. He wasn't himself, and sometimes he forgot who his real friends were and, instead of showing appreciation, took them for granted, like we all do. He was sick and feeling down. I explained that he needed to make an effort, to talk to others more, let it out. Masking his symptoms with booze wasn't helping him; although, I sometimes thought that weed might be a better way to ease the side effects of his treatments. I had been with David almost all the time since he took ill, but we rarely had serious discussions. He just couldn't deal with the reality of his situation—the possibility of dying was ever-present, even if we didn't talk about it directly. He kept his fear just below the surface to appear more masculine. I told him over and over again how much I loved him. He held back, afraid to tell me he loved me too because he became extremely emotional. At night before we slept, he would whisper, "I love you, Siskin'."

My heart broke. "I love you more." I tried reassuring him by saying that I would never leave him, that I would always stay. "Where you go, I will go, whether in body or soul," I told him.

Even though the Cape had been draining, Dave decided he wanted to go directly to the Brockton Fair; he had to challenge himself by going on the most jarring rides. First, we went back to his house so that he had a chance to shower and change clothes, and smoke half a joint. Bry left Perrii and Oscar behind and came along with us. After having a slice of pizza, we bought the tickets. Dave wanted to go on the gyrating ride. I had tried to talk him out of the pizza, and now the rides, but it was no use. I didn't want him to go on them, and I didn't want to go either, but he insisted and told me the rides weren't going to be that bad. "C'mon Lib," he said. "Let's have some fun! Live a little!"

"Will do..." We soon found out he was wrong. As the tiny cubicle twisted and spun around, he turned as white as a ghost, and—never mind him—I was sick as a dog! He was laughing hysterically to shake it off. It took me the entire evening to get over that one ride, and it took David about an hour to get rid of the shakes and get his color back. He ate junk food, and so did I: sausage sandwiches, fried dough, and Coke. Both of us felt like shit, but what the hell, he was happy. Then it started to rain in torrents, soaking everyone. After an hour of waiting out the deluge, Bry and Dave went to ride the bumper cars, wet clothes and all. He was so happy, I did not stop him. We went through the haunted house, which was laughable, walked around the park, and finally left. I dropped Dave and Bry off in Brockton. It was eleven thirty-five p.m. and I had to pick up R. Lee at twelve fifteen a.m., US Air. He was late by half an hour or so. I was still feeling sick from the twister ride—my head was killing me. David was hanging in there, denying how he really felt. I concluded that I was too old for going on rides. I swore I would never do it again. When we got back to the house, R. Lee and Dave decided to stay up playing backgammon with Bry. I was nervous, thinking that Dave should sleep, but he was wired and wanted to spend time with R. Lee. His anti-anxiety medicine didn't slow him down either. It was a busy day, but he was okay and didn't experience any setbacks that were noticeable. David missed R. Lee, whose visit buoyed up his spirits. It was a sad day when R. Lee went back on the plane.

The next trip David made was to the hospital. He was extremely ill on the way, confused, and drifted in and out of consciousness. As we found out, there was a problem with his blood. He needed to see the doctors, not only because he had to have a transfusion, but also to reassure him that he was going to be all right. My efforts to console him didn't always work, but he did become calmer when I told him I would be staying at the hospital with him day and night. His cousin called, and because Dave couldn't speak, I spoke for him, giving his cousin information about the bone marrow testing. The doctors said he needed to get a bone marrow transplant now. I located all of his family, but Dave's immediate family *wasn't* cooperating. It was petty and unfortunate that his brother and sister, who associated David with the black side of their family, didn't want to help him. We didn't have good news the day before on the preliminary tests either. I was hoping for different results, but when the echocardiogram was completed the tech said he had fluid around his heart, and the doctors said that he shouldn't drink anything liquid. Despite being swollen, he was resting comfortably. Then, when his air unit started acting up, making loud noises, I thought that they would move him to a quieter room, or at least fix the machine. The air units were randomly going on and off. I rang for the nurse, and she fixed it. I went out into the hall and spoke with the doctor, who told me that there was no infection around his heart or valves, but there was some swelling of the heart valve, and that he had to be monitored. They gave him something to take that increased his urination, and the pee was the right shade of yellow. David relaxed. The doctor said he would be in to see him again before he left the floor. The doctor did come back, and Dave felt reassured. Then he and I had a long talk about how death was calling him. He imagined that there were two lines of people, and he had only a split second to make a decision between the two: life or death. Dave said he chose life. He had experienced near-death episodes twice and he knew, as I knew, that death was imminent. I just wanted him to fight back as much as possible while everything was being done to keep him alive! If only I knew then what I know now! The doctors were administering morphine, which caused him to hallucinate. The stuffed Daffy Duck I gave him made him cuckoo—he thought Daffy was flying!

Since the chemotherapy in July, David had been staying with me. He was in and out of danger, and it wasn't too long before he was back in the hospital again. I ran to and fro between the hospital and the house to check on my business and make food to bring back to Dave while his sister stayed with him. His younger brother had relented and was seeing him too, but he had the nerve to argue with him. That was not cool!

August 23rd was a Wednesday. It was seven-fifteen a.m., and I hadn't heard from anyone at the hospital yet. I didn't want to call Dave in case he was sleeping, and I was hoping someone would be in touch soon. I was so uptight. His sister called at eight a.m. Dave was delirious and running a temperature of one hundred and four degrees from an infection. I vowed that once I was at the hospital I would not leave! Everyone who came into Dave's room had to wear a mask. I wore two masks because I was on an antibiotic for a sinus infection. I wished R. Lee would come back and stay for a while, and I called to let him know that it was an emergency and he should fly home. He agreed to come back on the next flight. He hated hospitals, but we feared David wasn't coming home again.

David was in danger; his white blood cell count was extremely high. He had a constant fever of one hundred and four point five degrees, pneumonia, and some kind of bacteria. His blood pressure was low. The blood and the antibiotics they had given him weren't working. They were growing the bacteria he had in the lab until they could identify what kind of infection he had. When they finally brought Dave back into his room, I had a headache and was so tired and sick I wasn't paying close attention, but for now, he was out of immediate danger and that was all that mattered. I told my foster sister that David was in bad shape, and she came to visit. She didn't have the time to stay long, and I understood when she left soon after. I couldn't sleep. R. Lee had arrived and spent the entire night with Dave and me. In the morning, my phone was ringing off the hook, and one of the doctors commented that I received more calls than he did, and he was on call! I told him I was on call too, and he laughed—little did he know that I wasn't joking. When David woke, he had pains in his chest and diarrhea. He was more swollen than he was the night before. They gave him two drips of morphine and two milligrams of Ativan, and he relaxed; Dave was panicky about the pneumonia. Trauma visits all of us in our lives at one time or another, but I had experienced more than my share. My greatest wish was for Dave to recover, but he needed help beyond what medicine could do for him. I went home for a short time while R. Lee stayed with him. I did some paperwork and took a shower. I couldn't sleep. I had to go back. I was too worried about what was going to happen!

Life had become a true stress test. Being a madam and running the girls who traveled in the Circuit was a full-time, twenty-four hour job. There were no problems with this system until approximately 1995, when it all started to change. The ladies were getting sloppy, and we were accepting new madams—mini-madams—and they were letting all kinds of girls into the circle. It was starting to get too big and out of control. The computer—1996-1997—was beginning to get noticed for business purposes. Clients and businessmen were recruiting girls themselves online, eliminating the madams, and seeing them on the side. This took away any protections for the girls and changed a very well-managed system to a dangerous one. Before all of this, we were well known in a positive way internationally. Yup, things were getting sloppy and there started to be too much talk about all of us, and information about the Circuit was being leaked.

That was not okay because the new mini-madams were not keeping things in control, as we soon found out in years to come. The computer and escort women, the ones who never worked the hard way to get this business, came in and began with big advertising for girls. The Circuit was getting bigger, but not better

We were talking too much on the phones, using codes less and open speech more. No one knew about us who should not have—until Ginny and her carelessness. She got herself busted after her client turned her in. And it tumbled to the end! Well, that was truly a big turn of events. The Circuit would never be the same again. But the business was nothing compared to what was happening with David.

I got as much done as I could before going back to the hospital; I felt that Dave was safe with R. Lee there. The first time R. Lee visited him in the hospital after Dave was diagnosed, he almost passed out, and the nurse had to give him orange juice! I was impressed by R. Lee's stamina. He called me early in the morning and told me David wanted to know where I was, so, of course, I went back right away, no problem. He calmed right down when he saw me walking into his room with a smile on my face. My body filled with joy seeing his smile! After a couple of hours, I asked the nurse to give him Ativan again so he would remain calm. I wanted him to move, regardless of what the doctors said. I got him up, danger or not, *he had to move.* And I believe it was because of that the fluid around his heart decreased. He was stable again. David had been close to dying three times now, and I hoped he would make it through another time. I had to believe he would. I needed him in my life, and in my son's life, forever.

CHAPTER EIGHTY-THREE

Autumn and Winter

The year 1995 was a year of sheer hell. Still, through the sadness and pain of watching David go up and down on the grand scale of life versus death, we had our moments, most of them experienced outside the hospital, at his house or mine, or on short trips. Because he couldn't manage on his own, he moved back to my house indefinitely, where he felt totally at ease. His red cell counts were low again, and the doctors suggested another round of chemotherapy but said that it was up to us. They knew he was terminal, and I couldn't watch him suffer the effects of having more poison pumped through his body anymore. There were no bone marrow donors, and though my son had the same blood type, their DNA did not match. My son wanted in the worst way to be a donor for his stepdad—R. Lee would risk his own life for the ones he loved, and it filled me with pride to be his mother. I could not love anyone more than him. I know that some people would say that I didn't deserve to have a child at all because of my lifestyle and my past, but those people cannot see below the surface. I deserve my son, my best friend; everyone deserves someone to love. Everyone. And now, during the worst time in one's life, what does it matter what any human does as long as it harms no one?

Despite the touch of pneumonia he still had, I made the decision to go away with David for Christmas. He wanted to travel and didn't care where he went, and I didn't blame him. The doctors were against it, saying that he could possibly die on this trip if his white count elevated and he got a fever. I told the doctors I would rather have him die happily on vacation in sunshine than in a bare, white hospital room. Against their judgment, I went ahead and made the reservations. David wanted to go to Puerto Rico, and that's where we were going to go. He wanted to see a rain forest and be in a warm climate. We would be there through Christmas and back for New Year's. I packed us up. David was thrilled! He had a persistent cough but was so excited! The hospital loaded me up with meds, and I carried them all with me. Also, I planned to make sure that Dave wore his mask in the airport and on the plane, just in case he might be susceptible to a bacteria or virus because of his pneumonia. A friend drove us to the airport, and Dave didn't stop smiling the whole way. I had him sit and rest while I got the tickets, and there seemed to be a lot of friendly people on the flight with us; he was talking to everyone, with his mask on, and the smile on his face showed through it. This trip was worth a million smiles. I watched him, his blue eyes sparkling, and the glow of his childlike being—he was a beautiful man who loved everyone.

The flight was peaceful. David ate while I wrote in my diary about our trip. Wanting to experience every moment, he fought against going to sleep, but then he took an Ativan, calmed down right away, and went to sleep on my shoulder with his blue bear, Randy. His tired body needed the rest. I held him, listening to his raspy breathing. When we landed, we were the last ones off the plane. We already had a driver a friend had recommended, and when he picked us up, I explained about David's condition so he would be aware that at some point we might need a hospital. We agreed that each day, for cash, he would take us to all the special places. Although he tried not to show it, the sympathy he felt for Dave was apparent. He was one hell of a guy, and we still exchange Christmas cards to this day. His nickname for David was "Jefe." David took to him immediately and bombarded him with questions about the rain forests and beaches.

We checked into the hotel on the beach, bottom floor, right on the water. We had two queen-size beds in case Dave needed to be in his own bed; he was used to our king-size bed at home. He took his meds, but he wanted to go out to have a beer. We went, and after one beer he was buzzed—his eyes appeared to be crossed. We planned out seven full days of vacation, his only disappointment being that he was too weak to go out on a boat to fish. We had dinner at a place where the casinos were, and, of course, David wanted to gamble. I didn't have a problem with the gambling; what bothered me was that he was coughing so badly from the thick smoke and his pneumonia that he had to put on a mask to breathe, and it didn't help at all. I could see he was exhausted.

We went back to our room early to prepare for our day trip in the morning. He was still coughing, and I went out to find some cough medicine and bring him warm herbal tea. It was a good thing I did because he needed to sleep. I doubled up on his antibiotics for insurance, and he passed right out! In the morning, he ate a huge breakfast. He felt better after having taken the higher dosage of antibiotics and the cough medicine the night before. Our driver took us to museums, to the countryside, and told David about the "chupacabra," an alien creature that was said to roam Puerto Rico, killing animals and sucking their blood like a vampire. David was intrigued. The driver's nickname "Jefe" stuck—I was calling him that now. When we came back to the hotel, we were told that a storm was coming in. They said it was supposed to be a bad one and to stay inside. Dave got a couple of beers and said he wanted to sit outside on the beach during the storm. "I want to see it up close," he said. I tried to convince him to stay inside, but he said, "Lib, what's the worst thing that could happen? I could die in a storm?" He was right; the storm couldn't be more devastating than the cancer that ravaged his body. I told him I would go out there with him. We were asked to get off the beach, but when I explained, they backed off. We sat through the wind and rain under a canopy umbrella that blew like crazy from side to side as we watched sand and small pieces of debris circulating around us. We were covered in sand. David had his mask on. When the storm was over, he was content. He loved being outside in the elements and always went for walks in the rain and snow back home. When we went to bed, we held each other tightly, and I could feel the love and fear coursing through his body and entering mine. The dread I felt was overwhelming; death was knocking on Dave's door.

The next day was calm, with clear blue skies. Of all things, David was curious about where the working girls were, and he wasn't shy to ask. And he did tell me he missed being home to pick them up and take them grocery shopping. Well, I knew that. The driver knew exactly where to go. He said men drove their cars into motel-type storage units, and when the door closed, they went inside to see the girls. We were both fascinated by the tour that day. We never told the driver what I did. We had to have a quiet night because the plans for the next day were to go to some mountainous areas and then see the rain forest, and perhaps the beach. We both had to get some rest to be up by five a.m. Dave's temperature was up and down, even with the double dose of antibiotics. When I asked him if he wanted to go home he said no, but he was extremely angry as if he were finally letting out all his fury at what he was going through. "I don't want to go back, ever!" he said. "I want to stay here by the water with you, Lib. Only you. And die in your arms—no more medicine!" We talked, and that helped him.

He said he wished we could stay for the winter, and I replied, "Me too, David. We can always come back. I'll save more money." There was a lengthy silence. We both knew what the future held. Looking back, I should have stayed with David in Puerto Rico, to die in the sunshine, lying on a warm sandy beach. Feeling responsible for him made me not go with my heart. *Never again!* I will go with the heart next time…if ever.

We went back to the hotel to get ready for dinner. The restaurant was romantic, high up, overlooking a bright tropical garden. Dave ordered a beer, as usual, and a steak with potatoes and vegetables. I was surprised when he ate all of it and asked for desert. Maybe the higher dosages of antibiotics were working; maybe the vacation was doing him some good. Whichever it was, or both, positive energy flowed in his treated veins.

While we sat for a bit to give Dave time to digest, we couldn't help but notice that the man sitting next to us had a newspaper with a picture of the chupacabra that our driver had told us about.

David asked the man if he could take a look at the creature, and after he handed him the newspaper, Dave started talking about how he wished he could see an alien. The man looked distinguished, like a professor…and was one! As we spoke, we found out he was in Puerto Rico to do research in the mountainous regions of the country to find the chupacabra and other exotic life forms. David listened and asked question after question. The professor said that there were other alien forms besides this one and he had been researching them for quite a while, sometimes in the mountains of Hawaii. David was deep into the conversation, but his coughing was becoming progressively worse with his excitement—it just would not stop. It was impossible for him to converse because of the constant coughing. He looked like he was having difficulty breathing as well. The professor was concerned and asked Dave if he was okay. I explained his illness to the professor, and he was sorry to hear what it was. He told David to keep his spirit up and take care, and then gave him his personal card. Dave was deeply touched. We had to go. The professor handed the newspaper to Dave to keep. As much as Dave wanted to continue, he had exhausted himself, and I had to get him back to the hotel to rest. When he could finally lie back and relax, he felt better and his coughing slowed down. To this day, I still have that newspaper.

The antibiotics had to be stronger, so I upped the dosage. The doctors said I could do that if I thought it was necessary, but if his fever rose above a certain point, he would have to go into the hospital. I hated to feed him the antibiotics because of his low immune system. I took his temperature, and his fever was hovering around one hundred degrees. Whew…not bad. Every day had been stressful in one way or another. David took off his shirt, and we stretched out in bed and watched TV. The Hickman line in his chest was in my view, a reminder of the severity of his illness. After a couple of hours, the coughing stopped. I kept on rubbing his back and legs with eucalyptus cream to help him. He slept soundly through the night, even late into the morning, peacefully. I told him we would be taking it nice and easy, and we were going to rest whenever he was tired—no more pushing. The driver said he'd return in a couple of hours, and I didn't care that we were off-schedule. I got eggs, toast, and juice for Dave, and he took his pills. "I feel better," he said. "Let's go!" We were off again. He did feel pretty well, no cough yet, and his fever was still down. His smile and attitude were super! We were on our way to the rain forest, David with his rain jacket and me with a poncho. This was the day he had been waiting for. The scenery on the drive there was beautiful, with the exception of the overflowing trash cans at the stops along the roadside, which attracted some menacing-looking vultures, standing with the people like they too were waiting for the same bus. David sat in the front, and I held his shoulders as I leaned over his seat. We arrived at the entrance, and the air was so clean and fresh! We climbed up to a tower that overlooked the magnificent trees. When Dave stepped in front of the oval-shaped window he was outlined, as in a silhouette, and I snapped a picture of him. The photograph captured that sad yet peaceful moment. It was a beautiful picture. I wished time would stop and I could keep this precious man here with me forever.

In my mind, I was bargaining for David to live, and I told myself I would give up everything if only he wouldn't die. None of the material things in life mean a thing—being alive and free, with good health, is all that matters. We took each other's hands as we walked down and entered the rain forest. We were connected. This was one of the last times we would be spending a vacation together, and it was our time, whatever was left of it. The moment felt like a miracle.

The sky opened up, and it started to pour. We ran to take shelter in one of those huts that are meant for protection, but on the way, David saw an elderly woman who was obviously chilled by the rain, and he took off his jacket and draped it around her shoulders. She thanked him profusely. "It's yours," he said, "I don't need it anymore."

"Thank you. You are so kind," her daughter said. She thanked us both. David refused my coat, saying, "I want to feel the rain, Lib. Please, it feels so good. I feel free."

"Okay, go for it…"

The sight of him in paradise drenched by the raindrops was sublime, his face smiling as he held up his arms toward the sky and let the rain fall on his face as he licked the raindrops with his tongue.

Oh, my god, why do people have to suffer to learn? Later, the driver took us to a beach where David laid out on a blanket to watch and listen to the sparkling ocean and soak in the warmth of the sun. The waves were like a healthy sedative. He ate some food and was content, lounging with me on the soft sand. I could see him savoring each moment, and I thought that this is why he wants to die by the water, I too would want the same one day.

We had a list of things left to do. David seemed to be better. There were sick days and nights, but overall the trip was unequivocally worth it. And I wouldn't change my life or Dave's life, or the life of anyone who is curious and wants to live until the last breath without doctors! We have only once to go around, and why not live life to the fullest? Whatever is beyond this life is unknowable, but I imagine it to be quiet and peaceful.

The only glitch of the trip happened on our way back. Our flight was cancelled at the last moment and our bags went on a different plane to Boston. Shit! Everyone was wearing summer clothing at the airport because we were going to be on a layover when we were still in a warm climate. We were supposed to get our bags and then change flights. That didn't happen, and instead we were laid over on another flight in a cold climate without sweaters or coats, and then were supposed to fly to Boston. People were in an uproar, including myself. I went off on the airline, telling them about David. There was a group of elderly people who had been on tour in Puerto Rico, and we were all complaining together. They overheard me saying some things and asked about David. I told them my husband had a fever from pneumonia and was sick with leukemia, and that he needed to have warmer clothing. David never wanted special treatment and didn't want anyone to know, but I had to tell them. He thought all I said was that he had a bad cold and a temperature…at least that's what I told him. David kept them all entertained, telling joke after joke, even laughing at his own jokes. They loved him. He truly was a Pied Piper! We all exchanged telephone numbers and addresses, and they peeled off the sweaters and jackets they were wearing and gave them to him. It was a touching moment, he almost broke down and cried, but he hung in there with his next joke! He was cold enough to accept two of the jackets. All of us stayed in communication with one another for years. That short moment connected us! When we arrived back in Boston, David was extremely sick and they admitted him to Tufts. I felt so badly, but he said, "Lib, we were together. It was all worth it. And I loved the rain forest! Remember that! I love you so much…you have always made my dreams come true!"

CHAPTER EIGHTY-FOUR

New Year's Eve

I regretted that David's condition had gotten worse after the trip, but at the same time I was happy! The doctors were surprised that he had done so well and stayed that long, and was still alive. As David put it, "I wouldn't have had it any other way, and I wanted to stay! So what if I'm sick? I'll be okay. I'd rather be sick on the beach than sick on a sheet." I sensed that his death was close. I supposed that he knew too, despite our optimism about him getting better. We didn't talk about it, only about coming home from the hospital. I begged the doctors to let him come home for New Year's Eve. And, again, they were against it, but they understood that Dave was not long for this world and they could not fight our decisions. I insisted I wanted him at home and not in the hospital unless he had to be there for appointments or treatment. No was not an option. I wasn't going to follow their rules; I had followed their recommendations at the beginning but not as time went on because it was the quality of David's life that concerned me more than the length of time he had on this earth. At least I had some control over his happiness. But, regardless, the illness was going to take him because of their poisonous treatments. David was coming home, and the doctors said that they would evaluate him again after New Year's Eve, and pumped him full of medicine. His pneumonia was in check for the time being. The leukemia was not the only thing killing him, the chemo was also because it compromised his immune system—it was a Catch-22. It was clear to me that it was a matter of days, maybe weeks, or with luck, perhaps longer. *Please,* I prayed for longer, *we need each other!*

At his request, I bought David his favorite champagne, Cristal. I got two bottles to share with his family and Bry when he came home for New Year's Eve. I felt that I couldn't refuse him. I made all his favorite foods, and his family came over. He had only wanted both of us, but I said, "Dave, it's your family." We didn't include anyone else. By the stroke of midnight, David had already drunk a half-bottle of the Cristal, and he took his next gulp without using a glass. We watched and listened as the Times Square bell struck midnight, and we entered a new year, 1996. David was hysterical with laughter and couldn't stop. He had made it to ring in another year! His face began to turn bluish, and I went over to him to calm him down, taking the bottle away and lying him down on his pillow to catch his breath. He was overexcited. I asked everyone to leave the room for a few minutes. It was pitiful, painful, and joyous. He had made it to 1996, and they had said he would not make it beyond three months after he was first diagnosed! He lived, and now we would see how much longer he could hang in there.

The time we spent together after New Year's was sporadic, a good day here and another there, for a couple of hours at a time. Dave's body was becoming thinner and fragile, and his pain was excruciating. He had undergone a number of transfusions during February. In March, after the last time we went to the hospital for a transfusion, he was bleeding out from his bowels so profusely that I had filled up an entire garbage bag with bloody diapers. When I changed the diaper he was wearing, I gave him the impression that he had gone to the bathroom rather than tell him he was bleeding because he wasn't aware he was that bad. The blood came out in large clots, and I was frightened! When I called the hospital, the doctor told me to bring him in immediately for a last transfusion. His last? He gave us the final word when we got there—they checked David out, there was nothing more they could do. His white cell count was astronomical. There would be no further chemo. They were giving him blood to stay alive. This was it. There was no way I would allow his death to be prolonged and miserable, staged in a hospital setting, *no* sterile room, *no* white sheets!

When they told David his prognosis, he did not answer, just turned his face and body to the wall as he lay on the hospital bed. I was heartbroken…I felt, like him, that all hope was gone. I walked to his bedside and said, "David, I love you. Come on, let's go home." Tears rolled down our cheeks. It took a few minutes, but he finally turned toward me and got into his wheelchair by himself, using every iota of strength that he had left. "I have to see Dr. Miller and Dr. Sprague by myself," he said. He wheeled himself down the corridor behind me to find them, and when we found Dr. Miller, he extended his hand to him and said, "Thanks, Doc. See ya soon."

"Yes, David. I'll see you soon." Dr. Sprague had tears in her eyes. She hugged him. "Take care, David. If you need us, call."

"Sure thing," he said with an uncomfortable laugh, tinged by sorrow.

"Are you ready, Dave?" I asked in a strained, upbeat tone. He shook his head yes. He had used whatever strength he had, and I pushed him the remainder of the way to the elevator. His sister was silently crying. No one had words, or answers.

We left to go to the car. When we got there his sister, still sobbing, got into the back seat. I looked at her, and we connected for a second or two. "We have to make a stop," I said.

"Where, Lib?" Dave asked, the weakness of his voice conveying how fragile he had become. His blood level was too low for him to be totally aware. It seemed as though his will had been drained from him. I held his hand. Arriving at the park in Brookline where we went the first time we got together, where we had that intimate moment, I pulled down the driveway and parked. I went over to Dave's side of the car, opened the door, and had him lean on me as we stood there recalling our time together on the lush grass. "Kiss me, David," I said, and we kissed passionately, though he was weak. He couldn't maintain his posture standing and asked if we could go. This really hurt, the emotions we felt were intense.

"We can go, David."

"Thanks, Lib, thanks…"

"Remember that we will always be a part of this park." He smiled at that and shook his head.

When we got home, Bry and our contractor friend L.S. greeted us at the sidewalk and carried David up the stairway; he could not walk, so they made a seat with their hands for him to sit down on. There were tears in his eyes as we lifted David up. He held his arms around their necks as if they were his brothers. We all ended up crying.

March was cold. Dave made it to his fortieth birthday on March 3, 1996, which we celebrated in our bedroom with balloons, cards, and gifts. It was his last week. There was a chill to the air, and there were ravens flying in dense flocks across the sky and perching on the wires outside our bedroom window on the opposite side of the street. It was like an Alfred Hitchcock movie. There were so many of them they covered the lines completely. David said they were there waiting for him to pass. With me bracing him, we walked into the bathroom for a moment alone. Holding the walls for support, and with great pain, he sat and rested on the toilet seat. He said, "Lib, I didn't want to talk to you with my family there. I wanted to speak to you alone. When I go, I want you there beside me. Lib, I'm not afraid to die…I'm afraid to leave you here without me. I wanted to die with you in my arms at the beach, but now it doesn't matter as long as we're together." I didn't want to agree, but the truth was that I had always needed him as much if not more than he needed me, and he was more afraid for me than he was for himself. How would I manage without him?

"You'll be with me, David. Your soul will go wherever I go, and we will always have that connection." We walked back to the bedroom arm in arm.

"Lib, I'll love you until my last breath and beyond." He lay down, his head and shoulders propped up with pillows, and I sat on the edge of the bed near him. I leaned across his legs and looked up at his face, crying.

"I love you too. I don't want you to go. Please hang in there, please!"

I had made arrangements for David's funeral with Barbara at Levine's Chapel, on Harvard Street in Brookline, the month before. I went all-out—I picked out one of the best caskets, the best of everything, even a state police escort and a guitar made of yellow roses. Although some people consider it foolish to pay exorbitant prices for those who are no longer living, I wanted him to be buried comfortably, not in a pine box like the one my father later chose to be buried in, with just a sheet covering him. The female rabbi I had found for him wasn't available at that time, so Barbara replaced her with another rabbi, a man.

After we went to bed for the night on the day we had the talk in the bathroom, David was never fully conscious again until the rabbi came. He didn't speak, but lay there trying to breath. The soft gurgle in his chest was the rattle, the sound of death. Days passed—his last fight for life. I called the rabbi, and he broke from what he was doing to come over right away. In the bedroom, you could see the jet-black ravens on the phone wires across the street in the gleaming bright sunlight, keeping their vigil. I had loved ravens since I was a child, from the time my mom brought the raven in to heal, but I wanted them to leave today. David had said that they were an omen, and as I looked out the window that day, I believed they were. I couldn't help but think of the week before his last visit to the hospital, when he woke in the night telling me the reaper was trying to take him by his legs! How awful that was! He cried out so with fever and pain.

The rabbi came into the bedroom. He said hello to all of us, then went to David's bedside. "Hello, David." David rose up off the pillows like magic. And, with a slight smile, said, "Hello, Rabbi."

"David, do you know the reason I'm here?"

"Yes, Rabbi, I know."

"Okay, David. I'm going to say a prayer for you." David sat up, his spine straight as if he were at attention, life flowing through his veins from the man with the prayer book. Just a moment ago, he had been oblivious to everything around him for days! I sat down next to Dave and held him—he was alive! But he was only aware of the rabbi and the words he was saying. When the rabbi had finished, he asked David if there was anything he wanted to say. His sister and younger brother watched; his other brother from out of town was there too, standing silently. We waited for his reply. He said, "No, Rabbi. Thank you." His voice was barely audible.

"Okay, David. You rest. You will be in good hands." The rabbi smiled warmly and touched David. He said his goodbyes to us, and the moment that he left the room I tried talking to David, but he wouldn't respond. He lay back down without any assistance and was no longer present in our space anymore. His mind was focused somewhere else. My son tried to get him to respond, and…nothing. He stared ahead like he was comatose. No response. The sound of the gurgling in his chest as the blood flooded his lungs was pronounced. I wanted to go with him! I had almost stopped breathing when the nurse had to pull me away. She needed space to care for David in his last moments and for me to breathe. He had his headphones on, listening to the Whispers, his favorite group, as he passed away. That was his send-off. That brilliant sun-filled March day was David's last, and as my son and I walked up the stairway from his room, we saw a rainbow on the hallway wall, a spectrum of colors reflected by the sun and David's life and death. I said it was a piece of heaven that had entered our home as David took his last breaths. R. Lee then asked, "Mom, are you all right?" I shook my head yes, and just said, "Rest in peace, David. I will miss your face. I will miss your ocean-blue eyes and your endless happiness." I will always love you.

CHAPTER EIGHTY-FIVE

Funeral

I felt numb. The shock of seeing him lying there lifeless hadn't fully hit me. We knew it was going to happen, however, nothing could have prepared me for viewing my loved one's dead body. I wasn't dealing with it yet. It was an upsetting scene for my son and I. The nurse needed complete silence while she made sure Dave had fully passed. And when she called us back downstairs, I entered the room and the woman, though black, looked pale grayish-white and was sweating. She said she actually saw David's form detach from his body and elevate in the air! I believed that his spirit had risen, and I lay down beside his body. I knew his presence was still there… She had to call the doctor to ask what she had witnessed. That nurse did the home care for Dave, she felt the pain and sorrow and saw his spirit.

The men from Levine's came in with a velvet burgundy body bag to pick up David's mortal remains. My son and I dressed him for his trip to the funeral home—the red velour Gap sweatshirt he loved and black sweat pants so he would be warm. We were both crying during the process. Days earlier, when he was suffering so, I wanted the doctors to give him a huge dose of morphine to stop his misery because I lacked the courage it would take to end his life myself. Now he was no longer in pain, and I was faced with his loss. Perrii, our cocker spaniel, was like Dave's child, and when they moved his body he went berserk, barking uncontrollably, screeching like a person, and circling around the dining room table until R. Lee had to pick him up and hold him. Oscar, on the other hand, was shaking, and hid, whimpering while they were moving Dave's body down our front steps. My son was so brave; this was a touching sight. David was his dad, in the true sense of the word, and he did more for R. Lee than any man ever had. He loved R. Lee!

The funeral was surreal. I went through the motions at the funeral home. Dave's family was low-key as the preparations for the funeral service were being made. Not one of them contributed anything to the funeral, and just as David and I had discussed earlier, none of them wanted to acknowledge their ethnic background and the black members of their family. As he lay there in horrific pain, their denial was very upsetting to David. His mother's family was black and proud of their heritage. David was proud as well, and when the relatives from his maternal side visited him in the hospital and at the house, he was so happy, unlike his siblings, who ignored them then, and afterward at the funeral, just because of the color of their skin.

Following Jewish tradition, the funeral took place as soon as possible after David's death. The crowd at the funeral was so large there were state troopers there to control it. After the viewing for the family and my shaky speech (given with the rabbi, who was outstanding, by my side for support while I spoke), the long procession of cars drove to Sharon Memorial Park. The guitar made of yellow roses was there as were so many more flowers that were transported from Levine's to the gravesite. My foster sister and her daughter took it hard—over time they had come to love David. Eric broke down, as did Rio and all my friends. Charlie, the madam from New York, came with her husband to pay their respects; she was the only one of the madams I was closely acquainted with who came. The rest, not even a card! But what should I have expected from them anyway… absolutely nothing.

At the gravesite, my son and I threw dirt and rocks over the casket, but I did not feel he was in the box. "I'm with you, David," I said, just before they buried his body in the ground. My son and

I stood together and wept. Our hearts were broken because he had been taken from us. It was difficult to remember just how many people there were at the funeral and then back at my house. Some of their faces did register despite the frame of mind I was in. And then, for a moment, my numbness gave way and I was lifted into a state of euphoria because I believed I was in touch with David's spirit. I seemed to float through my house, where David inhabited every corner as if he were there.

David was a man with a good heart. After he passed away, I asked myself why there are so many wonderful people who get sick and die while they are still so young. Perhaps it's fate. Eva, the fortune-teller, knew what the future held. When we first met, David prophetically told me he was going to die young. He was right, and really did know that, deep in his soul. He said that one of his brothers was going to die in an accident and another brother of a sickness, that his mother had told him these things when she was very sick, dying of cancer. All of them came true. Even Eva's reference to my accident was eerily accurate. David was diagnosed with cancer on March 13, 1995, and admitted into his room at Tufts on March 14th at three p.m., and died on March 14, 1996, at approximately three p.m.—was that mystical or what? He had foreseen his own destiny when he wagered he would live one year to the day of his diagnosis.

As I go back over my life, I believe that I have been lucky. Even now I am as lucky as hell. I lived, and I know my life could have been so much worse than it was. I knew David was my angel; even though it was only for a short time, he was sent here to be with me. His memory, and my mom's, and all of my friends' memories, stay close to me. Their spirits live on not only in my mind, but also in the routines of my daily life. I am blessed to have lived through so many near death experiences. I am truly blessed to have the drive to keep on going, no matter how far down I go.

I dove into my work the day after David's burial. My son flew back to Atlanta and called me at nine a.m. the next morning to tell me about a dream he had: David was in his living room and the casket was there, open. They both looked inside the casket, and R. Lee said, "How can you be here when you are there?" David was wearing his work clothes, and my son could see how well he appeared to be. He was okay, and talking with R. Lee. Whenever I brought up the subject of the dream after that morning, R. Lee couldn't remember it; the trauma of David's death and funeral probably blocked it from his consciousness at first. Eventually, he remembered the dream.

Every day was tough to get through without David, and at night, I had to drink one or two glasses of wine to be able to fall asleep. I slept in my regular spot next to where his body used to rest, putting my head down on his pillow with Randy, his blue teddy bear that was meant to give him comfort when he was sick, much as it now comforted me. Months passed, and I was still consumed by thinking about him. A girl from Framingham, who worked and answered my phones, convinced me to take a break and go out with her. This would be another new beginning in my life, one that was a total surprise!

CHAPTER EIGHTY-SIX

Sleazy Bar in Framingham

After the funeral, when I lay in our bed I could still breathe in David's scent. I believed that I was with him in his soul, and that his spirit remained and inhabited every inch of our home. I rarely left the house, working the phones day and night to pay off all of Dave's bills. I had many opportunities to be with wealthy men who were willing to support me. I wanted to be with the Jewish man with two kids, but the timing seemed off. It would have been great to have that security and love, but I wasn't ready. David was omnipresent in my life, and he blocked my view. I really thought I could be with this one client who was also a friend. He was successful and had a great business sense, which attracted me to him. I planned a trip with him, his daughter, R. Lee, and myself. Being around him during the day was fine, but spending the night with him was something altogether different. I didn't feel comfortable sleeping with him just yet. I let him go, and then thought about him constantly—too late! My head was still influenced by the street life, which taught me that customers weren't suitable for my personal world. I never thought I would change. Even though I understood I had to move on, I just couldn't get past that and Dave. I wanted love and security, but at the time didn't understand the reason I had such a difficult time choosing what would make me happy. I was battling with myself, and I would not be in this cell today if I weren't so hardheaded. I could have married him and gotten out of the life. I kicked myself in the ass big time for that. My son liked my client Rick, and told me that he would be good to me and I'd be happy doing the things I enjoyed: traveling, decorating, painting, writing, and gardening in my own rose garden. But I didn't listen to my son, or David for that matter. I chose to stay in my world beyond the rose garden, where I had resided for my entire adult life. Although I dreamed of having a perfect life one day, in my mind I was cynical, and believed that my chance for having that kind of life may have already passed. But no one knows what may happen in the future, and what is a perfect life anyway? It is just being happy with yourself and whatever you have, and if you are lucky enough to have a good mate who loves you.

****

I stayed in my pretty office at home, conducting business, alone as usual, madam after madam talking about all the old girls, and the new ones coming out who did not have the same experience. One night, my phone girl finally convinced me to go out with her. Okay, I'll go! I got ready to go out to a club I never heard of in Framingham Center. It was called Mr. G's, and from the sound of it I guessed there was something about the bar that wasn't kosher. I was overdressed, and when Shay came to get me, she said, "Oh, no. No. It's not a place like that. Jeans are okay." I changed my clothes, putting on heels, jeans, and a sequined vest, no jewelry except for my watch and David's Masada coin neckpiece. The outside appearance of the bar made me really want to leave.

"Hey, you know what, why don't we go to another bar?"

"No," she said, "it's cool!"

When we went inside, I saw that Mr. G's was exactly what the name implied…geez, why am I here? It felt like I was back in the Zone, but worse. It was a town bar, with a little bit of this and a little bit of that. *Damn,* I thought, *what have I gotten into now?* Going back home seemed like a good idea, especially because we had come in my car, but her car was parked at my house so I was stuck for as long as she wanted to stay. I hung in there and downed some bad liquor, one after another. Looking around, I knew this was not for me. There were small-time hustlers and pimps, some gay men, and a few lesbian women. Then Shay introduced me to her friends, and I noticed a man, casual in a sweat suit, and clean cut—not like the other wannabes. He was standing talking to a couple of girls, and I saw him look over at me. I was not in any state to deal with someone at this point. Shay said he was a family friend, her girlfriend Jaimie's godfather, and introduced us. I said hello and told him right off that this wasn't a good time for me to be meeting anyone. Shouting over the din in the bar, I explained the reason, and the conversation was short; it was almost closing time. He gave me his number and I gave him the number of the house phone, a line I rarely answered because I figured he wouldn't call. When we left, he came out of the bar and watched us drive off. He seemed to be nice enough, but then what was he doing in a bar like that? For that matter, what was I doing in a bar like that? Shay tried talking to me about her friend Russ, saying that she had known him for a long time and what a great guy he was, and I listened with her words going in one ear and out the other. I was way too drunk for anything. I figured she was trying to hook me up with her friend for points only.

Two weeks later, I was driving in my car while Shay answered the phones at the house. One line was for business, the other a private line. David had used it for his contracting business, and after he moved out of the house, the line remained hooked up to an answering machine. Shay called me on my cell phone and said that Russ had called and was on the other line.

"Who called?"

"Russ."

"Who's Russ? I don't know him," I said.

Shay said, "Yes you do…my friend from Mr. G's. Remember him now?"

"Yeah, the tall one, hanging out with the two girls by his side." I told Shay to take his phone number. "I'll call him later."

"He wants to know if he can call you now."

"I guess, give him my cell number. I'll talk to him." I wasn't quite sure about it, thinking that perhaps I should have waited. Looking back, there is no doubt in my mind that I did the right thing. I was on the rebound from losing someone and wasn't quite ready to see anyone else yet. But I took his call, and we made some plans to meet, along with Shay, at a restaurant on Beacon Street. That one meeting turned into several weekend meetings. Shit, why did I get myself involved so quickly…I didn't want him to know about my phone business and kept it to myself, although he noticed that I received a lot of calls and said so. I told him the calls were about antique furniture and jewelry. I was suspicious of his motives for wanting to be with me, as I was with every man. Was it because he liked me, or something else?

We continued dating. I was extremely vulnerable after losing David only half a year ago, and dating felt like I was caretaking again. With all that I had to do, I took on another man. We went to Provincetown with Shay and Jamie and stayed for the weekend. We had mad sex after I had been drinking, even kinky sex that involved some spanking. Sexually, there was a mutual attraction. Perhaps we both needed someone, and that was the reason we clicked. He had a good job at the time we met, and he was pleasant enough, but I had a private investigator check him out just to be sure. I felt a bit more at ease after that. He didn't have a record and appeared to be exactly what he said he was. He was divorced and had one child from the marriage. He was somewhat secretive and was living with his parents, which seemed strange to me. I was torn between Rick, who had known me for years and would have been a great choice for me, and Russ, who could never give me the security or love I craved. Slowly, over a period of time, I stopped calling Rick. He was very upset, really hurt, and angry that I was dating someone else. It nagged at me that I was making a mistake by letting him go; he would have loved me in every way. R. Lee encouraged me to go with Rick because he was afraid for me to take on a man who might prove to be a burden. I was caught between the two of them—Rick and Russ—and was at a loss for what to do. Things shifted when I didn't call Rick anymore. He wasn't interested in waiting for me any longer. I felt like I was still in the life on the streets, pressured to choose between one pimp or another. Rick's parting words to me were, "We could have rocked on the front porch together for the rest of our lives." I wish I had considered what he was offering me then, but I was living from moment to moment, not thinking in terms of the future. It was a bad move not to think wisely. I was acting on impulse, and the rest is history. Although I sometimes look back with some regret, I wasn't sorry about moving forward with Russ. I figured I could always survive on my own anyway, an independence that I developed from a very young age. Men supported women in the world in which I grew up; however, Russ wasn't big on money contributions, at least not yet.

****

I have given help to girls in the life and in the Circuit without receiving so much as a thank you, the same treatment I've received from some men in my life, with the exception of David. The last girl in the world of madams I helped after Dave's passing was a black girl from Philly, a selfish young woman who would have done anything for money and to be a part of the most prestigious league of madams. I should have known better than to help her. I introduced her to everyone so that she could establish herself with the madams on the Circuit, and even to my own girls. She stole them for herself, and I found out later that she had used her best friend, shafted her, to get to me. She would never help anyone else unless she benefited—she was a user. She was a reminder of just how ruthless people in any business can be; being nice gets you stepped on in life. I had as much money as I wanted, and concluded that money wasn't everything and that good relationships were more important. In my personal life I would not be with a man for money, nor would I use people for my own good then toss them aside. I believe a price is paid later in life for taking advantage of people, and we all suffer as a result. That was the last time I would help girls or madams beyond exchanging my girls for theirs. And now I want it all to disappear. I'm in jail because of a girl just like her who was too disloyal to take responsibility for her own actions and not pull in the Circuit that she was lucky to be on.

****

Russ and I had been together for a while. He began coming over to my house for dinner after he finished work; first one day a week, then sometimes for a weekend, and then additional days during the week. I wasn't certain about my future with him and didn't want to get involved more than I already was. I was focused on R. Lee, and spending our first Christmas without having David with us. After Dave died, I stayed mostly to myself. I saw who my friends were and weaned myself from the others, who weren't any good for me. Russ had close friends he talked about, but he only introduced me to a couple of them. He was close to his family, particularly his mother and his two nieces. When I first met them, they were not keen on me because I was white. Two of his sisters acted as though they liked me only because they found out I had money. It was obvious from the vibe I got from them that they were trouble.

He and I became closer over time. When Russ slept over during our first year together, I would go downstairs to the bedroom where David died, leaving him up in my son's room to sleep. I still hadn't let go of Dave. Russ said he understood. Still, I felt there was something about him that I didn't trust because he was so secretive, some aspect of his attitude and behavior that was extremely private and hard to pin down. He rarely revealed anything about himself or the people he knew—like 007!

The bedroom where David died was my comfort zone after he was gone. One night, I was tossing and couldn't relax enough to sleep with Russ so I went back downstairs to David's room, but instead of lying on my side next to him like I did when he died, I lay across the bottom of the bed where his feet would be. He always had sensitive feet. I looked at the clock by the TV and it said ten minutes to seven. I had been up all night and was exhausted. I had to go to sleep, even for a couple of hours. I closed my eyes, and just as I finally dozed off, I felt a tug on my hands, which were hung over the edge of the bed. "Lib, Lib! Wake up, Lib…" "Okay, okay, I'm awake." The pulling continued, and then I lifted my head to look at the wall by the doorway near the light switch. David was there, smiling at me. "Lib, c'mon! Come with me! C'mon!"

"Okay," I replied, then I looked at the clock behind me by the TV stand—it was five minutes to seven. I looked back and David was still standing there. He looked so handsome in his white shirt and pants, and that smile of his was perfect. I felt so serene…He kept pulling my hand, but I fell off to sleep. Then I was awakened again. "Lib, Lib, c'mon! Are you coming? You need to come now!"

"Yes, yes, I am!" I looked up again, drained and fatigued. David's eyes twinkled as he smiled, and his face was lit up like a star. He was beautiful. I sensed his smile touching my face as if he were kissing me with warm lips. "Lib, I have to go now!"

"Wait for me, David! Wait!"

And as he pulled his hand loose from mine, he said, "Have to go now."

I looked back at the clock. It was seven a.m. I fell asleep, and the next time I woke up it was nine a.m. on the nose. I got up slowly and looked around the bedroom. I smelled the air, sniffing madly, but his scent was gone. The density of the atmosphere had returned to normal. His presence had vanished. The house was clear of his spirit, but I was certain he had been there, briefly, to say goodbye. He knew I was okay and had left. My angel had left me. When I took one step beyond the threshold of the bedroom doorway and then stepped back inside the room, I felt no difference. I ran upstairs to wake Russ to tell him, and as he listened, I wondered if he thought I was crazy. "David was here!" I told him in my enthusiasm. Yes, I was sure it was real. He was standing there like an angel with no wings. Russ said he understood. I went downstairs to the bathroom on the second floor and didn't notice anything out of the ordinary except that the smell of witch hazel was no longer there. The air was clear, and the antiseptic smell that pervaded the atmosphere in the house—all these months after his death—had disappeared!

Not long after that, Russ moved in, and we stayed in the upstairs bedroom. It took a year for me to disassemble the shrine I had built to David in our bedroom. I waited even longer to purchase a new bedroom set. Dave's spirit will always remain part of my house; his presence still lives in the lumber holding up the walls. By living with Russ only eight months after David died, I hoped I was not being foolish and moving on too quickly. I wanted to be free for once in my life, yet I was catering to another man instead of having a man who cared for and catered to me. Maybe he'd be different after we lived together for a while. But in my heart, I knew better. And, of course, it never helps when I spoil men.

Business was booming. R. Lee was on his own and doing well. I was keeping to myself and weathering the ups and downs of my new relationship. Russ was rough around the edges and had some annoying habits, but I stuck in there as I usually did—it was my M.O. I still distrusted him because he was so closed and didn't express much. He did not share money or friends, nor did he extend himself for the sake of anyone besides himself. He was personable enough, though, and for the first three years we traveled and spent money. Somehow the time passed by. In 1999, I bought a house in Florida to have as a second home to rent out in the summer. It was a good investment. The price was reasonable, and I put in five thousand dollars worth of work, and spent two thousand dollars on furniture so that within a couple of years I could sell it with a gain of twenty-five thousand dollars plus if I chose to. I also furnished it with my own furniture from the house in Brookline, including the bedroom set David and I had shared. It was time to let that go. The house was cute. Russ loved it because it was in a warm climate and had a pool. I liked it for the same reasons but resented having to pay for the luxury of a second home by myself. I had opened another store and was working night and day. Russ hated the shitting ducks that came into the pool whenever I left the gate open. Oh well, shit happens.

During these years, I fell for Russ in a totally different way than I had loved David. Russ was aloof, and it was easy for me to be detached then. I wasn't going to give one hundred percent when he never gave fifty percent of himself; time, maybe with time…I was sure that I wouldn't ever marry him because I didn't feel secure in any way, and I was reconciling myself to the fact that I would always feel somewhat alone. Russ had his good sides at times, and he tried in small ways, but he was who he was. I had to accept that. I missed David's help, his personality and energy, and his constant smiles and laughter. We rode bikes, took walks, fed the ducks, went for long drives, sleeping in our car, huddled together under a blanket. We roughed it, and it was true happiness. Now is so different. Dave had been a good friend and lover, and supported me one hundred percent in whatever I chose to pursue. We talked together, cooked together… and he always thought of me. We went to Paris, Maine, to the Mount Mica Quarry, and dug large quartz and mica stones for the wall that remains in my Brookline home. His one bad habit was that he loved women too much and was easily tempted by them. I wasn't happy with that aspect of Dave's behavior, but he loved me and showed it in every other way; I never doubted that. Most people, including myself, accept less than one hundred percent in a relationship—I am still waiting for fifty-fifty. I want to be needed as much as I need someone else, and to share equally, not for someone only to take, but to give. I'd like a companion whose love would be the frosting on the cake. Dreams can come true, just ask for smaller portions and feel lucky about the good days.

Things in my life were transforming, and the Circuit was changing. Guys were trying to have the madams go on the internet, which changed the game by making it an impersonal transaction. They took girls onto their websites, exposing everyone's information. Would the madams be able to protect them in the reality of the big world where men were out there looking for solo girls to go after? I always made sure the girls were protected by screening the clients well myself, and relying on men who had been customers for years or were referrals. Mini-madams with no experience were popping up, taking the girls off the Circuit to expose them in ads over the internet, stealing them from the established madams, and exploiting the Circuit. My good, all-American girls were moving on, as did some of the best madams. I was losing the classier girls who had worked for me so long, and they were being replaced by seedier types. None of the so-called madams stuck together; they were cutthroats, wanting the profit all for themselves, and the old ones lost business. There were new and widespread issues in the brothels as the year 2000 approached. The trust the madams had once shared in the Circuit was disintegrating.

In late 1999, I opened a new store in Brookline with a one- to two-year lease. The store was small, and I knew at some point that I would have to expand. I was on my own, but hired David's friend Mr. L. to do the construction on the interior of the store. When he was dying, Dave had asked him to help me whenever I needed anything. The store was successful, and I could have taken another year's lease if I wanted to, but the space was too small and the basement flooded. I had to move, but didn't have another store yet. So I put up the sale signs and sold out some inventory. By the end of 2000, that store was closed.

Before his death, David and I had discussed going to Paris for my fiftieth birthday in November 2000, but rather than abandon the plans we had made entirely, R. Lee and I went to Paris together and celebrated the 10th of November in the city of love. The Eiffel Tower was lit up with the year 2000 written across it for the millennium. Despite the cold weather, we enjoyed ourselves at museums, parks, restaurants, burlesque shows, etc. I toasted David with glass after glass of wine on my birthday—until my son cut me off! We had such a great time in each other's company that we talked about making a trip again at least once every year after that. But now that things were so different financially, life wasn't that easy.

CHAPTER EIGHTY-SEVEN

A Disturbing Phone Call

I stopped giving parties at my house. Christmas was never the same after Dave died. For so many years, all I did was spend money for food and expensive gifts. I didn't feel the same satisfaction I used to in preparing for the holidays. Decorating was a lot of work, and it dawned on me that it was time to put an end to serving people—no one really appreciated it with the exception of my son and Russ. And R. Lee didn't come home as often after David died; he kept his distance. The truth was that he worried about my future all the time and hoped that I would someday have a good life with someone. He was skeptical of Russ and his intentions. He wanted me to be taken care of rather than me taking care of a man. I understood his wish for me and wanted the same for myself. I just continued wishing that with every year things with Russ would get better. It had been five years, and I was a bit impatient for things to change. He was in and out of jobs. It was a good thing I had my own money.

I was smiling and happy, recalling the trip to Paris with my son, when I received a disturbing phone call from two of my former girls. One of them, the older of the two, worked for me and one of my madams in New York. Whenever she had something to tell me it invariably was the truth. I knew her for years. I trusted her, and thought back to the time she called me from New York to tell me in a soft, hushed voice there was a dead man in the closet of her room at Nana's place and she had to keep working. "What happened?" I asked her.

"He was high and had a fucking heart attack on top of the girl, so we rolled him off her and put him in the closet. That's what Nana's orders were."

"Shit, you have to be kidding!" She was so freaked out because there were more customers coming in and she would have to see them with a corpse in the closet. She pictured the dead man falling out of the closet onto the floor while she was fucking the clients. I calmed her down best as I could. Nana—being the madam that she was—would never stop the money from flowing no matter who died, one of the girls or a client. She assured the girl that someone would be up there later to take him out. I couldn't envision doing that, ever. I'm not sure what I would have done, but calling the police was the most logical choice, letting the girls go beforehand, of course. He was high, and it was an accident, and people do die having sex. That's not the first time it's happened in this business. She told the truth to the very last word; I found out about what happened and how it ended up from Nana later. The man was an older gentleman, and the family hushed up the way he died to avoid any scandal. So when this girl told me it was time to shut down the apartments because something was in the air, I closed them immediately. I didn't have to be warned twice. She worked for me a lot, she was intelligent and astute. I would not have believed any other girls. Plus, many in Philly said they had heard rumors too, even from the low-end girls and madams.

Before Christmas, I called and asked the ladies in New York if they had heard anything, and they said no. But prior to the call I heard that one madam in New Orleans was working with my madam friend in New York because it was urgent that she raise some cash—she owed money to some client, or something to that effect. The story was bullshit. My inner voice was warning me against doing anything. Although I refused to work with the New Orleans mini-madam three times before because of her rep, the madam in New York persuaded me that she really needed to work and to give her a chance. "She good girl! You take her!" Nana said with her Chinese accent, telling me that her girls weren't making enough money in New Orleans, yeah, sure...the ones she stole from the Circuit for herself. I should have said no, and someone else advised me not to, but I said yes to help her out. I thought, "What if it were me and I needed help?" She came up from New Orleans, and I met her at the apartment I had sublet. That was a big mistake; it was rare to meet anyone from the Circuit face-to-face. There were only a handful of trustworthy girls and madams. One of these was Angie, in Atlanta. I met and hung out with her, but she was just like the Mayflower madam, she loved to show off with her girls, parading them in public like trophy bitches.

I fell for it hook, line, and sinker. It didn't matter that I was closed on Christmas, even though customers did call. So Miss New Orleans came in...she was there to make a full report on my business. My eyes were blinded to the reality of the situation. A snitch! She told them my address—everything—to get herself out of trouble. She smiled in my face, took the money, and squealed. She was not a genuine madam like the older ones I first knew in the Circuit who kept their mouths shut. She was a mini-madam, a rat without any loyalty. She didn't care about anyone but herself, so the unthinkable happened unexpectedly. I told Russ I needed a break from the cold weather and that we should pack up and go to the Florida house in April, after the snow had melted a bit and we could drive. He was fine with that. I wanted to go even sooner to get out of the cold, but procrastinated. I didn't want to involve him in my business, so I did not explain any of the facts about New Orleans or being in trouble with a client. He had to work until they could give him time off, and I was getting things rolling for the new store, scouting out possible locations. And then, before we had a chance to go, we got a complete surprise. It was April 2001. We were ready to go to my second home in Florida on the weekend, but it was too late! I was living in the town where, on Beals Street, John Kennedy, Robert, Eunice, and Patricia were born.

A wealthy, historical town with beautiful neighborhoods, and the federal case against me and others was about to be splashed all over the media...on September 11, 2001.

All the federal agents were busy watching and recording the women on the Circuit when they should have been spending their time watching for terrorists in our country. They continued watching and listening from 9/11 until April 18, 2002. By then, there was extensive fallout resulting from those resources being misdirected. The FBI's special agent in charge of the New Orleans office, Ken Kaiser, defended the brothel investigation and stated that it was an important criminal corruption case involving a national network and in no way interfered with counter-terrorism activities. Still, politicians, journalists, TV personalities, and news hosts mocked the FBI's actions. I watched Bill O'Reilly on TV derisively mention that there were FBI agents wasting time on brothels rather than terrorists. Suspiciously, the topic was dropped from news media conversations.

CHAPTER EIGHTY-EIGHT

April 18, 2002

Oh shit. I don't want a cellmate, but here she is—a cellmate, sitting on the other side of the jail cell, just in time to distract me from my train of thought. She walked in and sat on the bench facing me, crossing her legs. She looked like she was in her early twenties. The FBI lady said a few words to her, then turned to the door, keyed the lock, and pulled it closed behind her. "Ms. Siskind, you probably won't be here much longer," the attractive FBI lady said, standing at the jail entrance on the other side. "As soon as your bail is made, someone will be down for you." The door shut. "They're working on the final papers now." I thanked her. Finally. I sighed. Phew… All day, I had been lost in deep thought, going over my life and possible future, and I felt like I was waking from a long dream. Was it true? How did I get here after all my years of being so cautious? When Dave was in decline, he told me, "Please, get rid of the house and business! Go somewhere nice to live and be happy. Write your books and live your life, please. You and R. Lee should be around each other more often. Stop walking on eggshells." He had been right. I've been through so much in my life and now I find myself in a jail cell? I got here by being careless and not following my own rules. Not only had I been walking on eggshells, all this time I had been walking on thin ice.

"What did you do?" a voice asked.

"It's a long story and pretty boring. Sorry, can't go there, it's much too complicated," I told the young one.

"Why are you here?" I asked, immediately regretting the question.

Then she asked for my name.

"Leah," I said. I didn't want to use my real name even though they had already called me using my last name, Siskind. "What's your name?"

"Peaches."

Hmmm, of course, *I thought.*

"Sweet like fruit," I told her, and she smiled with pride. She obviously didn't want to use her real name either. Or was that her real name?

She was attractive in a way: olive skin, big brown eyes, and lush lips. But her hair needed some help—it was tangled and knotted as if she had just gotten out of bed. She had on a blue tee shirt with army-green cargo pants and white Converse high tops that were dirty and worn. After being strip-searched and questioned, I had been sitting in that cell for hours, running my life story through my mind like a feature film. Listening to this young woman who could have been me some thirty or so years ago was a nightmare. She went on and on; it felt like the longest hours of my life, almost like when Dave was dying, sitting with him, waiting for him to draw his last breath, or the nightmare of me sitting in this jail cell on a serious charge that took me by surprise. I had to go to the bathroom and had been holding it for an inordinate amount of time. There was no door, no stall, and a camera at the front to monitor every move. And now company…Peaches talked and talked and talked. I could hardly focus on anything. Thinking about my life helped me withstand the wait in the cell, and it abruptly stopped when Peaches came in. Peaches said, "They're trying to stick me with a charge of trafficking in painkillers—Oxy, Percocet, Vicodin—and they are so wrong. I didn't do it…I mean, I've done it before, but not this time…I'm innocent… Maybe at one time I did, but not now…no way…absolutely no way." She didn't have to convince me. Peaches could use some painkillers herself right now, right at this very moment—maybe a potent tranquilizer. She just did not shut up. For sure, Peaches and I were as innocent and pure as the driven snow, both facing felony convictions.

A generation or two separated us in age. I made good money, wore nice clothes, and lived in comfort in a large Victorian home in a fine neighborhood. Peaches' clothes were threadbare, and she probably lived in a couple of different homes a week, maybe one of them on the street.

Depending on what day it was, she might have a different job, selling drugs, or selling herself. This was obvious judging by the things she was saying. What a terrible life. Yes, I had been there. Funny thing was, I knew Peaches better than she knew herself. I never let on that I knew more. I stayed on her level to keep her comfortable in her space. I was happy I graduated from her class long ago, but I needed to get another degree now, being all the way straight so I could live my life in freedom.

She kept on. I was hearing her but not totally listening. I gave her the sandwich they had brought me to eat. I couldn't eat a thing. I kept thinking how familiar this is, this moment, exactly like my many past encounters with being arrested when I was younger. I needed to think about this now. I could go to jail! I asked myself if I could handle that—I decided that yes, I could. I could take lots of books that I never had time to read before, and write my own books every day and finally finish them. I would do all those things I'd never had enough time to do. I was sad though, not for me, but for my son. He is the only one who can make me feel so bad; to not be able to see or talk to him for any length of time would crush me. I would never let him or anyone else I loved come up to see me in a prison. I could not handle that. I prayed and prayed, hoping my angels above could help me out once again, one last big time.

****

All day, all morning long and into the afternoon, my legal counsel was working to get me released. I was sure Russ was back at my house in Brookline fielding phone calls from cities and towns across the nation, not knowing what to say, just retrieving messages from women and girls. The working girls and the madams who had not been arrested were dialing numbers and asking questions, at breakneck speed and with terrific urgency, about the ones that the FBI got. I'm sure they were scared. Madams called madams. Girls called madams. Girls called girls. Everyone was nervous; everyone needed information fast. The Circuit had become a gossip line for bitches. *Who got arrested? When? Where? What were the charges? Would there be any more arrests? Is anyone going to prison? Who will be next?* I learned later that they instructed Russ, "Call me as soon as possible," like he was their secretary.

There is something wonderfully democratic about the unease and paranoia generated when a big-time madam is arrested. It is a sort of discomfort and anxiety that afflicts the person of modest circumstances as well as the affluent. It puts fear into the hearts of blue-collar and white-collar workers alike. It doesn't matter if you are a bigwig or small fry, whether you have tons of cash or not much at all, if you were a customer of the madam, and she gets pinched, you start pacing the halls, nervously staring out the window, saying to yourself never again (of course, like the last snort of cocaine—never again if I make it through this—until you find another you believe is safe to see), fearfully picking up the newspaper, flipping through the news channels on TV, tossing and turning in your boxer shorts or cotton briefs in your sheets—and maybe even not getting an erection with your wife! You are wondering if she is going to let your secret out. And where is her client list? If she's stupid, it's where they can find it. The men were worried. I don't blame them, but I knew their secret was safe with me.

As word spread about the Circuit arrests, many, many men across our beautiful land were sweating buckets. My name began appearing in newspapers, and news station trucks with satellite dishes were about to be parked in rows on my street. The reporters questioned my neighbors, any new calls for my services dried up, and calls from spooked customers inquiring about what I was saying, and to whom, increased exponentially as my exposure grew broader.

****

My clients need not have worried. They were safe with me, unequivocally. They were my living and my lifeblood, and I would protect them. Protecting clients is what a madam is supposed to do, always, but not these other M's! Old rules were broken, and squealing became the thing to do—that's why I'm here today. And if I have to be here for some time, then so be it. You do the crime, you pay the price.

****

Worried people were not the only ones who called my house when my name came out and hit the press. For the first time in years, my adoptive family called, interested in my life and wanting to talk to me. Members of the family were not exactly happy to have their name made public in such a scandalous way. It was my name, and I felt a kind of retribution for all those years they had snubbed and overlooked me. They were wondering what was going on with the case, and if and when the whole thing might blow over. They offered me money, a charity I wasn't willing to take. In fact, the relatives from my father's side were royally upset. Well, they could stay upset. Why didn't they call when I needed a family? What was happening certainly wasn't my intention. I was resentful in a sense, and yet I was calm. I was finally having my day. I was able to be my real self, no more role-playing. Where were they all those years ago when I was hungry and alone? I could have used a telephone call or some concern. Where was my adopted family when Anita was beating me? Where were they when I needed to be saved from the abuse, and neglect, and starvation I endured for years? They were nowhere in sight. I owed them nothing. Where was my so-called adoptive family? Living with the rich, wearing earplugs.

My plan was to go home, lock the doors, close the curtains, and start selling off my properties to raise money to pay my legal fees. I intended to work fast—even if it was an overreaction—because I believed someone would come and take all that I had worked for from me. I paid my taxes, keeping my stores and flea market sales separate from my consulting sex business. I acquired my stores and homes legally and didn't hide anything. I really liked the house in Florida too. It was just starting to come around, and I dreamed that one day I could retire and move there to write my books. Selling that house was going to hurt but would not be nearly as painful as selling the house David and I built together, the house my son called home, and the home I cherished…

****

I wanted to disappear, hide, crumble, and weep, but there was nowhere to go. I had too much responsibility to just sit and cry. I held it in. I have never allowed myself to break down to the point of not functioning because that wouldn't get me anywhere. I didn't have the time to feel sorry for myself, now or ever; I had to think and move on. All the heartaches I have felt in my life converged when Dave died. It was the most I cried in years. Now I was suffering from embarrassment and fear for others. How was I going to feel when my son, or his friends and their families, found out what happened? That thought was enough to make me want to cry, like the day David's brother verbally stripped me naked and my past was revealed to my son—my child, my blood…And, of course, I was scared of what was going to happen to me. I prayed my neighbors wouldn't be judgmental and reject me, and that my store customers would remain loyal. I resolved that I would have the nerve to face all of them. Then—time seemed to stop. I would be getting out of this claustrophobic cell and away from my chatty roommate soon.

****

At about three-thirty in the afternoon, I was finally brought into the courtroom for arraignment. Throughout the day, the attorney had managed to represent me by phone; he was not actually present when the charges were formally read. I stood alone in this hall of so-called justice. The room was more like an auditorium, with beautiful woodwork; the layout was just as you'd see on TV, whether it was *Perry Mason*, *Judge Judy*, or *Law and Order*.

The judge sat in his black robe, elevated on his kingly throne in the front of the courtroom. I was a defendant without a lawyer present. To my right stood an assistant U.S. attorney general; he looked like a kid, a few years out of law school. He could never understand all of this. None of them could except for the men who knew madams or girls and once shared time and space with them. They were the ones who would understand. Then the judge read the charge, the one that had been recited to me back in my dining room at daybreak: "You are under arrest for conspiracy to travel in interstate commerce in aid of a prostitution enterprise out of New Orleans." Me, Libbe Siskind!

The man in the black robe was august-looking and silver-haired. He peered through thick eyeglasses at some sheets of paper that he held in his hand and looked up, first at the U.S. attorney, then at me.

"Ms. Siskind, are you entering a plea?" asked the judge.

"Yes, your honor, not guilty," I declared, plainly and confidently.

"Okay," he said, then turned to the U.S. attorney general.

"What has been decided in terms of bail?"

"Your honor, the defendant will be released on the recognizance of her counsel."

I wasn't a flight risk, and I wasn't violent. This arrangement appeared as if it might work for everyone. I was holding my breath, and had to remind myself to keep breathing. Lady FBI was at my side. "Ms. Siskind, we'll get you out of here in a few minutes." I felt comfortable with her as if she had a heart and was genuinely concerned. At least, that's what I wanted to believe. It was almost two hours more before all the paperwork and formalities were completed. And then I was released around five-thirty or six p.m. A weight was lifted off my chest!

Russ had made his way over and was waiting for me in the courthouse parking lot. I spotted him right away, ran over to him, hugged him, and held on to him; as I grew to know Russ, I had come to love him. He knew me, and I was not alone. After a good minute embracing each other, I stopped thinking of myself only and blurted, "Did you talk to my son? Did you talk to him? And are you okay?"

"Yes, Lib…yes, of course, don't worry. I called and spoke with R. Lee. He's cool. I explained everything and told him it was being taken care of. I told him you would be back home today and that you would call him to explain the best you could." My chest was tight again. They had given back my inhaler, and I took a quick puff. I had a lot to tell him.

As Russ drove us home, he filled me in on as much as he knew about what he was beginning to understand was a far-reaching federal sting, all of which seemed to be tied to M., and her apartment brothel on Canal Street in New Orleans. From what he told me, the sting had targeted the Circuit, and it was their intention to disrupt the fifty-plus-year-old, quasi-secret society and interstate network of top madams and high-priced call girls. On a national scale, this was unprecedented. Never had the world's oldest profession received such coordinated and focused attention from the law based on information given to them by a mini-madam and her client who turned her in. She knew nothing about how hard the madams worked to keep their businesses private, not exposed to the public and a subject of gossip. Protecting the privacy of the men who paid for services was uppermost in my mind, but not in hers; she exposed all her clients. The attention we were receiving was more glaring than ever; I should never have had anything to do with M. She was bad news, and my gut had told me not to, just as my friend had also advised me. I should have listened.

Over the next few days, through talks with my lawyer, I was able to get a fairly good handle on why I, along with so many others, was arrested. And why in the world so much effort and resources had been devoted to taking us down. It was crazy! The government and cops had long known about the Canal Street brothel and the Circuit, and did not do a thing right away. Why, for more than a year, did a coalition of law enforcement agencies—with the FBI spearheading the effort—spy on the sex trade using the naked eye, audio and visual taping and recording devices, and reviews of many personal and business records? This was not usual for them when it came to prostitution. Perhaps the nature of the Circuit, which involved interstate travel, was the basis for such an elaborate probe, and they thought we were a syndicate. Plus, a doctor's extortion of money had triggered it.

The answer was tied to an old story in crime and crime fighting: someone got arrested and was facing serious time, and he had information on some other criminal activity—information he would gladly share with the cops, FBI, whomever, in exchange for leniency in the charges filed and punishment handed down. In my case, that someone was a drug-addicted surgeon in New Orleans who, near the end of 2000, had been busted for Medicare fraud. When investigators went through his bank accounts, they found that he had spent close to three hundred fifty thousand dollars over a three-year period on the services of the Canal Street Brothel. With this info, the authorities asked the doctor if he would be willing to make a deal: provide intelligence to help take down the brothel and its connections, and in return, prosecutors and judges would go easy on him in sentencing. What a jerk he was—not a man, just a mouse wanting his own cheese. The doc said yes, and not only reported the real workings of the brothel, but also concocted fanciful stories as well, fiction that had to do with a massive drug business run out of the house of ill-repute on Canal Street. He said anything to get off the hook.

An investigation began, and ramped up as news came down the pike. The FBI operated as the general of the troops while other law enforcement agencies, variously and at different junctures, served as junior officers. As 2001 rolled along, all the necessary warrants and orders were obtained to allot the manpower and technology to snoop on the madams and girls. Many federal agents were assigned to protect America from consenting adults selling sex to other consenting adults. As the Islamic fanatics of Al Qaeda, directed by Osama bin Laden, learned how to fly passenger jets and managed to stay off the radar screen of the FBI, prostitutes across the nation were on the radar and received prime manpower attention from the feds. Even in the moment, the government neglected to detect the fact that the deadliest attack ever on American soil was in the works; multiple agents were monitoring phone calls between madams, call girls, and johns. Some of those monitored calls were made on the very date—September 11, 2001. Do you think the resources of the FBI could have been better directed that year? Why weren't these agents called off the phones? Our country needed more help than busting brothels.

Indeed, in a congressional hearing on terrorism held after the 9/11 attacks, U.S. Senator Patrick Leahy, chair of the Judiciary Committee, questioned the decision of the feds to spy on the Circuit, barking into the microphone, "It comes as an enormous revelation to the American public that there might have been prostitutes in New Orleans. I mean, who knew?"

I had one more close call. Springfield, Ohio. After everything was shut down, years after the case ended, my phones were still at the house, and a woman I knew who ran an older, low-end house, set me up once again, but over a small phone call. I had no girls. All I said was that if I could help find a number I would let her know. And that did it, second case over nothing. My lawyer joked that I was now a career criminal. We went to Springfield, Ohio. I could tell they wanted blood, but I was no longer trading on the Circuit. The prosecutor was out to nail my ass, but the judge ruled in my favor. The case was shut. Still, it was another charge. I was afraid to even answer the phones anymore, but I had to tell everyone I was done. For years, men and girls still called.

CHAPTER EIGHTY-NINE

Looking Ahead

I questioned the reasoning of the U.S. government to put their resources into breaking up the Circuit while there were major issues to deal with, like the terrorists on 9/11 who killed thousands, or the very real problem of the sexual slave trade in the U.S. My son's friend, an off-duty fireman, died in a fiery stairwell of the twin towers that bright September morning. He was a true hero, as were all the other men and women who perished. If the FBI had spent more of their time and resources tracking terrorists instead of crimes of sex or misdemeanors, perhaps this tragedy could have been averted. During the time I spent in the federal jail cell waiting, I made decisions about major issues in my life. It gave me motivation to do so much more in my remaining years. I made it through the ordeal of the trial without having to spend time in jail. When the case ended, I began a new chapter in my life. I relocated my store to Brighton, Massachusetts. Clients called who still wanted to do business, but I was not reopening that one—I'd had enough of being a career criminal...

The money coming in is legitimate, barely enough to pay my bills, but I am free and moving on. I write constantly. The store was doing okay, but not enough for luxuries in my life. My health is good, outside of the aching bones and back pains that have plagued me since the old car accident in 1980. I do not take any drugs except for Advil and herbs. I don't drink. I don't smoke. I smile every day and take a breath because I do not take life for granted, even when it's cloudy outside or inside my heart. I do not go a day without talking to all my angels. I talk to my son, who is in my corner, as often as I can. We speak constantly. And on every 9/11, I call him because I know he is thinking about his friend and all the others who passed on from that tragedy. I think of all the people I knew who have passed on. By believing in myself, I make things happen, whether big or small. I have published several books, both adult and children's stories, many of which convey experiences I didn't have as well as those I did, allowing for an often-joyful expression of my inner self to the outer world that is entirely separate from the criminal implications of previous parts of my life. I have notebooks filled with ideas for other books besides this one, and a stack of manuscripts at various stages of the writing process—children's books, novels, a fantasy trilogy, and a book about the Circuit, which follows this one. I invested in two cottages on Cape Cod, taking a loan from my big home to buy and then flip them. I sold both, but the crash in 2008 slowed business down. Even then, I wanted to go back in business. I missed my girls and my clients, but I felt like chains were around my neck.

The business in my retail store was like everyone's now; sales were slow more often than not due to the internet. I have a website for my store but don't sell on it yet, and advertise on Instagram and Facebook in an effort to keep up with the times. I closed my last store in Brighton in May of 2016. And sold my house! I am a bit slow when it comes to the internet; I do not like the world of computers because it makes people even more distant from one another. I refuse to write emails to my son. I want him to send cards and call so I can hear his voice and know he's happy and healthy. Although computers are a great resource for information, I do not want my life to depend on them. So many people are out of touch with reality, living by pressing keys. And as for the sex industry on the internet, it is out in the open without regulation, growing day by day for children to view—I believe that is at least ten times worse than any brothel ever was. I could not believe I really sold my house. It took three years to pack up before selling it. Collectibles, art, personal items, all so dear to me that they needed special care. It was heart-wrenching and highly emotional because I was leaving behind all my memories of that time and place, mostly of R. Lee and David. So much…so much to leave behind.

I loved walking up the stone stairway to my porch. I tended to my gardens; I wanted my roses to bloom long after I had gone. The cement pots of fresh flowers in front of my house meant so much to me. When I looked at my house I saw something I created, with dignity and the help of David and our friend L.S. (who did all of the finish work), to leave to my son…or so I thought. I felt deep sorrow in knowing that was time to let go of my home in Brookline in order to move on. That house is me! And will always be a part of me. R. Lee said, however, "Mom, it's only made of wood. Anywhere you are is home. We take our memories with us."

That was the hardest transition for me—letting go. I will miss writing during my down time at the store, sitting on a chair on the sidewalk, and the people in the area knew me, waved, said hello, and asked me how the books were coming along. I miss that. I am always thinking about new stories I want to publish someday soon, in addition to what is on Amazon now. I am very much into rebuilding broken-down homes and making them beautiful. I hope to keep doing that. I need to stay busy. That small Cape house, the one I sold last, was the best little second home—shabby chic, French doors that looked out over the water. That is one my next dreams, to have another one of those again. The more important dream is for my son to have his own home again.

Isn't life great? There are angels who have walked me, and others, through difficult times for sure, but just to be alive and not in jail, or a drunk or drug addict, is great. I have a special son who loves me no matter what I've done. R. Lee has truly been a gift. He did not like what he found out about me when he was younger, and was unsure of me because of things other people told him through the years, but he turned out to be a very spiritual man with an understanding heart who accepts me for who I am. It took years of work and talking to create a friendship between us. Besides being a mother to him, I am his friend. Watching him grow into the man he is has been fulfilling. He is a hard worker, and believes in marriage, but won't go there unless it's for keeps. He is careful, has no children, does not drink, do drugs, or smoke. I am blessed! I do miss the part of my life with my clients and my girls.

R. Lee lived with his dog, who recently passed on, which devastated him. The dog was named after his best friend, Manny, the firefighter who was killed on 9/11. They went to school together. This was an unquestionable tragedy, comparable to nothing else in life I could imagine. It was receiving the news about his death that day that stays foremost in my memory, not what happened to me on that date. My son went through a painful experience because of my arrest, and it looked like I might go to jail (at first they said possibly five years). He was in a bad way then. He has no other family; his father never paid attention to him until the year before he died, and now he is gone too. Dave was dear to my son and was like a real father to him. His presence will always be with us, even if it is just in spirit.

My cocker spaniel Perrii died in 2006. My last moments with him, holding him as he died in pain, destroyed me. Oscar, my old dachshund, died in 2008. I had to put him down but, thankfully, he was not in pain. They were great dogs, and I loved them dearly. I miss the old boys, and want to have dogs when I retire. But I have not retired just yet. I reopened a new store in 2018. Sometimes I wonder which madams survived. I do know that Charlie passed on, just like so many others I knew. I have not spoken to any of them in years. My friend Eric passed away in 2013 of unknown causes, although I suspect it was drug-related. Rio's wife died a horrible death, when she was fifty-two, from brain cancer.

J.N. was diagnosed with stage four lung cancer in 2008, and passed away on April 28, 2018. In an odd coincidence of timing, J.N. passed just before his birthday, and David died soon after his. J.N. had five sons, but only four that he connected with because one was put up for adoption and, sadly, he had never met him. He expressed that he wanted the four to keep in touch, but did not get his last wish. J. N. never had a chance to write the note he intended to for this book because the cancer took him away first, but these are words written to me from him before he passed that I would like to share (the spacing and punctuation is exactly as he typed it):

> Moonbeams lit the night and a symphony
> of stars played a melody only I could hear
> I thought of you and the sky grew wild
> with visions of you being near
>
> When I took your hand in mine the galaxy
> exploded into crystals of venus colors
>
> We laughed so hard that our tears became
> rivers we floated away on
>
> You walked barefoot across my soul and
> left your soft imprints in the sandy
> beaches of my mind
>
> We filled each imprint with cups of love
> and together we drank to us and to our
> infinite time

We had FaceTimed a few days prior to the end. R. Lee was with him at his bedside just before his final days. J.N. passed early in the evening, and I sent this text to his phone later that night: "Rest. You are at peace. Love to you…we were friends for a long time, now you can visit David…we will all be angels in heaven one day…my last text… Libbe."

What happens in life is often so unexpected. But life has been good to me, and I will never hide who I am again. I am comfortable, even proud, of myself. I understand that because I was an abused child, placed in foster care, a prostitute, and then a madam that some people will view me as a victim and feel pity for me, others will judge me harshly—but I don't go there, I move forward. I hope my past will not affect people's desire to read the books for children that I have written. I built my own life and continue learning every day from what I have experienced. I treat others as I want to be treated. I receive respect from my neighbors and the customers who come into my store. I love the house that David and I put our hearts and souls into, and I will always cherish the fulfillment of the dream of having my own home. But now I have a new house, it's made of wood too. I've also raised a wonderful son who loves me unconditionally, and have a beautiful daughter, who is now in my life—I finally found my little girl! I cherish and love them both. In a very odd coincidence, when I first met David he told me that he went to a Shawmut Bank in Kenmore Square where he used to see a girl there all the time, and that she looked just like me; she could have been my clone. When he told me that, I didn't take it seriously. Years later, when I told my daughter that story she confirmed it, she was that girl! I have never met my other son, but when I reached out to his father, he thanked me for the gift of his wonderful boy, who has a good life, is happy, but was not ready to meet me. I'm okay with that, and am content just knowing that he is well. I will always have a place in my heart for him.

I wish I could share my knowledge of many issues having to do with prostitution with those who are vulnerable, and one day do what I can to make some contribution to the betterment of the foster care system. I would like to be able to do something in life to help others when I retire. I have dedicated this book to my son, and although I prefer that he never reads it, I hope that if he does, he will still, after all, love me no matter what. Now that I'm in my early seventies, I want to let it all go and be who I am—a real person—take it or leave it. Does anyone know what it feels like to spend your whole life as an object, not as a person…as Libbe the satisfaction machine, not Libbe the human being? You build a shell around yourself believing that there is no choice, but *you* live inside—disconnected from all others. I did, I hope you don't ever have to.

Am I happy? Yes, I'm happy to be alive. David foresaw my future on his deathbed when he advised me "to live life." He didn't want me to keep the Pink Lady. He knew the house would be a never-ending drain on my wallet and didn't want all my money going toward its care and maintenance, leaving me with little cash to enjoy life. I have fulfilled his wish. I sold the house in July of 2016, walking away without locking the door because it was too emotional. My memories came with me. I will miss that life, yes, I admit that! We packed up all my stuff and Russ and I drove a 26-foot truck to Florida, thinking I would move there. He flew back and I left a month and a half later, packing everything back up again and driving another 26-foot truck by myself. A friend of mine from Ohio took the ride with. Florida was not the place for me to live, I was uncomfortable being away from Boston. I moved to another city in Massachusetts, bought a fixer-upper, and am still working on it. I opened a retail store nearby in 2018. My lifestyle is radically different from what it once was, yet I am not discouraged, instead I roll with the punches. I'm quite sure my life is as stressful as the lives of the majority of Americans. What separates us is the world of "the life" and the perspective I've developed as a result of participating in an activity deemed illegal by the system. The future for each of us is an unknown, but one thing is for certain: I am free to look beyond my rose garden to a flourishing balance of life, no matter where my roses may grow in the future. If the fates allow, this is not the end.

My story still continues. Some of the true old madams of the Circuit may have passed on, and a few may still be here. I have spoken to some who retired or still have a little bit going on, but I never went back to join the bunch that was left. Yes, madams do still trade off, but it's not the same. The internet took over the old way. I am still involved in selling antiques, collectibles, and vintage items. And I hope to finish writing my story about the Circuit by the end of 2022—a world of its own.

Libbe Leah Siskind

AUTHOR'S NOTE

I told the story of my early childhood in my first book, *A Thorn in Rose's Garden*. Since then, I have written several novels and children's books. I am now working on a fantasy trilogy and a sequel to *In the Room Beyond the Rose Garden*, tentatively titled *The Circuit.* Never has any author or madam written about the Circuit before. My insight into the workings of this infamous prostitution ring was gained as I lived it, through my relationships with the other madams and the girls. There are no tales naming clients. Rather, the privacy of the men who were involved is maintained. In this respect, *The Circuit* will stand by itself among all the other books written about the subject of prostitution.

In the Room Beyond the Rose Garden tells my personal story with facets of the business of prostitution—a tease, a glimpse of the life. *The Circuit* is going to explain the actual structure, function, and details of the massive network of what is a world-wide profession. This will be the reality of a down and dirty situation, from the streets on up, not the glamorized version seen in movies and television. You will read about the real people, not the stereotypes usually presented. Unless you've lived it, travelled the road, you cannot know what the actual people face, their lives, their families, their health, their internal conflicts and the mayhem of their reality. Mind you, some people in the life are more than happy to be doing what they do, others are conflicted but enmeshed by circumstances. There should be no blame on anyone in life for decisions that only hurt themselves. We make our choices and choose that path, whether in the world of everyday people, in Hollywood with celebrities, or on the Circuit. You will see the true facts—the reality—not a cinematic portrayal. *The Circuit* will be for you, for me, for everyone who wants to know the truth.

Goldie (Stella), Libbe's biological mother

Joseph, Libbe's biological father

Rose and Freddy's baby picture of Libbe

Mommy Rose in the 1950's

Freddy (on the left), a daredevil wing walker, was the mechanic and pilot of this plane

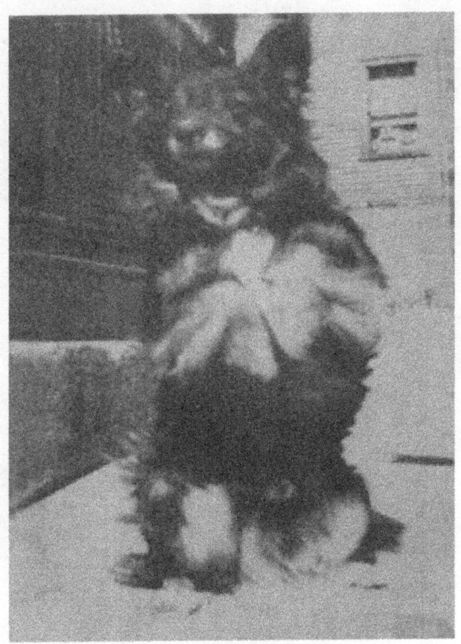

Buddy

Libbe at 5 years old with curls trimmed for a portrait

Stoneham Sanitarium and the White House on the left

Freddy's truck

Anita and Fred

1950's in Stoneham with the pixie cut

Fred with Anita as a shadow

Libbe at 12 living in a foster home

Libbe at 15 still at the same foster home

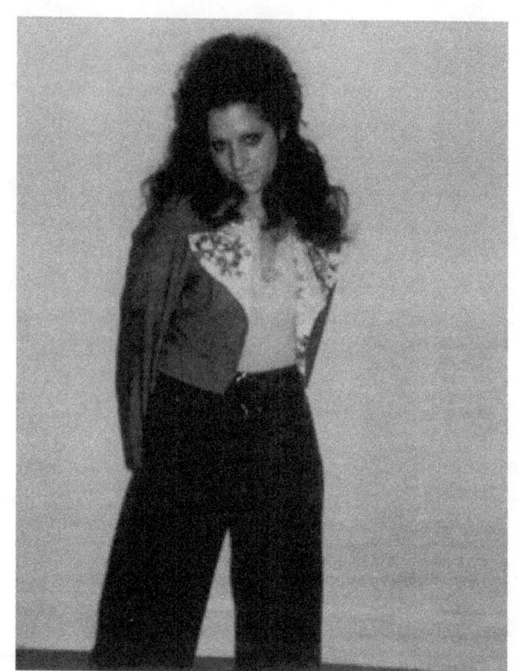

Libbe at 18 working the Combat Zone

1974, Jimmy at Tennis Road

Libbe and Ruthie (Robin) at the kite festival at Franklin Park

Ruthie (Robin) and Eric

R. Lee's birthday party

Libbe and R. Lee before she went out to work

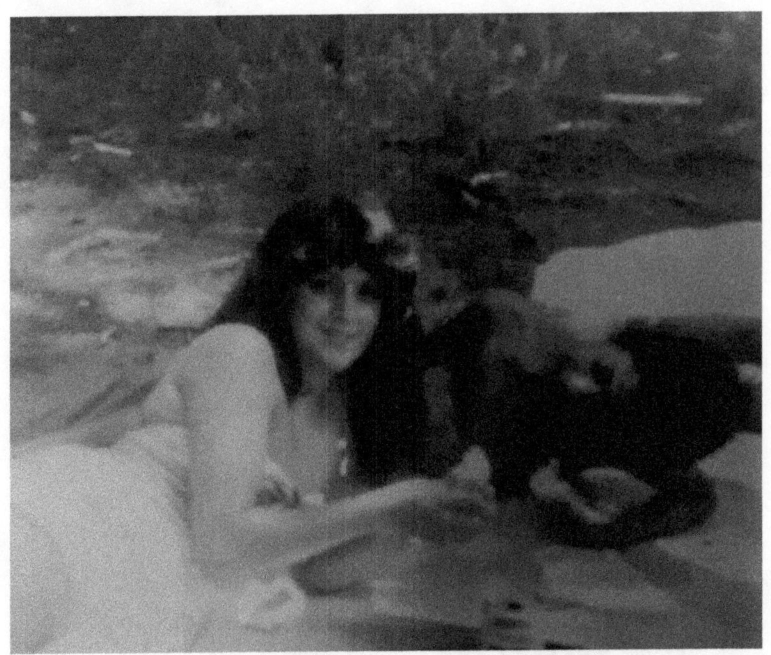

Libbe and R. Lee at summer camp

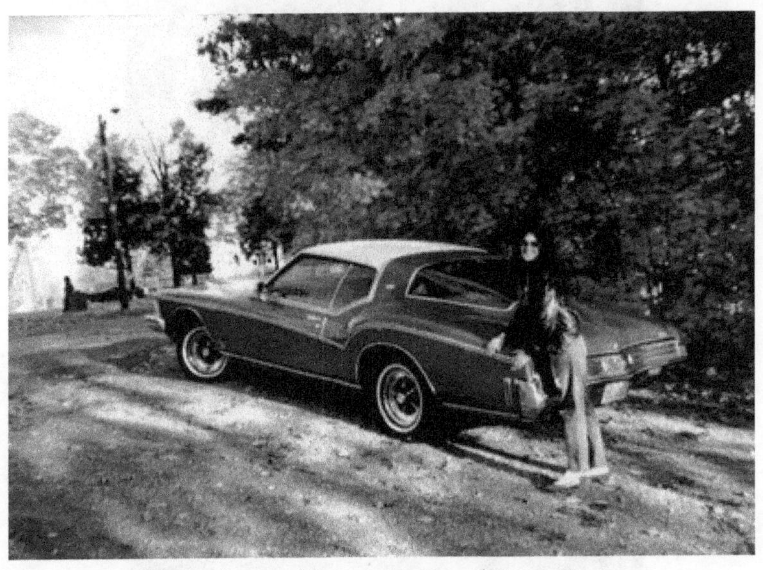

Libbe and one of her 1973 Grand Sport Rivieras

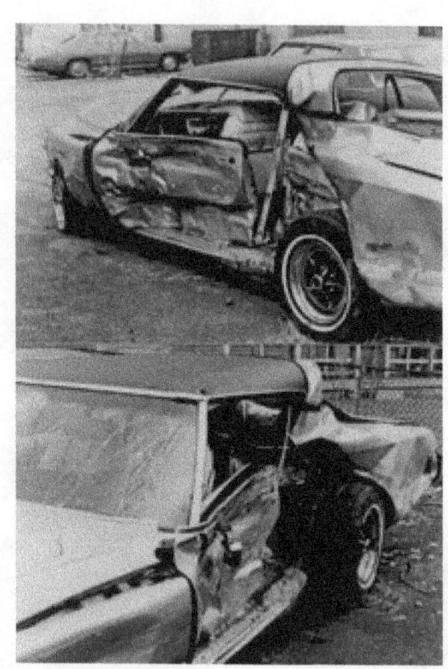

1971 Riviera after the January 1980 car accident

Atherton Road from start in 1981 as a green house to finish as the Pink Lady

Libbe and David

Oscar and Perrii

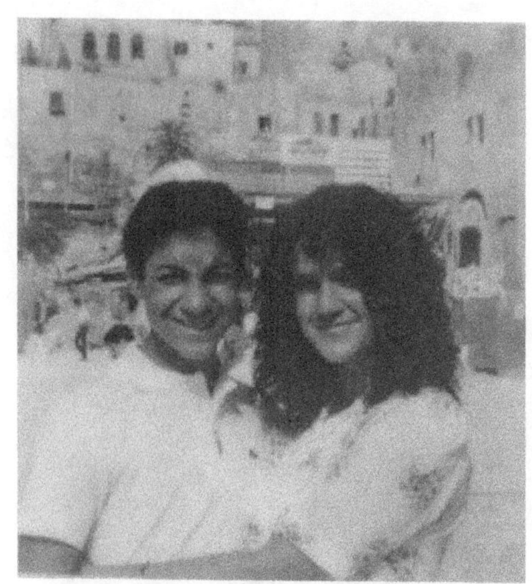

R. Lee and Libbe in Israel

Together in Israel

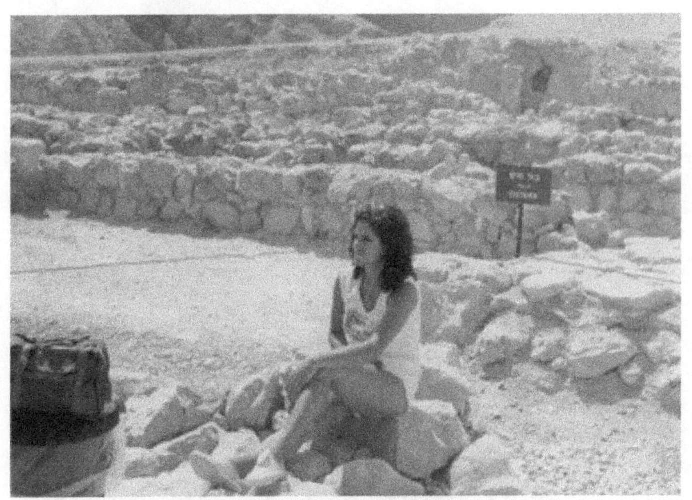

Libbe in Israel at Masada

December 1995, David at the rain forest in Puerto Rico

1996, In Remembrance of David

www.townonline.com/brookline

Atherton Road woman may be Hub madam

By Doug Hanchett
BOSTON HERALD

A nationwide bust of brothels led from New Orleans to a pastel Victorian home on Atherton Road.

Sitting high above the quiet street, resplendent in hot pink, the stately manse looks like it could indeed be Brookline's very own bordello.

But those who know owner Libbe Siskind say it's hard to believe allegations that she's really a madam, one who may have turned her home into a cathouse as part of a national network of high-class brothels.

"It doesn't make any sense at all," said a man who has lived across the street for 13 years. "She's just been a wonderful neighbor. It's very baffling to me."

The 51-year-old Siskind was indicted in New Orleans last week on one count of prostitution conspiracy, which carries a maximum five years in prison. Authorities say she was the madam for Boston, hosting prostitutes who rotated among brothels in New Orleans, Pittsburgh, New York City, Atlanta and Chicago.

Siskind didn't answer the door over the weekend, but a woman who answered her phone said she wasn't around and sounded surprised about charges.

A tenant of Siskind, who wouldn't divulge his name, said he's never seen any sign of hanky-panky. "I can pretty much guarantee you that there's nothing going on in the house ... unless they're helicoptering [johns] to the roof," said the man, who described Siskind as a "wonderful" landlady. "We were just blown away," by the allegations, he said. "We were shocked."

Until recently, Siskind owned A Piece of Heaven, a small collectibles shop on Cypress Street. A fellow shopkeeper in the block of stores said the business abruptly shut down two months ago.

"[Siskind] was here on a Saturday and then when I came in on [the following] Monday, she was gone," said the man, who didn't want his name used.

Siskind was described as quiet, but the shopkeeper said she was rarely at the store. And when she was — mostly on Saturdays — she spent a lot of time on the phone.

The shopkeeper said a mutual friend once told him that A Piece of Heaven was a "front" for Siskind. But the friend refused to elaborate, saying "you don't want to know."

"I didn't know what he meant," said the shopkeeper. "Now I think I know."

BOSTON HERALD SATURDAY, APRIL 6, 2002

Fed brothel bust ID's Brookline woman as alleged Hub madam

2002 prostitution ring bust articles

Neighbors shocked at charge of catting under hot pink roof

By DOUG HANCHETT

Sitting high above Atherton Road, resplendent in hot pink, the stately Victorian manse looks like it could indeed be Brookline's very own bordello.

But those who know owner Libbe Siskind say it's hard to believe allegations that she's really a madam, one who may have turned her painstakingly restored home into a Coolidge Corner cathouse as part of a national network of high-class brothels.

"It doesn't make any sense at all," said a man who has lived across the street for 13 years. "She's just been a wonderful neighbor. It's very baffling to me."

The 51-year-old Siskind was indicted in New Orleans last week on one count of prostitution conspiracy, which carries a maximum five years in prison. Authorities say she was the madam for Boston, hosting prostitutes who rotated among brothels in New Orleans, Pittsburgh, New York City, Atlanta and Chicago.

Siskind didn't answer the door yesterday. A woman who answered her phone said she wasn't around and sounded surprised about charges.

"Libbe's not in town this week," said the woman. "I don't even know about this."

Siskind's house is just up the hill from bustling Coolidge Corner, and sits high above the street. An elaborate fieldstone stairway leads up to the covered front porch, with a lovely ceiling fan above the doorway.

In the front door was a sign that asked visitors to take off their shoes before entering.

A tenant of Siskind, who wouldn't divulge his name, said he's never seen any sign of hanky-panky.

"I can pretty much guarantee you that there's nothing going on in the house ... unless they're helicoptering (johns) to the roof," said the man.

The man said there's never any "foot traffic" in the house and described Siskind as a "wonderful" landlady.

"We were just blown away," by the allegations, he said. "We were shocked."

Siskind's neighbor, who didn't want his name used, said she has had various tenants over the years, but that he also never noticed anything out of the ordinary.

Like some of those who know Siskind, the neighbor didn't believe the allegations until they were shown a story in yesterday's Herald.

But a few passers-by had no trouble believing the Victorian could be part of a thriving call-girl ring.

"Well, it's pink. It's kind of appropriate," said one woman.

Until recently, Siskind owned A Piece of Heaven, a small collectibles shop on Cypress Street in Brookline that sold porcelain dolls and small gifts. A fellow shopkeeper in the single-story block of stores said the business abruptly shut down two months ago.

"(Siskind) was here on a Saturday and then when I came in on (the following) Monday, she was gone," said the man, who didn't want his name used.

Siskind was described as quiet, but the shopkeeper said she was rarely at the store. And when she was — mostly on Saturdays — she spent a lot of time on the phone.

The shopkeeper said a mutual friend once told him that A Piece of Heaven was a "front" for Siskind. But the friend refused to elaborate, saying "you don't want to know."

"I didn't know what he meant," said the shopkeeper. "Now I think I know."

A number of businesses have been listed at Siskind's address over the years, including A Piece of Heaven, Diamond Detailing and Emilie's Sweets & Gifts.

The latter was owned by a relative of Siskind's, Rae and Janice Litwack of Brockton, who yesterday denied knowing Libbe Siskind.

"Sorry, can't help you. Thanks for calling," she said before quickly hanging up the phone.

APRIL 7, 2002 BOSTON SUNDAY HERALD

April 2002, Boston Sunday Herald article

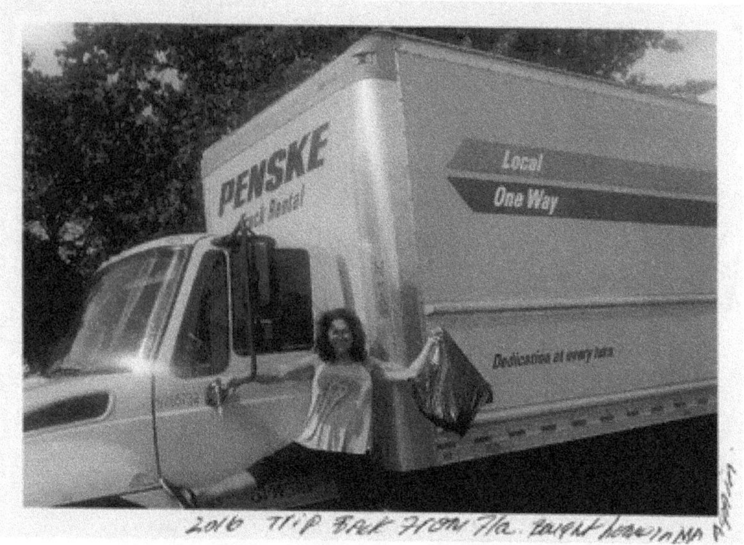

2016, Libbe and the 25' truck she drove from Florida to Boston

2018, Libbe in her new retail store

2021, Libbe at 70 years old and still in her store

The Story of the Birthmother

THE ADOPTION CONNECTION, INC
11 Peabody Square, Room #6
Peabody, MA 01960
May 27, 1983

Libbe Siskind
66 A Rd.
Brookline, MA 02146

Dear Libbe:

I wanted to get back to you and let you know exactly what we have found so far. Things are looking good and developing on the right track, but I wanted to give you a breakdown on what we have found so far and where we are going from here.

We started with the birth of your birthmother. Goldie P (***last names have been redacted for privacy-Ed***), born Chelsea, Mass., 2/26/1916. Father was Louis F. P, Mother Dora B P and both of her parents were born in Russia and at the time of Goldie's birth they resided at 150 Bloomingdale. Goldie's father's occupation was a cigar maker.

On March 21, 1937 Goldie P, age 29, residing at 79 Savin St., Boston married George W. At the time of the marriage George was 23 years old and he was residing at 1107 Blue Hill Ave., Boston. It was his first marriage and his occupation was a locksmith and he too was born in Boston. George W parents were Max and Annie W.

I know that you mentioned that someone told you that they had divorced and that Goldie had remarried. So far we have checked marriages in Mass. from 1950 through 1976 and found no remarriage on a Goldie P W. I guess it is possible that they married out-of-state. However going over the information that you received from Sheila F of the Dept. of Social

Services, I noted that it mentioned that the Ws had two daughters, one born in 41 and one in 45. I was able to locate the information on one of those daughters. I found that on March 5, 1945 one was born. Her Mother was Goldie P W, her Father was George. At the time of her birth George and Goldie resided at 106 Brunwick. I feel that the information we found will definitely put us on the right track and I have now gone and searched for a marriage on the daughter and see what direction that takes us in.*

I am also trying to locate deaths on Goldie's parents feeling that we know that her Mother died before the time of your birth, but at the time of your birth her father and brother were still alive and still in this area. If you have any questions regarding this information please give me a call. However, I will get back to you as soon as possible probably within the next two to three weeks. Hope you are pleased with what you are learning so far.

Sincerely,
(*signed*) S. D.
Director

*the other sister died in a car accident on the way to Florida

Excerpts from Jewish Family and Children's Services

Circa 1960

I. TESTS ADMINISTERED:

Wechler Intelligence Scale for Children
Bender-Gestalt Test
Figure Drawings
Rorschach
Thematic Apperception Test

II. PARENTAL OBSERVATIONS

The Siskind family consist of: Mr. Fred Siskind a fifty-nine year old Jewish truck driver; Mrs. Anita Siskind, a fifty-nine year old housewife and their only child Libbe.

Adoptive father denies any problems. Stepmother complains of lying, stealing, disobedience, sex play and instigating trouble between parents. It's felt that stepmother exaggerates Libbe's problems.

According to Mrs. Anita Siskind, Libbe has poor eating habits. She does not have good table manners and, on occasion, hoards food. From the few hoarding incidents described to me (Mrs. Frances Ackerman, Caseworker), it appears that Libbe might have hid food that Mrs. Siskind wanted her to eat in spite of Libbe's not wanting it. (Libbe) held food in her mouth and did not swallow, complained about the food Mrs. Siskind prepared and threw away the sandwiches she gave her. Mrs. Siskind told the worker at Mass.

Mental Health Center that she knew how much Libbe should eat and insisted that she eat the amount that was put on her plate. Libbe often threatened to vomit.

Libbe wanders. Mrs. Siskind relates an incident in which Libbe was brought home by a policeman who she had told the following: her mother was deceased and she was looking for an aunt. At the Mass Mental Health Center, Mrs. Siskind complained that Libbe kept her room poorly, messed up her drawers and destroyed her toys. Mrs. Siskind told the worker at Mass. Mental Health Center that Libbe has no friends because she was so unpleasant to be with. Mr. Siskind reported, however, that his wife was so strict with Libbe that she would not allow Libbe to have friends in the house, and since Mrs. Siskind took pride in her garden, they could not play in the yard.

The three of them form an unusual triangle in which there is a great deal of deceit, which Libbe often uses quite manipulatively. For example, after Libbe had lied , mother told father to hit her. Libbe and father went to the basement where Mr. Siskind hit the chair while Libbe screamed. (…) Mrs. Siskind expressed resentment over her husband's preference for Libbe. She contrasts his indulgence of Libbe with what she considers his neglect for her.(…) [Mrs. Siskind] told the Mass Mental Health Centre worker that Libbe caused the first Mrs. Siskind to have cancer.

In July 1962, Libbe was sent to friends of the family in Florida who complain of many problems. Applicant(father) feels that this is not a good placement and is urging that she return to Boston. However adoptive father's home is out of the question for Libbe. Applicant is requesting temporary shelter at New Englsnd Home to enable Jewish Family and Children's Service to find a suitable home for Libbe.

III. BEHAVIORAL OBSERVATIONS:

Libbe is a thin little girl with an alert expression on her face, whose hair and clothing look always somewhat disarranged.

She behaves in a pseudo-mature and somewhat ingratiating manner towards one but on the whole is quite pleasant and compliant.

However, she appears to be a rather manipulative child. For example, she would convey a message to her step-mother which was not given to her, etc. I found her to be a likeable girl and on the whole quite cooperative.

Libbe is a fearful, anxious girl who has a slightly ingratiating manner and shows evidence of having considerable feelings of underlying aggression. Her anxiety appears to be centered around her marked feelings of insecurity. She is inhibited and repressed and seems to be expressing her aggression indirectly by her "manipulative" behavior and possibly through her "enuresis".

There are no indications of organicity and her reality testing appears to be adequate.

Libbe and her parents were seen weekly at Mass Mental Health Center in 1960 and 1961. It was felt that Libbe was not psychotic and not unmanageable and that parents were quite disturbed and not workable.

Aydin Cankardas-Wysocki, PhD.
Principal Psychologist
Child Psychiatry Unit
Mass. Mental Health Center

So many people and memories have left my doorstep. I hope that everyone I met in my lifetime has had health and happiness.

Until we meet again . .

CPSIA information can be obtained
at www.ICGtesting.com
Printed in the USA
LVHW111644131122
732905LV00001B/1

9 781956 096088